T0203000

Lecture Notes in Artificial Intelligence   12978

Subseries of Lecture Notes in Computer Science

More information about this subseries at http://www.springer.com/series/1244

Yuxiao Dong · Nicolas Kourtellis ·
Barbara Hammer · Jose A. Lozano (Eds.)

Machine Learning and Knowledge Discovery in Databases

Applied Data Science Track

European Conference, ECML PKDD 2021
Bilbao, Spain, September 13–17, 2021
Proceedings, Part IV

 Springer

Editors
Yuxiao Dong
Facebook AI
Seattle, WA, USA

Nicolas Kourtellis
Torre Telefonica
Barcelona, Spain

Barbara Hammer
Bielefeld University, CITEC
Bielefeld, Germany

Jose A. Lozano (iD)
Basque Center for Applied Mathematics
Bilbao, Spain

ISSN 0302-9743   ISSN 1611-3349   (electronic)
Lecture Notes in Artificial Intelligence
ISBN 978-3-030-86513-9   ISBN 978-3-030-86514-6   (eBook)
https://doi.org/10.1007/978-3-030-86514-6

LNCS Sublibrary: SL7 – Artificial Intelligence

This Springer imprint is published by the registered company Springer Nature Switzerland AG
The registered company address is: Gewerbestrasse 11, 6330 Cham, Switzerland

Preface

This edition of the European Conference on Machine Learning and Principles and Practice of Knowledge Discovery in Databases (ECML PKDD 2021) has still been affected by the COVID-19 pandemic. Unfortunately it had to be held online and we could only meet each other virtually. However, the experience gained in the previous edition joined to the knowledge collected from other virtual conferences allowed us to provide an attractive and engaging agenda.

ECML PKDD is an annual conference that provides an international forum for the latest research in all areas related to machine learning and knowledge discovery in databases, including innovative applications. It is the leading European machine learning and data mining conference and builds upon a very successful series of ECML PKDD conferences. Scheduled to take place in Bilbao, Spain, ECML PKDD 2021 was held fully virtually, during September 13–17, 2021. The conference attracted over 1000 participants from all over the world. More generally, the conference received substantial attention from industry through sponsorship, participation, and also the industry track.

The main conference program consisted of presentations of 210 accepted conference papers, 40 papers accepted in the journal track and 4 keynote talks: Jie Tang (Tsinghua University), Susan Athey (Stanford University), Joaquin Quiñonero Candela (Facebook), and Marta Kwiatkowska (University of Oxford). In addition, there were 22 workshops, 8 tutorials, 2 combined workshop-tutorials, the PhD forum, and the discovery challenge. Papers presented during the three main conference days were organized in three different tracks:

- Research Track: research or methodology papers from all areas in machine learning, knowledge discovery, and data mining.
- Applied Data Science Track: papers on novel applications of machine learning, data mining, and knowledge discovery to solve real-world use cases, thereby bridging the gap between practice and current theory.
- Journal Track: papers that were published in special issues of the Springer journals Machine Learning and Data Mining and Knowledge Discovery.

We received a similar number of submissions to last year with 685 and 220 submissions for the Research and Applied Data Science Tracks respectively. We accepted 146 (21%) and 64 (29%) of these. In addition, there were 40 papers from the Journal Track. All in all, the high-quality submissions allowed us to put together an exceptionally rich and exciting program.

The Awards Committee selected research papers that were considered to be of exceptional quality and worthy of special recognition:

- Best (Student) Machine Learning Paper Award: Reparameterized Sampling for Generative Adversarial Networks, by Yifei Wang, Yisen Wang, Jiansheng Yang and Zhouchen Lin.

- First Runner-up (Student) Machine Learning Paper Award: "Continual Learning with Dual Regularizations", by Xuejun Han and Yuhong Guo.
- Best Applied Data Science Paper Award: "Open Data Science to fight COVID-19: Winning the 500k XPRIZE Pandemic Response Challenge", by Miguel Angel Lozano, Oscar Garibo, Eloy Piñol, Miguel Rebollo, Kristina Polotskaya, Miguel Angel Garcia-March, J. Alberto Conejero, Francisco Escolano and Nuria Oliver.
- Best Student Data Mining Paper Award: "Conditional Neural Relational Inference for Interacting Systems", by Joao Candido Ramos, Lionel Blondé, Stéphane Armand and Alexandros Kalousis.
- Test of Time Award for highest-impact paper from ECML PKDD 2011: "Influence and Passivity in Social Media", by Daniel M. Romero, Wojciech Galuba, Sitaram Asur and Bernardo A. Huberman.

We would like to wholeheartedly thank all participants, authors, Program Committee members, area chairs, session chairs, volunteers, co-organizers, and organizers of workshops and tutorials for their contributions that helped make ECML PKDD 2021 a great success. We would also like to thank the ECML PKDD Steering Committee and all sponsors.

September 2021

Jose A. Lozano
Nuria Oliver
Fernando Pérez-Cruz
Stefan Kramer
Jesse Read
Yuxiao Dong
Nicolas Kourtellis
Barbara Hammer

Organization

General Chair

Jose A. Lozano   Basque Center for Applied Mathematics, Spain

Research Track Program Chairs

Nuria Oliver   Vodafone Institute for Society and Communications,
         Germany, and Data-Pop Alliance, USA
Fernando Pérez-Cruz   Swiss Data Science Center, Switzerland
Stefan Kramer   Johannes Gutenberg Universität Mainz, Germany
Jesse Read   École Polytechnique, France

Applied Data Science Track Program Chairs

Yuxiao Dong   Facebook AI, Seattle, USA
Nicolas Kourtellis   Telefonica Research, Barcelona, Spain
Barbara Hammer   Bielefeld University, Germany

Journal Track Chairs

Sergio Escalera   Universitat de Barcelona, Spain
Heike Trautmann   University of Münster, Germany
Annalisa Appice   Università degli Studi di Bari, Italy
Jose A. Gámez   Universidad de Castilla-La Mancha, Spain

Discovery Challenge Chairs

Paula Brito   Universidade do Porto, Portugal
Dino Ienco   Université Montpellier, France

Workshop and Tutorial Chairs

Alipio Jorge   Universidade do Porto, Portugal
Yun Sing Koh   University of Auckland, New Zealand

Industrial Track Chairs

Miguel Veganzones   Sherpa.ia, Portugal
Sabri Skhiri   EURA NOVA, Belgium

Award Chairs

Myra Spiliopoulou   Otto-von-Guericke-University Magdeburg, Germany
João Gama   University of Porto, Portugal

PhD Forum Chairs

Jeronimo Hernandez   University of Barcelona, Spain
Zahra Ahmadi   Johannes Gutenberg Universität Mainz, Germany

Production, Publicity, and Public Relations Chairs

Sophie Burkhardt   Johannes Gutenberg Universität Mainz, Germany
Julia Sidorova   Universidad Complutense de Madrid, Spain

Local Chairs

Iñaki Inza   University of the Basque Country, Spain
Alexander Mendiburu   University of the Basque Country, Spain
Santiago Mazuelas   Basque Center for Applied Mathematics, Spain
Aritz Pèrez   Basque Center for Applied Mathematics, Spain
Borja Calvo   University of the Basque Country, Spain

Proceedings Chair

Tania Cerquitelli   Politecnico di Torino, Italy

Sponsorship Chair

Santiago Mazuelas   Basque Center for Applied Mathematics, Spain

Web Chairs

Olatz Hernandez   Basque Center for Applied Mathematics, Spain
   Aretxabaleta
Estíbaliz Gutièrrez   Basque Center for Applied Mathematics, Spain

ECML PKDD Steering Committee

Andrea Passerini   University of Trento, Italy
Francesco Bonchi   ISI Foundation, Italy
Albert Bifet   Télécom ParisTech, France
Sašo Džeroski   Jožef Stefan Institute, Slovenia
Katharina Morik   TU Dortmund, Germany
Arno Siebes   Utrecht University, The Netherlands
Siegfried Nijssen   Université Catholique de Louvain, Belgium

Luís Moreira-Matias	Finiata GmbH, Germany
Alessandra Sala	Shutterstock, Ireland
Georgiana Ifrim	University College Dublin, Ireland
Thomas Gärtner	University of Nottingham, UK
Neil Hurley	University College Dublin, Ireland
Michele Berlingerio	IBM Research, Ireland
Elisa Fromont	Université de Rennes, France
Arno Knobbe	Universiteit Leiden, The Netherlands
Ulf Brefeld	Leuphana Universität Lüneburg, Germany
Andreas Hotho	Julius-Maximilians-Universität Würzburg, Germany
Ira Assent	Aarhus University, Denmark
Kristian Kersting	TU Darmstadt University, Germany
Jefrey Lijffijt	Ghent University, Belgium
Isabel Valera	Saarland University, Germany

Program Committee

Guest Editorial Board, Journal Track

Richard Allmendinger	University of Manchester
Marie Anastacio	Leiden University
Ana Paula Appel	IBM Research Brazil
Dennis Assenmacher	University of Münster
Ira Assent	Aarhus University
Martin Atzmueller	Osnabrueck University
Jaume Bacardit	Newcastle University
Anthony Bagnall	University of East Anglia
Mitra Baratchi	University of Twente
Srikanta Bedathur	IIT Delhi
Alessio Benavoli	CSIS
Viktor Bengs	Paderborn University
Massimo Bilancia	University of Bari "Aldo Moro"
Klemens Böhm	Karlsruhe Institute of Technology
Veronica Bolon Canedo	Universidade da Coruna
Ilaria Bordino	UniCredit R&D
Jakob Bossek	University of Adelaide
Ulf Brefeld	Leuphana Universität Luneburg
Michelangelo Ceci	Universita degli Studi di Bari "Aldo Moro"
Loïc Cerf	Universidade Federal de Minas Gerais
Victor Manuel Cerqueira	University of Porto
Laetitia Chapel	IRISA
Silvia Chiusano	Politecnico di Torino
Roberto Corizzo	American University, Washington D.C.
Marco de Gemmis	Università degli Studi di Bari "Aldo Moro"
Sébastien Destercke	Università degli Studi di Bari "Aldo Moro"
Shridhar Devamane	Visvesvaraya Technological University

Carlotta Domeniconi	George Mason University
Wouter Duivesteijn	Eindhoven University of Technology
Tapio Elomaa	Tampere University of Technology
Hugo Jair Escalante	INAOE
Nicola Fanizzi	Università degli Studi di Bari "Aldo Moro"
Stefano Ferilli	Università degli Studi di Bari "Aldo Moro"
Pedro Ferreira	Universidade de Lisboa
Cesar Ferri	Valencia Polytechnic University
Julia Flores	University of Castilla-La Mancha
Germain Forestier	Université de Haute Alsace
Marco Frasca	University of Milan
Ricardo J. G. B. Campello	University of Newcastle
Esther Galbrun	University of Eastern Finland
João Gama	University of Porto
Paolo Garza	Politecnico di Torino
Pascal Germain	Université Laval
Fabian Gieseke	University of Münster
Josif Grabocka	University of Hildesheim
Gianluigi Greco	University of Calabria
Riccardo Guidotti	University of Pisa
Francesco Gullo	UniCredit
Stephan Günnemann	Technical University of Munich
Tias Guns	Vrije Universiteit Brussel
Antonella Guzzo	University of Calabria
Alexander Hagg	Hochschule Bonn-Rhein-Sieg University of Applied Sciences
Jin-Kao Hao	University of Angers
Daniel Hernández-Lobato	Universidad Autónoma de Madrid
Jose Hernández-Orallo	Universitat Politècnica de València
Martin Holena	Institute of Computer Science, Academy of Sciences of the Czech Republic
Jaakko Hollmén	Aalto University
Dino Ienco	IRSTEA
Georgiana Ifrim	University College Dublin
Felix Iglesias	TU Wien
Angelo Impedovo	University of Bari "Aldo Moro"
Mahdi Jalili	RMIT University
Nathalie Japkowicz	University of Ottawa
Szymon Jaroszewicz	Institute of Computer Science, Polish Academy of Sciences
Michael Kamp	Monash University
Mehdi Kaytoue	Infologic
Pascal Kerschke	University of Münster
Dragi Kocev	Jozef Stefan Institute
Lars Kotthoff	University of Wyoming
Tipaluck Krityakierne	University of Bern

Peer Kröger	Ludwig Maximilian University of Munich
Meelis Kull	University of Tartu
Michel Lang	TU Dortmund University
Helge Langseth	Norwegian University of Science and Technology
Oswald Lanz	FBK
Mark Last	Ben-Gurion University of the Negev
Kangwook Lee	University of Wisconsin-Madison
Jurica Levatic	IRB Barcelona
Thomar Liebig	TU Dortmund
Hsuan-Tien Lin	National Taiwan University
Marius Lindauer	Leibniz University Hannover
Marco Lippi	University of Modena and Reggio Emilia
Corrado Loglisci	Università degli Studi di Bari
Manuel Lopez-Ibanez	University of Malaga
Nuno Lourenço	University of Coimbra
Claudio Lucchese	Ca' Foscari University of Venice
Brian Mac Namee	University College Dublin
Gjorgji Madjarov	Ss. Cyril and Methodius University
Davide Maiorca	University of Cagliari
Giuseppe Manco	ICAR-CNR
Elena Marchiori	Radboud University
Elio Masciari	Università di Napoli Federico II
Andres R. Masegosa	Norwegian University of Science and Technology
Ernestina Menasalvas	Universidad Politécnica de Madrid
Rosa Meo	University of Torino
Paolo Mignone	University of Bari "Aldo Moro"
Anna Monreale	University of Pisa
Giovanni Montana	University of Warwick
Grègoire Montavon	TU Berlin
Katharina Morik	TU Dortmund
Animesh Mukherjee	Indian Institute of Technology, Kharagpur
Amedeo Napoli	LORIA Nancy
Frank Naumann	University of Adelaide
Thomas Dyhre	Aalborg University
Bruno Ordozgoiti	Aalto University
Rita P. Ribeiro	University of Porto
Pance Panov	Jozef Stefan Institute
Apostolos Papadopoulos	Aristotle University of Thessaloniki
Panagiotis Papapetrou	Stockholm University
Andrea Passerini	University of Trento
Mykola Pechenizkiy	Eindhoven University of Technology
Charlotte Pelletier	Université Bretagne Sud
Ruggero G. Pensa	University of Torino
Nico Piatkowski	TU Dortmund
Dario Piga	IDSIA Dalle Molle Institute for Artificial Intelligence Research - USI/SUPSI

Gianvito Pio	Università degli Studi di Bari "Aldo Moro"
Marc Plantevit	LIRIS - Université Claude Bernard Lyon 1
Marius Popescu	University of Bucharest
Raphael Prager	University of Münster
Mike Preuss	Universiteit Leiden
Jose M. Puerta	Universidad de Castilla-La Mancha
Kai Puolamäki	University of Helsinki
Chedy Raïssi	Inria
Jan Ramon	Inria
Matteo Riondato	Amherst College
Thomas A. Runkler	Siemens Corporate Technology
Antonio Salmerón	University of Almería
Joerg Sander	University of Alberta
Roberto Santana	University of the Basque Country
Michael Schaub	RWTH Aachen
Lars Schmidt-Thieme	University of Hildesheim
Santiago Segui	Universitat de Barcelona
Thomas Seidl	Ludwig-Maximilians-Universitaet Muenchen
Moritz Seiler	University of Münster
Shinichi Shirakawa	Yokohama National University
Jim Smith	University of the West of England
Carlos Soares	University of Porto
Gerasimos Spanakis	Maastricht University
Giancarlo Sperlì	University of Naples Federico II
Myra Spiliopoulou	Otto-von-Guericke-University Magdeburg
Giovanni Stilo	Università degli Studi dell'Aquila
Catalin Stoean	University of Craiova
Mahito Sugiyama	National Institute of Informatics
Nikolaj Tatti	University of Helsinki
Alexandre Termier	Université de Rennes 1
Kevin Tierney	Bielefeld University
Luis Torgo	University of Porto
Roberto Trasarti	CNR Pisa
Sébastien Treguer	Inria
Leonardo Trujillo	Instituto Tecnológico de Tijuana
Ivor Tsang	University of Technology Sydney
Grigorios Tsoumakas	Aristotle University of Thessaloniki
Steffen Udluft	Siemens
Arnaud Vandaele	Université de Mons
Matthijs van Leeuwen	Leiden University
Celine Vens	KU Leuven Kulak
Herna Viktor	University of Ottawa
Marco Virgolin	Centrum Wiskunde & Informatica
Jordi Vitrià	Universitat de Barcelona
Christel Vrain	LIFO – University of Orléans
Jilles Vreeken	Helmholtz Center for Information Security

Willem Waegeman	Ghent University
David Walker	University of Plymouth
Hao Wang	Leiden University
Elizabeth F. Wanner	CEFET
Tu Wei-Wei	4paradigm
Pascal Welke	University of Bonn
Marcel Wever	Paderborn University
Man Leung Wong	Lingnan University
Stefan Wrobel	Fraunhofer IAIS, University of Bonn
Zheng Ying	Inria
Guoxian Yu	Shandong University
Xiang Zhang	Harvard University
Ye Zhu	Deakin University
Arthur Zimek	University of Southern Denmark
Albrecht Zimmermann	Université Caen Normandie
Marinka Zitnik	Harvard University

Area Chairs, Research Track

Fabrizio Angiulli	University of Calabria
Ricardo Baeza-Yates	Universitat Pompeu Fabra
Roberto Bayardo	Google
Bettina Berendt	Katholieke Universiteit Leuven
Philipp Berens	University of Tübingen
Michael Berthold	University of Konstanz
Hendrik Blockeel	Katholieke Universiteit Leuven
Juergen Branke	University of Warwick
Ulf Brefeld	Leuphana University Lüneburg
Toon Calders	Universiteit Antwerpen
Michelangelo Ceci	Università degli Studi di Bari "Aldo Moro"
Duen Horng Chau	Georgia Institute of Technology
Nicolas Courty	Université Bretagne Sud, IRISA Research Institute Computer and Systems Aléatoires
Bruno Cremilleux	Université de Caen Normandie
Philippe Cudre-Mauroux	University of Fribourg
James Cussens	University of Bristol
Jesse Davis	Katholieke Universiteit Leuven
Bob Durrant	University of Waikato
Tapio Elomaa	Tampere University
Johannes Fürnkranz	Johannes Kepler University Linz
Eibe Frank	University of Waikato
Elisa Fromont	Université de Rennes 1
Stephan Günnemann	Technical University of Munich
Patrick Gallinari	LIP6 - University of Paris
Joao Gama	University of Porto
Przemyslaw Grabowicz	University of Massachusetts, Amherst

Eyke Hüllermeier	Paderborn University
Allan Hanbury	Vienna University of Technology
Daniel Hernández-Lobato	Universidad Autónoma de Madrid
José Hernández-Orallo	Universitat Politècnica de València
Andreas Hotho	University of Wuerzburg
Inaki Inza	University of the Basque Country
Marius Kloft	TU Kaiserslautern
Arno Knobbe	Universiteit Leiden
Lars Kotthoff	University of Wyoming
Danica Kragic	KTH Royal Institute of Technology
Sébastien Lefèvre	Université Bretagne Sud
Bruno Lepri	FBK-Irst
Patrick Loiseau	Inria and Ecole Polytechnique
Jorg Lucke	University of Oldenburg
Fragkiskos Malliaros	Paris-Saclay University, CentraleSupelec, and Inria
Giuseppe Manco	ICAR-CNR
Dunja Mladenic	Jozef Stefan Institute
Katharina Morik	TU Dortmund
Sriraam Natarajan	Indiana University Bloomington
Siegfried Nijssen	Université catholique de Louvain
Andrea Passerini	University of Trento
Mykola Pechenizkiy	Eindhoven University of Technology
Jaakko Peltonen	Aalto University and University of Tampere
Marian-Andrei Rizoiu	University of Technology Sydney
Céline Robardet	INSA Lyon
Maja Rudolph	Bosch
Lars Schmidt-Thieme	University of Hildesheim
Thomas Seidl	Ludwig-Maximilians-Universität München
Arno Siebes	Utrecht University
Myra Spiliopoulou	Otto-von-Guericke-University Magdeburg
Yizhou Sun	University of California, Los Angeles
Einoshin Suzuki	Kyushu University
Jie Tang	Tsinghua University
Ke Tang	Southern University of Science and Technology
Marc Tommasi	University of Lille
Isabel Valera	Saarland University
Celine Vens	KU Leuven Kulak
Christel Vrain	LIFO - University of Orléans
Jilles Vreeken	Helmholtz Center for Information Security
Willem Waegeman	Ghent University
Stefan Wrobel	Fraunhofer IAIS, University of Bonn
Min-Ling Zhang	Southeast University

Area Chairs, Applied Data Science Track

Francesco Calabrese	Vodafone
Michelangelo Ceci	Università degli Studi di Bari "Aldo Moro"
Gianmarco De Francisci Morales	ISI Foundation
Tom Diethe	Amazon
Johannes Frünkranz	Johannes Kepler University Linz
Han Fang	Facebook
Faisal Farooq	Qatar Computing Research Institute
Rayid Ghani	Carnegie Mellon Univiersity
Francesco Gullo	UniCredit
Xiangnan He	University of Science and Technology of China
Georgiana Ifrim	University College Dublin
Thorsten Jungeblut	Bielefeld University of Applied Sciences
John A. Lee	Université catholique de Louvain
Ilias Leontiadis	Samsung AI
Viktor Losing	Honda Research Institute Europe
Yin Lou	Ant Group
Gabor Melli	Sony PlayStation
Luis Moreira-Matias	University of Porto
Nicolò Navarin	University of Padova
Benjamin Paaßen	German Research Center for Artificial Intelligence
Kitsuchart Pasupa	King Mongkut's Institute of Technology Ladkrabang
Mykola Pechenizkiy	Eindhoven University of Technology
Julien Perez	Naver Labs Europe
Fabio Pinelli	IMT Lucca
Zhaochun Ren	Shandong University
Sascha Saralajew	Porsche AG
Fabrizio Silvestri	Facebook
Sinong Wang	Facebook AI
Xing Xie	Microsoft Research Asia
Jian Xu	Citadel
Jing Zhang	Renmin University of China

Program Committee Members, Research Track

Hanno Ackermann	Leibniz University Hannover
Linara Adilova	Fraunhofer IAIS
Zahra Ahmadi	Johannes Gutenberg University
Cuneyt Gurcan Akcora	University of Manitoba
Omer Deniz Akyildiz	University of Warwick
Carlos M. Alaíz Gudín	Universidad Autónoma de Madrid
Mohamed Alami	Ecole Polytechnique
Chehbourne Abdullah Alchihabi	Carleton University
Pegah Alizadeh	University of Caen Normandy

Reem Alotaibi	King Abdulaziz University
Massih-Reza Amini	Université Grenoble Alpes
Shin Ando	Tokyo University of Science
Thiago Andrade	INESC TEC
Kimon Antonakopoulos	Inria
Alessandro Antonucci	IDSIA
Muhammad Umer Anwaar	Technical University of Munich
Eva Armengol	IIIA-SIC
Dennis Assenmacher	University of Münster
Matthias Aßenmacher	Ludwig-Maximilians-Universität München
Martin Atzmueller	Osnabrueck University
Behrouz Babaki	Polytechnique Montreal
Rohit Babbar	Aalto University
Elena Baralis	Politecnico di Torino
Mitra Baratchi	University of Twente
Christian Bauckhage	University of Bonn, Fraunhofer IAIS
Martin Becker	University of Würzburg
Jessa Bekker	Katholieke Universiteit Leuven
Colin Bellinger	National Research Council of Canada
Khalid Benabdeslem	LIRIS Laboratory, Claude Bernard University Lyon I
Diana Benavides-Prado	Auckland University of Technology
Anes Bendimerad	LIRIS
Christoph Bergmeir	University of Granada
Alexander Binder	UiO
Aleksandar Bojchevski	Technical University of Munich
Ahcène Boubekki	UiT Arctic University of Norway
Paula Branco	EECS University of Ottawa
Tanya Braun	University of Lübeck
Katharina Breininger	Friedrich-Alexander-Universität Erlangen Nürnberg
Wieland Brendel	University of Tübingen
John Burden	University of Cambridge
Sophie Burkhardt	TU Kaiserslautern
Sebastian Buschjäger	TU Dortmund
Borja Calvo	University of the Basque Country
Stephane Canu	LITIS, INSA de Rouen
Cornelia Caragea	University of Illinois at Chicago
Paula Carroll	University College Dublin
Giuseppe Casalicchio	Ludwig Maximilian University of Munich
Bogdan Cautis	Paris-Saclay University
Rémy Cazabet	Université de Lyon
Josu Ceberio	University of the Basque Country
Peggy Cellier	IRISA/INSA Rennes
Mattia Cerrato	Università degli Studi di Torino
Ricardo Cerri	Federal University of Sao Carlos
Alessandra Cervone	Amazon
Ayman Chaouki	Institut Mines-Télécom

Paco Charte	Universidad de Jaén
Rita Chattopadhyay	Intel Corporation
Vaggos Chatziafratis	Stanford University
Tianyi Chen	Zhejiang University City College
Yuzhou Chen	Southern Methodist University
Yiu-Ming Cheung	Hong Kong Baptist University
Anshuman Chhabra	University of California, Davis
Ting-Wu Chin	Carnegie Mellon University
Oana Cocarascu	King's College London
Lidia Contreras-Ochando	Universitat Politècnica de València
Roberto Corizzo	American University
Anna Helena Reali Costa	Universidade de São Paulo
Fabrizio Costa	University of Exeter
Gustavo De Assis Costa	Instituto Federal de Educação, Ciência e Tecnologia de Goiás
Bertrand Cuissart	GREYC
Thi-Bich-Hanh Dao	University of Orleans
Mayukh Das	Microsoft Research Lab
Padraig Davidson	Universität Würzburg
Paul Davidsson	Malmö University
Gwendoline De Bie	ENS
Tijl De Bie	Ghent University
Andre de Carvalho	Universidade de São Paulo
Orphée De Clercq	Ghent University
Alper Demir	İzmir University of Economics
Nicola Di Mauro	Università degli Studi di Bari "Aldo Moro"
Yao-Xiang Ding	Nanjing University
Carola Doerr	Sorbonne University
Boxiang Dong	Montclair State University
Ruihai Dong	University College Dublin
Xin Du	Eindhoven University of Technology
Stefan Duffner	LIRIS
Wouter Duivesteijn	Eindhoven University of Technology
Audrey Durand	McGill University
Inês Dutra	University of Porto
Saso Dzeroski	Jozef Stefan Institute
Hamid Eghbalzadeh	Johannes Kepler University
Dominik Endres	University of Marburg
Roberto Esposito	Università degli Studi di Torino
Samuel G. Fadel	Universidade Estadual de Campinas
Xiuyi Fan	Imperial College London
Hadi Fanaee-T.	Halmstad University
Elaine Faria	Federal University of Uberlandia
Fabio Fassetti	University of Calabria
Kilian Fatras	Inria
Ad Feelders	Utrecht University

Songhe Feng	Beijing Jiaotong University
Àngela Fernández-Pascual	Universidad Autónoma de Madrid
Daniel Fernández-Sánchez	Universidad Autónoma de Madrid
Sofia Fernandes	University of Aveiro
Cesar Ferri	Universitat Politécnica de Valéncia
Rémi Flamary	École Polytechnique
Michael Flynn	University of East Anglia
Germain Forestier	Université de Haute Alsace
Kary Främling	Umeå University
Benoît Frénay	Université de Namur
Vincent Francois	University of Amsterdam
Emilia Gómez	Joint Research Centre - European Commission
Luis Galárraga	Inria
Esther Galbrun	University of Eastern Finland
Claudio Gallicchio	University of Pisa
Jochen Garcke	University of Bonn
Clément Gautrais	KU Leuven
Yulia Gel	University of Texas at Dallas and University of Waterloo
Pierre Geurts	University of Liège
Amirata Ghorbani	Stanford University
Heitor Murilo Gomes	University of Waikato
Chen Gong	Shanghai Jiao Tong University
Bedartha Goswami	University of Tübingen
Henry Gouk	University of Edinburgh
James Goulding	University of Nottingham
Antoine Gourru	Université Lumière Lyon 2
Massimo Guarascio	ICAR-CNR
Riccardo Guidotti	University of Pisa
Ekta Gujral	University of California, Riverside
Francesco Gullo	UniCredit
Tias Guns	Vrije Universiteit Brussel
Thomas Guyet	Institut Agro, IRISA
Tom Hanika	University of Kassel
Valentin Hartmann	Ecole Polytechnique Fédérale de Lausanne
Marwan Hassani	Eindhoven University of Technology
Jukka Heikkonen	University of Turku
Fredrik Heintz	Linköping University
Sibylle Hess	TU Eindhoven
Jaakko Hollmén	Aalto University
Tamas Horvath	University of Bonn, Fraunhofer IAIS
Binbin Hu	Ant Group
Hong Huang	UGoe
Georgiana Ifrim	University College Dublin
Angelo Impedovo	Università degli studi di Bari "Aldo Moro"

Nathalie Japkowicz	American University
Szymon Jaroszewicz	Institute of Computer Science, Polish Academy of Sciences
Saumya Jetley	Inria
Binbin Jia	Southeast University
Xiuyi Jia	School of Computer Science and Technology, Nanjing University of Science and Technology
Yuheng Jia	City University of Hong Kong
Siyang Jiang	National Taiwan University
Priyadarshini Kumari	IIT Bombay
Ata Kaban	University of Birmingham
Tomasz Kajdanowicz	Wroclaw University of Technology
Vana Kalogeraki	Athens University of Economics and Business
Toshihiro Kamishima	National Institute of Advanced Industrial Science and Technology
Michael Kamp	Monash University
Bo Kang	Ghent University
Dimitrios Karapiperis	Hellenic Open University
Panagiotis Karras	Aarhus University
George Karypis	University of Minnesota
Mark Keane	University College Dublin
Kristian Kersting	TU Darmstadt
Masahiro Kimura	Ryukoku University
Jiri Klema	Czech Technical University
Dragi Kocev	Jozef Stefan Institute
Masahiro Kohjima	NTT
Lukasz Korycki	Virginia Commonwealth University
Peer Kröger	Ludwig Maximilian University of München
Anna Krause	University of Würzburg
Bartosz Krawczyk	Virginia Commonwealth University
Georg Krempl	Utrecht University
Meelis Kull	University of Tartu
Vladimir Kuzmanovski	Aalto University
Ariel Kwiatkowski	Ecole Polytechnique
Emanuele La Malfa	University of Oxford
Beatriz López	University of Girona
Preethi Lahoti	Aalto University
Ichraf Lahouli	Euranova
Niklas Lavesson	Jönköping University
Aonghus Lawlor	University College Dublin
Jeongmin Lee	University of Pittsburgh
Daniel Lemire	LICEF Research Center and Université du Québec
Florian Lemmerich	University of Passau
Elisabeth Lex	Graz University of Technology
Jiani Li	Vanderbilt University
Rui Li	Inspur Group
Wentong Liao	Lebniz University Hannover

Jiayin Lin	University of Wollongong
Rudolf Lioutikov	UT Austin
Marco Lippi	University of Modena and Reggio Emilia
Suzanne Little	Dublin City University
Shengcai Liu	University of Science and Technology of China
Shenghua Liu	Institute of Computing Technology, Chinese Academy of Sciences
Philipp Liznerski	Technische Universität Kaiserslautern
Corrado Loglisci	Università degli Studi di Bari "Aldo Moro"
Ting Long	Shanghai Jiaotong University
Tsai-Ching Lu	HRL Laboratories
Yunpu Ma	Siemens AG
Zichen Ma	The Chinese University of Hong Kong
Sara Madeira	Universidade de Lisboa
Simona Maggio	Dataiku
Sara Magliacane	IBM
Sebastian Mair	Leuphana University Lüneburg
Lorenzo Malandri	University of Milan Bicocca
Donato Malerba	Università degli Studi di Bari "Aldo Moro"
Pekka Malo	Aalto University
Robin Manhaeve	KU Leuven
Silviu Maniu	Université Paris-Sud
Giuseppe Marra	KU Leuven
Fernando Martínez-Plumed	Joint Research Centre - European Commission
Alexander Marx	Max Plank Institue for Informatics and Saarland University
Florent Masseglia	Inria
Tetsu Matsukawa	Kyushu University
Wolfgang Mayer	University of South Australia
Santiago Mazuelas	Basque center for Applied Mathematics
Stefano Melacci	University of Siena
Ernestina Menasalvas	Universidad Politécnica de Madrid
Rosa Meo	Università degli Studi di Torino
Alberto Maria Metelli	Politecnico di Milano
Saskia Metzler	Max Planck Institute for Informatics
Alessio Micheli	University of Pisa
Paolo Mignone	Università degli studi di Bari "Aldo Moro"
Matej Mihelčić	University of Zagreb
Decebal Constantin Mocanu	University of Twente
Nuno Moniz	INESC TEC and University of Porto
Carlos Monserrat	Universitat Politécnica de Valéncia
Corrado Monti	ISI Foundation
Jacob Montiel	University of Waikato
Ahmadreza Mosallanezhad	Arizona State University
Tanmoy Mukherjee	University of Tennessee
Martin Mundt	Goethe University

Mohamed Nadif	Université de Paris
Omer Nagar	Bar Ilan University
Felipe Kenji Nakano	Katholieke Universiteit Leuven
Mirco Nanni	KDD-Lab ISTI-CNR Pisa
Apurva Narayan	University of Waterloo
Nicolò Navarin	University of Padova
Benjamin Negrevergne	Paris Dauphine University
Hurley Neil	University College Dublin
Stefan Neumann	University of Vienna
Ngoc-Tri Ngo	The University of Danang - University of Science and Technology
Dai Nguyen	Monash University
Eirini Ntoutsi	Free University Berlin
Andrea Nuernberger	Otto-von-Guericke-Universität Magdeburg
Pablo Olmos	University Carlos III
James O'Neill	University of Liverpool
Barry O'Sullivan	University College Cork
Rita P. Ribeiro	University of Porto
Aritz Pèrez	Basque Center for Applied Mathematics
Joao Palotti	Qatar Computing Research Institute
Guansong Pang	University of Adelaide
Pance Panov	Jozef Stefan Institute
Evangelos Papalexakis	University of California, Riverside
Haekyu Park	Georgia Institute of Technology
Sudipta Paul	Umeå University
Yulong Pei	Eindhoven University of Technology
Charlotte Pelletier	Université Bretagne Sud
Ruggero G. Pensa	University of Torino
Bryan Perozzi	Google
Nathanael Perraudin	ETH Zurich
Lukas Pfahler	TU Dortmund
Bastian Pfeifer	Medical University of Graz
Nico Piatkowski	TU Dortmund
Robert Pienta	Georgia Institute of Technology
Fábio Pinto	Faculdade de Economia do Porto
Gianvito Pio	University of Bari "Aldo Moro"
Giuseppe Pirrò	Sapienza University of Rome
Claudia Plant	University of Vienna
Marc Plantevit	LIRIS - Universitè Claude Bernard Lyon 1
Amit Portnoy	Ben Gurion University
Melanie Pradier	Harvard University
Paul Prasse	University of Potsdam
Philippe Preux	Inria, LIFL, Universitè de Lille
Ricardo Prudencio	Federal University of Pernambuco
Zhou Qifei	Peking University
Erik Quaeghebeur	TU Eindhoven

Tahrima Rahman	University of Texas at Dallas
Herilalaina Rakotoarison	Inria
Alexander Rakowski	Hasso Plattner Institute
María José Ramírez	Universitat Politècnica de València
Visvanathan Ramesh	Goethe University
Jan Ramon	Inria
Huzefa Rangwala	George Mason University
Aleksandra Rashkovska	Jožef Stefan Institute
Joe Redshaw	University of Nottingham
Matthias Renz	Christian-Albrechts-Universität zu Kiel
Matteo Riondato	Amherst College
Ettore Ritacco	ICAR-CNR
Mateus Riva	Télécom ParisTech
Antonio Rivera	Universidad Politécnica de Madrid
Marko Robnik-Sikonja	University of Ljubljana
Simon Rodriguez Santana	Institute of Mathematical Sciences (ICMAT-CSIC)
Mohammad Rostami	University of Southern California
Céline Rouveirol	Laboratoire LIPN-UMR CNRS
Jože Rožanec	Jožef Stefan Institute
Peter Rubbens	Flanders Marine Institute
David Ruegamer	LMU Munich
Salvatore Ruggieri	Università di Pisa
Francisco Ruiz	DeepMind
Anne Sabourin	Télécom ParisTech
Tapio Salakoski	University of Turku
Pablo Sanchez-Martin	Max Planck Institute for Intelligent Systems
Emanuele Sansone	KU Leuven
Yucel Saygin	Sabanci University
Patrick Schäfer	Humboldt Universität zu Berlin
Pierre Schaus	UCLouvain
Ute Schmid	University of Bamberg
Sebastian Schmoll	Ludwig Maximilian University of Munich
Marc Schoenauer	Inria
Matthias Schubert	Ludwig Maximilian University of Munich
Marian Scuturici	LIRIS-INSA de Lyon
Junming Shao	University of Science and Technology of China
Manali Sharma	Samsung Semiconductor Inc.
Abdul Saboor Sheikh	Zalando Research
Jacquelyn Shelton	Hong Kong Polytechnic University
Feihong Shen	Jilin University
Gavin Smith	University of Nottingham
Kma Solaiman	Purdue University
Arnaud Soulet	Université François Rabelais Tours
Alessandro Sperduti	University of Padua
Giovanni Stilo	Università degli Studi dell'Aquila
Michiel Stock	Ghent University

Lech Szymanski	University of Otago
Shazia Tabassum	University of Porto
Andrea Tagarelli	University of Calabria
Acar Tamersoy	NortonLifeLock Research Group
Chang Wei Tan	Monash University
Sasu Tarkoma	University of Helsinki
Bouadi Tassadit	IRISA-Université Rennes 1
Nikolaj Tatti	University of Helsinki
Maryam Tavakol	Eindhoven University of Technology
Pooya Tavallali	University of California, Los Angeles
Maguelonne Teisseire	Irstea - UMR Tetis
Alexandre Termier	Université de Rennes 1
Stefano Teso	University of Trento
Janek Thomas	Fraunhofer Institute for Integrated Circuits IIS
Alessandro Tibo	Aalborg University
Sofia Triantafillou	University of Pittsburgh
Grigorios Tsoumakas	Aristotle University of Thessaloniki
Peter van der Putten	LIACS, Leiden University and Pegasystems
Elia Van Wolputte	KU Leuven
Robert A. Vandermeulen	Technische Universität Berlin
Fabio Vandin	University of Padova
Filipe Veiga	Massachusetts Institute of Technology
Bruno Veloso	Universidade Portucalense and LIAAD - INESC TEC
Sebastián Ventura	University of Cordoba
Rosana Veroneze	UNICAMP
Herna Viktor	University of Ottawa
João Vinagre	INESC TEC
Huaiyu Wan	Beijing Jiaotong University
Beilun Wang	Southeast University
Hu Wang	University of Adelaide
Lun Wang	University of California, Berkeley
Yu Wang	Peking University
Zijie J. Wang	Georgia Tech
Tong Wei	Nanjing University
Pascal Welke	University of Bonn
Joerg Wicker	University of Auckland
Moritz Wolter	University of Bonn
Ning Xu	Southeast University
Akihiro Yamaguchi	Toshiba Corporation
Haitian Yang	Institute of Information Engineering, Chinese Academy of Sciences
Yang Yang	Nanjing University
Zhuang Yang	Sun Yat-sen University
Helen Yannakoudakis	King's College London
Heng Yao	Tongji University
Han-Jia Ye	Nanjing University

Kristina Yordanova	University of Rostock
Tetsuya Yoshida	Nara Women's University
Guoxian Yu	Shandong University, China
Sha Yuan	Tsinghua University
Valentina Zantedeschi	INSA Lyon
Albin Zehe	University of Würzburg
Bob Zhang	University of Macau
Teng Zhang	Huazhong University of Science and Technology
Liang Zhao	University of São Paulo
Bingxin Zhou	University of Sydney
Kenny Zhu	Shanghai Jiao Tong University
Yanqiao Zhu	Institute of Automation, Chinese Academy of Sciences
Arthur Zimek	University of Southern Denmark
Albrecht Zimmermann	Université Caen Normandie
Indre Zliobaite	University of Helsinki
Markus Zopf	NEC Labs Europe

Program Committee Members, Applied Data Science Track

Mahdi Abolghasemi	Monash University
Evrim Acar	Simula Research Lab
Deepak Ajwani	University College Dublin
Pegah Alizadeh	University of Caen Normandy
Jean-Marc Andreoli	Naver Labs Europe
Giorgio Angelotti	ISAE Supaero
Stefanos Antaris	KTH Royal Institute of Technology
Xiang Ao	Institute of Computing Technology, Chinese Academy of Sciences
Yusuf Arslan	University of Luxembourg
Cristian Axenie	Huawei European Research Center
Hanane Azzag	Université Sorbonne Paris Nord
Pedro Baiz	Imperial College London
Idir Benouaret	CNRS, Université Grenoble Alpes
Laurent Besacier	Laboratoire d'Informatique de Grenoble
Antonio Bevilacqua	Insight Centre for Data Analytics
Adrien Bibal	University of Namur
Wu Bin	Zhengzhou University
Patrick Blöbaum	Amazon
Pavel Blinov	Sber Artificial Intelligence Laboratory
Ludovico Boratto	University of Cagliari
Stefano Bortoli	Huawei Technologies Duesseldorf
Zekun Cai	University of Tokyo
Nicolas Carrara	University of Toronto
John Cartlidge	University of Bristol
Oded Cats	Delft University of Technology
Tania Cerquitelli	Politecnico di Torino

Prithwish Chakraborty   IBM
Rita Chattopadhyay   Intel Corp.
Keru Chen   GrabTaxi Pte Ltd.
Liang Chen   Sun Yat-sen University
Zhiyong Cheng   Shandong Artificial Intelligence Institute
Silvia Chiusano   Politecnico di Torino
Minqi Chong   Citadel
Jeremie Clos   University of Nottingham
J. Albert Conejero Casares   Universitat Politécnica de Vaécia
Evan Crothers   University of Ottawa
Henggang Cui   Uber ATG
Tiago Cunha   University of Porto
Padraig Cunningham   University College Dublin
Eustache Diemert   CRITEO Research
Nat Dilokthanakul   Vidyasirimedhi Institute of Science and Technology
Daizong Ding   Fudan University
Kaize Ding   ASU
Michele Donini   Amazon
Lukas Ewecker   Porsche AG
Zipei Fan   University of Tokyo
Bojing Feng   National Laboratory of Pattern Recognition, Institute of Automation, Chinese Academy of Science
Flavio Figueiredo   Universidade Federal de Minas Gerais
Blaz Fortuna   Qlector d.o.o.
Zuohui Fu   Rutgers University
Fabio Fumarola   University of Bari "Aldo Moro"
Chen Gao   Tsinghua University
Luis Garcia   University of Brasília
Cinmayii Garillos-Manliguez   University of the Philippines Mindanao
Kiran Garimella   Aalto University
Etienne Goffinet   Laboratoire LIPN-UMR CNRS
Michael Granitzer   University of Passau
Xinyu Guan   Xi'an Jiaotong University
Thomas Guyet   Institut Agro, IRISA
Massinissa Hamidi   Laboratoire LIPN-UMR CNRS
Junheng Hao   University of California, Los Angeles
Martina Hasenjaeger   Honda Research Institute Europe GmbH
Lars Holdijk   University of Amsterdam
Chao Huang   University of Notre Dame
Guanjie Huang   Penn State University
Hong Huang   UGoe
Yiran Huang   TECO
Madiha Ijaz   IBM
Roberto Interdonato   CIRAD - UMR TETIS
Omid Isfahani Alamdari   University of Pisa

Guillaume Jacquet	JRC
Nathalie Japkowicz	American University
Shaoxiong Ji	Aalto University
Nan Jiang	Purdue University
Renhe Jiang	University of Tokyo
Song Jiang	University of California, Los Angeles
Adan Jose-Garcia	University of Exeter
Jihed Khiari	Johannes Kepler Universität
Hyunju Kim	KAIST
Tomas Kliegr	University of Economics
Yun Sing Koh	University of Auckland
Pawan Kumar	IIIT, Hyderabad
Chandresh Kumar Maurya	CSE, IIT Indore
Thach Le Nguyen	The Insight Centre for Data Analytics
Mustapha Lebbah	Université Paris 13, LIPN-CNRS
Dongman Lee	Korea Advanced Institute of Science and Technology
Rui Li	Sony
Xiaoting Li	Pennsylvania State University
Zeyu Li	University of California, Los Angeles
Defu Lian	University of Science and Technology of China
Jiayin Lin	University of Wollongong
Jason Lines	University of East Anglia
Bowen Liu	Stanford University
Pedro Henrique Luz de Araujo	University of Brasilia
Fenglong Ma	Pennsylvania State University
Brian Mac Namee	University College Dublin
Manchit Madan	Myntra
Ajay Mahimkar	AT&T Labs
Domenico Mandaglio	Università della Calabria
Koji Maruhashi	Fujitsu Laboratories Ltd.
Sarah Masud	LCS2, IIIT-D
Eric Meissner	University of Cambridge
João Mendes-Moreira	INESC TEC
Chuan Meng	Shandong University
Fabio Mercorio	University of Milano-Bicocca
Angela Meyer	Bern University of Applied Sciences
Congcong Miao	Tsinghua University
Stéphane Moreau	Université de Sherbrooke
Koyel Mukherjee	IBM Research India
Fabricio Murai	Universidade Federal de Minas Gerais
Taichi Murayama	NAIST
Philip Nadler	Imperial College London
Franco Maria Nardini	ISTI-CNR
Ngoc-Tri Ngo	The University of Danang - University of Science and Technology

Anna Nguyen	Karlsruhe Institute of Technology
Hao Niu	KDDI Research, Inc.
Inna Novalija	Jožef Stefan Institute
Tsuyosh Okita	Kyushu Institute of Technology
Aoma Osmani	LIPN-UMR CNRS 7030, Université Paris 13
Latifa Oukhellou	IFSTTAR
Andrei Paleyes	University of Cambridge
Chanyoung Park	KAIST
Juan Manuel Parrilla Gutierrez	University of Glasgow
Luca Pasa	Università degli Studi Di Padova
Pedro Pereira Rodrigues	University of Porto
Miquel Perelló-Nieto	University of Bristol
Beatrice Perez	Dartmouth College
Alan Perotti	ISI Foundation
Mirko Polato	University of Padua
Giovanni Ponti	ENEA
Nicolas Posocco	Eura Nova
Cedric Pradalier	GeorgiaTech Lorraine
Giulia Preti	ISI Foundation
A. A. A. Qahtan	Utrecht University
Chuan Qin	University of Science and Technology of China
Dimitrios Rafailidis	University of Thessaly
Cyril Ray	Arts et Metiers Institute of Technology, Ecole Navale, IRENav
Wolfgang Reif	University of Augsburg
Kit Rodolfa	Carnegie Mellon University
Christophe Rodrigues	Pôle Universitaire Léonard de Vinci
Natali Ruchansky	Netflix
Hajer Salem	AUDENSIEL
Parinya Sanguansat	Panyapiwat Institute of Management
Atul Saroop	Amazon
Alexander Schiendorfer	Technische Hochschule Ingolstadt
Peter Schlicht	Volkswagen
Jens Schreiber	University of Kassel
Alexander Schulz	Bielefeld University
Andrea Schwung	FH SWF
Edoardo Serra	Boise State University
Lorenzo Severini	UniCredit
Ammar Shaker	Paderborn University
Jiaming Shen	University of Illinois at Urbana-Champaign
Rongye Shi	Columbia University
Wang Siyu	Southwestern University of Finance and Economics
Hao Song	University of Bristol
Francesca Spezzano	Boise State University
Simon Stieber	University of Augsburg

Laurens Stoop	Utrecht University
Hongyang Su	Harbin Institute of Technology
David Sun	Apple
Weiwei Sun	Shandong University
Maryam Tabar	Pennsylvania State University
Anika Tabassum	Virginia Tech
Garth Tarr	University of Sydney
Dinh Van Tran	University of Padova
Sreekanth Vempati	Myntra
Herna Viktor	University of Ottawa
Daheng Wang	University of Notre Dame
Hongwei Wang	Stanford University
Wenjie Wang	National University of Singapore
Yue Wang	Microsoft Research
Zhaonan Wang	University of Tokyo and National Institute of Advanced Industrial Science and Technology
Michael Wilbur	Vanderbilt University
Roberto Wolfler Calvo	LIPN, Université Paris 13
Di Wu	Chongqing Institute of Green and Intelligent Technology
Gang Xiong	Chinese Academy of Sciences
Xiaoyu Xu	Chongqing Institute of Green and Intelligent Technology
Yexiang Xue	Purdue University
Sangeeta Yadav	Indian Institute of Science
Hao Yan	Washington University in St. Louis
Chuang Yang	University of Tokyo
Yang Yang	Northwestern University
You Yizhe	Institute of Information Engineering, Chinese Academy of Sciences
Alexander Ypma	ASML
Jun Yuan	The Boeing Company
Mingxuan Yue	University of Southern California
Danqing Zhang	Amazon
Jiangwei Zhang	Tencent
Xiaohan Zhang	Sony Interactive Entertainment
Xinyang Zhang	University of Illinois at Urbana-Champaign
Yongxin Zhang	Sun Yat-sen University
Mia Zhao	Airbnb
Tong Zhao	University of Notre Dame
Bin Zhou	National University of Defense Technology
Bo Zhou	Baidu
Louis Zigrand	Université Sorbonne Paris Nord

Sponsors

Contents – Part IV

E-commerce and Finance

Healthcare and Medical Applications (including Covid)

Mobility and Transportation

Anomaly Detection and Malware

Example Introduction and Overview

Anomaly Detection: How to Artificially Increase Your F1-Score with a Biased Evaluation Protocol

Damien Fourure$^{(\boxtimes)}$ ⓘ, Muhammad Usama Javaid ⓘ, Nicolas Posocco ⓘ, and Simon Tihon ⓘ

EURA NOVA, Mont-St-Guibert, Belgium
{damien.fourure,muhammad.javaid,nicolas.posocco,simon.tihon}@euranova.eu

Abstract. Anomaly detection is a widely explored domain in machine learning. Many models are proposed in the literature, and compared through different metrics measured on various datasets. The most popular metrics used to compare performances are F1-score, AUC and AVPR. In this paper, we show that F1-score and AVPR are highly sensitive to the contamination rate. One consequence is that it is possible to artificially increase their values by modifying the train-test split procedure. This leads to misleading comparisons between algorithms in the literature, especially when the evaluation protocol is not well detailed. Moreover, we show that the F1-score and the AVPR cannot be used to compare performances on different datasets as they do not reflect the intrinsic difficulty of modeling such data. Based on these observations, we claim that F1-score and AVPR should not be used as metrics for anomaly detection. We recommend a generic evaluation procedure for unsupervised anomaly detection, including the use of other metrics such as the AUC, which are more robust to arbitrary choices in the evaluation protocol.

Keywords: Anomaly detection · One-class classification · Contamination rate · Metrics

1 Introduction

Anomaly detection has been widely studied in the past few years, mostly for its immediate usability in real-world applications. Though there are multiple definitions of anomalies in the literature, most definitions agree on the fact that anomalies are data points which do not come from the main distribution. In the setting of unsupervised anomaly detection, the goal is to create a model which can distinguish anomalous samples from normal ones without being given such label at train time. In order to do so, most approaches follow a one-class classification framework, which models the normal data from the train set, and predicts as anomalous any point which does not fit this distribution of normal samples.

D. Fourure, M. U. Javaid, N. Posocco and S. Tihon—Equal contribution.

Y. Dong et al. (Eds.): ECML PKDD 2021, LNAI 12978, pp. 3–18, 2021.
https://doi.org/10.1007/978-3-030-86514-6_1

Such prediction needs some prior knowledge provided through a contamination rate on the test set, which is the ratio of anomalous data within. This ratio is used to build the model's decision rule.

In this setting, a lot of the literature uses the F1-score or the average precision (AVPR) to evaluate and compare models. In this paper we show that the evaluation protocol (train-test split and contamination rate estimation) has a direct influence on the contamination rate of the test set and the decision threshold, which in turn has a direct influence on these metrics. We highlight a comparability issue between results in different papers based on such evidence, and suggest an unbiased protocol to evaluate and compare unsupervised anomaly detection algorithms.

After an extensive study of the unsupervised anomaly detection field and of previous analyses of the evaluation methods (Sect. 2), we study the impact of the evaluation procedure on commonly used metrics (Sect. 3). Identified issues include a possibility to artificially increase the obtained scores and a non-comparability of the results over different datasets. Taking these into account, we suggest the use of a protocol leading to a better comparability in Sect. 4.

2   Related Work

Anomaly detection has been heavily dominated by unsupervised classification settings. One very popular approach in unsupervised anomaly detection is one-class classification, which refers to the setting where at train time, the model is given only normal samples to learn what the normal distribution is. The goal is to learn a scoring function to assign each data point an abnormality score. A threshold is then calculated from either a known or estimated contamination rate to turn scores into labels, samples with higher scores being considered as anomalies. In the literature different scoring functions have been used:

Proximity-based methods use heuristics based on distances between samples in some relevant space. These algorithms estimate the local density of data points through distances, and point out the most isolated ones. Legacy approaches include a simple distance to the Kth neighbour [2], Angle-Based Outlier Detection (ABOD) [11], which uses the variance over the angles between the different vectors to all pairs of points weighted by the distances between them, Local Outlier Factor (LOF) [3], which measures the local deviation of a given data point with respect to its neighbours, Connectivity-based Outlier Factor (COF) [23], which uses a ratio of averages of chaining distances with neighbours and Clustering-Based Local Outlier Factor (CBLOF) [10], which clusters the data and scores samples based on the size of the cluster they belong to and the distance to the closest big cluster. More recent approaches include DROCC [8], which makes the assumption that normal points lie on a well-sampled, locally linear low dimensional manifold and abnormal points lie at least at a certain distance from this manifold.

Reconstruction-based approaches use notions of reconstruction error to determine which data points are anomalous, the reconstruction of the densest parts of the distribution being easier to learn in general. In [17] for instance, the projection of each point on the main PCA axes is used to detect anomalies. As for [28], a GAN with a memory matrix is presented, each row containing a memorised latent vector with the objective to enclose all the normal data, in latent space, in between memorised vectors. The optimisation introduces a reconstruction error.

Representation-based approaches attempt to project the data in a space in which it is easy to identify outliers. Following this idea, One-Class SVM (OC-SVM) [22] uses a hypersphere to encompass all of the instances in the projection space. [12] proposed a neural network with robust subspace recovery layer. IDAGMM [13] presents an iterative algorithm based on an autoencoder and clustering, with the hypothesis that normal data points form a cluster with low variance. OneFlow [16], is a normalising-flow based method which aims at learning a minimum enclosing ball containing most of the data in the latent space, the optimisation ensuring that denser regions are projected close to the origin.

Adversarial scoring use the output of a discriminator as a proxy for abnormality, since it is precisely the goal of a discriminator to distinguish normal samples from other inputs. Driven by the motivation, an ensemble gan method is proposed in [9]. GANomaly [1] presents a conditional generative adversarial network with a encoder-decoder-encoder network to train better on normal images at training, and [27] presents Adversarially Learned Interface method with cycle consistency to ensure good reconstruction of normal data in one-class setting. [29] presents a gan network with autoencoder as generator for anomaly detection on images datasets.

Feature-level approaches try to detect anomalies at feature-level, and aggregate such information on each sample to produce an abnormality score at sample level. HBOS [7] assumes feature independence and calculates the degree of abnormality by building histograms. RVAE [5] uses a variational autencoder to introduce cell abnormality, which is converted into sample anomaly detection.

All of these categories are of course non-exclusive, and some approaches, as the very popular Isolation Forest [15], which uses the mean depth at which each sample is isolated in a forest of randomly built trees, do not fall in any of these. On the opposite, some recent methods combine multiple of such proxies for abnormality to reach better performances, each one using different hypotheses to model anomalies. For example [31] presents an end-to-end anomaly detection architecture. The model uses an autoencoder to perform dimensionality reduction to one or two dimensions and calculates several similarity errors, feeding then both latent representation and reconstruction errors to the gaussian mixture model. AnoGAN [21], which uses both a reconstruction error and a discriminator score to detect anomalies, also falls in this category.

Even if the original one-class setting requires data to be all normal at train time (which makes one-class approaches not strictly unsupervised) some approaches do not require clean data at train time, since they use what they learn about normal data to reduce as much as possible the impact of anomalies [13,16].

For all these settings, the main evaluation metrics used in the literature are the F1-score, the AUC (area under ROC curve) and the AVPR (average precision). The link between sensitivity, specificity and F1-score has been studied in [14], providing thresholding-related insights. In this work, we highlight the heterogeneity of current evaluation procedures in unsupervised anomaly detection performed in a one-class framework, would it be in terms of metrics or contamination-rate determination. For instance, many papers do not provide complete information about how the train-test splits are made [5,16]. For the same datasets, some papers re-inject the train anomalies in the test set [9,24,31][1] and some others do not [30,31]. In some cases, it is not clear which contamination rate was used to compute the threshold [9,16,28,29,31], and some approaches prefer evaluating their model with multiple thresholds [12]. Different metrics are used to evaluate performences - F1-score [8,9,13,27,29,31], precision [9,27,31], recall [9,27,31], sensitivity [21], specificity [21], AUC [1,5,6,8,9,12,13,21,25,27–29], AVPR [5,12,13,25]. Finally many papers report directly the results from other papers and do not test the associated algorithms in their particular evaluation setting.

We show that all above-mentioned setup details have a direct impact on the F1-score and the AVPR. Since such heterogeneity leads to reproducibility and comparability issues, we suggest the use of an evaluation protocol with a robust metric which allows comparison.

3   Issues When Using F1-Score and AVPR Metrics

In this section, we analyse the sensitivity of the F1-score and AVPR metrics with respect to the contamination rate of the test set. First, we define the problem and different metrics and explain the impact of the estimation of the contamination rate. Then, we analyse the evolution of the metrics according to the true contamination rate of the test set. After having explained different evaluation protocols used in the literature, we show how they can be used to produce artificially good results using the F1-score and AVPR metrics. Finally, we show that these two metrics are also unsuitable for estimating the difficulty of datasets.

3.1   Formalism and Problem Statement

Consider a dataset $\mathbf{D} = \{(\mathbf{x}_1, y_1), \ldots, (\mathbf{x}_N, y_N)\} \subset \mathbb{R}^d \times \{0,1\}$, with $\mathbf{x}_i$ the d-dimensional samples and y_i the corresponding labels. We assume both classes are composed of i.i.d. samples. We also assume the normal class labeled 0 outnumbers the anomaly class labeled 1. Therefore, we choose the anomaly class as

---

[1] [31] do not publish their code but an unofficial implementation widely used (264 stars and 76 forks at the time of writing) is available at https://github.com/danieltan07/dagmm.

	Actual Anomaly	Actual Normal
Predicted Anomaly	tp	fp
Predicted Normal	fn	tn

(a) Confusion Matrix

$$precision = \frac{tp}{tp + fp}$$

$$recall = \frac{tp}{tp + fn}$$

$$F1\text{-}score = \frac{2}{precision^{-1} + recall^{-1}}$$

(b) Metrics based on binary predictions

Fig. 1. Metrics definitions.

positive class and use $^+$ to refer to it, while using $^-$ to refer to the normal class. This dataset is split into a train set $\mathbf{D}^{train} \subset \mathbf{D}$ and a test set $\mathbf{D}^{test} = \mathbf{D} \backslash \mathbf{D}^{train}$. Different procedures are used in the anomaly-detection community to perform this split, as detailed in Sect. 3.3. We denote N_t^+ (resp. N_t^-) the number of anomalous (resp. normal) samples in the test set.

We consider one-class classifiers, which are models learning an anomaly-score function f based only on clean samples $\mathbf{X}^{clean} = \{\mathbf{x} \; \forall (\mathbf{x}, y) \in \mathbf{D}^{train} \mid y = 0\}$. The anomaly-score function returns, for a given sample $\mathbf{x}$, an anomaly score $\hat{s} = f(\mathbf{x}) \in \mathbb{R}$ such that the higher the score, the more likely it is that $\mathbf{x}$ is an anomaly. We define $P^+(\hat{s})$ (resp. $P^-(\hat{s})$) the probability that an anomaly (resp. a clean sample) obtains an anomaly-score $\hat{s}$ with the trained model.

To get a binary prediction $\hat{y}$ for a sample $\mathbf{x}$ with anomaly score $\hat{s}$, we need to apply a threshold t to the anomaly score such that $\hat{y} = 1$ if $\hat{s} \geq t$ else $\hat{y} = 0$. Different ways to compute this threshold are used in the literature. A common approach is to choose it according to an estimation $\hat{\alpha}$ of the contamination rate α. The contamination rate is the proportion of anomalous samples in the dataset. It can be taken as domain knowledge, estimated on the train set or, for evaluation purposes only, on the test set directly.

3.2 Definition of the Metrics

Using the final prediction and the ground truth labels, we can count the *true positives tp, true negatives tn, false positives fp* and *false negatives fn*, as shown in Fig. 1a. The *precision, recall* and *F1-score* are computed using these quantities as shown in the equations of Fig. 1b. An example of these metrics applied with a varying contamination rate estimation $\hat{\alpha}$, inducing a varying threshold, is shown in Fig. 2. It is interesting to note that, if the estimated contamination rate $\hat{\alpha}$ is equal to the true contamination rate α, we have *precision = recall = F1-score*. This can be easily explained: if the estimated contamination rate is the true contamination rate, the threshold is computed such that the number of samples predicted as anomalous is equal to the number of true anomalies in the set. Thus, if a normal sample is wrongly predicted as anomalous (i.e. is a false positive), it necessarily means that an anomalous sample has been predicted as normal (i.e. is a false negative). That is, $fp = fn$. Given the formulas of precision and recall

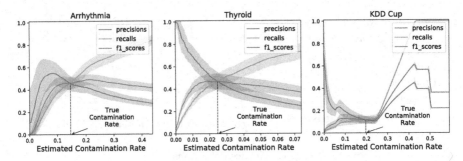

Fig. 2. Evolution of the *Precisions*, *Recalls* and *F1-scores* according to the estimated contamination rate on three different datasets. The curves are obtained using the Algorithm 1 introduced in Sect. 3.3.

(see equations of Fig. 1b) we have *precision* = *recall*. As the F1-score is the harmonic mean of precision and recall, we have *precision* = *recall* = *F1-score*. Inversely, if this equality can be observed in reported results, it is safe to assume the estimation of the contamination rate is equal to the true contamination rate.

We also include the AUC and AVPR in our analysis. These metrics are obtained by analysing the results with different thresholds. The AUC is defined through the receiver-operator characteristic (ROC) curve, a curve of the true positive rate over the false positive rate for various thresholds. Therefore, we redefine tp, fp, fn and tn as functions depending on the threshold. The area under the ROC curve AUC, sometimes written $AUROC$, is the total area under this curve, that is:

$$AUC = \int_{t=-\infty}^{\infty} \frac{tp(t)}{tp(t) + fn(t)} \frac{d}{dt} \left(\frac{fp}{fp + tn} \right)\Big|_t dt. \tag{1}$$

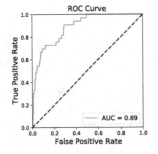
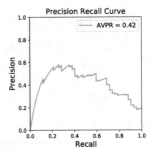

Fig. 3. Example of ROC curve and precision recall curve obtained on the Arrhythmia dataset. The scores are obtained using the Algorithm 1 introduced in Sect. 3.3.

Similarly, the AVPR is defined through the precision-recall (PR) curve, a curve of precision over recall for different thresholds. The area under this curve is referred to as the average precision (AVPR) metric, as it can be seen as a weighted average of the precision for different recall. We have

$$AVPR = \int_{t=-\infty}^{\infty} precision(t)\frac{d}{dt}(recall)\Big|_t dt. \tag{2}$$

An example of a ROC curve and a precision recall curve is given in Fig. 3.

We show in this paper that the F1-score and AVPR metrics are highly sensitive to the true contamination rate of the test set. We show this sensitivity has a negative impact on the comparison of different classifiers or datasets, especially when using different protocols.

3.3   Evaluation Protocols: Theory vs Practice

Machine learning theory tells us that the evaluation of an algorithm should be done on a test set completely separated from the train set. Algorithm 1 presents the unbiased procedure to train and evaluate an anomaly detection model. A dataset (containing both normal and anomalous samples) is split into a train set and a test set. The anomalous samples from the train set are removed to get a clean set that is used to train a model. The train set is also used to compute the contamination rate and fix the threshold, for example using a threshold such that the train set has as many anomalies as predicted anomalies, i.e. $fp = fn$. This threshold is finally used on the predictions made on the new (unseen) samples composing the test set to measure the F1-score. The AUC and AVPR are computed using the predicted scores directly. Even though this procedure is theoretically the correct way to evaluate a model, it has a significant drawback in practice. The anomalous samples in the train set are used only to compute the threshold for the F1-score and are then thrown away. Because there are, by definition, few anomalies in a dataset, one could be tempted to use these samples in the test set. Indeed, as visible in Fig. 4, the more anomalous samples we can use to evaluate a model, the more precise the evaluation.

To make full use of the anomalous samples, the procedure described in Algorithm 2 recycles the anomalous samples contained in the train set. The threshold is then computed on the test set as there are no anomalies left in the train set to estimate it. This leads to a situation where $precision = recall = F1\text{-}score$ as described in Sect. 3.1. This recycling procedure makes sense in the context of anomaly detection as it obtains more precise results, and can be found in the literature [24,31].

Algorithms 1 and 2 take as input any dataset and any trainable anomaly-score function. For the dataset, if not specified otherwise, we use the Arrhythmia and Thyroid datasets from the ODDS repository [20] and the Kddcup dataset from the UCI repository [4]. These datasets are often used in the anomaly-detection literature, and are therefore all indicated for our analysis. They have respectively 452, 3772 and 494020 samples, with a contamination rate of respectively 14.6%,

---

Algorithm 1: Theoretically unbiased evaluation protocol

Input:

$\mathbf{D} \subset \mathbb{R}^d \times \{0,1\}$ a set of N d-dimensional input samples and their corresponding labels (1 = anomaly, 0 = normal)

β the amount of data used for the test set

f a trainable anomaly-score function

Output:

F1-score, AUC and AVPR

Procedure:

$\mathbf{D}^{train}, \mathbf{D}^{test} = \text{split\_train\_test}(\mathbf{D}, \beta)$

$\mathbf{X}^{clean} = \{\mathbf{x} \; \forall(\mathbf{x}, y) \in \mathbf{D}^{train} \mid y = 0\}$

Normalise the data based on $\mathbf{X}^{clean}$ if necessary

Train f using $\mathbf{X}^{clean}$

$\hat{\mathbf{s}}^{train} = \{(f(\mathbf{x}), y) \; \forall(\mathbf{x}, y) \in \mathbf{D}^{train}\}$

Compute estimated contamination rate $\hat{\alpha} = \frac{|\{(\mathbf{x},y) \; \forall(\mathbf{x},y)\in\mathbf{D}^{train}|y=1\}|}{|\mathbf{D}^{train}|}$

Compute threshold t such that $\frac{|\{(\hat{s},y) \; \forall(\hat{s},y)\in\hat{\mathbf{s}}^{train}|\hat{s}\geq t\}|}{|\hat{\mathbf{s}}^{train}|} = \hat{\alpha}$

$\hat{\mathbf{s}}^{test} = \{(f(\mathbf{x}), y) \; \forall(\mathbf{x}, y) \in \mathbf{D}^{test}\}$

$\hat{\mathbf{y}}^{test} = \{(\hat{y}, y) \; \forall(\hat{s}, y) \in \hat{\mathbf{s}}^{test} \; \forall \hat{y} \in \{0,1\} \mid \hat{y} = 1 \text{ if } \hat{s} \geq t \text{ else } \hat{y} = 0\}$

Compute F1-score using $\hat{\mathbf{y}}^{test}$

Compute AUC and AVPR using $\hat{\mathbf{s}}^{test}$

Algorithm 2: *Recycling* evaluation protocol for anomaly detection

---

Input:

$\mathbf{D} \subset \mathbb{R}^d \times \{0,1\}$ a set of N d-dimensional input samples and their corresponding labels (1 = anomaly, 0 = normal)

β the amount of data used for the test set

f a trainable anomaly-score function

Output:

F1-score, AUC and AVPR

Procedure:

$\mathbf{D}^{train}, \mathbf{D}^{test} = \text{split\_train\_test}(\mathbf{D}, \beta)$

$\mathbf{X}^{clean} = \{\mathbf{x} \; \forall(\mathbf{x}, y) \in \mathbf{D}^{train} \mid y = 0\}$

Add $\{(\mathbf{x}, y) \; \forall(\mathbf{x}, y) \in \mathbf{D}^{train} \mid y = 1\}$ to $\mathbf{D}^{test}$

Normalise the data based on $\mathbf{X}^{clean}$ if necessary

Train f using $\mathbf{X}^{clean}$

$\hat{\mathbf{s}}^{test} = \{(f(\mathbf{x}), y) \; \forall(\mathbf{x}, y) \in \mathbf{D}^{test}\}$

Compute contamination rate $\alpha = \frac{|\{(\mathbf{x},y) \; \forall(\mathbf{x},y)\in\mathbf{D}^{test}|y=1\}|}{|\mathbf{D}^{test}|}$

Compute threshold t such that $\frac{|\{(\hat{s},y) \; \forall(\hat{s},y)\in\hat{\mathbf{s}}^{test}|\hat{s}\geq t\}|}{|\hat{\mathbf{s}}^{test}|} = \alpha$

$\hat{\mathbf{y}}^{test} = \{(\hat{y}, y) \; \forall(\hat{s}, y) \in \hat{\mathbf{s}}^{test} \; \forall \hat{y} \in \{0,1\} \mid \hat{y} = 1 \text{ if } \hat{s} \geq t \text{ else } \hat{y} = 0\}$

Compute F1-score using $\hat{\mathbf{y}}^{test}$

Compute AUC and AVPR using $\hat{\mathbf{s}}^{test}$

2.5% and 19.7%. For Kddcup, as done in the literature, the samples labeled as *"normal"* are considered as anomalous and, for computational reasons, only

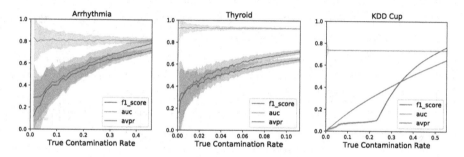

Fig. 4. F1-Score, AUC and AVPR versus the number of anomalies in the test set for three different datasets.

10% are used. For the trainable anomaly-score function, if not specified otherwise, we use OC-SVM [22] with its default hyper-parameters, as implemented in `sklearn` [18]. We choose this model as it has proven its worth and is often used as a baseline in the literature. We run all our experiments 100 times to report meaningful means and standard deviations. The code to reproduce all our figures and results is available at https://github.com/euranova/F1-Score-is-Biased.

3.4   Metrics Sensitivity to the Contamination Rate of the Test Set

We analyse the effect of the contamination rate of the test set on the F1-score and AVPR metrics. To do so, we use a variant of Algorithm 2 with a 20–80 train-test split on the clean samples only. We then re-inject a varying number of anomalous samples in the test set, from none to all of them. Figure 4 shows that F1-score and AVPR improve as more anomalies are added to the test set. Because the train set is fixed, this clearly shows that the F1-score and AVPR metrics are biased by the amount of anomalous samples in the test set. This sensitivity can be analysed theoretically.

First, note that the contamination rate $\alpha = \frac{N_t^+}{N_t^+ + N_t^-} = \frac{N_t^+}{N_t^-} / \left(\frac{N_t^+}{N_t^-} + 1 \right)$ is increasing with $\frac{N_t^+}{N_t^-}$. We start the analysis in a constant-threshold setting where the threshold t does not depend on the test set, e.g. as in Algorithm 1. In this setting, we can compute $p^- = \int_{\hat{s}=-\infty}^{t} P^-(\hat{s})d\hat{s}$ the probability that the model classifies correctly a normal sample and $p^+ = \int_{\hat{s}=t}^{\infty} P^+(\hat{s})d\hat{s}$ the probability that the model classifies correctly an anomalous sample (the recall). We observe that $tn = N_t^- * p^-$ and $fp = N_t^- * (1 - p^-)$ are directly proportional to N_t^-, while $tp = N_t^+ * p^+$ and $fn = N_t^+ * (1 - p^+)$ are directly proportional to N_t^+. As such, the recall p^+ does not depend on α while the precision ($= \frac{N_t^+ * p^+}{N_t^+ * p^+ + N_t^- * p^-} = \frac{\frac{N_t^+}{N_t^-} p^+}{\frac{N_t^+}{N_t^-} p^+ + p^-}$) increases with $\frac{N_t^+}{N_t^-}$ and therefore with α. This proves the AVPR increases with α as the only value changing in Eq. 2 is the increasing precision.

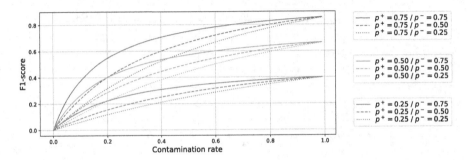

Fig. 5. Theoretical F1-score for varying contamination rates of the test set, anomaly-detection capabilities p^+ and normal-detection capabilities p^-.

This also proves the F1-score with a fixed threshold is increasing with α, as it is the harmonic mean of a constant and an increasing value. This theoretical variation of the F1-score is shown in Fig. 5.

We now analyse the case where the threshold t for the F1-score is computed using the test set as done in Algorithm 2. As we use a perfect estimation of the contamination rate, we have $recall = precision = F1\text{-}score$. Let us analyse this quantity in the view of the recall and compare it to the constant-threshold setting. If we add an anomaly to the test set, there are two possibilities:

- It is at the right side of the threshold, hence the threshold stays constant as there are still as many samples detected as anomalies as there are anomalies.
- It is at the wrong side of the threshold. The threshold therefore decreases to include one more sample as a predicted anomaly. There are two possibilities:
  - This additional sample is an anomaly, in which case the recall increases, whereas it would have decreased in the constant-threshold setting.
  - This additional sample is a clean sample, in which case the recall decreases the same way it would have decreased in the constant-threshold setting.

Compared to the constant-threshold setting, the only difference is the case where the recall is better than expected thanks to the shift of the threshold. Therefore, adding anomalies increases the F1-score even more than in the constant-threshold setting, meaning the variable-threshold setting is even more biased by the contamination rate of the test set. More formally, if we add anomalies without changing the number of clean samples, the new threshold t' will be smaller (or equal in the case of a perfect classifier) than the old one t, as we want to select more samples as being anomalies. The recall, precision and F1-score therefore increase from $\int_{\hat{s}=t}^{\infty} P^+(\hat{s})d\hat{s}$ (i.e. p^+ in the previous demonstration) to $\int_{\hat{s}=t'}^{t} P^+(\hat{s})d\hat{s} + \int_{\hat{s}=t}^{\infty} P^+(\hat{s})d\hat{s}$, which is greater or equal as a probability is always positive. Thus, if the classifier is not a perfect classifier, the F1-score increases with the contamination rate of the test set.

This concludes our demonstration that both the AVPR and the F1-score metrics are biased by the contamination rate of the test set.

Table 1. Demonstration of the sensitivity of the metrics to the evaluation protocol. Optimal threshold is the threshold computed on the test set to obtain the best F1-score possible (unapplicable to AUC and AVPR).

	Split procedure	Algorithm 1	Algorithm 2	Algorithm 2	Algorithm 2
	Test size	20%	20%	5%	5%
	Threshold	Estimated	Estimated	Estimated	Optimal
F1	arrhythmia	$0.451_{(\pm\ 0.103)}$	$0.715_{(\pm\ 0.025)}$	$0.867_{(\pm\ 0.021)}$	$0.888_{(\pm\ 0.012)}$
	kddcup	$0.102_{(\pm\ 0.025)}$	$0.762_{(\pm\ 0.004)}$	$0.940_{(\pm\ 0.002)}$	$0.971_{(\pm\ 0.001)}$
	thyroid	$0.446_{(\pm\ 0.110)}$	$0.647_{(\pm\ 0.022)}$	$0.781_{(\pm\ 0.021)}$	$0.803_{(\pm\ 0.017)}$
AVPR	arrhythmia	$0.481_{(\pm\ 0.116)}$	$0.770_{(\pm\ 0.041)}$	$0.924_{(\pm\ 0.028)}$	$0.924_{(\pm\ 0.029)}$
	kddcup	$0.299_{(\pm\ 0.017)}$	$0.653_{(\pm\ 0.015)}$	$0.872_{(\pm\ 0.008)}$	$0.873_{(\pm\ 0.007)}$
	thyroid	$0.488_{(\pm\ 0.113)}$	$0.719_{(\pm\ 0.020)}$	$0.880_{(\pm\ 0.017)}$	$0.881_{(\pm\ 0.017)}$
AUC	arrhythmia	$0.809_{(\pm\ 0.065)}$	$0.806_{(\pm\ 0.020)}$	$0.803_{(\pm\ 0.042)}$	$0.799_{(\pm\ 0.042)}$
	kddcup	$0.736_{(\pm\ 0.007)}$	$0.735_{(\pm\ 0.007)}$	$0.735_{(\pm\ 0.011)}$	$0.737_{(\pm\ 0.011)}$
	thyroid	$0.935_{(\pm\ 0.027)}$	$0.931_{(\pm\ 0.005)}$	$0.929_{(\pm\ 0.009)}$	$0.929_{(\pm\ 0.009)}$

3.5   How to Artificially Increase Your F1-Score and AVPR

Combining the previous results and algorithms, we can define an algorithm to get an arbitrarily good F1-score or AVPR on any dataset. As shown in Sect. 3.4, the F1-score and AVPR are sensitive to the contamination rate of the test set. Using the Algorithm 2 from Sect. 3.3, we can make this contamination rate vary. To do so, we only have to modify β, the amount of data used for the test set. Indeed, it modifies the number of normal samples N_t^- in the test set while the number of anomalies N_t^+ stays the same. Pushed to the extreme, we can have near to no clean samples in the test set, resulting in a near-to-perfect F1-score and AVPR. This phenomenon is shown in Table 1. We can see that, by using the Algorithm 2 the F1-score increases for all three datasets. This is because the anomalous sample of the train set are re-injected and thus the contamination rate of the test set increases. Then, using 5% of the data for the test set instead of 20% increase again the F1-score and AVPR.

Another interesting observation is that fixing the threshold according to the contamination rate does not give the optimal F1-score [14]. In practice, using a threshold smaller than this one often results in a better F1-score, as visible in Fig. 2 and shown in Fig. 6. As a consequence, we can artificially increase the F1-scores even more by computing the optimal threshold. This is shown in the last two columns of Table 1.

This proves that, with the exact same model and seemingly identical metrics, the F1-score can be greater and greater. This clearly supports the importance of specifying in detail the train-test split used and the way the threshold is computed. We observe in the literature that this part of the evaluation protocols is often missing or unclear [5,9,29,31], and the reported results are therefore impossible to compare with. This is part of the reproducibility problem observed in

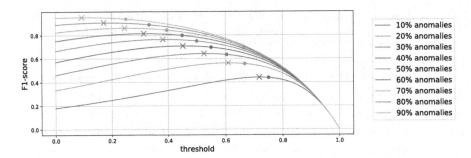

Fig. 6. Theoretical example of the evolution of the F1-score for different thresholds and contamination rates of the test set. The model used is a toy model having $P^+(\hat{s}) = 2 * \hat{s}$ and $P^-(\hat{s}) = 2 * (1 - \hat{s})$ for $0 \leq \hat{s} \leq 1$. Dots are the $fp = fn$ thresholds and crosses are the optimal thresholds.

the machine learning community. More importantly, some papers report results computed using different evaluation protocols [9, 24], leading to meaningless comparisons that are nonetheless used to draw arbitrary conclusions.

3.6   F1-Score Cannot Compare Datasets Difficulty

Another shortcoming of the F1-score and AVPR metrics is the comparison between datasets. One may be tempted to conclude that a dataset on which an approach has a higher F1-score is easier to model than another dataset with a lower score. However, this intuition is flawed when using these metrics as they strongly depend on the contamination rate of these datasets.

Figure 7 highlights the dataset comparison problem. Figure 7d shows the F1-score and AUC obtained on two toy datasets, an easy one (with a big radius) and a hard one (with a small radius). We show that we can obtain a better F1-score on a hard dataset (Fig. 7c) than on an easy dataset (Fig. 7a) just by changing the contamination rate. With an equal contamination rate (Fig. 7b) we can see that the easy dataset is indeed easier to model.

This situation also appears in real-world datasets. Indeed, in Table 1 with Algorithm 1, the *kdd cup* dataset appears harder than *arrhythmia* and *thyroid* as it obtains a worse F1-score. However, if we compare them with Algorithm 2, the *kdd cup* dataset obtains better results than the other two. The comparison of the datasets difficulty is inconsistent and therefore unreliable.

4   Call for Action

Given the instability shown in Sect. 3, we suggest the anomaly-detection community to use the evaluation protocol described in Algorithm 2 but using only the AUC metric. Other approaches could be adopted, but this one will give better comparability between reported results and these results will have lower variances.

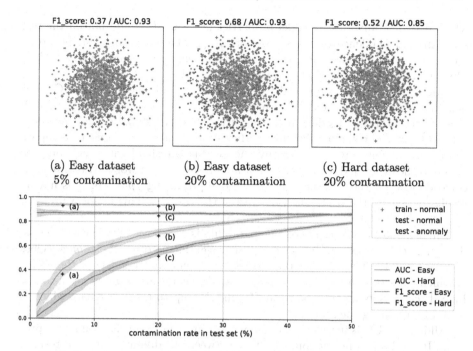

(a) Easy dataset
5% contamination

(b) Easy dataset
20% contamination

(c) Hard dataset
20% contamination

(d) Performances comparison between easy toy dataset and hard toy dataset

Fig. 7. Analysis of the dataset comparison through different metrics. We randomly draw normal samples from a standard gaussian distribution, and anomalous samples from a noisy a around the mean. By varying the radius of the circle - 2.5 for the *easy* case, 2.1 for the *hard* one - we change the difficulty of the dataset. The greater the radius, the easier it is to separate both distributions. A simple gaussian is used as model.

4.1   Use AUC

We have demonstrated in Sect. 3 how the F1-score and AVPR metrics can be tricky to use and lead to wrong conclusions, slowing down the research in the field. To avoid these pitfalls, we recommend using the AUC metric. First of all, AUC is not sensitive to the contamination rate of the test set, as shown in Fig. 4. This can be proven by developing Eq. 1:

$$AUC = \int_{t=-\infty}^{\infty} \frac{tp(t)}{tp(t) + fn(t)} \frac{d}{dt}\left(\frac{fp}{fp + tn}\right)\Big|_t dt \tag{3}$$

$$= \int_{t=-\infty}^{\infty} \int_{\hat{s}=t}^{\infty} P^+(\hat{s})d\hat{s} \frac{d}{dt}\left(\int_{\hat{s}'=-\infty}^{t} P^-(\hat{s}')d\hat{s}'\right)\Big|_t dt \tag{4}$$

$$= \int_{\{(\hat{s},t)\in\mathbb{R}^2|\hat{s}\geq t\}} P^+(\hat{s})P^-(t)\ d\hat{s}\ dt \tag{5}$$

which depends only on the model properties (P^+ and P^-) and not on the test set. This independence prevents most of the problems identified in the previous section. As illustrated in Fig. 7, datasets are more comparable using AUC. Moreover, Table 1 highlights the stability of the AUC.

Additionally, there is no need to define a threshold when using AUC. This is a good thing as the choice of a threshold can prevent comparability. Indeed, most of the proposed models in the literature [9,16,19,29,31] do not include a way to train a threshold. Therefore, arbitrary thresholds are used to compute the F1-score. The way to arbitrarily choose this threshold can vary from one paper to the other and lead to incomparable results. Even worse, this threshold could depend on the test set, such as the one producing $fp = fn$, thus having results biased by the contamination rate of the test set. This is not a problem with the AUC as it does not need a threshold.

Finally, another source of non-comparability is the choice of the positive class. Some may choose the *normal* class as positive [8,19] and other the *anomaly* class as positive [9,12,26]. AUC has the advantage of being independent of the choice of which class is seen as positive, as long as the scores are negated accordingly. Indeed, Eq. 5 is symmetric between P^+ and P^- up to the $\hat{s} \geq t$ part which is solved by negating the scores.

All in all, AUC is insensitive to many arbitrary choices in the evaluation protocol. It results in a better comparability between the different reported results.

4.2 Do Not Waste Anomalous Samples

As, by definition, anomalous samples are rare, it is important to re-inject them in the test set, as described in Algorithm 2. Indeed, by using more anomalous samples in the test set, the variance in the metrics is lower.

As shown in Table 1, when using AUC, Algorithm 2 gives the same mean result than Algorithm 1, but with a better precision (lower standard deviation). This is easily explained by the fact that there are more anomalies in the test set, increasing the applicability of the law of large numbers. This increased precision can be useful to obtain significant results rather than random-looking ones. Algorithm 2 can be used as long as the metric used is not biased by the contamination rate of the test set. It is therefore compatible with the AUC metric.

5 Conclusion

The literature in the field of anomaly detection lacks precision in describing evaluation protocols. Because of the sensitivity of the F1-score and AVPR metrics to the contamination rate of the test set, this results in a reproducibility issue of the proposed works as well as a comparison problem between said works. Moreover, we observe that some works do the subtle mistake of comparing results produced with different evaluation protocols and draw arbitrary conclusions from it. To solve this problem, we suggest the anomaly-detection community to use the AUC, which is insensitive to most arbitrary choices in the evaluation protocol. Moreover, we propose to use a *recycling* algorithm (Algorithm 2) for the train-test split to make the most of anomalies in each dataset. These two actions will result in more comparable and more precise results across research teams.

References

1. Akcay, S., Atapour-Abarghouei, A., Breckon, T.P.: GANomaly: semi-supervised anomaly detection via adversarial training. In: Jawahar, C.V., Li, H., Mori, G., Schindler, K. (eds.) ACCV 2018. LNCS, vol. 11363, pp. 622–637. Springer, Cham (2019). https://doi.org/10.1007/978-3-030-20893-6_39
2. Angiulli, F., Pizzuti, C.: Fast outlier detection in high dimensional spaces. In: Elomaa, T., Mannila, H., Toivonen, H. (eds.) PKDD 2002. LNCS, vol. 2431, pp. 15–27. Springer, Heidelberg (2002). https://doi.org/10.1007/3-540-45681-3_2
3. Breunig, M.M., Kriegel, H.P., Ng, R.T., Sander, J.: LOF: identifying density-based local outliers. In: Proceedings of the 2000 ACM SIGMOD International Conference on Management of Data, pp. 93–104 (2000)
4. Dua, D., Graff, C.: UCI machine learning repository (2017). http://archive.ics.uci.edu/ml
5. Eduardo, S., Nazábal, A., Williams, C.K., Sutton, C.: Robust variational autoencoders for outlier detection and repair of mixed-type data. In: International Conference on Artificial Intelligence and Statistics, pp. 4056–4066. PMLR (2020)
6. Ergen, T., Kozat, S.S.: Unsupervised anomaly detection with LSTM neural networks. IEEE trans. Neural Netw. Learn. Syst. **31**(8), 3127–3141 (2019)
7. Goldstein, M., Dengel, A.: Histogram-based outlier score (HBOS): a fast unsupervised anomaly detection algorithm. KI-2012: Poster and Demo Track, pp. 59–63 (2012)
8. Goyal, S., Raghunathan, A., Jain, M., Simhadri, H.V., Jain, P.: DROCC: deep robust one-class classification. In: International Conference on Machine Learning, pp. 3711–3721. PMLR (2020)
9. Han, X., Chen, X., Liu, L.P.: GAN ensemble for anomaly detection. arXiv preprint arXiv:2012.07988 (2020)
10. He, Z., Xu, X., Deng, S.: Discovering cluster-based local outliers. Pattern Recogn. Lett. **24**(9–10), 1641–1650 (2003)
11. Kriegel, H.P., Schubert, M., Zimek, A.: Angle-based outlier detection in high-dimensional data. In: Proceedings of the ACM SIGKDD International Conference on Knowledge Discovery and Data Mining, pp. 444–452, August 2008. https://doi.org/10.1145/1401890.1401946
12. Lai, C.H., Zou, D., Lerman, G.: Robust subspace recovery layer for unsupervised anomaly detection. In: International Conference on Learning Representations (2020). https://openreview.net/forum?id=rylb3eBtwr
13. Li, T., Wang, Z., Liu, S., Lin, W.Y.: Deep unsupervised anomaly detection. In: Proceedings of the IEEE/CVF Winter Conference on Applications of Computer Vision (WACV), pp. 3636–3645, January 2021
14. Lipton, Z.C., Elkan, C., Naryanaswamy, B.: Optimal thresholding of classifiers to maximize F1 measure. In: Calders, T., Esposito, F., Hüllermeier, E., Meo, R. (eds.) ECML PKDD 2014. LNCS (LNAI), vol. 8725, pp. 225–239. Springer, Heidelberg (2014). https://doi.org/10.1007/978-3-662-44851-9_15

15. Liu, F.T., Ting, K.M., Zhou, Z.H.: Isolation forest. In: Proceedings of the 2008 Eighth IEEE International Conference on Data Mining, ICDM 2008, pp. 413–422. IEEE Computer Society, USA (2008). https://doi.org/10.1109/ICDM.2008.17
16. Maziarka, Ł., Śmieja, M., Sendera, M., Struski, Ł., Tabor, J., Spurek, P.: Flow-based anomaly detection (2020)
17. Parra, L., Deco, G., Miesbach, S.: Statistical independence and novelty detection with information preserving nonlinear maps. Neural Comput. **8** (1997). https://doi.org/10.1162/neco.1996.8.2.260
18. Pedregosa, F., et al.: Scikit-learn: machine learning in Python. J. Mach. Learn. Res. **12**, 2825–2830 (2011)
19. Perera, P., Nallapati, R., Xiang, B.: Ocgan: One-class novelty detection using gans with constrained latent representations. In: Proceedings of the IEEE/CVF Conference on Computer Vision and Pattern Recognition (CVPR), June 2019
20. Rayana, S.: ODDS library (2016). http://odds.cs.stonybrook.edu
21. Schlegl, T., Seeböck, P., Waldstein, S.M., Schmidt-Erfurth, U., Langs, G.: Unsupervised anomaly detection with generative adversarial networks to guide marker discovery. In: Niethammer, M., et al. (eds.) IPMI 2017. LNCS, vol. 10265, pp. 146–157. Springer, Cham (2017). https://doi.org/10.1007/978-3-319-59050-9_12
22. Schölkopf, B., Williamson, R.C., Smola, A.J., Shawe-Taylor, J., Platt, J.C., et al.: Support vector method for novelty detection. In: NIPS, vol. 12, pp. 582–588. Citeseer (1999)
23. Tang, J., Chen, Z., Fu, A.W., Cheung, D.W.: Enhancing effectiveness of outlier detections for low density patterns. In: Chen, M.-S., Yu, P.S., Liu, B. (eds.) PAKDD 2002. LNCS (LNAI), vol. 2336, pp. 535–548. Springer, Heidelberg (2002). https://doi.org/10.1007/3-540-47887-6_53
24. Wang, J., Sun, S., Yu, Y.: Multivariate triangular quantile maps for novelty detection. In: Advances in Neural Information Processing Systems, vol. 32. Curran Associates, Inc. (2019)
25. Wang, S., et al.: Effective end-to-end unsupervised outlier detection via inlier priority of discriminative network. In: NeurIPS, pp. 5960–5973 (2019)
26. Xu, X., Liu, H., Yao, M.: Recent progress of anomaly detection. Complexity **2019**, 1–11 (2019). https://doi.org/10.1155/2019/2686378
27. Yang, Z., Bozchalooi, I.S., Darve, E.: Regularized cycle consistent generative adversarial network for anomaly detection (2020)
28. Yang, Z., Zhang, T., Bozchalooi, I.S., Darve, E.: Memory augmented generative adversarial networks for anomaly detection (2020)
29. Zaigham Zaheer, M., Lee, J.H., Astrid, M., Lee, S.I.: Old is gold: redefining the adversarially learned one-class classifier training paradigm. In: 2020 IEEE/CVF Conference on Computer Vision and Pattern Recognition (CVPR), pp. 14171–14181 (2020). https://doi.org/10.1109/CVPR42600.2020.01419
30. Zhai, S., Cheng, Y., Lu, W., Zhang, Z.: Deep structured energy based models for anomaly detection. In: International Conference on Machine Learning, pp. 1100–1109. PMLR (2016)
31. Zong, B., et al.: Deep autoencoding gaussian mixture model for unsupervised anomaly detection. In: International Conference on Learning Representations (2018)

Mining Anomalies in Subspaces of High-Dimensional Time Series for Financial Transactional Data

Jingzhu He[1($\boxtimes$)], Chin-Chia Michael Yeh[2], Yanhong Wu[2], Liang Wang[2], and Wei Zhang[2]

[1] North Carolina State University, Raleigh, NC, USA
jhe16@ncsu.edu
[2] Visa Research, Palo Alto, CA, USA
{miyeh,yanwu,liawang,wzhan}@visa.com

Abstract. Anomaly detection for high-dimensional time series is always a difficult problem due to its vast search space. For general high-dimensional data, the anomalies often manifest in subspaces rather than the whole data space, and it requires an $O(2^N)$ combinatorial search for finding the exact solution (i.e., the anomalous subspaces) where N denotes the number of dimensions. In this paper, we present a novel and practical unsupervised anomaly retrieval system to retrieve anomalies from a large volume of high dimensional transactional time series. Our system consists of two integrated modules: subspace searching module and time series discord mining module. For the subspace searching module, we propose two approximate searching methods which are capable of finding quality anomalous subspaces orders of magnitudes faster than the brute-force solution. For the discord mining module, we adopt a simple, yet effective nearest neighbor method. The proposed system is implemented and evaluated on both synthetic and real-world transactional data. The results indicate that our anomaly retrieval system can localize high quality anomaly candidates in seconds, making it practical to use in a production environment.

Keywords: Unsupervised anomaly retrieval · High-dimensional time series · Subspace searching · Data mining

1 Introduction

Time series anomaly detection is important for building automatic monitoring systems. Although anomaly detection in time series data has been extensively studied in literature for decades, the majority of prior work only detects anomalies on either one or all dimensions. While searching anomalies in subspaces is commonly studied in vector space-based methods [4,11], nearly no work has been done in searching anomalies in subspaces of multidimensional time series. If the system does not retrieve anomalies from the correct subspace, it often results

© Springer Nature Switzerland AG 2021
Y. Dong et al. (Eds.): ECML PKDD 2021, LNAI 12978, pp. 19–36, 2021.
https://doi.org/10.1007/978-3-030-86514-6_2

in producing undesirable results due to false dismissals similar to the case of multidimensional motif discovery [35].

Let us consider an example as shown in Fig. 1 where we have a three-dimensional time series and aim to identify the days containing anomalies. The state-of-the-art discord mining-based methods [4, 17] generally compare the distances between time series associated with each pair of days and generate anomaly alerts once the nearest neighbor distances exceed certain thresholds. If we apply these methods independently on each dimension (dim. 0, 1, or 2), as every daily pattern occurs twice, all nearest neighbor distances between the days are low and no alert will be generated on any of these dimensions. These results also hold if we apply the same algorithm to the combined time series (all dim.). Only if we combine dimension 0 and dimension 1 (dim. 0 + 1), the anomaly, which occur on day one, can be detected by the discord mining-based method. In other words, the anomaly detection system will falsely dismiss the anomalies if it does not exhaustively search anomalies in *all* possible combinations of dimensions (i.e., subspaces).

Detecting anomalies in subspaces is crucial in many domains. In this paper, we focus on finding anomalies in financial transaction data, a particular area where a failed detection strategy may cause multi-million-dollar losses. For example, during the 2013 ATM cyber looting attack, US$2.4 million was looted from about 3,000 ATMs in New York City [27]. The attackers evenly distributed looting to the targeted ATMs so that only an extra US$800 was withdrawn from each ATM. Given that such a small amount of perturbation can be considered as a normal daily fluctuation, this attack is not discoverable by monitoring ATM's associated time series[1] individually. Meanwhile, this attack

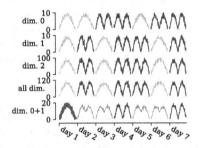

Fig. 1. The anomalous patterns (red/bold) are detectable only when dimension 0 and dimension 1 are combined. The blue/thin lines are recurrent (i.e., normal) patterns. (Color figure online)

can neither be detected by monitoring the aggregated transaction volume of all the ATMs in the U.S. as the targeted ATMs represent only 5% of the total ATMs [32]. Although some pre-defined rules (e.g., detecting withdrawals with the same dollar amount that occurred at multiple ATMs within a short time) can capture the anomalies in this case, attackers can quickly learn the rules and adapt their behaviors accordingly. Therefore, we need to develop an algorithm to detect the "correct" combinations of time series associated with each ATM without relying on simple rules.

A simple solution is exhaustive search (i.e., brute-force), by examining anomalies in all possible subspaces (i.e., combination of dimensions), potential anomalies manifested in subspaces can be identified. However, such brute-force solution is not scalable: searching all possible dimension combinations requires an

---

[1] The time series is generated by hourly withdrawn amount.

$O(2^N)$ time complexity where N denotes the number of dimensions. Such complexity is infeasible for most real-world data, especially for transactional data. Collectively, a typical global payment company generates hundreds of millions of transaction records per day and each transaction record is typically associated with hundreds of attributes, representing different characteristics, such as transaction type, zipcode, and transaction amount. By aggregating statistics for transaction records associated with different common categorical attributes (e.g., a particular zipcode) hourly, we can generate *multidimensional time series* from transactional data. As anomalies may manifest in subspaces of the multi-dimensional time series, the anomaly retrieval system needs to quickly identify the potential most suspicious subspaces.

This paper presents a novel unsupervised anomaly retrieval system on multi-dimensional time series data. We design the anomaly retrieval system with two modules, i.e., *subspace searching* and *time series discord mining*. We present and evaluate two alternative approaches to perform approximate subspace search, i.e., *greedy search* and *evolutionary search*. The proposed approximate subspace searching methods are capable of finding quality anomalies with their runtime being an order of magnitude faster than the brute-force solution. For time series discord mining, we design a nearest neighbor-based method with Dynamic Time Warping (DTW) to locate and score the anomalies. We outline two different advanced implementations of the discord mining method with 86% runtime reduction over the naive implementation. Adopting improvements proposed for both modules, the proposed system is practical for deployment in the production environment for monitoring transactional data. Our paper makes the following contributions.

1. We investigate the unsupervised anomaly retrieval problem on multidimensional time series. We divide the problem into two sub-problems and design an anomaly retrieval system with two modules: subspace searching and discord mining.
2. We propose two different approaches to find the most anomalous subspace from an $O(2^N)$ search space for financial transactional data.
3. We design an efficient discord mining method based on DTW distances to identify the temporal location of the anomalies and evaluate the anomalous degree of the anomalies.
4. We implement our algorithm and conduct comprehensive experiments on both synthetic data and real-world transactional data. The experiment results show that our system outperforms all alternative approaches and it is practical for applications in real-world products.

2   Related Work

The anomaly detection problem has been extensively studied for over a decade, and there are many variants of the problem [2,4,11,12]. In this section, we focus on two variants that are mostly relevant to this work: *high-dimensional data anomaly detection* and *time series anomaly detection*.

High-Dimensional Data Anomaly Detection: The proposed methods for high-dimensional data anomaly detection problem usually attempt to solve the curse of dimensionality associated with high-dimensional data and find anomalies that manifest in subspace span by a subset of dimensions [12]. These methods either use alternative anomaly scores to combat the curse of dimensionality or define/search for a subspace where the anomalies are most likely to manifest. For example, angle-based methods solve the curse of dimensionality by mining anomalies based on angles between the vector space representation of the data instead of Euclidean distance [12,18,38,39]. The hyperplane-based method proposed in [19] defines subspaces with respect to each data point's neighbors. The UBL [5] method performs anomaly detection on all dimensions of system metrics based on neural networks. To search the subspaces where anomalies may manifest, various approaches have been explored such as bottom-up search [23,34], dependency among different dimensions [16], dimensionality unbiasedness [31], set enumeration tree [6], evolutionary algorithm [1] and domain knowledge [33]. Nevertheless, existing work typically identifies anomalous records in a database using the associated attributes represented as high-dimensional feature vectors. Even in the works that deal with streaming data [37–39], time series view of the data is not considered for the anomaly detection problem. To the best of our knowledge, our work is the first one to adopt time series representation of high dimensional data for anomaly detection.

Time Series Anomaly Detection: Various techniques like Markov models, dynamic Bayesian networks, and neural networks are explored for time series anomaly detection [11], and different techniques are proposed to capture different types of anomalies. For example, Siffer et al. [29] designed an extreme value detection system based on extreme value theory for streaming time series data without requiring any manually-determined thresholds. Both DILOF [24] and MiLOF [26] detect time series anomaly based on the Local Outlier Factor (LOF) scores. Existing work such as [21] and [10] defines the anomaly based on data density. Another simple yet effective definition for time series anomaly is time series discord [4,17]. It defines time series anomalies as the most unusual subsequences (subsets of consecutive data points) in time series. Besides these studies, many efforts have been made to apply deep learning-based anomaly detection on time series in various domains [3,8,15]. Malhotra et al. [20] and Su et al. [30] detect time series anomalies based on the reconstructed error computed from recurrent neural networks. The TScope method [13] adopts a unique feature extraction method and a customized Self-Organizing Map-based score to detect anomalies in system call traces. Most of the aforementioned work either considers each data point independently [10,21,24,26,29], or does not consider the fact that anomalies could manifest in subspace instead of full space [3,8,13,15,17,20,30]. As a result, to the best of our knowledge, our method is the only method that is capable of identifying anomalies based on time series discord definition in high-dimensional data.

3 Definitions and Notation

Definition 1 (Transaction record). Each record is formulated as $D = [d_1, d_2, d_3, ..., d_n, t, a]$, where each d_i represents a discrete attribute that has a finite set of possible values. n is the number of discrete attributes. Besides these discrete attributes, each transaction record has a timestamp t indicating the occurring time of the transaction and the transaction amount a, which is a numerical value.

Definition 2 (Transaction database). A transaction database $\mathbf{D}$ stores a collection of transaction records.

An example of a transaction database, consisting of four transaction records, is shown in Table 1. Three individuals (Alice, Bob, and Carlos) have transactions at three different merchants (eBay, Amazon, and Walmart) in two different states (California and Washington).

Table 1. Four records from an example transaction database.

Customer	Merchant	Location	Timestamp	Amount
Alice	eBay	CA	1559854527	35
Bob	eBay	CA	1559854635	35
Alice	Amazon	WA	1559854800	50
Carlos	Walmart	CA	1559859053	38

To account for temporal variations of the transaction database, we generate a time series from the database using a *sliding aggregator*.

Definition 3 (Sliding aggregator). Given a transaction database $\mathbf{D}$, a sliding aggregator $A(\cdot)$ is an aggregating function that generates a time series by summarizing the statistics of transactions satisfied given conditions with a sliding window of window size w and hop size h.

For example, we want to look at the per hour transaction amounts in California for a database D. Then we apply the sliding aggregator $A(count(), w = 1\,\text{hour}, h = 1\,\text{hour}, Location = \text{CA})$ on D. Using the example database shown in Table 1, the first two transaction records, i.e., Alice and Bob, are fed into the $count()$ function as they satisfy the condition $Location = \text{CA}$ and occur within the same hour-long window. The function output is a time series that includes the aggregated transaction amounts of each sliding window.

Applying a single sliding aggregator only creates one view of the transaction database. To represent the database more holistically, we define the subspace set of a given transaction database as follows.

Definition 4 (Subspace set). Given a transaction database $\mathbf{D}$, the corresponding subspace set $\mathbf{S_D} = [T_1, T_2, T_3, ..., T_m]$ is a set of m univariate time series, where each $T_i \in \mathbf{S_D}$ is generated by applying different sliding aggregators and is considered as one of m subspaces.

As each $T_i \in \mathbf{S_D}$ stores one view of the database D, we regard each T_i as a subspace of $\mathbf{S_D}$. Continuing with the example shown in Table 1, by simply calculating the hourly counts for *all* combinations of locations, the total number of subspaces (i.e., number of $T_i \in \mathbf{S_D}$) will be $2^{50} - 1 \approx 1$ quadrillion. To help us explain our subspace search methodology, we further define the concept of *unit subspace*.

Definition 5 (Unit subspace). Given a subspace set $\mathbf{S_D}$, a unit subspace is a subspace that cannot be obtained through a combination of other subspaces within $\mathbf{S_D}$.

Let us say that the $\mathbf{S_D}$ consists of the aforementioned one quadrillion subspaces generated by selecting all combinations of locations, a unit subspace is a subspace associated with a single location. For instance, the subspace $T_{CA} = A(Location = \text{CA})^2$ is a unit subspace while the subspace $T_{CA,WA} = A(Location = \text{CA} \vee Location = \text{WA})$ is *not* a unit subspace as $T_{CA,WA}$ can be generated by combining T_{CA} and T_{WA}. Throughout the paper, we use the term "dimension" and "unit subspace" interchangeably. Therefore, each dimension of the multivariate time series shown in Fig. 1 is a unit subspace, and the overall subspace set includes both the unit subspaces and all possible combinations of the unit subspaces.

With all the essential concepts associated with subspace defined, we are at the stage of defining concepts associated with time series discord mining.

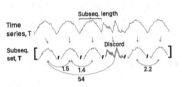

Definition 6 (Time series discord). Given a time series T, the time series discord is the subsequence with maximum *dynamic time warping* (DTW) distance with its nearest neighbor, and the anomaly score is the DTW distance between the discord and its nearest neighbor.

Fig. 2. The discord (red) is the subsequence with the largest distance with its nearest neighbor. Each subsequence's nearest neighbor is indicated by the curved arrow and the curved arrow is pointed *toward* its neighbor. The distances are shown next to the curved arrow. (Color figure online)

In order to identify the discord, we search for the nearest neighbor of each subsequence based on the z-normalizing DTW distance within $\mathbf{T}$; then, store the distance between each subsequence and its nearest neighbor (see Fig. 2). Based on the stored distance values, we identify the discord from $\mathbf{T}$ in Fig. 2 by locating the subsequence with largest nearest neighbor distance.

4   System Architecture

In Fig. 3, we provide an overview of the proposed anomaly retrieval system. First, a set of sliding aggregators are applied to the transaction database to extract unit subspaces. We then feed the unit subspaces into the *Subspace Searching Module* (see Sect. 4.1). The *Subspace Searching Module* executes iteratively and

---

[2] Other inputs (i.e., $count()$, $w = 1\,\text{h}$ and $h = 1\,\text{h}$) of $A()$ are omitted for brevity.

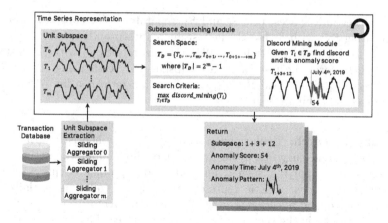

Fig. 3. The architecture of the proposed anomaly search system.

searches for the subspace(s) with the largest possibility of being anomalous. The set of suggested subspace(s) is sent to *Discord Mining Module* for evaluating the anomaly score of the subspaces. The results of *Discord Mining Module* are then sent back to the *Subspace Searching Module* to guide the search direction in the next iteration. The goal of the *Subspace Searching Module* is to suggest the next anomalous subspace in each iteration and the goal of the *Discord Mining Module* is to evaluate the anomaly scores of the identified subspaces output by the *Subspace Searching Module*. Finally, once the iterative process is done (i.e., convergence is reached), a ranked list containing the identified anomalous subspaces, anomaly scores, temporal location of the anomalies, and the anomaly patterns are returned to the user for further investigation. The ranked list is formed by storing all the evaluated anomalies during the search process.

4.1 Subspace Searching Module

As we describe in Sect. 3, it is impossible to perform discord mining on all the combinations of unit subspaces for real-world transactional data because the size of search space is exponential with respect to the number of unit subspaces. We design two heuristic searching algorithms for the subspace search problem: greedy search and evolutionary search.

Greedy Search: The greedy search method finds the most anomalous subspace by making a greedy choice at each iteration. We demonstrate the greedy search method with an example. Assume we have four unit subspaces (i.e., S_1, S_2, S_3, and S_4) initially. In the first step, we evaluate each unit subspace individually and find out that S_2 has the largest anomaly score. Next, we evaluate the combined subspace of S_2 with S_1, S_3, and S_4, separately. Let us say the combined subspace of S_2 and S_3 has the largest anomaly score; we aggregate them together ($S_2 + S_3 = S_{2,3}$). For the next step, we evaluate the aggregated spaces by combining

$S_{2,3}$ with other unit spaces, i.e., S_1 and S_4, separately. The subspace produced by aggregating $S_{2,3}$ with S_1 has the largest anomaly score; therefore, we proceed with $S_{1,2,3}$ for the next iteration. Finally, we aggregate $S_{1,2,3}$ with the last unit subspace S_4 to form the last candidate subspace. By comparing the anomaly scores of S_2, $S_{2,3}$, $S_{1,2,3}$, and $S_{1,2,3,4}$, the algorithm returns a list of subspaces ordered based on anomaly scores.

Evolutionary Search: Evolutionary search [7,14] is a heuristic optimization method. As its name suggests, evolutionary algorithms mimic the natural selection process, and applying such a method to our problem requires defining the following functions: genetic representation, fitness function, initialization, crossover, mutate, and selection strategy. We use a bit vector to represent a subspace, where the 1's in the vector indicating the presence of a unit subspace. The length of the bit vector is equal to the number of unit subspaces. For example, if we have unit subspaces S_1, S_2 and S_3, we use [101] to represent a particular subspace that is generated by combining S_1 and S_3. The fitness function is the anomaly score generated from the Discord Mining Module.

For the initialization, each individual within the population can be produced by generating a random binary vector. Given two parent binary vectors for the crossover, for every position of the offspring's binary vector, we randomly copy the value from one of the parents. If a mutation occurs, we randomly flip the mutated bit in the binary vector. For selection strategy, we use the tournament selection method with three tournament participants. The particular evolutionary algorithm we used is the $(\mu + \lambda)$ algorithm [9], and a ranked list of the individuals (subspaces) ordered based on anomaly scores is returned.

There are several hyperparameters in the evolutionary search method (i.e., population size per generation μ, number of offspring λ, probability of crossover p_{cx}, and number of generation n), and the time complexity is determined based on the hyperparameter setting. Specifically, the time complexity is $O(n\lambda)$ where n is the number of generations and λ is the number of offsprings. There are two major factors that users need to consider when deciding hyperparameter settings: the runtime requirement and the domain knowledge about the potential solution. Other model hyperparameters can be set based on the user's domain knowledge. For example, if users believe the solution should only consist of different unit subspaces, users should initialize the initial population with binary vectors with higher sparsity.

Greedy Versus Evolutionary Search: There is no clear winner when comparing the greedy search method with the evolutionary search method. The decision on which method to adopt should be decided in a case-by-case fashion. To help the decision process, we show the cost comparison between the two approaches in Table 2.

The major differences between the two methods are
1) flexibility in computational
cost and 2) the number of
hyperparameters. The greedy
search method has a fixed time
complexity of $O(n^2)$ where n is
the number of unit subspace.
The time complexity is sub-

Table 2. Comparison between greedy and evolutionary search.

	Advantages	Disadvantages
Greedy	Fixed time complexity $O(n^2)$ No hyperparameter	Inflexible cost
Evolutionary	Flexible computational cost	Hyperparameters

stantially better than the naive approach of $O(2^n)$, but it still could be too
expensive for problems that demand a faster algorithm. Because the time complexity of the evolutionary search method only depends on the hyperparameter
setting, the evolutionary search method can be parameterized in a way that the
required speed can be achieved. The adjustable time complexity associated with
evolutionary search comes with a disadvantage: it requires users to provide a set
of hyperparameters while greedy search requires no hyperparameters. In other
words, the greedy search method is much easier to use compared to the evolutionary algorithm. We perform an empirical comparison of the two methods in
Sect. 5.2.

4.2   Discord Mining Module

For the Discord Mining Module, we apply a nearest neighbor searching strategy
based on DTW distances. The brute-force method computes the distances of
all pairs of subsequences. The output is the subsequence with the largest DTW
distance with the nearest neighbor. We call this method Discord Mining V0
(DM-V0).

Can We Do Better Than DM-V0? Since computing the Euclidean distance
is an order of magnitude faster than the DTW distance, it is possible to derive a
faster discord mining algorithm using the fact that the z-normalized Euclidean
distance for a pair of subsequences is always greater than their z-normalized
DTW distance. We only need to evaluate the DTW distance of a subsequence
pair when their Euclidean distance is greater than the current solution (i.e.,
the pair with the largest DTW distance in the current iteration of the search
process); therefore, we can avoid unnecessary DTW distance computation using
precomputed Euclidean distances. On top of that, we can also guide the search
process using the precomputed Euclidean distances by evaluating the pair with
the largest Euclidean distances first because the pair is more likely to contain the
discord. We call the improved version Discord Mining V1 (DM-V1). The time
complexity of DM-V1 is still $O(n^2m^2)$ where n is the number of subsequences
and m is the length of a subsequence, but empirically it has a smaller runtime
comparing to DM-V0 (see Fig. 4).

Can We Do Even Better Than DM-V1? Many existing time series data mining algorithms take advantage of the fact that subsequences could be overlapped with each other [22,25,40]. Their superior computational speed is achieved by avoiding redundant computation for the overlapped regions. It has been shown by Zhu et al. [40] that computing pairwise z-normalized Euclidean distance for every subsequence in a time series can be reduced from $O(n^2 m)$ with naive implementation to $O(n^2)$ using a more optimal implementation. Using the $STOMP$ algo-

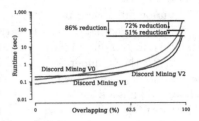

Fig. 4. The runtime of DM-V0, DM-V1, and DM-V2 under different overlapping condition. Note, the y-axis is runtime on a logarithmic scale.

rithm introduced in [40], we further improve the efficiency of DM-V1. Note, the original purpose of the $STOMP$ is to compute the matrix profile [36]. We modify the algorithm to return the pairwise distance matrix (i.e., all computed distance profiles [36]) instead of the matrix profile. We call the newly-introduced algorithm, Discord Mining V2 (DM-V2).

When Do We Use DM-V2 Versus V1? DM-V2 takes advantage of the fact that subsequences within the subsequence set are overlapped with each other. However, the runtime of the $STOMP$ algorithm is longer than pair-wise Euclidean distance computation when the overlap between subsequences is small. To study the relationship between the runtime of different discord mining methods and the overlap ratio, we have performed experiments on a synthetic random walk time series ($|T| = 2,880$). We set the subsequence length to 48, and the overlap between consecutive subsequences are varied from 0 to 47. The experiment is repeated 100 times and the average value is reported; the result is presented in Fig. 4.

DM-V1 is faster than DM-V0 which shows how precomputing the z-normalized Euclidean distance can indeed reduce the search time. When the overlap is close to 100% of the subsequence length, the runtime reduction is 72% by replacing DM-V0 with DM-V1. When DM-V2 is adopted, the runtime reduction is 86% comparing to DM-V0, and the runtime reduction is 51% comparing to DM-V1. On the contrary, when the subsequences have zero overlaps, the runtime of DM-V1 is the shortest compared with the alternatives, and the runtime for DM-V2 requires an extra 119 ms compared to DM-V1 and 58 milliseconds compared to DM-V0. The runtime for DM-V1 and DM-V2 intersect when the overlap of subsequence is around 63.5%. In other words, to achieve the optimal performance under this particular experiment setup, we should use DM-V1 when the overlap between subsequence is less than or equal to 63.5% and DM-V2 when the overlap is greater than 63.5%.

4.3 Discussion

The goal of our anomaly retrieval system is to obtain a list of anomalies ordered based on their corresponding anomaly scores, and the anomaly with the highest anomaly score may not be a true anomaly from the user's standpoint. However, by providing users a list of anomaly candidates with its contextual information (i.e., which subspace the candidate is from, the candidate's temporal location, the shape of the anomaly pattern), the user can investigate further using the contextual information of each candidate. Such interaction is similar to how people use an online search engine.

Our two-module design can be easily extended for different applications. Currently, we use a nearest neighbor-based method to mine time series discord since we find it is suitable for finding anomalies (e.g., extreme values, abnormal trends, and sudden changes) in transactional time series data. In other applications, the Discord Mining Module can be replaced by a more suitable anomaly mining method for the application. As a result, we fix the Discord Mining Module design to the time series discord-based method and focus on comparing different subspace searching methods in Sect. 5.

5 Evaluation

The experiments are all conducted on a Linux server with Intel Xeon CPU E5-2650 v4. We present several alternative algorithms for subspace searching to compare with our system firstly. We then perform a stress test with synthetic transactional data to understand our system's runtime and output quality under different scenarios. Finally, we evaluate our anomaly retrieval system on real transactional data to show its effectiveness in real-world scenarios.

5.1 Alternative Approaches

Now, we introduce several alternative algorithms for the Subspace Searching Module to compare with greedy and evolutionary search.

- **All-dimension:** The method returns the subspace that consists of all dimensions, i.e., it aggregates all the unit subspaces then returns it as the output.
- **One-best dimension:** The method computes the anomaly score associated with each dimension (i.e., unit subspace), then returns the dimension (i.e., unit subspace) with the largest anomaly score.
- **Hierarchical clustering:** The method performs hierarchical clustering on dimensions, which means that dimensions with similar time series are clustered together. Suppose we have n dimensions, the clustering process groups the dimensions in $n - 1$ steps. In each step, the hierarchical clustering algorithm merges either a dimension or a pre-existing cluster (i.e., grouped dimensions) with another dimension or pre-existing cluster. We consider each cluster of dimensions as a subspace, and we evaluate each subspace then return the ranked list of subspaces ordered by the anomaly scores. This method explores the possibility of using the similarity among dimensions for reducing the search space.

5.2 Synthetic Data

Methodology: Since it is beyond the modern computers' capability to obtain the optimal solution on real-world transactional data, we generate a set of synthetic data where the set of all possible combinations of unit subspaces is small enough for the brute-force subspace searching. Additionally, we generate the time series for each unit subspace directly instead of raw transactional data to streamline the data generation process as both the Subspace Searching Module and the Discord Mining Module work on time series representation of a transaction database. The synthetic data generated using the default experiment setting consists of 8 unit subspaces, and each unit subspace consists of 30 days of transactional data where each day is represented with 48 data points.

To study the effect of various variables associated with the synthetic dataset on the runtime and quality of the solution, we have varied one variable in the default experiment setting for each set of experiments. We generate 100 synthetic data points using different random seeds for each experiment setting to minimize the randomness effect.

To obtain the optimal solution, we generate all the subspaces $\mathbf{S}_{bf}$ (i.e., all combinations of the unit subspaces) by brute force. Figure 5 shows the most anomalous subspace and the least anomalous subspace. The anomalies are highlighted in red.

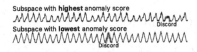

Fig. 5. The time series data of the most and least anomalous subspace.

Aside from the runtime, we also measure the performance of our system with *averaged rank* which captures the quality of the approximated solution. The averaged rank is computed as follows: given a subspace S discovered by an approximated algorithm, we find the rank of S in $\mathbf{S}_{bf}$. Because we repeat the experiment on 100 synthetic data points generated using different random seeds (with the same experiment setting), we compute the average of these 100 ranks and report the averaged rank as the performance measurement of the solution quality.

In addition to the two subspace search approaches, we also include the result of a random baseline. The random baseline returns a random subspace as the solution. Out of all the alternative approaches, we only include the hierarchical clustering-based method because all the other approaches are only capable of returning subspaces that consist of either one unit subspace or all unit subspaces. For all the experiments, we use multi-thread implementation with the number of threads set to 48. We use DM-V1 in all experiments as there is no overlap between subsequences.

Results: The experiment result is summarized in Fig. 6. The first row of Fig. 6 shows the averaged rank (i.e., quality of solution) under different Subspace Searching Modules. The number of unit spaces ranges from 4 to 16, constituting $2^4 - 1$ to $2^{16} - 1$ subspaces. As the number of unit subspace increases exponentially, the ranks of all the subspace searching methods increase correspondingly. All three subspace searching methods grow at a much slower rate compared to the exponential growth of the random baseline. We also observe that the performance of the

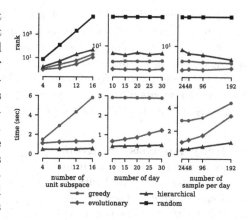

Fig. 6. Experiment result on synthetic data. Note that the y-axis of the plot in the first row is on a logarithmic scale.

proposed methods (i.e., greedy and evolutionary) is better than the hierarchical clustering-based method. On the contrary, the variable of the number of days does not have any correlation with the average rank: increasing or decreasing the number of days does not change the search space for anomaly retrieval. When the number of samples per day increases, the average ranks of the proposed algorithms slightly improve.

The second row of Fig. 6 depicts the runtime under different Subspace Searching Modules. We do not include the runtime of the random baseline in this study because there is no subspace search operation in the random baseline. When we change the number of unit subspaces, the size of the search space explored by the Subspace Searching Module is changed, thus varying such a variable could influence the runtime of the Subspace Searching Module. For the greedy method, the result shows that the computational cost is linear to the number of unit subspaces. For the evolutionary method, the time complexity only depends on the hyperparameter settings of the algorithm. Since we use the same hyperparameter setting (i.e., the default setting presented in the next section) throughout the experiment, the runtime is not affected by the change in the number of unit subspaces. Note that though the runtime of the greedy method more than triples when the number of subspaces grows from 4 to 16, it is still much faster than the brute force method as the brute force method requires a whopping 33 min to find the solution compared to the six seconds for the greedy method.

When we change either the number of days or the number of samples per day, the module that is mostly affected by the change is the Discord Mining Module. Increasing either of these variables, in theory, should increase the computational time quadratically of the Discord Mining Module. Nevertheless, the number of days has a limited effect on the greedy search method and the growing trend of the evolutionary search method suggests a quadratic growth rate. The number of samples per day has a similar impact on the runtime of both the greedy search method and the evolutionary search method. The trend suggests a quadratic growth in both methods' runtime with respect to the number of samples per day. Overall, the hierarchical clustering-based method is faster than the other methods due to its smaller search space; however, it also has the worst averaged rank for the same reason. We also generated figures with other common performance measurements for retrieval systems (i.e., MAP and NDCG [28]). Because the conclusion remains the same, we omit those figures for brevity.

Sensitivity Analysis for Evolutionary Search: As there are many hyperparameters associated with the evolutionary search method, we perform sensitivity analysis using synthetic data with 12 unit subspaces, 30 days of transactional data, and 48 data points per day. This analysis also compares greedy search with evolutionary search under different hyperparameter settings to help users decide on which subspace searching method to use. The result is shown in Fig. 7. Similar to Fig. 6, the y-axis indicates performance measurements like rank and time while the x-axis indicates varied hyperparameters. The "default" hyperparameter setting is: $\mu = 64$, $\lambda = 32$, $p_{cx} = 0.7$, and $n = 8$ where μ is population size per generation, λ is number of offspring, p_{cx} is probability of crossover, and n is number of generation.

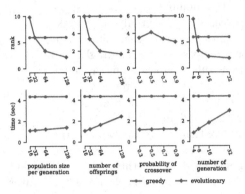

Fig. 7. Performance of evolutionary search under different hyperparameter settings.

First of all, the runtime mostly depends on λ and n. When we increase either λ or n, the runtime also increases linearly and the rank improves considerably before saturation. The value associated with μ also has a positive correlation with the runtime, but the growth rate is much less than λ and n while the improvement in rank remains prominent. On the contrary, p_{cx} does not affect the runtime, and setting it to 0.9 gives us the best result comparing to other p_{cx} settings. Note, although the evolutionary search method almost always outperforms the greedy search throughout the sensitivity analysis, there are still cases where the evolutionary search method is surpassed by the greedy search method when the hyperparameter setting is not ideal. This demonstrates the benefit of the greedy search method: there is no sensitivity analysis required for using greedy search because there are no hyperparameters associated with the greedy search method. Similar to previous experiments, the figures with other performance measurements are omitted for brevity.

5.3   Real-World Transactional Data

Data Collection: We collect all the California state transactional data in July 2018 from a payment company. Each transaction is associated with tens of attributes. Particularly, we determine that the unit subspaces are defined by Merchant Category Code (MCC). The MCC is the code used to determine the business type (e.g., department store, clothing store, and grocery) of a merchant. When transactions of different MCC are analyzed together (i.e., combining their corresponding unit subspace to form a subspace), it could reveal valuable information regarding certain business sectors. Discovered anomalous MCC subspaces can be interpreted and used as guidance for designing business strategies. For example, let's say MCC_1 stands for department stores, and MCC_2 stands for clothing stores. If an anomalous event with unusual rising transaction volume is detected in the subspace (MCC_1, MCC_2) on a specific date, such an event could indicate that there could be a big sale on the date for stores that sell garments.

The dataset is 70 GB and consists of over 600 million transactions from 415 MCCs. In each trial of the experiment, we randomly select one day and a subset of MCCs (1% of the MCCs) in the transaction database; we then randomly add synthesized transactions belonging to the selected MCCs to the day and randomly remove transactions from the selected MCCs occurring on that day. We repeat the experiment 16 times. When we apply the sliding aggregator, we use a sliding window of a half-hour and a hop size of the same length. The particular statistics we compute with the sliding aggregator is the sum of the transaction amounts spent in the window.

Since we have the ground truth about the temporal location of the anomalies, we return the averaged rank of the *real* anomalous day in the ranked list returned by different anomaly retrieval systems over the 16 trials. To obtain the ranked list, the anomaly score associated with each day in the subspace returned by each system is computed; then the computed scores are used as the sorting criteria. Because the tested systems are retrieval systems, we measure the performance of the systems using information retrieval performance measures like MAP [28] and NDCG [28] to evaluate the quality of the ranked list in addition to the averaged rank. Note, for the averaged rank, a lower number means better performance; for MAP and NDCG, a higher number means better performance.

Table 3. Experiment results with real transactional data.

Method	Average rank	MAP	NDCG	Runtime (Sec)
Random	15.50	0.63	0.34	–
All-dimension	20.75	0.36	0.24	0.02
One-best dimension	17.31	0.47	0.28	9.58
Hierarchical clustering	17.31	0.47	0.28	4.17
Greedy search	**5.94**	**0.86**	**0.46**	1,345.50
Evolutionary search	8.63	0.72	0.39	87.62

Results: The experiment results are shown in Table 3. All alternative approaches listed in Sect. 5.1 are examined. The proposed system, either with greedy search or evolutionary search, considerably outperforms the baseline methods with the greedy search being slightly better than the evolutionary search. On the contrary, either the one dimension or all dimension system fails to reliably detect the injected anomalies as their corresponding performance is even worse than the random baseline. The use of all dimension system fails because the injected anomalies only affect 1% of the unit subspace. Additionally, the one dimension system fails because it cannot locate the anomaly when only one dimension is considered. The anomaly on one dimension is too small to be captured. The hierarchical clustering-based system also produces poor results as the assumption that the anomalous space consists of similar unit subspaces does not hold for our database. In terms of the runtime, the proposed system, even with the slower greedy search method, is capable of running in real-time as the runtimes are all less than the data sampling period (i.e., 1,800 s). Similar to the results we present in Fig. 6, the evolutionary search method is capable of finding a solution that has a comparable quality with the solution located by greedy search with a shorter runtime.

6   Conclusion

In this paper, we propose an anomaly retrieval system for high-dimensional time series. The proposed system consists of two integrated modules, i.e., subspace searching module and discord mining module. We implement the proposed system and perform a comprehensive evaluation with synthetic data and real-world transactional data. Our experimental results show that our system outperforms the baseline algorithms with an execution time suitable for real-time analysis in the production environment. It only takes 22 min to process one month of transaction records (i.e., 600 million records) with the greedy search variant of the proposed system, and 1.5 min for the evolutionary search variant.

References

1. Aggarwal, C.C., Yu, P.S.: Outlier detection for high dimensional data. In: ACM Sigmod Record (2001)
2. Breunig, M.M., Kriegel, H.P., Ng, R.T., Sander, J.: LOF: identifying density-based local outliers. In: ACM Sigmod Record (2000)
3. Chakraborty, K., Mehrotra, K., Mohan, C.K., Ranka, S.: Forecasting the behavior of multivariate time series using neural networks. Neural Netw. **5**, 961–970 (1992)
4. Chandola, V., et al.: Anomaly detection: a survey. ACM Comput. Surv. **41**, 1–58 (2009)
5. Dean, D.J., Nguyen, H., Gu, X.: UBL: Unsupervised behavior learning for predicting performance anomalies in virtualized cloud systems. In: ICAC (2012)
6. Duan, L., et al.: Mining outlying aspects on numeric data. DMKD **29**, 1116–1151 (2015)
7. Eiben, A.E., et al.: Introduction to Evolutionary Computing. Springer, Heidelberg (2003). https://doi.org/10.1007/978-3-662-05094-1
8. Faruk, D.Ö.: A hybrid neural network and ARIMA model for water quality time series prediction. Eng. Appl. Artif. Intell. **23**, 586–594 (2010)
9. Fortin, F.A., et al.: DEAP: evolutionary algorithms made easy. JMLR **13**, 2171–2175 (2012)
10. Gong, S., Zhang, Y., Yu, G.: Clustering stream data by exploring the evolution of density mountain. VLDB **11**, 393–405 (2017)

11. Gupta, M., et al.: Outlier detection for temporal data: a survey. IEEE TMKD **26**, 2250–2267 (2013)

12. Han, J., Pei, J., Kamber, M.: Data Mining: Concepts and Techniques. Elsevier, Amsterdam (2011)

13. He, J., et al.: TScope: automatic timeout bug identification for server systems. In: ICAC (2018)

14. Holland, J.H.: Genetic algorithms. Sci. Am. **267**, 66–73 (1992)

15. Kaastra, I., Boyd, M.: Designing a neural network for forecasting financial and economic time series. Neurocomputing **10**, 215–236 (1996)

16. Keller, F., Muller, E., Bohm, K.: HICS: high contrast subspaces for density-based outlier ranking. In: ICDE (2012)

17. Keogh, E., Lin, J., Lee, S.H., Van Herle, H.: Finding the most unusual time series subsequence: algorithms and applications. KIS **11**, 1–27 (2007)

18. Kriegel, H.-P., Kröger, P., Schubert, E., Zimek, A.: Outlier detection in axis-parallel subspaces of high dimensional data. In: Theeramunkong, T., Kijsirikul, B., Cercone, N., Ho, T.-B. (eds.) PAKDD 2009. LNCS (LNAI), vol. 5476, pp. 831–838. Springer, Heidelberg (2009). https://doi.org/10.1007/978-3-642-01307-2_86

19. Kriegel, H.P., Schubert, M., Zimek, A.: Angle-based outlier detection in high-dimensional data. In: SIGKDD (2008)

20. Malhotra, P., Vig, L., Shroff, G., Agarwal, P.: Long short term memory networks for anomaly detection in time series. In: Proceedings. Presses universitaires de Louvain (2015)

21. Manzoor, E., Lamba, H., Akoglu, L.: xStream: outlier detection in feature-evolving data streams. In: SIGKDD (2018)

22. Mueen, A., et al.: Time series join on subsequence correlation. In: ICDM (2014)

23. Müller, E., Schiffer, M., Seidl, T.: Statistical selection of relevant subspace projections for outlier ranking. In: ICDE (2011)

24. Na, G.S., Kim, D., Yu, H.: DILOF: effective and memory efficient local outlier detection in data streams. In: SIGKDD (2018)

25. Rakthanmanon, T., et al.: Searching and mining trillions of time series subsequences under dynamic time warping. In: SIGKDD. ACM (2012)

26. Salehi, M., Leckie, C., Bezdek, J.C., Vaithianathan, T., Zhang, X.: Fast memory efficient local outlier detection in data streams. TKDE **28**, 3246–3260 (2016)

27. Santora, M.: In hours, thieves took $45 million in A.T.M. scheme (2013). https://www.nytimes.com/2013/05/10/nyregion/eight-charged-in-45-million-global-cyber-bank-thefts.html

28. Schütze, H., Manning, C.D., Raghavan, P.: Introduction to Information Retrieval, vol. 39. Cambridge University Press, Cambridge (2008)

29. Siffer, A., Fouque, P.A., Termier, A., Largouet, C.: Anomaly detection in streams with extreme value theory. In: SIGKDD. ACM (2017)

30. Su, Y., Zhao, Y., Niu, C., Liu, R., Sun, W., Pei, D.: Robust anomaly detection for multivariate time series through stochastic recurrent neural network. In: SIGKDD (2019)

31. Vinh, N.X., et al.: Discovering outlying aspects in large datasets. DMKD **30**, 1520–1555 (2016)

32. World Bank Group: World bank open data (2019). https://data.worldbank.org/

33. Wu, T., et al.: Promotion analysis in multi-dimensional space. VLDB **2**, 109–120 (2009)

34. Ye, M., Li, X., Orlowska, M.E.: Projected outlier detection in high-dimensional mixed-attributes data set. Expert Syst. Appl. **36**, 7104–7113 (2009)

35. Yeh, C.C.M., Kavantzas, N., Keogh, E.: Matrix profile VI: Meaningful multidimensional motif discovery. In: ICDM (2017)

36. Yeh, C.C.M., et al.: Matrix profile I: all pairs similarity joins for time series: a unifying view that includes motifs, discords and shapelets. In: ICDM (2016)

37. Zhang, J., Gao, Q., Wang, H.: SPOT: a system for detecting projected outliers from high-dimensional data streams. In: ICDE (2008)

38. Zhang, L., Lin, J., Karim, R.: An angle-based subspace anomaly detection approach to high-dimensional data: with an application to industrial fault detection. Reliabil. Eng. Syst. Saf. **142**, 482–497 (2015)

39. Zhang, L., Lin, J., Karim, R.: Sliding window-based fault detection from high-dimensional data streams. IEEE Trans. Syst. Man Cybern.: Syst. **47**, 289–303 (2016)

40. Zhu, Y., et al.: Matrix profile II: exploiting a novel algorithm and GPUs to break the one hundred million barrier for time series motifs and joins. In: ICDM (2016)

AIMED-RL: Exploring Adversarial Malware Examples with Reinforcement Learning

Raphael Labaca-Castro[1,2]([✉]), Sebastian Franz[3], and Gabi Dreo Rodosek[1,2]

[1] Research Institute CODE, 81739 Munich, Germany
[2] Universität der Bundeswehr München, 85577 Neubiberg, Germany
raphael.labaca@unibw.de
[3] Technische Universität München, 85748 Munich, Germany

Abstract. Machine learning models have been widely implemented to classify software. These models allow to generalize static features of Windows portable executable files. While highly accurate in terms of classification, they still exhibit weaknesses that can be exploited by applying subtle transformations to the input object. Despite their semantic-preserving nature, such transformations can render the file corrupt. Hence, unlike in the computer vision domain, integrity verification is vital to the generation of adversarial malware examples. Many approaches have been explored in the literature, however, most of them have either overestimated the semantic-preserving transformations or achieved modest evasion rates across general files. We therefore present AIMED-RL, Automatic Intelligent Malware modifications to Evade Detection using Reinforcement Learning. Our approach is able to generate adversarial examples that lead machine learning models to misclassify malware files, without compromising their functionality. We implement our approach using a Distributional Double Deep Q-Network agent, adding a penalty to improve diversity of transformations. Thereby, we achieve competitive results compared to previous research based on reinforcement learning while minimizing the required sequence of transformations.

Keywords: Adversarial learning · Reinforcement learning · Malware

1 Introduction

Malicious software, known as malware, has been a prevalent digital threat. Large efforts have been conducted to correctly and efficiently detect malicious applications using Machine Learning (ML) [1,2]. However, ML models can be fooled by tricking the classifier into returning the incorrect label [3]. Subtle transformations, referred to as perturbations, inserted into the file can be responsible for

S. Franz—Work done at Research Institute CODE while a student at LMU Munich.
This research is partially supported by EC H2020 Project CONCORDIA GA 830927.

Y. Dong et al. (Eds.): ECML PKDD 2021, LNAI 12978, pp. 37–52, 2021.
https://doi.org/10.1007/978-3-030-86514-6_3

misclassification. For this reason, the generation of adversarial malware examples has become an intensive area of research in the last decade [4]. Unlike in the computer vision domain, where images can be randomly modified with adversarial perturbations, Windows Portable Executable (PE) files can lose their integrity and functionality following a series of too many or strong injections [5].

Recent advances have shown that ML-based malware classifiers report weaknesses when confronted with gradient-based attacks [6]. Generative Adversarial Networks (GAN) were also successful in generating adversarial examples. In this case, a surrogate model was trained based on the target malware classifier. Both approaches rely heavily on feature-space adversarial examples, thus merely producing a representation of the input object rather than a real file [7,8].

Conversely, further research has been looking at the problem-space on the Windows platform. Anderson et al. [9] were one of the first to show that reinforcement learning (RL) can be successfully used to generate adversarial examples in the problem space for Windows PE. Yet, the use of semantic-preserving perturbations can still lead to corrupt adversarial examples. Hence, an integrity verification is paramount to ensure functionality. Further approaches, including Labaca-Castro et al. [10], explored Genetic Programming (GP) with integrity verification that outperforms similar strategies without rendering the files corrupt. However, the inherent issue of getting stuck in local-minima may prevent the system from finding the best sequence of adversarial transformations.

We, therefore, present **AIMED-RL**: Automatic Intelligent Malware modifications to Evade Detection with Reinforcement Learning. This approach combines integrity analysis with improved reinforcement learning techniques. We assume that an attacker use a toolbox with a set of transformations, which can be injected into an original malware file and prevent a ML-based model from properly classifying it as malicious. Our approach shows that RL can be implemented to increase the success rate of such attacks against malware classifiers and is able to outperform previous research in the field by significantly reducing the efforts. This paper is structured as follows: In Sect. 2, we take an extensive look at the existing literature about adversarial machine learning in the malware domain focusing mainly on RL. Next, we describe the methodology in Sect. 3 and illuminate the design of our reinforcement learning approach. In Sect. 4 we present the results and further explores the experiments conducted. Finally, we conclude this work with a short summary in Sect. 6.

2   Related Work

Here we evaluate the existing literature about adversarial machine learning in the malware domain. We discuss related research and elaborate on the current state of the field.

2.1   Reinforcement Learning

Reinforcement learning has become an increasing area of scientific interest in the past decade. The usage of RL has extended beyond traditional applications and entered new fields, such as networking and security [11–14].

One of the first attempts to generate adversarial malware examples using RL was presented by Anderson et al. [9]. The authors implemented ten different perturbations designed to be semantic- and functionality-preserving; that is, they do not negatively affect the structure of the actual code. A maximum budget of ten turns, equivalent to ten injected perturbations, was allowed before the attempt was cancelled and the next episode was started. The reward function only consisted of the detection result by the classifier, where 0 stands for a detected file and 10 for an evasive. The environment was based on the OpenAI gym framework [15]. The article reports an evasion rate of up to 24%, and an average rate of 16.25% over 200 holdout malware examples. According to the authors, the results must be seen as modest in comparison to white-box based gradient attacks or grey-box attempts. Although the perturbations were intended to be functionality-preserving, they did, in fact, hamper the integrity of the adversarial examples since no integrity verification took place.

Building on the same idea, Fang et al., [16] undertook a similar approach using different parameters. The state input was reduced to 513 dimensions and consisted only of byte and entropy histograms. The authors assumed that a smaller and thus more comprehensive input could simplify the training of the agent. The action space was also decreased to four actions, which were expected to maintain improved functionality-preserving properties. A value-based Double Deep Q-Network (DDQN) was trained. In addition, it is reported the use of integrity verification to validate that the created examples remained functional [17]. An evasion rate of 46.56% was reported, which can be considered a strong improvement compared to previous approaches. However, the use of 80 injections based on only four different perturbations could potentially make it easier to detect and identify files that have been respectively modified.

Fang, Zeng, et al., [18] criticized that previous work [9] claimed to use a black-box scenario, while using the same feature-space for the reinforcement learning agent as well as for the detection engine, resembling more a grey-box attack. To avoid this problem, they trained their own classifier to detect PE files using 2,478 dimensions. Still, it remains unclear if this solves the issue since attackers usually have domain knowledge and could be able to anticipate which features are likely to be used by a static malware classifier. They further suggested that the high amount of randomness in the perturbations used in previous work [9, 16] could lead to instability during the training process. Instead of picking an import function at random, for instance, they crafted an individual perturbation for each import function. These alterations led to a significantly increased action space with 218 dimensions, which raises the question about whether the agent is able to explore the possible states satisfactorily and register the small differences between the many individual perturbations. A DDQN model in combination with a Dueling DQN (DuDDQN) was implemented and the agent was trained for 3,000 episodes, which then reported an evasion rate of 19.13%.

2.2 Further Approaches

In a stochastic approach [5] perturbations were randomly injected into the malware to explore the potential of automated malware manipulation. An integrity test was implemented using a sandbox [17] to check whether the malware is still functional after the injections. It was reported that an increasing number of injected perturbations reduced the number of functional examples considerably, ranging from 50% functionality for three injected perturbations to only 7.5% for 25. Overall, 18% of manipulated files were reported to be functional on average. The detection was tested by malware scanners on VirusTotal [19]. The best manipulated and functional examples achieved a reduction in the detection rate by about 80%. Interestingly, examples using only five perturbations showed similar results as those relying on an extreme number of 500 perturbations. Moreover, the length of the perturbation sequence proved to be less important than the order of the injected perturbations. However, the approach was slow to find adversarial examples when scaling and, hence, optimization techniques will be needed to improve efficiency.

To address the limitations discussed, another strategy was proposed [10]. This time, a genetic programming algorithm was implemented to find adversarial malware examples. Unlike reinforcement learning, this technique does not require any training time. The fitness function was composed of four parameters, namely functionality, detection, similarity (to the original file on byte-level) and distance (number of generations). Compared to previous approach [5], the current solution was significantly faster, thus requiring less processing time to create files. It also produced fewer corrupted, non-functioning examples. Probing the functional examples against four classifiers, evasion rates of about 24% were reported.

In [20], another similar genetic programming approach to evade static detection was introduced. In this case, the authors only used two perturbations, both of which were meant to be functionality-preserving by design. They, therefore, did not employ an integrity step to check the generated examples for functionality. The perturbations were *padding* (adding bytes at the end of the file) and *section injection*, which were previously used by Anderson et al. and Labaca-Castro et al., among other perturbations. By removing the functionality check, the process of generating adversarial malware was sped up significantly, thus avoiding the most limiting factor regarding the performance in previous approaches [5,10]. However, no evidence was presented to confirm the functionality of the malware, as the files did not appear to be verified a posteriori. In fact, the original perturbations used in [9] were also declared to be functionality-preserving, but turned out to produce corrupted malware as it was acknowledged in the article. Nonetheless, the authors reported that the approach managed to evade, on average, a considerable amount of 12 commercial classifiers.

3   AIMED-RL

In this section, we present how the experiments using reinforcement learning for adversarial malware have been designed. We start providing the theoretical context and continue defining the experimental settings and environment of our approach.

3.1   Framework and Notation

The idea behind reinforcement learning is to find the best decision or action for a given input *state*. Because every state will be linked to a certain *reward*, a machine learning model based on reinforcement learning is programmed to maximize this reward over a sequence of states. The entity that is deciding and executing the actions is called *agent* in RL-terms. By exploring a lot of possible states over the course of many *episodes*, the agent will eventually learn to link actions and states to some amount of reward. After the exploratory *training* stage, it should now be able to perform the best possible action for each state, leading to the highest reward. This process can be formalized as a *Markov Decision Process* (MDP), consisting of a 4-tuple:

$$MDP := (S, A, \gamma, R(S, A)) \tag{1}$$

For S being a finite set of possible states, A the set of possible actions, γ a discount factor for future rewards and $R(S, A)$ the reward function. A transition from one state to another can formally be described as:

$$(s_t, a_t, r_{t+1}, s_{t+1}) \tag{2}$$

This makes clear that for every timestep (*turn*) t an action has to be chosen by the agent to transition to the next state s. The rule by which the agent decides which action to take is called the *policy* of the agent. It can be formalized as a probability distribution over the available set of actions given a certain state:

$$\pi(a|s) = P[A_t = a | S_t = s] \tag{3}$$

It is necessary to describe the policy of the agent as non-deterministic, because it has some random component in the training stage.

After all, the most important goal in reinforcement learning is for the agent to learn a (near) optimal policy.

Q-Learning and Deep Q-Learning. Q-learning has already been introduced in the early 1990s [21]. Following the reinforcement learning process described in Eq. 1–3, it becomes clear that each different state has its own value determined by its current reward and the possible future reward that the next states can deliver. The function that ascribes these values to the state is called the *value* function $V(s)$. However, for practical reasons, it is simpler to consider the actions associated with the state transitions. This relation is defined by the eponymous Q-function:

$$Q(s, a) = r(s, a) + \gamma \max_{a' \in A} Q(s', a') \tag{4}$$

The discount factor γ controls hereby, how much the agent is grinding for a long-term reward (high value for γ), or is just greedily considering the current reward (low value for γ). This means that the Q-value is the expected discounted reward for executing action a at state s and following policy π thereafter [21].

To track and update the Q-values, they have to be stored together with their associated state and action pair. In a simple case, with only few states and actions available, a 2D table can be used to accomplish the task. This approach can be regarded similarly to dynamic programming. Even if one only stores the visited and thus relevant states, complexity and storage limits are exceeded very fast. The application of deep neural networks allows to handle this problem.

Instead of directly calculating the Q-values and storing them, a deep neural network with weights θ can be used as a non-linear function approximator. The network can be trained by minimizing the loss function $L(\theta)$ over the course of training episodes with stochastic gradient descent. The size of the output layer of the network must match the number of possible actions. This mimics a supervised learning process, where the reward defines the labeled data for a state. The network has to learn to predict these rewards correctly in order to minimize the loss function. From these predictions, the optimal actions to achieve the highest reward can eventually be inferred [22].

3.2   Experimental Setting

Attacker Knowledge. Following previous work [4,23], training data knowledge is defined by $\mathcal{D}$ and feature set $\mathcal{X}$, algorithm g, and hyperparameters w.

Limited Knowledge (LK). Based upon $\theta_{LK} = \{\hat{\mathcal{D}}\}$, attackers can query the model in unlimited fashion and receive binary outputs labelling the adversarial examples into malicious or benign. Moreover, they could also transfer the results of the queries into a surrogate classifier in case the attackers have additional knowledge of the learning algorithm and feature set $\theta_{LK} = \{\hat{\mathcal{D}}, \hat{\mathcal{X}}, \hat{g}, \hat{w}\}$. In our scenario, the LK capability fits the situation appropriately since the agent is only able to assign a reward based on the output of the classifier. None of the underlying architecture from the model nor its training set are relevant for the attackers.

Target Model. A LightGBM [24] model is implemented, which was trained on 600,000 benign and malicious software files. In terms of performance, the model scores an ROC-AUC of 0.993 [9]. After analyzing an input file, the classifier returns a value between 0 and 1 for benign or malicious examples respectively. Ergo, a larger value corresponds to a higher confidence in the examined file being malicious. As used in the literature [5,9], for the evaluation, we keep the threshold set to 0.9 to label a file as malware and, hence, be able to benchmark performance against different approaches. Regarding the training stage however, we decided to lower the confidence rate to 0.8, providing a bigger challenge for the RL agent. Note that this threshold is only known to the detection model and is not used by the RL agent, in order to keep the characteristics of a black-box scenario and attack.

Injection Strategy. Within the literature, a number of publications used varying numbers to define the maximum of allowed perturbations for the agent, ranging from 10 [9] to 100 [18]. However, in [10] the authors suggested that a smaller number of around five perturbations showed similar results and that the order of perturbations could be more relevant than the actual quantity. We therefore limited the number of allowed injections to five perturbations.

Furthermore, we introduced an additional *reset* strategy to enhance the idea of *order* matters more than *numbers*. Our environment is allowed to reset the malware example back to its original state if the classifier is still able to detect it after five perturbations. This allows the agent a second shot at the same file, if the first attempt failed to successfully generate an adversarial example.

3.3   Environment

State. The state input for the agent presented by the environment consists of both, handcrafted PE features extracted from the bytes of the binary file as well as structure-agnostic byte(-entropy) histograms. To extract the PE-specific information, the LIEF library [25] is employed. The state relies on the feature space defined by [9]:

PE-Specific Features. i) *Metadata from PE header file information* (62 dim.): Extracted features from the PE header, such as OS information, linker version or the magic number. ii) *Metadata about the PE sections* (255 dim.): Stores information about section names, sizes and entropy. A hash function is used to compress these values into 255 dimensions for every PE file. iii) *Metadata about Import Table* (1280 dim.): Contains information about the names of imported functions and libraries in the import table of the data directory. The names are stored up to a maximum amount of 10,000 characters. iv) *Metadata about Export Table* (128 dim.): Stores the names of exported functions. The length of the stored value is also limited to 10,000 characters. v) *Counts of human-readable strings* (104 dim.): Counts the number of certain strings like URLs (*https*), registry entries (*HKEY_*) or paths (*c:/*), and creates a histogram that stores the distribution of characters within the strings. vi) *General file information* (10 dim.): General metadata about the file. For instance, whether it has a debug section or a signature, and the length of export and import tables. It also stores the size of the whole file.

Structure-Independent Features. i) *Byte histogram* (256 dim.): Creates a histogram with byte occurrences over the whole binary file. ii) *2D byte-entropy histogram* (256 dim.): To compute the byte-entropy histogram, windows with size 2048 bytes are slided over the raw bytes from the file with a step size of 1024 bytes. For every block created in this way, the entropy is calculated as the base 2 logarithm of the bytes in the block. After that, the byte-entropy histogram is created with these computed values and flattened into a 256 dimensional feature vector. The method is based on the work by [26]; this original work used both a smaller window (1024 bytes) and step size (256 bytes) than applied here.

Both, PE-specific and structure-independent information sum up to a 2,351 dimensional feature vector.

Reward. The reward is one of the most important aspects of the environment, as it directly influences the policy of the agent. In our implementation, the reward consists of a linear function of three individual parameters. We hereby decided to set $R_{max} = 10$ as the maximum reward for each.

In [9], only *detection* R_{det} was used to calculate the reward R, returning $R_{det} = 0$ for detected and $R_{det} = 10$ for adversarial examples.

More recent approaches [5,16,18], also included the *distance* R_{dis} from the original file in their reward function. R_{dis} is expressed by the number of turns that have passed. We multiplied it with a factor that gives the maximum number of allowed perturbations $t_{max} = 5$ the highest reward. Thus we incentivised our agents to use our domain knowledge that five perturbations seem to be the most promising in terms of evasion and functionality. R_{dis} can therefore be defined as follows:

$$R_{dis} = \frac{R_{max}}{t_{max}} * t \tag{5}$$

This work further includes the *similarity* R_{sim} of a manipulated file compared to the original one for the reward function, which is inspired by a genetic programming approach [10]. The similarity value is calculated based on a byte-level comparison of the two respective files. A bigger distance between the two files results in a larger value, leading to a higher diversity caused by the injected perturbation.

Given that the value can vary within a larger range, we decided to calculate a ratio between the modified file size, S_{mod}, and the original, S_{orig}, aiming to maintain consistency across the adversarial examples. Based on empirical examination, we determined that a percentage value of $S_{best} = 40\%$ should work best to create the most promising modifications. That is why we calculated R_{sim} according to the difference to this value:

$$R_{sim} = (1 - |S_{best} - \frac{S_{mod}}{S_{orig}}|) * R_{max} \tag{6}$$

In order to be able to tune the model based on importance of each parameter, we introduced weights, ω, for each of the rewards. We therefore present the different weight distributions in Table 1.

The following equation summarizes the reward, R, for our environment:

$$R = R_{det} * \omega_{det} + R_{sim} * \omega_{sim} + R_{dis} * \omega_{dis} \tag{7}$$

Table 1. Weight distribution strategies for the reward function. Standard sets the same weight to each parameter whilst Incremental shifts the attention towards detection.

R_{det}	R_{sim}	R_{dist}	STRATEGY
0.33	0.33	0.33	Standard
0.50	0.20	0.30	Incremental

We have established that agents tend to inject the same perturbation repeatedly and, thus, we introduced a penalization to the reward function. The change consists in a *reward penalty* if the agent uses duplicated perturbations, ρ, within the same file:

$$R = \begin{cases} R & \text{for } \rho = 0 \\ R * 0.8 & \text{for } \rho = 1 \\ R * 0.6 & \text{for } \rho > 1 \end{cases} \tag{8}$$

Actions. The agent's task is to decide on each turn which perturbation should be injected into the PE file. The actions are injected sequentially, so that every turn builds on the modified file from the previous injection. The perturbations injected [9], with the exception of *identity* and *create_new_entry_point*, which were left out because of technical problems [5], are described as follows: i) *overlay_append*: Appends a sequence of bytes at the end of the PE file (overlay); length and entropy are random. ii) *imports_append*: Adds an unused function to the import table in the data directory. The function is chosen randomly from a predefined list of DLL imports. iii) *section_rename*: Manipulates an existing section name. For all section perturbations the section name is chosen at random from a list of known benign section names. iv) *section_add*: Creates a new unused section in the section table. v) *section_append*: Appends bytes at the end of a section. The length and entropy of the injected bytes is again chosen at random. vi) *upx_pack*: Uses the UPX [27] packer to pack the whole PE file. Note that the compression level (between 1 and 9) is also chosen at random. vii) *upx_unpack*: Unpacks the file using the UPX packer. viii) *remove_signature*: Removes the signer information in the certificate table of the data directory. ix) *remove_debug*: Manipulates the debug information in the data directory. x) *break_optional_header_checksum*: Modifies and thus breaks the optional header checksum by setting it to 0. Note that the first six perturbations use randomization. The implications of this have already been discussed in section Sect. 2.1.

Agent. While an Actor Critic model with Experience Replay (ACER) has been used [9] as a policy-based approach for generating adversarial malware examples, it has been shown [16,18] that value-based networks are also suited for RL problems in the malware context. Hence, we implement *Deep Q-Networks* with additional enhancements [28] that account for data efficiency and performance as can be observed in Table 2.

Table 2. Overview of RL-based approaches and its parameters. While related work implemented ACER, DDQN and Dueling DDQN (DuDDQN), we use a Distributional DDQN (DiDDQN) agent and Noisy Nets as exploration strategy.

APPROACH	AGENT	OPTIMIZER	D. FACTOR	EXPLORATION
Fang et al., 2019	DDQN	Adam	0.99	$\epsilon - greedy$
F., Zeng et al., 2020	DuDDQN	RMSProp	N/A	Boltzmann
Anderson et al., 2018	ACER	Adam	0.95	Boltzmann
AIMED-RL	**DiDDQN**	**Adam**	**0.95**	**Noisy Nets**

Our experiments with baseline DQN showed a concentrated distribution of Q-values whilst Distributional DQN allowed more precise decisions and improvements in the learning process.

Instead of a regular DQN, we used a *Distributional DQN* [29] with two hidden layers and 64 nodes each and $V_{min} = -10$, $V_{max} = 10$, $N_{atoms} = 51$ that focus in learning the distribution of rewards rather than the expected reward value.

In addition, we implemented a *Double DQN* [30], which is a well-known extension to Q-Learning that solves the problem of action-value overestimation. The neural network uses *Adam* [31] as optimizer with the following parameters: $\alpha = 0.001, \beta_1 = 0.9, \beta_2 = 0.999$ and $\epsilon = 0.01$. Another enhancement was to apply *prioritized experience replay* [32] with $\alpha = 0.6, \beta_0 = 0.4, betasteps = t_{max} * episodes, capacity = 1,000$, instead of usual replay buffers. This allows to select episodes from the replay buffer with higher information for the agent more often, which leads to a more efficient training process. For exploration, we chose *Noisy Nets* [33] with $\sigma = 0.5$ since it allowed for better exploration of the action space and more diversified transformation vectors.

4   Experimental Results

In this section we discuss the results from the experiments. Motivated by limitations from previous work, we focus on answering the following research questions:

RQ1: Is it possible to *increase diversity* in the sequence of adversarial perturbations? (Sect. 4.1)

RQ2: Can RL-based agents *efficiently* learn to evade *malware classifiers* with shorter sequences of perturbations? (Sect. 4.2)

During the training stage of our agents, we sampled 4,187 portable executable files from VirusShare [34]. The experiments have been evaluated on a holdout set of 200 malware examples that were not included in the training set. The integrity is verified by executing the adversarial example in a protected environment [17].

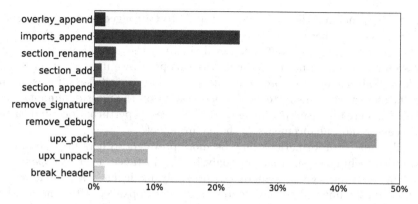

Fig. 1. Usage of perturbations of best agent to create adversarial files. While two perturbations are particularly dominant, a broad range of actions can be observed.

4.1   Diversity of Perturbations

As we can observe in Fig. 1, the agent employs a broad variety of perturbations throughout the evaluation to generate adversarial examples. In line with previous research [9,18,20], *upx_pack* turned out to be the most dominant perturbation in our environment.

Table 3. Comparison of evasion rates among agents using two different strategies: incremental and standard weights with (WP) and with no penalty (NP). An additional set was included to compare RL-based agents with random results.

STRATEGY	EPISODES	AVG. EVASION	BEST AGENT
Incremental (WP)	1000	23.52%	40.00%
	1500	20.35%	33.84%
Incremental (NP)	1000	18.78%	30.81%
	1500	23.06%	35.35%
Standard (WP)	1000	21.07%	35.86%
	1500	26.29%	43.15%
Standard (NP)	1000	21.6%	30.0%
	1500	23.74%	41.41%
Random Agent	–	21.21%	24.62%

Since packing strongly impacts the structure of the file and this is an important feature for static malware classifiers, its dominance over other perturbations appears reasonable. In fact, packing is a common practice amongst commercial (benign) software vendors to obfuscate their code or to reduce the size of their executable files. Further research [20] suggests that these kind of perturbations (i.e., packing) increase the probability of a file to be flagged as malicious. However, from the classifier perspective, considering compressing with UPX packing a malicious behavior itself would necessarily increase the number of false-positive results and is therefore not encouraged. At this point, we must note that some attacks will always be more prominent and, therefore, we advise to focus on the diversity of perturbations instead of concentrating on the most dominant. Most of the agents created used heterogeneous sequences of perturbations, indicating the success of our enhancements to the environment.

While some transformations may be more prevalent, others may be flagged by security techniques such as pre-analysis. For instance, *overlay_append* can indeed be a strong sign of a modified, probably malicious, file. For a benign PE it would be unusual to have bytes randomly appended after the overlay, as these would only increase its file size without adding any value. Packing or unpacking the file before presenting it to the ML-model could also be applied as a pre-analysis technique to avoid packers to fool the classifier.

4.2 Evasion Rate

In Table 3 we observe the comparison of evasion results among agents taking into account different strategies. In each case, 10 agents were trained for 1000 and 1500 episodes respectively. A random agent has also been added to compare the generation of adversarial examples with the use of reinforcement learning. Note that some combinations of perturbations can render the adversarial examples corrupt. These files were excluded from both the training and the evaluation sets, resulting in non-uniform values for some evasion rates. While the best *average evasion rate* improvement scores 7%, the best *agent* is improved by more than 20%. Both weight distributions returned agents that scored significantly better than a purely random approach. The best agents, however, were trained with the help of our reward penalty strategy. In fact, the agents implementing the penalty technique always outperform their non-penalized counterparts, as depicted in Fig. 2 where a comparison among four different configuration of agents is displayed.

The best agent, trained within $1,500$ episodes using *standard* strategy with penalty, managed to score an evasion rate of 43.15% on the holdout set. The adversarial examples created were 97.64% functional, leading to an overall evasion rate of 42.13%. Even considering the reset strategy that de-facto doubles the amount of episodes to $3,000$, this number of episodes is still arguably small. In fact, the agent was updated only about 13,900 times during training. This is equivalent to the number of modifications created during training and is considerably lower than the budget of 50,000 modifications used by [9] in their previous approach. Thus, such an agent can be trained without highly powerful hardware in a short period of time.

Table 4 summarizes the results of AIMED-RL compared to previous work. While Fang et al. [16] report a higher evasion rate of 46.56% with functional files, it is important to note that we were not able to reproduce these results given that no artifact was made available.

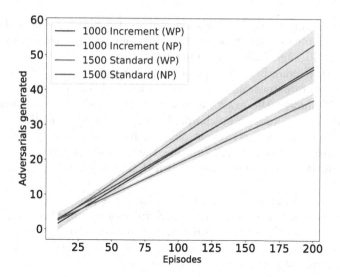

Fig. 2. Comparing our best results regarding the reward penalty strategy. The lines represent the average of generated adversarial files over ten trained agents. For both numbers of training episodes, the agents with the penalty outperform their counterparts. This concerns both the best and the average evasion rate.

We experienced a similar situation with F., Zeng et al. [18]. In this case only the malware set was published.

Table 4. Comparison of evasion results of AIMED-RL against different approaches in the literature. The LGBM model is employed widely across the literature and serves as a benchmark. Only one approach implemented DeepDetectNet (DDNet), which makes their evasion rates less comparable. The functionality test (FT) returns a binary output.

APPROACH	SPACE	REWARD	PERTS.	MODEL	FT	EVASION
Fang et al., 2019	4	R_{det}, R_{dist}	80	LGBM	Yes	46.56%
F., Zeng et al., 2020	218	R_{det}, R_{dist}	100	DDNet	Yes	19.13%
Anderson et al., 2018	11	R_{det}	10	LGBM	No	16.25%
AIMED-RL	**10**	$R_{det}, R_{dist}, R_{sim}$	**5**	**LGBM**	**Yes**	**42.13%**

Therefore, in order to evaluate the data, we proceeded to acquire their pool of malware files and modified them with our best agent. By adding only five perturbations we were able to get 42 out of 50 to be functional, ergo 84%. In their work, however, they were injecting up to 100 transformations. Even if their results keep the functionality rate that we had with five perturbations, the evasion rate with our integrity tests would be around 16.07%. Since this is an extrapolation we do not strive for formal comparison. Nevertheless, we believe these reproducible steps are important given that highly-perturbed PE files are reported to break after a large number of modifications [5]. This argument similarly applies to [16] which also used a high budget of 80 perturbations.

On the other hand, further approaches [16,18] also reported the use of IDA Pro [35] to generate control flow graphs as a means of checking whether the examples still showed the exact same behavior. Although this approach may seem compelling, in order to be thoroughly implemented, it is likely to require manual verification and, therefore, strongly increase the cost of generating fully-functional adversarial examples. Regarding the remaining approach by Anderson et al. [9], while the environment was published, integrity verification did not take place.

With respect to the reward, the distribution of the parameters contributed in different degrees towards the total reward. *Similarity* accounts for 24%, *Detection* 32%, and *Distance* 44%. In our approach, distance is updated on every turn and hence has stronger role. However, further room for optimization may still be available in terms of how parameters are updated.

Overall, the agent that reports the best evasion result on the holdout dataset needs $1,500$ episodes of training with *standard* strategy and *penalization* activated. Unlike what can generally be observed in the literature, the evasion rate for successful adversarial examples seems to improve by a better combination of small factors rather than a larger sequence of adversarial perturbations.

5   Availability

In order to foster further research in this area we are releasing AIMED-RL[1]. While we are aware that the work could be misused by adversaries, we believe that enforcing security to protect from adversarial examples outweighs the potentially negative impact. Malicious actors have available resources to generate sophisticated attacks and even legitimate software can be exploited by committed adversaries. However, releasing the code to the community can enable researchers to protect towards adaptive attacks and therefore increase the level of defenses against adversarial malware.

6   Conclusion

In this paper we presented AIMED-RL, which aims to extend the capabilities of existing approaches to generate fully functional adversarial examples in the malware domain. We redefined the reward function and evaluated different weight strategies to maximize the output. To address the limitation of homogeneous sequences of perturbations, which are a widely discussed limitation in reinforcement learning approaches, we introduced and demonstrated the importance of a penalty technique. Moreover, we showed that is possible to train a competitive agent that generates adversarial examples with a shorter sequence of transformations, which leads to less manipulated adversarial malware, without compromising its functionality.

---

[1] https://github.com/zRapha/AIMED.

References

1. Ucci, D., Aniello, L., Baldoni, R.: Survey of machine learning techniques for malware analysis. Comput. Secur. **81**, 123–147 (2019)
2. Raff, E., Nicholas, C.: Survey of machine learning methods and challenges for windows malware classification. arXiv:2006.09271 (2020)
3. Szegedy, C., et al.: Intriguing properties of neural networks. arXiv (2013)
4. Biggio, B., Roli, F.: Wild patterns: ten years after the rise of adversarial machine learning. Pattern Recogn. **84**, 317–331 (2018)
5. Labaca-Castro, R., Schmitt, C., Rodosek, G.D.: ARMED: how automatic malware modifications can evade static detection? In: 2019 5th International Conference on Information Management (ICIM), pp. 20–27 (2019)
6. Labaca-Castro, R., Biggio, B., Rodosek, G.D.: Poster: attacking malware classifiers by crafting gradient-attacks that preserve functionality. In: Proceedings of the 2019 ACM SIGSAC Conference on Computer and Communications Security, pp. 2565–2567 (2019)
7. Hu, W., Tan, Y.: Generating adversarial malware examples for black-box attacks based on GAN. ArXiv (2017)
8. Castro, R.L., Schmitt, C., Rodosek, G.D.: Poster: training GANs to generate adversarial examples against malware classification. IEEE Secur. Priv. (2019)
9. Anderson, H.S., Kharkar, A., Filar, B., Evans, D., Roth, P.: Learning to evade static PE machine learning malware models via RL. ArXiv (2018)
10. Labaca-Castro, R., Schmitt, C., Rodosek, G.D.: AIMED: evolving malware with genetic programming to evade detection. In: 2019 18th IEEE International Conference on Trust, Security and Privacy in Computing and Communications/13th IEEE International Conference On Big Data Science And Engineering (TrustCom/BigDataSE), pp. 240–247 (2019)
11. Chen, T., Liu, J., Xiang, Y., Niu, W., Tong, E., Han, Z.: Adversarial attack and defense in reinforcement learning-from AI security view. Cybersecurity **2**(1), 11 (2019)
12. Luong, N.C., et al.: Applications of deep reinforcement learning in communications and networking: A survey. IEEE Commun. Surv. Tutor. **21**(4), 3133–3174 (2019)
13. Nguyen, T.T., Reddi, V.J.: Deep reinforcement learning for cyber security. arXiv preprint arXiv:1906.05799 (2019)
14. Qian, Y., Wu, J., Wang, R., Zhu, F., Zhang, W.: Survey on reinforcement learning applications in communication networks. J. Commun. Inform. Netw. **4**(2), 30–39 (2019)
15. Brockman, G., et al.: OpenAI gym. ArXiv (2016)
16. Fang, Z., Wang, J., Li, B., Wu, S., Zhou, Y., Huang, H.: Evading anti-malware engines with deep reinforcement learning. IEEE Access **7**, 48867–48879 (2019)
17. Guarnieri, C., Tanasi, A., Bremer, J., Schloesser, M.: Cuckoo sandbox - automated malware analysis. Cuckoo (2021)
18. Fang, Y., Zeng, Y., Li, B., Liu, L., Zhang, L.: DeepDetectNet vs RLAttackNet: an adversarial method to improve deep learning-based static malware detection model. PLOS One **15**(4), e0231626 (2020)
19. VirusTotal. Analyze suspicious files and URLs to detect types of malware, automatically share them with the security community (2021). https://virustotal.com. Accessed 25 Feb 2021
20. Demetrio, L., Biggio, B., Lagorio, G., Roli, F., Armando, A.: Functionality-preserving black-box optimization of adversarial windows malware. ArXiv (2020)

21. Christopher, J.C.H.: Watkins and Peter Dayan. Q-learning. Mach. Learn. **8**(1992), 279–292 (1992)
22. Mnih, V., et al.: Playing atari with deep reinforcement learning. ArXiv (2013)
23. Carlini, N., et al.: On evaluating adversarial robustness. CoRR, abs/1902.06705 (2019)
24. Ke, G., et al.: LightGBM: a highly efficient gradient boosting decision tree. In: Guyon, I., et al. (eds.) Advances in Neural Information Processing Systems, vol. 30, pp. 3146–3154. Curran Associates Inc. (2017)
25. Quarkslab: LIEF: library to instrument executable formats. QuarksLab (2020)
26. Saxe, J., Berlin, K.: Deep neural network based malware detection using two dimensional binary program features. ArXiv (2015)
27. Oberhumer, M.F.X.J., Molnár, L., Reiser, J.F.: UPX: the ultimate packer for executables - homepage. GitHub (2020)
28. Hessel, M., et al.: Rainbow: combining improvements in deep reinforcement learning. Proceedings of the AAAI Conference on Artificial Intelligence, vol. 32, no. 1, pp. 3215–3222 (2018)
29. Bellemare, M.G., Dabney, W., Munos, R.: A distributional perspective on reinforcement learning. ArXiv, 21 July 2017
30. van Hasselt, H., Guez, A., Silver, D.: Deep reinforcement learning with double q-learning. In: Proceedings of the AAAI Conference on Artificial Intelligence, vol. 30, no. 1 (2016)
31. Kingma, D.P., Ba, J.: Adam: a method for stochastic optimization. ArXiv (2014)
32. Schaul, T., Quan, J., Antonoglou, I., Silver, D.: Prioritized experience replay. ArXiv (2015)
33. Fortunato, M., et al.: Noisy networks for exploration. In: Proceedings of the International Conference on Representation Learning (ICLR 2018), Vancouver, Canada (2018)
34. VirusShare. VirusShare: a repository of malware samples for security researchers (2021). https://virusshare.com. Accessed 12 Mar 2021
35. Hex-Rays. IDA Pro: A powerful disassembler and a versatile debugger (2021). https://www.hex-rays.com/products/ida/. Accessed 29 Mar 2021

Learning Explainable Representations of Malware Behavior

Paul Prasse[1]([✉]), Jan Brabec[2], Jan Kohout[2], Martin Kopp[2], Lukas Bajer[2], and Tobias Scheffer[1]

[1] Department of Computer Science, University of Potsdam, Potsdam, Germany
{prasse,scheffer}@uni-potsdam.de
[2] Cisco Systems, Cognitive Intelligence, Prague, Czech Republic
{janbrabe,jkohout,markopp,lubajer}@cisco.com

Abstract. We address the problems of identifying malware in network telemetry logs and providing *indicators of compromise*—comprehensible explanations of behavioral patterns that identify the threat. In our system, an array of specialized detectors abstracts network-flow data into comprehensible *network events* in a first step. We develop a neural network that processes this sequence of events and identifies specific threats, malware families and broad categories of malware. We then use the *integrated-gradients* method to highlight events that jointly constitute the characteristic behavioral pattern of the threat. We compare network architectures based on CNNs, LSTMs, and transformers, and explore the efficacy of unsupervised pre-training experimentally on large-scale telemetry data. We demonstrate how this system detects njRAT and other malware based on behavioral patterns.

Keywords: Neural networks · Malware detection · Sequence models · Unsupervised pre-training

1 Introduction

Toady's malware can exhibit different kinds of malicious behaviour. Malware collects personal and financial data, can encrypt users' files for ransom, is used to commit click-fraud, or promotes financial scams by intrusive advertising. Client-based antivirus tools employ signature-based analysis, static analysis of portable-executable files, emulation, and dynamic, behavior-based analysis to detect malware [34]. Systems that analyze network telemetry data complement antivirus software and are widely used in corporate networks. They allow organizations to enforce acceptable-use and security policies throughout the network and minimize management overhead. Telemetry analysis makes it possible to encapsulate malware detection into network devices or cloud services [6,17].

Research on applying machine learning to malware detection is abundant. However, the principal obstacle that impedes the deployment of machine-learning solutions in practice is that computer-security analysts need to be able

© Springer Nature Switzerland AG 2021
Y. Dong et al. (Eds.): ECML PKDD 2021, LNAI 12978, pp. 53–68, 2021.
https://doi.org/10.1007/978-3-030-86514-6_4

to validate and confirm—or overturn—decisions to block software as malware. However, machine-learning models usually work as black boxes and do not provide a decision rationale that analysts can understand and verify. In computer security, *indicators of compromise* refer to specific, observable evidence that indicates, with high confidence, malicious behavior. Security analysts consider indicators of compromise to be grounds for the classification of software as malware. For instance, indicators of compromise that identify software as variants of the *WannaCry* malware family include the presence of the WannaCry ransom note in the executable file and communication patterns to specific URLs that are used exclusively by a kill-switch mechanism of the virus [3].

In recent years, machine-learning models have been developed that emphasize *explainability* of the decisions and underlying representations. For instance, *Shapley values* [22], and the *DeepLift* [32] and *integrated gradients* methods [33] quantify the contribution of input attributes to the model decision. However, in order to be part of a comprehensible explanation of why software is in fact malicious, the importance weights would have to refer to events that analysts can relate to specific behavior of malicious software.

In this paper, we first discuss a framework of classifiers that detect a wide range of intuitively meaningful network events. We then develop neural networks that detect malware based on behavioral patterns composed of these behaviors. We compare network architectures based on CNNs, LSTMs, and transformers. In order to address the relative scarcity of labeled data, we investigate whether initializing the models by unsupervised pre-training improves their performance. We review how the model detects the njRAT and other malware families based on behavioral indicators of compromise.

2   Related Work

Prior work on the analysis of *HTTP logs* [25] has addressed the problems of identifying command-and-control servers [24], unsupervised detection of malware [7,19], and supervised detection of malware using domain blacklists as labels [6,8,13]. HTTP log files contain the full URL string, from which a wide array of informative features can be extracted [6].

A body of recent work has aimed at detecting Android malware by network-traffic analysis. Arora *et al.* [5] use the average packet size, average flow duration, and a small set of other features to identify 48 malicious Android apps. Lashkari *et al.* [20] collect 1,500 benign and 400 malicious Android apps, extract flow duration and volume feature, and apply several machine-learning algorithms from the Weka library. They observe high accuracy values on the level of individual flows. Demontie *et al.* [10] model different types of attacks against such detection mechanisms and devise a feature-learning paradigm that mitigates these attacks. Malik and Kaushal [23] aggregate the VirusTotal ranking of an app with a crowd-sourced domain-reputation service (Web of Trust) and the app's resource permission to arrive at a ranking.

Prior work on *HTTPS logs* has aimed at identifying the application layer protocol [9,12,37]. In order to cluster web servers that host similar applications, Kohout *et al.* [18] developed features that are derived from a histogram of observable time intervals and data volumes of connections. Using this feature representation, Lokoč *et al.* [21] introduced an approximate k-NN classifier that identifies servers which are contacted by malware.

Graph-based classification methods [4] have been explored, but they can only be applied by an agent that is able to perceive a significant portion of the global network graph—which raises substantial logistic and privacy challenges. By contrast, this paper studies an approach that relies only on the agent's ability to observe the traffic of a single organization.

Prior work on neural networks for network-flow analysis [26] has worked with labels for client computers (infected and not infected)—which leads to a multi-instance learning problem. CNNs have also been applied to analyzing URLs which are observable as long as clients use the HTTP instead of the encrypted HTTPS protocol [30]. Malware detection from HTTPS traffic has been studied using a combination of word2vec embeddings of domain names and long short term memory networks (LSTMs) [27] as well as convolutional neural networks [28]. Since the network-flow data only logs communication events between clients and hosts, these models act as black boxes that do not provide security analysts any verifiable decision rationale. Since we collected data containing only specific network events without the information of the used domain names, we are not able to apply these models to our data.

Recent findings suggest that the greater robustness of convolutional neural networks (CNNs) may outweight the ability of LSTMs to account for long-term dependencies [14]. This motivates us to explore convolutional architectures. Transformer networks [36] are encoder-decoder architectures using multi-head self-attention layers and positional encodings widely used for NLP tasks. GPT-2 [29] and BERT [11] show that transformers pre-trained on a large corpus learn representations that can be fine-tuned for classification problems.

3 Problem Setting and Operating Environment

This section first describes the operating environment and the first stage of the *Cisco Cognitive Intelligence* system that abstracts network traffic into *network events*. Section 3.2 proceeds to define the threat taxonomy and to lay out the problem setting. Section 3.3 describes the data set that we collect for the experiments described in this paper.

3.1 Network Events

The *Cisco Cognitive Intelligence (CI)* [35] intrusion detection system monitors the network traffic of the customer organization for which it is deployed. Initially, the traffic is captured in the form of web proxy logs that enumerate which users connect to which servers on the internet, and include timestamps and the data volume sent and received. The CI engine then abstracts log entries into a set of *network events*—high-level behavioral indicators that can be interpreted by security analysts. Individual network events are not generally suspicious by themselves, but specific *patterns of network events* can constitute *indicators of compromise* that identify threats. In total, CI distinguishes hundreds of events; their detection mechanisms fall into four main categories.

- *Signature-based events* are detected by matching behavioral signatures that have been created manually by a domain expert. This includes detection based on known URL patterns or known host names.
- *Classifier-based events* are detected by special-purpose classifiers that have been trained on historical proxy logs. These classifiers included models that identify specific popular applications.
- *Anomaly-based events* are detected by a multitude of statistical, volumetric, proximity-based, targeted, and domain-specific anomaly detectors. Events in this category include, for example, contacting a server which is unlikely for the given user, or communication patterns that are too regular to be caused by a human user using a web browser.
- *Contextual events* capture various network behaviors to provide additional context; for instance, file downloads, direct access of a raw IP address without specified host name, or software updates.

For purposes of the work, each interval of five minutes in which at least one network flow is detected, the *set of network events* is timestamped and logged. Events are indexed by the *users* who sent or received the traffic. No data are logged for intervals in which no event occurs. The resulting data structure for each organization is a sparse sequence of sets of network events for each user within the organization.

3.2   Identification of Threats

We use a malware taxonomy with three levels: *threat ID, malware family, and malware category*. The *threat ID* identifies a particular version of a malware product, or versions that are so similar that a security analyst cannot distinguish them. For instance, a threat ID can correspond to a particular version of the njRAT malware [1], all instances of which use the same user-agent and URL pattern for communication. The *malware family* entails all versions of a malware product—for instance, WannaCry is a malware family of which multiple versions are known to differ in their communication behavior. Finally, the *malware category* broadly characterizes the monetization scheme or harmful behavior of a wide range of malware products. For instance, *advertisement injector, information stealer*, and *cryptocurrency miner* are malware categories.

Labeled training and evaluation data consist of sets of network events of five-minute intervals associated with a particular user in which threats have been identified by security analysts. In order to determine threat IDs, malware families, and categories, security analysts inspect network events and any available external sources of information about contacted servers. In some cases, hash keys of the executable files are also available and can be matched against databases of known malware to determine the ground truth. Due to this involvement of qualified experts, labeled data are valuable and relatively scarce.

Table 1. Data set statistics for malware category evaluation.

Malware category	Training instances	Test instances
Potentially unwanted application	14,675	10,026
Ad injector	14,434	17,174
Malicious advertising	3,287	1,354
Malicious content distribution	2,232	9,088
Cryptocurrency miner	1,114	1,857
Scareware	198	398
Information stealer	128	131

The *problem setting* for the malware-detection model is to detect for each organization, user, and each five-minute interval in which at least one network event has occurred, which threat ID, malware family, and malware category the user has been exposed to. That is, each *instance* is a combination of an organization, a user and a five-minute time interval. Threats are presented to security analysts on the most specific level on which they can be detected. Specific threat IDs provide the most concrete actionable information for analysts. However, for unknown or unidentifiable threats, the malware family or category provides a lead which an analyst can follow up on. In addition to the threat, *indicators of compromise* in the form of the relevant network events that identify the threat have to be presented to the analysts for review.

The analysis of this paper focuses on distinguishing between different threat IDs, malware families, and categories, and offering comprehensive indicators of compromise. The equally important problem of distinguishing between malware and benign activities has, for instance, been studied by Prasse *et al.* [28]. The majority of benign network traffic is not included in our data because only time intervals in which network events occur are logged.

We will measure precision-recall curves, the multi-class accuracy, and the macro-averaged AUC to evaluate the models under investigation. The average AUC is calculated as the mean of the AUC values of the individual classes. Precision—the fraction of alarms that are not false alarms—directly measures the amount of unnecessary workload imposed on security analysts, while recall quantifies the detection rate. We also compare the models in terms of ROC cuves because these curves are invariant to class ratios.

3.3   Data Collection and Quantitative Analysis

We collected the entire network traffic of 348 companies for one day in June 2020 as training data, and for one day in July 2020 as evaluation data. The training data contain the network traffic of 1,506,105 users while the evaluation data contain the traffic of 1,402,554 unique users. In total, the data set consists of 9,776,911 training instances and 9,970,560 test instances, where each instance is a combination of an organization, a user, and a five-minute interval in which

Table 2. Data set statistics for malware family evaluation.

Malware family	Training	Test	Malware category
ArcadeYum	12,051	6,231	Potentially unwanted application
Malicious Android firmware	38	30	Information stealer
njRAT	15	37	Information stealer
WannaCry	4	7	Ransomware

Table 3. Data set statistics for threat ID evaluation.

Threat ID	Training instances	Test instances	Malware category
Threat ID 1	8,900	9,710	Ad injector
Threat ID 2	900	924	Potentially unwanted application
Threat ID 3	11,894	6,075	Potentially unwanted application
Threat ID 4	641	783	Potentially unwanted application
Threat ID 5	606	425	Ad injector
Threat ID 6	392	567	Malicious advertising
Threat ID 7	2,099	9,027	Malicious content distribution
Threat ID 8	119	54	Typosquatting
Threat ID 9	282	193	Phishing

at least one network event was observed. In total, 216 distinct network events occur at least once in training and evaluation data—most of these events occur frequently. On average, 2.69 network events are observed in each five-minute interval in the training data and 2.73 events in the test data.

Table 1 shows the seven malware categories that occur in the data at least 100 times. *Potentially unwanted applications (PUAs)* are the most frequent class of malware; these free applications are mostly installed voluntarily for some advertised functionality, but then cannot be uninstalled without expert knowledge and expose the user to intrusive advertisements or steal user data. Table 2 shows all malware families that analysts have identified in our data. Most malware families fall into the category of PUA, but analysts have been able to identify a number of high-risk viruses. Comparing Tables 1 and 2 shows that for many threats, analysts are able to determine the malware category, but not the specific malware family.

Finally, Table 3 shows those threat IDs for which at least 100 instances occur in our data. In many cases, analysts identify a specific threat which is assigned a threat ID based on the malware's behavior, without being able to ultimately determine which malware family it has been derived from.

4   Models

This section develops the neural network architectures that we will explore in the experimental part of this paper. All networks process the sequence of network

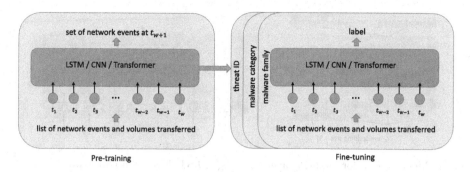

Fig. 1. Model architecture.

events provided by the detector array. In one version of the networks, we employ unsupervised pre-training of the models—see Fig. 1. We will compare the pre-trained models to reference versions without pre-training.

4.1 Architectures

Here we develop three different model architectures: an *LSTM* model using several bidirectional LSTM layers [16], a *CNN* model using stacked one-dimensional CNN layers [14], and a *transformer* model that uses multiple multi-head attention blocks [36]. We also implement a random forest baseline.

The input to the different model architectures consists of a window of w five-minute intervals, each of which is represented by a set of network events, a timestamp, and the numbers of bytes sent and received. The width w of the window is a tunable hyperparameter. The set of network events for each time step are processed by an embedding layer followed by an averaging layer that computes the mean embedding for all the network events for the current five-minute interval (see Fig. 2a). The mean embedding is than concatenated with the log transformed time differences between subsequent elements in the window and the log-transformed number of bytes sent and received.

The LSTM model consists of multiple layers of bidirectional LSTM units, followed by a number of dense layers with a dropout rate of 0.1. The number of layers of each type and the number of units per layer for each of the models are hyperparameters that we will tune in Sect. 5; see Table 4. The output layer consists of a softmax layer with the number of units equal to the number of different classes (see Fig. 2b). The CNN model starts off with a concatenation layer that combines the elements in the input window. The next layers are multiple pairs of a one-dimensional convolutional layer followed by a max-pooling layer. The last CNN layer is connected to an average-pooling layer and a number of dense layers on top of it. The last layer is a softmax layer with one unit per output classes (see Fig. 2c).

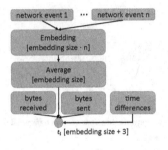

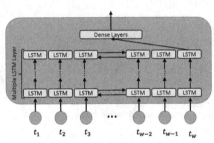

(a) Model input for a single five-minute interval.

(b) LSTM model architecture.

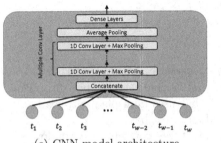

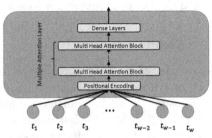

(c) CNN model architecture.

(d) Transformer model architecture.

Fig. 2. Model input and models.

The transformer model consists of an absolute positional encoding layer that outputs the sum of the positional encoding and the concatenated input sequence [31]. The output of the positional encoding layer is fed into multiple attention layers [36]. The output of the last multi-head attention layer is fed into a sequence of dense layers. The last layer consists of a softmax layer with one unit per output class (see Fig. 2d).

The random forest (RF), which serves as natural baseline, consumes the one-hot encodings of all network events within the window and the concatenated list of all log transformed bytes sent, log-transformed bytes received, and the time differences between susequent elements within the window.

Table 4. Best hyperparameters found using grid search.

	Hyperparameter	Parameter range	Best value
LSTM	embedding size	$\{2^6, \ldots, 2^8\}$	128
	# LSTM layers	$\{1, \cdots, 4\}$	1
	LSTM units	$\{2^3, \ldots, 2^{11}\}$	1024
	# Dense layers	$\{1, \ldots, 3\}$	2
	# Dense units	$\{2^6, \ldots, 2^{10}\}$	256
CNN	embedding size	$\{2^6, \ldots, 2^8\}$	128
	# CNN layers	$\{1, \cdots, 4\}$	3
	kernel size	$\{2^1, \ldots, 2^3\}$	4
	# filters	$\{2^2, \ldots, 2^7\}$	32
	# Dense layers	$\{1, \ldots, 3\}$	2
	# Dense units	$\{2^6, \ldots, 2^{10}\}$	256
Transformer	embedding size	$\{2^6, \ldots, 2^8\}$	128
	# attention blocks	$\{1, \cdots, 4\}$	2
	# attention heads	$\{2^2, \ldots, 2^7\}$	8
	# Dense attention units	$\{2^2, \ldots, 2^7\}$	512
	# Dense layers	$\{1, \ldots, 3\}$	2
	# Dense units	$\{2^6, \ldots, 2^{10}\}$	512
RF	# trees	$\{10, 100, 1000\}$	100
	# max depth	$\{2, 10, 100, None\}$	10

4.2 Unsupervised Pre-training

Since labeling training data requires highly-trained analysts to identify and analyze threats, labeled data are relatively scarce. While the number of labels is in the tens of thousands in our study, the number of unlabeled instances collected over two days is around 20 millions. Unsupervised pre-training offers the potential for the network to learn a low-level representation that structures the data in such a way that the subsequent supervised learning problem becomes easier to solve with limited labeled data.

To pre-train the models, we use all 9,776,911 training instances. The training objective is to predict the set of network events present at time step t_{w+1} given the sets of events of previous time steps $t_1, \ldots t_w$ (see Fig. 1). This is a multi-label classification problem, since we want to predict all present network events at time step t_{w+1}. This model serves as a "language model" [11,29] for network events that learns an internal representation which is able to predict the next network events given their context. For the pre-training step, we add a fully connected dense layer with sigmoid activation function to the models. We train these models using the binary cross entropy loss function. We will compare the *pre-trained* models to their counterparts that have been trained *from scratch* with Glorot initialization [15].

5 Experiments

This section reports on malware-detection performance of the models under investigation, and on the interpretability of the indicators of compromise. We split the data into a training part that we acquired in June 2020 and an evaluation part acquired in July 2020.

5.1 Hyperparameter Optimization

We optimize the width of the window of five-minute time intervals w used to train the models by evaluating values from 3 to 41 with a nested training-test split on the training part of the data using the threat-ID classification task. In the following experiments, we fix the number of used five-minute intervals w to 21 (see Fig. 2). That is, each training and test instance is a sequence of 21 five-minute intervals; training and test sequences are split into overlapping sequences of that length. We tune the number of layers of each type, and the number of units per layer for all models using a 5-fold cross-validation on the training part of the data using the threat-ID classification task. The grid of parameters and the best hyperparameters can be found in Table 4. The optimal parameters for the random forest baseline are found using a 5-fold cross-validation on the training data of the given task.

We train all models on a single server with 40-core Intel(R) Xeon(R) CPU E5-2640 processor and 512 GB of memory. We train all neural networks using the Keras and Tensorflow libraries on a GeForce GTX TITAN X GPU using the NVidia CUDA platform. We implement the evaluation framework using the scikit-learn machine learning package. The code can be found online[1].

5.2 Malware-Classification Performance

In the following we compare the classification performance of the different models for the tasks of detecting threat IDs, malware categories, and malware families. We compare neural networks that are trained from scratch using Glorot initialization and models initialized with pre-trained weights as described in Sect. 4.2. We also investigate how the number of training data points per class effects the performance. To do so, we measure the accuracy acc@n and average AUC@n after the models have been trained on n instances per class. Since obtaining malware labels is time consuming and costly, this gives us an estimation of how the models behave in a few-shot learning scenario.

Table 5 shows the overall results for all described models and all the different levels of the threat taxonomy on the evaluation data. We see that the transformer outperforms CNN and LSTM most of the time, and that the pre-trained models almost always significantly outperform their counterparts that have been trained from scratch, based on a two-sided, paired t test with $p < 0.05$. Only the LSTM models are in some cases not able to benefit from pre-training. We also see that the neural network architectures outperform the random forest baseline in all settings, so we conclude that using the sequential information and sequential patterns can be exploited to classify different malware types. Using more training instances nearly always boosts the overall performance. Only for the detection

---

[1] https://github.com/prassepaul/Learning-Explainable-Representations-of-Malware-Behavior.

of different malware families the performance in terms of the average AUC is lower when training with the full data set. We think this is caused by highly imbalanced class distribution pushing the models to favor for specific classes.

From Table 5, we conclude that in almost all cases the transformer model with unsupervised pre-training is the overall best model. Because of that, the following detailed analysis is performed using only the transformer model architecture.

Additional experiments in which we determine the ROC and precision-recall curves that the transformer with pre-training achieves for individual threats, malware families, and malware categories can be found in an online appendix[2]. From these experiments, we can furthermore conclude that threat IDs that have a one-to-one relationship with a malware family are the easiest ones to identify, and that broad categories such as PUA that include a wide range of different threats are the most difficult to pin down.

Table 5. Accuracy and AUC for the detection of threat IDs, malware families, and categories, after training on some or all training data, with and without pre-training. Acc@n and AUC@n refer to the accuracy and AUC, respectively, after training on up to n instances per class. For results marked "*", the accuracy of pre-trained models is significantly better ($p < 0.05$) compared to the same model trained from scratch. Results marked "†" are significantly better ($p < 0.05$) than the next-best model.

		CNN		LSTM		Transformer		Random Forest
		Scratch	Pre-tr.	Scratch	Pre-tr.	Scratch	Pre-tr.	Scratch
Threat ID	acc@10	0.394	0.437*	0.314	0.375*	0.352	**0.559*†**	0.413
	acc@50	0.618	0.648*	0.567	0.478	0.612	**0.731*†**	0.57
	acc@100	0.666	0.689*	0.624	0.54	0.685	**0.759*†**	0.614
	acc	0.785	0.799	0.806	**0.843*†**	0.769	0.776	0.809
	AUC@10	0.794	0.773	0.75	0.698	0.748	**0.848***	0.832
	AUC@50	0.889	0.893	0.874	0.807	0.893	**0.941*†**	0.902
	AUC@100	0.906	0.914*	0.897	0.829	0.902	**0.948*†**	0.912
	AUC	0.937	**0.952***	0.935	0.942	0.915	0.95*	0.925
Malware category	acc@10	0.23	0.396*	0.196	0.312*	0.228	**0.456*†**	0.338
	acc@50	0.524	0.598*	0.515	0.485	0.575	**0.652*†**	0.54
	acc@100	0.618	0.669*	0.597	0.539	0.652	**0.703*†**	0.606
	acc	0.77	0.785*	0.769	0.772	0.771	**0.802*†**	0.73
	AUC@10	0.752	0.813*	0.73	0.728	0.747	**0.821***	0.819
	AUC@50	0.86	0.901*	0.861	0.808	0.879	**0.924*†**	0.889
	AUC@100	0.881	0.91*	0.877	0.831	0.914	**0.938*†**	0.907
	AUC	0.917	0.937*	0.908	0.902	0.912	**0.96*†**	0.916
Malware family	acc@10	0.439	**0.91***	0.01	0.894*	0.322	0.893*	0.846
	acc@50	0.839	0.939*	0.592	0.923*	0.808	**0.946***	0.923
	acc@100	0.87	0.959	0.875	0.952	0.866	**0.977*†**	0.962
	acc	0.929	0.993*	0.889	**0.995*†**	0.954	0.992	0.994
	AUC@10	0.886	**0.985***	0.785	0.964*	0.855	0.983*	0.106
	AUC@50	0.96	0.992*	0.832	0.982*	0.967	**0.993***	0.199
	AUC@100	0.96	0.993*	0.922	0.983	0.969	**0.995***	0.199
	AUC	0.921	**0.983***	0.923	0.983*	0.486	0.947*	0.322

---

[2] https://www.uni-potsdam.de/fileadmin/projects/cs-ml/media/prasse_ecml2021_appendix.pdf.

5.3 Indicators of Compromise

This section explores the interpretablility of the indicators of compromise inferred from the transformer model. We use the *integrated gradients* method to highlight the most important features for a given input sequence [33]. Integrated gradients can compute the contribution of each network event when classifying a given input sequence. We calculate the impact of all input features using

$$IG_i(x) = (x_i - x_i') \times \int_{\alpha=0}^{1} \frac{\partial F(x' + \alpha \times (x - x'))}{\partial x_i} d\alpha, \tag{1}$$

where i denotes the i-th feature, x the input to the model, x' the baseline, and α the interpolation constant for the perturbation of the features. The term $(x_i - x_i')$ denotes the difference between original input and "baseline". Similar to the all-zeros baseline that is used for input images, we set the baseline to the instance with all zero-embeddings and original numerical features. The baseline input is needed to scale the integrated gradients. In practice we approximate this integral by the numerical approximation

$$IG_i^{approx}(x) = (x_i - x_i') \times \sum_{k=1}^{m} \frac{\partial F(x' + \frac{k}{m} \times (x - x'))}{\partial x_i} \times \frac{1}{m}, \tag{2}$$

where k is the number of approximation steps.

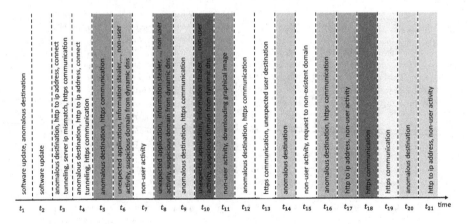

Fig. 3. Feature importance for detection of njRAT using *integrated gradients* for a single instance. The intensity of the red hue indicates the importance of network events.

Single-Instance Evaluation. Using the Integrated Gradients from Eq. 2, we determine which input time steps contributed to which extend to the overall classification. Figure 3 shows an example output for an instance classified as *njRAT*. The njRAT malware family, also called Bladabindi, is a widespread remote access trojan (RAT). It allows attackers to steal passwords, log keystrokes, activate webcam and microphone, give access to the command line, and allows attackers to remotely execute and manipulate files and system registry.

It uses the HTTP user-agent field (this is reflected in the event *unexpected application* in Fig. 3) to exfiltrate sensitive information (event *information stealer* in Fig. 3) from the infected machine. The communication with C&C server uses dynamic DNS with string patterns such as *maroco.dyndns.org/is-rinoy* or *man2010.no-ip.org/is-ready* and specifically crafted host names. This usage of dynamic DNS is reflected in event *suspicious domain from dynamic DNS* in Fig. 3, the specific host names as event *anomalous destination*. These characteristic features of njRAT are also the most important features for the transformer. We conclude that this explanation matches known behavior of njRAT.

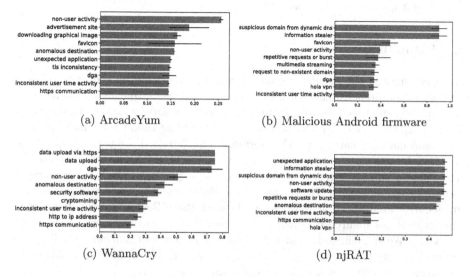

(a) ArcadeYum

(b) Malicious Android firmware

(c) WannaCry

(d) njRAT

Fig. 4. Feature importances of the top 10 features for detection of different malware families. The width of the bar is computed by using the *integrated gradients* method for each positively classified instance and averaging the obtained values for all network events. Error bars denote the standard deviation.

Feature Importance. We add the feature importance values for all the instances classified as a particular malware family. Figure 4 shows the feature importance for different families. For *njRAT*, we see that the top four features captured in Fig. 4d match the behavior of njRAT described above. The *ArcadeYum* family is a typical example of the PUA/adware category. When installed, it starts to download large amounts of advertisement and present it as additional banners rendered on top of legitimate websites or as pop-up windows. The advertisement images are downloaded on the background without users knowledge and often from hosts that may be a source of additional infections. This behaviour is again captures by the most important features in Fig. 4a.

Most of the *WannaCry* samples that we were able to detect are older versions that use DGA domains as a kill switch—see [3] for details. The behavioral indicators *dga, non-user activity, anomalous destination, inconsistent user time activity* in Fig. 4c are related to the regular attempt to contact these DGA domains. Some of the identified samples are actually *WannaMine* [2], a crypto-mining modification of the original WannaCry malware. Their activity is captured by the *cryptomining* event as well as the *http to IP address*, which is the mechanism through which WannaMine downloads additional modules. *Malicious Android firmware*, Fig. 4b, is known for gathering and exfiltrating sensitive user information and using dynamic DNS to avoid blacklists. Both behaviors are represented as the top two features. The further actions depend on the type and version of the infected device. Usually, an advertisement auction service is contacted and advertisement images or videos are being displayed (*multimedia streaming, repetitive requests, non-user activity, dga*).

6   Conclusion

We have studied the problem of identifying threats based on sequences of sets of human-comprehensible network events that are the output of a wide array of specialized detectors. We can conclude that the *transformer* architecture outperforms both the CNN and LSTM models at identifying threat IDs, malware families, and malware categories. Furthermore, unsupervised pre-training improves the transformer's performance over supervised learning from scratch. We use the *integrated gradients* method to determine the sequence of the most important network events that constitute *indicators of compromise* which can be verified by security analysts. Our detailed analysis of the njRAT malware shows that the sequence of highly important events corresponds to the known behavior of the virus. We can conclude that for the four most frequent malware families, the network events that reach the highest aggregated feature importance across all occurrences match known indicators of compromise.

References

1. MSIL/Bladabindi. https://www.microsoft.com/en-us/wdsi/threats/malware-encyclopedia-description?name=MSIL/Bladabindi. Accessed 31 Mar 2021
2. Wannamine cryptominer that uses eternalblue still active. https://www.cybereason.com/blog/wannamine-cryptominer-eternalblue-wannacry. Accessed 31 Mar 2021
3. Indicators associated with wannacry ransomware (2017). https://us-cert.cisa.gov/ncas/alerts/TA17-132A. Accessed 24 Mar 2021
4. Anderson, B., Quist, D., Neil, J., Storlie, C., Lane, T.: Graph-based malware detection using dynamic analysis. J. Comput. Virol. **7**(4), 247–258 (2011)
5. Arora, A., Garg, S., Peddoju, S.K.: Malware detection using network traffic analysis in android based mobile devices. In: International Conference on Next Generation Mobile Apps, Services and Technologies, pp. 66–71 (2014)

6. Bartos, K., Sofka, M.: Robust representation for domain adaptation in network security. In: Bifet, A., et al. (eds.) ECML PKDD 2015. LNCS (LNAI), vol. 9286, pp. 116–132. Springer, Cham (2015). https://doi.org/10.1007/978-3-319-23461-8_8

7. Bartoš, K., Sofka, M., Franc, V.: Optimized invariant representation of network traffic for detecting unseen malware variants. In: USENIX Security Symposium, pp. 807–822 (2016)

8. Brabec, J., Machlica, L.: Decision-forest voting scheme for classification of rare classes in network intrusion detection. In: 2018 IEEE International Conference on Systems, Man, and Cybernetics (SMC), pp. 3325–3330 (2018)

9. Crotti, M., Dusi, M., Gringoli, F., Salgarelli, L.: Traffic classification through simple statistical fingerprinting. ACM SIGCOMM Comput. Commun. Rev. **37**(1), 5–16 (2007)

10. Demontis, A., et al.: Yes, machine learning can be more secure! a case study on Android malware detection. IEEE Trans. Dependable Secure Comput. 1 (2018)

11. Devlin, J., Chang, M.W., Lee, K., Toutanova, K.: BERT: pre-training of deep bidirectional transformers for language understanding. arXiv preprint arXiv:1810.04805 (2018)

12. Dusi, M., Crotti, M., Gringoli, F., Salgarelli, L.: Tunnel hunter: detecting application-layer tunnels with statistical fingerprinting. Comput. Netw. **53**(1), 81–97 (2009)

13. Franc, V., Sofka, M., Bartos, K.: Learning detector of malicious network traffic from weak labels. In: Bifet, A., et al. (eds.) ECML PKDD 2015. LNCS (LNAI), vol. 9286, pp. 85–99. Springer, Cham (2015). https://doi.org/10.1007/978-3-319-23461-8_6

14. Gehring, J., Auli, M., Grangier, D., Yarats, D., Dauphin, Y.N.: Convolutional sequence to sequence learning. In: International Conference on Machine Learning, pp. 1243–1252. PMLR (2017)

15. Glorot, X., Bengio, Y.: Understanding the difficulty of training deep feedforward neural networks. In: Teh, Y.W., Titterington, M. (eds.) Proceedings of the Thirteenth International Conference on Artificial Intelligence and Statistics. Proceedings of Machine Learning Research, vol. 9, pp. 249–256. Chia Laguna Resort, Sardinia, Italy, 13–15 May 2010

16. Hochreiter, S., Schmidhuber, J.: Long short-term memory. Neural Comput. **9**(8), 1735–1780 (1997)

17. Karim, M.E., Walenstein, A., Lakhotia, A., Parida, L.: Malware phylogeny generation using permutations of code. J. Comput. Virol. **1**(1–2), 13–23 (2005)

18. Kohout, J., Pevný, T.: Automatic discovery of web servers hosting similar applications. In: Proceedings of the IFIP/IEEE International Symposium on Integrated Network Management (2015)

19. Kohout, J., Pevný, T.: Unsupervised detection of malware in persistent web traffic. In: Proceedings of the IEEE International Conference on Acoustics, Speech and Signal Processing (2015)

20. Lashkari, A., Kadir, A., Gonzalez, H., Mbah, K., Ghorbani, A.: Towards a network-based framework for Android malware detection and characterization. In: Proceedings International Conference on Privacy, Security, and Trust (2015)

21. Lokoč, J., Kohout, J., Čech, P., Skopal, T., Pevný, T.: k-NN classification of malware in HTTPS traffic using the metric space approach. In: Chau, M., Wang, G.A., Chen, H. (eds.) PAISI 2016. LNCS, vol. 9650, pp. 131–145. Springer, Cham (2016). https://doi.org/10.1007/978-3-319-31863-9_10

22. Lundberg, S.M., Lee, S.I.: A unified approach to interpreting model predictions. In: Guyon, I., Luxburg, U.V., Bengio, S., Wallach, H., Fergus, R., Vishwanathan, S., Garnett, R. (eds.) Advances in Neural Information Processing Systems 30, pp. 4765–4774 (2017)

23. Malik, J., Kaushal, R.: CREDROID: Android malware detection by network traffic analysis. In: Proceedings of the First ACM Workshop on Privacy-Aware Mobile Computing, pp. 28–36. ACM (2016)

24. Nelms, T., Perdisci, R., Ahamad, M.: ExecScent: mining for new C&C domains in live networks with adaptive control protocol templates. In: Proceedings of the USENIX Security Symposium (2013)

25. Nguyen, T., Armitage, G.: A survey of techniques for internet traffic classification using machine learning. IEEE Commun. Surv. Tutor. **10**(4), 56–76 (2008)

26. Pevný, T., Somol, P.: Discriminative models for multi-instance problems with tree structure. In: Proceedings of the International Workshop on Artificial Intelligence for Computer Security (2016)

27. Prasse, P., Machlica, L., Pevný, T., Havelka, J., Scheffer, T.: Malware detection by analysing network traffic with neural networks. In: Proceedings of the European Conference on Machine Learning (2017)

28. Prasse, P., Knaebel, R., Machlica, L., Pevný, T., Scheffer, T.: Joint detection of malicious domains and infected clients. Mach. Learn. **108**(8), 1353–1368 (2019)

29. Radford, A., et al.: Better language models and their implications. OpenAI Blog (2019). https://openai.com/blog/better-language-models

30. Saxe, J., Berlin, K.: eXpose: a character-level convolutional neural network with embeddings for detecting malicious URLs, file paths and registry keys. arXiv preprint arXiv:1702.08568 (2017)

31. Shaw, P., Uszkoreit, J., Vaswani, A.: Self-attention with relative position representations. arXiv preprint arXiv:1803.02155 (2018)

32. Shrikumar, A., Greenside, P., Shcherbina, A., Kundaje, A.: Not just a black box: learning important features through propagating activation differences. arXiv preprint arXiv:1605.01713 (2016)

33. Sundararajan, M., Taly, A., Yan, Q.: Axiomatic attribution for deep networks. In: International Conference on Machine Learning, pp. 3319–3328. PMLR (2017)

34. Swinnen, A., Mesbahi, A.: One packer to rule them all: empirical identification, comparison and circumvention of current antivirus detection techniques. BlackHat USA (2014)

35. Valeros, V., Somol, P., Rehak, M., Grill, M.: Cognitive threat analytics: turn your proxy into security device. Cisco Security Blog (2016). https://blogs.cisco.com/security/cognitive-threat-analytics-turn-your-proxy-into-security-device. Accessed 24 Mar 2021

36. Vaswani, A., et al.: Attention is all you need. arXiv preprint arXiv:1706.03762 (2017)

37. Wright, C.V., Monrose, F., Masson, G.M.: On inferring application protocol behaviors in encrypted network traffic. J. Mach. Learn. Res. **7**, 2745–2769 (2006)

Strategic Mitigation Against Wireless Attacks on Autonomous Platoons

Guoxin Sun[1]([✉]), Tansu Alpcan[1], Benjamin I. P. Rubinstein[1],
and Seyit Camtepe[2]

[1] University of Melbourne, Parkville, Australia
`guoxins@student.unimelb.edu.au`,
{`tansu.alpcan,brubinstein`}`@unimelb.edu.au`
[2] CSIRO Data61, Eveleigh, Australia
`seyit.camtepe@data61.csiro.au`

Abstract. With the increased demand for connected and autonomous vehicles, vehicle platoons will play a significant role in the near future, enhancing traffic efficiency and safety. However, their reliance on wireless communication channels makes such systems susceptible to a range of cyber-attacks. An intelligent adversary could target the platoon through message falsification between vehicles to carry out high-impact attacks. This would create persistent degradation of platoon stability or even cause catastrophic collisions. In this paper, we present a novel, end-to-end attack detection and mitigation framework. We use a deep neural network as an example anomaly detector tuned to reduce false alarm rate. We then model the interactions between the imperfect detector, the intelligent adversary and the defense system as a non-cooperative security game with imperfect information. In this setting, the adversary performs a test-time boiling frog attack against the detector. The Nash-equilibrium solution considers the downstream effects of the test-time attack, to guide the control system reconfiguration for the vehicles to mitigate communication-based attacks. The simulations conducted in a sophisticated simulator demonstrate the potential for real-world online deployment in a distributed manner. Results show that our approach outperforms baseline methods by up to 30% in terms of increase of defense utilities, leading up to 176% increase in minimum inter-vehicle distances for collision avoidance under attacks.

1 Introduction

Connected and autonomous vehicles have emerged as an extensive and promising research area over the past two decades [11]. As a closely related topic, vehicular platooning earns its reputation by providing driver/passenger comfort, improved energy efficiency, pollution reduction as well as increase of traffic

We gratefully acknowledge support from the DSTG Next Generation Technology Fund and CSIRO Data61 CRP 'Adversarial Machine Learning for Cyber', and a CSIRO Data61 PhD scholarship.

Y. Dong et al. (Eds.): ECML PKDD 2021, LNAI 12978, pp. 69–84, 2021.
https://doi.org/10.1007/978-3-030-86514-6_5

throughput. The platooning concept involves a group of vehicles travelling in a tightly coupled manner from an origin to a destination as a single unit. A platoon member receives other vehicles' dynamics and maneuver-related information via a vehicle-to-vehicle (V2V) communication network to compute control commands accordingly and maintain platoon stability, i.e., to maintain a narrow inter-vehicle distance and relative velocity.

However, such V2V communication implementations also expose novel attack vectors, which increase security vulnerabilities and highlight vehicle platoons as an appealing target for cyber-physical attacks. Adversaries could inject multiple falsified vehicle nodes into the platoon remotely. This allows them to publish carefully crafted beacon messages to gain the privilege of the road or to cause traffic congestion and even serious collisions [3]. There is a growing body of literature that recognises the effectiveness of machine learning based anomaly detection algorithms applied on vehicular platooning [1,6,18]. Even though such studies aim to maximise their detection performance, inevitable false alarm and miss rates still limit the possibility of real-world deployment where hundreds of thousands of detections may be required per second. Yet, attack detection is barely the first step. How to react upon a detection report is still an essential and open research problem that remains to be answered. Furthermore, an intelligent adversary could reconnoitre the platoon system and the deployed defense measures for a period of time to launch stealthy attacks. Unlike traditional adversaries, they leverage knowledge of defense actions and detector characteristics to adapt attack strategies, thereby evading detection.

Our work aims to answer the following questions to improve the security and safety of vehicle platoons: **(1)** How to overcome the limitations of the state-of-the-art anomaly detection algorithms especially those purposely tuned to decrease the false positive rate? **(2)** How to use the detection report to mitigate a potential attack? **(3)** How to defend against intelligent adversaries who leverage their prior knowledge about the defense system? **(4)** How to acquire adequate data for detector training and to evaluate the performance of the proposed approach applied on complex platoon systems?

In this paper, we propose an end-to-end attack detection and mitigation framework to answer these questions. We firstly construct a vehicle platoon and traffic flows on a highway segment in a sophisticated simulator *Webots* [16]. Two control policies are implemented for each platoon member: one sensor-based controller using local measurements from embedded sensor modules and one communication-based controller using messages transmitted via V2V communication network. Secondly, we investigate a particular type of data corruption attack and with this solid simulation foundation, we collect data to train a deep neural net (DNN) model as an anomaly detector. The detector tuning process is in favour of low false positives to increase its real-world usability and public acceptance. Thirdly, we model the interactions between the imperfect detector, the intelligent adversary and defense vehicle as a security game with imperfect information and use the Nash-equilibrium solution to guide control system reconfiguration for the vehicle to mitigate the attack. Lastly, we test our proposed system under different simulation scenarios to demonstrate its effectiveness and potential for real-world online deployment in a distributed manner. The contributions of this paper include:

(1) We propose a novel attack detection and mitigation framework that intelligently switches between two platoon control policies to improve the security level of vehicle platoons against intelligent communication-based attacks.

(2) We develop a unique approach that uses game theory to guide the controller switching process.

(3) Our security game formulation captures imperfect detectors as a chance node in our security game structure, and takes detection errors (e.g., false alarms and misses) into account. We consider a boiling frog attack and its downstream effects on the platoon – far beyond the typical myopic focus on accuracy.

(4) The results are illustrated using sophisticated, system-level simulations, where our approach outperforms baseline methods by 30% in terms of increase of defense utilities, leading up to 176% increase in minimum inter-vehicle distances under attacks.

The rest of the paper is organised as follows. The next subsection summarizes related work. Section 2 describes the considered platoon control policies, attack model as well as the anomaly detector. Section 3 presents the details of our proposed defense framework. Simulation setup and training procedures are presented in Sect. 4. Results and discussions are covered in Sect. 5. Lastly, Sect. 6 outlines some concluding remarks.

1.1 Related Work

Sumra *et al.* [15] provide a comprehensive survey of the attacks on major security goals, i.e., confidentiality, integrity and availability. Malicious attackers can breach privacy by attempting an eavesdropping attack to steal and misuse confidential information [17]. The use of vehicular botnets to attempt a denial-of-service (DoS) or distributed denial-of-service (DDoS) attack may cause serious network congestion or disruption [19]. The attacker may disrupt the platoon operation by hijacking the sensors to conduct the replay attack with the aim to feed the control system with outdated signals generated previously by the system [10]. Therefore, there is urgent need to address the safety risks caused by such communication-based attacks.

Several attempts have been made to detect communication-based attacks. In [6], authors compare the effectiveness of deep neural net and convolutional neural net models in the identification of a malicious insider who tries to cause collisions by altering the controller gains. Yang *et al.* [18] propose an ensemble learning model that consists of 4 tree-based ML algorithms to improve detection accuracy against attacks on Controller Area Network (CAN) bus. Alotibi *et al.* [1] combine a data driven anomaly detection algorithm based on generalized extreme studentized deviate (ESD) with the physical laws of kinematics to perform real-time detection. Although these methods provide reasonably good attack detection performance, how to respond to the imperfect detection reports still remains an open research question.

Game-theoretic analysis has become a popular tool in adversarial machine learning and cybersecurity analysis [2]. Extensive research has examined problems of allocating limited defense resources (e.g., energy [13], manpower [5], communication bandwidth [14]) against intelligent adversaries in a network. The present work builds on these existing advancements in machine learning as well as game theory and introduces a novel, end-to-end attack detection and mitigation framework to improve platoon security in an online and distributed manner.

2   Message Falsification Attacks Against Platoons

2.1   Vehicular Platoon Control Policy

In the present work, we consider a vehicle platoon traveling on a straight highway segment. We start by implementing a popular platoon control policy – cooperative adaptive cruise control (CACC [12]) on each platoon member. In particular, data packets containing location, speed and acceleration information of the lead vehicle and the preceding vehicle are transmitted periodically to each vehicle via V2V communication, based on which longitudinal control decisions are made to maintain platoon stability. Adaptive cruise control (ACC) is a relatively mature control policy widely deployed in many modern vehicles. It performs the longitudinal following control task using measurements from sensors like a Radar. With the aid of V2V communication, CACC is expected to have a smaller distance headway and an increase in control bandwidth and reliability compared to sensor-based ACC [8]. Besides, long time operation of ACC controller will destroy so-called string stability of the vehicle platoon [12]. Therefore, we treat CACC as the primary controller and ACC as the supplementary controller activated only when a communication attack is expected to happen.

2.2   Attack Model

As a starting point, we consider the attacker compromises the communication link between two consecutive vehicles and performs messages falsification attacks [11]. By continuously monitoring the communication network, the adversary may change the content of transmitted messages and inserts them back into the network. The presence of this type of attack could cause instabilities to the vehicle platoon or even collisions. For the rest of the paper, we consider the attacker modifies the velocity messages in a subtle way before broadcasting to the following vehicle by adopting a **boiling frog attack strategy.** In such attacks, the attacker progressively increases the falsified velocity magnitude aiming to evade detection. The modified messages are very similar to the original ones at the beginning of the attack. It might be already too late when the control centre or a detector notices this attack leading to very short respond time or collision. The falsified velocity $v_{false}(t)$, assuming attack starts at time $t = 0$, can be expressed as:

$$v_{false}(t) = \max \left\{ v_{orig}(t) + \sum_{t'=0}^{t'=t} \gamma \cdot V_{max}, \ v_{orig}(t) + V_{max} \right\}, \qquad (1)$$

where V_{max} is the maximum velocity modification set by the attacker, $v_{orig}(t)$ is the current original velocity, $\gamma \in [0, 1)$ is the incremental gradient.

2.3 Attack Detection Algorithm

Our defense framework builds upon recent advances in anomaly detection [4]. We treat it as a classification problem and train the anomaly detection model through supervised learning on class-imbalanced data sets. Although supervised learning is often more accurate than semi-supervised and unsupervised approaches, the exact type of training approaches and anomaly detectors are not key factors in our proposed defense framework. Any types of detectors could easily fit in with only minor parameter changes of the framework.

We demonstrate the proposed defense framework with DNN based anomaly detectors. Apart from the input layer, we choose to have three hidden layers activated by Rectified Linear (Relu) function and one output layer activated by sigmoid function to return the probability of a received message being malicious. There are two dropout layers (having rate equal 0.3) after the second and third hidden layers respectively to reduce overfitting. Optimizer, learning rate and objective function are key hyperparameters used to adjust the weight update process of neurons in hidden layers. The optimizer used in this analysis is Adam with 0.01 as the learning rate. Binary crossentropy is chosen to be the objective function and the whole training process is divided to 50 batches of size 2048 with 20% of the training data-set used for validation.

3 Security Game-Based Mitigation Framework

We model the interactions between the imperfect anomaly detector, the intelligent adversary (i.e., the *Attacker*) and the defense system (i.e., the *Defender*) as a non-cooperative cybersecurity game in extensive form. In formulating our game-theoretic defense framework, we adopt the following commonly accepted definitions from game theory [2]: **(1)** *Chance node*: A chance node can be seen as a fictitious (virtual) player who performs actions according to a probability distribution. **(2)** *Information set*: An information set is a collection of decision nodes of one player. As the game reaches the information set, the player cannot distinguish the nodes within the information set.

The game begins with the Attacker deciding whether to initiate the boiling frog attack or not. Regardless of whether transmitted messages have been maliciously modified, each vehicle performs anomaly detection upon receiving the messages. Each detection report is associated with a certain probability of error (i.e., false alarms and misses) and we use *chance nodes* to model the uncertainty of detection results. Consequently, once the Defender obtains the detection results, it is still unclear whether an attack has been actually carried out or not. This unique situation is captured by two information sets for the Defender: one indicating an attack and one for no attack. This essentially means the Defender must consider the consequences of both an actual attack having occurred, and no attack having occurred, when an attack has been reported by the detector.

Eventually, after considering a rational Attacker's actions and the chances of detection errors, the Defender decides whether to downgrade the CACC controller to the ACC controller or remain with the CACC controller based on Nash equilibrium solution of the game.

Formally, we model the game with the following components: **(a)** Attacker's action space $\mathcal{A}^A := \{a:$ boiling frog attack; $na:$ not attacking$\}$ **(b)** Chance nodes $C := \{r:$ reporting an attack; $nr:$ not reporting an attack$\}$ **(c)** Defender's action space $\mathcal{A}^D := \{acc:$ local sensor-based controller (ACC); $cacc:$ collaborative communication-based controller (CACC)$\}$

The strategy profile is modeled as $\langle a, c, d \rangle$ for $a \in \mathcal{A}^A$, $c \in C$ and $d \in \mathcal{A}^D$. In this work, we focus on Nash equilibrium as the solution concept in which there is no profitable deviation of rational player's chosen strategy after considering their opponent's choice. This is based on a reasonable assumption of rationality that each player acts for their best interests. Other solution concepts exist for players with different levels of rationality. The pseudo-code for our defense framework is presented in Algorithm 1.

Algorithm 1: End-to-end Anomaly Detection and Mitigation

---

initialization;
while *Destination is not reached* **do**
> Platoon progresses on the road;
> Vehicle receives message S;
> Detection result $R \leftarrow$ Anomaly Detection(S);
> Utility value $U \leftarrow$ Utility(S);
> Nash Equilibrium, Decision $\leftarrow$ Game Solver(R, U);
> **if** *Decision is acc* **then**
> > | Activate ACC;
>
> **else**
> > | Activate CACC;
>
> **end**

end

Utilities of the Players. The utility functions $U^D(a, c, d)$ and $U^A(a, c, d)$ (of strategy profiles) are essential to represent the preference over every outcome for the Attacker and the Defender respectively. In our framework, each utility function consists of two components represented in matrix form to capture different cases:

$$U^D(a, c, d) = U_1^D(a, d) + U_2(c, d), \tag{2}$$

$$U^A(a, c, d) = U_1^A(a, d) - U_2(c, d), \tag{3}$$

$$U_1^D(a, d) = \begin{bmatrix} \alpha_d & -\alpha_f \\ -\alpha_m & 0 \end{bmatrix} \begin{matrix} (acc) \\ (cacc) \end{matrix}, \quad U_1^A(a, d) = \begin{bmatrix} -\alpha_d & 0 \\ \alpha_m & 0 \end{bmatrix} \begin{matrix} (acc) \\ (cacc) \end{matrix}, \tag{4}$$

with column labels (a) (na) above each matrix.

$$U_2(c,d) = \begin{matrix} (r) & (nr) \\ \begin{bmatrix} \beta_t & \beta_s \\ \beta_s & \beta_t \end{bmatrix} & \begin{matrix} (acc) \\ (cacc) \end{matrix} \end{matrix}, \tag{5}$$

where α's and β's are integers and terms in parentheses are the actions available for different players. The first utility component U_1 is with respect to the Attacker and the Defender's actions. The parameter α_d quantifies the Defender's gain for correctly deploying ACC controller to mitigate the attack a, whose negation is assumed as the Attacker's loss. The quantities $-\alpha_f$ and $-\alpha_m$ are the costs of a false alarm and missing an attack for the Defender respectively. For instance, the Defender may downgrade to ACC controller with higher chance when the cost of a miss outweigh a false alarm. There is a cost of missing an attack for the Defender, however, false alarms cost nothing to the Attacker, which is denoted by zero entry in (4).

The second utility component $U_2(c,d)$ captures how trustworthy the deployed detector is from the Defender's prospective. For instance, if the Defender trusts heavily in the detector then the gain β_t is very large to represent the large benefits of performing actions based on the detection results or similarly the gain of discarding the detection results β_s from this detector is very small or even negative. When the inter-vehicle distance reduces abnormally but there is still no attacks being reported, this indicates that the deployed detector becomes less trustworthy, so that the gain of performing actions irrespective of the detection reports increases. Note that utility values have a meaning only relative to each other since any affine transformation of the utilities would result in the same strategy profile. Therefore, we fix β_t and set β_s as an adaptive quantity utilizing sensor readings to incorporate the system dynamics.

$$\beta_s = \begin{cases} \lfloor k_s \log_2 (k_u \cdot \epsilon_{radar}) \rfloor, & \text{if } \epsilon_{radar} > \epsilon_{max}, \\ -k_c, & \text{otherwise}, \end{cases} \tag{6}$$

where $k's$ and ϵ_{max} are positive constants. k_s and k_u adjust the growth speed and x-axis intersection of the logarithm respectively. ϵ_{radar} is the inter-vehicle spacing error with respect to a prefixed desired inter-vehicle distance calculated based on Radar measurements. Under normal platoon operation where ϵ_{radar} is small, the deployed detector is trustworthy from the Defender's viewpoint. This is represented by a large constant k_c. When $\epsilon_{radar} > \epsilon_{max}$, the gain of discarding detection results increases gradually with logarithmic growth. In the simulation, the desired inter-vehicle distance is set to be $2\,\text{m}$ and ϵ_{max} is $0.1\,\text{m}$.

3.1 Numerical Example

We present one instance of the game shown graphically as in Fig. 1 to further explain our proposed game-theoretic framework. Both players' actions and detection reports are represented as edges and the resulting states are represented as nodes in the game tree. The utilities of each strategy profile are at the leaves highlighted in red for the Attacker and blue for the Defender. The example anomaly detector 85% of the time correctly reports benign data when there is no attack; it makes false alarms for the remaining 15% of the time. When an attack has truly occurred, this detector correctly reports it 65% of the time and misses for the remaining 35% of the time. We use a popular open-source game solver *Gambit* [9] to find Nash equilibrium solutions. The probability distribution of each player's actions is shown under the respective branches. A path from left to right in the figure follows the order of players' actions. For instance, the Attacker will attack with 73.91% of the chance and if the Detector reports no attack being detected, the Defender would still choose to downgrade to sensor based ACC controller 11.24% of the chance to react to this high attack intention and imperfect detection results. Code is available at https://garrisonsun.github.io/End-to-end-atttack-detection-and-mitigation-framework/.

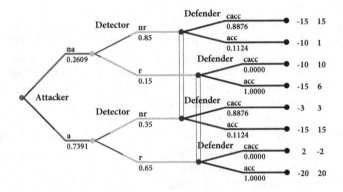

Fig. 1. An example game structure: the attacker's actions are in red, detection results are in green, and defender's controller switching decisions are in blue. (Color figure online)

4   Simulation Setup

Platoon and Traffic Simulation. To simulate the vehicle platoon, we use *Webots* [16], which is a multi-purpose simulator that provides a wide variety of virtual vehicle models, sensor modules including camera, radar, etc. as well as static objects and materials to construct different simulation circumstances. The simulation for our vehicle platoon use case can be divided into two major components: (1) vehicle platoon simulation; and (2) traffic flow simulation. For *vehicle platoon simulation*, we simulate a highway driving scenario in which a vehicle platoon consisting of 4 identical *BMW X5* vehicles driving along a highway segment of 5 km length in total. *BMW X5* is one of the built-in vehicle models in *Webots* with vehicle properties calibrated based on real-world vehicle dynamics. There are also multiple sensors equipped on different sensor slots to measure, receive and transmit critical driving information. For instance, location and acceleration are obtained from GPS and accelerometer readings respectively.

Speed information can be read directly from the speedometer on each vehicle. These vehicle dynamic messages are transmitted and received by its emitter and receiver modules as an approximation of Vehicular Ad hoc Network (VANET). We implement both CACC and ACC controllers in Python for each vehicle, which take the transmitted messages and sensor measurements as inputs to compute high level control outputs respectively.

For *traffic flow simulation*, we use Simulation of Urban MObility (SUMO) [7] to generate a large number of vehicles in real-time in order to construct a more realistic driving environment. 4 types of vehicles (i.e., motorcycles, light-weight vehicles, trucks, and trailers) with different moving characteristics are simulated. Different drivers also have different driving characteristics (cooperative or competitive) and intentions to merge introducing many random situations. The complete explanation and default parameter values are available in SUMO's documentation.

Detector Training. We next use the simulation platform to prepare data sets for detector training and testing purposes. At each simulation step, each vehicle receives critical dynamic information such as position, velocity and acceleration from its immediate predecessor and the lead vehicle, which correspond to the input variables of the CACC controller. These variables are combined as an input feature vector to the neural networks. We implement the proposed defense framework on each vehicle in a distributed manner. Therefore, without loss of generality, we demonstrate its performance by defending the third vehicle of the platoon with the communication channel established from the second vehicle being compromised by intelligent adversaries.

To prepare training and testing data sets, the platoon accelerates from stationary position to reach a desired velocity set by the platoon leader based on traffic conditions while maintaining a prefixed inter-vehicle distance and relative velocity. Once the platoon has driven 4900 m, message falsification attack initiates from the second vehicle against the third. The attacker maliciously adds an extra term to the original speed as shown in (1) with 10 km/h as the maximum altered speed and gradient $\gamma = 0.001$. An entire run of the simulation generates 18000 feature vectors on average, among which only 500 feature vectors belong to the attack class. Due to the imbalanced nature of the collected data, we assign weights as the inverse number of data samples to both benign class and attack class so as to heavily weight the few attack examples that are available.

To train a more robust detector applicable to various types of driving conditions, we investigate the vehicle driving characteristics with CACC controller under different traffic conditions. Heavy traffic condition leads to more frequent merging behaviour from other vehicles. Note that, the vehicle platoon adapts the disturbance introduced by different traffic conditions with only minimum variation of inter-vehicle distance as shown in Fig. 2a (zoomed-in view). Despite its performance in maintaining platoon stability, heavy traffic condition causes more acceleration and breaking maneuvers as shown in Fig. 2b and 2c. To balance the effects of traffic conditions, we train the network with 6 runs of simulation

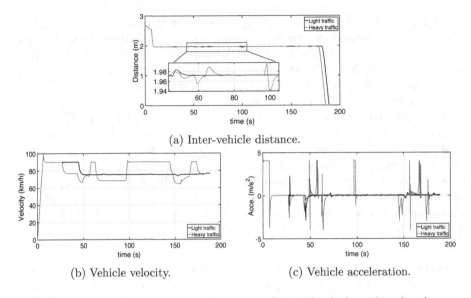

(a) Inter-vehicle distance.

(b) Vehicle velocity.   (c) Vehicle acceleration.

Fig. 2. Impact of different traffic conditions on the third vehicle within the platoon, showing inter-vehicle distance (a), vehicle velocity (b), and acceleration (c).

including 3 runs each for light and heavy traffic conditions respectively. There are 108534 feature vectors in total consisting of 104020 benign data samples and 4514 data samples with attack.

All hyperparameters (see Sect. 2.3) are tuned in a way that favours low false alarm rate to increase the usability and public acceptance of such defense method. We also set a high classification threshold. The detector reports a feature vector as malicious only if the malicious score form the output layer is greater than 0.9. The testing process involves 26 runs of simulation (half for each traffic condition) with 448744 benign samples and 19505 attack samples, based on which false alarm rate and miss rate are computed. As a result, this detector achieves a recall of 1 on benign samples but only 0.34 on attack samples, which defines the probability distribution of the chance node in the game tree. The downside of this detector is the increased detection miss rate, which is handled by the proposed game-theoretic model.

5   Simulation Results and Discussion

We consider three scenarios next to demonstrate that the proposed framework achieves the three primary goals of the paper. As an illustration, the same message falsification attack targets the second platoon member in a way causing the third vehicle to accelerate and collide. In the first two scenarios, we simulate a highway segment of 1 km length without traffic for simple illustration. The attack initiates once the platoon has driven for 500 m. We show its performance in a more realistic environment (i.e., longer operation time and disturbance from other vehicles) in the last scenario. We use inter-vehicle distance as a metric to show the mitigation effects in each of these scenarios. In addition, we also compare their corresponding utilities to show the effectiveness of our proposed approach from another viewpoint.

The built-in Radar module in *Webots* simulates sensor noise with a Gaussian distribution. We set its standard deviation as 0.3 with zero mean. However, the exact noise level depends on individual sensors and ambient environment. Due to limitations of the current simulation setup however, other disadvantages of ACC such as string stability violation is not explicitly shown.

Comparison of Defense Strategies. Figure 3 shows the inter-vehicle distance and the corresponding probability of downgrading from communication-based controller CACC to sensor-based controller ACC of vehicle 3 under different scenarios. To show our approach provides superior attack effect reduction and collision avoidance compared to a popular mitigation approach, we consider the following cases as indicated by the legend of the figure:

Ideal case: This is used for ease of comparison which indicates what happens if there is no attack and disturbance from traffic.

No attack mitigation: This indicates what happens if an attack is initiated but the platoon member is not equipped with any mitigation approaches.

Rule-based mitigation: The vehicle downgrades from CACC to ACC only if the anomaly score from the anomaly detector is greater than a predetermined threshold.

Low cost of miss: Cost of miss is a hyperparameter of our proposed approach indicating the cost of not responding to an attack.

High cost of miss: In this case, the cost of miss is set to a larger value.

The platoon starts to move from a stationary position with initial inter-vehicle distance of more than 2.5 m at time $t = 0$ s. This distance eventually reduces to the desired inter-vehicle spacing (2 m) as the platoon reaches steady (or equilibrium) state. If there is no attack or disturbance from other vehicles (i.e., the ideal case), platoon stability is maintained throughout the whole simulation as shown with pink dashed lines in the figure. There is also no need to deploy ACC controller so the probability of controller switching remains at zero as shown in Fig. 3b. After reaching steady driving state, the attack begins at time $t = 19.4$ s right after the platoon has moved 500 m. If no attack mitigation strategies are deployed, vehicle 3 will slowly move towards its predecessor leading to a collision (inter-vehicle distance equals zero) at $t = 27$ s as indicated by black dotted lines. If the defender chooses to follow a rule-based attack mitigation strategy as suggested in the existing literature, the collision is avoided as the backup controller kicks in at $t = 25.1$ s but the minimum inter-vehicle distance almost reaches 0.58 m (red triangle in Fig. 3a), which is very dangerous given all vehicles are driving at significant highway speeds.

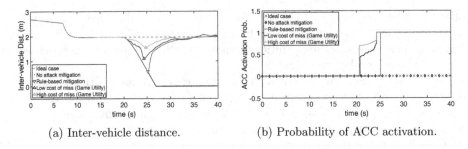

(a) Inter-vehicle distance.   (b) Probability of ACC activation.

Fig. 3. Comparison of different attack detection and mitigation approaches. Two realisations of our approach (in blue and green) result in a safer minimum inter-vehicle distance as marked by triangles in (a). (Color figure online)

With our proposed defense framework, the situation is greatly improved and the minimum inter-vehicle distance is increased to a much safer value. Under normal platoon operation conditions (where ϵ_{radar} is tiny), the gain β_t of responding according to detection results dominates its counterpart β_s. The trustworthiness of the detection results reduces dynamically as the inter-vehicle distance reduces abnormally. After passing the warning distance error set by ϵ_{max}, the gain β_s starts to increase and the resulting utility values would in favour the vehicle of activating ACC even though the detected anomaly probability of the received beacon message is still low. As vehicle 3 moves closer toward its preceding vehicle, this gain value β_s keeps increasing. As a result, the probability of deploying ACC increases, which coincides with the intuition that it is more likely to require mitigation acts as the situation is getting worse. In Figs. 3a and 3b, results from two utility settings are presented. With lower cost of a miss $-\alpha_m = -10$, the minimum inter-vehicle distance increases to 1.1 m (blue triangle in Fig. 3a). And this number increases to 1.6 m (green triangle in Fig. 3a) when the cost of missing an attack is high as $-\alpha_m = -30$. Note that, we are able to increase the minimum inter-vehicle distance by 90% and 176% respectively compared to the one (0.58 m) resulting from the rule-based mitigation approach. Higher α_m value increases the starting controller switching probability from 0.43 to 0.70 after the inter-vehicle distance passes the preset warning distance as indicated by green and blue plots at $t = 20.6$ s in Fig. 3b.

While higher α_m improves safety in this attack mitigation simulation, it is not always beneficial. High missing cost α_m leads to higher chance of early-stage ACC controller intervention. However, in comparison with CACC, ACC controller has disadvantages in distance headway, control bandwidth and reliability. Moreover, ACC controller fails to guarantee the string stability of vehicle platoon, which results in undesirable disturbance recovery characteristics. By altering the utility values such as α_m and α_f, the defender may trade off between the use of the sensor-based and communication-based controllers. The tuning process of this hyperparameter depends on factors such as the confidence in equipped sensors, the desired gap distance, vehicle characteristics, etc.

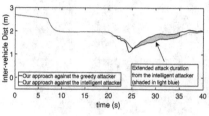

(a) Inter-vehicle distance.

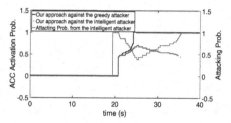

(b) ACC activation probability (left y-axis) and attacking probability from the intelligent attacker (right y-axis).

Fig. 4. Comparison of different types of attackers. The intelligent attacker keeps adjusting its attacking strategies shown by the dark green line in (b). This results in a slightly increased minimum inter-vehicle distance but allows the attack effects last much longer as shown by the shaded area in (a). (Color figure online)

Defense Against Greedy and Rational Attackers. An intelligent attacker may leverage knowledge about the platoon and deployed defense measures to perform targeted and stealthy attacks. In this subsection, we consider: **(1)** Greedy attacker: Once it decides to attack, it attacks the system all the time. **(2)** Intelligent attacker: It randomises its attack strategies based on the solution of the security game. In particular, once it senses being detected, it may suspend the attack behaviour.

Figure 4a presents the resulting inter-vehicle distance by our proposed defense framework against two types of attackers. Figure 4b contains the corresponding probability of controller switching (in orange) and probability of attacking (in dark green) based on the solution of the security game. The attacking probability of the greedy attacker is neglected in the figure. As shown in Fig. 4b, the attacker attacks with full intensity between 19.4 s and 20.75 s. Instead of maintaining this attacking intensity all the way till the end of the simulation, the game-instructed attacker reduces the probability of attacking after the preset suspicious gap error ϵ_{max} has been reached in order to avoid detection. The reduced attacking probability decreases the probability of controller switching and delays the time when the sensor based controller is fully activated. This effectively benefits the attacker with extended duration of the attacking effects as seen between 25 s and 35 s in Fig. 4a. Nevertheless, the proposed framework is still capable of improving the system's safety and reliability.

5.1 Realistic Driving Scenario

The simulation shown in Fig. 5 considers realistic driving environment (e.g., traffic) to demonstrate that our proposed approach can tolerate normal vehicle maneuvers such as breaking resulting from merging behaviour of other vehicles. In this simulation, the platoon aims to maintain a desired inter-vehicle distance of 2 m driving at 90 km/h for 5 km. Traffic could cause fluctuations in vehicle

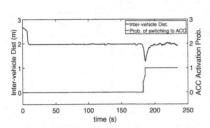

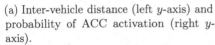

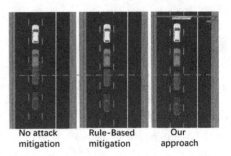

(a) Inter-vehicle distance (left y-axis) and probability of ACC activation (right y-axis).

(b) *Webots* simulation screenshots. The green line indicates the desired inter-vehicle spacing.

Fig. 5. Our proposed defense framework in realistic driving environment, with statics shown in (a) and simulation screenshots in (b).

dynamics, for example at time $t = 125$ s and $t = 170$ s in Fig. 5a, but such disturbances do not trigger undesired control system reconfiguration. The same type of boiling frog attack starts right after the platoon drove 4 km at time $t = 180$ s. Simulation comparison of different mitigation approaches is presented in Fig. 5b. As expected, our approach successfully mitigated the attack effects and hold the attacked vehicle at a relatively safe minimum inter-vehicle distance.

Comparison of Players' Utilities. In the previous subsections, we have shown the effectiveness of our proposed approach in terms of the increase of minimum inter-vehicle distance and the probability of ACC controller activation. We now illustrate its effectiveness from another viewpoint, namely in terms of utility values under different scenarios. We consider two specific Attacker behaviour, greedy and intelligent (adopting game solution) and two Defender types, adopting Rule-based mitigation and our security game-based mitigation as defined in earlier subsections. We record their interactions within a time window of 200 simulation steps and present their average utilities in Table 1. The Attacker's utility is negative in the left of the parentheses and the other positive value is the Defender's utility. Note that the game played is not a zero-sum game and players' utilities do not necessarily add up to zero.

Table 1. Average utility values of four combinations of attack-defence strategies with negative values for the Attacker and positive values for the Defender. The higher the value the better the outcome for that player.

Attacker	Defender	
	Rule-based	Our approach
Greedy	$(-7.1, 7.1)$	$(-11.0, 9.3)$
Intelligent	$(-8.8, 8.8)$	$(-10.4, 9.0)$

It is important to note that in Table 1, the nominal utility values are not important and relative values highlight players' outcomes based on their strategies. For example, our defense approach receives utilities of 9.3 and 9.0 instead of 7.1 and 8.8 against greedy and intelligent attackers respectively. This demonstrates that our approach outperforms the rule-based method up to 30% against both types of attackers. Unsurprisingly, if the Attacker happens to be greedy in against our defense approach, the Defender will gain more. On the other hand, both types of attackers will have less utilities against our proposed defense approach compared to against the rule-based one. Yet, an attacker may choose to be greedy instead of intelligent to gain more if they know the defense side is deployed with the rule-based method, which is less capable of defending the system. Different solution concepts other than the Nash equilibrium could be explored in the future to capture different assumptions on players' common knowledge and rationality.

6   Conclusion

In this paper, we have presented a novel approach for detecting and mitigating attacks against vehicle platoons, thereby enhancing system safety in an adversarial environment. Our approach uniquely combines the advancements of machine learning and game theory, where the interactions between an intelligent attacker, defense system in possession of an imperfect detector have been investigated. In this setting, the attacker launches a boiling frog test-time attack against the learner. The Nash equilibrium solution guides control system reconfiguration, in which the benefits of a communication-based and a sensor-based controller are optimised. Evaluating in a sophisticated simulation, our approach successfully avoids a collision, and outperforms the rule-based mitigation method by significantly increasing the worse-case inter-vehicle distance. It also defeats an intelligent adversary although the duration of the attack effects has been extended. Furthermore, the defense framework can be deployed on each platoon member operating in an online manner, which demonstrates its potential for real-world deployment. These results provide fresh insights and help answer the questions set out in this paper. Further research will explore the robustness of the proposed method against other types of attacks (e.g., position or acceleration falsification) initiated from different communication channels and against different types of anomaly detectors.

References

1. Alotibi, F., Abdelhakim, M.: Anomaly detection for cooperative adaptive cruise control in autonomous vehicles using statistical learning and kinematic model. IEEE Trans. Intell. Transp. Syst. (2020)
2. Alpcan, T., Başar, T.: Network Security: A Decision and Game-Theoretic Approach. Cambridge University Press, Cambridge (2010)

3. Boeira, F., Barcellos, M.P., de Freitas, E.P., Vinel, A., Asplund, M.: Effects of colluding sybil nodes in message falsification attacks for vehicular platooning. In: 2017 IEEE Vehicular Networking Conference (VNC), pp. 53–60. IEEE (2017)

4. Chalapathy, R., Chawla, S.: Deep learning for anomaly detection: a survey. arXiv preprint arXiv:1901.03407 (2019)

5. Fang, F., et al.: Deploying paws: field optimization of the protection assistant for wildlife security. In: AAAI, vol. 16, pp. 3966–3973 (2016)

6. Khanapuri, E., Chintalapati, T., Sharma, R., Gerdes, R.: Learning-based adversarial agent detection and identification in cyber physical systems applied to autonomous vehicular platoon. In: 2019 IEEE/ACM 5th International Workshop on Software Engineering for Smart Cyber-Physical Systems (SEsCPS), pp. 39–45. IEEE (2019)

7. Lopez, P.A., et al.: Microscopic traffic simulation using sumo. In: The 21st IEEE International Conference on Intelligent Transportation Systems. IEEE (2018). https://elib.dlr.de/124092/

8. Lu, X.Y., Hedrick, J.K., Drew, M.: ACC/CACC-control design, stability and robust performance. In: Proceedings of the 2002 American Control Conference (IEEE Cat. No. CH37301), vol. 6, pp. 4327–4332. IEEE (2002)

9. McKelvey, R.D., McLennan, A.M., Turocy, T.L.: Gambit: software tools for game theory (2006)

10. Merco, R., Biron, Z.A., Pisu, P.: Replay attack detection in a platoon of connected vehicles with cooperative adaptive cruise control. In: 2018 Annual American Control Conference (ACC), pp. 5582–5587. IEEE (2018)

11. Qayyum, A., Usama, M., Qadir, J., Al-Fuqaha, A.: Securing connected & autonomous vehicles: challenges posed by adversarial machine learning and the way forward. IEEE Commun. Surv. Tutor. **22**(2), 998–1026 (2020)

12. Rajamani, R.: Vehicle Dynamics and Control. Springer, Heidelberg (2011)

13. Sedjelmaci, H., Senouci, S.M., Al-Bahri, M.: A lightweight anomaly detection technique for low-resource IoT devices: a game-theoretic methodology. In: 2016 IEEE International Conference on Communications (ICC), pp. 1–6. IEEE (2016)

14. Subba, B., Biswas, S., Karmakar, S.: A game theory based multi layered intrusion detection framework for wireless sensor networks. Int. J. Wirel. Inf. Netw. **25**(4), 399–421 (2018)

15. Sumra, I.A., Hasbullah, H.B., AbManan, J.B.: Attacks on security goals (confidentiality, integrity, availability) in VANET: a survey. In: Laouiti, A., Qayyum, A., Mohamad Saad, M.N. (eds.) Vehicular Ad-hoc Networks for Smart Cities. AISC, vol. 306, pp. 51–61. Springer, Singapore (2015). https://doi.org/10.1007/978-981-287-158-9_5

16. Webots: http://www.cyberbotics.com. Open-source Mobile Robot Simulation Software

17. Wiedersheim, B., Ma, Z., Kargl, F., Papadimitratos, P.: Privacy in inter-vehicular networks: why simple pseudonym change is not enough. In: 2010 Seventh International Conference on Wireless on-Demand Network Systems and Services (WONS), pp. 176–183. IEEE (2010)

18. Yang, L., Moubayed, A., Hamieh, I., Shami, A.: Tree-based intelligent intrusion detection system in internet of vehicles. In: 2019 IEEE Global Communications Conference (GLOBECOM), pp. 1–6. IEEE (2019)

19. Zhang, D., Shen, Y.P., Zhou, S.Q., Dong, X.W., Yu, L.: Distributed secure platoon control of connected vehicles subject to dos attack: theory and application. IEEE Trans. Syst. Man Cybern. Syst. (2020)

DeFraudNet: An End-to-End Weak Supervision Framework to Detect Fraud in Online Food Delivery

Jose Mathew, Meghana Negi, Rutvik Vijjali$^{(\boxtimes)}$, and Jairaj Sathyanarayana

Swiggy, Bangalore, India
{jose.matthew,meghana.negi,vijjali.reddy,jairaj.s}@swiggy.in

Abstract. Detecting abusive and fraudulent claims is one of the key challenges in online food delivery. This is further aggravated by the fact that it is not practical to do reverse-logistics on food unlike in e-commerce. This makes the already-hard problem of harvesting labels for fraud even harder because we cannot confirm if the claim was legitimate by inspecting the item(s). Using manual effort to analyze transactions to generate labels is often expensive and time-consuming. On the other hand, typically, there is a wealth of 'noisy' information about what constitutes fraud, in the form of customer service interactions, weak and hard rules derived from data analytics, business intuition and domain understanding.

In this paper, we present a novel end-to-end framework for detecting fraudulent transactions based on large-scale label generation using weak supervision. We directly use Stanford AI Lab's (SAIL) Snorkel and tree based methods to do manual and automated discovery of labeling functions, to generate weak labels. We follow this up with an auto-encoder reconstruction-error based method to reduce label noise. The final step is a discriminator model which is an ensemble of an MLP and an LSTM. In addition to cross-sectional and longitudinal features around customer history, transactions, we also harvest customer embeddings from a Graph Convolution Network (GCN) on a customer-customer relationship graph, to capture collusive behavior. The final score is thresholded and used in decision making.

This solution is currently deployed for real-time serving and has yielded a 16% points' improvement in recall at a given precision level. These results are against a baseline MLP model based on manually labeled data and are highly significant at our scale. Our approach can easily scale to additional fraud scenarios or to use-cases where 'strong' labels are hard to get but weak labels are prevalent.

Keywords: Automated labelling functions · Snorkel · Class-specific autoencoders · LSTM · Graph Convolution Network

© Springer Nature Switzerland AG 2021
Y. Dong et al. (Eds.): ECML PKDD 2021, LNAI 12978, pp. 85–99, 2021.
https://doi.org/10.1007/978-3-030-86514-6_6

1   Introduction

At hyperlocal online food delivery platforms, the prevalence of fraud and abuse necessitates strong prevention systems that can identify and alert other systems and humans. Since most online food ordering platforms are three-sided marketplaces, abuse can originate from customers, delivery partners, restaurants and collusion between any combination of these entities.

Typically, a combination of online and offline ML models is at play in most fraud detection systems. When a customer makes a claim against a delivered order, real-time models kick in and offer fraud decisioning which is, in turn, used by a customer-service agent or a bot to make the final decision. Supervised models rely on labels and signals harvested from transactions from the past. While there is, typically, plenty of data available on the signals' side, generating labels is a time-consuming and expensive process. However, to achieve reasonable coverage over fraud modus operandi (MOs), the training data needs to be exhaustive, requiring a broad set of labels. Given that fraud is ever-evolving and dynamic, it makes it even more difficult to rely solely on manual labeling. Hence the need to complement human labeling with label generation at scale using other ML methods.

Our baseline is an MLP based discriminator model built on a limited set of 'strongly' labeled data from human experts. In this work, we start with insights and intuitions from the way human experts label transactions and convert them to 'labeling functions' (LFs). These LFs label a data point as either fraud or non-fraud or abstain from assigning any label. These labels (and features) are then fed to a Snorkel [1] generative model which synthesizes a single weak label for each data point. We then introduce a class-specific autoencoder based method to further 'denoise' these weak labels. Lastly, we fit a discriminator model (ensemble of a shallow MLP and an LSTM) to produce the final fraud score. In addition to the usual set of cross-sectional and longitudinal features, we also use embeddings harvested from a Graph Convolution Network (GCN) built on a customer-customer relationship graph. This helps us encapsulate connectedness and collusive behavior.

The final, winning pipeline is currently in production and has yielded a 16pp improvement in recall at a given precision level, which is highly significant at our scale. Additionally, this method saved us about 1.5 million person-hours worth of manual labeling effort.

In summary, our contributions are listed below.

1. We propose a novel end-to-end pipeline for real-time fraud detection based on a weak supervision framework consisting of the Snorkel generative model followed by a class specific autoencoder. A MLP/LSTM based discriminator model built on features spanning user/restaurant/delivery partner history, transaction details and entity-relationship graph based embeddings constitute the inferencing pipeline.
2. We report results from an extensive ablation study where we progressively evaluate a) flavors of LFs (handcrafted vs. decision-tree generated vs. combined), b) various features (historical cross-sectional, sequence, graph based,

near & real time), c) modeling methodologies, and arrive at an optimized configuration that provides 16pp improvement in recall for a given precision.
3. We have deployed the DeFraudNet model in production where it currently provides real-time decisions for hundreds of thousands of claims per week.

The remainder of the paper is organized as follows. In Sect. 2, we discuss related work. In Sect. 3, we introduce the end-to-end pipeline. Sections 4, 5, 6, 7 provide details about individual components of the pipeline and production deployment. We present the experiments and results from the ablative study in Sect. 8 followed by a summary and directions for future work in Sect. 9.

2   Related Work

We build a part of our work upon SAIL's Snorkel [1] data programming approach. Snorkel uses an ensemble of weak heuristics and rules based on domain knowledge to create a generative algorithm and apply it to an unlabelled dataset. As an extension of this work, in [2], the authors present a tree based modeling technique wherein the end-to-end process of weak label generation is automated. We take inspiration from this to automate and remove human bias from the process of creating LFs. We further take inspiration from [3] to use a class-specific autoencoder based method to reduce noise from the weak labels.

A vast majority of the published literature in the domain of fraud detection centers around credit cards and other financial instruments. [4] describes the use of Random Forests in credit card fraud detection while [5] compares and contrasts trees and SVMs for the same task. [6] proposes a deep learning model for identifying fraud in card payments while [7] shows the utility of sequential data to extract temporal patterns using RNNs. The authors use sequences of sessions and encode using an LSTM to predict a risk score. A GAN based denoising autoencoder architecture was implemented by Zheng et al. [15] for fraud detection in the telecom domain. Deng et al. [16] developed a methodology for fraud detection in online payment platforms where the availability of labelled customer data is limited, by learning latent representations based on adversarial autoencoders.

Recent works have also focussed on fraud detection using graph based approaches. The authors in [8] used a combination GCNs as well as processing meta information of nodes for generating combined representations and training from their labels.

In practice, efficient fraud detection systems operate by integrating several individual working pieces to form a whole pipeline. The authors of [9] propose a real time fraud detection pipeline that can flag multiple transactions using a combination of graph based embeddings and a decision tree based classifier. [10] makes use of a multi-graph framework where embeddings are used in conjunction with raw features cleaned using autoencoder, are fed into a gradient boosted tree parameter server for classification. [11] predicts fraud using interleaved transactions and processes them as a batch in multi-sequence RNNs with stacked GRUs, storing intermediate hidden states in a cache database.

Irrespective of the algorithm used or the domain, the common bottleneck is the availability of reliable labels and most literature that we have surveyed presumes the existence of labeled data.

3   The Framework: DeFraudNet

3.1   Problem Definition

We use the term order to represent a customer's transaction with our platform. Customers who have completed an order can raise a request for claiming issues with food delivery like food spillage, missing item, order delivered late, etc. If a claim is found to be genuine then a restitution of some sort is made to the customer. While the majority of claims are genuine, a small but significant minority is abusive. With millions of orders in a month, it is impossible to do manual adjudication of claims. It easily takes 45–60 min for a human expert to evaluate a claim by looking at a battery of signals across all the actors (customer, restaurant, delivery-partner, platform issues, collusions) involved.

Hence the problem definition is two-fold: *a) Augment strong labels with a large number of weak labels and use historical and transactional data to design a training pipeline, b) design an inference pipeline to predict whether a claim is fraudulent or not in real time.*

3.2   Fraud Detection Pipeline

Most existing fraud detection research presumes the existence of labeled data and reliability of these labels and emphasizes ML techniques to better predict fraud. To the best of our knowledge, DeFraudNet is the first end-to-end system that combines label generation to model serving in a unified framework. Our system consists of 4 stages (Fig. 1).

1. **Data and feature pipeline:** This is responsible for building the features that go into the training, validation and 'golden' datasets (Sect. 4).
2. **Label generation pipeline:** This contains the components to generate weak labels for all data points in the training and validation datasets (Sect. 5).
3. **Discriminator pipeline:** This trains the final discriminator models on features and labels from the previous stages (Sect. 6).
4. **Evaluation:** This facilitates ongoing evaluation of the fraud detection system by sending a sample of claims to human evaluators and using their judgment to compute precision, recall and related health-check metrics.

4   Data and Feature Processing

4.1   Dataset

Initially the dataset consists of all unclassified claims U. A small random sample from U is sent to the Risk Management Team (RMT) which manually adjudicates cases to generate 'strong' labels. We call this the 'golden' dataset G.

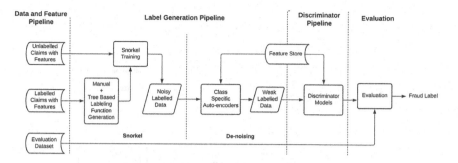

Fig. 1. DeFraudNet end to end framework

This dataset is inherently expensive and slow to generate (a few hundred labels per week) and we accumulate this across several months. We further split the human-labeled set G into D_{label_gen} and Deval around an arbitrary date t, to generate a training dataset and an out-of-time evaluation dataset, respectively. D_{label_gen} is used to learn decision tree-based LFs (interchangeably called auto LFs) while D_{eval} (or a random subsample) is used to evaluate all the models.

After isolating G from U, we create D_{ul_train} by sampling a large portion of U. D_{ul_train} and D_{label_gen} are inputs to the label generation pipeline. The output of this pipeline is a denoised, weak-labeled training dataset D_{train}.

Fig. 2 shows how these datasets are created and Table 1 represents the number of samples in these datasets over a period of 4 months which are used in our study.

Table 1. Overview of the datasets

	Number of samples
Unlabelled training data(D_{ul_train})	1.5 M
Golden label generation dataset(D_{label_gen})	6000
De-noised labelled Training dataset(D_{train})	1.48 M
Golden evaluation dataset(D_{eval})	5407

4.2 Feature Engineering

The features we use can be categorized into 4 types (Fig. 3):

a) F1: historical cross-sectional for all entities (i.e., customer, restaurant, delivery-partner, geolocation) involved in the claim (for example, customer tenure, restaurant's popularity, delivery-partner's experience level). These help encode medium to longer term behavior of the entities involved.

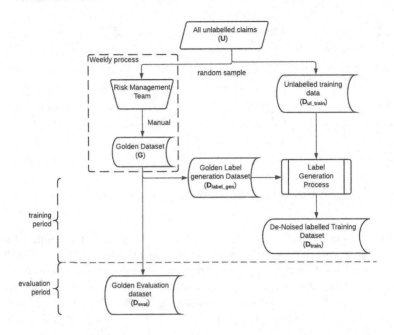

Fig. 2. Datasets

b) F2: real time & near real time (for example, current order's details like bill amount, number of claims in the last 15 min, time-of-day, claim type). These help capture the here & now information.

c) F3: customer's orders-sequence related information (cross-sectional and real time features at the time-steps of current and previous k orders). F3 when fed into an LSTM help capture the sequential nature which F1 and F2 do not fully encapsulate.

d) F4: customer graph embeddings. This is motivated by the insight that some fraudsters fly below the radar when looked at in isolation but patterns emerge when analyzed in conjunction with their 'neighbors' in some space. We found that shared payment instruments are one of the most common links in fraud rings. We use embeddings from a GCN learned on the customer-payment instrument graph, to capture this connectedness.

e) F5: Additionally, we take a subset of F1– mainly features focused on the restaurant and the delivery-partner. These help in learning the attribution of 'responsibility' to the restaurant and/or delivery-partner in a claim. For example, in a claim about a missing-item in the order, the restaurant may have missed packing the item and/or the delivery-partner may have dropped the item (irrespective of intention). We call these 'negative features' since they lead to bad customer experience.

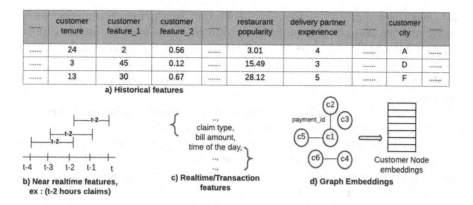

	customer tenure	customer feature_1	customer feature_2		restaurant popularity	delivery partner experience		customer city	
....	24	2	0.56	....	3.01	4	....	A	....
....	3	45	0.12	....	15.49	3	....	D	....
....	13	30	0.67	....	28.12	5	....	F	....

a) Historical features

b) Near realtime features, ex : (t-2 hours claims)

c) Realtime/Transaction features

d) Graph Embeddings

Fig. 3. Categories of features

5 Label Generation

5.1 Generating Noisy Labels Using LFs

We generate LFs via two methods: manually and using decision trees. Hand-crafted LFs are a direct, best-effort encapsulation of domain expertise and tend to be fairly simple rules based on, typically, 2–3 features. However, hard-coded thresholds on features in these LFs can make them brittle. If the business changes or new fraud patterns emerge, while human evaluators can make mental adjustments to their judgments, the LFs need to be revisited. Decision-tree derived (auto) LFs help alleviate these shortcomings because they learn feature combinations and thresholds from the (human-labeled D_{label_gen}) data. However, also because of this dependency, the extent of patterns they can learn is limited by the patterns covered in human labels. Hence we combine both the approaches resulting in a corpus of 45 handcrafted LFs and 150 auto LFs.

Following is an example of a hypothetical LF using two features.

```
@labeling_function()
def Fraud_Rule_1(x):
    """"if feature1 > X and feature2 = 1 then the request is Not Fraud:"""
    return Negative if ((x[feature1]>X) & (x[feature2] == 1)) else Abstain
```

In general, all LFs have the following properties: a) An LF can either assign or abstain from generating a label, b) LF decisions can overlap or conflict with other LFs.

5.2 Snorkel Generative Model

Once the LFs are created, we synthesize labels using Snorkel over D_{ul_train}. Internally, the Snorkel generative model creates a label matrix by applying LFs over each data point and formulates label generation as a matrix completion problem to produce noise-aware, confidence-weighted labels with 3 possible values–$0, 1, -1$ (abstain). In our case, $<1\%$ of labels were of the type abstain and we chose to drop the corresponding data points from further training process. Additionally, Snorkel emits several statistics for LFs, like coverage, conflicts, overlap and accuracy.

We tested the hypothesis of whether more LFs are always better. We experimented by a) pruning LFs at different accuracy thresholds, b) learning a discriminator model over the new labeled dataset (say, D'_{train}), c) testing final performance on D_{eval}. We found that a model using roughly 70% of all LFs had 3.3% better F1-score compared to a model using all the LFs. We hypothesize that this could be due to the dynamic nature of fraud patterns leading to volatility in the effectiveness of LFs and that the full set of LFs may not always be needed.

5.3   Class-Specific Autoencoders for Denoising

While Snorkel emits a consolidated label for each sample, our analysis showed that some labels were still noisy. For example, we observed that, among cases which had very similar features, a small minority had opposing labels due to the fact that just one or two minor (in terms of their intuitive contribution towards fraud) features were different. One way to approach cleaning these labels would be to look at individual feature distributions for each class and consider samples with highly deviant features as outliers. However, there may be conflicting samples wherein one feature might be deviant for one class and flipping the label might cause another feature to be deviant for that label's distribution. This requires generating representations that capture overall distributions of samples belonging to a particular class. We use class-specific autoencoder networks for cleaning the labels. The hypothesis is that, for a given class, the majority of data is correctly labelled by the generative model hence an autoencoder can be learned to reconstruct the correctly-labelled data with low error, and will reconstruct outliers with high error.

Two autoencoder models were trained, let's call them model_a (trained with samples labeled 0) and model_b (trained with samples labeled 1). Several architectures for autoencoders were explored and verified by examining the separation of reconstruction errors between same-class samples and opposite-class samples against D_{eval}. The architecture that achieved maximum separation in terms of median values of reconstruction errors with early stopping, was an expansive (latent dimension > input dimension) autoencoder with latent dimension (128) being roughly 2X the size of input dimension (54). We visualize the separation of classes in the validation dataset through box plots (Fig. 4).

As seen in Fig. 4, the models learn to separate the classes at roughly the 75th percentile boundary (where the two boxes roughly 'meet'). Based on this, we set two thresholds, threshold_a, the 75th percentile reconstruction error of 0-labeled samples on model_a and threshold_b equivalently for model_b. To achieve denoising we use the following logic: if reconstruction error of a sample on model_a is greater than threshold_a and less than threshold_b, we assign the sample a label

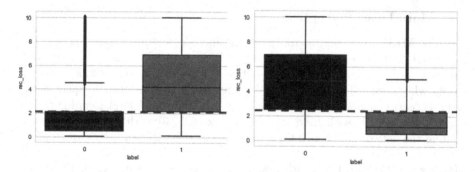

Fig. 4. a. Box plot visualization for model_a. **b.** Box plot visualization for model_b

of 1 and vice versa. Once the training data is cleaned using this denoising logic, we retrain the autoencoders with cleaned data and all steps are repeated. No new labels were flipped after two iterations.

6   Discriminator Models

We use Neural Network (NN) based methods as the final discriminator model. All discriminator models detailed below use weak labels of D_{train} and reduce the categorical cross entropy loss. Figure 5 illustrates how combinations of features and models are put together to predict the fraud decision.

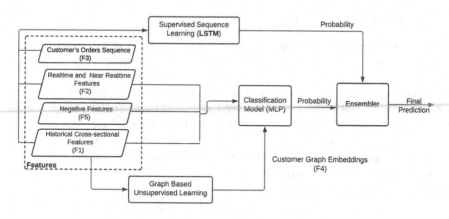

Fig. 5. Discriminator pipeline

6.1 Multi Layer Perceptron

Vanilla MLP. The inputs to the MLP include features from F1, F2 and F5. Each feature is transformed depending on how it is originally distributed. For example, normally-distributed features are transformed into z-scores while power-law-distributed features are log-transformed, specifically, $ln((1 + feature\_value)/(1 + feature\_median))$. The final model configuration was a 2-layer MLP with hidden layers of size (25, 3) with ReLu activations. Making the network deeper did not improve the downstream metric of recall.

MLP with Graph Embeddings. We experimented with augmenting the inputs to the MLP with the graph embeddings (F4). We construct a customer graph g defined as

$g = (V,E)$, $V= \{customer_1, customer_2, ...customer_n\}$, E = customer to customer link with same payment_id.

As is evident, g is a homogenous graph with a single edge-type. Each customer node is decorated with a subset of features from F1. A GCN was learned using the Deep Graph Infomax method on D_{train} (without the labels) and fine-tuned using D_{label_gen}. Customer node embeddings of size 128 are extracted from the final layer of the GCN. These embeddings are concatenated to F1, F2 and F5 and the MLP is retrained. The final MLP-with-graph-embeddings model had 3 layers of size (80,15,3) with ReLu activation.

The ablation study in Sect. 8 illustrates the lift in recall due to this change.

6.2 LSTM Sequence Model

Previous research like [7] and [11] have shown that learning from activity sequences is more effective in identifying fraud patterns than hand-engineered features. Hence, we develop a sequence prediction model that uses F3 as features (i.e.,customer's last k orders, their sequence and the (k+1)th (current) order's transactional features). We arrived at k = 20 by evaluating the F1-score for different values of k. We use a multi-layer stacked LSTM and the averaged representation of all hidden states is fed to the final softmax layer. We landed on the final architecture of an LSTM with 4 layers and 128 hidden units each followed by 2 dense layers with 256 and 64 hidden units respectively with ReLU activation using the Xavier initializer.

7 Deployment and Serving Infrastructure

All streaming logs, fact tables and entity data are available in our Hive based data warehouse. Most historical features are generated by Spark jobs while the near real-time features are generated using SQL-like queries on streaming data using Flink. All features are written to two sinks: to S3 for periodic retraining of models and to Amazon DynamoDB-DAX (DDB-DAX) for online inference of the production model.

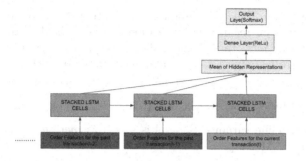

Fig. 6. LSTM architecture

At inference time, when a claim is made, the fraud detection microservice calls the model API hosted using Tensorflow Serving (TFS). The request consists of transaction details and real-time features. TFS fetches other feature values from the DDB-DAX cache. The TF model pipeline transforms features using tf.feature_columns, runs model predictions, ensembles and returns the final prediction to the client. We implemented custom transformers to do data transformations not natively available in TFS.

For model training, we used Tensorflow and p2.2xlarge GPU instances on AWS. Model decisions are evaluated on a weekly basis by RMT using a random sample.

The flow of the training and serving architecture is illustrated in Fig. 7.

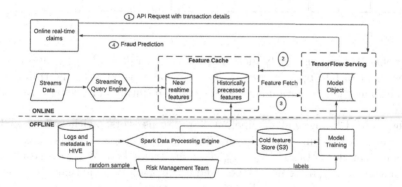

Fig. 7. Training and serving infrastructure

8   Ablation Experiments

8.1   Setup and Baseline

Most consumer-facing fraud detection systems are precision-first. Meaning, the downside of calling a 'good' customer fraudulent is asymmetrically high compared to the opposite. Hence we designed the ablation study to quantify impact of various pipelines on recall where precision has been fixed at the same, high value for all the variants. Table 2 shows the various pipelines studied. Our baseline is an MLP trained over D_{label_gen} and is evaluated over D_{eval}.

8.2 Experiments

In all the non-baseline variants, Snorkel is used to generate labels for D_{ul_train} spanning about 1.5 M samples.

Table 2. Results for different architectures

Pipeline	Handcrafted LFs	Auto LFs	Snorkel	Autoencoder based denoising	Graph embeddings	MLP	LSTM	Absolute recall improvement vs. baseline
1 (baseline)						✔		
2	✔		✔			✔		6.63%
3	✔	✔	✔			✔		2.3%
4	✔	✔	✔	✔		✔		10.43%
5	✔	✔	✔	✔			✔	8.61%
6	✔	✔	✔	✔	✔	✔		11.42%
7 (winner)	✔	✔	✔	✔	✔	✔	✔	16.01%

Pipeline 2, which uses only the labels from handcrafted LFs generates a recall improvement of 6.63 pp vs. baseline. This can be attributed to the training for pipeline 2 happening over a much larger dataset resulting in more patterns being learned.

The auto LF-augmented pipeline 3 performs worse with only a 2.3 pp improvement in recall. Auto LFs are limited by decision tree performance as well as the smaller dataset (D_{label_gen}) they are trained on. We hypothesize that auto LFs are adding more noisy labels and it is not always true that adding more LFs will improve performance. But since the manual curation of LFs is not scalable as fraud patterns frequently drift with time, we keep the auto LFs and add a denoising component resulting in pipeline 4. The results from denoising the weak labels is shown in Fig. 8. Here, dark blue colored nodes in Fig. 8.a and red coloured in Fig. 8.b represent samples originally labelled 0 and 1 respectively, that remained unchanged. Light blue coloured nodes represent the samples that were originally labelled 0 but flipped to 1 and pink coloured nodes represent the samples originally labelled 1 but flipped to 0. This resulted in 8% of label-1 and 11% of label-0 samples being flipped. The MLP discriminator model trained on these 'cleaned' labels showed a 10.43 pp recall improvement vs. the baseline.

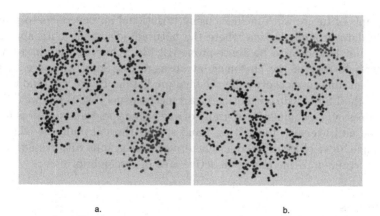

a.   b.

Fig. 8. t-SNE visualisation of latent representation for **a.** model_a and **b.** model_b

As explained in Sect. 6, we experimented with different modeling techniques to improve the performance of the discriminator. We keep the label generation components the same in the subsequent pipelines to measure incremental value of the different modelling techniques or feature generation methods. In pipeline 5, we replace the MLP with an LSTM as the discriminator. With an 8.61 pp improvement in recall, LSTM was not able to best the MLP discriminator. However, we should point out that the LSTM only used features from F3 and we couldn't use features from F1, F2 and F4 due to cost and infrastructural limitations. However, we qualitatively observed that the LSTM performed better than the MLP in cases where the customer's recent behavior was 'bursty'.

Pipeline 6 builds on pipeline 4 by adding the graph embeddings. This improves the recall by 11.42 pp (and 1 pp over pipeline 4, demonstrating the additional value-add from graph embeddings). Customers that were identified as fraudulent by pipeline 6 and not by pipeline 4 had one or more edges with a fraudulent claim rate that was 3× higher than the median.

Finally, we combine all components into pipeline 7 and ensemble the predictions from the MLP and the LSTM to achieve a 16 pp improvement in recall. This winning pipeline is currently deployed in production serving real-time decisions in milliseconds on hundreds of thousands of claims per week.

9   Conclusion

This work demonstrated the effectiveness of a pipeline consisting of handcrafted and auto-generated LFs followed by class-specific denoising autoencoders, to build effective supervised models when strongly labeled data is scarce. We show through our experiments how each step in the pipeline improves the evaluation metrics and propose a final multi-stage architecture for fraud detection. Our final model achieved a 16 pp improvement in recall when compared to the baseline MLP trained on limited, manually annotated data. This approach can easily scale to additional fraud scenarios and to use-cases where labeled data is sparse.

A sample of future work includes using variational autoencoders to generate synthetic data around pockets where the naturally-occurring data appears to be sparse but is known to be abuse-prone [12,13]. While we take into account longer term history of the customer, at an aggregate level, the recent bursty behavior can sometimes overwhelm the final prediction. Hence we could focus on extending the LSTM using attention based mechanisms [14]. While we explored connectedness via a homogeneous graph of one edge-type, fraud patterns usually tend to be multi-tenant. Identifying fraud spread through multiple edge types (for example, deviceIDs/wifiIDs) and heterogeneous graphs with restaurant and delivery partners into the mix is an active area of research for us.

References

1. Ratner, A., Bach, S.H., Ehrenberg, H., Fries, J., Wu, S., Ré, C.: Snorkel: rapid training data creation with weak supervision. In: VLDB Endow 11, 3, 269–282 (2017). https://doi.org/10.14778/3157794.3157797
2. Varma, P., Ré, C.: Snuba: automating weak supervision to label training data. In: VLDB Endow 12, 3, 223–236 (2018). https://doi.org/10.14778/3291264.3291268
3. Zhang, W., Wang, D., Tan, X.: Robust class-specific autoencoder for data cleaning and classification in the presence of label noise. Neural Process. Lett. **50**(2), 1845–1860 (2018). https://doi.org/10.1007/s11063-018-9963-9
4. Xuan, S., Liu, G., Li, Z., Zheng, L., Wang, S., Jiang, C.: Random forest for credit card fraud detection. In: 2018 IEEE 15th International Conference on Networking, Sensing and Control (ICNSC), Zhuhai, pp. 1–6 (2018). https://doi.org/10.1109/ICNSC.2018.8361343
5. Sahin, P.Y., Duman, E.: Detecting credit card fraud by decision trees and support vector machines. In: IMECS 2011 - International Multi Conference of Engineers and Computer Scientists, 1, 442–447 (2011)
6. Gomez, J.A., Arevalo, J., Paredes, R., Nin, J.: End-to-end neural network architecture for fraud scoring in card payments. Pattern Recogn. Lett. **105**, 175–181 (2018)
7. Wang, S., Liu, C., Gao, X., Qu, H., Xu, W.: Session-based fraud detection in online e-commerce transactions using recurrent neural networks. In: Altun, Y., Das, K., Mielikäinen, T., Malerba, D., Stefanowski, J., Read, J., Žitnik, M., Ceci, M., Džeroski, S. (eds.) ECML PKDD 2017. LNCS (LNAI), vol. 10536, pp. 241–252. Springer, Cham (2017). https://doi.org/10.1007/978-3-319-71273-4_20
8. Jiang, J., et al.: Anomaly detection with graph convolutional networks for insider threat and fraud detection. In: MILCOM 2019–2019 IEEE Military Communications Conference (MILCOM), Norfolk, VA, USA, pp. 109–114 (2019). https://doi.org/10.1109/MILCOM47813.2019.9020760
9. Cao, S., Yang, X., Chen, C., Zhou, J., Li, X., Qi, Y.: TitAnt: Online Real-time Transaction Fraud Detection in Ant Financial (2019)
10. Chen, C., et al.: InfDetect: a Large Scale Graph-based Fraud Detection System for E-Commerce Insurance (2020)
11. Branco, B., Abreu, P., Gomes, A., Almeida, M., Ascensão, J., Bizarro, P.: Interleaved sequence RNNs for fraud detection. In: Proceedings of the 26th ACM SIGKDD International Conference on Knowledge Discovery and Data Mining (2020)

12. Kingma, D.P., Welling, M.: Auto-Encoding Variational Bayes (2014)
13. Im, D., Ahn, S., Memisevic, R., Bengio, Y.: Denoising criterion for variational auto-encoding framework. In: Proceedings of the Thirty-First AAAI Conference on Artificial Intelligence, pp. 2059–2065 (2017). AAAI Press
14. Guo, J., Liu, G., Zuo, Y., Wu, J.: Learning sequential behavior representations for fraud detection. In: 2018 IEEE International Conference on Data Mining (ICDM), Singapore, pp. 127–136 (2018). https://doi.org/10.1109/ICDM.2018.00028
15. Zheng, Y.J., Zhou, X.H., Sheng, W.G., Xue, Y., Chen, S.Y.: Generative adversarial network based telecom fraud detection at the receiving bank. Neural Netw. **102**, 78–86 (2018)
16. Deng, R., Rua, N., Zhang, G., Zhang, X.: FraudJudger: Fraud Detection on Digital Payment Platforms with Fewer Labels, arXiv:1909.02398 (2019)

Spatio-Temporal Data

Time Series Forecasting with Gaussian Processes Needs Priors

Giorgio Corani[1]([✉]) [ID], Alessio Benavoli[2] [ID], and Marco Zaffalon[1] [ID]

[1] Istituto Dalle Molle di Studi sull'Intelligenza Artificiale (IDSIA), USI - SUPSI,
Lugano, Switzerland
`{giorgio.corani,marco.zaffalon}@idsia.ch`
[2] School of Computer Science and Statistics, Trinity College Dublin, Dublin, Ireland
`alessio.benavoli@tcd.ie`

Abstract. Automatic forecasting is the task of receiving a time series
and returning a forecast for the next time steps without any human
intervention. Gaussian Processes (GPs) are a powerful tool for modeling
time series, but so far there are no competitive approaches for automatic
forecasting based on GPs. We propose practical solutions to two problems: automatic selection of the optimal kernel and reliable estimation of
the hyperparameters. We propose a fixed composition of kernels, which
contains the components needed to model most time series: linear trend,
periodic patterns, and other flexible kernel for modeling the non-linear
trend. Not all components are necessary to model each time series; during
training the unnecessary components are automatically made irrelevant
via automatic relevance determination (ARD). We moreover assign priors
to the hyperparameters, in order to keep the inference within a plausible range; we design such priors through an empirical Bayes approach.
We present results on many time series of different types; our GP model
is more accurate than state-of-the-art time series models. Thanks to the
priors, a single restart is enough the estimate the hyperparameters; hence
the model is also fast to train.

1 Introduction

Automatic forecasting [14] is the task of receiving a time series and returning a
probabilistic forecast for the next time steps without any human intervention.
The algorithm should be both accurate and fast, in order to scale on a large
number of time series,

Time series models such as exponential smoothing (*ets*, [12]) and automated
arima procedures (*auto.arima* [14]) are strong baselines on monthly and quarterly time series, which contain limited number of samples. In these cases they
generally outperform recurrent neural networks [11], which are also much more
time-consuming to train.

Time series which are sampled at higher frequency generally contain multiple
seasonal patterns. For instance, a time series of hourly data typically contains

© Springer Nature Switzerland AG 2021
Y. Dong et al. (Eds.): ECML PKDD 2021, LNAI 12978, pp. 103–117, 2021.
https://doi.org/10.1007/978-3-030-86514-6_7

a daily and a weekly seasonal pattern. This type of time series can be forecast with models such as *tbats* [5] and *Prophet* [27].

Gaussian Processes (GPs) [21] are a powerful tool for modeling correlated observations, including time series. The GP provides a prior over functions, which captures prior beliefs about the function behavior, such as smoothness or periodicity. Given some observations, the prior is updated to form the posterior distribution over the functions. Dealing with Gaussian noise, this posterior distribution is again a GP. The posterior GP is used to predict the value of the function in points which have yet to be sampled; this prediction is accompanied by a principled quantification of the uncertainty. GPs have been used for the analysis of astronomical time series (see [7] and the references therein), forecasting of electric load [17] and analysis of correlated and irregularly-sampled time series [22].

Within a GP model, the kernel determines which functions are used for curve fitting. Complex functions can be obtained by summing or multiplying basic kernels; this is called *kernel composition*. In some cases the composition can be based on physical considerations [7] or personal expertise [17]. However algorithms which automatically optimize the kernel composition [6,15,19] do not scale, given the need for training a large number of competing GP models, each with cubic complexity. Moreover, there is no result showing that this strategy can forecast as accurately as the best time series models.

Summing up, there are currently no competitive approaches for automatic forecasting based on Gaussian Processes. In this paper we fill this gap, proposing a GP model which is accurate, fast to train and suitable for different types of time series.

We propose a kernel composition which contains useful components for modeling time series: linear trend, periodic patterns, and other flexible kernel for modeling the non-linear trend. We keep this composition fixed, thus avoiding kernel search. When dealing with a specific time series, some components might be unnecessary; during training they are made automatically irrelevant by *automatic relevance determination* (ARD) [18]. Indeed, ARD yields automatic feature selection for GPs.

We then consider how to reliably estimate the hyperparameters even on short time series. We keep their inference within a reasonable range by assigning priors to them. We define the parameters of such priors by means of a Bayesian hierarchical model trained on a separate subset of time series.

Extensive results show that our model is very accurate and versatile. It generally outperforms the state-of-the-art competitors on monthly and quarterly time series; moreover, it can be easily extended to model time series with double seasonality. Also in this case, it compares favorably to specialized time series models. A single restart is enough to sensibly estimate the hyperparameters; hence the model is also fast to train.

The paper is organized as follows: in Sect. 2 we introduce GPs; in Sect. 2.2 we present our kernel composition and the definition of the priors; in Sect. 3 we present the experiments.

2   Gaussian Processes

We cast time-series modeling as a regression problem:

$$y = f(\mathbf{x}) + v, \tag{1}$$

where $\mathbf{x} \in \mathbb{R}^p$, $f : \mathbb{R}^p \to \mathbb{R}$ and $v \sim N(0, s_v^2)$ is the noise. We assume a Gaussian Process (GP) as a prior distribution about function f:

$$f \sim GP(0, k_\theta),$$

where k_θ denotes the kernel with hyperparameters $\boldsymbol{\theta}$. It is common to adopt the zero function as a mean function, since a priori we do not know whether at any point the trend will be below or above the average [22].

The kernel defines the covariance between the value of the function in different locations: $Cov(f(\mathbf{x}), f(\mathbf{x}^*)) = k_\theta(\mathbf{x}, \mathbf{x}^*)$, $k_\theta : \mathbb{R}^p \times \mathbb{R}^p \to \mathbb{R}^+$ and thus it determines which functions are likely under the GP prior.

The most common kernel is the *squared exponential*, also referred to as radial basis funcion (RBF):

$$\text{RBF}: \; k_\theta(x_1, x_2) = s_r^2 \exp\left(-\frac{(x_1 - x_2)^2}{2\ell_r^2}\right),$$

whose hyperparameters are the variance s_r^2 and the lengthscale ℓ_r. Longer lengthscales yields smoother functions and shorter lengthscales yields wigglier functions. A limit of the RBF kernel is that, once conditioned on the training data, it does not extrapolate more than ℓ units away from the observations.

The periodic (PER) kernels yields periodic functions which repeat themselves exactly. Such function correspond to the sum of infinite Fourier terms [4,26] and hence the PER kernel can represent any periodic function. It is defined as:

$$\text{PER}: \; k_\theta(x_1, x_2) = s_p^2 \exp\left(-\frac{(2\sin^2(\pi|x_1 - x_2|/p_e)}{\ell_p^2}\right),$$

where ℓ_p^2 controls the wiggliness of the functions, p_e denotes the period and s_p^2 the variance.

Notice that in general, when the lengthscale of a kernel tends to infinity, or its variance tends to zero, the kernel yields functions that vary less and less as a function of x.

The linear kernel, which yields linear functions, is:

$$\text{LIN} : k_\theta(x_1, x_2) = s_b^2 + s_l^2 x_1 x_2,$$

A GP with LIN kernel is equivalent [21] to a Bayesian linear regression.

The white noise (WN) kernel, which is used to represent the noise of the regression, is:

$$\text{WN} : k_\theta(x_1, x_2) = s_v^2 \delta_{x_1, x_2}.$$

The above expressions are valid for $p = 1$, which is the case of a univariate time series; see [21] for the case $p > 1$ and further kernels.

2.1   Kernel Compositions

Positive definite kernels (i.e., those which define valid covariance functions) are closed under addition and multiplication [21]. Hence, complex functions can be modeled by adding or multiplying simpler kernels; this is called composition.

There are algorithms which iteratively train and compare GPs equipped with different kernel compositions [6,19], but they are characterized by large computational complexity. Even if recent works have made the procedures more scalable [15,28], they are still not comparable to lighting-fast time series model.

The *spectral mixture* kernel [30] allows the GP to fit complex functions without kernel search. It is defined as the sum of Q components, where the i-th component is:

$$\text{SM}_i : k_\theta(x_1, x_2) = s_{m_i}^2 \exp\left(-\frac{(x_1 - x_2)^2}{2\ell_{m_i}^2}\right) \cos\left(\frac{x_1 - x_2}{\tau_{m_i}}\right),$$

with hyperparameters are s_{m_i}, ℓ_{m_i} and τ_{m_i}. It also corresponds to the product of a RBF kernel and another kernel called cosine kernel. Estimating the hyperparameters of the SM kernel is however challenging: the marginal likelihood is highly multimodal and it is unclear how to initialize the optimization. In [31] Bayesian optimization is used for deciding the initialization at each restart. This is effective but requires quite a few restarts.

2.2   The Composition

We propose the following kernel composition:

$$K = \text{PER} + \text{LIN} + \text{RBF} + \text{SM}_1 + \text{SM}_2, \tag{2}$$

which arguably contains the most important components for forecasting.

The periodic kernel (PER) models the seasonal pattern; for monthly and quarterly time series, we assume a period of one year and we set $p_e = 1$. Time series with a double seasonality can be modeled by adding a second periodic kernel, as we do in Sect. 4.

The LIN kernel provides the linear trend. This is an important component: for instance, auto.arima [14] adds a linear trend (by applying first differences) to about 40% of the monthly time series of the M3 competition. The RBF and the two SM kernels are intended to model non-linear trends which might characterize the time series.

Automatic Relevance Determination. Some components of the composition might be unnecessary when fitting a certain time series: for instance, a time series might show no seasonal pattern or no linear trend. This is automatically managed via *automatic relevance determination* (ARD) [18]. When fitting the hyperparameters, the unnecessary components are given long lengthscale and/or small variance; in this way they are made irrelevant within the curve being fitted.

2.3 Training Strategy

Reliably estimating the hyperparameters of the GP can be challenging (see e.g. [31]), especially when dealing with small data sets such as monthly and quarterly time.

We keep the inference of the hyperparameters within a plausible range by assigning priors to them. Variances and lengthscales are non-negative parameters, to which we assign log-normal priors:

$$s_l^2, s_r^2, s_p^2, s_{m_1}^2, s_{m_2}^2, s_v^2 \sim \mathrm{LogN}(\nu_s, \lambda_s) \tag{3}$$

$$\ell_r \sim \mathrm{LogN}(\nu_r, \lambda_\ell) \tag{4}$$

$$\ell_p \sim \mathrm{LogN}(\nu_p, \lambda_\ell) \tag{5}$$

$$\ell_{m_1} \sim \mathrm{LogN}(\nu_{m_1}, \lambda_\ell) \tag{6}$$

$$\ell_{m_2} \sim \mathrm{LogN}(\nu_{m_2}, \lambda_\ell) \tag{7}$$

$$\tau_{m_1} \sim \mathrm{LogN}(\nu_{t_1}, \lambda_\ell) \tag{8}$$

$$\tau_{m_2} \sim \mathrm{LogN}(\nu_{t_2}, \lambda_\ell), \tag{9}$$

where $\mathrm{LogN}(\nu, \lambda)$ denotes the distribution with mean ν and variance λ.

According to Eq. (3), all components share the same prior on the variance. This assign to every component the same prior probability of being irrelevant, as a component can be made irrelevant by pushing its variance to zero. We assign moreover a shared variance λ_ℓ to all lengthscales, in order to simplify the numerical fitting of the hierarchical model described in the next section.

We manage time such that time increases of one unit when one year has passed. The lengthscales can be readily interpreted; for instance an RBF kernel with lengthscale of 1.5 years is able to forecast about 1.5 years in the future before reverting to the prior mean.

Hierarchical GP Model. To numerically define the priors (3)–(9), we adopt an empirical Bayes approach. We select a set of B time series and we fit a *hierarchical GP model* to extract distributional information about the hyperparameters. The hierarchical Bayes model allows learning different models from different related data sets [8, Chap. 5]. Example of hierarchical GP models, not related to time series, are given in [16] and [25].

We assume the hyperparameters of the different time series to be drawn from higher-level priors (*hyperprior*). For instance the lengthscales of the RBF kernel $(\ell_r^{(1)}, \ell_r^{(2)}, ..., \ell_r^{(B)})$ are all drawn from the same hyperprior.

The generative model for the j-th time series is hence:

$$s_l^{2(j)}, s_r^{2(j)}, s_p^{2(j)}, s_{m_1}^{2(j)}, s_{m_2}^{2(j)}, s_v^{2(j)} \sim \mathrm{LogN}(\nu_s, \lambda_s)$$
$$\ell_r^{(j)} \sim \mathrm{LogN}(\nu_r, \lambda_\ell)$$
$$\ell_p^{(j)} \sim \mathrm{LogN}(\nu_p, \lambda_l),$$
$$\ell_{m_1}^{(j)} \sim \mathrm{LogN}(\nu_{m_1}, \lambda_\ell)$$
$$\ell_{m_2}^{(j)} \sim \mathrm{LogN}(\nu_{m_2}, \lambda_\ell),$$
$$\tau_{m_1}^{(j)} \sim \mathrm{LogN}(\nu_{\tau_1}, \lambda_\ell)$$
$$\tau_{m_2}^{(j)} \sim \mathrm{LogN}(\nu_{\tau_2}, \lambda_\ell),$$
$$\mathbf{y}^{(j)} \sim N(0, K_\theta^{(j)}(X^{(j)}, X^{(j)})),$$

where K denotes our kernel composition, instantiated with the hyper-parameters of the j-th time series; $\theta^{(j)}$ denotes the hyper-parameters of the j-th time series.
We assign weakly-informative priors to the ν, λ parameters:

$$\nu_s, \nu_p, \nu_r, \nu_{m_2} \sim N(0, 5) \tag{10}$$
$$\nu_{m_1} \sim N(-1.5, 5) \tag{11}$$
$$\lambda_s, \lambda_l \sim \mathrm{Gamma}(1, 1). \tag{12}$$

The lower prior mean for ν_{m_1} is helpful for differentiating the estimation of SM_1 and SM_2 towards shorter-term and longer-term trends respectively.

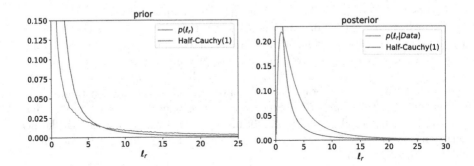

Fig. 1. Left: prior on ℓ_r induced by the hierarchical model. Right: posterior on ℓ_r estimated by the hierarchical model using 350 time-series. The Half-Cauchy distribution (with scale = 1) is shown for comparison. In this paper we represent time such that, when one year has passed, x increases of one unit.

We implemented the model in PyMC3 [24]. We use automatic differentiation variational inference to approximate the posterior distribution of the ν's and λ's. We fit the hierarchical model on 350 monthly time series from the M3 competition. Before fitting the hierarchical model, we standardize each time series to have mean 0 and variance 1. Moreover, we manage time such that time increases of one unit when one year has passed.

The priors induced by the hierarchical model have fat tails. Consider for instance the prior induced on ℓ_r, which according to Eq. (10)–(12) is: $p(\ell_r) = \iint \mathrm{LogN}(\ell_r; \nu_r, \lambda_\ell) N(\nu_r; 0, 5) \mathrm{Gamma}(\lambda_l; 1, 1) d\nu_r d\lambda_l$. It is shown in the left plot of Fig. 1, and its tails are actually fatter than those of the Half-Cauchy distribution.

Figure 1(right) shows instead the distribution on ℓ_r obtained using the posterior means of ν_r and λ_l, estimated by the hierarchical model. This yields a distribution on ℓ_r which we use as prior when fitting the GP. This prior has fat tails too, see the comparison with the half-Cauchy; nevertheless, it does inform the optimizer about the order of magnitude of ℓ_r. The median and the 95-th percentile of the prior of each hyperparameter are given in Table 1.

Table 1. Quantiles on the hyperparameters implied by the lognormal priors and parameters (ν, λ) of the lognormal priors. By design, the λs are equal for all lengthscales.

parameter	median	95th	ν	λ
variance	0.2	1.2	−1.5	1.0
std_periodic	1.2	6.3	0.2	1.0
rbf	3.0	15.4	1.1	1.0
SM_1 (rbf)	0.5	2.5	−0.7	1.0
SM_1 (cos)	1.7	8.6	0.5	1.0
SM_2 (rbf)	3.0	15.4	1.1	1.0
SM_2 (cos)	5.0	25.8	1.6	1.0

The prior on the variance is coherent with the fact that we work with standardized time series, whose variance is one.

The priors over the lengthscales also yield plausible ranges, every component having a median lengthscale comprised between 0.5 and 3 years, with long tails arriving up to 25 years.

All the experiments of this paper are thus computed using the priors of Table 1. To remove any danger of overfitting, we remove the 350 time series used to fit the hierarchical model from our experiments.

Further Considerations. In the jargon of time series, models which are fitted to a set of time series are referred to as *global* models, see for instance [20, 23]. The hierarchical model is a global model, as it jointly analyzes different time series. Global models can be more accurate than univariate models, if the time series are characterized by some common patterns. Yet, they are also more complicated to fit. In this paper we do not consider global models. We use the hierarchical model only for defining the priors on the hyperparameters of the GP.

2.4   MAP Estimation

We estimate the hyperparameters by computing the maximum a-posteriori (MAP) estimate of $\boldsymbol{\theta}$, thus approximating the marginal of $\mathbf{f}^*$ with (14). We thus maximize w.r.t. $\boldsymbol{\theta}$ the joint marginal probability of $\mathbf{y}, \boldsymbol{\theta}$, which is the product of the prior $p(\boldsymbol{\theta})$ and the marginal likelihood [21, Ch.2]:

$$p(\mathbf{y}|X, \boldsymbol{\theta}) = N(\mathbf{y}; 0, K_{\boldsymbol{\theta}}(X, X)). \tag{13}$$

Using a single restart, MAP estimation is generally accomplished in less than a second (on a standard computer) on monthly and quarterly time series, yielding thus quick training times.

2.5   Forecasting

Based on the training data $X^T = [\mathbf{x}_1, \ldots, \mathbf{x}_n]$, $\mathbf{y} = [y_1, \ldots, y_n]^T$, and given m test inputs $(X^*)^T = [\mathbf{x}_1^*, \ldots, \mathbf{x}_m^*]$, we wish to find the posterior distribution of $\mathbf{f}^* = [f(\mathbf{x}_1^*), \ldots, f(\mathbf{x}_m^*)]^T$.

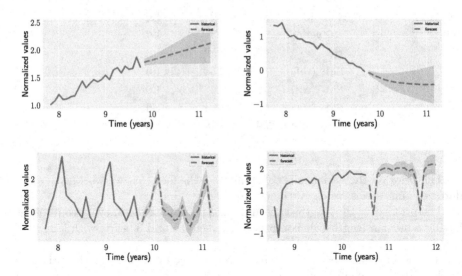

Fig. 2. Examples of GP forecasts on monthly time series, computed up to 18 months ahead.

From (1) and the properties of the Gaussian distribution,[1] the posterior distribution of $\mathbf{f}^*$ is [21, Sec. 2.2]:

$$p(\mathbf{f}^*|X^*, X, \mathbf{y}, \boldsymbol{\theta}) = N(\mathbf{f}^*; \hat{\boldsymbol{\mu}}_{\boldsymbol{\theta}}(X^*|X, \mathbf{y}), \hat{K}_{\boldsymbol{\theta}}(X^*, X^*|X)), \tag{14}$$

---

[1] In the paper, we incorporate the additive noise v into the kernel by adding a White noise kernel term.

with mean and covariance given by:

$$\hat{\mu}_\theta(\mathbf{f}^*|X, \mathbf{y}) = K_\theta(X^*, X)(K_\theta(X, X))^{-1}\mathbf{y},$$
$$\hat{K}_\theta(X^*, X^*|X) = K_\theta(X^*, X^*) \qquad (15)$$
$$- K_\theta(X^*, X)(K_\theta(X, X))^{-1}K_\theta(X, X^*).$$

Our kernel composition, trained using the proposed priors, yields sensible forecasts in very different contexts, as in Fig. 2.

3 Experiments

We run experiments on the monthly and quarterly time series of the M1 and M3 competitions, available from the package Mcomp [13] for R. The original 1428 time series of the M3 competition drop to 1078 once we remove the 350 time series used to fit the hierarchical model. Overall we consider about 959 quarterly time series (203 from M1, 756 from M3) and 1695 monthly time series (617 from M1 and 1078 from M3). The test set of monthly time series contains 18 months; the test set of quarterly time series contains 8 quarters. We standardize each time series to have mean 0 and variance 1 on the training set (Table 2).

Table 2. Main characteristics of the M1 and M3 data sets.

	quarterly		monthly	
	M1	M3	M1	M3
number of time series	203	756	617	1078
median training length	40	44	66	115
Test set length	8	8	18	18

We denote by GP our model trained *with* priors and by GP_0 our model trained *without* priors, i.e., by maximizing the marginal likelihood. We use a single restart when training both GP and GP_0; on these time series, which contain around 100 observations, the average training is generally less than one second on a standard laptop.

As competitors we consider *auto.arima* and *ets*, both available from the forecast package [12] for R. We tried also Prophet [27], but its accuracy was not competitive. We thus dropped it; we will consider it later in experiments with different types of time series.

Indicators

Let us denote by y_t and $\hat{y}_t$ the actual and the expected value of the time series at time t; by σ_t^2 the variance of the forecast at time t; by T the length of the test set. The mean absolute error (MAE) on the test set is:

Table 3. Median results on M1 and M3 time series. The best-performing model is boldfaced. Starred results correspond to the GP yielding a significant improvement over the competitor (95%, Bayesian signed-rank test).

competition	freq	score	GP	ets	arima	GP₀
M1	monthly	MAE	**0.58**	0.59	0.62*	0.72*
M1	monthly	CRPS	**0.41**	0.45*	0.45*	0.53*
M1	monthly	LL	**−1.13**	−1.27*	−1.28*	−1.67*
M1	quarterly	MAE	**0.57**	0.63*	0.62*	0.75*
M1	quarterly	CRPS	**0.39**	0.47*	0.44*	0.59*
M1	quarterly	LL	**−1.07**	−1.41*	−1.44*	−2.66*
M3	monthly	MAE	**0.48**	0.51*	0.51*	0.59*
M3	monthly	CRPS	**0.35**	0.38*	0.37*	0.42*
M3	monthly	LL	**−1.01**	−1.05*	−1.06*	−1.23*
M3	quarterly	MAE	0.42	**0.41**	**0.41**	0.54*
M3	quarterly	CRPS	**0.30**	0.31	0.31	0.40*
M3	quarterly	LL	**−0.85**	−0.90*	−0.94*	−1.61*

$$\text{MAE} = \sum_{t=1}^{T} |y_t - \hat{y}_t|$$

The continuous-ranked probability score (CRPS) [9] is a proper scoring rule which generalizes MAE to probabilistic forecasts. Let us denote by F_t the cumulative predictive distribution at time t and by z the variable over which we integrate. The CRPS is:

$$\text{CRPS}(F_t, y_t) = -\int_{-\infty}^{\infty} (F_t(z) - \mathbb{1}\{z \geq y_t\})^2 dz.$$

The log-likelihood of the test set (LL) is defined as:

$$\text{LL} = \frac{1}{T}\left(-\frac{1}{2}\sum_{t=1}^{T} \log(2\pi\sigma_t^2) - \frac{1}{2\sigma_t^2}\sum_{t=1}^{T}(y_t - \hat{y}_t)^2 \right)$$

MAE and CRPS are loss functions, hence the lower the better; instead for LL, the higher the better.

In Table 3 we report the median results for each indicator and each data set. In each setting the GP yields the best median on almost all indicators. However GP₀ is instead clearly outperformed by both ets and auto.arima. Hence, our GP model needs priors on the hyperparameters to produce highly accurate forecasts.

We then check the significance of the differences on the medians via the Bayesian signed-rank test [3], which is a Bayesian counterpart of the Wilcoxon signed-rank test. It returns posterior probabilities instead of the p-value. An advantage of this test over the frequentist one is that we can set a region of practical equivalence (rope) between the two algorithms being compared. When comparing algorithms A and B, the test returns three posterior probabilities: the probability of the two algorithms being practically equivalent, i.e., the probability of the median difference belonging to the rope; the probability of A being significantly better than B, and vice versa. As already pointed out, better means lower MAE, lower CRPS, higher LL. We considered a rope of ±0.01 on each indicator, similarly to [2]. We consider as significant the differences in which the probability of an algorithm being better than another is at least 95%. The improvement yielded by the GP over the competitors are significant in most cases; see the starred entries in Table 3. When the median of some competitor was better than that of the GP, the difference was not statistically significant.

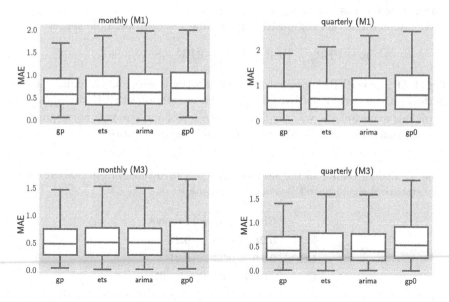

Fig. 3. Distribution of MAE on the monthly and quarterly time series of the M1 and M3 competition.

The improvement is not only on the medians, but it also involve the distribution across time series, as shown by the boxplots of MAE (Fig. 3). Similar results hold also for the distribution of the other indicators, which we do not show for reasons of space.

4 Dealing with Multiple Seasonalities

We then test the versatility of our GP model, by considering time series with multiple seasonalities. We consider the electricity data set[2], which contains 370 time series regarding electricity demand for different Portuguese households.

Each time series covers the period January 2011–September 2015 with a sampling frequency of 15 mins, totaling 140k points. To have a more manageable data set we aggregate the data to 6-h steps. We consider a training set containing of 250 days (1000 points) and a test set of 10.5 days (42 steps).

Such time series have a daily and a weekly seasonal pattern. This can be addressed by approaches which model seasonality using Fourier terms. For instance TBATS [5] introduces Fourier terms within an exponential smoothing state space model. Prophet [27] is a decomposable Bayesian time series model, whose final forecast is the sum of different functions, which account for different effects. The seasonality function is modeled by Fourier terms. Prophet however is not very effective on time series with simpler seasonality, such as monthly and quarterly time series, as we have already seen.

We adapt the kernel composition by adding a second periodic kernel:

$$K = PER_w + PER_d + LIN + RBF + SM_1 + SM_2,$$

where PER_w and PER_d represents respectively the weekly and the daily pattern. We thus set the period of PER_w to $\frac{1}{52.18}$ and the period of PER_d to $\frac{1}{(365.25)}$ As in previous experiments, we standardize time series and one year corresponds to time increasing of one unit. We can keep unchanged the priors.

Table 4. Median results on the electricy data sets (370 time series). Starred results imply statistical significance (Bayesian signed rank test).

	GP	Tbats	Prophet
MAE	**0.26**	0.30*	0.29*
CRPS	**0.19**	0.23*	0.21*
LL	**−0.37**	−0.60*	−0.49*

In Table 4 we report the median results across the 370 time series; the GP delivers the best performance on all indicators. The GP model compares favorably to the competitors also as for the distribution of the MAE (Fig. 4) across time series.

---

[2] https://archive.ics.uci.edu/ml/datasets/ElectricityLoadDiagrams20112014.

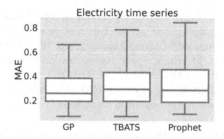

Fig. 4. Boxplot of MAE on the 370 electricity time series.

5   Code and Replicability

We make available our code and the data of M1 and M3 time series at the link: https://github.com/IDSIA/gpforecasting/. Our implementation is based on the GPy library [10].

6   Conclusions

As far as we know, these are the best results obtained so far in automatic forecasting with Gaussian processes. Our model is competitive with the best time series models on different types of time series: monthly, quarterly and time series with multiple seasonalities.

The model is fast to train, at least on time series containing less than 500 data points. Recent computational advances with GPs in time series [1,26] could allow the application of our methodology also to time series thousands of observations.

Our GP model yields both good point forecast and a reliable quantification of the uncertainty, as shown by the CRPS and LL indicators. It is thus an interesting candidate for problems of hierarchical forecasting [29], which require forecasts with a sound quantification of the uncertainty.

Due to the general properties of the GP, the model can be learned also from irregularly sampled or incomplete time series.

Acknowledgments. Work for this paper has been partially supported by the Swiss NSF grant n. 167199 of the funding scheme *NRP 75 Big Data*.

We thank David Huber for polishing our initial implementation and helping with the experiments.

References

1. Ambikasaran, S., Foreman-Mackey, D., Greengard, L., Hogg, D.W., O'Neil, M.: Fast direct methods for gaussian processes. IEEE Trans. Pattern Anal. Mach. Intell. **38**(2), 252–265 (2015)
2. Benavoli, A., Corani, G., Demšar, J., Zaffalon, M.: Time for a change: a tutorial for comparing multiple classifiers through Bayesian analysis. J. Mach. Learn. Res. **18**(1), 2653–2688 (2017)

3. Benavoli, A., Corani, G., Mangili, F., Zaffalon, M., Ruggeri, F.: A Bayesian Wilcoxon signed-rank test based on the Dirichlet process. In: Proceedings of the International Conference on Machine Learning, pp. 1026–1034 (2014)
4. Benavoli, A., Zaffalon, M.: State Space representation of non-stationary Gaussian processes. arXiv preprint arXiv:1601.01544 (2016)
5. De Livera, A.M., Hyndman, R.J., Snyder, R.D.: Forecasting time series with complex seasonal patterns using exponential smoothing. J. Am. Stat. Assoc. **106**(496), 1513–1527 (2011)
6. Duvenaud, D., Lloyd, J., Grosse, R., Tenenbaum, J., Zoubin, G.: Structure discovery in nonparametric regression through compositional kernel search. In: Proceedings of the International Conference on Machine Learning, pp. 1166–1174 (2013)
7. Foreman-Mackey, D., Agol, E., Ambikasaran, S., Angus, R.: Fast and scalable Gaussian process modeling with applications to astronomical time series. Astron. J. **154**(6), 220 (2017)
8. Gelman, A., Carlin, J., Stern, H., Dunson, D., Vehtari, A., Rubin, D.: Bayesian Data Analysis, 3rd edn. Chapman and Hall/CRC, Boca Raton (2013)
9. Gneiting, T., Raftery, A.E.: Strictly proper scoring rules, prediction, and estimation. J. Am. Stat. Assoc. **102**(477), 359–378 (2007)
10. GPy: GPy: A Gaussian process framework in Python (since 2012). http://github.com/SheffieldML/GPy
11. Hewamalage, H., Bergmeir, C., Bandara, K.: Recurrent neural networks for time series forecasting: Current status and future directions. Int. J. Forecast. **37**(1), 388–427 (2021)
12. Hyndman, R.J., Athanasopoulos, G.: Forecasting: Principles and Practice, 2nd edn. OTexts: Melbourne (2018). OTexts.com/fpp2
13. Hyndman, R.: Mcomp: Data from the M-Competitions (2018). https://CRAN.R-project.org/package=Mcomp, r package version 2.8
14. Hyndman, R.J., Khandakar, Y.: Automatic time series forecasting: the forecast package for R. J. Stat. Softw. **26**(3), 1–22 (2008). http://www.jstatsoft.org/article/view/v027i03
15. Kim, H., Teh, Y.W.: Scaling up the automatic statistician: scalable structure discovery using Gaussian processes. In: International Conference on Artificial Intelligence and Statistics, pp. 575–584. PMLR (2018)
16. Lawrence, N.D., Platt, J.C.: Learning to learn with the informative vector machine. In: Proceedings of the Twenty-First International Conference on Machine Learning, p. 65 (2004)
17. Lloyd, J.R.: GEFCom2012 hierarchical load forecasting: gradient boosting machines and Gaussian processes. Int. J. Forecast. **30**(2), 369–374 (2014)
18. MacKay, D.J.: Introduction to Gaussian processes. NATO ASI Ser. F Comput. Syst. Sci. **168**, 133–166 (1998)
19. Malkomes, G., Schaff, C., Garnett, R.: Bayesian optimization for automated model selection. In: Hutter, F., Kotthoff, L., Vanschoren, J. (eds.) Proceedings of the Workshop on Automatic Machine Learning, vol. 64, pp. 41–47 (2016)
20. Montero-Manso, P., Athanasopoulos, G., Hyndman, R.J., Talagala, T.S.: FFORMA: feature-based forecast model averaging. Int. J. Forecast. **36**(1), 86–92 (2020)
21. Rasmussen, C., Williams, C.: Gaussian Processes for Machine Learning (2006)
22. Roberts, S., Osborne, M., Ebden, M., Reece, S., Gibson, N., Aigrain, S.: Gaussian processes for time-series modelling. Philos. Trans. R. Soc. A: Math. Phys. Eng. Sci. **371**(1984), 20110550 (2013)

23. Salinas, D., Flunkert, V., Gasthaus, J., Januschowski, T.: DeepAR: probabilistic forecasting with autoregressive recurrent networks. Int. J. Forecast. **36**(3), 1181–1191 (2020)
24. Salvatier, J., Wiecki, T.V., Fonnesbeck, C.: Probabilistic programming in Python using PyMC3. PeerJ Comput. Sci. **2**, e55 (2016)
25. Schwaighofer, A., Tresp, V., Yu, K.: Learning gaussian process kernels via hierarchical Bayes. In: Advances in Neural Information Processing Systems, pp. 1209–1216 (2005)
26. Solin, A., Särkkä, S.: Explicit link between periodic covariance functions and state space models. In: Artificial Intelligence and Statistics, pp. 904–912. PMLR (2014)
27. Taylor, S.J., Letham, B.: Forecasting at scale. Am. Stat. **72**(1), 37–45 (2018)
28. Teng, T., Chen, J., Zhang, Y., Low, B.K.H.: Scalable variational Bayesian kernel selection for sparse Gaussian process regression. In: Proceedings of the AAAI Conference on Artificial Intelligence, vol. 34, pp. 5997–6004 (2020)
29. Wickramasuriya, S.L., Athanasopoulos, G., Hyndman, R.J.: Optimal forecast reconciliation for hierarchical and grouped time series through trace minimization. J. Am. Stat. Assoc. **114**(526), 804–819 (2019)
30. Wilson, A., Adams, R.: Gaussian process kernels for pattern discovery and extrapolation. In: Proceedings of the International Conference on Machine Learning, pp. 1067–1075 (2013)
31. Wu, J., Poloczek, M., Wilson, A.G., Frazier, P.: Bayesian optimization with gradients. In: Advances in Neural Information Processing Systems, pp. 5267–5278 (2017)

Task Embedding Temporal Convolution Networks for Transfer Learning Problems in Renewable Power Time Series Forecast

Jens Schreiber$^{(\boxtimes)}$ ⓘ, Stephan Vogt ⓘ, and Bernhard Sick ⓘ

University of Kassel, Wilhelmshöher Allee 71, 34121 Kassel, Germany
{j.schreiber,stephan.vogt,bsick}@uni-kassel.de

Abstract. Task embeddings in multi-layer perceptrons (MLP) for multi-task learning and inductive transfer learning in renewable power forecasts is an exciting new technique. In many cases, this approach improves the forecast error and reduces the required training data. However, it does not take the periodic influences in power forecasts within a day into account, i.e., the diurnal cycle. Therefore, we extended this idea to temporal convolutional networks to consider those in tasks of day-ahead power forecasts for renewables. We propose transforming the embedding space, which contains the latent similarities between tasks, through convolution and providing these results to the network's residual block. The proposed architecture significantly improves the forecast accuracy up to 25% for multi-task learning for power forecasts on the open EuropeWindFarm and GermanSolarFarm datasets compared to the MLP approach. Based on the same data, we achieve a ten percent improvement for the wind datasets and more than 20% in most cases for the solar dataset for inductive transfer learning without catastrophic forgetting. Finally, we are the first to propose zero-shot learning for renewable power forecasts. The proposed architecture achieves an error as good as the task embedding MLP with a full year of training data in the respective experiments.

Keywords: Transfer learning · Time series · CNN · Renewables · TCN

1 Introduction

The Paris commitment demands to limit human-induced global warming below 2 °C above pre-industrial levels to reduce the impact of the climate crisis. To achieve the commitment, renewable energy resources need to increase their share from 14% in 2015 to 63% in 2050 in the worldwide energy production [1]. To assure grid stability, energy suppliers require reliable power forecasts based on numerical weather predictions (NWPs) as input due to the weather dependency. These predicted weather features, such as wind speed or radiation, are the input to models predicting the expected power generation in *day-ahead* forecasts between 24 and 48 h into the future.

© Springer Nature Switzerland AG 2021
Y. Dong et al. (Eds.): ECML PKDD 2021, LNAI 12978, pp. 118–134, 2021.
https://doi.org/10.1007/978-3-030-86514-6_8

Another problem is that each of those parks typically has individual characteristics to learn by the forecast models. Therefore, a single forecast model is learned per park or even for a single wind turbine in practice. Assuming there are 30,000 wind facilities with an average number of 10,000 parameters per model solely in Germany, this makes a total of 300 million parameters to train. Additionally, the hyperparameters need to be optimized.

The training of those models contradicts the Paris commitment, as the training and even the inference themselves have an extensive energy demand and cause a considerable amount of carbon emmission [2]. To reduce the number of models that need to be optimized, while leveraging knowledge between parks, [3] proposed to utilize multi-task learning (MTL) approaches. In their task embedding multi-layer perceptron (MLP) the discrete task information, *which task is to be predicted*, is encoded through an embedding layer and concatenated with other input features. However, this approach still requires a reasonable amount of training data in the task of day-ahead power forecasts for renewables. This training data is often not available for new parks. Therefore, in [4], the task embedding MLP extracts knowledge from a set of source tasks, e.g., several known wind parks. This knowledge is adapted to unseen target tasks, during initial training, with limited training instances. In their approach, a Bayesian variant of the task embedding MLP leads to the best results for wind parks with limited training data.

However, there are periodic patterns, i.e., the diurnal cycle, within day-ahead forecasts affecting the forecast error [5]. Those are not considered within an MLP, even though the substantial benefits of time series forecasts through convolutional neural networks (CNNs) are known [6]. Further, ideally, we can forecast parks without any historical power measurements. This zero-shot learning paradigm is essential to assure reasonable forecasts from the beginning of a new park. Therefore, we are interested in answering the following research questions:

Question 1. Can an MTL CNN architecture improve the forecast error for wind and photovoltaic (PV) parks compared to a similar MLP MTL architecture?

Question 2. Are CNN based MTL architectures capable of providing good forecasts in zero-shot learning for renewable power forecasts?

Question 3. Are CNN based MTL architectures beneficial during inductive transfer learning (TL) compared to a similar MLP MTL approach?

To answer those questions, we propose task-*temporal convolution network (TCN)*, see Fig. 1. *Task-TCN* encodes task-specific information through an embedding layer. Thus, each park gets an *increasing* task ID ($m \in \mathbb{N}^+$) assigned as input to the embedding layer. We assure that the TCN learns relations between tasks during training by adding the encoded task information in a residual block. By encoding the task ID through an embedding layer, we can extend the network to new parks while avoiding catastrophic forgetting of previous parks. We utilize the idea of task embeddings in our proposed method as

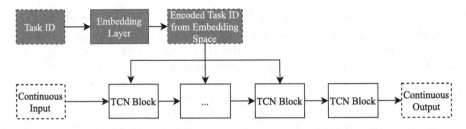

Fig. 1. Task-TCN encodes a task ID, for each task, through an embedding layer. The learned encoding from the embedding space is *added* in the residual block to provide task-specific forecasts.

well in our baseline to assure a comparison of similar MTL architectures. Evaluation of the task-TCN on the open EuropeWindFarm and GermanSolarFarm[1], in comparison to the Bayesian task embedding MLP as the baseline, leads to the following contributions:

- The proposed task-TCN architecture, for MTL renewable power forecasts, leads to improvements of up to 25%.
- The proposed task-TCN leads to improvements of more than ten percent for wind and up to 40% for the solar dataset for inductive ML problems.
- We are the first to propose zero-shot learning for renewables and the task-TCN achieves an error as good as the task embedding MLP with a full year of training data in the respective experiments.

The source code and supplementary material of the experiments are openly accessible[2]. The remainder of this article is structured as follows. Section 2 describes related work. The following Sect. 3 introduces relevant definitions and details the proposed approach. We describe the datasets, discuss the experiment and most essential findings in Sect. 4. In the final section, we summarize our work and provide insides for future work.

2   Related Work

To answer our research question, we review related work in the field of MTL, (inductive) TL, and zero-shot learning focusing on power forecasts for wind and PV. Formal definitions of those topics are given in Sect. 3.1. For comprehensive surveys on TL and MTL, outside the domain of renewables, refer to [7,8].

Most of the related work applying TL focuses on utilizing neural networks. However, the study of [9] proposes an MTL strategy for Gaussian processes to forecast PV targets. By clustering wind parks through their distribution, a weighting scheme provides predictions for a new park in [10]. The approach of [11] utilizes an auxiliary dataset, created through k-nearest neighbors, to improve the

---

[1] https://www.uni-kassel.de/eecs/ies/downloads, accessed 2021-06-30.
[2] https://github.com/scribbler00/task-TCN, accessed 2021-06-30.

forecasts error in short-term wind power predictions. This data driven method is in principle adaptable to our approach but is outside the focus of our work. The same argument holds for the instance-based TL for day-ahead solar power forecasts proposed in [12].

To find a suitable representation for (inductive) TL and MTL various articles utilize autoencoders, e.g., [13,14] and more recently a self-attention based encoder-decoder structure [15]. One problem with autoencoders is that the information extraction is typically limited to the input space and neglects knowledge shared between tasks in the target space, which is, e.g., achieved through hard parameter sharing (HPS). Further, all of those articles consider (ultra) short-term forecasts and do not examine the more difficult day-ahead predictions. Most of the previously mentioned work utilizing neural networks focuses on feed forward networks neglecting the time series problem at hand. However, more recent work also considers recurrent networks and finetuning to achieve good results for ultra-short-term forecast horizon of PV [16]. Moreover, the article [17] provides a strategy for quantile regression for day-ahead solar power forecasts using CNNs and finetuning. But both articles are missing out on making use of multiple targets, which we consider in our approach.

The authors of [3] utilize a task embedding for encoding of task-specific information in a HPS network. This approach is similar to *word2vec* [18] and encoding of categorical features to replace one-hot encodings in [19]. The task embedding improves the forecast error with a minimal amount of parameters for day-ahead wind and solar power forecasts in a MTL setting. A thorough evaluation of inductive TL for day-ahead wind power forecast is given in [4]. Furthermore, a Bayesian task embedding assures that similar tasks are close to one another in case of limited data. The Bayesian task embedding is superior to models learned from scratch and a traditional HPS. The task embedding can be considered state of the art due to their excellent results with minimal parameters even when trained with limited data. Further, the approach of task embedding avoids catastrophic forgetting. However, both of the articles utilizing task embeddings neglect to extend this approach to CNNs that we address.

Overall, the related work shows limited research on TL and MTL for day-ahead power forecasts. Furthermore, none of those approaches provide a framework for wind as well as PV power forecasts. Moreover, there is limited research in addressing TL challenges through recent work in time series forecasts [20]. Note, due to the recent success and benefits of CNNs over recurrent networks [20,21] we focus on the former. Further, to the best of our knowledge, there has been no attempt to provide zero-shot forecasts in the field of renewable energies. Besides, none of those proposals consider a unified framework that takes recent advances in time series forecast into account, such as TCN, while being applicable to MTL, inductive TL, and zero-shot learning.

3   Proposed Method

In the following, we detail essential definitions, relate the task embedding MLP to MTL, and describe our proposed architecture.

3.1 Definition of MTL, TL, and Zero-Shot Learning

The following definitions have been introduced in [7,8]. We slightly modified them for a consistent formulation of multi-source TL and MTL.

Definition 1 (Domain). *A domain is defined by $\mathcal{D} = \{\mathcal{X}, P(X)\}$, where $\mathcal{X}$ is the feature space and $P(X)$ is the marginal distribution with $X = \{\mathbf{x} \mid \mathbf{x}_i \in \mathcal{X}, i = 1, \ldots, N\}$.*

Definition 2 (Task). *The task of a domain is defined with $\mathcal{T} = \{\mathcal{Y}, f(\cdot)\}$, where the function is defined by $f : \mathcal{X} \to \mathcal{Y}$. The function $f(\cdot)$ is learned by training instances $\{\mathbf{x}_i, y_i\}$ with $\mathbf{x}_i \in X$ and $y_i \in Y$, where $Y = \{y \mid y_i \in \mathcal{Y}, i = 1, \ldots, N\}$. The function $f(\cdot)$ describes characteristics of the distribution $P(Y \mid X)$. In a Bayesian approach those are samples and the expectation in a frequentist view.*

Note, in these definitions, $\mathbf{x}_i$ are available weather predictions and y_i are historical power measurements of a park. We assume that X and Y are ordered sets for the required time series forecasts for simplicity.

Definition 3 (Inductive Transfer Learning). *Inductive Transfer Learning has the goal to transfer knowledge from source (S) tasks $\{\mathcal{T}_{S_m}\}_{m=1}^{m=M}$ to a target (T) task $\mathcal{T}_T$. Therefore, we use $M \in \mathbb{N}^+$ source domains $\{(\mathcal{D}_{S_m}, \mathcal{T}_{S_m}) \mid m = 1, \ldots, M\}$ and (limited) training instances $\{\mathbf{x}_{T_i}, y_{T_i}\}$ with $\mathbf{x}_{T_i} \in X_T$ and $y_{T_i} \in Y_T$ to learn a function $f_T(\cdot)$.*

In contrast to transductive TL, labeled training data in the target domain is available in inductive TL.

Definition 4 (Zero-shot learning). *Zero-shot learning can be interpreted as unsupervised transductive TL [22]. In this setting, meta-information from source and target tasks is used to select an appropriate prediction function $f_{S_m}(\cdot)$ to predict the target task.*

In comparison to transductive TL, zero-shot learning is not using a domain adaptation approach between the source(s) and the target. This unsupervised approach makes it an even more challenging problem as no assumptions are made of the source and target domain [22].

Definition 5 (Multi-Task Learning). *In MTL approaches, each task is accompanied by a domain $\mathcal{D}_m$ with $i \in \{1, \ldots, N\}$ training instances $(\mathbf{x}_i^m, y_i^m)$, where $\mathbf{x}_i^m \in X^m$, $y_i^m \in Y^m$, $m \in 1, \ldots, M$, and $M \in \mathbb{N}^+$ tasks.*

In contrast to inductive transfer and zero-shot learning, all tasks have a sufficient amount of training data in MTL problems. Furthermore, in MTL we are typically interested in improving all tasks' forecast errors simultaneously.

3.2   Proposed Method

Typically, in MTL, there are two approaches to share knowledge and improve the forecasts error: soft parameter sharing (SPS) and HPS. In HPS architectures, there are predominantly common layers that are the same for all tasks and few task-specific layers. In SPS, each task has an individual model and similarity is enforced through regularization [8]. As SPS requires additional parameters compared to HPS, due to the separate networks for each task, we focus on the latter to reduce the energy demand by the additional parameters.

Previously, we argued that the function $f(\cdot)$ describes the conditional distribution $P(Y \mid X)$, where Y is a set of observed power generations and X are observations of the numerical weather prediction. However, this description neglects the possibility to model individual forecasts for different parks in MTL settings. Therefore, we describe how to model this dependency through an embedding layer in an MLP as suggested in [3,4]. By doing so, we are the *first to provide a mathematical description* between the task embedding and the MTL definition. Afterward, we explain the Bayesian embedding layer and detail how our approach extends the idea of task embeddings to TCNs.

Task-Embedding for MLPs encodes an increasing (discrete) task ID about *which task $m \in \mathbb{N}^+$ is to be predicted* through an embedding layer and concatenates results of this embedding space with other continuous input features [3,4]. In the following we connect embedding layers to the MTL definition. Therefore, consider a common function $h(\cdot)$ for all M tasks that approximates $P(y_m \mid X_m, g(m))$, where m is the discrete information whose task is to be predicted with $m \in 1, \ldots, M$ and $M \in \mathbb{N}^+$. $g(m)$ is then a transformation into an arbitrary real valued dimension.

Assuming we have such a transformation, the conditional modeling allows us to develop a model without task-specific layers. The required information on the task is given through $g(m)$. Therefore, the function $h(\cdot)$ for MTL has the training instances $\{\mathbf{x}_i^m, y_i^m, g(m)\}$. Ideally, we want a mapping g that is beneficial for the MTL problems, e.g., similar tasks are close to another in the embedding space. Respectively, an MTL approach needs to learn this mapping function during training. For such a problem, the authors of [19] propose the following equation of an embedding layer:

$$g(m) = \sum_{\alpha=1}^{M} \mathbf{w}_{\alpha\beta}\boldsymbol{\delta}_{m\alpha} = \mathbf{w}_{m\beta}, \qquad (1)$$

where $\boldsymbol{\delta}_{m\alpha}$ is the Kronecker delta. Therefore, $\boldsymbol{\delta}_{m\alpha}$ is a vector of length M (M tasks), where only the entry with $\alpha = m$ is non-zero and $\mathbf{w}_{\alpha\beta} \in \mathbb{R}^D$ is the learnable vector at this position. Respectively, the function g maps the discrete value m of a task ID through a one-hot encoding to a trainable vector.

This transformation is then concatenated with other (continuous) features. Due to the joint training for multiple tasks, e.g., within one batch we have various tasks, it is beneficial for the network to learn a mapping where similar

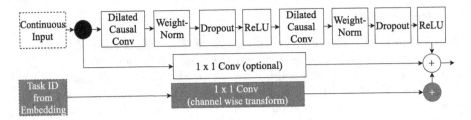

Fig. 2. Residual block of the task-TCN. The encoded task ID, from the embedding space, is transformed through a 1D convolution. The transformed task ID is then added to the results of the original TCN residual block.

tasks have a similar vector $\mathbf{w}_{\alpha\beta}$. This mapping allows the utilization of a similar transformation in later layers for similar domains and targets.

Bayesian Task-Embeddings are especially interesting in the scenario where limited data for a (single) task is available. If a limited amount of data is available, e.g., in the inductive transfer learning problem, a Bayesian approach allows placing an identical, independent prior on $\mathbf{w}_{m\beta}$. This prior ensures that indistinguishable tasks, due to limited data, are within a similar neighborhood. At the same time, tasks with sufficient data have an encoding that is different from other tasks. We apply *Bayes by backprop* solely on the embedding layer. By using a standard normal distribution and sampling weights solely from the embedding, to minimize the expected lower bound (ELBO) [23], we limit the training effort for the number of additional parameters and benefit from the embedding space's Bayesian approach.

Task-Embedding for Temporal Convolution Neural Networks are a way to take advantage of periodic patterns, e.g., the diurnal cycle, in *day-ahead* forecasts [5] in an MTL architecture. In MTL day-ahead power forecast problems, we forecast the expected power $y_{24}^m, \ldots, y_{48}^m$ for $m \in 1, \ldots, M$ parks. In contrast to intra-day forecasts between 0 and 23 hours into the future, day-ahead forecasts are more challenging as the forecast error increases with an increasing forecast horizon [24]. We have the numerical weather features $\mathbf{x}_{24}^m, \ldots, \mathbf{x}_{48}^m$ from a weather prediction originating from t_0 (e.g. originating from 0 o'clock UTC) as input. The fundamental building block of task-TCN is the *TCN* [21], a CNN architecture for time series. In this architecture, the residual blocks limit the problem of vanishing gradients, see Fig. 2.

In the previously discussed task embedding for MLPs, the embedding is concatenated with the continuous weather input features to provide task-specific forecasts. However, simply concatenating the embedding output along the time axis in CNNs leads to additional channels with the same information for each time step. Respectively, having redundant information along the time axis. We found this not to work well in preliminary experiments due to the redundant information causing a plateau in the training error.

Instead, we propose to *add* the result from $g(m_i)$ at the end of the residual block, see Fig. 2. Therefore, we first transform the encoded task ID through a 1-D convolution layer with a kernel size of one. The transformation gives the network the possibility to learn an encoding that is different in each channel. Effectively, this allows the network to adjust each feature (channel) specifically for the task at hand. For instance consider, that the output of the first residual block has 100 channels of 24 time steps. For a single sample, the dimension will be $1 \times 100 \times 24$. Also, consider that each task has an embedding vector of dimension 1×10. The embedding tensor will then be $1 \times 10 \times 24$. After applying the transformation, through the 1D convolution, the transformed embedding tensor will also be of dimension $1 \times 100 \times 24$. By adding this tensor in the residual block, we provide distinct task related information in each channel, giving the network the possibility to learn task specific features in each channel while limiting redundant information in contrast to a concatenation. This principle applies to any residual block within the network. A study on the diverse learned similarities of tasks per channel is presented in the supplementary material.

4   Experimental Evaluation of the Task-Temporal Convolution Network

To answer our research questions, we conducted one experiment for each of the three research questions. We evaluate each of these experiments on the datasets explained in Sect. 4.1. Sect. 4.2 lists relevant evaluation measures. The design of experiments and the evaluations are detailed in Sect. 4.3, 4.4, and 4.5. The models detailed in Sect. 4.3 are the source models for the other experiments. The description also includes the Bayesian MLP that is the baseline in all experiments. All models are similar in the sense that they share the task embedding architecture and hyperparameters are identical. We refer to *TCN first* and *MLP first* when the encoded information is considered only in the first layer and *TCN all* when the task information is added in all, except the last, residual blocks.

4.1   GemanSolarFarm and EuropeWindFarm Dataset

In the GermanSolarFarm and the EuropeWindFarm dataset, the uncertainty of the NWP makes it challenging to predict the generated power. We refer to these as wind and solar datasets in the following. This mismatch between the weather forecast and power can be seen in Fig. 3 and Fig. 4. As weather forecasts are valid for a larger area, a mismatch between the forecast horizon and the placement of a park causes uncertainty. The uncertainty also increases with the increasing forecast horizon of the weather prediction [5].

The solar dataset consists of 21 parks, while the wind dataset consists of 45 parks. Both datasets include day-ahead weather forecasts, between 24 and 48 h into the future, of the European center for medium-range weather forecast

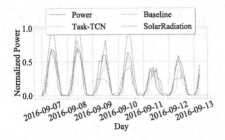
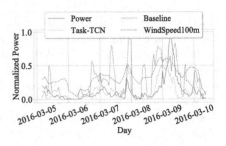

Fig. 3. Forecasts of a solar park with 30 days training data.

Fig. 4. Forecasts of a wind park with 30 days training data.

model [25]. The data also includes the normalized historical power measurements. The solar dataset has a three-hourly resolution for two years and two months. We linearly interpolate the data to have a resolution of one hour to increase the number of samples, especially for the inductive TL problem. The wind dataset has data from two years with an hourly resolution. The data is linearly interpolated to have a 15-min resolution. Respectively, the PV dataset has 24 timestamps per day and 96 for the wind dataset. Days not fulfilling these criteria are neglected. The first year is considered for training while the remaining data is used for testing. Weather features are standardized on the training data. This process results in about 8200 samples per park for training and 9400 for testing in the solar dataset. The wind dataset has about 28400 training and 27400 test samples. The solar dataset contains 38 features, such as sun position and solar radiation. The wind dataset contains seven features, such as wind speed and wind direction. To test the algorithm for inductive TL and zero-shot learning, we split the parks through five-fold cross-validation so that each park is a target task once while having different source tasks.

One disadvantage of these two datasets is that they do not contain any meta-information directly, not even the location. Typically, the meta-information in zero-shot learning is used as a proxy to find a similar source task. However, this information is also not available in other open datasets for renewable power forecasts. Therefore, we create meta-information through the input space, see Sect. 4.4. One advantage of the datasets is that they are distributed throughout Germany and even Europe. This distribution makes the MTL, inductive TL, and zero-shot learning more realistic as one cannot assume that parks are nearby in practice.

4.2   Evaluation Measures

In all experiments, we are considering the normalized root-mean-squared error (nRMSE). A significant difference between a (reference) model and the baseline is tested through the Wilcoxon test (with $\alpha = 0.05$), by comparing the nRMSE of a park from the baseline and a reference model. To calculate improvements against the baseline, we consider the mean skill of all m parks by

$$\text{skill}_m = 1 - \frac{\text{nRMSE}_{\text{reference}_m}}{\text{nRMSE}_{\text{baseline}_m}} \text{ and skill} = \frac{1}{M} \sum_{m=1}^{m=M} \text{skill}_m, \tag{2}$$

where values larger than zero indicate an improvement upon the baseline.

4.3 MTL Experiment

In this section, we conduct an experiment to answer the research question:

Question 1. Can an MTL CNN architecture improve the forecast error for wind and PV parks compared to a similar MLP MTL architecture?

Findings: The proposed task-TCN improves the baseline up to 18% for the solar dataset and 13% for the wind dataset.

Design of Experiment: Ten percent of the training data is validation data for hyperparameter optimization. Details on the grid search for hyperparameter optimization are available in the supplementary material. Due to the five-fold cross-validation, each park is trained four times, see Sect. 4.1. We calculate the mean nRMSE of a park for these runs. In total, we train six models and evaluate them through the nRMSE and the skill. The first two are the task embedding MLP (*MLP first*) and the Bayesian variant of the embedding layer, where the latter is considered the baseline. Both MLP variants can be considered as state of the art, see Sect. 2. For the TCN we provide the encoded task ID from the embedding once only to the *first* residual block (*TCN first*) and in the other variant to *all* except the last layer (*TCN all*). We exclude the last layer as we assume that sufficient information from the embedding is available at this point in the network. Afterward, only a transformation to the power of a specific task is required. For each of those two models, we consider a Bayesian and a non-Bayesian variant. We do not consider an ablation study without the task embedding as the architecture would then no longer be extendable to new tasks without catastrophic forgetting for inductive TL. Further, the improvement through the embedding over single-task learning is also shown in [3,4].

Detailed Findings: All variants of the TCN lead to a significant improvement compared to the Bayesian *MLP first* as the baseline, see Table 1. The non-Bayesian *MLP first* has significantly worse results than the baseline for both datasets. In the case of the PV dataset, the non-Bayesian *TCN all* has the smallest mean nRMSE (0.071), std, and best skill. It is essential to consider that probably due to the larger correlation between PV parks in this dataset, as described in [3], it is beneficial for the TCN to share information in *all* residual blocks. In contrast, the wind dataset tasks are less correlated compared to the PV dataset [3]. Therefore, the non-Bayesian *TCN first* has the best results with a mean nRMSE of 0.136.

Table 1. Evaluation results for the wind and PV dataset for the mean nRMSE and standard deviation (std) from all parks. The asterisk symbol marks significantly different nRMSE values of reference (Ref.) models than the baseline (BS). The significance is tested through the Wilcoxon signed-rank test with $\alpha = 0.05$. In case that the skill is larger than zero, this indicates a significant improvement upon the baseline.

Model	Type	DataType	PV			Wind		
		EmbPos	Skill	nRMSE	std	Skill	nRMSE	std
MLP	Bayes	First (BS)	0.000	0.087	0.005	0.000	0.184	0.007
	Normal	First (Ref.)	−0.087	0.095*	0.015	−0.239	0.229*	0.047
TCN	Bayes	All (Ref.)	0.092	0.079*	0.002	0.092	0.169*	0.005
		First (Ref.)	0.098	0.078*	0.002	0.089	0.169*	0.007
	Normal	All (Ref.)	**0.181**	**0.071***	**0.001**	0.254	0.137*	0.002
		First (Ref.)	0.174	0.072*	0.001	**0.258**	**0.136***	**0.002**

Interestingly, for both datasets, the Bayesian TCN perform substantially worse than their non-Bayesian variants. However, the Bayesian *MLP first* error is significantly better than the non-Bayesian approach. In the case of the Bayesian *MLP first*, the prior probably allows the model to better learn the commonalities and differences between tasks, especially in case of insufficient data [4]. However, in the case of the TCN, the additional channel wise transform allows the network to learn an encoding that is different in each channel. Due to this possibility of learning a vast amount of features that reflect different amounts of similarities between tasks, it makes the benefits of a Bayesian approach dispensable, especially since they are sensitive to the selection of the prior, which is constant in all experiments. Nonetheless, the results are promising for the following experiments, as the Bayesian *MLP first* baseline improves upon the non-Bayesian MLP similar to [4] and the proposed task-TCN improves upon the baseline.

4.4   Zero-Shot Learning Experiment

In this section, we conduct an experiment to answer the research question:

Question 2. Are CNN based MTL architectures capable of providing good forecasts in zero-shot learning for renewable power forecasts?

Findings: The best TCN models achieve excellent forecast errors for PV and wind as these models have a similar mean nRMSE compared to the baseline from the previous experiment with a full year of data. However, outliers for the wind dataset are present that need to be considered in future work.

Design of Experiment: In this experiment, we use the same model as described in the previous section. Initially, we need to find a suitable source task applicable to an unknown task. As stated earlier in Sect. 4.1, the two datasets do not have meta-information directly applicable to select an appropriate source task. However, a common approach in TL for time series is to use dynamic time warping (DTW) as a similarity measure in the feature space between the source and the target [20]. We assume that a similar park type, e.g., the same rotor diameter, is placed in similar regions with identical weather features. Even though this is not optimal, it is still a reasonable assumption to make. For instance, wind parks near coasts typically have larger rotor diameters than parks placed in a forest. To determine the most similar wind or PV park, we calculate the mean squared difference through DTW between the source and the target. In the case of the wind dataset, we use the wind speed at 100 m height. For the solar dataset, we utilize direct radiation, as those two are the most relevant features to forecast the expected power [24]. We calculate the similarity based on the first year's training data of the source and target task. Using the entire year is possible, as the input features are themselves forecasts and are extractable for the past. After finding the most prominent candidate through the training data, we forecast on the test dataset. Based on these forecasts, we calculate the nRMSE for each park and the skill to measure the improvement.

Detailed Findings: Table 2 summarizes the respective results. For the PV dataset, the non-Bayesian *TCN all* achieves the best mean nRMSE of 0.081. All other TCN models have a similar mean nRMSE of 0.082. This zero-shot learning result is outstanding since it is still better than the baseline from the previous experiment with a mean nRMSE of 0.087 with a full year of training data.

The Bayesian *TCN all* and *TCN first* have the best mean nRMSE with 0.182 and improvements above 10% compared to the zero-shot baseline of this experiment for the wind dataset. The non-Bayesian TCNs have a similar nRMSE of 0.188. Again, the result of the best TCNs is less than the mean nRMSE (0.184) of the baseline from the previous experiment.

Nonetheless, there are two interesting observations. First, for all models on the wind dataset, outliers above an nRMSE of 0.5 are present. As the wind dataset has parks spread throughout Europe with distinct topographies and weather situations, these outliers are not surprising. Furthermore, the source task selection is solely based on DTW, as a proxy for the missing meta-information. Respectively, these outliers need to be considered in future work, e.g., through additional meta-information. Second, for the wind dataset, the Bayesian TCN variants are better than their non-Bayesian counterparts. This effect is surprising, as their basis from the previous experiment behaves inversely. We can assume that due to the prior, acting as a regularizer, in Bayesian TCNs we have fewer outliers for indistinguishable tasks. However, this should be considered in future work.

4.5   Inductive TL Experiment

In this section, we conduct an experiment to answer the research question:

Table 2. Result for zero-shot learning, cf. with Table 1.

Model	Type	DataType	PV			Wind		
		EmbPos	Skill	nRMSE	std	Skill	nRMSE	std
MLP	Bayes	First (BS)	0.000	0.093	**0.018**	0.000	0.202	**0.071**
	Normal	First (Ref.)	−0.055	0.098	0.028	−0.159	0.226*	0.082
TCN	Bayes	All (Ref.)	0.123	0.082*	0.018	**0.109**	**0.182***	0.076
		First (Ref.)	0.123	0.082*	0.019	0.104	0.182*	0.073
	Normal	All (Ref.)	**0.129**	**0.081***	0.020	0.058	0.188	0.078
		First (Ref.)	0.127	0.082*	0.019	0.059	0.188	0.077

Question 3. Are CNN based MTL architectures beneficial during inductive TL compared to a similar MLP MTL approach?

Findings: With only 90 days of training data, the nRMSE of the TCN architecture is similar to the TCN with an entire year of training data. This result shows that the proposed model is extendable to new tasks having a similar error while avoiding catastrophic forgetting with improvements above 25% compared to the baseline.

Design of Experiment: As seasonal influences affect the forecast error [24], we test how the different seasons as training data result in other target errors. Further, to test the influence of the amount of available training data, we train with data from 7, 14, 30, 60, 90 and additionally 365 days. To avoid catastrophic forgetting, we only finetune the embedding layer. In this way, the network needs to learn a transformation of the task ID similar to previous source parks and use this encoding. Finally, we tested two methods to initialize the embedding of the new task. The first one uses the *default* initialization strategy of pytorch. The second one *copies* the task embedding based on the most similar task through the smallest mean squared error on 10% of the training data.

Detailed Findings: In the following, we show exemplary results of the spring season for both datasets. Those lead to the best results compared to other seasons for training. When comparing models with another, observations are similar to those presented in the following also for other seasons. The results with a year of training data and other seasons are available in the supplementary material.

The results for the wind dataset are summarized in Table 3. For all except one case, copying the task ID leads to an improved mean nRMSE compared to the default initialization strategy for all models and available training amounts. All TCN variants achieve a significant improvement upon the baseline for all different numbers of training data. The non-Bayesian *TCN all*, where we *copy* the most similar embedding vector, has the best mean nRMSE for most training

Table 3. Mean nRMSE for spring of wind data set. Significant differences of the reference (Ref.) compared to the baseline (BS) is tested through the Wilcoxon signed-rank test with $\alpha = 0.05$ and marked with *.

Model	Embedding Type	Embedding Position	DaysTraining	nRMSE				
			Embedding Initialization	7	14	30	60	90
MLP	Bayes	First	Copy (Ref.)	0.233	0.229	0.213	0.206	0.186
			Default (BS)	0.234	0.229	0.213	0.205	0.186
	Normal	First	Copy (Ref.)	0.237	0.233	0.212	0.200	0.181
			Default (Ref.)	0.255	0.247*	0.229*	0.217*	0.200*
TCN	Bayes	All	Copy (Ref.)	0.178*	0.192*	0.171*	0.170*	0.162*
			Default (Ref.)	0.186*	0.200*	0.177*	0.173*	0.163*
		First	Copy (Ref.)	0.177*	0.195*	0.176*	0.172*	0.165*
			Default (Ref.)	0.184*	0.202*	0.180*	0.175*	0.165*
	Normal	All	Copy (Ref.)	**0.161***	**0.173***	0.152*	**0.141***	**0.137***
			Default (Ref.)	0.179*	0.188*	0.155*	0.146*	0.139*
		First	Copy (Ref.)	0.163*	0.181*	**0.148***	0.142*	0.137*
			Default (Ref.)	0.187*	0.199*	0.162*	0.152*	0.142*

amounts. The non-Bayesian *MLP first* is either significant worse or has a similar nRMSE than the Bayesian MLP.

Table 4 summarizes the same results for the solar dataset. Again, copying the task ID leads to an improved mean nRMSE for all models, compared to the default initialization strategy, except in one case. A significant improvement is achieved through the non-Bayesian *MLP first* and *copying* the encoded task ID. All TCN models achieve a significant improvement upon the baseline. In most cases, the *TCN first* that *copies* the embedding vector has the best or at least a similar result. Interestingly, the non-Bayesian *MLP first* is significantly better than the Bayesian baseline, which contrasts with the results from the MTL experiment. Potentially, this contradiction is caused by an insufficient amount of training epochs during inductive TL for the Bayesian model that is required to reduce the ELBO.

Due to these results, we can summarize that the TCN models achieve significant improvements compared to the MLP baselines. This result is not surprising, as, also in other research domains [20], the hierarchical learning structure of CNNs is beneficial for TL in time series. In our cases, the best PV results are when considering the embedding vector solely at the first residual block. It is probably sufficient since the network can bypass information to later layers, without losing information, due to the residual block. However, for the more non-linear problem of wind power forecasts, it is also beneficial to consider the encoded task ID in all residual blocks.

Table 4. Mean nRMSE for spring of pv data set, cf. with Table 3.

Model	Embedding Type	Embedding Position	Days Training	nRMSE				
			Embedding Initialization	7	14	30	60	90
MLP	Bayes	First	Copy (Ref.)	0.305	0.204	0.167	0.110	0.116
			Default (BS)	0.305	0.204	0.167	0.110	0.116
	Normal	First	Copy (Ref.)	0.170*	0.192	0.096*	0.086*	0.089*
			Default (Ref.)	0.263	0.199	0.132	0.093*	0.097*
TCN	Bayes	All	Copy (Ref.)	**0.094***	0.100*	0.097*	0.083*	0.084*
			Default (Ref.)	0.095*	0.098*	0.097*	0.083*	0.084*
		First	Copy (Ref.)	0.106*	0.104*	0.091*	0.084*	0.084*
			Default (Ref.)	0.106*	0.104*	0.092*	0.084*	0.084*
	Normal	All	Copy (Ref.)	0.096*	0.083*	0.078*	0.076*	**0.077***
			Default (Ref.)	0.106*	0.105*	0.117	0.079*	0.078*
		First	Copy (Ref.)	0.106*	**0.081***	**0.076***	**0.076***	0.078*
			Default (Ref.)	0.117*	0.090*	0.099*	0.078*	0.080*

5   Conclusion and Future Work

We successfully showed the applicability of the proposed task TCN for wind and PV day-ahead power forecasts. The proposed architecture provides the possibility to solve critical real-world challenges in renewable power forecasts. It provides a framework for MTL, inductive TL, and zero-shot learning and improves the forecast error significantly compared to the Bayesian MLP task embedding as the baseline in all three domains. However, some results of the Bayesian architecture for the inductive TL are contradictory. Those contradictions are probably caused by insufficient training epochs to reduce the ELBO that should be investigated in future work. The most intriguing result for future work concerns the zero-shot learning experiment as the proposed TCN architecture achieves at least a similar low forecast error, without training data, as the Bayesian MLP with a full year of training data. Even though we achieve excellent results for the PV and wind dataset, the wind dataset led to some outliers that can be considered by taking additional meta-information into account in future work.

Acknowledgments. This work results from the project TRANSFER (01IS20020B) funded by BMBF (German Federal Ministry of Education and Research).

References

1. Gielen, D., Boshell, F., Saygin, D., et al.: The role of renewable energy in the global energy transformation. Energy Strategy Rev. **24**, 38–50 (2019)
2. Schwartz, R., Dodge, J., Smith, N.A., et al.: Green AI. CoRR, pp. 1–12 (2019). arXiv: 1907.10597
3. Schreiber, J., Sick, B.: Emerging relation network and task embedding for multi-task regression problems. In: ICPR (2020)

4. Vogt, S., Braun, A., Dobschinski, J., et al.: Wind power forecasting based on deep neural networks and transfer learning. In: 18th Wind Integration Workshop, pp. 8 (2019)

5. Schreiber, J., Buschin, A., Sick, B.: Influences in forecast errors for wind and photovoltaic power: a study on machine learning models. In: INFORMATIK 2019, pp. 585–598. Gesellschaft für Informatik e.V. (2019)

6. Solas, M., Cepeda, N., Viegas, J.L.: Convolutional neural network for short-term wind power forecasting. In: Proceedings of the ISGT-Europe 2019 (2019)

7. Fuzhen, Z., Zhiyuan, Q., Keyu, D., et al.: A comprehensive survey on transfer learning. Proc. IEEE **109**(1), 43–76 (2021)

8. Zhang, Y., Yang, Q.: A survey on multi-task learning. IEEE TKDE, 1–20 (2021, early access)

9. Shireen, T., Shao, C., Wang, H., et al.: Iterative multi-task learning for time-series modeling of solar panel PV outputs. Appl. Energy **212**, 654–662 (2018)

10. Tasnim, S., Rahman, A., Oo, A.M.T., et al.: Wind power prediction in new stations based on knowledge of existing Stations: A cluster based multi source domain adaptation approach. Knowl.-Based Syst. **145**, 15–24 (2018)

11. Cao, L., Wang, L., Huang, C., et al.: A transfer learning strategy for short-term wind power forecasting. In: Chinese Automation Congress, pp. 3070–3075. IEEE (2018)

12. Cai, L., Gu, J., Ma, J., et al.: Probabilistic wind power forecasting approach via instance-based transfer learning embedded gradient boosting decision trees. Energies **12**(1), 159 (2019)

13. Qureshi, A.S., Khan, A.: Adaptive transfer learning in deep neural networks: Wind power prediction using knowledge transfer from region to region and between different task domains. Comput. Intell. **35**(4), 1088–1112 (2019)

14. Liu, X., Cao, Z., Zhang, Z.: Short-term predictions of multiple wind turbine power outputs based on deep neural networks with transfer learning. Energy **217**, 119356 (2021)

15. Ju, Y., Li, J., Sun, G.: Ultra-short-term photovoltaic power prediction based on self-attention mechanism and multi-task learning. IEEE Access **8**, 44821–44829 (2020)

16. Zhou, S., Zhou, L., Mao, M., et al.: Transfer learning for photovoltaic power forecasting with long short-term memory neural network. In: Proceedings of the BigComp 2020, pp. 125–132 (2020)

17. Zang, H., Cheng, L., Ding, T., et al.: Day-ahead photovoltaic power forecasting approach based on deep convolutional neural networks and meta learning. Int. JEPE **118**, 105790 (2020)

18. Mikolov, T., Chen, K., Corrado, G., et al.: Distributed representations of words and phrases and their compositionality. In: NIPS, pp. 3111–3119 (2013)

19. Guo, C., Berkhahn, F.: Entity embeddings of categorical variables. CoRR, pp. 1–9 (2016). arXiv: 1604.06737

20. Fawaz, H.I., Forestier, G., Weber, J., et al.: Transfer learning for time series classification. In: 2018 IEEE BigData, pp. 1367–1376 (2019)

21. Yan, J., Mu, L., Wang, L., Ranjan, R., Zomaya, A.Y.: Temporal convolutional networks for the advance prediction of ENSO. Sci. Rep. **10**(1), 1–15 (2020)

22. Reis, J., Gonçalves, G.: Hyper-process model: a zero-shot learning algorithm for regression problems based on shape analysis. JMLR **1**, 1–36 (2018)

23. Blundell, C., Cornebise, J., Kavukcuoglu, K., et al.: Weight uncertainty in neural networks. In: 32nd ICML 2015, vol. 37, pp. 1613–1622 (2015)

24. Schreiber, J., Siefert, M., Winter, K., et al.: Prophesy: Prognoseunsicherheiten von Windenergie und Photovoltaik in zukünftigen Stromversorgungssystemen. German National Library of Science and Technology, p. 159 (2020)
25. European centre for medium-range weather forecasts (2020). http://www.ecmwf.int/. Accessed 30 Mar 2021

Generating Multi-type Temporal Sequences to Mitigate Class-Imbalanced Problem

Lun Jiang, Nima Salehi Sadghiani[✉], Zhuo Tao, and Andrew Cohen

Unity, San Francisco, CA 94103, USA
{lun,nimas,zhuo,andrew.cohen}@unity3d.com

Abstract. From the ad network standpoint, a user's activity is a multi-type sequence of temporal events consisting of event types and time intervals. Understanding user patterns in ad networks has received increasing attention from the machine learning community. Particularly, the problems of fraud detection, Conversion Rate (CVR), and Click-Through Rate (CTR) prediction are of interest. However, the class imbalance between major and minor classes in these tasks can bias a machine learning model leading to poor performance. This study proposes using two multi-type (continuous and discrete) training approaches for GANs to deal with the limitations of traditional GANs in passing the gradient updates for discrete tokens. First, we used the Reinforcement Learning (RL)-based training approach and then, an approximation of the multinomial distribution parameterized in terms of the softmax function (Gumble-Softmax). Our extensive experiments based on synthetic data have shown the trained generator can generate sequences with desired properties measured by multiple criteria.

Keywords: Multi-type sequences · Temporal events · Generative adversarial network · Reinforcement learning

1 Introduction

Game developers can monetize their games by selling in-game ad placements to advertisers. Ads can be integrated in multiple ways such as a banner in the background or commercials during breaks (when a specific part of the game is completed). There are four main elements in the game advertising ecosystem: publishers or developers, advertisers, advertising networks, and users [21]. Game advertising networks connect advertisers with game developers and serve billions of ads to user devices, triggering enormous ad events. For example, Unity Ads reports 22.9B+ monthly global ad impressions, reaching 2B+ monthly active end-users worldwide[1].

---

[1] https://www.businesswire.com/news/home/20201013005191/en/.

L. Jiang, N. S. Sadghiani and Z. Tao—Authors contributed equally.

© Springer Nature Switzerland AG 2021
Y. Dong et al. (Eds.): ECML PKDD 2021, LNAI 12978, pp. 135–150, 2021.
https://doi.org/10.1007/978-3-030-86514-6_9

An ad event is a user interaction e.g. request, start, view, click, and install. Each type stands for one specific kind of ad-related user action happening at a specific time. A complete ad life cycle consists of a temporal sequence of ad events, each of which is a tuple of event types with corresponding time intervals. Click and install are two kinds of ad events commonly associated with ad revenue. Pay-Per-Click [17] and Pay-Per-Install [27] are the most widely used advertising models for pricing.

Unlike traditional advertising, online advertising offers services that link user interactions to conversions or clicks. Due to this, predicting a user's probability of clicking or conversion rate has become one of the most important problems in online advertising [4]. Predicting Conversion Rate (CVR) and Click-Through Rate (CTR) are usually treated as supervised learning problems [7]. For example, in CTR prediction, the labels are click/not-click an ad for every user. The sequence of events before a click/not-click response are used as features of the supervised learning model.

Unfortunately, as advertisers allocate more of their budget into this ecosystem, there is more incentive to abuse the advertising networks and defraud advertisers of their money [22]. Fraudulent ad activity aimed at generating illegitimate ad revenue or unearned benefits are one of the major threats to online advertising models. Common types of fraudulent activities include fake impressions [14], click bots [13,19], or click farms [24].

Given the massive ad activity data in-game advertising networks, machine learning-based approaches have become popular in the industry. However, it is not a straightforward task to train machine learning models directly on the sequences collected from ad activities [5].

The primary issue in these problems is class imbalance. By definition, the ratio of typical user behavior to anomalous will heavily favor typical. For example, the CVR can be as low as 0.01% for game ads. Similarly, most ad traffic is non-fraudulent, and data labeling by human experts is time-consuming. In these scenarios, label sparsity leads to low availability of labeled sequences for the minor class. Simply oversampling the minority class can cause significant overfitting, while undersampling the majority may lead to information loss and yield a tiny training dataset [1]. In this study, we present a novel method to generate synthetic data to mitigate class imbalance.

The main contributions of our work can be summarized as follows:

1. A novel reinforcement learning formulation that trains a generator to generate multi-type temporal sequences with non-uniform time intervals.
2. A novel training method for sequence GAN that uses a critic network.
3. A new application for event-based sequence GAN in game advertising.

2   Related Work

Generative Adversarial Networks (GANs) [11] have drawn significant attention as a framework for training generative models capable of producing synthetic data with desired structures and properties [18]. It was proposed to use GANs to generate data that mimics training data as an augmented oversampling method with an application in credit card fraud. The generated data is used to assist the classification of credit card fraud [1].

2.1 GAN for Sequence Data

Despite the remarkable success of GANs in generating synthetic data, very few studies focus on generating sequential data. This is due to additional challenges in generating temporally dependent samples. Recurrent Neural Network (RNN) solutions are state-of-the-art in modeling sequential data. Recurrent Conditional GAN (RCGAN) generates real-valued multi-dimensional time series and then uses the generated series for supervised training [10]. The time series data in their study were physiological signals sampled at specific fixed frequencies. However, ad event data has higher complexity due to non-uniform time intervals and discrete event types and thus can not be modeled as wave signals. In ad event sequences, two events with a short time interval tend to be more correlated than events with larger time intervals.

A GAN-based generative model for DNA along with an activation maximization technique for DNA sequence data is proposed by [18]. Their experiments have shown that these generative techniques can learn the important structure from DNA sequences and can be used to design new DNA sequences with desired properties. Similarly to the previous study, their focus is on fixed interval sequences.

The Long Short-Term Memory (LSTM)-Autoencoder is used to encode the benign users into a latent space [30]. They proposed using One-Class Adversarial Network (OCAN) for the training process of the GAN model. In their training framework, the discriminator is trained to be a classifier for distinguishing benign users, and the generator produces samples that are complementary to the representations of benign users.

2.2 RL for GANs with Sequences of Discrete Tokens

When generating continuous outputs, gradient updates can be passed from the discriminator to the generator. However, for discrete outputs, this is not straightforward due to a lack of differentiability. The issue of training GAN models to generate sequences of discrete tokens is addressed in [28]. They proposed a sequence generation framework called SeqGAN that models the data generator as a stochastic policy learned via Reinforcement Learning (RL) [26]. SeqGAN learns a policy using the vanilla policy gradient and Monte Carlo (MC) rollouts to approximate the advantage. MC rollouts are a computationally expensive process in the training loop. Moreover, SeqGAN is limited to discrete token generation. In our work, we propose a modified version of SeqGAN that can generate both discrete tokens and continuous time-intervals. Additionally, to efficiently train the policy network, we employ a Critic network to approximate the return given a partially generated sequence to speed up the training process. This approach also brings the potential to use a trained Critic network for early fraud detection from partial sequences.

An application of SeqGAN in recommendation systems is presented in [29]. The paper solves the slow convergence and unstable RL training by using the Actor-Critic algorithm instead of MC roll-outs. Their generator model produces the entire recommended sequences given the interaction history while the discriminator learns to maximize the score of ground-truth and minimize the score of generated sequences. In each step, the generator G generates a token by top-k beam search based on the model distribution. In our work, we directly sample from the distribution of the output probabilities of the tokens. While our methodologies are close, we are aiming for different goals. We optimize the generated data to solve the sample imbalance problem while they optimize for better recommendations. Therefore, different evaluation metrics are needed. Our methodologies also differ in the training strategy. For example, we used a Critic network as the baseline, whereas they used Temporal-Difference bootstrap targets. They pre-trained the discriminator on the generated data to reduce the exposure bias, while we pre-trained the discriminator on the actual training data for improving the metrics we use in our experiments. More importantly, they do not include time intervals as an attribute in their model while we have time intervals in our models.

The idea of using SeqGan to adversarially learn the output sequences while optimizing towards chemical metrics with the algorithm REINFORCE [26] is proposed in [12]. They have shown that it is often advantageous to guide the generative model towards some desirable characteristics, while ensuring that the samples resemble the initial distribution.

2.3 Gumbel-Softmax Distribution for GANs with Sequences of Discrete Tokens

The Gumbel-Softmax distribution is proposed in [20] to address the limitation of GANs for generating sequences of discrete tokens. The Gumbel-Softmax is a continuous approximation to a multinomial distribution parameterized over a softmax function. This approximation is differentiable thus enabling backpropagation through an approximation of a discrete sampling procedure. A temperature parameter can be used to controll the degree of approximation [16]. When the temperature is lower, the approximation is closer to the one hot distribution; when it is higher, the approximation is closer to a uniform distribution.

Another application of Gumbel-Softmax distributions is proposed in [6] for generating small molecular graphs.

3 Methodology

In this section, we introduce a new methodology to generate multi-type sequences using GAN, which can be trained by using RL and Gumbel-Softmax reparametrization.

3.1 Definitions

The sequence of an ad event with length L is composed of two sub-sequences, the sub-sequence of event types x and the sub-sequence of time stamps. First, we

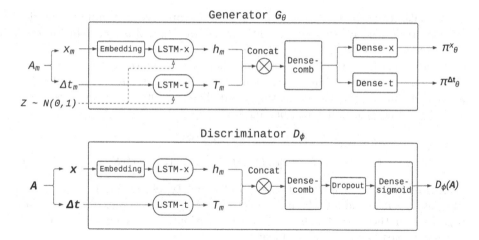

Fig. 1. Architecture of the Generator and the Discriminator.

transform the time stamps t into time intervals $\boldsymbol{\Delta t}$ and $\Delta t_m = t_m - t_{m-1}, \forall m \in [1, L]$, and $\Delta t_1 = t_1 - 0$. Then, we combine the event types and time intervals into a joint multi-type sequence $\boldsymbol{A}$:

$$\boldsymbol{A} = \boldsymbol{A}_{1:L} = \{(x_1, \Delta t_1), (x_2, \Delta t_2), \ldots, A(x_m, \Delta t_m), \ldots, (x_L, \Delta t_L)\}$$

where a bold $\boldsymbol{A}_{1:m}$ denotes a partial sequence from step 1 to step m, and a non-bold $A_m = (x_m, \Delta t_m)$ denotes a single pair in the sequence.

3.2 RL and Policy Improvement to Train GAN

We implemented a modified version of SeqGAN model to generate multi-type temporal sequences. The architecture is shown in Fig. 1.

The sequence generation process of our generator G can be modeled as a sequential decision process in RL. h_m and T_m are the hidden states of LSTM cells, and $Z \sim \mathcal{N}(0,1)$ is the normal noise used to initialize h_m and T_m at the beginning of each generation process.

From the perspective of RL, at each step m, we define the state S_m as the partial sequence $\boldsymbol{A}_{1:m}$, a.k.a,

$$S_m = \boldsymbol{A}_{1:m} \tag{1}$$

During the generation process, at each step m, a new pair

$$A_{m+1} = (x_{m+1}, \Delta t_{m+1}) \tag{2}$$

is appended to the current partial sequence $\boldsymbol{A}_{1:m}$ to formulate a new partial sequence $\boldsymbol{A}_{1:m+1}$, and thus transit to a new state S_{m+1}, based on the definition of state in (1). This process repeats step by step, until a complete sequence $\boldsymbol{A}$ of length L described in (Sect. 3.1) is fully constructed.

To make decisions in this sequence generation process, we employ a hybrid policy to represent action spaces with both continuous and discrete dimensions (similar to the idea in [23]). This policy is designed to choose discrete event types and continuous time intervals, assuming their action spaces are independent. Then we use a categorical distribution and a Gaussian distribution to model the policy distributions for the event types and the time intervals respectively. So the hybrid generator policy can be defined as:

$$G_\theta(a_m|S_m) = \pi_\theta^x(a_m^x|S_m) \cdot \pi_\theta^{\Delta t}(a_m^{\Delta t}|S_m)$$
$$= Cat(x|\alpha_\theta(S_m)) \cdot \mathcal{N}(\Delta t|\mu_\theta(S_m), \sigma_\theta^2(S_m)) \tag{3}$$

where $x \in \boldsymbol{K}, \Delta t \in R_{\geq 0}$. $\boldsymbol{K}$ is the set of all event types. Then an action a_m is taken at step m to sample the next event type x_{m+1} and the next time interval Δt_{m+1} given the hybrid policy (3). So the action has discrete part and the continuous part sampled independently:

$$a_m = \{a_m^x, a_m^{\Delta t}\} \tag{4}$$
$$a_m^x = x_{m+1} \sim Cat(x|\alpha_\theta(S_m)) \tag{5}$$
$$a_m^{\Delta t} = \Delta t_{m+1} \sim \mathcal{N}(\Delta t|\mu_\theta(S_m), \sigma_\theta^2(S_m)) \tag{6}$$

where a_m^x is the action to find the next event type x_{m+1} and $a_m^{\Delta t}$ is the action to find the next time interval Δt_{m+1}.

When generating a new event type and time interval at each step, we follow the generator policy and sample from categorical and Gaussian distributions independently and concatenate them to obtain the action vector a_m, then append them to the current partial sequence $\boldsymbol{A}_{1:m}$ to obtain a new partial sequence $\boldsymbol{A}_{1:m+1}$. Once a complete sequence of length L has been generated, we pass the sequence $\boldsymbol{A}$ to the Discriminator D which predicts the probability of the sequence to be real against fake:

$$D_\phi(\boldsymbol{A}) = Pr(Y = 1|\boldsymbol{A}; \phi) \tag{7}$$

The feedback from D can be used to train G to generate sequences similar to real training data to deceive D. Because the discrete data is not differentiable, gradients can not passed back to generator like in image-base GANs.

The original SeqGAN training uses Policy Gradient method with MC roll-out to optimize the policy [28]. In order to reduce variance in the optimization process, SeqGAN runs the roll-out policy starting from current state till the end of the sequence for multiple times to get the mean return. Here we use an Actor-Critic method with a Critic network instead of MC roll-out to estimate the value of any state, which is computationally more efficient [2].

The critic network models a state-dependent value $\hat{V}_\psi^{G_\theta}(S_m)$ for a partially generated sequence $\boldsymbol{A}_{1:m}$ under policy G_θ. The output of the critic is defined as the expected future return for the current state $S_m = \boldsymbol{A}_{1:m}$, which will be given by the discriminator D when a complete sequence $\boldsymbol{A}$ is generated.

$$\hat{V}_\psi^{G_\theta}(S_m) = \mathbb{E}_{\boldsymbol{A}_{m+1:L} \sim G_\theta(S_m)}[D_\phi(\boldsymbol{A})] \tag{8}$$

The parameters in the critic value function $\hat{V}_\psi^{G_\theta}(S_m)$ are updated during training by minimizing the mean squared error between the true return $D_\phi(\boldsymbol{A})$ and the critic value:

$$J(\psi) = \mathbb{E}[(D_\phi(\boldsymbol{A}) - \hat{V}_\psi^{G_\theta}(S_m))^2] \tag{9}$$

The difference between them, $D_\phi(\boldsymbol{A}) - \hat{V}_\psi^{G_\theta}(S_m)$, is named the advantage function, which can be used in G training and helps to reduce variance.

The goal of G training is to choose actions based on a policy that maximizes expected return. The object function of G follows Policy Gradient method [26] which can be derived as:

$$\nabla_\theta J(\theta) = \sum_{m=0}^{L-1} \mathbb{E}_{a_m \sim G_\theta(a_m|S_m)}[\nabla_\theta \log G_\theta(a_m|S_m) \cdot (D_\phi(\boldsymbol{A}) - \hat{V}_\psi^{G_\theta}(S_m))] \tag{10}$$

Because of the independence assumption we made, the policy gradient term can be broken down and written into a categorical cross-entropy and a Gaussian log-likelihood as follows:

$$\nabla_\theta \log G_\theta(a_m|S_m)$$
$$= \nabla_\theta[\log Cat(x = x_{m+1}|\alpha_\theta(S_m)) + \log \mathcal{N}(\Delta t = \Delta t_{m+1}|\mu_\theta(S_m), \sigma_\theta^2(S_m))]$$
$$= \nabla_\theta[\mathbb{E}_{x \in K} \mathbb{1}_x(x_{m+1}) \Pr(x = x_{m+1}) - \frac{(\Delta t_{m+1} - \mu_\theta(S_m))^2}{2\sigma_\theta^2(S_m)} - \frac{1}{2}\log(2\pi\sigma_\theta^2(S_m))]$$
$$\tag{11}$$

The goal of D training to use distinguish generated sequences with true sequences from training data. D_ϕ is updated through minimizing binary cross-entropy loss. G and D alternatively in GAN training.

The training data are taken from the positive class $\boldsymbol{\Omega}^+$ of our synthetic Ad event dataset $\boldsymbol{\Omega}$, which are shown in the Sect. 4.1.

Before GAN training, We pre-train G with Maximum Likelihood Estimation (MLE) self-regression on the sequences and pre-train D with binary classification for better convergence. Details about pre-training and GAN training The Pseudo code of the entire process is shown in Algorithm 1.

3.3   An Approximation with Gumbel-Softmax Distribution

Beside RL, we also tried to overcome the gradient updates problem for discrete token in GAN using Gumbel-Softmax reparametrization. We use the same generator G and discriminator D setups as described in Sect. 3.2, except that the generator policy $G_\theta(a_m|S_m)$ is different from that in (3). For the continuous part, we no longer sample time intervals from a parametrized Normal distribution, but directly take G outputs as the next time interval.

$$a_m^{\Delta t} = \Delta t_{m+1} = \Delta t_\theta(S_m) \tag{12}$$

Algorithm 1. Sequence Generative Adversarial Nets Training with RL

Require: training dataset $\boldsymbol{\Omega}^+$, generator G_θ, discriminator D_ϕ, critic $\hat{V}_\psi^{G_\theta}$.

1: Initialize G_θ, D_ϕ, $\hat{V}_\psi^{G_\theta}$ with random weights θ, ϕ, ψ
2: Pre-train G_θ with MLE self-regression on $\boldsymbol{\Omega}^+$.
3: Generate fake dataset $\boldsymbol{\Omega}^{+fake}$ using pre-trained G_θ.
4: Pre-train D_ϕ via minimizing binary cross-entropy on $\boldsymbol{\Omega}^+ \cup \boldsymbol{\Omega}^{+fake}$
5: **repeat**
6:     **for** G-steps **do**
7:         Generate a batch of fake sequences $\boldsymbol{A}^{fake} \sim G_\theta$
8:         Get true rewards $D_\phi(\boldsymbol{A})$ from discriminator
9:         **for** m in $1:L$ **do**
10:            $S_m \leftarrow \boldsymbol{A}_{1:m}^{fake}$
11:            $a_m \leftarrow (x_{m+1}, \Delta t_{m+1}) \in \boldsymbol{A}^{fake}$
12:            $\alpha_\theta(S_m), \mu_\theta(S_m), \sigma_\theta(S_m) \leftarrow G_\theta(S_m)$
13:            Compute policy gradient as shown in Eq. (11)
14:            Compute value estimate $\hat{V}_\psi^{G_\theta}(S_m)$ by Eq. (8)
15:            Compute the advantage $(D_\phi(\boldsymbol{A}) - \hat{V}_\psi^{G_\theta}(S_m))$
16:        Update critic param. ψ by minimizing Eq. (9)
17:        Update generator param. θ via Eq. (10)
18:    **for** D-steps **do**
19:        Generate a batch of sequences $\boldsymbol{A}^{fake} \sim G_\theta$
20:        Sample a batch of sequences $\boldsymbol{A}^{true}$ from $\boldsymbol{\Omega}^+$
21:        Train discriminator D_ϕ on $\boldsymbol{A}_{fake} \cup \boldsymbol{A}_{true}$ and update param. ϕ via minimizing binary cross-entropy
22: **until** terminate condition satisfied

For the discrete part, in the forward pass of training the generator G, we add a Gumbel noise to the probability distribution of event types at each step m, and use argmax operator to sample the next event type x_{m+1}:

$$a_m^x = x_{m+1} = \arg \max_i (\log(\alpha_\theta(S_m)_i) + g_i) \quad \text{for} \quad i = 1, \ldots, |\boldsymbol{K}| \qquad (13)$$

where τ is the temperature and g is a random variable with a standard Gumbel distribution:

$$g = -\log(-\log(U)), \quad \text{where} \quad U \sim \text{Uniform}([0,1]) \qquad (14)$$

In the backward pass of G training, we reparametrize the categorical distribution using a Gumbel random variable g to create a differentiable approximation of the discrete representation of a_m^x to calculate gradients:

$$\Pr(a_m^x = x_i, x_i \in \boldsymbol{K} | S_m) = \frac{\exp\left((\log(\alpha_\theta(S_m)_i) + g_i)/\tau\right)}{\sum_{j=1}^k \exp\left((\log(\alpha_\theta(S_m)_j) + g_j)/\tau\right)} \qquad (15)$$
$$\text{for} \quad i = 1, \ldots, |\boldsymbol{K}|$$

After the Gumbel-Softmax reparametrization, we can train the multi-type GAN with discrete event types using a similar approach in [20].

4   Data Experiments

Due to data privacy laws (e.g. GDPR[2], CCPA[3]), and to protect confidential details of the Unity Ads Exchange and Fraud Detection service, we opt not to use real-world ad events data in this study to avoid releasing user behavior patterns to the public. While anonymizing the real-world dataset can hide users' identities, it cannot disguise the users' behavior patterns and distributions. Fraudsters can easily employ bots to simulate the features of real users to bypass fraud detection systems, if given access to the real data.

Instead, we conduct our experiments on a synthetic dataset, which contains simplified data patterns we observed and abstracted from real-world ad events. The design philosophy is explained in Sect. 4.1. The synthetic dataset and code used to generate it are publicly available[4].

4.1   Synthetic Dataset

We define the synthetic dataset as Ω. There are 4 types of hypothetical ad events in Ω, shown as $K = \{a, b, c, d\}$. Each sequence in the synthetic dataset Ω has a uniform length $L = 20$. A step at m corresponds to a tuple of event type and time interval, $(x_m, \Delta t_m)$, where x_m is sampled uniformly from K, and Δt_m is sampled from a Chi-Square distribution with the degree of freedom conditioned on x_m, i.e.:

$$x_m \sim \text{Uniform}\{a, b, c, d\} \quad \Delta t_m \sim \mathcal{X}^2(k), \quad k = \begin{cases} 10 & \text{if} \quad x_m = a \\ 20 & \text{if} \quad x_m = b \\ 40 & \text{if} \quad x_m = c \\ 80 & \text{if} \quad x_m = d \end{cases} \quad (16)$$

One example of a complete synthetic sequence is as below:

$$\begin{aligned} A_{e.g.} = [&(a, 5), (a, 22), (b, 27), (c, 44), (c, 43), \\ &(d, 87), (b, 30), (c, 36), (d, 75), (c, 28), \\ &(a, 9), (b, 24), (a, 9), (c, 40), (b, 29), \\ &(c, 37), (a, 10), (b, 19), (c, 26), (b, 7)] \end{aligned}$$

---

[2] General Data Protection Regulation.
[3] California Consumer Privacy Act.
[4] https://github.com/project-basileus/multitype-sequence-generation-by-tlstm-gan.

There are two classes in Ω, the positive class Ω^+ and the negative class Ω^-. As the two classes can be highly imbalanced in real-world Ad events data (e.g. fraud/non-fraud, buyer/non-Buyer, conversion/non-conversion, etc.), the positive class is the minority in Ω, with a positive-to-negative ratio of 1 : 500. A positive sequence has the following properties:

1. The time delay between any two consecutive events of the same event type is greater than or equal to 20.
2. Each d event is paired with one and only one previous c event. Each c event can be paired with at most one d event after it.
3. The time delay between any two paired c and d events is smaller than or equal to 200.

Sequences failing to have all 3 properties above are considered negative. The positive class Ω^+ is the training dataset. We train a GAN to generate data points from the minority class with the above properties. We will employ them as an oracle to evaluate the quality of GAN-generated sequences, as described in Sect. 4.2.

The design philosophy of the synthetic dataset is to simulate real-world patterns with as much fidelity as possible while hiding real parameters to prevent reverse-engineering by fraudsters. Specifically, the hypothetical ad events $\{a, b, c, d\}$ mimic four typical real ad events: starts, views, clicks, and installs. Real-world time delay between ad events follows a long-tail distribution, while in the synthetic dataset, it is modeled with a Chi-Square distribution conditioned on the preceding event type. Moreover, the three properties of a positive sequence are also abstracted from real-world data patterns: property 1 detects high-frequency attacks; property 2 describes the ad attribution process between clicks and installs; property 3 checks the validity of an attribution window. Ad attribution refers to the process of determining the user actions that led to the desired outcome between the click of the ad and the conversion.

4.2   Evaluation Metric

In the last few years, several different evaluation metrics for GANs have been introduced in the literature. Among them, Fréchet Inception Distance (FID) [15] has been used extensively [8]. However, this only captures the numerical part of a sequence, but our sequences are multi-type containing both the discrete categorical part (event type) and the continuous numerical part (time interval). Thus, we propose using multiple metrics to measure the quality of generated sequences. We use Mean Absolute Deviation (MAD) to measure the discrete event types, and use FID to evaluate the continuous time intervals. In addition, we employ an oracle score based on the known properties in the training data to

Table 1. Oracle metrics calculated using Ω^+ as base

Samp.	Reinforcement Learning (RL)			Gumbel-Softmax (GS)		
	MAD ↓	FID ↓	Oracle ↑	MAD ↓	FID ↓	Oracle ↑
G0	0.8265	19892.4782	0.0015	0.7368	10045.2759	0.1477
G1	0.6622	**101.7972**	0.0820	0.6399	10455.6409	0.3600
G2	**0.2849**	6495.2955	**0.5407**	**0.5427**	**9111.5298**	**0.55875**

measure the similarity between generated sequences and the training data. The arrows (↑↓) show the improvement directions.

MAD ↓. We propose using MAD to evaluate the statistical dispersion between the categorical part (i.e., the event types) of the generated multi-type sequences and that of the training data. We use the training dataset Ω^+ as the comparison base, and then one-hot encode the event types of training sequences to calculate the medians at each step m. Median is known to be more robust to noise and fits our need to have categorical values as opposed to mean.

The MAD score of any batches of generated sequences B is computed as the mean absolute deviation of each sequence from the base medians, shown as below as MAD can be computed using:

$$MAD(B) = \frac{1}{|B|} \sum_{A \in B} \sum_{m=1}^{L} \left| x_m^A - \tilde{E}_m(\Omega^+) \right| \tag{17}$$

where B is a batch of generated sequences, $|B|$ is the batch size, A is a sequence of length L in B, x_m^A is the event type of step m in A, $\tilde{E}_m(\Omega^+)$ is the base median of the event types at step m across the training dataset Ω^+.

FID ↓. Similarly to MAD, we use FID to measure the distance between the numerical part (i.e., the time intervals) of the multi-type sequences and that of the training data. This score focuses on capturing certain desirable properties including the quality and diversity of the generated sequences. FID performs well in terms of robustness and computational efficiency [3]. The Fréchet distance between two Gaussians is defined as:

$$FID(x, g) = \left\| \mu_x - \mu_g \right\|_2^2 + Tr\left(\Sigma_x + \Sigma_g - 2\left(\Sigma_x \Sigma_g\right)^{\frac{1}{2}} \right) \tag{18}$$

where (μ_x, Σ_x) and (μ_g, Σ_g) are the means and covariances for the training and generated data distribution, respectively.

Oracle ↑. One of the most direct ways to measure the quality of a generated sequence is to check whether it has the known data properties of the positive class (described in Sect. 4.1). For a batch of generated sequences, we calculate the percentage of sequences having all 3 properties of the positive class over all sequences, and then use this ratio as the oracle score. For example, for a data batch from the training dataset Ω^+, the oracle score is 1. The oracle score is a metric taking both the continuous and discrete part of a sequence into consideration.

4.3   Experiment Setup

We take 4000 samples from the Ω^+ dataset defined in Sect. 4.1 for model training. As is described in Algorithm 1, we first pre-train G and D and then start GAN training from the pre-trained G and D. We define the following terms to describe the generator at different training phases:

- $G0$: Generator with initial random model parameters.
- $G1$: Generator pre-trained using MLE self-regression.
- $G2$: Generator after GAN training.

The ratio between G training steps and D training steps is set to 1 : 1. Both G and D have the same batch size 256, and use the Adam optimizer with learning rate 10^{-4}.

During the pre-training and training processes, we evaluated the performance of the trained generator G after some steps. The trained generator was then used to generate a batch of data points and the batch evaluated according to the metrics defined in Sect. 4.2.

To avoid mode collapse and convergence problems, we used several techniques including label smoothing and noisy labels [25] in GAN training. In RL training, we added entropy regularizers [9] to the reward for discrete token and continuous time interval generation to avoid over-fitting.

4.4   Experiment Results

Table 1 shows the evaluation metric values of the sequences generated by G at different phases of training. The MAD, FID score are calculated respectively using data sampled from Ω^+ as the base for the comparisons.

The curves of evaluation metrics during pre-training and training are shown in Fig. 2 and Fig. 3, respectively.

The results in Table 1 demonstrate that the sequences generated by GAN-trained $G2$ have a significantly higher oracle score than that generated by the MLE pre-trained generator $G1$ and randomly initialized generator $G0$, for both RL and Gumbel-Softmax training. This indicates that the generator is able to learn the intrinsic patterns and properties in the training data Ω^+, and is able to mimic these patterns to deceive the discriminator.

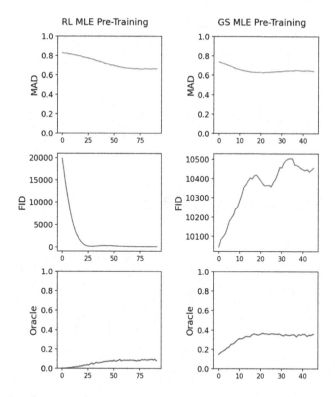

Fig. 2. Metrics of generated sequences over pre-training steps for Reinforcement Learning (RL) and Gumbel-Softmax (GS).

From the perspective of metric curves, we noticed that in the pre-training of RL, the FID score of the generator decayed sharply from around $20,000$ to around 100, while the improvements of MAD score and oracle score were stalling. It suggested that the MLE training was over-fitting in learning the continuous distribution of the time interval Δt, while paying much less effort to learn the patterns in the discrete event type x, and the relationships and hidden connections between the continuous and the discrete parts.

Comparing the performance of RL and Gumbel-Softmax training approaches, we found that the RL approach converged faster in pre-training and training with smoother metrics curves, but it was vulnerable to over-fitting and Gaussian model collapsing. Meanwhile, the Gumbel-Softmax approach converged slower with more curve oscillations, but it was less prone to over-fitting, even with the entropy regularizers in reward.

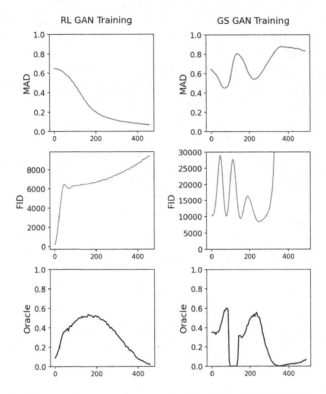

Fig. 3. Metrics of generated sequences over training steps for Reinforcement Learning (RL) and Gumbel-Softmax (GS).

5   Conclusions

In this paper, we have described, trained, and evaluated a novel methodology for generating artificial sequences with multi-type tokens. As this task poses new challenges, we have presented and compared the policy gradient (RL) and Gumbel-Softmax approaches for training a multi-type GAN. The generator proposed in this paper is capable of generating multi-type temporal sequences with non-uniform time intervals. We have also proposed using multiple criteria to measure the quality of the generated sequences. Experiments demonstrate that the generated multi-type sequences contain the desired properties.

Furthermore, we compared the performance of our generator for both RL and GS approaches with data from our carefully designed synthetic dataset. We concluded that the SeqGAN-trained generator has a higher performance compared to pre-trained generators using self-regression MLE, measured by multiple criteria including MAD, FID, oracle scores that are appropriate for evaluating multi-type sequences.

Acknowledgments. The authors would like to thank Unity for giving the opportunity to work on this project during Unity's HackWeek 2020.

References

1. Ba, H.: Improving detection of credit card fraudulent transactions using generative adversarial networks. arXiv preprint arXiv:1907.03355 (2019)
2. Bhatnagar, S., Sutton, R.S., Ghavamzadeh, M., Lee, M.: Natural gradient actor-critic algorithms. Automatica (2007)
3. Borji, A.: Pros and cons of GAN evaluation measures. Comput. Vis. Image Underst. **179**, 41–65 (2019)
4. Chapelle, O., Manavoglu, E., Rosales, R.: Simple and scalable response prediction for display advertising. ACM Trans. Intell. Syst. Technol. (TIST) **5**(4), 1–34 (2014)
5. Choi, J.A., Lim, K.: Identifying machine learning techniques for classification of target advertising. ICT Express (2020)
6. De Cao, N., Kipf, T.: MolGAN: an implicit generative model for small molecular graphs. arXiv preprint arXiv:1805.11973 (2018)
7. Deng, C., Wang, H., Tan, Q., Xu, J., Gai, K.: Calibrating user response predictions in online advertising. In: Dong, Y., Mladenić, D., Saunders, C. (eds.) ECML PKDD 2020. LNCS (LNAI), vol. 12460, pp. 208–223. Springer, Cham (2021). https://doi.org/10.1007/978-3-030-67667-4_13
8. DeVries, T., Romero, A., Pineda, L., Taylor, G.W., Drozdzal, M.: On the evaluation of conditional GANs. arXiv preprint arXiv:1907.08175 (2019)
9. Dieng, A.B., Ruiz, F.J., Blei, D.M., Titsias, M.K.: Prescribed generative adversarial networks. arXiv preprint arXiv:1910.04302 (2019)
10. Esteban, C., Hyland, S.L., Rätsch, G.: Real-valued (medical) time series generation with recurrent conditional GANs. arXiv preprint arXiv:1706.02633 (2017)
11. Goodfellow, I., et al.: Generative adversarial nets. In: Advances in Neural Information Processing Systems, pp. 2672–2680 (2014)
12. Guimaraes, G.L., Sanchez-Lengeling, B., Outeiral, C., Farias, P.L.C., Aspuru-Guzik, A.: Objective-reinforced generative adversarial networks (organ) for sequence generation models. arXiv preprint arXiv:1705.10843 (2017)
13. Haddadi, H.: Fighting online click-fraud using bluff ads. ACM SIGCOMM Comput. Commun. Rev. **40**(2), 21–25 (2010)
14. Haider, C.M.R., Iqbal, A., Rahman, A.H., Rahman, M.S.: An ensemble learning based approach for impression fraud detection in mobile advertising. J. Netw. Comput. Appl. **112**, 126–141 (2018)
15. Heusel, M., Ramsauer, H., Unterthiner, T., Nessler, B., Hochreiter, S.: GANs trained by a two time-scale update rule converge to a local Nash equilibrium. In: Advances in Neural Information Processing Systems, pp. 6626–6637 (2017)
16. Jang, E., Gu, S., Poole, B.: Categorical reparameterization with gumbel-softmax. arXiv preprint arXiv:1611.01144 (2016)
17. Kapoor, K.K., Dwivedi, Y.K., Piercy, N.C.: Pay-per-click advertising: a literature review. Mark. Rev. **16**(2), 183–202 (2016)
18. Killoran, N., Lee, L.J., Delong, A., Duvenaud, D., Frey, B.J.: Generating and designing DNA with deep generative models. arXiv preprint arXiv:1712.06148 (2017)
19. Kudugunta, S.: Deep neural networks for bot detection. Inf. Sci. **467**, 312–322 (2018)
20. Kusner, M.J., Hernández-Lobato, J.M.: GANs for sequences of discrete elements with the gumbel-softmax distribution. arXiv preprint arXiv:1611.04051 (2016)
21. Mouawi, R., Elhajj, I.H., Chehab, A., Kayssi, A.: Crowdsourcing for click fraud detection. EURASIP J. Inf. Secur. **2019**(1), 11 (2019)

22. Nagaraja, S., Shah, R.: Clicktok: click fraud detection using traffic analysis. In: Proceedings of the 12th Conference on Security and Privacy in Wireless and Mobile Networks, pp. 105–116 (2019)
23. Neunert, M., et al.: Continuous-discrete reinforcement learning for hybrid control in robotics. arXiv preprint arXiv:2001.00449 (2020)
24. Oentaryo, R., et al.: Detecting click fraud in online advertising: a data mining approach. J. Mach. Learn. Res. **15**(1), 99–140 (2014)
25. Salimans, T., Goodfellow, I., Zaremba, W., Cheung, V., Radford, A., Chen, X.: Improved techniques for training GANs. In: Advances in Neural Information Processing System, vol. 29, pp. 2234–2242 (2016)
26. Sutton, R.S., Barto, A.G.: Reinforcement Learning: An Introduction. MIT Press, Cambridge (2018)
27. Thomas, K., et al.: Investigating commercial pay-per-install and the distribution of unwanted software. In: 25th USENIX Security Symposium (USENIX Security 2016), pp. 721–739 (2016)
28. Yu, L., Zhang, W., Wang, J., Yu, Y.: SeqGAN: sequence generative adversarial nets with policy gradient. In: Thirty-First AAAI Conference on Artificial Intelligence (2017)
29. Zhao, P., Shui, T., Zhang, Y., Xiao, K., Bian, K.: Adversarial oracular seq2seq learning for sequential recommendation. In: Proceedings of the Twenty-Ninth International Joint Conference on Artificial Intelligence, IJCAI, pp. 1905–1911 (2020)
30. Zheng, P., Yuan, S., Wu, X., Li, J., Lu, A.: One-class adversarial nets for fraud detection. In: Proceedings of the AAAI Conference on Artificial Intelligence, vol. 33, pp. 1286–1293 (2019)

Recognizing Skeleton-Based Hand Gestures by a Spatio-Temporal Network

Xin Li(i), Jun Liao(i), and Li Liu(✉)(i)

School of Big Data and Software Engineering, Chongqing University,
Chongqing 401331, China
{cquxinli,liaojun,dcsliuli}@cqu.edu.cn

Abstract. A key challenge in skeleton-based hand gesture recognition is the fact that a gesture can often be performed in several different ways, with each consisting of its own configuration of poses and their spatio-temporal dependencies. This leads us to define a spatio-temporal network model that explicitly characterizes these internal configurations of poses and their local spatio-temporal dependencies. The model introduces a latent vector variable from the coordinates embedding to characterize these unique fine-grained configurations among joints of a particular hand gesture. Furthermore, an attention scorer is devised to exchange joint-pose information in the encoder structure, and as a result, all local spatio-temporal dependencies are globally consistent. Empirical evaluations on two benchmark datasets and one in-house dataset suggest our approach significantly outperforms the state-of-the-art methods.

Keywords: Hand gesture recognition · Skeleton data · Spatio-temporal dependency · Feature consistency

1 Introduction

Hand gesture recognition has become an active research field, given its role in facilitating a broad range of applications in human-computer interaction such as touchless interfaces [13] and human behavior understanding [12]. Computer vision-based approaches have been at the forefront of this field. In particular, current techniques are becoming mature to recognize static hand poses from 3D skeleton collection devices like the Leap Motion Controller. Compared with RGB-D images, skeleton-based approaches have the advantages of smaller data size, leading to less computational costs, and are robust to complex phenomena such as variable lighting effects and occlusions. For example, hand poses like grasp can be collected by depth sensors with their 3D skeleton data recording the locations of hand joints. Such *pose* consists of a fixed number of hand bones and joints and can be inferred from a single video frame.

The main focus of this paper is on dynamic hand gesture recognition, where a *gesture* is a collection of spatio-temporally related hand poses, with each being detected in a single frame. However, a key challenge in hand gesture recognition

© Springer Nature Switzerland AG 2021
Y. Dong et al. (Eds.): ECML PKDD 2021, LNAI 12978, pp. 151–167, 2021.
https://doi.org/10.1007/978-3-030-86514-6_10

is the fact that a hand gesture can often be performed in several different ways, with each consisting of its own configuration of poses and their spatio-temporal dependencies. For instance, it is found that there are 17 different hand shapes to perform a grasp [8]. In addition, individuals often possess diverse styles of performing the same hand gestures, and consequently, it is rather challenge to manage similar or intricate relations with skeleton data that only involves simple coordinate information. Accordingly, understanding hand gestures requires not only the detection of hand poses, but also the interpretation of their rich spatio-temporal dependencies. That is to say, a dynamic hand gesture recognition model should capture inherent structures associated with individual poses as well as their spatio-temporal dependencies.

Despite being a very challenging problem, in recent years there has been a rapid growth of interest in modeling and recognizing articulated hand gestures. Traditional approaches have gained attention in recent years for addressing hand gesture recognition problems. These approaches are often rich in modeling internal relations among poses by leveraging expert knowledge about kinematics and employing hand-crafted features of 3D joint positions like Fisher Vector [5], SPD matrices [18], joint distances [23] to characterize gesture sequences. These approaches have the advantages of being semantically clear, logically elegant, and reusable. However, these manually encoded features need to be carefully defined by domain experts, which could be rather difficult to scale up and is almost impossible for many practical scenarios where spatio-temporal relations among poses are intricate. In addition, they can only manage the connections between joints but often ignore the useful information from a single joint, and as a result, it would be fairly limited to build a unified model for representing these various features.

On the other hand, the most popular modeling paradigm might be that of the deep neural networks, which include techniques such as recurrent neural network (RNN), long short-term memory model (LSTM) and gated recurrent unit (GRU). Due to the capacity of generating high-level semantic features in the latent space, it is not surprising that these neural network-based models generally surpass their conventional counterparts that only consider utilizing joint-level information by a large margin. However, they have difficulties in capturing rich fine-grained (low-level or joint-level) spatial relationships among joints [11]. In fact, these models mostly focus on coarse-grained (high-level or pose-level) spatial information (e.g. taking all the joints as a whole in a pose and describing their relations between two adjacent frames on pose level), ignoring internal joint dependency within a single frame and external joint relations among different frames. As a result, only spatial relations associated with entire hand can be sufficiently captured. They often cannot distinguish between two similar gestures like *grab* and *pinch*, which only differ in the degrees of bending of the fingers, as illustrated in Fig. 1. Moreover, most of the existing approaches adopt *shake* gesture, which only repeats a fixed style of regular movements, to demonstrate their superiority on dynamic recognition. However, we found these models can only perform well on such simple gestures but not others (e.g. *Danbian* in Tai Chi gestures, which contains complex grasping and rotating movements), especially for the gestures with complicate discipline.

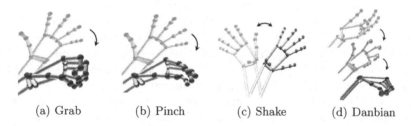

(a) Grab   (b) Pinch   (c) Shake   (d) Danbian

Fig. 1. Visualization of different skeleton-based hand gestures. Note that *Danbian* is a Tai Chi gesture from our in-house dataset TaiChi2021 collected by ourself.

To address the above issues in hand gesture recognition, we present a skeleton-based spatio-temporal network to explicitly model the skeletal context of spatio-temporal relations. In particular, our approach considers a principled way of dealing with the inherit structural variability in hand gestures. Briefly speaking, to describe an articulated hand, we first propose to introduce a set of latent vector variables, named coordinates embedding, to represent several separate kinematic locations of hand joints. Now each resulting vector from the coordinates embedding representation contains its unique set of high-level poses together with their low-level joint features of spatial information. To fully characterize a certain cluster of instances that possess similar hand gestures and their spatio-temporal dependencies, a spatio-temporal network is devised to encode the spatial relationships along with the temporal relations. Specifically, a unit variable that represents a joint in a frame is updated by exchanging information with other unit variables from the same frame and different frames, allowing our model to manage both spatial and temporal dependencies among joints from various frames. In addition, an attention scorer is incorporated into the units in each layer to capture pose-level spatio-temporal relations, and subsequently it ensures feature consistency between the high-level pose space and the low-level joint space without loss of their internal spacial relations. In this way, our network-based approach is more capable of characterizing the inherit spatio-temporal structural variability in hand gestures when compared to existing methods, which is also verified during empirical evaluations on two publicly-available datasets and one in-house dataset (Tai Chi gestures) collected by ourselves, which will be detailed in later sections.

2   Related Work

2.1   Hand Pose and Gesture Representation

There are typically three categories to represent hand poses and gestures: sensor-based representation, RGB-based representation and skeleton-based representation. We refer the interested readers to the excellent literatures [14,20] for the first two approaches. Here we mainly focus on skeleton-based representation, which has attracted a lot of attentions owing to its robustness against viewpoint change and the geometric description of rigid body. Such representation regards skeleton as a set of independent joint points with 3D coordinates to represent a hand pose. Besides, gesture representation is also very important that it should effectively capture the spatio-temporal dynamic characteristics of joints from a collection of time-ordered coordinates. Three most common methods are Euler angle representation, unit quaternion representation and manifold-based representation. However, they suffers from their unique challenges: the Euler angle representation is subjected to non-intrinsic singularity or gimbal lock issue, which leads to numerical and analytical difficulty; the unit quaternions approach leads to singularity-free parametrization of rotation matrices, but at the cost of one additional parameter; and the manifold-based approaches such as Lie group-based representation was found that their relative geometry provides a more sensible description compared to absolute locations of one joint. Moreover, most of existing approaches are specifically designed for human body representation, which is hard to deploy in hand scenarios where the structure of hand joints cannot be duplicated directly from that of full body. This inspires us to employ the coordinates embedding to describe an articulated hand to retain its skeletal location restrictions on hand joints.

2.2 Hand Gesture Recognition

Many studies focus on encoding input motion sequences to characterize the kinematic features for enhancing hand gesture recognition. As aforementioned in the introduction section, conventional approaches such as SVM and HMM [1,5,9] need to be handcrafted from domain knowledge. Therefore, deep neural networks are commonly used to detect motions in recent years. RNN-based approaches were widely implemented for motion modeling, which were adopted to capture the temporal features. Chen et al. [2] used bidirectional LSTM to model hand motion features (rotation and translation), while Maghoumi et al. [16] chose GRU to directly process raw skeleton data for gesture recognition. However, neither of them takes into account the spatio-temporal connections between joints, and they are computationally expensive and difficult for parallel computing due to the sequential structure of RNN. In such cases CNN-based methods like STA-Res-TCN [10] are introduced to address such issues of managing spatial relationship and improving the training speed for skeleton-based gesture recognition. DD-Net [23] employs 1D CNN with two embedded features (one between joint points and one between frames, both of which require manual calculation) without considering the connection between various joints on different frames. Liu et al. [15] combines 3D CNN and 2D CNN to characterize spatial and temporal features for hand poses and movements separately, but neglects the connection between the two features. TCN, a variant of CNN, is used to capture the spatio-temporal relationship in skeleton data [10]. All of these models are capable of handling coarse-grained spatial relationships, but unfortunately they are weak in maintaining fine-grained spatial information sufficiently.

To fully exploiting spatio-temporal features, geometric deep learning such as manifolds and graphs [17,22] is applied to skeleton-based gesture recognition. DG-STA [3] constructs a fully-connected graph from the hand skeleton, representing the spatio-temporal relations by connecting the joint points in the same frame and between adjacent frames. ST-TS-HGR-NET [17] uses SPD matrices to represent temporal relationships of hand joints in the graph. However, these approaches are limited to capture the local spatio-temporal features of joints interactively among different frames. To address the problems in these models (as mentioned in the introduction section), we present the spatio-temporal network to explicitly capture the inherent structural varieties of skeleton motions with spatio-temporal dependencies.

3 Problem Formulation

3.1 Definition

Give a dataset $\mathcal{D}$ of M samples from a set of C hand gestures, a spatio-temporal neural network is constructed with respect to the spatial and temporal relations among low-level joints and high-level poses. Each sample is a sequence of T frames measured in time and spaced at uniform time intervals. In the field of skeleton-based hand gesture recognition, it is usually described as a sequence of hand poses in ordered frames, with each being consisting of a collection of hand joints' position information (such as 3D Cartesian coordinates) at a certain frame. Formally, given a sample of hand gesture $\mathbf{g} = <\mathbf{p}_t | t = 1, 2, \ldots, T>$, a pose $\mathbf{p}_t$ is associated with a certain joints' configuration of the hand skeleton at the t-th frame, which is composed of the 3D coordinates of joints. We denote it as $\mathbf{p}_t = \{\mathbf{j}_{tn} | n = 1, 2, \ldots, N\}$, where $\mathbf{j}_{tn}$ is a 3-dimensional vector representing the 3D coordinates of the n-th joint at the t-th frame, i.e., $\mathbf{j}_{tn} = [x_{tn}, y_{tn}, z_{tn}]$. N is the number of joints, and here, $N = 22$ in hand skeleton.

3.2 Embedding Representation for Skeletal Data

It is hardly to represent the spatial relations directly within a joint by only using such simple and raw 3-dimensional coordinates. To further characterize the internal spatial features of a hand joint, there are typically two types of embedding representations, i.e., *interaction embedding*, where interactive relations between any two coordinates of a joint are embedded into the skeleton-based feature space, thereby describing local spatial dependencies of the coordinates in the same joint at a certain frame such as $x_{tn} \oplus y_{tn}$ ($\oplus$ refers to a binary operation such as addition, subtraction, multiplication), and *polynomial embedding*, which may simply power the feature to form a new one, e.g., x_{tn}^2 and x_{tn}^3, or to further complicate the matter, $\sum_{i,j,k=0}^{\infty} \theta_{ijk} x_{tn}^i y_{tn}^j z_{tn}^k$ (θ is a constant parameter).

However, these two embedding representations suffer from catastrophic error degradation when the raw coordinates exists bias. They will exaggerate such errors, and thus they are not robust to hand motion drifts, which often occurs in skeleton-based hand gesture recognition. Furthermore, their new generated features are built though the joint compensation of the effects of all monomials or polynomials of different order, and because these are unbounded, a slight deviation over that range will surely break such joint compensation and some term will dominate over the other, leading to rapid deviation, which is unsuitable for extrapolation. In addition, the number of monomials and their composition mechanisms should be manually formulated, which is impractical in the scenarios of complex hand gesture recognition. This inspires us to introduce in what follows a novel embedding representation, named *coordinates embedding*, which can be automatically learned through a spatio-temporal neural network defined in the next section.

Coordinates Embedding. Different from other embedding representations, our approach aims to map the three-dimensional coordinates of a joint into a higher-dimensional vector in a simple but effective way, rather than merely increasing the number of features. Formally, the coordinates embedding maps each $\mathbf{j}_{tn}$ into a latent vector of size λ, as defined as follows:

$$\hat{\mathbf{j}}_{tn} = \mathbf{W}^{(0)} \times \mathbf{j}_{tn} + \mathbf{B}^{(0)} = \begin{bmatrix} w_{1x} & w_{1y} & w_{1z} \\ \vdots & \vdots & \vdots \\ w_{\lambda x} & w_{\lambda y} & w_{\lambda z} \end{bmatrix} \cdot \begin{bmatrix} x_{tn} \\ y_{tn} \\ z_{tn} \end{bmatrix} + \begin{bmatrix} b_1 \\ \vdots \\ b_\lambda \end{bmatrix}, \qquad (1)$$

where $\mathbf{W}^{(0)}$ is a weight matrix of size 3λ, and $\mathbf{B}^{(0)}$ is a bias vector of size λ. $\hat{\mathbf{j}}_{tn}$ is the new coordinates embedding features of the joint n at the frame t, which can fully characterize the internal spatial dependencies on the low-level coordinates in any joint. In the end, the skeleton are mapped to a series of coordinates embedding vectors: $\hat{\mathbf{J}} = [\hat{\mathbf{j}}_{11}, \hat{\mathbf{j}}_{12}, \ldots, \hat{\mathbf{j}}_{1N}, \ldots, \hat{\mathbf{j}}_{T1}, \hat{\mathbf{j}}_{T2}, \ldots, \hat{\mathbf{j}}_{TN}]$.

In this way, all the generated features can form a joint network-based feature space that describes a unique hand gesture. This inspires us to present in what follows a spatio-temporal model where these joint-pose feature-based networks can be systematically constructed to characterize the hand gestures of interests.

4   Our Model

It is known that the spatio-temporal relations of joint-pose dependencies can be described by an encoder-decoder structure in hand gesture recognition. Given a hand gesture sample consisting of a sequence of poses $\mathbf{g} = <\mathbf{p}_1, \mathbf{p}_2, \ldots, \mathbf{p}_T>$, the spatio-temporal relationship among various joints in the same frame or among different frames can be characterized by leveraging the coordinates embedding in our encoder-classifier structure, which a spatio-temporal neural network that can be divided into two parts: a *spatio-temporal feature encoder* and a *network-based classifier*, as illustrated in Fig. 2. In summary, we employ the feature encoder to map both the raw skeletal data $\mathbf{J}$ and its corresponding coordinates embedding $\hat{\mathbf{J}}$ into a unified spatio-temporal feature space that characterizes gesture motions. It is also worth noting that an attention scorer is incorporated to ensure feature

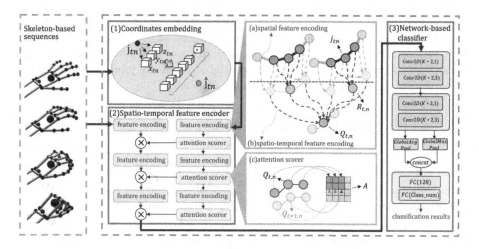

Fig. 2. The framework of our approach.

consistency between the high-level pose space and the low-level joint space. As for decoder, a simple network-based classifier is constructed with a collection of 2D convolutional layers and fully-connected layers.

4.1 Spatio-Temporal Feature Encoder

We argue that encoding raw skeletal data and their corresponding embedded data should facilitate learning a certain of information in their own latent space simultaneously. To this end, our model contains two streams that maintain their respective private features separately. Without loss of generality, we define a gesture sample **g** contains N joints in a time frame, with each joint being composed of a K-dimensional vector (e.g., $K = 3$ for raw data, and $K = \lambda$ for embedded data). It is worth noting that the private feature space can be easily extended to other embedding data such as interaction embedding and polynomial embedding in our model. For the convenience of understanding, **g** can be regarded as an image of size $T \times N \times K$, where K is considered as the number of channels. An element at location (t, n, k) in the image refers to the data point of joint n at frame t with the k-th information about the gesture. For each private encoder, our model divides the feature encoding procedure into two stages, namely, *spatial feature encoding* which discovers the interactions of adjacent joints within a certain frame, and *spatio-temporal feature encoding* which explicitly captures the temporal connections of spatial features among successive frames, and as a result can learn the fined-grained (or joint-level) features of the gesture **g**.

Spatial Feature Encoding. In this stage, we encode the spatial relations among adjacent joints in each frame to form a *spatial feature map* (Fig. 3). In details, take the raw feature space as an example, the feature map of raw skeletal data is denoted by $\mathbf{R}$, which has T frames, with each containing N *spatial states*, i.e., the spatial relations among U adjacent joints ($1 < U \le N$). Formally, $\mathbf{R} = \{\mathbf{R}_{t,n}|t = 1, \dots, T; n = 1, \dots, N\}$, where $\mathbf{R}_{t,n} = \{r_{t,n,k}|k = 1, 2, \dots, K\}$ is K-dimensional vector representing the spatial state of the joint n at the frame t. Its element $r_{t,n,k} \in \mathbf{R}$ can be calculated as follows:

$$r_{t,n,k} = \mathbf{J}_{t,n,U} * \mathbf{W}_k^{(11)} = \sum_{i=1}^{U}\sum_{j=1}^{K}\mathbf{j}_{t,n-1+i,j} \times w_{k,i,j}^{(11)}, \tag{2}$$

where $*$ means the convolutional product. $\mathbf{J}_{t,n,U}$ is a $U \times K$ matrix of the coordinates from the n-th joint to the $(n+U-1)$-th joint at the t-th frame, and $\mathbf{W}_k^{(11)}$ is a filtering matrix of size $U \times K$. Similarly, in the embedded feature space, the feature map of spatial states is denoted by $\hat{\mathbf{R}}$, where $\hat{r}_{t,n,k} = \hat{\mathbf{J}}_{t,n,U} * \mathbf{W}_k^{(12)}$. It is worth mentioning that to keep the same shape as the skeletal data (i.e., $N \times T \times K$) in these new feature maps, we set all the coordinates data $J_{t,n-1+i,j} = 0$ or $\hat{J}_{t,n-1+i,j} = 0$ when $n - 1 + i > N$.

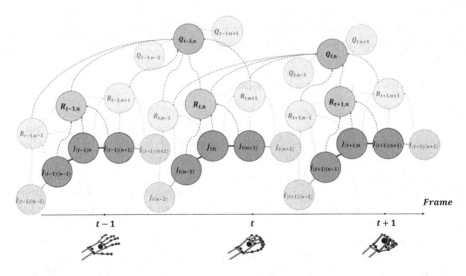

Fig. 3. Illustration of dataflows that update spatial feature states and spatio-temporal feature states in our model. The spatial state $\mathbf{R}_{t,n}$ is updated by exchanging information with the states of multiple joints (blue dashed line), while the spatio-temporal state $\mathbf{Q}_{t,n}$ is updated according to multiple spatial states $\mathbf{R}_{t,n}$ in different time frames (red dashed line). (Color figure online)

Spatio-Temporal Feature Encoding. To further capture the spatio-temporal relations among joints from different frames, we continue to generate the *spatio-temporal feature map* based on the spatial feature map (Fig. 3). It maps the spatial states into a spatio-temporal space of N spatial relations among V

adjacent joints $(1 < V \leq N)$ in H successive frames $(1 < H \leq T)$ over all the T frames. We call such features as *spatio-temporal states*. Mathematically, $\mathbf{Q} = \{\mathbf{Q}_{t,n}|t = 1, \ldots, T; n = 1, \ldots, N\}$, where $\mathbf{Q}_{t,n} = \{q_{t,n,k}|k = 1, \ldots, K\}$, representing the spatio-temporal states of joint n at frame t. In details, $q_{t,n,k}$ is computed by:

$$q_{t,n,k} = \mathbf{R}_{t,n,V} * \mathbf{W}_k^{(21)} = \sum_{h=1}^{H}\sum_{i=1}^{V}\sum_{j=1}^{K} r_{t-1+h,2n-2+i,j} \times w_{k,h,i,j}^{(21)}, \qquad (3)$$

where $\mathbf{R}_{t,n,V}$ is a $H \times V \times K$ matrix of the spatial states indicating the V adjacent joints among the H successive frames in $\mathbf{R}$, and $\mathbf{W}_k^{(21)}$ is a filtering matrix of size $H \times V \times K$. Likewise, we can also obtain the spatio-temporal feature map in embedded feature space denoted by $\hat{\mathbf{Q}}$, where $\hat{q}_{t,n,k} = \hat{\mathbf{R}}_{t,n,V} * \mathbf{W}_k^{(22)}$.

4.2   Attention Scorer

It is straightforward to obtain final features by adding an attention mechanism, which can capture long-term dependencies during our encoding process. We consider the pyramid contextual attention from PEN-Net [24], which uses attention at different joints. However, it is computationally expensive to calculate attention scores of feature states for all the joints. Inspired by DG-STA [3], we further adopt a shared attention scores to reduce the computational cost.

To reduce the number of trainable parameters and interchange the features between raw data and embedded data, we combine $\mathbf{Q}$ in the raw feature space and $\hat{\mathbf{Q}}$ in the embedded feature space by defining a *feature weight matrix*. Specifically, a scoring function is designed to calculate the attention weight of each spatio-temporal state in the raw skeletal feature map $\mathbf{Q}$ to determine the importance of each state, thereby obtaining the feature weight matrix of $T \times N$, represented by $\mathbf{A} = \{a_{t,n}|t = 1, \ldots, T; n = 1, \ldots, N\}$, with each $a_{t,n}$ being calculated as follows:

$$a_{t,n} = \frac{1}{1 + e^{-\sum_{k=1}^{K}(w_k^{(3)} \times q_{t,n,k} + b_k^{(3)})}}, \qquad (4)$$

where $w_k^{(3)} \in \mathbf{W}^{(3)}$ is the weight parameter for the k-th channel and $b_k^{(3)} \in \mathbf{B}^{(3)}$ is the bias.

By adhering to the principle that the importance of features will be enlarged or reduced by weight, we combine the embedded feature maps with the feature weight matrix to get a final spatio-temporal feature map $\mathbf{M}$ that is capable of highlighting the most critical features with a shape of $T \times N \times K$. Here, $\mathbf{M} = \{m_{t,n,k}|t = 1, \ldots, T; n = 1, \ldots, N; k = 1, \ldots, K\}$, where

$$m_{t,n,k} = \hat{q}_{t,n,k} \times a_{t,n}. \qquad (5)$$

In this way, the shared space generated by the attention scorer ensures feature consistency between the raw skeleton space and the embedded coordinate space without loss of their internal spacial relations at joint level.

4.3   Network-Based Classifier

Now we are ready to build a dynamic hand gesture recognition classifier by treating these encoded feature maps as new inputs. In particular, during the training stage, we put all the generated features together to form a joint skeleton-based feature space. Within this joint skeleton-based feature space, each sample **g** from the c-th type of hand gesture in the training set can be represented by a feature map of size $T \times N \times K$, and each entry in the feature map represents a spatio-temporal weight value of the corresponding joint at a certain frame. Since neural network-based models are capable of learning high-level (or pose-level) spatial information, we can feed these low-level (or joint-level) feature maps into any appropriate network-based models for the recognition task. Here we train a simple neural network model as shown in Fig. 2, which consists of two convolutional blocks and one fully-connected block to achieve the tasks of hand gesture recognition. In our model, global average pooling and global maximum pooling are respectively used and concatenated to regularize the entire network structure to prevent overfitting.

For simplicity, we choose categorical cross-entropy as the loss function which is commonly used during network training:

$$Loss(\varphi, \hat{\varphi}) = -\sum_{c=1}^{C} \varphi_c \cdot \log \hat{\varphi}_c, \qquad (6)$$

where C is the number of classes, φ is the ground truth and $\hat{\varphi}$ is the prediction. Finally, the parameters $\mathbf{W} = \{\mathbf{W}^{(0)}, \mathbf{W}^{(11)}, \mathbf{W}^{(12)}, \mathbf{W}^{(21)}, \mathbf{W}^{(22)}, \mathbf{W}^{(3)}, \mathbf{W}^{(4)}, \mathbf{B}^{(0)}, \mathbf{B}^{(3)}\}$ in our encoder-classifier model can be estimated by optimizing the following objective over the dataset $\mathcal{D}$:

$$\hat{\mathbf{W}} = \underset{\mathbf{W}, \mathcal{D}}{\arg \min} \, Loss(\varphi, \hat{\varphi}), \qquad (7)$$

where $\mathbf{W}^{(4)}$ is the parameters in the network-based classifier. There are probably a number of $(2U + 2VH + 1)K^2 + 5K$ training parameters on $\mathbf{W}$, which is acceptable for dynamic hand gesture in practice.

5   Experiments

5.1   Datasets and Preprocessing

Three skeleton-based hand gesture datasets are considered in our experiments, including two publicly-available benchmark datasets and one in-house dataset on Tai Chi gestures collected by ourselves.

DHG14/28 [5]. This publicly-available dataset contains 2,800 samples, including 14 gestures. Each gesture is performed five times in two finger configurations by 20 participants, and thus it can also be divided into 28 categories to discriminate such fine-grained finger gestures. We applied the same leave-one-subject-out training as that in [3,5,17] for fair comparison.

SHREC2017 [6]. It consists of 14 hand gestures performed by 28 individuals with a number of $2,800$ samples in two ways: using one finger, or the whole hand. The ratio of training and testing sequences is $7:3$.

TaiChi2021. To our best knowledge, the two above mentioned datasets are so far the only ones publicly available for the field of skeleton-based hand gesture recognition. In particular, the instances of these gestures are relatively simple without considering the fine-grained joint-level actions. To this end, we propose a new dataset about Tai Chi gestures on Leapmotion, which is an ongoing effort, and at the moment it contains $3,600$ annotated samples of nine gestures performed by 10 participants (five males and five females) on 20 hand joints. Each gesture is performed 20 runs by each participant with each hand. Considering the difference between left-hand and right-hand actions, the dataset was divided into 18 categories in our experiment. The ratio of training and testing sequences is $7:3$.

5.2   Experimental Set-Ups and Baselines

Our model is implemented by Keras with backend of Tensorflow. It is optimized by Adam optimizer ($\beta_1 = 0.9$ and $\beta_2 = 0.999$) with the learning rate of 1×10^{-3} and the step size of $e^{-0.1}$ on one GeForce GTX 750Ti GPU. We set the hyper-parameters $T = 32$, $\lambda = 32$, $U = 3$, $V = 9$ and $H = 3$. The batch size is fixed to 256. All the skeletal sequences are resampled with the same length of T by employing median filtering.

The classification performance of our model is compared 2 conventional methods and 13 network-based methods. For fair comparison, we did not apply any data augmentation or pre-trained weights to boost the performance. *Accuracy* is employed as the evaluation metric, which is computed as the proportion of true results among the total number of samples.

5.3   Comparison Results on Publicly-Available Datasets

Table 1 depicts the comparison results with Accuracy. Our model clearly outperforms the other models with a large margin on all two datasets. This is mainly due to their abilities to take advantage of the rich spatio-temporal dependency information among both low-level joints and high-level poses. Notably, although network-based models such as GCN family encode spatio-temporal information, during training they neglect all the low-level relations among joints at the same frame and among different frames. This might explain why STA-GCN performs slightly better than our model on SHREC2017(14) involving simple spatial relations, but most of such models give much worse performance on 28 gestures than that on 14 gestures where more complicate relationships are required to be handled at joint level. Unfortunately, these models are rather limited in characterizing such fine-grained information.

Table 1. Accuracy comparisons on DHG14/28 and SHREC2017. The percentage in the bracket shows the accuracy change taken our approach as a baseline. − means not applicable in this case.

Methods	Accuracy (%)			
	DHG(14)	DHG(28)	SHREC(14)	SHREC(28)
SoCJ+HoHD+HoWR [5]	83.1(−10.2)	80.0(−11.8)	88.2(−7.1)	81.9(−11.7)
GST+AG [4]	82.5(−10.8)	68.1(−23.7)	88.2(−7.1)	81.9(−11.7)
CNN+LSTM [19]	85.6(−7.7)	81.1(−10.7)	−	−
MF-RNN [2]	84.6(−8.7)	80.4(−11.4)	−	−
DPTC [21]	85.8(−7.5)	80.2(−11.6)	−	−
Res-TCN [10]	86.9(−6.4)	83.6(−8.2)	91.1(−4.2)	87.3(−6.3)
STA-Res-TCN [10]	89.2(−4.1)	85.0(−6.8)	93.6(−1.7)	90.7(−2.9)
P-CNN [7]	91.2(−2.1)	84.3(−7.5)	−	−
DeepGRU [16]	−	−	94.5(−0.8)	91.4(−2.2)
ST-GCN [22]	91.2(−2.1)	87.1(−4.7)	92.7(−2.6)	87.7(−5.9)
DG-STA [3]	91.9(−1.4)	88.0(−3.8)	94.4(−0.9)	90.7(−2.9)
ST-TS-HGR-NET [17]	87.3(−6.0)	83.4(−8.4)	94.2(−1.1)	89.4(−4.2)
DD-Net [23]	−	−	94.6(−0.7)	91.9(−1.7)
STA-GCN [25]	91.5(−1.8)	87.7(−4.1)	**95.4(+0.1)**	91.8(−1.8)
HPEV-HMM-NET [15]	92.5(−0.8)	88.8(−3.0)	94.8(−0.5)	92.2(−0.7)
Ours	**93.3**	**91.8**	95.3	**93.6**

5.4   Comparisons Results on TaiChi2021

Unlike the two publicly-available datasets, TaiChi2021 dataset is more challenging due to its stochastic nature which causes difficulties to category its gestures. The quantitative results of the comparison with other competing models as well as the performance of our model on each Tai Chi gestures are reported in Fig. 4. It can be observed that our model is relative more accurate to distinguish among these hand gestures than other three competing models. It also can be seen that our model is faster than other methods on convergence, and consequently facilitates the training optimization process. For instance, *Grasp* and *Danbian* are more challenging than others because they contain more finger movements than hand movements. Fortunately, our model can effectively encode fingers' joint relations and hand's pose relations simultaneously. In contrast, other models encode high-level sequential relations between poses only. In addition, it is clear that our model performs better than other models on distinguishing between two similar gestures *Rise* and *Up*, which only differ in the bending degrees of the fingers. This might be that some Tai Chi gestures only change their finger motions slightly. It can verify our conjecture that our spatio-temporal learning network can capture these fine-grained changes, but others may suffer from the similarity indistinguishability issue. Also, we compared the convergence speed

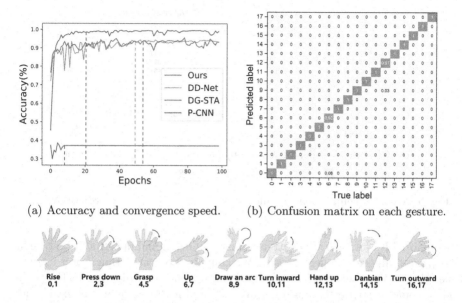

(a) Accuracy and convergence speed.   (b) Confusion matrix on each gesture.

Fig. 4. Comparisons of the competing methods on TaiChi2021 dataset. The odd (resp. even) labels indicate left-hand (resp. right-hand) gestures.

of our model against that of P-CNN as the baseline. For the sake of fairness, they are trained under the same settings on the parameters such as batch sizes. Figure 4(a) shows the comparison results of their performance metrics in the first 100 epochs. It can be seen that our model is faster than other competing models on convergence, and consequently facilitates the training optimization process.

5.5 Ablation Study

In this section, we conduct two ablation studies to measure the effectiveness of the modules in our model. It is worth noting that we show the results on SHREC2017 here, and the studies from other datasets are not shown due to page limitation, but similar results are obtained in our experiment.

Coordinates Embedding. We evaluate the effectiveness of coordinates embedding by varying the size of embedded features λ. We used the same parameter settings depicted in Sect. 5.2. As shown in Fig. 5(a), it is obvious that there is an improvement in accuracy when λ grows to 32, and a slight decline when λ is larger than 128. This is mainly because the duration of poses in a gesture is very short. For instance, *Tap*, which happens rapidly, are only associated with a handful of frames. Consequently, the coordinates embedding vector is overfitted when a large feature size is set, leading to fake relations remained in the spatio-temporal network, which is harmful to the model training. In addition, a very large value of λ may result in computational burden.

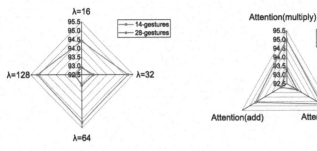

(a) Changes on different λ.   (b) Changes on different attention mechanisms.

Fig. 5. Accuracy comparisons of different settings of our model on SHREC2017.

Attention Mechanism. The attention mechanism is an important structure in our spatio-temporal feature encoder. We compared our attention scorer against other three commonly used structures, the difference of which lies in the ways how to combine spatio-temporal feature map and feature weight matrix, including multiplication, connection, and addition. Figure 5(b) reports the comparison results of average accuracy on all the gestures. It can be found that the multiplication performs slightly better than other two mechanisms due to its capability of reducing encoder states $\mathbf{R}_{t,n}$ and $\mathbf{Q}_{t,n}$ into attention scores, by applying simple matrix multiplications. In general, the performance of multiplicative and additive functions are similar but the multiplicative function is faster and more space-efficient.

Component Effectiveness. We separately evaluate the effects of different components in our network by removing modules or replacing them with conventional methods. They are evaluated by testing for two types of investigations that are common with neural network models: coordinates embedding effects (i.e. remove coordinates embedding features and only remain raw skeletal features) and encoder component effects (i.e. replace our structured spatio-temporal encoder with a naïve CNN of two layers). Table 2 reports the comparison results on SHREC2017, which can be clearly seen that changing the components may lead to negative effects on the performance of our model. It is clear that when removing coordinates embedding features $\hat{\mathbf{J}}$, the performance drops faster than that changing other components. This might be due to the low-level encoding of fine-grained spatial information in our model. Besides, when using the naïve CNN encoder, the model gives worse performance than that using our spatio-temporal decoder, which indicates that our model is more effective to recognize joints, fingers, and hand gradually than obtaining them at the same time.

Table 2. Investigation of the impact of the components in our model. × refers to no such component, while √ means the reservation of it.

No.	Embedding	Encoder	14-gestures	28-gestures
1	×	×	94.8	93.0
2	√	×	95.2	93.2
3	×	√	95.0	93.3
4	√	√	**95.3**	**93.6**

6 Conclusion

In this paper, we present a spatio-temporal neural network with a coordinates embedding representation for skeletal data, which can capture the inherit spatial and temporal varieties of hand gestures at both joint and pose levels simultaneously. It is more efficient and flexible than existing methods on hand gesture recognition. As for future work, we will explore the applications of our model on raw image videos, and we will consider detecting multiple hand motions with probabilities and will instead learn a network recognizing gestures under uncertainty.

Acknowledgement. This work was supported by grants from the National Major Science and Technology Projects of China (grant no. 2018AAA0100703) and the National Natural Science Foundation of China (grant no. 61977012).

References

1. Canavan, S., Keyes, W., Mccormick, R., Kunnumpurath, J., Hoelzel, T., Yin, L.: Hand gesture recognition using a skeleton-based feature representation with a random regression forest. In: 2017 IEEE International Conference on Image Processing (ICIP), pp. 2364–2368. IEEE (2017)
2. Chen, X., Guo, H., Wang, G., Zhang, L.: Motion feature augmented recurrent neural network for skeleton-based dynamic hand gesture recognition. In: 2017 IEEE International Conference on Image Processing (ICIP), pp. 2881–2885. IEEE (2017)
3. Chen, Y., Zhao, L., Peng, X., Yuan, J., Metaxas, D.N.: Construct dynamic graphs for hand gesture recognition via spatial-temporal attention. arXiv preprint arXiv:1907.08871 (2019)
4. De Smedt, Q., Wannous, H., Vandeborre, J.-P.: 3D hand gesture recognition by analysing set-of-joints trajectories. In: Wannous, H., Pala, P., Daoudi, M., Flórez-Revuelta, F. (eds.) UHA3DS 2016. LNCS, vol. 10188, pp. 86–97. Springer, Cham (2018). https://doi.org/10.1007/978-3-319-91863-1_7
5. De Smedt, Q., Wannous, H., Vandeborre, J.P.: Skeleton-based dynamic hand gesture recognition. In: Proceedings of the IEEE Conference on Computer Vision and Pattern Recognition Workshops, pp. 1–9 (2016)
6. De Smedt, Q., Wannous, H., Vandeborre, J.P., Guerry, J., Le Saux, B., Filliat, D.: Shrec'17 track: 3D hand gesture recognition using a depth and skeletal dataset. In: 3DOR-10th Eurographics Workshop on 3D Object Retrieval, pp. 1–6 (2017)

7. Devineau, G., Moutarde, F., Xi, W., Yang, J.: Deep learning for hand gesture recognition on skeletal data. In: 2018 13th IEEE International Conference on Automatic Face & Gesture Recognition (FG 2018), pp. 106–113. IEEE (2018)
8. Feix, T., Pawlik, R., Schmiedmayer, H.B., Romero, J., Kragic, D.: A comprehensive grasp taxonomy. In: Robotics, Science and Systems: Workshop on Understanding the Human Hand for Advancing Robotic Manipulation, Seattle, WA, USA, vol. 2, pp. 2–3 (2009)
9. Ghotkar, A., Vidap, P., Deo, K.: Dynamic hand gesture recognition using hidden Markov model by Microsoft Kinect sensor. Int. J. Comput. Appl. **150**(5), 5–9 (2016)
10. Hou, J., Wang, G., Chen, X., Xue, J.H., Zhu, R., Yang, H.: Spatial-temporal attention res-TCN for skeleton-based dynamic hand gesture recognition. In: Proceedings of the European Conference on Computer Vision (ECCV) Workshops, pp. 273–286 (2018)
11. Hu, J.F., Fan, Z.C., Liao, J., Liu, L.: Predicting long-term skeletal motions by a spatio-temporal hierarchical recurrent network. In: the 24th European Conference on Artificial Intelligence (ECAI), pp. 2720–2727 (2020)
12. Sharath Kumar, Y.H., Vinutha, V.: Hand gesture recognition for sign language: a skeleton approach. In: Das, S., Pal, T., Kar, S., Satapathy, S.C., Mandal, J.K. (eds.) Proceedings of the 4th International Conference on Frontiers in Intelligent Computing: Theory and Applications (FICTA) 2015. AISC, vol. 404, pp. 611–623. Springer, New Delhi (2016). https://doi.org/10.1007/978-81-322-2695-6_52
13. Lee, D.H., Hong, K.S.: Game interface using hand gesture recognition. In: 5th International Conference on Computer Sciences and Convergence Information Technology, pp. 1092–1097. IEEE (2010)
14. Lin, H.I., Hsu, M.H., Chen, W.K.: Human hand gesture recognition using a convolution neural network. In: 2014 IEEE International Conference on Automation Science and Engineering (CASE), pp. 1038–1043. IEEE (2014)
15. Liu, J., Liu, Y., Wang, Y., Prinet, V., Xiang, S., Pan, C.: Decoupled representation learning for skeleton-based gesture recognition. In: Proceedings of the IEEE/CVF Conference on Computer Vision and Pattern Recognition, pp. 5751–5760 (2020)
16. Maghoumi, M., LaViola, J.J.: DeepGRU: deep gesture recognition utility. In: Bebis, G., et al. (eds.) ISVC 2019. LNCS, vol. 11844, pp. 16–31. Springer, Cham (2019). https://doi.org/10.1007/978-3-030-33720-9_2
17. Nguyen, X.S., Brun, L., Lézoray, O., Bougleux, S.: A neural network based on SPD manifold learning for skeleton-based hand gesture recognition. In: Proceedings of the IEEE/CVF Conference on Computer Vision and Pattern Recognition, pp. 12036–12045 (2019)
18. Nguyen, X.S., Brun, L., Lezoray, O., Bougleux, S.: Skeleton-based hand gesture recognition by learning SPD matrices with neural networks. In: 2019 14th IEEE International Conference on Automatic Face & Gesture Recognition (FG 2019), pp. 1–5. IEEE (2019)
19. Nunez, J.C., Cabido, R., Pantrigo, J.J., Montemayor, A.S., Velez, J.F.: Convolutional neural networks and long short-term memory for skeleton-based human activity and hand gesture recognition. Pattern Recogn. **76**, 80–94 (2018)
20. Pezzuoli, F., Corona, D., Corradini, M.L.: Recognition and classification of dynamic hand gestures by a wearable data-glove. SN Comput. Sci. **2**(1), 1–9 (2021)
21. Weng, J., Liu, M., Jiang, X., Yuan, J.: Deformable pose traversal convolution for 3D action and gesture recognition. In: Proceedings of the European Conference on Computer Vision (ECCV), pp. 136–152 (2018)

22. Yan, S., Xiong, Y., Lin, D.: Spatial temporal graph convolutional networks for skeleton-based action recognition. In: Proceedings of the AAAI Conference on Artificial Intelligence, vol. 32 (2018)
23. Yang, F., Wu, Y., Sakti, S., Nakamura, S.: Make skeleton-based action recognition model smaller, faster and better. In: Proceedings of the ACM Multimedia Asia, pp. 1–6 (2019)
24. Zeng, Y., Fu, J., Chao, H., Guo, B.: Learning pyramid-context encoder network for high-quality image inpainting. In: Proceedings of the IEEE/CVF Conference on Computer Vision and Pattern Recognition, pp. 1486–1494 (2019)
25. Zhang, W., Lin, Z., Cheng, J., Ma, C., Deng, X., Wang, H.: STA-GCN: two-stream graph convolutional network with spatial-temporal attention for hand gesture recognition. Vis. Comput. **36**(10), 2433–2444 (2020)

E-commerce and Finance

Smurf-Based Anti-money Laundering in Time-Evolving Transaction Networks

Michele Starnini[1]([✉]), Charalampos E. Tsourakakis[1,4], Maryam Zamanipour[1], André Panisson[1], Walter Allasia[2], Marco Fornasiero[2], Laura Li Puma[3], Valeria Ricci[3], Silvia Ronchiadin[3], Angela Ugrinoska[2], Marco Varetto[2], and Dario Moncalvo[2]

[1] ISI Foundation, via Chisola 5, 10126 Turin, Italy
{michele.starnini,babis.tsourakakis,maryam.zamanipour}@isi.it
[2] Intesa Sanpaolo, Corso Inghilterra 3, 10138 Turin, Italy
{walter.allasia,dario.moncalvo}@intesasanpaolo.com
[3] Intesa Sanpaolo Innovation Center, Corso Inghilterra 3, 10138 Turin, Italy
silvia.ronchiadin@intesasanpaolo.com
[4] Boston University, 111 Cummington Mall, Boston, MA 02215, USA

Abstract. Money laundering refers to the criminal attempt of concealing the origins of illegally obtained money, usually by passing it through a complex sequence of seemingly legitimate financial transactions through several financial institutions. Given a large time-evolving graph of financial transactions, how can we spot money laundering activities? In this work, we focus on detecting smurfing, a money-laundering technique that involves breaking up large amounts of money into multiple small transactions. Our key contribution is a method that efficiently finds suspicious smurf-like subgraphs. Specifically, we find that the velocity characteristics of smurfing allow us to find smurfs by using a standard database join, thus bypassing the computational complexity of the subgraph isomorphism problem. We apply our method on a real-world transaction graph spanning a period of six months, with more than 180M transactions involving more than 31M bank accounts, and we verify its efficiency. Finally, by a careful analysis of the suspicious motifs found, we provide a classification of smurf-like motifs into categories that shed light on how money launderers exploit geography, among other things, in their illicit transactions.

Keywords: Anti-money laundering · Graph mining · Subgraph isomorphism · Data mining

1 Introduction

Money laundering is an umbrella term, that captures the processing of criminal proceeds to disguise their illegal origin in order to legitimize the ill-gotten gains

---

M. Starnini, C. E. Tsourakakis and M. Zamanipour—Equal contribution.

© Springer Nature Switzerland AG 2021
Y. Dong et al. (Eds.): ECML PKDD 2021, LNAI 12978, pp. 171–186, 2021.
https://doi.org/10.1007/978-3-030-86514-6_11

of crime [12]. While this definition may not include money related to terror financing, which does not necessarily have a criminal origin, it is broad enough to cover all possible activities aimed at hiding the origin of illicitly gained assets. Money laundering has three well-defined stages: (i) placement, (ii) layering, and (iii) integration. Ebikake [10] describes in great detail how money launderers adapt to reality. In the placement stage, illicitly gained assets are introduced into the legitimate financial system while being cleansed of the most obvious traces of illegality. For example, forged documentation can be used to justify the money introduced as a legitimate receipt from the sales of real estate or interest in a business. In this phase, many different bank accounts across different banks can be used, or front companies that can belong even to high net-worth people. Once the money is deposited and its origin successfully explained, the placement stage is complete. In the layering phase, money-launders move around the money through a series of transactions that have no real purpose other than hiding the criminal nature of the money. For layering, money-launders may use banks in countries with poor law enforcement, or which do not cooperate with international financial authorities. Possible layering activities include investment in financial products which have good liquidity or which can be bought and sold easily with limited tracking (e.g. unlisted stocks and shares), real estate, fake loans that allow transfer of money to a business when in reality there is no loan, sending money overseas for education purposes, donations, and transferring money to shell companies [10]. Finally, in the integration stage, these assets are integrated into the legal economy and other assets can be legally purchased.

Despite the worldwide efforts against it, it is estimated that money laundering involves from 2% to 5% of the world's domestic product [13,29]. Fighting organized crime is of paramount importance for financial institutions: Failures in anti-money laundering (AML) controls may result in huge fines for financial institutions by national and foreign authorities. For example, Danske bank, the major Danish bank, faces a possible fine of around 2 billions euros for a money-laundering case of about 200 billions euros occurring through Danske's branch in Estonia, from 2007 to 2015 [15]. Recently, US authorities fined HSBC by 1.9 billion US dollars in a settlement over missing money laundering controls [19]. In order to comply with the current legislation, financial institutions generally follow several guidelines and recommendation, either official [3,12] or informal and internal best practices [20,21] that impose specific controls to be carried out on customers and on their activities/operations. These money-laundering controls have been historically implemented as a set of rules, such as fixed threshold flagging suspicious transactions, or transactions through countries considered at high risk, which are later manually inspected. Note that due to the heterogeneous financial services landscape and transaction means, there is no regulator guidance so technically detailed to play a standard-setting role. Each financial institution has thus the freedom and the responsibility to implement the controls with the techniques it deems most useful and efficient for the purpose. Such implementations are often made with deterministic approaches based on fixed rules and conditions to be calibrated over time and adapted to the various cases.

Rule-based approaches are simple to implement, but suffer from several drawbacks: rules need to be constantly updated, and performance of single rules is very difficult to disentangle. Furthermore, rule-based systems perform badly on unstructured data and expert knowledge is needed to design rules. Finally, as a result of poor rule-based system design and data quality issues, classifiers for spotting alerts tend to aim for high recall by introducing a large number of false positives, that have to be manually inspected later on.

Therefore, there is a need for new data-driven tools for anti-money laundering able to overcome rule-based approaches. In this paper, we will focus on the central stage of money-laundering, i.e. layering, to detect suspicious transactions aimed at hiding the real origin and target of money transfers. A common method used by money-launders is to break down the amount of money to launder into smaller amounts and through various entities. This structuring technique is known as "smurfing", where smurfs are the financial actors (either companies or physical persons) responsible for organizing money transfers. These multiple intermediaries make small cash deposits or buy assets in amounts under a certain threshold, which is thought to be relevant and more likely to be reported by the banks to financial authorities. In this way, they try to avoid raising suspicions. The detection of smurfs in financial transactions is a pivotal task in the financial industry [37]. Smurfs naturally translate into specific subgraph structures within transaction graphs, where nodes are financial actors (i.e. bank accounts) and links represent money transfers between accounts. It is worth mentioning that, in a completely different field, smurf-like structures play an important role in security applications, e.g., [8].

Here, we focus on the two smurf-like motifs shown in Fig. 1.

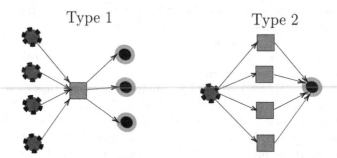

Fig. 1. Type 1 (left) and type 2 (right) smurf-like motifs. Source (red dotted circles), middle (squares), and target (green circles) are shown from left to right. (Color figure online)

The first motif consists of a set of source nodes that send money to a middle node, who then sends that money to a set of target nodes. The second motif consists of a single source, sending money to multiple middle nodes, who then send money to a single target node. We refer to these two subgraphs, as motif type 1, and motif type 2. We outline that the number of source and target nodes in motif type 1, and similarly the number of middle nodes in motif type 2 may vary. While prior domain knowledge gives certain bounds on these node counts, searching for each possible motif instantiation using a state-of-the-art subgraph isomorphism algorithm is computationally expensive, and infeasible on large-scale transaction graphs. Our contributions include the following:

- We propose a pipeline that efficiently finds suspicious smurf-like subgraphs as shown in Fig. 1. Our pipeline exploits the *velocity* of real-world money laundering transactions, and allows us to bypass the computational complexity lower bound of subgraph isomorphism. Perhaps surprisingly, our pipeline is based on a standard database join, and careful pre-, and post-processing filtering.
- We evaluate our pipeline on a large real-world transaction network with more than 184 million transactions using the financial services of a major Italian bank (from now on just referred as MIB). We observe that our pipeline allows us to find suspicious smurfs efficiently.
- We analyze the output motifs, and provide a systematic classification of suspicious motifs. For instance, we observe that certain suspicious motifs have a *u-turn* form. The source(s) and the target(s) are MIB bank accounts, whereas the middle node(s) is (are) non-MIB account(s), that may exist in high risk countries. Our classification sheds light into money launderers behavior, especially regarding how they exploit geography.

2   Related Work

For a general overview of machine learning, and data-driven techniques used for anti-money laundering, see the recent survey by Chen et al. [7]. Here, we briefly review work that lies close to ours.

Flowscope is a novel tool for discovering dense flows from sources to untraceable destinations via many middle accounts that on purpose create chains to avoid getting flagged. The key intuition behind Flowscope is that large amounts of money need to be transferred through "dummy" accounts that serve as intermediaries before the dirty money reaches the final destination(s). The authors focus on detecting dense multi-partite subgraphs. While the Flowscope formulation and the proposed algorithm are important contributions towards AML, there exist important money laundering schemes that use few intermediary accounts, and thus do not induce dense subgraphs. Furthermore, Flowscope relies on the assumption that intermediate accounts have low balance, namely, they receive a certain amount and transfer it almost entirely. Real bank transaction data available to MIB indicate that intermediary nodes may transfer an amount only approximately similar to the one received from the source. For the aforementioned reasons, Weber et al. use graph convolutional networks [23] for fighting money laundering in bitcoin transactions [36]. Their method takes as input the transaction network, possibly node features, and some labels that are used to train the neural network. Lee et al. [24] propose a minimum description length approach to reorder the node ids in order to reveal all smurf-like subgraphs in a transaction network. However, many of these smurf-like subgraphs do not correspond to money laundering activities. Such false positives have an immense cost. The false positives are between 75% and 99% of the total alerts issued. This consumes bank resources, and places in inconvenient spot entities and people that abide by the law.

Isomorphism. Graph isomorphism is the problem of determining whether two graphs G_1 and G_2 are isomorphic. Formally, this is equivalent to determining if there exists a bijective mapping f from the set of the nodes of G_1 to the node set of G_2 such that any two nodes u, v of G_1 are adjacent in G_1 if and only if $f(u)$ and $f(v)$ are adjacent in G_2. The state-of-the-art algorithm is due to Babai and Luks [2], and despite the recent progress made by Babai it is not yet clear whether the problem is solvable in polynomial time or not [1].

The subgraph isomorphism problem asks whether a *pattern graph H* appears as a subgraph of a *target graph G*. This problem is known to be NP-complete as it generalizes well-known NP-complete problems including the *Maximum Clique*, and the *Hamiltonian Cycle* [14]. Formally, a subgraph isomorphism is an injective map f from the vertices of H to the vertices of G such that if two vertices u and v are adjacent in H, then $f(u)$ and $f(v)$ are adjacent in G. In our work, we focus on the variant of the subgraph isomorphism that aims to list the occurrences of the pattern H in the target graph G, rather than just decide if any occurrence of H exists in G. In general, searching for a motif with k nodes requires $O(n^k)$ time. Despite this asymptotic tight lower bound, there exist many algorithms that perform significantly better in practice compared to brute force. The classic algorithm is Ullman's backtracking algorithm with a look ahead function [35]. Given the importance of subgraph isomorphism in mining networks and graph databases, a lot of research has focused on efficient algorithm design. Notable algorithms include VF2 [9], GraphQL [16], QuickSI [32], GADDI [38], SPath [39]. ISMAGS is a recent algorithm that provides one solution per symmetry group [18]. This algorithm is particularly valuable when there is an exponential number of isomorphisms that are symmetrically equivalent. Another line of research has focused on designing efficient algorithms for special classes of graphs. A recent notable algorithm is due to Bressan et al. [6] that finds all occurrences of an induced k-vertex subgraph in a d-degenerate graph. Their algorithm runs in $O(f(k, d) \cdot n^\ell)$ where ℓ is the size of the largest induced matching in the motif to be searched. It is worth mentioning that subgraph isomorphism lies at the heart of frequent pattern discovery [22].

3 Dataset Description

In this section we describe in detail the dataset of financial transactions we used in our experiments. The dataset encompass all wire transfers performed by the Head Office services of MIB in a period of six months, from August 1st, 2020 to January 31st, 2021 thus including SEPA [11] SCT and SWIFT-enabled

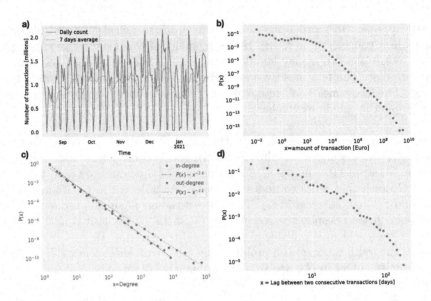

Fig. 2. Some empirical properties of the dataset: (a) Number of transactions in time, on a daily basis. (b) Probability distribution of the amount transferred in euros (log-log scale). (c) Probability distribution of the in- and out-degree (log-log scale). (d) Probability distribution of the time interval τ between two consecutive transactions involving the same sender and/or receiver (log-log scale).

[34] national and international wire transfers. Data were made available to the research team in a fully anonymized form respecting the strictest privacy and security requirements.

The average monthly volume is close to 30 million transactions. Figure 2(a) shows the number of transactions in time, aggregated on a daily basis. One can see that the number of transactions monitored is more than one million per day, excluded weekends. There is a considerable decrease in activity around the middle of August and during Christmas break. Each data entry includes a set of features, regarding both the sender/receiver parties and the transaction characteristics. For sender/receiver parties, data includes their anonymized bank account number, anonymized bank's BIC, party's and bank's country of residence (both at ISO alpha 2 level), and if the party is legal or physical person. For each transaction, features include timestamp, amount transferred, currency used, and transaction means (SEPA or SWIFT).

Figure 2(b) plots the empirical probability distribution of the amount transferred within the whole data set, in euros. One can see that most transactions regard an amount between few hundreds and few thousands euros. However, much larger amounts are present in the data set, up to a few billions euros. After a few thousands euros, the amount distribution decays as power-law function, indicating that very large transactions occur with very small probability, yet different than zero.

Table 1. Approximate number of nodes, edges, and weakly connected components of the entire dataset, and broken down by month.

Time period	N	E	# WCCs
Aug. 1st, 2020 -Jan. 31st, 2021	31M	184M	847K
Aug. '20	16M	26M	859K
Sep. '20	17M	31M	853K
Oct. '20	17M	33M	829K
Nov. '20	18M	32M	831K
Dec. '20	18M	33M	1073K
Jan. '21	17M	30M	869K

The dataset is naturally modeled as a time-evolving, directed multi-graph, a special instance of temporal networks [17]. In such graphs, nodes are a static collection of elements, edges are dynamic. In our dataset, nodes represent bank accounts while edges transactions. Table 1 shows the number of nodes N, edges E, and number of weakly connected components (WCCs), for graphs reconstructed from the whole dataset and from single months. Out of the 847 092 connected components of the whole dataset graph, the giant component spans 29 693 858 nodes whereas the second largest contains only 304 nodes. We represent the information that a node i sent $w(i,j)$ financial amount to node j at time t as the quadruplet (i,j,w,t). We denote by n_{ij} and W_{ij} the number of transactions and the total amount of money transferred from node i to node j, respectively. The in-degree (out-degree) of node i, k_i^{in} (k_i^{out}), corresponds to the total number of counter-parties sending (receiving) money from (to) node i, over the whole time interval under consideration. The total amount of money sent (received) by node i, W_i^{out} (W_i^{in}) is obtained by summing all outgoing (incoming) transactions involving node i, $W_i^{out} = \sum_j W_{ij}$ ($W_i^{in} = \sum_j W_{ji}$).

Figure 2(c) shows the in-degrees and out-degrees of the whole transaction graph in the 6-month period in log-log scale. Both distributions are heavy-tailed, compatible with a power-law function $P(k) \sim k^{-\gamma}$, with similar exponents $\gamma_{in} \simeq 2.6$ and $\gamma_{out} \simeq 2.2$. This indicates that most actors are involved in transactions with few counter-parties, only very few parties engage with many others. However, a typical scale for the number of counter-parties is missing: in the data set there are present actors receiving money from up to one thousands different peers, and sending money to up ten thousands different parties. Nodes with large in- or out-degree typically correspond to companies that are not suspicious of money laundering activities; this could involve transferring money to a large number of employees, and receiving money from numerous business partners. As we will see in the following, we are interested in spotting actors interacting with relatively few counterparties. Figure 2(c) shows that, despite highly-connected nodes being a tiny fraction of the network, their presence is non-negligible. The scale-free form of the degree distribution suggests that pruning hubs might be effective in reducing the amount of data to monitor, as we will see. Indeed, removing a hub implies to remove all connected edges and this might affect the network's connectivity, possibly breaking the graph into disconnected components and thus making the motifs extraction easier [30]. This theoretical observation has been also specifically validated in empirical transaction networks [31]. A different result would hold if the network had an homogeneous degree distribution (e.g. Erdos–Renyi graphs).

The time-varying graph representation allows us to take into account the activation dynamics of nodes and edges, corresponding to the dynamical features of sender/receiving parties [17]. Figure 2(d) shows the inter-transaction time distribution $P(\tau)$ between two consecutive activation of the same node, i.e. the time interval τ between two consecutive transactions involving the same sender and/or receiver, aggregated over the whole data set, expressed in hours. The inter-transaction time distribution $P(\tau)$ is heavy-tailed, indicating that the transaction dynamics follows a bursty behavior, as common in several human and natural contexts [33]: most transactions involving the same parties occur at small timescales, while large time intervals are increasingly less likely. Here, we are interested in spotting transactions occurring within a relatively small time interval, like a few days. Figure 2(d) shows that, accordingly to the bursty nature of the transaction dynamics, these kind of transactions represent a large fraction of the total. For instance, 85% of consecutive transactions involving the same parties occur within 7 days. Therefore, an a priori filter aimed at pruning transactions occurring within large time-intervals would not be effective in significantly reducing the amount of data to monitor, as we will see in the following.

Note that one can generate synthetic time-evolving graphs with properties similar to the original data, by means of the probability density functions showed in Figs. 2(b),(c),(d). The degree distribution $P(k)$ (Fig. 2(c)) can be exploited to generate a directed network by means of the so-called configuration model [5], allowing the possibility of multiple edges between nodes. The distribution of amounts (Fig. 2(b)) can be used to generate weights for each edge. The dynamics of the network can be taken into account by recent modelling frameworks developed to generate temporal networks, such as activity-driven networks [28]. Finally, the broad-tailed form of the inter-transaction time distribution (Fig. 2(d)) can be reproduced by using models for bursty temporal networks [27], in which the link activation dynamics follows a non-Poissonian process.

4   Extraction of Smurf-Like Motifs from Transaction Graph

In this Section we exactly define the problem of interest and propose a framework to efficiently solve it. Then, we show the motifs extracted by our method, classified from the perspective of anti-money laundering stakeholders.

4.1   Proposed Pipeline

Problem Definition. Figure 1 shows type 1 and type 2 subgraphs that we wish to extract efficiently from a large transaction graph. Observe that when there is one source and one target in motif 1, and one middle node in motif 2, the two motif types coincide. We are interested in finding a set of motifs as shown in Fig. 1, that may have varying number of nodes, but involve few bank accounts (less than 20 in total), and are suspicious. The key characteristic we encode as suspiciousness is the velocity that the transactions within the motif take place. We state this as the following problem:

> *Problem 1.* Given a time-evolving transaction network, find all motifs of type 1 and type 2, that involve at least 3 nodes, and at most k nodes, and all transactions take place within a time window of ΔT days.

Typically all the transactions from the source(s) to the middle node(s), take place before the transactions from the latter to the target(s). However, there can exist some asynchrony. From now on, let $\mathcal{S}, \mathcal{M}, \mathcal{T}$ be the sets of sources, middle nodes, and targets in motifs type 1, and type 2 respectively. Let $s = |\mathcal{S}|, t = |\mathcal{T}|$. We outline that existing anti-money laundering tools based on graph mining, including Flowscope [25] and AutoAudit [24], are not satisfactory formulations in our application. Perhaps, the most appropriate formulation is to cast the aforementioned problem as a subgraph isomorphism problem. Specifically, we can create a dictionary of motifs that we are interested in, and roll a time window spanning over the dataset to search for each motif using an efficient subgraph isomorphism algorithm, e.g., [35]. Unfortunately, this formulation is computationally expensive and does not scale well to large networks.

Proposed Framework. Before we delve into the details of our proposed framework, it is worth summarizing our key contributions. Our framework consists of a pipeline that involves few, computationally inexpensive steps, that pre-process the graph, perform simple database joins, and post-process the output, and is able to find suspicious subgraphs. Furthermore, by mining the output, we classify the motifs into categories that are of independent interest to anti-financial crime investigators and practitioners.

The pre-processing part removes nodes and edges that the bank knows or believes with high confidence that are not involved in money laundering. This part imposes the following constraints on the graph: edges whose weight is less than a certain threshold are removed, nodes with in-degree and out-degree above a certain threshold are removed. Transactions involving a small amount are indeed not suspicious for money laundering, as well as bank accounts with very large activity. Furthermore, we ensure that each path of length 2 involves at least one cross-border transaction. Since most bank accounts are Italian, this implies that in each three-nodes path at least one node is non-Italian. Table 2 shows an example (by using data from the month of November) of how the pre-processing steps greatly reduce the graph's size. For instance, even if nodes with in- or out-degree above 50 are just 0.2% of the transaction network, these account for almost 50% of edges. Altogether, the pre-processing constraints reduce the graph's size of about 1000 times.

Table 2. Effects of the 3 pre-processing steps (highlighted in Table 3) on the graph's number of nodes N and edges E. At each pre-processing step the graph's size significantly decreases. As an example, we show data from November.

Graph	N	E
Original	18M	26M
Min Edge Weight	1.22M	1.28M
Max k^{in}, k^{out}	152K	125K
Min cross-border transactions	21K	46K

Table 3. Values of constraints applied in the pipeline.

Pipeline	Constraint	Values
Pre-processing	Min Edge weight	Non-disclosed threshold
Pre-processing	Max k^{in}, k^{out}	50
Pre-processing	Min cross-border transactions	1
Motifs extraction	Motif 1	$s, t > 1$
Motifs extraction	Motif 2	$s = t = 1$
Motifs extraction	Max inter-transaction time ΔT	Non-disclosed threshold
Post-processing	Min total flow	Non-disclosed threshold
Post-processing	Flow ratio	Non-disclosed thresholds

Our search step is a standard graph database join that finds common neighbors between different pairs of nodes within the time window ΔT we are interested in. For instance for motif type 2, for a given ordered pair of nodes (u, v) we find the set of nodes that is out-going neighbors of u, and in-coming neighbors of v. The perhaps surprising finding is that this naive search algorithm that bypasses the constraint that the middle nodes should not have any edges between them (or induce few in general) is *automatically* satisfied by most of the output of the search step, due to our pre-processing step, and due to enforcing the velocity constraint. Furthermore, we find that one large motif may unpack into several smaller suspicious motifs, where the source, and target nodes remain the same, and the set of intermediary nodes may change over time.

Finally, motifs extracted are post-processed, in order to respect some additional constraints related to nodes and edges features. For each motif, the total incoming and outgoing flow can be computed, as the sum of the amount transferred through incoming and outgoing edges of the middle nodes, respectively. Similarly, the total flow transferred from source to target nodes is equal to the minimum between incoming and outgoing flows. Motifs must have a total flow transferred above a certain threshold, and the ratio between outgoing and incoming flows between a certain interval. The topological, dynamical, and additional constraints applied to extract the suspicious subgraph are summarized in Table 3. Note that for security reasons, we do not disclose the exact values used in the pipeline.

Table 4. Running times in seconds of ISMAGS [18] for searching an induced path $i \rightarrow j \rightarrow k$ (column 1), a motif of type 1 with $s = t = 3$ (column 2), and our proposed method on searching *all* motifs of type 1 where $1 \leq s, t \leq 6$ over five different three-day windows (one per row). Running ISMAGS for searching a motif with $s = t = 3$ requires hours.

ISMAGS ($s = t = 1$)	ISMAGS ($s = t = 3$)	Proposed method
88.0 s	>1 h	84.0 s
30.4 s	>1 h	43.3 s
94.0 s	>1 h	87 s
38.4 s	>1 h	44.3 s
15.6 s	>1 h	26.9 s
73 s	>1 h	69 s

4.2 Results

Here we show the results of our pipeline. First, we compare the efficiency of our method with a state of the art algorithm for subgraph isomorphism search, ISMAGS [18]. Then, we highlight a few interesting motifs extracted from the transaction network. Finally, we provide a systematic classification of motifs found according to the geography of countries involved.

Comparison to Subgraph Isomorphism. Table 4 compares the running time of ISMAGS [18] and our proposed method on five different time-windows of length ΔT for finding efficiently motif type 1. ISMAGS runs efficiently only when $s = t = 1$. Even when $s = 2$, ISMAGs may require more than an hour for certain time windows. When $s = t = 3$, for all considered time-windows, ISMAGS consistently requires time at the order of hours to find the motifs. This comes in sheer contrast to our proposed method, that forgets the constraint of finding induced subgraphs. Once we find a set of candidate subgraphs, our method checks which ones are isomorphic to the desired motif. We find all 36 possible instatiations of induced motifs of type 1 with $1 \leq s, t \leq 6$. The running time is always less than a minute and half. This happens since the time constraint we impose by looking into time-windows biases the dataset towards having this property, i.e., our proposed method finds induced subgraphs even if it is not explicitly searching for such. Furthermore, the number and size of subgraphs extracted is relatively small, so it is possible to check a posteriori if these subgraphs are induced.

Anomalous Subgraphs. Figure 3 shows a subset of the output of our pipeline, colored accordingly to the geographical risk of each country involved: green for Italian bank accounts (considered non risky), orange for medium risk countries, yellow for low risk countries, and red for the high risk countries. Figure 3(a) shows a type 1 motif, with $s = 1, t = 8$. The middle node receives on day 1 a large amount of money from a German (DE) account, and then within the next couple of days distributes it in smaller amounts to 8 different bank accounts, all

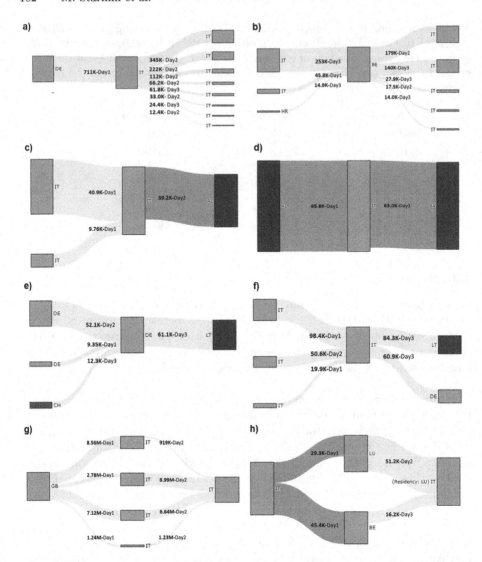

Fig. 3. Different groups of transactions extracted from the platform that are classified as suspicious due to their smurf-like behaviour. For each motif, nodes are colored
accordingly to the geographical risk of each country involved: green for Italian bank
accounts (considered non risky), orange for medium risk countries, yellow for low risk
countries, and red for the high risk countries. Edge thickness indicates the amount
transferred, also labeled on top of the edges. (Color figure online)

within Italy (IT). Figures 3(b), (c) show two more motifs of type 1 that involves
multiple countries. In Fig. 3(b), the middle node resides in Belgium (BE), while
source and target nodes are in Italy and Croatia (HR), while in Fig. 3(c) the
amount is transferred entirely outside Italy. Figure 3(d) shows an induced path

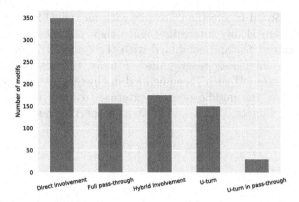

Fig. 4. Number of motifs extracted from the whole data set for each class, defined in the main text.

of length 2 where the source and target nodes reside in Albania and Bosnia, respectively, while the middle node in Italy. Note that the two transactions take place within a single day. It is worth outlining that Albania is ranked as one of two of the countries most at risk from money laundering according to the Money Laundering and Terrorist Financing Index, published by the Basel Institute [4]. Similarly, Figs. 3(e),(f) show two more suspicious motifs, involving Germany (DE), Switzerland (CH), Italy (IT), and Lithuania (LT) Figs. 3(g), (h) show two examples of type 2 motifs: in Fig. 3(e) the source node resides in Great Britain (GB), in Fig. 3(e) both middle nodes are outside Italy while source and target nodes are in Italy.

Motif Classification. The motifs extracted can be classified according to the needs of further manual inspection, to be performed by anti-financial crime specialists. Figure 4 shows the distribution of the motifs detected according to our classification, which relies on the geography of the bank accounts involved. This classification is performed from the point of view of the financial institutions monitoring transactions (MIB in this case), but it can be generalized to any financial institution. The largest share of the motifs extracted can be classified as "direct involvement". In these motifs, MIB customers are engaged as pivotal figures (i.e. middle nodes), while being both beneficiary as well as ordering party of conspicuous transactions in the velocity schema. Another substantial share of motifs are classified as "full pass-through". In these motifs, MIB is supporting the payment delivery of others banks, so all the nodes involved are not MIB customer. Another case can be classified as "hybrid involvement", in which, while the pivotal middle node is external to MIB, some of the wire transfers start from or are directed to MIB customers. In this case, we have MIB nodes only in one side of the motif. An example of this class are motifs sketched in Fig. 3(c). Another important category is the one in which all source and target nodes belong to MIB customer base, while the middle node is external to the bank. This case is defined as "U-turn" in the literature [26]. The middle node is frequently located abroad in specific countries with inexplicable business reasons. Those cases are remarkably interesting since they present an enhanced "lack of economic purpose" feature, combined with the typical triggering red flag of "money laundering high risk geographies". Finally, the last class is composed by motifs in which the "U-turn" is embedded in clusters of "pass-through" payments. In this case, the middle node is external to MIB, as well as a subset of sources and/or targets, thus we label it as a specific class "U-turn in pass-through".

5 Conclusion

In this work we have proposed a practical pipeline for finding sets of transactions suspicious of money laundering. We show that our method scales gracefully with the size of the dataset, and bypasses the computational complexity lower bound of subgraph isomorphism by exploiting the high velocity characteristics of smurf-like transactions. Specifically, we show that simple database joins when combined with prior knowledge result in efficiency, which is crucial for real-time detection of such illicit activities. Furthermore, by studying the output of our pipeline, we provide a novel characterization of smurf-like motifs that is of independent interest to anti-money laundering practitioners and financial crime units. The latter provides insights on how money launderers use geography and the efficiency limitations of real-world transaction monitoring systems to perform their activities. An interesting open direction is learning more complex motifs that money launderers form by leveraging labeled transactions.

According to the perspective of anti-financial crime stakeholders, mainly interested into the practical monitoring power of the tools regardless the underlying mathematical approach, it is to be stressed that the "direct involvement" schema may be, at least in a partial manner, spotted with traditional rule-based algorithms based on counters and thresholds applied to wire transfers involving the customer base. These methods rely on relational databases only and are largely popular inside the banking industry. However, they present relevant limitations intrinsic to the fact that they do not consider the features of the whole transaction graph. Such limitations become almost a state of blindness for the cases "full pass-through", "hybrid involvement", "U-turn", and "U-turn in pass-through". These cases are to be taken into account when not only the customer base of bank but also counter-parties partially or totally external to it are to be considered. In this line of work, the presented results are a seminal contribution far from being maturely exploited in improving transaction monitoring systems.

Acknowledgements. The research was conducted under a cooperative agreement between ISI Foundation, Intesa Sanpaolo Innovation Center, and Intesa Sanpaolo. The authors would like to thank Paolo Baracco, Piero Boccassino, Valerio Cencig, Raffaele Cosimo, Guido de Vecchi, Emmanuele Di Fenza, Maurizio Montagnese, Alessandro Raso, Mauro Ronzano and Luigi Ruggerone for their useful comments.

Data Availability Statement. The data supporting the findings of this study is available from Intesa Sanpaolo upon request to Intesa Sanpaolo Innovation Center (`innovationcenter@pec.intesasanpaolo.com`). Please note that restrictions for data availability apply. Researchers interested in having access to data for academic purposes will be asked to sign a non-disclosure agreement.

References

1. Babai, L.: Graph isomorphism in quasipolynomial time. In: Proceedings of the Forty-Eighth Annual ACM Symposium on Theory of Computing, pp. 684–697 (2016)
2. Babai, L., Luks, E.M.: Canonical labeling of graphs. In: Proceedings of the Fifteenth Annual ACM Symposium on Theory of Computing, pp. 171–183 (1983)
3. Banca d'Italia - Unita di Informazione Finanziaria per l'Italia. Rapporto annuale 2019 (12) (2020)
4. Basel institute on Governance. Basel AML index: 9th public edition ranking money laundering and terrorist financing risks around the world (2020)
5. Bender, E.A., Canfield, E.: The asymptotic number of labeled graphs with given degree sequences. J. Comb. Theory Ser. A **24**(3), 296–307 (1978)
6. Bressan, M., Roth, M.: Counting homomorphisms, subgraphs, and induced subgraphs in degenerate graphs: new hardness results and complete complexity classifications. arXiv preprint arXiv:2103.05588 (2021)
7. Chen, Z., Khoa, L.D., Teoh, E.N., Nazir, A., Karuppiah, E.K., Lam, K.S.: Machine learning techniques for anti-money laundering (AML) solutions in suspicious transaction detection: a review. Knowl. Inf. Syst. **57**(2), 245–285 (2018). https://doi.org/10.1007/s10115-017-1144-z
8. Choudhury, S., Holder, L., Chin, G., Ray, A., Beus, S., Feo, J.: StreamWorks: a system for dynamic graph search. In: Proceedings of the 2013 ACM SIGMOD International Conference on Management of Data, pp. 1101–1104 (2013)
9. Cordella, L.P., Foggia, P., Sansone, C., Vento, M.: A (sub) graph isomorphism algorithm for matching large graphs. IEEE Trans. Pattern Anal. Mach. Intell. **26**(10), 1367–1372 (2004)
10. Ebikake, E.: Money laundering: an assessment of soft law as a technique for repressive and preventive anti-money laundering control. J. Money Laund. Control. **19**(4), 346–375 (2016). https://doi.org/10.1108/JMLC-07-2015-0029
11. European Payments Council (EPC). Sepa single euro payment area
12. FATF, Financial Action Task Force. International standards on combating money laundering and the financing of terrorism & proliferation (2012–2020)
13. Financial Intelligence Group. From suspicion to action, converting financial intelligence into greater operational impact. Financial intelligence group (2017). https://www.europol.europa.eu/publications-documents/suspicion-to-action-converting-financial-intelligence-greater-operational-impact
14. Garey, M.R., Johnson, D.S.: Computers and intractability. A Guide to the Theory of Np-Completeness (1979)
15. Guardian. Danske bank money laundering is biggest scandal in Europe (2018). https://www.theguardian.com/business/2018/sep/20/danske-bank-money-laundering-is-biggest-scandal-in-europe-european-commission
16. He, H., Singh, A.K.: Graphs-at-a-time: query language and access methods for graph databases. In: Proceedings of the 2008 ACM SIGMOD International Conference on Management of Data, pp. 405–418 (2008)

17. Holme, P., Saramäki, J. (eds.): Temporal Networks. Springer, Berlin (2013). https://doi.org/10.1007/978-3-642-36461-7
18. Houbraken, M., Demeyer, S., Michoel, T., Audenaert, P., Colle, D., Pickavet, M.: The index-based subgraph matching algorithm with general symmetries (ISMAGS): exploiting symmetry for faster subgraph enumeration. PloS One 9(5), e97896 (2014)
19. Huang, J.: Effectiveness of US anti-money laundering regulations and HSBC case study. J. Money Laund. Control. 18, 525–532 (2015). https://doi.org/10.1108/JMLC-05-2015-0018
20. IntesaSanpaolo. Anti-money laundering rulebook, international branches (2019). Internal document (restricted)
21. IntesaSanpaolo. Guidelines for combating money laundering and terrorist financing and for managing embargoes (2019). Internal document (restricted)
22. Jiang, C., Coenen, F., Zito, M.: A survey of frequent subgraph mining algorithms. Knowl. Eng. Rev. 28(1), 75–105 (2013)
23. Kipf, T.N., Welling, M.: Semi-supervised classification with graph convolutional networks. arXiv preprint arXiv:1609.02907 (2016)
24. Lee, M.-C., et al.: AutoAudit: mining accounting and time-evolving graphs. arXiv preprint arXiv:2011.00447 (2020)
25. Li, X., et al.: FlowScope: spotting money laundering based on graphs. In: AAAI, pp. 4731–4738 (2020)
26. MAS – Monetary authority of Singapore. Red flag indicators for banks (2015)
27. Moinet, A., Starnini, M., Pastor-Satorras, R.: Burstiness and aging in social temporal networks. Phys. Rev. Lett. 114, 108701 (2015)
28. Perra, N., Gonçalves, B., Pastor-Satorras, R., Vespignani, A.: Activity driven modeling of time varying networks. Sci. Rep. 2(1), 469 (2012)
29. Schott, P.A.: Reference guide to anti-money laundering and combating the financing of terrorism (2006). https://openknowledge.worldbank.org/bitstream/handle/10986/6977/350520Referenc1Money01OFFICIAL0USE1.pdf;sequence=1
30. Schwartz, N., Cohen, R., Ben-Avraham, D., Barabási, A.-L., Havlin, S.: Percolation in directed scale-free networks. Phys. Rev. E 66(1), 15104 (2002)
31. Semeraro, A., Tambuscio, M., Ronchiadin, S., Li Puma, L., Ruffo, G.: Structural inequalities emerging from a large wire transfers network. Appl. Netw. Sci. 5(1), 1–35 (2020). https://doi.org/10.1007/s41109-020-00314-x
32. Shang, H., Zhang, Y., Lin, X., Yu, J.X.: Taming verification hardness: an efficient algorithm for testing subgraph isomorphism. Proc. VLDB Endow. 1(1), 364–375 (2008)
33. Song, C., Koren, T., Wang, P., Barabasi, A.-L.: Modelling the scaling properties of human mobility. Nat. Phys. 6(10), 818–823 (2010)
34. S.W.I.F.T. Society for worldwide interbank financial telecommunication
35. Ullmann, J.R.: An algorithm for subgraph isomorphism. J. ACM (JACM) 23(1), 31–42 (1976)
36. Weber, M., et al.: Scalable graph learning for anti-money laundering: a first look. arXiv preprint arXiv:1812.00076 (2018)
37. Welling, S.N.: Smurfs, money laundering and the federal criminal law: the crime of structuring transactions. Fla. Law Rev. 41, 287–343 (1989)
38. Zhang, S., Li, S., Yang, J.: GADDI: distance index based subgraph matching in biological networks. In: Proceedings of the 12th International Conference on Extending Database Technology: Advances in Database Technology, pp. 192–203 (2009)
39. Zhao, P., Han, J.: On graph query optimization in large networks. Proc. VLDB Endow. 3(1–2), 340–351 (2010)

Spatio-Temporal Multi-graph Networks for Demand Forecasting in Online Marketplaces

Ankit Gandhi[1]([✉]), Aakanksha[2], Sivaramakrishnan Kaveri[1], and Vineet Chaoji[1]

[1] Amazon – India Machine Learning, Bengaluru, India
{ganankit,kavers,vchaoji}@amazon.com
[2] Microsoft, Hyderabad, India
aakanksha@microsoft.com

Abstract. Demand forecasting is fundamental to successful inventory planning and optimisation of logistics costs for online marketplaces such as Amazon. Millions of products and thousands of sellers are competing against each other in an online marketplace. In this paper, we propose a framework to forecast demand for a product from a particular seller (referred as offer/seller-product demand in the paper). Inventory planning and placements based on these forecasts help sellers in lowering fulfilment costs, improving instock availability and increasing shorter delivery promises to the customers. Most of the recent forecasting approaches in the literature are one-dimensional, i.e., during prediction, the future forecast mainly depends on the offer i.e. its historical sales and features. These approaches don't consider the effect of other offers and hence, fail to capture the correlations across different sellers and products seen in situations like, (i) competition between sellers offering similar products, (ii) effect of a seller going out of stock for the product on competing seller, (iii) launch of new competing products/offers and (iv) cold start offers or offers with very limited historical sales data. In this paper, we propose a general demand forecasting framework for multivariate correlated time series. The proposed technique models the homogeneous and heterogeneous correlations between sellers and products across different time series using graph neural networks (GNN) and uses state-of-the-art forecasting models based upon LSTMs and TCNs for modelling individual time series. We have experimented with various GNN architectures such as GCNs, GraphSAGE and GATs for modelling the correlations. We applied the framework to forecast the future demand of products, sold on Amazon, for each seller and we show that it performs ∼16% better than state-of-the-art forecasting approaches.

Keywords: Demand forecasting in e-commerce · Time-series forecasting · Graph neural networks · Correlated multivariate time series

Aakanksha—Work was done as part of internship at Amazon.

Y. Dong et al. (Eds.): ECML PKDD 2021, LNAI 12978, pp. 187–203, 2021.
https://doi.org/10.1007/978-3-030-86514-6_12

1 Introduction

Forecasting product demand for different sellers is important for e-commerce marketplaces for successful inventory planning and optimizing supply chain costs. These forecasted demand recommendations are then used by sellers to stock inventory in their warehouses or fulfilment centres. In online marketplaces such as Amazon, there are hundreds of thousands of sellers offering millions of products. A single product can be offered by multiple sellers and a seller can sell multiple products. Demand for a particular offer not only depends on its historical sales but also on other factors such as competition with other sellers, other sellers offering same/similar product going out of stock, other sellers increasing or decreasing the price, launch of new competing products, etc. In order to accurately predict offer level demand, it is imperative to capture the correlations between different offers in the model.

In e-commerce, the demand is highly dynamic and often fluctuating because of holidays, deals, discounts, intermittent offer campaigns, competitor trends, etc. Recent works for e-commerce demand forecasting based on neural networks [19–21,25] have shown that they significantly outperform traditional forecasting models such as ARIMA [4,5] and exponential smoothing [13]. The traditional methods are univariate and forecast for each time series in isolation. Whereas in e-commerce, products are often related in terms of grouping, categories or sub-categories, and hence, their demand patterns are correlated. Neural networks take into account these correlations using dynamic historical attributes and static covariates to extract higher order features, and identify complex patterns within and across time series.

Even though these deep models are trained on all offers to capture these correlations, during prediction they only focus on using an offer's historical time series data to predict the future time series. However, for offer demand forecasting, looking into other time series may be useful during prediction time, for instance, it might be beneficial to look at (i) out of stock status for the same product from other sellers, (ii) launch of competing/similar products, (iii) price increase/decrease from other sellers offering same product, (iv) performance of competing seller going up/down suddenly (rating, shipping, reviews, etc.). In the past, authors in [15], proposed a combination of convolution and recurrent connections that takes multiple time series as input to the network, thus capturing some of the above scenarios during prediction. However, it doesn't scale beyond a few time series as the input layer size grows. In [22], authors propose a scalable network that can leverage both local and global patterns during training and prediction. They combine a global matrix factorization model over all time series regularized by a temporal convolution network with another temporal network to capture local properties of each time-series and associated covariates. In this paper, we propose a more systematic method of modelling the correlation between different entities across time series using GNNs.

Graphs are an extremely powerful tool to capture and represent interactions between entities in a seamless manner. The entities (sellers and products) can be represented as nodes of a graph and their direct correlation can be represented by edges (refer to Sect. 3.2 for graph construction). This results in a multi-modal[1] and multi-relational[2] graph. In addition, nodes and edges can be represented using a set of historical features, characterizing their intrinsic properties. Recently, researchers have proposed various methods that are capable of learning from graph-structured data [6,10–12,14,18,23,27,28,30]. All of these methods are based on Graph Convolutional Networks (GCNs) and its extensions. GCNs learn to aggregate feature information from local graph neighborhoods using neural networks. These methods have been shown to boost the performance of many graph-level tasks such as node classification, link prediction, graph classification, subgraph classification, etc.

In this work, we propose a framework for performing demand forecasting in multivariate correlated time series data. We model the homogeneous and heterogeneous correlations between different sellers and products across time series at the time of training as well as prediction, and inject the learned representations into state-of-the-art neural network architectures [1,8,25] for demand forecasting. At each time step, we define a graph structure based on seller attributes, product attributes, offer demand, product similarity/substitute [17,24], and obtain the seller and product representations. The edge structure in the graph vary over time based upon demand and other connections. Thus, an unrolled version of the network comprises of multiple graphs (referred to here as multi-graph networks) sharing the same parameters (refer to Fig. 1). The sequence of representations from GNNs along with historical demand is then fed into sequential neural model such as LSTMs, TCNs, etc., to forecast the future demand. We experiment with different variations of GNN architectures such as GCNs [14], GraphSAGE [11], GAT [23], etc. by incorporating various node and edge features to learn the seller and product embeddings at each time step. While the LSTM/TCN modules make use of just the sequential information present in the data, our aim is to augment these modules with correlations across time series learnt using GNNs. We train the complete spatio-temporal multigraph network in an end-to-end fashion, where embeddings from the GNN layer are fed into the sequential model to make demand forecasts, and the loss is optimized over the entire network. Following are the main contributions of the paper – (i) a generic framework for handling competing/correlated time series in demand forecasting, (ii) use of GNNs for modelling the effect of sellers and products on each other in online marketplaces during training and prediction, (iii) the framework can be plugged into any state-of-the-art sequential model for better demand forecasts, (iv) extension of standard GNN architectures to heterogeneous graphs by leveraging edge features and (v) empirical evaluation of framework using real world marketplace data from Amazon against other forecasting techniques.

We evaluate the framework for forecasting demand of offers sold on Amazon marketplace on a dataset comprising of $21K$ sellers and $1.89MM$ products, and show that the proposed models have $\sim16\%$ lower mean absolute percentage error (MAPE) than state-of-the-art demand forecasting approaches used in e-commerce. For products that are sold by more than one seller, the improvement is

---

[1] Graph having different kinds of nodes (sellers, products).

[2] Graph having multiple types of edges between nodes (in-stock, product substitute).

~30%, and for cold and warm start offers (that has history of less than 3 months), the improvement is ~25%. The rest of the paper is organized as follows. Section 2 provides an overview of the extensive literature on forecasting models, especially for e-commerce and correlated time series. In Sect. 3, we present the proposed framework of spatio-temporal multi-graph networks for demand forecasting. In Sect. 4, we compare the performance of the proposed model and its variants with the state-of-the-art approaches for demand forecasting as well as some of the implementation details. We conclude with the final remarks in Sect. 5.

2   Prior Work

Time series forecasting is a key component in many industrial and business decision processes, and hence, a wide variety of different forecasting methods have been developed in the past. ARIMA models [4,5] and state space models [9,13] have been well established de-facto forecasting models in the industry. However, for retail demand forecasting they don't seem to work well as they cannot infer shared patterns from a dataset of similar time series. Deep neural network based forecasting solutions provide an alternative [1,20–22,25]. In this section, we mostly focus on recent deep learning approaches. Benidis et al. provide an excellent summary and review of various neural forecasting approaches in [3]. DeepAR [21] proposed an auto regressive recurrent neural network model on a large number of related time series to estimate the probability distribution of future demand. DeepState [20] models time series forecasting by marrying state space models with deep recurrent neural networks to learn complex patterns from data while retaining the interpretability. Wen et al. [25] proposed a multi-horizon quantile recurrent forecaster where the time series history is modelled using LSTMs, and an MLP is used to decode the input into multi horizon demand forecasts. LSTNet [15] uses a combination of CNN and RNN to extract short-term temporal patterns as well as correlations among variables. Chen et al. [8] proposed a probabilistic framework with temporal convolutional neural networks for forecasting based on dilated causal convolutions. DeepGLO [22] is a hybrid model that combines a global matrix factorization model regularized by a temporal convolution network and another temporal network to capture the local properties of time series and associated covariates. There have been methods to take into account correlation between time series like DeepGLO [22], LSTNet [15], etc., however, we provide a more systematic method of modelling the correlations between different entities in the time series using GNNs.

There have been few works in the past focusing specifically on retail demand forecasting. Mukherjee et al. [19] developed an MLP and LSTM based architecture for the eRetail company – Flipkart, and outputs the probability distribution of future demand as a mixture of Gaussians. Bandara et al. [2] built an LSTM based network for forecasting on real world dataset from Walmart. However, none of the previous works focus on demand forecasting for 'marketplaces', where multiple sellers are involved and explicitly model the correlations in their time-series.

There are also a few prior works that use GNNs for demand forecasting focusing mainly on the application of traffic forecasting. DCRNN [16] incorporates

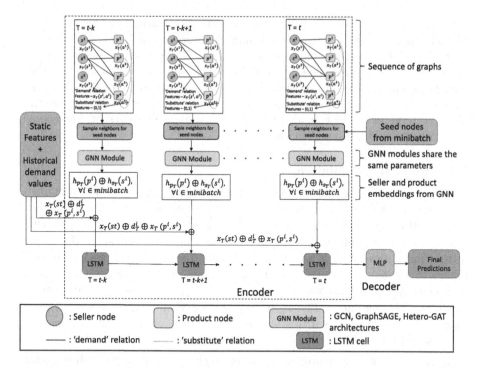

Fig. 1. Training architecture of the demand forecasting model for online marketplaces. At each time-step, a graph is defined between seller and product nodes that models the correlation between them using 'demand' and 'substitute' relations. From these graphs, product and seller embeddings are learned using GNN layer. The embeddings from GNN are then concatenated with static features and demand value for that time-step, and fed into the sequential model (in this case, LSTM) to forecast offer-level demand.

both spatial and temporal dependency in the traffic flow using diffusion convolution and RNNs for traffic forecasting. ST-GCN [29] is a deep learning framework that integrates graph convolution and gated temporal convolution through spatio-temporal convolutional blocks for traffic forecasting. GraphWaveNet [26] captures spatio-temporal dependencies by combining graph convolution with dilated casual convolution. StemGNN [7] is a spectral temporal GNN that captures inter series correlations and temporal dependencies jointly in the spectral domain for demand forecasting. To the best of our knowledge, this is the first work, that predicts offer demand for online marketplaces by explicitly modelling the correlations between different sellers and products in the time series, and accounting for their effects on each other.

3   Proposed Method

This section describes the problem formulation and the technical details of the network architecture employed to solve the problem of demand forecasting in online marketplaces. We start with the problem formulation, and by describing the general graph structure for modelling the correlations between time series containing different sellers and products. In Sect. 3.3, we describe various GNN architectures to produce node (seller and product) representations and how they have been adapted for our problem. Finally, we describe some of the sequential models that have been considered for the experimentation for extracting the temporal patterns in the historical time series data. Figure 1 represents the overall architecture of the proposed method.

3.1   Problem Formulation

Let $\mathcal{S}$ denote the set of sellers and $\mathcal{P}$ denote the set of products in the marketplace. Given a set of N time series, each series comprising of a seller, a product and historical demand, $<s^i, p^i, [y^i_{t-k,t}]>^N_{i=1}$, where $y^i_{t-k,t} = [d^i_{t-k}, d^i_{t-k+1}, \ldots d^i_t]$, d^i_t denotes the demand for a seller-product at time t, k represents the length of the time series, $s^i \in \mathcal{S}$ and $p^i \in \mathcal{P}$ denotes the seller and product respectively for i^{th} time series, and N is the number of time series. Our goal is to predict $[\hat{y}^i_{t+1,t+K}]^N_{i=1}$, where $\hat{y}^i_{t+1,t+K} = [\hat{d}^i_{t+1}, \hat{d}^i_{t+2}, \ldots \hat{d}^i_{t+K}]$, the demand for future K time steps. Let x^i_t be the feature vector for i^{th} time series at time t. We can break down this feature vector into four different components, $x^i_t = [x_t(p^i), x_t(s^i), x_t(p^i, s^i), x_t(st)]-$

(i) $x_t(p^i)$ denotes the features specific to product only such as product brand, product category, total product sales in trailing months, total product gross merchandise sales (GMS) in trailing months, product shipping charges, number of product views/clicks in trailing months, etc.,

(ii) $x_t(s^i)$ denotes the features specific to seller only such as seller rating, seller performance metrics, seller reviews, total GMS in trailing months for the seller, total sales by the seller in trailing months, total views of all the products offered by a seller in trailing months, etc.,

(iii) $x_t(p^i, s^i)$ denotes the features dependent on both seller and product of the time series such as total views of p^i offered by s^i in trailing months, total sales of p^i offered by s^i in trailing months, total GMS of p^i offered by s^i in trailing months, whether product belongs to seller's main category/subcategory, out of stock history of p^i from s^i, etc., and

(iv) $x_t(st)$ denotes static features independent of the seller as well as product such as the number of days to the nearest holidays that have significant impact on the future demand, bank related offers and cashbacks on the platform, etc.

We formulate the demand forecasting for an offer as a regression problem where we have to predict the future demand ($\hat{y}^i_{t+1,t+K}$) given the historical demand ($y^i_{t-k,t}$), and the time series features ($x^i_{t-k:t}$).

3.2   Graph Construction

We represent correlation between different sellers and products across time series using graphs. Sellers and products are represented as nodes, and their interactions are represented as edges in the graph. For instance, products can be correlated to each other in terms of their similarity or substitutability; sellers can be correlated to each other if they are selling similar products, their shipping channels are same (self-fulfilled vs marketplace-fulfilled), primary category of the products offered by them is same, etc. The goal is to generate accurate embeddings or representations of the sellers and products, in order to use them effectively to predict their demand for a specified period in the future. To learn these embeddings for time t, in this work, we construct a graph $\mathcal{G}_t = ([\mathcal{P}, \mathcal{S}], \mathcal{E}_t)$ consisting of nodes in two disjoint sets, namely, $\mathcal{S}$ (representing sellers) and $\mathcal{P}$ (representing the products they offer), and the set of edges $\mathcal{E}_t$ with following connections to capture their correlatedness:

(i) Demand edge: It is defined between seller s^i and product p^i, $1 \leq i \leq N$, at time t, if there exists a demand for product p^i from seller s^i at time t. This edge models the dynamic connections in the graphs.

(ii) Substitute edge: It is defined between two products, p^i and p^j, representing their similarity or substitutability. This edge models the static connections in the graphs and is not dependent on time.

These graphs are constructed for each time step of the historical data, i.e., there are as many graphs as the number of time steps $(\mathcal{G}_{t-k}, \mathcal{G}_{t-k+1}, \ldots, \mathcal{G}_t)$. In addition to the graph structure, we utilise x_t^i (defined in Sect. 3.1) as the input features of the nodes and edges in the graph $\mathcal{G}_t$. The seller node i in the graph $\mathcal{G}_t$ is initialized with seller specific feature – $x_t(s^i)$, the product node i is initialized with product specific feature – $x_t(p^i)$, demand edges (if exist) are initialized with seller-product features – $x_t(p^i, s^i)$, whereas the substitute edges are just binary connections with no features. Hence, we efficiently utilise the seller and product characteristics in conjunction with the graphical information and edge features to produce high-quality embeddings. These embeddings are then fed into a time series model for the generation of accurate forecasts. Figure 1 represents the sequence of graphs constructed for modelling the correlation between sellers and products over time.

3.3   Graph Neural Networks

In this section, we present the details of various GNN architectures and their adaptations that we have employed to generate representations for seller and product nodes in our graphs. The basic unit for all the architectures is GCN, which uses localized convolutional modules that capture information from the node's neighborhood. Following subsections describe all the architectures in detail. We empirically evaluate each of these methods in Sect. 4 on a real-world online marketplace dataset. We create graph for each timestep t separately, hence, dropping the subscript t from the notation in this section.

Graph Convolutional Networks: Using GCNs, we capture the homogeneous correlations in the graph. In this case, we construct a graph with only one type of node and edge. Since, we have two types of nodes in the graph – sellers and products, a 2-layer MLP is used for the input features to map them to the same dimension before GCN layer, so that the nodes can be treated homogeneously. Also, we consider only the demand relation in this homogeneous graph. The idea behind GCNs is that it learns how to transform and propagate information across the graph, captured by node feature vectors [14]. To generate embedding for a node, it uses the localized convolutional module that captures information from the node's neighborhood. In GCNs, we stack multiple such convolutional modules to capture information about the graph topology. Initial node features are provided as input to the GCN and then, the node embeddings are computed by applying the series of convolutional modules.

Let $h^l(i)$ denote the embedding of ith node at l^{th} layer from graph $\mathcal{G}$. Then, $h^l(i)$ can be computed as follows -

$$h^l(i) = \sigma \left(\frac{1}{|\mathcal{N}(i)|} \sum_{u \in \mathcal{N}(i)} W^l h^{l-1}(u) \right) \tag{1}$$

where, $\mathcal{N}(i)$ denotes the neighborhood of node i, and W^l is the learnable weight for layer l that is shared across nodes. This technique is referred as Homo-GCN in the paper. Edge features $(x_t(p^i, s^i))$ are not used in this formulation, only a binary relation is considered.

GraphSAGE (GS): A seller can offer thousands of products. And if the seller has demand for all the products, then it is very inefficient to take the full size of a seller's neighborhood for learning its representation as is done in GCN. In GS [11], a sampling mechanism is adopted to obtain a fixed number of neighbors for each node, which makes it suitable for representation learning in such large graphs. This technique also captures only the homogeneous correlations. It performs graph convolutions and obtains the node embeddings in the following manner –

$$h^l(i) = \sigma \left(W'^l h^{l-1}(i) + \frac{1}{|S_{\mathcal{N}(i)}|} \sum_{u \in S_{\mathcal{N}(i)}} W^l h^{l-1}(u) \right) \tag{2}$$

where, $S_{\mathcal{N}(i)}$ is a random sample of the ith node neighbors, and W^l & W'^l are the learnable weights shared across all the nodes. Note that we perform aggregation on neighborhood information using the mean function. However, any alternate function can be employed for this operation. For GS formulation also, we ignore the edge features, and map the seller and product features using a 2-layer MLP network to the same dimension, to treat the nodes homogeneously. We refer to this method as Homo-GS.

Heterogeneous GraphSAGE with Edge Features: The graphs built in Sect. 3.2 to capture the correlatedness are inherently heterogeneous in nature (attributing to the presence of two node types – 'sellers' and 'products', and two relation types – 'demand' and 'substitute'). Homo-GCN and Homo-GS methods considered above treat the neighborhood of seller and product nodes in a similar manner. In this formulation, we extend Homo-GS to heterogeneous graphs where a separate convolutional module for each relation type is learned. Let us denote the hidden representation of ith seller node at layer l by $h_s^l(i)$ and i^{th} product node at layer l by $h_p^l(i)$. Then, we obtain the seller representations using following –

$$h_s^l(i) = \sigma(W_s^{'l} h_s^{l-1}(i) + \frac{1}{|S_{\mathcal{N}_s(i)}|} \sum_{u \in S_{\mathcal{N}_s(i)}} W_p^l [h_p^{l-1}(u) \overbrace{\oplus x(u,i)}^{\text{edge features}}]) \quad (3)$$

$$\underbrace{\hspace{6cm}}_{\text{aggregation under relation demand}}$$

where, $S_{\mathcal{N}_s(i)}$ is a random sample of the ith seller node neighbors under relation 'demand' (neighbors for seller nodes would be product nodes), W_p^l is the learnable weight matrix under relation demand and $W_s^{'l}$ is the learnable self weight matrix for seller nodes. Before performing the aggregation over product nodes, we also concatenate (denoted by $\oplus$) the edge features $x(u,i)$ with the product embeddings.

Product representations are computed by aggregation under two relations – demand and substitute, using the following equation –

$$h_p^l(i) = \sigma \left(W_p^{'l} h_p^{l-1}(i) + \underbrace{\frac{1}{|S_{\mathcal{N}_p(i)}|} \sum_{u \in S_{\mathcal{N}_p(i)}} W_s^l [h_s^{l-1}(u) \oplus x(i,u)]}_{\text{aggregation under relation demand}} \right.$$

$$\left. + \underbrace{\frac{1}{|S_{\mathcal{N}_p''(i)}|} \sum_{u \in S_{\mathcal{N}_p''(i)}} W_p^{''l} h_p^{l-1}(u)}_{\text{aggregation under relation substitute}} \right) \quad (4)$$

where, $S_{\mathcal{N}_p(i)}$ is a random sample of the ith product node neighbors under relation 'demand' (neighbors of product nodes would be seller nodes), W_s^l is the learnable weight matrix under relation demand, $W_p^{'l}$ is the learnable self weight matrix for product nodes, $S_{\mathcal{N}_p''(i)}$ is a random sample of the ith product node neighbors under relation 'substitute' (neighbors for product nodes would be product nodes), and $W_p^{''l}$ is the learnable weight matrix under relation 'substitute'. Here also, we concatenate the 'demand' edge features as explained above. This architecture is referred as Hetero-GS-Demand-Substitute.

Heterogeneous Graph Attention Networks with Edge Features: In all the above architectures, we compute hidden representations of seller and product nodes by assigning equal importance to all their neighboring nodes. In the context of demand forecasting, we may want to assign higher weight to more similar products or to products that have higher demand in the neighborhood while learning the representation, as that will help in capturing the correlation between nodes in a better way and accurately predicting the future demand. GAT [23] networks allow us to compute the hidden representation of each node in the graph by attending over its neighbors, following a self-attention strategy. As opposed to GCN or GS, GAT allows for implicitly assigning different importances to neighboring nodes. We compute the seller embeddings by extending Hetero-GS-Demand-Substitute architecture using attention weights –

$$h_s^l(i) = \sigma \left(W_s^{'l} h_s^{l-1}(i) + \frac{1}{|S_{\mathcal{N}_s(i)}|} \sum_{u \in S_{\mathcal{N}_s(i)}} \alpha_{iu}^l W_p^l [h_p^{l-1}(u) \oplus x(u,i)] \right) \quad (5)$$

where α_{iu}^l denotes the attention weights for l^{th} layer and is computed as follows –

$$e_{iu}^l = LeakyReLU(a^{l^T}.[h_p^{l-1}(u) \oplus h_s^{l-1}(i) \oplus x(u,i)]), \quad \alpha_{iu}^l = \frac{\exp(e_{iu}^l)}{\sum_{v \in S_{\mathcal{N}_s(i)}} \exp(e_{iv}^l)} \quad (6)$$

where a^l is the shared learnable linear transformation applied to every node. Attention scores are computed by utilizing source node embeddings, destination node embeddings and the edge features between source and destination as shown in Eq. 6.

Likewise, by modifying the Eq. 4, we obtain the product representations as follows –

$$h_p^l(i) = \sigma \left(W_p^{'l} h_p^{l-1}(i) + \frac{1}{|S_{\mathcal{N}_p(i)}|} \sum_{u \in S_{\mathcal{N}_p(i)}} \alpha_{iu}^{'l} W_s^l [h_s^{l-1}(u) \oplus x(i,u)] \right.$$
$$\left. + \frac{1}{|S_{\mathcal{N}_p''(i)}|} \sum_{u \in S_{\mathcal{N}_p''(i)}} \alpha_p^{''l} W_p^{''l} h_p^{l-1}(u) \right) \quad (7)$$

where $\alpha_{iu}^{'l}$ and $\alpha_p^{''l}$ denote the attention weights and are computed in a similar manner as shown in Eq. 6. This architecture is referred as Hetero-GAT-Demand-Substitute in the experimental section.

3.4 Sequential Model

The seller and product representations are obtained from the above GNN module for each timestep of the time series data. Given the tuple $<s^i, p^i, y_{t-k,t}^i>$ (refer to Sect. 3.1), the sequence of ith product and i^{th} seller representations – $(h_{p_{t-k}}(i), h_{p_{t-k+1}}(i), \ldots, h_{p_t}(i))$ and $(h_{s_{t-k}}(i), h_{s_{t-k+1}}(i), \ldots, h_{s_t}(i))$ is obtained from the GNN module using graphs $\mathcal{G}_{t-k}, \mathcal{G}_{t-k+1}, \ldots, \mathcal{G}_t$ respectively. These embeddings are aggregated with the demand, static features and the available seller-product features, which are then fed into the sequential model for predicting the future demand. The final input to the sequential model is given by –

$$\left(h_{p_{t-k}}(i) \oplus h_{s_{t-k}}(i) \oplus x_{t-k}(p^i, s^i) \oplus x_{t-k}(st) \oplus d_{t-k}^i, \right.$$
$$\left. \ldots, h_{p_t}(i) \oplus h_{s_t}(i) \oplus x_t(p^i, s^i) \oplus x_t(st) \oplus d_t^i \right)_{i=1}^N \quad (8)$$

This module consists primarily of a sequential network to capture the temporal characteristics of the historical demand data. We employ an encoder-decoder based Seq2Seq model for this purpose which has shown to outperform other models for e-commerce forecasting [2, 19, 25]. The sequential model we experimented with resembles the one used by Wen et al. [25], where a vanilla LSTM is used to encode the history into hidden state and an MLP is used as a decoder for predicting the future demand. Furthermore, MLP is used instead of LSTM as a decoder to avoid feeding predictions recursively as surrogate of ground truth, since it leads to error accumulation. Figure 1 represents the complete architecture of the model pictorially.

We also employed TCN [1] architecture for modelling the above sequential data. In the past, TCNs have been shown to outperform recurrent architectures across a broad range of sequence modelling tasks, and we observed the same for our task. TCNs perform dilated causal convolutions, and a key characteristic is that the output at time t is only convolved with the elements that occurred before t so that there is no information leakage. Some of the key advantages of TCNs are that they are easily parallelisable because of convolutional architecture, require less memory as compared to recurrent architectures and have flexible receptive field making them easy to adapt to different domains.

Note that in this work, we conducted our experiments using mainly LSTMs and TCNs. However, the GNN module can easily extend to any other suitable and relevant network for sequence modelling.

4   Experimental Results

This section outlines our experiments using different GNN architectures for demand forecasting in online marketplaces. We validate the proposed framework on a real-world dataset from Amazon for forecasting product demand for different sellers.

Dataset Details: We use a random sample of the demand data (weekly sales of products from sellers) on Amazon from January 2016 to July 2018 for evaluating our models. For training the models, we use the demand data from January 2016 to July 2017 (~1.5 years). For validation and testing, we use the demand data from August 2017 to Jan 2018 (6 months) and Feb 2018 to July 2018 (6 months) respectively to perform out of window evaluation. Table 1 shows the statistics on number of sellers and number of products on the random sample of demand data used for experimentation. We organize the time-series at weekly level, i.e., a single time-step in our models corresponds to demand for 1 week. We use the historical demand data for the last 2 years (104 weeks) for a seller and a product, to predict the future demand for next 4 weeks. Therefore, the length of our time series is $k = 104$ and we predict the demand for future $K = 4$ weeks in all our experiments.

Metrics: We mainly use mean absolute percentage error (MAPE) to compare our models. We compute the MAPE metric over a span of four weeks after

Table 1. Statistics on the train, validation and test dataset used for the experimentation

Dataset	No. of time series	No. of sellers	No. of products
Train	6,411,000	21,020	1,889,908
Validation	2,136,002	22,476	1,801,478
Test	2,154,694	23,700	1,812,206

skipping the week of forecast creation date. MAPE is defined as the average of absolute percentage errors over all time series in the test set, i.e.,

$$MAPE = \frac{1}{M}\left(\sum_i L(\sum_{j=2}^{5} d_{t+j}^i, \sum_{k=2}^{5} \hat{d}_{t+j}^i)\right)$$

where, $M = \#$time series in test set

$$L(d, \hat{d}) = 1, \text{ if } d = 0 \text{ and } \hat{d} \neq 0, \quad L(d, \hat{d}) = 0, \text{ if } d = 0 \text{ and } \hat{d} = 0,$$

$$L(d, \hat{d}) = \frac{||d - \hat{d}||}{d}, \text{ otherwise}$$

Loss Function: We train our multi-graph network in an end-to-end supervised manner using the quantile loss at the 50th percentile, also known as the P50 loss. A quantile is the value below which a certain fraction of samples in the distribution fall. The quantile loss can be defined as:

$$Loss = \sum_i \sum_{j=2}^{5} q \times \max(0, d_{t+j}^i - \hat{d}_{t+j}^i) + (1 - q) \times \max(0, \hat{d}_{t+j}^i - d_{t+j}^i)$$

where q is the required quantile (between 0 and 1). Here, q = 0.5.

4.1   Implementation Details

We use DGL and PyTorch for implementing all our architectures. We train our networks in a minibatch fashion. In each minibatch, we take 1048 ($= batch\ size$) time series, identify the unique sellers and products in them (seed nodes), perform sampling in all the graphs to identify the neighbors for these seed nodes, compute embeddings for the seed nodes from each of the sampled graphs, feed it into a sequential network for generating predictions, and finally back-propagate the loss to train the network. A 2-layer GNN network (16 hidden units) followed by a 2-layer LSTM network (16 hidden units) is used in all the variants. For decoder, an MLP with 2-layers, having 512 hidden units each is used. All the variants converge after 8–10 epochs of training with *learning rate = 0.003*. We finetune these hyparameters by optimizing the performance on the validation set. For TCNs, we use an 8-layer network with kernel size as 7. For training multi-graph networks, we make use of a multi-GPU approach using Torch's DistributedDataParallel library. The main computational bottleneck while training such a huge network is the sampling mechanism. And, the sampling has to be done for all the graphs at each minibatch, based on the sellers and products in that minibatch. Presently, sampling in DGL is implemented in CPU and consumes a large amount of time. For example, in an p3.8x AWS instance, LSTM takes 30 min/epoch for training whereas Homo-GCN and Homo-GS take 1.5 h/epoch and 3 h/epoch respectively for training. The feature dimension of our input features is as follows – $x_t(s^i) = 26$, $x_t(p^i) = 16$, $x_t(p^i, s^i) = 83$, and $x_t(st) = 8$.

4.2 Comparison with Baseline

We perform the exhaustive evaluation of various GNN architectures proposed in the Sect. 3.3. The methods under contention are –

1. **LSTM:** This is our baseline method. This architecture resembles the one proposed by Wen et al. [25], where a vanilla LSTM is used to encode all history into hidden state and an MLP is used as a decoder for predicting the future demand. At each time-step, we concatenate the features x_t^i with the demand value d_t^i and provide it as an input to the LSTM.
2. **Homo-GCN:** In this architecture, GCN is applied to homogeneous graph without considering the edge features in the graph.
3. **Homo-GS:** In this architecture, GS is applied to homogeneous graph without considering the edge features in the graph.
4. **Homo-GAT:** This is an extension of Homo-GCN or Homo-GS to GAT networks. For this method also, we convert the graph into a homogeneous graph, and ignore the edge related features in the graph.
5. **Homo-GS-Demand**: This architecture is an extension of Homo-GS. Along with the input node features, we also add the demand relation features in the homogeneous graph.
6. **Homo-GAT-Demand**: This architecture is an extension of Homo-GAT. In the homogeneous graph, demand relation features are added.
7. **Hetero-GS-Demand-Substitute**: This architecture is proposed in Sect. 3.3. It includes both demand and substitute relations in the graph along with their features.
8. **Hetero-GAT-Demand-Substitute**: This architecture is also proposed in Sect. 3.3. It includes both demand and substitute relations in the graph along with their features.

Table 2 summarizes the performance of above models relative to an LSTM model based baseline. As it can be seen, the best performing GNN model results in ~16% improvement in MAPE as compared to LSTM model. Hence, there is a merit in modelling correlations in the times series using GNNs. The GNN

Table 2. Improvement in MAPE metric for different variants of GNN architectures relative to an LSTM model based baseline. We also report improvement in MAPE for two special cases – (i) when a product is being sold by more than one seller (multi-seller products), (ii) cold/warm start offers, and show that the performance improvement is even more significant in these cases.

Method	MAPE (all offers)	MAPE (multi-seller products)	MAPE (cold start offers)
Homo-GCN	4.08%	4.91%	10.20%
Homo-GS	9.33%	12.60%	17.41%
Homo-GAT	10.13%	14.78%	17.54%
Homo-GS-Demand	13.05%	20.51%	20.72%
Homo-GAT-Demand	14.82%	25.48%	21.51%
Hetero-GS-Demand-Substitute	14.34%	27.43%	23.56%
Hetero-GAT-Demand-Substitute	16.30%	29.43%	24.43%

module allows us to capture the homogeneous and heterogeneous correlations residing in the time series data of online marketplaces in a principled manner. In all the experiments, on expected lines, we see that GAT performs significantly better than the GCN and GS variants, and GS performs better than the GCN. Also, adding the features for demand relation in the graph improves the performance by ~3.7% and ~4.7% for Homo-GS and Homo-GAT respectively. Finally, moving to a heterogeneous setup with multiple kinds of relation (demand and substitute), further improves the performance by ~1.5% and yields the best model.

As discussed in Sect. 3.4, we have also experimented with TCNs as the sequential model. We plugged the GNN modules into TCN network and trained the complete network in an end-to-end fashion. With Homo-GS, we observed that the MAPE improves by 5.43% and with Homo-GAT, the MAPE improves by 6.65% relative to an TCN baseline.

4.3 Demand Forecasting for Multi-seller Products and Cold Start Offers

The idea behind using GNNs with sequential model is to model the homogeneous and heterogeneous correlations in the multivariate time series data. Intuitively, the correlation is high when a single product is being offered by multiple sellers on the platform due to competition, being out of stock, price increase/decrease by other sellers, etc. In order to validate this, we filter out the time series from the test set that contain products being offered by more than one seller. There are 505,485 such time series in the test data. We evaluate the MAPE on this set explicitly and show that the best GNN model performs 29.34% better than the LSTM model (refer to Table 2). This improvement is much higher than the improvement on the full test set (16.30%), thereby, highlighting the fact that the selected subset of the data has more correlations and the proposed framework is able to capture them across different time series using GNNs.

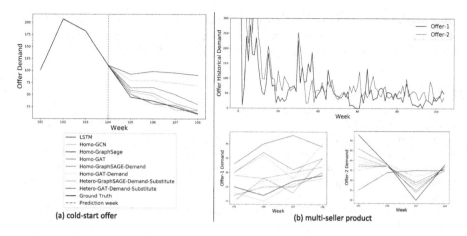

Fig. 2. Future forecast for (a) a cold-start offer and (b) a multi-seller product (from 2 sellers) from our dataset using different techniques. Note that the cold start offer has historical demand for 3 weeks only (101, 102 and 103) whereas for multi-seller offer, there are 2 sellers offering the same product, and history is available for both the offers for 104 weeks. The task is to predict the demand for future 4 weeks. As the LSTM architecture looks only at the offer sales and features to forecast the demand, it performs much worse than the GNN based techniques. GNN techniques leverage other correlated time series also for predicting the future demand.

Another scenario that can greatly benefit with the modelling of correlations is the problem of forecasting demand for cold-start or warm-start offers. The cold/warm-start offers do not have enough history to predict their future demand accurately. This happens quite often in online marketplaces when a seller launches a new product or a new seller starts offering any of the existing products on the platform. In such cases, the proposed framework can be leveraged to derive their demand from other correlated time series in the data. To empirically validate this, we filter out the time series from the test data that contain offers which have less than 3 months (12 weeks) of history. On this set, the best performing GNN model improves MAPE by ~24.43% which is again much higher than the improvement on the overall test set. Figure 2 shows the actual forecast values using different methods for a cold-start offer and a multi-seller product.

5   Conclusion

In this work, we propose a generic framework for handling competing/correlated time series in demand forecasting. We evaluated the framework for the task of demand forecasting in online marketplaces. We capture the correlation between sellers and products using different variants of GNN, and show that it can be plugged into any sequential model for demand prediction. The proposed technique improves the MAPE on a real-world marketplace data by ~16% by capturing the homogeneous and heterogeneous correlations across multivariate time series using GNNs. We also extended various standard GNN architectures to utilise edge features as well for updating the node embeddings.

References

1. Bai, S., Kolter, J.Z., Koltun, V.: An empirical evaluation of generic convolutional and recurrent networks for sequence modeling (2018)
2. Bandara, K., et al.: Sales demand forecast in e-commerce using a long short-term memory neural network methodology. In: Neural Information Processing (2019)
3. Benidis, K., Rangapuram, S.S., Flunkert, V., et. al.: Neural forecasting: introduction and literature overview (2020)
4. Box, G.E.P., Cox, D.R.: An analysis of transformations. J. Roy. Stat. Soc.: Ser. B (Methodol.) **26**, 211–243 (1964)
5. Box, G.E.P., Jenkins, G.M., Reinsel, G.C., Ljung, G.M.: Time Series Analysis: Forecasting and Control. Wiley, New York (2015)
6. Bronstein, M.M., Bruna, J., LeCun, Y., Szlam, A., Vandergheynst, P.: Geometric deep learning: going beyond Euclidean data. CoRR (2016)
7. Cao, D., Wang, Y., Duan, J., Zhang, C., Zhu, X., et al.: Spectral temporal graph neural network for multivariate time-series forecasting. In: NeurIPS (2020)
8. Chen, Y., Kang, Y., Chen, Y., Wang, Z.: Probabilistic forecasting with temporal convolutional neural network (2020)
9. Durbin, J., Koopman, S.J.: Time Series Analysis by State Space Methods, 2nd edn. Oxford University Press, Oxford (2012)
10. Ghorbani, M., Baghshah, M.S., Rabiee, H.R.: Multi-layered graph embedding with graph convolutional networks. CoRR (2018)
11. Hamilton, W.L., Ying, R., Leskovec, J.: Inductive representation learning on large graphs. CoRR (2017)
12. Hamilton, W.L., Ying, R., Leskovec, J.: Representation learning on graphs: methods and applications. CoRR (2017)
13. Hyndman, R., Koehler, A.B., Ord, J.K., Snyder, R.D.: Forecasting with Exponential Smoothing: The State Space Approach. Springer Series in Statistics, Springer, Heidelberg (2008). https://doi.org/10.1007/978-3-540-71918-2
14. Kipf, T.N., Welling, M.: Semi-supervised classification with graph convolutional networks. CoRR (2016)
15. Lai, G., Chang, W., Yang, Y., Liu, H.: Modeling long- and short-term temporal patterns with deep neural networks. CoRR (2017)
16. Li, Y., Yu, R., Shahabi, C., Liu, Y.: Diffusion convolutional recurrent neural network: data-driven traffic forecasting. In: ICLR (2018)
17. McAuley, J., Pandey, R., Leskovec, J.: Inferring networks of substitutable and complementary products. In: KDD (2015)
18. Monti, F., Bronstein, M.M., Bresson, X.: Geometric matrix completion with recurrent multi-graph neural networks. CoRR (2017)
19. Mukherjee, S., Shankar, D., Ghosh, A., et al.: ARMDN: associative and recurrent mixture density networks for eRetail demand forecasting. CoRR (2018)
20. Rangapuram, S.S., Seeger, M.W., Gasthaus, J., Stella, L., Wang, Y., Januschowski, T.: Deep state space models for time series forecasting. In: NeurIPS (2018)
21. Salinas, D., Flunkert, V., Gasthaus, J.: DeepAR: probabilistic forecasting with autoregressive recurrent networks (2019)

22. Sen, R., Yu, H.F., Dhillon, I.S.: Think globally, act locally: a deep neural network approach to high-dimensional time series forecasting. In: NeurIPS (2019)
23. Veličković, P., Cucurull, G., Casanova, A., Romero, A., Liò, P., Bengio, Y.: Graph attention networks. In: ICLR (2018)
24. Wang, Z., Jiang, Z., Ren, Z., et al.: A path-constrained framework for discriminating substitutable and complementary products in e-commerce. In: WSDM (2018)
25. Wen, R., Torkkola, K., Narayanaswamy, B., Madeka, D.: A multi-horizon quantile recurrent forecaster (2018)
26. Wu, Z., Pan, S., Long, G., Jiang, J., Zhang, C.: Graph WaveNet for deep spatial-temporal graph modeling. In: IJCAI-2019 (2019)
27. Ying, R., He, R., Chen, K., Eksombatchai, P., Hamilton, W.L., Leskovec, J.: Graph convolutional neural networks for web-scale recommender systems. CoRR (2018)
28. You, J., Ying, R., Ren, X., Hamilton, W.L., Leskovec, J.: GraphRNN: a deep generative model for graphs. CoRR (2018)
29. Yu, B., Yin, H., Zhu, Z.: Spatio-temporal graph convolutional networks: a deep learning framework for traffic forecasting. In: IJCAI (2018)
30. Zitnik, M., Agrawal, M., Leskovec, J.: Modeling polypharmacy side effects with graph convolutional networks. CoRR (2018)

The Limit Order Book Recreation Model (LOBRM): An Extended Analysis

Zijian Shi$^{(\boxtimes)}$ and John Cartlidge

Department of Computer Science, University of Bristol, Bristol BS8 1UB, UK
{zijian.shi,john.cartlidge}@bristol.ac.uk

Abstract. The limit order book (LOB) depicts the fine-grained demand and supply relationship for financial assets and is widely used in market microstructure studies. Nevertheless, the availability and high cost of LOB data restrict its wider application. The LOB recreation model (LOBRM) was recently proposed to bridge this gap by synthesizing the LOB from trades and quotes (TAQ) data. However, in the original LOBRM study, there were two limitations: (1) experiments were conducted on a relatively small dataset containing only one day of LOB data; and (2) the training and testing were performed in a non-chronological fashion, which essentially re-frames the task as interpolation and potentially introduces lookahead bias. In this study, we extend the research on LOBRM and further validate its use in real-world application scenarios. We first advance the workflow of LOBRM by (1) adding a time-weighted z-score standardization for the LOB and (2) substituting the ordinary differential equation kernel with an exponential decay kernel to lower computation complexity. Experiments are conducted on the extended LOBSTER dataset in a chronological fashion, as it would be used in a real-world application. We find that (1) LOBRM with decay kernel is superior to traditional non-linear models, and module ensembling is effective; (2) prediction accuracy is negatively related to the volatility of order volumes resting in the LOB; (3) the proposed sparse encoding method for TAQ exhibits good generalization ability and can facilitate manifold tasks; and (4) the influence of stochastic drift on prediction accuracy can be alleviated by increasing historical samples.

Keywords: Limit order book · Time series prediction · Financial machine learning

1 Introduction

The majority of financial exchange venues utilise a continuous double auction (CDA) mechanism [11] for matching orders. Under CDA formation, both *ask* orders (orders to sell a given quantity at a given price) and *bid* orders (orders to buy a given quantity at a given price) arrive at the venue continuously, with no minimum time interval limit. When a new order arrives, if it does not immediately execute, it will enter the limit order book (LOB); which contains a list of

© Springer Nature Switzerland AG 2021
Y. Dong et al. (Eds.): ECML PKDD 2021, LNAI 12978, pp. 204–220, 2021.
https://doi.org/10.1007/978-3-030-86514-6_13

current bids and a list of current asks, both sorted by price-time priority. There-fore, the LOB contains valuable information on the instantaneous demand and supply for a particular financial asset (e.g., a stock, a commodity, a derivative, etc.). For this reason, LOB data has been used for many and various studies, including exploration of the price formation mechanism [20], market anomaly detection [26], and testing of trading algorithms [1].

However, there remain some obstacles for the wider application of LOB data. Firstly, LOB data subscription fees are usually high, sometimes amounting to tens of thousands of dollars per annum.[1] This might be a trivial sum for an insti-tutional subscriber, however for individual investors and researchers this signif-icant expense can hold them back. Further, LOB data is entirely unavailable in venues that deliberately do not make order information public, for instance some e-commercial markets and *dark pools* (e.g., see [6,7]). This challenge attracts researchers to consider the possibility of recreating the LOB from a more easily available source, such as *trades and quotes* (TAQ) data. TAQ data contains the *top price level* information of a LOB (the lowest-priced ask and highest-priced bid), together with a history of transactions. It is published to the public for free in most venues. Blanchet et al. [5] have previously demonstrated that it is possible to predict daily average order volumes resting at different price levels of the LOB, using only TAQ data for parameter estimation. More recently, from a deep learning perspective, the LOB recreation model (LOBRM) was proposed to formalize the task as a time series prediction problem, and an ensembled recurrent neural network (RNN) model was successfully used to predict order volumes in a high frequency manner for the first time [23]. Nevertheless, there exist two key restrictions in the LOBRM study: (1) The original LOBRM study was conducted in an interpolation style on only one day's length of LOB data, for two stocks. For the model to be applied in a real world application scenario, such as online prediction of market price movements, LOBRM performance requires evaluation on an extended multi-day dataset, with chronological training and testing such that there is no possibility of lookahead bias; (2) The ordinary dif-ferential equation (ODE) kernel used in the original LOBRM model has high computation complexity and is therefore inefficient for more realistic application scenarios when large amounts (weeks or months) of training data is used.

Contributions:

1. We advance the workflow and structure of the LOBRM model, such that: (i) a time-weighted z-score standardization for LOB features is used to enhance the model's generalization ability; and (ii) the original ODE kernel is substituted for an exponential decay kernel to enable faster inference of latent states, greater runtime efficiency, and a reduction in overfitting.
2. We use chronological training and testing to conduct experiments on an extended LOBSTER dataset that is an order of magnitude larger than the original dataset. We find that: (i) LOBRM with continuous decay kernel

---

[1] http://www.nasdaqtrader.com/Trader.aspx?id=DPUSdata.

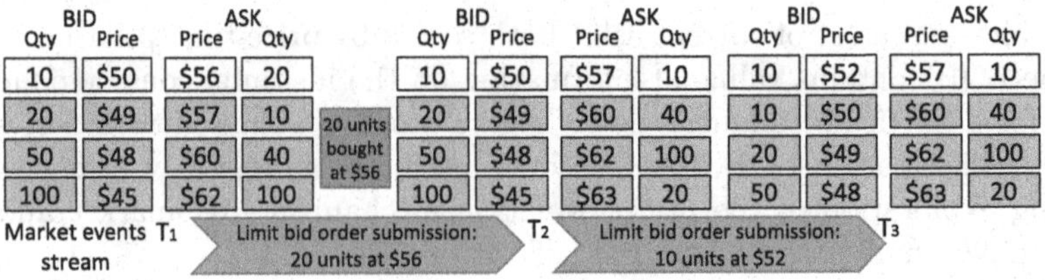

BID Qty	BID Price	ASK Price	ASK Qty		BID Qty	BID Price	ASK Price	ASK Qty		BID Qty	BID Price	ASK Price	ASK Qty
10	$50	$56	20		10	$50	$57	10		10	$52	$57	10
20	$49	$57	10	20 units bought at $56	20	$49	$60	40		10	$50	$60	40
50	$48	$60	40		50	$48	$62	100		20	$49	$62	100
100	$45	$62	100		100	$45	$63	20		50	$48	$63	20

Market events stream T₁ Limit bid order submission: 20 units at $56 T₂ Limit bid order submission: 10 units at $52 T₃

Fig. 1. A LOB of four price levels evolving with time. White and blue boxes indicate the top level and deeper levels of the LOB. Grey boxes indicate market events stream. Orange box indicates trade records. White and orange boxes together form TAQ. (Color figure online)

is superior in modelling the irregularly sampled LOB; and (ii) the module ensembling of LOBRM is effective.

3. We draw new empirical findings that further enrich the current literature: (i) the proposed sparse encoding method for TAQ data has good generalization ability and can facilitate manifold tasks including LOB prediction and price trend prediction; (ii) prediction accuracy of the LOBRM is negatively related to volume volatility at unseen price levels; and (iii) the influence of stochastic drift on model performance can be alleviated by increasing the amount of historical training samples.

2   Background and Related Work

2.1   The Limit Order Book (LOB)

In a CDA market, bids and asks with specified price and quantity (or *volume*) are submitted, cancelled, and transacted continuously. The LOB contains an ask side and a bid side, with ask orders arranged in price ascending order and bid orders arranged in price descending order. Ask orders with the lowest price (*best ask*) and bid orders with the highest price (*best bid*) form the top level of a LOB, and their respective prices are called *quotes*. If a newly submitted ask (or bid) price is not higher (or lower) than the best bid (or ask), a trade happens. TAQ data contains all historical quotes and trades in the venue. That is, LOB data contains strictly more information than TAQ data. Figure 1 provides a visual illustration of a LOB and the relationship between the LOB and the TAQ data.

Traditional statistical models of the LOB assume that LOB evolution follows the rules of a Markovian system, with market events (order submission, cancellation, and transaction) following stochastic point processes, such as a Hawkes process or a Poisson process [2,10]. This formulation generalizes a LOB market of high complexity to a dynamic system controlled by a few parameters, where probabilistic theorems like the law of large numbers [12] and stationary equilibrium in a Markovian system [5] can be utilized to draw long-term empirical conclusions. However, while statistical modelling can capture long term behaviour patterns of the LOB, these models cannot consistently perform well in a high frequency domain. In recent years, there has been an emergence of research using deep learning approaches to model and exploit the LOB. Sirignano et al. [24] performed a significant study on a comprehensive pool of 500 stocks. They revealed that features learned by a Long Short-Term Memory (LSTM) network can be utilized to predict next mid-price movement direction {*up, down*} with accuracy range [0.65, 0.76] across all 500 stocks. Their study also demonstrated that deep learning models suffer less from problems such as stochastic drift that exist in statistical models of the LOB. Other deep learning studies of the LOB include extracting high frequency indicators [21,25], predicting future stock price movement [16,27], and training reinforcement trading agents [13,18].

2.2   Generating Synthetic LOB Data

Synthetic LOB data, generated by models that learn from the real LOB or imitate the *stylized facts* of a CDA market, has been used as an alternative when real LOB data is unavailable. The advantages of using synthetic LOB data lie in its low cost and infinite availability. It has been widely adopted to backtest trading algorithms, explore market dynamics, and facilitate teaching activities.

Synthetic LOB data can be generated using three mainstream methodologies. **Agent-based models** have been well studied and are the most popular approach for generating a synthetic LOB. By configuring agents that trade using common strategies, such as market makers, momentum traders, and mean reversion traders, the synthetic LOB can closely approximate the stylised facts of a real LOB [17]. Stock market simulators have a long history, from the Santa Fe artificial stock exchange [3] to recent multi-agent exchange environments [4]. **Generative models** attempt to learn regularities embedded in market event streams or the LOB directly. One representative research by Li et al. [15] utilized generative adversarial networks to learn and replicate the historical dependency among orders. The synthesised order stream and resulting LOB were found to closely resemble the real market data.

We consider the aforementioned two approaches as *unsupervised*, since no real LOB data is used to verify the authenticity of the generated data. Model quality can only be verified by testing whether certain *stylized facts* exist in the synthetic data. In contrast, **supervised models** use real LOB data as ground truth. As indicated in [5], TAQ data is informative of LOB volumes for small-tick stocks. By modelling the tail probability of price change per trade in a Markovian LOB, daily average order volumes at unseen price levels can be estimated by the steady-state distribution of the infinite server queue. Shi et al. [23] further formulate the task of generating a synthetic LOB as a time series prediction problem using a continuous RNN. The proposed model (LOBRM) is able to predict LOB order volumes using a defined length of TAQ data as input. As long as a historical TAQ trajectory is available, the model is able to produce a historical replay of the LOB based on the knowledge it learned from supervised training. This paper concentrates on a further exploration of the LOBRM model presented in [23].

3 Model Formulation

3.1 Motivation

The LOBRM model represents the first attempt to synthesize LOB data from a supervised deep learning perspective [23]. LOBRM is essentially an ensemble of RNNs that take TAQ data as input and produce LOB volume predictions as output. However, in the original study, there were three restrictions present: (1) Experiments were performed using a relatively small LOB dataset consisting of only one day's LOB data for two small-tick stocks. To verify its generalization ability, LOBRM requires testing on multi-day LOB data for a variety of stocks. (2) Experiments adopted a non-chronological approach to the formation of time series samples, such that samples were shuffled before splitting into training and testing sets. We intend to test model performance using a strictly chronological approach to ensure that LOBRM is applicable to real world online scenarios, with no possibility of introducing lookahead bias. Specifically, we use the first three days' data for training, the fourth day's data for validation, and the fifth day's data for testing. Time series samples are not shuffled, thus ensuring that chronological ordering is preserved. (3) The core module of the original LOBRM made use of an ODE-RNN, a RNN variant with ODE kernels to derive fine-grained time-continuous latent states [22]. As the computational complexity of ODE-RNN is n times that of a vanilla RNN – where n is the granularity of the latent state – it is not efficient for training data of large size. Therefore, we substitute the ODE-RNN for an RNN-decay module [8], which has been shown to be a more time-efficient model for irregularly sampled time series [14].

3.2 Problem Description

To simplify the problem of recreating the LOB, we make the same assumptions proposed in [23]: (1) Following common practice (e.g., [5,12]), the bid and ask sides of the LOB are modelled separately; (2) We only consider instantaneous LOB data at the time of each trade event, and ignore the LOB for all other events, such as order submission and cancellation; (3) We only consider the top five price levels of the LOB; (4) We assume that the price interval between each price level is exactly one *tick* – the smallest increment permitted in quoting or trading a security at a particular exchange venue – which is supported by empirical evidence that orders in the LOB for small-tick stocks tend to be densely distributed around the top price levels [5]. Following these assumptions, the price at different LOB levels can be directly deduced from the known quote price at target time. Therefore, the LOB recreation task resolves to the simpler problem of only predicting order volumes resting at each price level.

For generalization, we denote trades and quotes streams as $\{TD_i\}_{i\in n}$ and $\{QT_i\}_{i\in n}$ respectively, and trajectories of time points for TAQ records as $\{T_i\}_{i\in n}$ indexed by $n = \{1,\ldots,N\}$, where N equals the number of time points in TAQ. The LOB sampled at $\{T_i\}_{i\in n}$ are denoted as $\{LOB_i\}_{i\in n}$. For each record at time T_i, $QT_i = \left(p_i^{a(1)}, v_i^{a(1)}, p_i^{b(1)}, v_i^{b(1)}\right)$, where $p_i^{a(1)}, v_i^{a(1)}, p_i^{b(1)}, v_i^{b(1)}$ denote best ask price, order volume at best ask, best bid price, and order volume at best bid, respectively. $TD_i = \left(p_i^{td}, v_i^{td}, d_i^{td}\right)$, where $p_i^{td}, v_i^{td}, d_i^{td}$ denote price, volume, and direction of the trade, with $+1$ and -1 indicating orders being sold or bought. $LOB_i = (p_i^{a(l)}, v_i^{a(l)}, p_i^{b(l)}, v_i^{b(l)})$ depicts the price and volume information at all price levels, with $l \in (1, ..., L)$, here $L = 5$. From the aforementioned model assumptions, we have $p_i^{a(l)} = p_i^{a(1)} + (l-1)\tau$ and $p_i^{b(l)} = p_i^{b(1)} - (l-1)\tau$, where τ is the minimum tick size (1 cent in the US market). For a single sample, the model predicts $(v_I^{a(2)}, ..., v_I^{a(L)})$ and $(v_I^{b(2)}, ..., v_I^{b(L)})$ conditioned on the observations of $\{QT_i\}_{I-S:I}$ and $\{TD_i\}_{I-S:I}$, with S being the time series sample size, i.e., the maximum number of time steps that the model looks back in TAQ data history.

3.3   Formalized Workflow of LOBRM

LOB Data Standardization. As we intend to apply the LOBRM model on LOBs of five days' length for different financial assets, data standardization is necessary for the model's understanding of data of various numerical scales. We perform time-weighted z-score standardization on all LOB volumes, based on the fact that the LOB is a continuous dynamic system with uneven time intervals between updates. We use $\left\{v_n^{(l)}\right\}_{0:N}$ and $\{T_n\}_{0:N}$ to indicate volume trajectory on price level l, and affiliated timestamps N as the total number of LOB updates for training. Time-weighted mean and standard deviation are calculated as:

$$\text{Mean}^{(l)} = \sum_{i=0}^{N-1} (T_{i+1} - T_i) v_i^{(l)} / (T_N - T_0) \tag{1}$$

$$\text{Std}^{(l)} = \left(\sum_{i=0}^{N-1} (T_{i+1} - T_i) \left(v_i^{(l)} - \text{Mean}^{(l)} \right)^2 / (T_N - T_0) \right)^{\frac{1}{2}} \tag{2}$$

From empirical observation, we witness that the volume statistics on deeper price levels $\left\{v_n^{(2-5)}\right\}_{0:N}$ have similar patterns, while those statistics deviate from volume statistics on the top price level $\left\{v_n^{(1)}\right\}_{0:N}$. In particular, the top level tends to have much lower mean and much higher standard deviation (e.g., see later Table 1). Thus, we treat 'top' and 'deeper' levels as two separate sets to standardize. As trade volumes $\{v_n^{tq}\}_{0:N}$ are discrete events and do not persist in time, we use a normal z-score standardization for trade data. To avoid lookahead bias, statistics are calculated without considering test data. Finally, using these statistics, LOBs for training, validation, and testing are standardized.

Sparse Encoding for TAQ. TAQ data contains multi-modal information, including order type (*bid* or *ask*), price, and volume. While under the formulation of LOBRM, only order volumes at derived price levels (i.e., *deeper* levels 2–5) are predicted. We use a one-hot positional encoding, such that only volume information is encoded explicitly; while price is indicated by the position of non-zero elements in the one-hot vector.

Take the encoding of an ask quote as an example. Conditioned on current best ask price $p_I^{a(1)}$ and best bid price $p_I^{b(1)}$ at T_I, we represent the ask quote record $(p_{I-s}^{a(1)}, v_{I-s}^{a(1)})$ and bid quote record $(p_{I-s}^{b(1)}, v_{I-s}^{b(1)})$ at T_{I-s}, $s \in \{0, \dots, S\}$ as:

$$\begin{cases} O_{2k-1}^{aq}, \text{where } o_{k+sp_s^a} = v_{I-s}^{a(1)} \\ O_{2k-1}^{bq}, \text{where } o_{k+sp_s^b} = v_{I-s}^{b(1)} \end{cases} \tag{3}$$

where $k \in R$, $sp_s^a = (p_{I-s}^{a(1)} - p_I^{a(1)})/\tau$ and $sp_s^b = (p_{I-s}^{b(1)} - p_I^{b(1)})/\tau$. O_{2k-1} is a one-hot vector with dimension $1 \times (2k-1)$; and o_{sp} denotes the sp-th element of the vector. The value of k is chosen to cover more than 90% of past quote price fluctuations, relative to the current quote price. Here $k = 8$, which means historical quotes with relative price $[-7, +7]$ ticks are encoded into feature vectors. Then, a trade record $(p_{I-s}^{td}, v_{I-s}^{td}, d_{I-s}^{td})$, is represented as:

$$\begin{cases} O_{2k-1}^{td}, \text{where } o_{p_{I-s}^{td} - p_I^{a(1)}} = v_{I-s}^{td} \text{ if } d_{I-s}^{td} < 0 \\ O_{2k-1}^{td}, \text{where } o_{p_{I-s}^{td} - p_I^{b(1)}} = v_{I-s}^{td} \text{ if } d_{I-s}^{td} > 0 \end{cases} \tag{4}$$

Finally, those three features are concatenated into (O^{aq}, O^{bq}, O^{td}) and are used as input. It can also be a concatenation of four features, with ask and bid trade represented separately. Later, in experiment Sect. 4.4, we show this sparse encoding method can achieve enhanced robustness in LOB volume prediction and price trend prediction.

Market Event Simulator Module (ES). The ES module models the overall net order arrivals as inhomogeneous poisson processes, and predicts LOB volumes from a dynamic perspective. If an RNN structure is used to iteratively receive encoded LOB features at every timestep, its latent state can be deemed as reflective of market microstructure condition over a short historical time window. A multi-layer perceptron (MLP) layer can then be used to decode latent states directly into vectors representing net order arrival rates at each price level.

The original LOBRM model uses ODE-RNN, a continuous RNN variant that learns fine-grained latent state between discrete inputs in a data-driven manner, to model the continuous evolution of market conditions. In ODE-RNN, a hidden state $h(t)$ is defined as a solution to an ODE initial value problem. The latent state between two inputs can then be derived using an ODE solver as:

$$\frac{dh(t)}{dt} = f_\theta(h(t), t) \text{ where } h(t_0) = h_0 \tag{5}$$

$$h_i' = \text{ODEsolver}(f_\theta, h_{i-1}, (t_{i-1}, t_i)) \tag{6}$$

in which function f_θ is a separate neural network parameterized by θ.

Even though ODE-RNN contributes most to prediction accuracy, it is of high computation complexity (see Sect. 3.1). Therefore, for an efficient use of LOBRM, especially when trained on large amounts of data, or used for online prediction, the ODE-RNN is unsuitable. Also, we find in chronological experiments that the ODE-RNN tends to cause overfitting due to the fully flexible latent states.

Faced with these challenges, we propose the use of a pre-defined exponential decay kernel [8,14], instead of the ODE kernel in the ES module. The inference of latent states between discrete inputs is denoted as:

$$h_i' = h_{i-1} * exp\left(-f_\theta\left(h_{i-1}\right) * \Phi\left(t_{i-1}, t_i\right)\right) \tag{7}$$

$$h_i = \text{GRUunit}\left(h_i', x_i\right) \tag{8}$$

where f_θ is a separate neural network parameterized by θ, and Φ is a smoothing function for time intervals to avoid gradient diminishing. A GRU unit [9] is then used for instant updating of the latent state at input timesteps. The advantages of employing an exponential decay kernel are threefold: (1) It allows for efficient inference of latent states; (2) It is a continuous RNN that imitates continuity of market evolution and includes temporal information within the model structure itself, sharing the advantages of continuous RNN in modelling irregularly sampled time series; (3) It is less likely to cause overfitting as the kernel form is predefined, whereas the latent state evolution in ODE-RNN is fully flexible.

We derive the vector of net order arrival rates $\Lambda_{I-s} = [\lambda_{I-s}^{a(2)}, ..., \lambda_{I-s}^{a(L)}]$ at time T_{I-s} directly from the latent state h_{I-s}, using an MLP layer as:

$$\Lambda_{I-s} = \text{MLP}\left(h_{I-s}\right) \tag{9}$$

After acquiring the trajectory of Λ at all trade times over the defined length of time steps, we calculate the accumulated order volumes between $[T_{I-S}, T_I]$ as:

$$\sum_{i=I-S}^{I} \Lambda_i \times \Phi\left(T_{i+1} - T_i\right) \tag{10}$$

History Compiler Module (HC). The HC module predicts LOB volumes from a historical perspective. It concentrates on historical quotes that are most relevant to current LOB volumes at deeper price levels. More precisely, for an ask side model the volumes to be predicted at target time are of prices $\{p_I^{a(1)} + \tau, ..., p_I^{a(1)} + (L-1)\tau\}$. Only historical ask quotes with price within this range are used as inputs into the HC module. As one-hot encoded ask quotes fall within the price range of $\{p_I^{a(1)} - k\tau, ..., p_I^{a(1)} + k\tau\}$, vectors need to be trimmed to remove verbose information and retain the most relevant information. Formally, we represent a trimmed ask quote record $(p_{I-s}^{a(1)}, v_{I-s}^{a(1)})$ as:

$$\begin{cases} O_{L-1}, \text{where } o_{sp_s^a} = v_{I-s}^{a(1)} \text{ if } sp_s^a \in [1, L-1] \\ Z_{L-1} \qquad\qquad \text{otherwise} \end{cases} \tag{11}$$

where O_{L-1} is a one-hot vector of dimension $1 \times (L-1)$; $o_{sp_s^a}$ denotes the sp_s^a-th element of the vector; and Z_{L-1} denotes a zero vector of the same dimension. The intention of the HC module is to look back in history to check how many orders were resting at price levels we are interested in at target time. Thus, we manually trim input feature vectors to leave out verbose information. A discrete GRU unit is used to compile trimmed features and generate volume predictions which are used as supplements to ES predictions.

Weighting Scheme Module (WS). This module is designed to combine the predictions from the ES and HC modules into a final prediction. We follow the intuition that if the HC prediction for a particular price level is reliable from a historical perspective, a higher weight will be allocated to it, and *vice versa*. If quote history for a target time price level is both abundant and recent, we weight the information provided on current LOB volumes as more reliable. The abundancy and timing of historical quotes are denoted by the masking sequence of HC inputs. Formally, we represent the mask of an ask side HC input as:

$$\begin{cases} O_{L-1}, \text{where } o_{sp_s^a} = 1 \text{ if } sp_s^a \in [1, L-1] \\ \qquad Z_{L-1} \qquad \text{otherwise} \end{cases} \tag{12}$$

A GRU unit is used to receive the whole masking sequence to generate a weighting vector of size $1 \times (L-1)$ to combine predictions from ES and HC modules.

4 Experiment and Empirical Analysis

In this section, experiments are conducted on the extended LOBSTER dataset. These data were kindly provided by lobsterdata.com for academic research. The stocks and time periods were not selected by the authors. The dataset contains LOB data of five days' length for three small-tick stocks (Microsoft, symbol MSFT; Intel, INTC; and JPMorgan, JPM). To ensure that there is no selection bias or "cherry-picking" of data, all three available small-tick stocks were used in this study. The extended dataset is approximately ten times the size of the dataset used in [23] and is a strict superset, therefore enabling easier results comparison.

Model Specification: The **ES module** consists of a GRU with 64 units, a two layered MLP with 32 units and ReLU activation for deriving parameters of the decay kernel, and a two layered MLP decoder with 64 units and Tanh activation. The **HC module** consists of a GRU with 64 units, and a two layered MLP decoder with 64 units and LeakyReLU activation. The latent state size is set at 32 in ES and HC modules. The **WS module** consists of a GRU with 16 units, and a one-layered MLP decoder with 16 units and Sigmoid activation. The latent state size is set at 16 in the WS module. L1 loss is used as the loss function; and all models are trained for 150 iterations, with a learning rate of 2e−4. Model parameters are chosen based on the lowest loss on the validation set.

4.1 Data Preprocessing

We clean the dataset by retaining only LOB updates at trade times, and removing LOB data during the first half-hour after market open and the last half-hour before market close as these periods tend to be volatile. To alleviate the effect of outliers, we divide all volume numbers by 100 and winsorize the data by the range $[0.005, 0.995]$. Then, the standardization method proposed in Sect. 3.3 is applied to the cleansed LOB data. Data statistics are illustrated in Table 1.

Table 1. Volume statistics before standardization, showing time-weighted mean volume and standard deviation on the top level and deep levels (levels 2 to 5).

	MSFT		INTC		JPM	
	Bid	Ask	Bid	Ask	Bid	Ask
Top	119.7/89.1		127.1/98.3		32.7/38.5	
Deep	189.6/51.7	192.7/53.4	185.6/62.3	178.9/51.4	61.3/23.9	63.4/40.5

We use the first three days' data for training, the fourth day's data for validation, and the fifth day's data for testing. This is a significantly different approach to that taken in [23], in which the task was essentially interpolation, as all time series samples were shuffled before splitting into training and testing sets (i.e., training and testing sets were not ordered chronologically). We extract TAQ data and labels directly from the standardized LOB. These data are then converted to time series samples using a rolling window of size S, such that the first sample consists of TAQ histories at timesteps 1 to S and is labeled by LOB volume at deep price levels at time step S. The second sample consists of TAQ history at timesteps 2 to $S + 1$ and is labeled using LOB at time step $S + 1$, *etc.* We set parameters $S = 100$ and $k = 8$, as in the original LOBRM model [23].

4.2 Model Comparison

In this section, we illustrate training results on generating synthetic LOB using mainstream regression and machine learning methods: (1) Support Vector Machine Regression with linear kernel (LSVR); (2) Ridge Regression (RR); (3) Single Layer Feedforward Network (SLFN); and (4) XGBoost Regression (XGBR). We then evaluate the performance of LOBRM with either discrete RNN or Continuous RNN module: (1) GRU; (2) GRU-T, with time concatenated input; (3) Decay; and (4) Decay-T, with time concatenated input. Two criteria are used: (1) L1 loss on test set. As all labels are standardized into z-score, the loss indicates the multiple of standard deviations between prediction and ground truth; (2) R-squared, calculated on the test data using the method presented by Blanchet et al. [5], to enable us to perform a strict comparison with the existing literature.

Table 2 presents evaluation results. Judging from both criteria, we observe that non-linear models outperform linear models (LSVR and RR). The LOBRM family also outperforms traditional non-linear models (especially in terms of R-squared) by effective ensembling of RNNs. This indicates that the recurrent structure of RNNs can facilitate the model's capability in explaining temporal variance in LOB volume. Further, LOBRMs with a continuous RNN module exhibit superior performance over those with a discrete RNN module in 4 out of 6 experiments. LOBRM (Decay-T) achieves the lowest average L1 test loss and highest average R-squared, indicating that incorporating temporal information in both feature vectors and latent state dynamics is the most suitable approach to

Table 2. Model comparison. Criteria shown in format: test loss/R-squared; all numbers are in 1e−1. The lowest test loss and highest R-squared in each set are underlined.

Model	MSFT		INTC		JPM	
	Bid	Ask	Bid	Ask	Bid	Ask
LSVR	10.00/0.29	9.74/0.36	8.72/0.21	10.30/0.14	6.91/0.54	3.96/0.51
RR	7.90/0.55	7.70/0.67	6.18/0.53	7.00/0.40	6.86/0.65	4.10/0.46
SLFN	7.06/0.68	6.88/0.88	5.55/0.86	5.88/0.53	6.61/0.71	3.69/0.62
XGBR	6.50/0.43	6.91/0.80	5.21/0.82	5.93/0.83	6.81/0.76	3.73/0.69
LOBRM (GRU)	6.44/1.24	6.44/1.55	5.34/1.05	5.70/0.53	6.27/1.17	3.30/1.25
LOBRM (GRU-T)	6.45/1.38	6.45/1.56	5.36/1.06	5.65/0.84	6.13/1.48	3.34/1.73
LOBRM (Decay)	6.54/1.30	6.47/1.49	5.33/1.11	5.52/0.73	6.35/1.20	3.29/1.37
LOBRM (Decay-T)	6.28/1.58	6.15/1.77	5.33/1.07	5.64/0.82	6.18/1.54	3.32/1.65

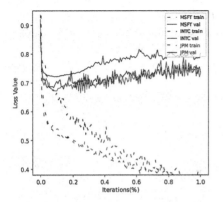

Fig. 2. Training (dash) and validation (line) loss curves for bid-side models.

Fig. 3. Hourly test loss plotted against hourly volume standard deviation.

capture the model's dependence on time. Meanwhile we find the model tends to be overfitting, with validation loss starting to rise before training loss converges. Figure 2 shows loss curves for LOBRM (Decay-T) trained with a higher learning rate of 2e-3. The phenomenon of overfitting also explains why we use a predefined exponential decay kernel instead of a fully flexible ODE kernel involving a lot more parameters to model temporal dependence. Thus, in the following experiments, we continue using LOBRM (Decay-T) as the main model.

As shown in Table 2, test losses across 6 sets of experiments fluctuate in the range [0.332, 0.628] for LOBRM (Decay-T). To test whether this fluctuation results from order volume volatility, we use the pre-trained model to calculate the correlation of (hourly) test L1 loss across all experiments against the (hourly) standard deviation of non-standardized volume resting at deep price levels (see Fig. 3). We find that the correlation between hourly L1 loss and volume volatility

Table 3. Ablation study: test loss.

	MSFT		INTC		JPM		Avg.
	Bid	Ask	Bid	Ask	Bid	Ask	
HC	6.79	7.42	5.47	6.78	6.22	3.86	6.09
ES	6.31	6.99	5.94	5.70	6.04	3.36	5.72
HC+ES	6.26	6.45	5.40	5.50	6.02	3.32	5.49
HC+ES+WS	6.28	6.15	5.33	5.64	6.18	3.38	5.49

is significant (p-value < 0.01) with a correlation coefficient of $\rho = 0.48$. Thus, we conclude that LOB prediction accuracy is negatively related to volume volatility.

Compared with the original LOBRM study, which uses a non-chronological training and testing method, we find that the performance of LOBRM trained in a chronological manner is weakened. In order to make the criteria comparable, we first transform the L1 loss in z-score into L1 loss on volume as a percentage of average volume, using $(zscore * std_i)/mean_i$ for each dataset i. The transformed loss on LOBRM (Decay-T) ranges in $[16.1\%, 24.1\%]$ with a mean value of 18.9%, whereas this criteria in non-chronological experiments has an average of 6.9%. The main reason lies in that, in non-chronological experiments the model attempts to predict the volume at a target timestep when both volumes at past and future timesteps are known and used for training. This leakage of information from the future introduces a form of lookahead bias into the model that tends to increase the prediction accuracy. In the experiments presented here, no future labels are used for training, thus lookahead bias is eliminated.

We further compare our results of R-squared with results from the statistical model approaching a similar task proposed in [5], in which presented R-squared values ranged in $[0.81, 0.88]$ for daily average volume at different price levels. However, in comparison, our R-squared values presented in Table 2 are regressed against the ground truth with no averaging procedure. As we have only one-day length of data for training, we cannot generate daily average volume prediction for R-squared calculation. When we average volume predictions into hourly frequency, the value of R-squared across 6 experiments ranges in $[0.48, 0.88]$ with an average value of 0.71. We find our results comparable to the existing literature, even though those results are not measured using identical conditions.

4.3   Ablation Study

We conduct an ablation study to demonstrate the effectiveness of module ensembling. Four experiments are conducted: HC, using only the history compiler; ES, using only the market events simulator; HC+ES, which includes the history compiler and event simulator, using a pre-defined weight to combine outputs; and HC+ES+WS, which is the full LOBRM with adaptive weighting scheme.

Results are shown in Table 3. We see that predictions from the HC alone have the highest test error, as the inputs it receives are trimmed to contain

Table 4. LOBRM test loss comparison of explicit and sparse encodings of TAQ data.

	MSFT		INTC		JPM		Avg.
	Bid	Ask	Bid	Ask	Bid	Ask	
Explicit	6.87	6.43	6.80	9.95	7.60	4.14	6.97
Sparse	6.31	6.99	5.94	5.70	6.04	3.36	5.72

only the most relevant data for current LOB volume prediction. ES module, by receiving complete TAQ data input and modelling market events as a stochastic process using a continuous RNN, achieves a lower error than HC module and is the dominant module that contributes to prediction accuracy. Combining both HC and ES modules, either using a predefined or adaptive weight, achieves the best performance, which suggests that the predictions from HC and ES are complementary and can be effectively combined to gain a higher accuracy prediction. The purpose of the WS module in the original LOBRM study is to facilitate the model's use in transfer learning and it does not contribute to prediction accuracy when tested on the same stock that it was trained, as is the case here.

4.4 Superiority of Sparse Encoding for TAQ

LOB Volume Prediction. In sparse encoding, only volume information in TAQ is encoded explicitly and price information are embedded implicitly by positions of non-zero elements in one-hot vectors. In explicit encoding, information including price, volume, and trade direction are encoded directly as non-zero elements in feature vectors. Here we use the ES module in LOBRM (Decay-T) as the main model and tested the model prediction accuracy when these two different encoding methods are used. We don't choose the full model as explicitly encoded input cannot be trimmed so HC module is not used. Results are shown in Table 4. We see that the model with sparse encoding achieves lower test loss error in 5 out of 6 experiments. The average test loss for the model with sparse encoding is 17.9% lower than the model with explicit encoding.

Price Trend Prediction. We compare the sparse encoding method with the convolution method proposed in [27] for quotes data in the task of stock price trend prediction. On the basis of explicit encoding, the convolution encoding method applies two convolution layers with filters of size $[1 \times 2]$ and stride $[1 \times 2]$ on quote data. This structure first convolutionalize price and volume information at ask and bid sides respectively and then convolutionalize two sides' information together. We approach a similar task presented in [27] but simplify the model structure to concentrate on the prediction accuracy variation brought by different encoding methods. We set length of time series samples as $S = 50$. For sparse encoding, we set $k = 5$. For convolution encoding, we use 16 $[1 \times 2]$ kernels with stride $[1 \times 2]$ followed by LeakyReLU activation. We standardize features using

Table 5. Future price prediction: validation/test accuracy.

	Sparse (implicit price)	Convolution (explicit price)	Convolution (no price)
Min-max	59.8%/55.2%	55.9%/54.4%	57.2%/53.9%
Z-score	60.2%/57.4%	57.1%/54.0%	58.3%/55.0%

Table 6. LOBRM (Decay-T) test loss against training size.

	MSFT		INTC		JPM		Avg.
	Bid	Ask	Bid	Ask	Bid	Ask	
Day3	7.15	7.15	6.05	6.18	6.29	3.33	6.03
Day2+3	6.25	6.58	5.86	5.73	6.40	3.32	5.69
Day1+2+3	6.28	6.15	5.33	5.64	6.18	3.32	5.48

min-max or z-score standardization. Encoded data are passed to an MLP with ReLU activation. A GRU unit is used to receive iterative inputs and the final latent state is connected with an MLP with Softmax activation to generate a possibility distribution over three labels $\{down, same, up\}$. We test the model on MSFT five-day dataset, using first three days for training, the fourth day for validation, and the fifth day for testing. We run a rolling average of five timesteps to alleviate label imbalance [19], with 29%, 40%, and 31% for *up*, *same*, and *down*. We train the model with cross entropy loss for 50 iterations and choose the model with highest validation accuracy.

Results are shown in Table 5. We can see that the sparse encoding method with two different standardization methods has superior performance in the task of price trend prediction, compared with convolution encoding either with or without price information. Thus, we draw the conclusion that the sparse encoding method for TAQ data can not only benefit the task of LOB volume prediction, but also other tasks including stock price trend prediction.

4.5   Is the Model Well-Trained?

As financial time series suffer from stochastic drift, in the sense that the distribution of data is unstable and tends to vary temporarily, large amounts of data is needed for model training. For example, the LOB used in [5] and [24] is of one month's and seventeen month's length. Here, for all six sets of experiments (3 stocks × 2 sides) we use three days' LOB data for training, one day's data for validation, and one day's data for testing. We would like to test whether this amount of training data is abundant enough for out-of-sample testing.

As the dataset we possess contains five consecutive trading days' LOB data, we leave out the fourth day's and fifth day's LOB data for validation and testing. We first use the third day's data for training and then iteratively add in the second and the first day's historical data to observe how the validation and testing loss change. Results are shown in Table 6. We can see that there is a downward tendency in average test loss as more historical data is used for training. This is especially true for `MSFT` ask, `INTC` bid, and `INTC` ask. This phenomenon suggests that the influence of stochastic drift may be alleviated by exposing the model to more historical samples. Therefore, we would expect even lower out-of-sample errors if more historical data can be used for training.

5   Conclusion

We have extended the research on the LOBRM, the first deep learning model for generating synthetic LOB data. Two major revisions were proposed: standardizing LOB data with time-weighted z-score to improve the model's generalization ability; and substituting the original ODE kernel with an exponential decay kernel (Decay-T) to improve time efficiency. Experiments were conducted on an extended LOBSTER dataset, a strict superset of the data used in the original study, with size approximately ten times larger. Using a fully chronological training and testing regime, we demonstrated that LOBRM (Decay-T) has superior performance over traditional models, and showed the efficacy of module ensembling. We further found that: (1) LOB volume prediction accuracy is negatively related to volume volatility; (2) sparse one-hot positional encoding of TAQ data can benefit manifold tasks; and (3) there is some evidence that the influence of stochastic drift can be alleviated by increasing the number of historical samples. As a whole, this study validates the use of LOBRM in demanding application scenarios that require efficient inference and involve large amounts of data for training and predicting.

Acknowledgements. Zijian Shi's PhD is supported by a China Scholarship Council (CSC)/University of Bristol joint-funded scholarship. John Cartlidge is sponsored by Refinitiv.

References

1. Abergel, F., Huré, C., Pham, H.: Algorithmic trading in a microstructural limit order book model. Quant. Finance **20**(8), 1263–1283 (2020)
2. Abergel, F., Jedidi, A.: Long-time behavior of a Hawkes process-based limit order book. SIAM J. Financ. Math. **6**(1), 1026–1043 (2015)
3. Arthur, W.B., Holland, J.H., LeBaron, B., Palmer, R., Tayler, P.: Asset Pricing Under Endogenous Expectations in An Artificial Stock Market. The Economy as an Evolving Complex System II 27 (1996)
4. Belcak, P., Calliess, J.P., Zohren, S.: Fast agent-based simulation framework of limit order books with applications to pro-rata markets and the study of latency effects (2020). arXiv preprint. https://arxiv.org/abs/2008.07871
5. Blanchet, J., Chen, X., Pei, Y.: Unraveling limit order books using just bid/ask prices (2017). https://web.stanford.edu/~jblanche/papers/LOB_v1.pdf. Unpublished preprint

6. Cartlidge, J., Smart, N.P., Talibi Alaoui, Y.: MPC joins the dark side. In: ACM Asia Conference on Computer and Communications Security, pp. 148–159 (2019)
7. Cartlidge, J., Smart, N.P., Talibi Alaoui, Y.: Multi-party computation mechanism for anonymous equity block trading: a secure implementation of Turquoise Plato Uncross (2020). Cryptology ePrint Archive. https://eprint.iacr.org/2020/662
8. Che, Z., Purushotham, S., Cho, K., Sontag, D., Liu, Y.: Recurrent neural networks for multivariate time series with missing values. Sci. Rep. **8**(1), 1–12 (2018)
9. Cho, K., et al.: Learning phrase representations using RNN encoder-decoder for statistical machine translation. In: Conference on Empirical Methods in Natural Language Processing, pp. 1724–1734 (2014)
10. Cont, R., De Larrard, A.: Price dynamics in a Markovian limit order market. SIAM J. Financ. Math. **4**(1), 1–25 (2013)
11. Friedman, D.: The double auction market institution: a survey. In: The Double Auction Market: Institutions, Theories, and Evidence, vol. 14, pp. 3–25 (1993)
12. Horst, U., Kreher, D.: A weak law of large numbers for a limit order book model with fully state dependent order dynamics. SIAM J. Financ. Math. **8**(1), 314–343 (2017)
13. Kumar, P.: Deep reinforcement learning for market making. In: 19th International Conference on Autonomous Agents and MultiAgent Systems, pp. 1892–1894 (2020)
14. Lechner, M., Hasani, R.: Learning long-term dependencies in irregularly-sampled time series. In: Annual Conference on Advances in Neural Information Processing Systems (2020, preprint). https://arxiv.org/abs/2006.04418
15. Li, J., Wang, X., Lin, Y., Sinha, A., Wellman, M.: Generating realistic stock market order streams. In: 34th AAAI Conference on Artificial Intelligence, pp. 727–734 (2020)
16. Mäkinen, Y., Kanniainen, J., Gabbouj, M., Iosifidis, A.: Forecasting jump arrivals in stock prices: new attention-based network architecture using limit order book data. Quant. Finance **19**(12), 2033–2050 (2019)
17. McGroarty, F., Booth, A., Gerding, E., Chinthalapati, V.L.R.: High frequency trading strategies, market fragility and price spikes: an agent based model perspective. Ann. Oper. Res. 217–244 (2018). https://doi.org/10.1007/s10479-018-3019-4
18. Nevmyvaka, Y., Feng, Y., Kearns, M.: Reinforcement learning for optimized trade execution. In: 23rd International Conference on Machine Learning (ICML), pp. 673–680 (2006)
19. Ntakaris, A., Magris, M., Kanniainen, J., Gabbouj, M., Iosifidis, A.: Benchmark dataset for mid-price forecasting of limit order book data with machine learning methods. J. Forecast. **37**(8), 852–866 (2018)
20. Parlour, C.A.: Price dynamics in limit order markets. Rev. Financ. Stud. **11**(4), 789–816 (1998)
21. Passalis, N., Tefas, A., Kanniainen, J., Gabbouj, M., Iosifidis, A.: Temporal logistic neural bag-of-features for financial time series forecasting leveraging limit order book data. Pattern Recogn. Lett. **136**, 183–189 (2020)
22. Rubanova, Y., Chen, T.Q., Duvenaud, D.K.: Latent ordinary differential equations for irregularly-sampled time series. In: Annual Conference on Advances in Neural Information Processing Systems, pp. 5321–5331 (2019)
23. Shi, Z., Chen, Y., Cartlidge, J.: The LOB recreation model: Predicting the limit order book from TAQ history using an ordinary differential equation recurrent neural network. In: 35th AAAI Conference on Artificial Intelligence, pp. 548–556 (2021)
24. Sirignano, J., Cont, R.: Universal features of price formation in financial markets: perspectives from deep learning. Quant. Finance **19**(9), 1449–1459 (2019)

25. Tsantekidis, A., Passalis, N., Tefas, A., Kanniainen, J., Gabbouj, M., Iosifidis, A.: Using deep learning for price prediction by exploiting stationary limit order book features. Appl. Soft Comput. **93**, 106401 (2020)
26. Ye, Z., Florescu, I.: Extracting information from the limit order book: new measures to evaluate equity data flow. High Freq. **2**(1), 37–47 (2019)
27. Zhang, Z., Zohren, S., Roberts, S.: DeepLOB: deep convolutional neural networks for limit order books. IEEE Trans. Signal Process. **67**(11), 3001–3012 (2019)

Taking over the Stock Market: Adversarial Perturbations Against Algorithmic Traders

Elior Nehemya$^{(\boxtimes)}$, Yael Mathov , Asaf Shabtai , and Yuval Elovici

Department of Software and Information Systems Engineering,
Ben-Gurion University of the Negev, Beer-Sheva 8410501, Israel
{nehemya,yaelmath}@post.bgu.ac.il, {shabtaia,elovici}@bgu.ac.il

Abstract. In recent years, machine learning has become prevalent in numerous tasks, including algorithmic trading. Stock market traders utilize machine learning models to predict the market's behavior and execute an investment strategy accordingly. However, machine learning models have been shown to be susceptible to input manipulations called adversarial examples. Despite this risk, the trading domain remains largely unexplored in the context of adversarial learning. In this study, we present a realistic scenario in which an attacker influences algorithmic trading systems by using adversarial learning techniques to manipulate the input data stream in real time. The attacker creates a universal adversarial perturbation that is agnostic to the target model and time of use, which remains imperceptible when added to the input stream. We evaluate our attack on a real-world market data stream and target three different trading algorithms. We show that when added to the input stream, our perturbation can fool the trading algorithms at future unseen data points, in both white-box and black-box settings. Finally, we present various mitigation methods and discuss their limitations, which stem from the algorithmic trading domain. We believe that these findings should serve as a warning to the finance community regarding the threats in this area and promote further research on the risks associated with using automated learning models in the trading domain.

Keywords: Adversarial examples · Algorithmic trading

1 Introduction

In recent history, stock markets have been a significant vehicle for personal and institutional investing. When buying or selling financial assets via the stock exchange, traders gain or lose money based on changes in the assets' value. To maximize his/her profits, the trader needs to accurately predict changes in the market. Yet, predicting the prices of financial assets is a challenging task, due to

---

E. Nehemya and Y. Mathov—Both authors contributed equally.

© Springer Nature Switzerland AG 2021
Y. Dong et al. (Eds.): ECML PKDD 2021, LNAI 12978, pp. 221–236, 2021.
https://doi.org/10.1007/978-3-030-86514-6_14

the complex dynamics of the market's behavior. To do so, a trader processes a vast amount of market data and uses it to try to predict the value of a specific stock. Based on this prediction, the trader develops an investment strategy concerning the stock, which results in one of the following actions: (1) selling the stock, (2) buying more of the stock, or (3) holding his/her assets intact.

To gain a possible advantage, traders use computers to analyze financial market data quickly and execute trades automatically; known as algorithmic trading (AT), this is the most common form of stock trading performed today [28]. Most AT systems use a similar process, consisting of three main steps: data preprocessing, applying prediction model, and investment strategy execution. The preprocessed data is used to predict the market's behavior using a prediction unit known as the alpha model, and based on this prediction, the best investment strategy is chosen and executed. In the past, a set of predefined rules was used to calculate the market predictions and choose the investment strategy [8], but today, the popularity of machine learning is changing the picture. More traders are relying on machine learning-based alpha models, such as support vector machine (SVM) and artificial neural network (ANN) architectures [15], which can automatically make multiple predictions in milliseconds based a large amount of data; the edge they provide is especially useful in high-frequency trading (HFT). However, since most of the methods used to choose the investment strategy are still rule-based, the alpha model has become the heart of AT systems.

In recent years, hackers have profited from the stock market by spreading fake news [10] or published stolen sensitive information [4,9] on companies as a means of decreasing their stock price. Additionally, cyber attacks can be used to compromise various players in the market to affect the market directly (e.g., by hacking traders' accounts and performing transactions on their behalf [20,24]). Since no one is safe from those threats [21], regulatory authorities fight them by monitoring the stock market to identify fraudulent activity performed by malicious or compromised entities. However, the nature of AT makes it challenging to monitor and understand the bots' behaviors, especially in HFT systems that perform many transactions in a short period of time, making it difficult to identify real-time changes in their operation. Therefore, changes regarding the behavior of an AT bot can only be identified retrospectively, which may be too late. Moreover, AT bots can use complex learning algorithms (i.e., ANNs), which remain a focus of research due to their lack of explainability [14].

Along with the potential cyber attacks and the monitoring challenges mentioned above, a new threat has emerged from the rapid technological improvements seen in recent years: Machine learning models have been shown to be vulnerable to adversarial inputs known as adversarial examples, which are maliciously modified data samples that are designed so that they will be misclassified by the target model [27]. This vulnerability threatens the reliability of machine learning models and could potentially jeopardize sensitive applications, such as those used in the trading domain. By exploiting the existence of adversarial examples, an attacker can gain control of an AT bot's alpha model and, as a result, influence the system's actions. Moreover, by gaining control of multiple

AT systems, an attacker could put the entire stock market at risk. Yet, adversarial perturbations in AT are rare, mainly due to the data, which is extremely dynamic, unpredictable, and heavily monitored by law enforcement agencies; thus, state-of-the-art attacks successfully used in other domains may be ineffective in the trading realm. Unlike images, where the features are pixels that can be easily perturbed, AT data is extracted from a live stream of the stock market, with numeric features that are inclined to change rapidly and sometimes in a chaotic manner. Additionally, since AT alpha models use real-time data, crafting a perturbation for a specific data point in advance is challenging. Due to the frequent changes in the data, by the time the attacker has crafted the adversarial perturbation, the data may have changed completely. Since the attacker cannot predict the market's behavior, he/she cannot craft a perturbation in real time.

In this study, we investigate the existence of adversarial perturbations in the AT domain, taking all of the aforementioned challenges into account. We present a realistic scenario where an attacker who manipulates the HFT data stream can gain control of an AT bot's actions in real time. To achieve this goal, we present an algorithm that utilizes known market data to craft a targeted universal adversarial perturbation (TUAP), which can fool the alpha model. The algorithm is designed to create a small, imperceptible TUAP to avoid detection; the TUAP created is agnostic to the target alpha model, as well as to the unseen data samples to which it is added. Our method is evaluated using real-world stock data and three different prediction models in both white-box and black-box settings. We also demonstrate different mitigation methods against our attack and discuss their limitations when used to protect AT systems. Our results suggest that the risk of adversarial examples in the trading domain is significantly higher than expected. Based on our review of the literature, it seems that adversarial learning in the trading domain largely remains an unexplored field of research. Therefore, we encourage both regulators and traders to address this concern and implement the methods needed to reduce the risk caused by the use of vulnerable models for algorithmic trading.

2   Background

2.1   Algorithmic Trading

Algorithmic trading refers to the use of computer programs that perform trading transactions based on an analysis of the stock market. Both human and AT system traders aim to maximize their profit by perfecting their ability to predict a stock's future price, use it to define an investment strategy, and perform beneficial transactions [28]. Since an accurate prediction results in a more profitable investment, the AT system maintains an alpha model that models the market's behavior. The system also has an execution logic unit which turns the prediction into a transaction based on risk management policies. A popular type of AT is HFT, where traders perform a large number of transactions in a short period of time [28]. Since HFT requires split-second decisions, it relies solely on automated software [5], and thus, we focus on this type of trading in this paper.

To predict the future stock price, the alpha model obtains data from an online broker or other external sources. There are two main types of features used for stock market prediction [15]: fundamental indicators and technical indicators, which are used for fundamental and technical analysis, respectively. Fundamental analysis focuses on macro factors that might correlate with the stock's price, such as financial records, economic reports, and balance sheets. Conversely, technical analysis assumes that all of the relevant information is factored into the stock's price. More than 80% of alpha models use technical indicators as input features [15]. Since the AT system's decisions are based on the market prediction, traders are constantly seeking new methods to improve their alpha models. In the past, traders made predictions by manually building trading strategies based on known patterns in the market data stream [8]. However, increases in computational capabilities caused traders to switch to sophisticated statistical methods, which were later replaced by machine learning-based alpha models that were shown to better estimate the market's behavior. The emergence of the big data era introduced new models, and traders requiring rapid analysis of the massive amount of market data began to use ANNs [11], such as deep neural networks (DNNs) [1,7], and recurrent neural networks (RNNs) [6,23].

2.2   Adversarial Learning

The term adversarial example was first used in [27] to describe a well-crafted perturbation added to an input sample that fools a target DNN. Crafting an adversarial example is done by adding an imperceptible perturbation to an input sample, resulting in misclassification by the model. Additionally, adversarial perturbations can fool other models, even those trained on different training sets, which is known as the transferability property of adversarial examples [27]. Those findings caused the research community to delve deeper in order to better understand this vulnerability and develop new methods for crafting adversarial perturbations [13,16]. To use adversarial examples in more realistic scenarios, some studies utilized the transferability property to perform an attack in black-box settings. The attacker creates adversarial examples for a surrogate model and then transfers them to the target model, which he/she knows little about. Initially, adversarial perturbations were crafted based on a specific data sample; this changed when the universal adversarial perturbation (UAP) was presented [19]. The UAP is a single perturbation that can fool a learning model when added to both the samples in the training set and unseen data samples and is also transferable to other neural networks. Since this method allows an attacker to craft one perturbation and use it against unseen samples, it can be used in domains where the data is unknown (e.g., AT).

Initial research targeted images, but recent studies have expanded to other domains, yet the AT domain remained unexplored. While the simple attacks targeting AT presented in [2] can easily be identified by regulation authorities, they demonstrate how AT increases volatility in the market. Therefore, it is reasonable to suspect that adversarial examples could be used in the trading domain since it increasingly relies on machine learning models. An adversarial

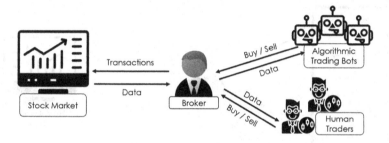

Fig. 1. A simplified illustration of the HFT ecosystem. All traders (humans and AT bots) collect market data and send transaction requests to the broker. The broker executes the transaction and sends the market data to the trader.

learning-based attack was demonstrated with a UAP that was used to identify transactions that manipulate the limit order book data and, as a result, cause the target AT bot to change its behavior [12]. However, this method is limited to stocks with low trading volume because by the time the attacker finalizes the transactions, the limit order book can completely change, which can make the malicious transactions less effective or not effective at all.

3   Problem Description

3.1   Trading Setup

We assume the simplified HFT environment presented in Fig. 1, with the following entities: a broker, traders (humans or AT bots), and the stock market. Stock market transactions are limited to trusted members only, which may limit the traders' ability to exchange assets in the market [25]. Therefore, a broker is a trusted entity that connects traders and the stock market by receiving and executing buy and sell requests on behalf of the traders. Each transaction changes the market's supply and demand, thus affecting the stock price. Information about the market changes, including changes in stock prices, is sent to the traders via the broker. However, data anomalies are common in HFT due to software bugs, errors in transaction requests, environmental conditions, and more [18]. Thus, some AT systems embed anomaly detection filters during preprocessing and ignore abnormal changes in the data. In this work, we focus on discount brokers who play a major role in HFT by providing online trading platforms to encourage frequent trade execution. The target AT system receives data from the broker, in the form of one-minute intraday stock prices, and processes and feeds it to a machine learning-based alpha model, which tries to predict whether the stock price will increase or decrease. Based on the prediction, the AT system chooses an investment strategy and performs the corresponding action.

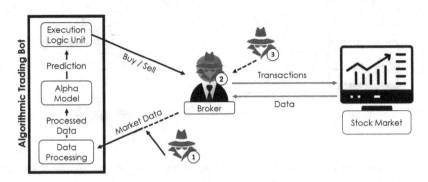

Fig. 2. An illustration of the attack flow. The attacker can be one of the following: (1) A cyber attacker that targets a specific AT bot, (2) a malicious broker, or (3) a compromised broker. While (1) manipulates just the data feed for one AT bot, (2) and (3) perturb the data to all traders that collect data from the broker.

3.2   Threat Model

Since fraudulent behavior or cyber crimes performed by any entity in the stock market can result in significant financial gain [21], we can assume that even a broker cannot be trusted. Therefore, we consider the three threat models shown in Fig. 2: a cyber attacker performs a man-in-the-middle attack on the data stream sent from the broker to the bot and gains control of the data sent to the alpha model; a malicious broker manipulates the data he/she sends to the traders to personally benefit from the effects of the perturbed data on the traders; and a compromised broker unknowingly sends the traders data that was manipulated by an attacker. In all cases, the attacker's goal is to profit financially or personally by sabotaging one or more AT systems. We assume that the attacker can manipulate the market stream and send it to the AT system, which uses the data as an input. Additionally, the attacker is aware of the existence of regulatory monitoring and the possibility that an anomaly detector might be used to filter significant changes in the data, and wants to bypass both by performing minor changes in the data stream. We start by assuming that the attacker has complete knowledge of the target model, and later this assumption will be dropped. Since the three threat models share similar characteristics, we examine our solution under a single scenario in which the attacker can manipulate the input to the AT system in real time.

4   Proposed Attack

As illustrated in Fig. 2, the attacker wants to perturb the market data stream to fool the alpha model and control the AT system's behavior. However, the trading domain introduces new challenges that need to be addressed to build a realistic attack against AT systems. First, stock market data rapidly changes over time, and by the time the attacker crafts the perturbation, it may be no longer relevant since the prices have likely changed. Second, the attacker does not know the true label ahead of time, and perturbing the data might create an undesired outcome; if at a specific time both the target and true labels are 'increase,' adding a perturbation might cause the undesired effect in which the sample is classified as 'decrease.' To address those challenges, we suggest a targeted version of a UAP [19]. Since the perturbation is effective when added to unseen data, the attacker can craft one TUAP in advance and apply it to the data stream in real time. We craft the TUAP using past data samples with equal representation of all classes to ensure that input samples that were originally classified as the target class will output the same result after applying the TUAP.

We define f to be the AT system's alpha model, which receives a snapshot x of a stock's price for a period of k minutes and outputs an estimation $f(x)$ for the price behavior in the next few minutes ('increase' or 'decrease'). For a set of snapshots of stock prices X, a target label y, and an alpha model f, the attacker aims to craft a TUAP v, such that the number of $x \in X$, where $f(x + v) = y$, is maximal. Therefore, we define a successful attack using the targeted fooling rate (*TFR*): the *percentage* of $x \in X$ such that $f(x + v) = y$. To maintain the imperceptibility and make the TUAP look like a normal price fluctuation, the size of v, $\|v\|_2$, should be minimal. Thus, the attacker chooses two thresholds that determine the attack's requirements: δ denotes the minimal TFR value for $f(x + v)$ with regard to y, while ϵ defines the maximal perturbation size.

To craft the TUAP, Algorithm 1 receives a set of data points X, a target label y, a classifier f, a minimal TFR δ threshold, and a maximal perturbation size ϵ, and iteratively crafts a TUAP v such that $TFR(f(X + v), y) \geq \delta$ and $\|v\|_2 \leq \epsilon$. Thus, the TUAP is smaller than ϵ, yet it fools f for at least $\delta\%$ of X. To calculate the TUAP, we initialize v to a zero vector (line 1) and split X into batches to improve the convergence time of the optimization process. Next, we iteratively calculate TUAP v by checking each batch X_B in X, and if $TFR(f(X_B + v), y) \geq \delta$ (line 4), we update v as follows: First, we compute a perturbation v_i with minimal size and maximal TFR (line 5) using a modified version of projected gradient descent [16], which we chose due to its simplicity, short runtime, and reliable results. Then, to update v (line 6), we use *Projection* to project $v + v_i$ into an epsilon ball under the L_2 distance; thus ensuring that $\|v\|_2 \leq \epsilon$. If the algorithm finds a TUAP where $TFR(f(X + v), y) \geq \delta$ (line 9), then it returns v. Otherwise, the loop ends after E iterations without finding a result, and the attacker should consider changing the constraints (i.e., δ or ϵ).

5   Evaluation Setup

5.1   Dataset

We use real intraday market data from the S&P 500 index from Kaggle [22]. For each stock, the dataset contains the open-high-low-close data at one-minute intervals between 11/9/2017-16/2/2018. We define an input sample as a stream of 25 continuous one-minute records, where each record consists of the opening price, high price, low price, closing price, and the traded stock volume at

---

Algorithm 1: Crafting a targeted universal adversarial perturbation.

---

input   : Dataset X, target class y, alpha model f, maximal perturbation size ϵ,
           minimal expected TFR δ, and maximal number of iterations E.

output: A targeted universal adversarial perturbation v.

initialize $v \leftarrow 0$

for $k = 1$ *up to* E **do**

    foreach *batch* X_B *in* X **do**

        if $TFR(f(X_B + v), y) < \delta$ **then**

            $v_i \leftarrow \arg\min_r \|r\|_2$ *s.t.* $TFR(f(X_B + v + r), y) \geq \delta$

            $v \leftarrow Projection(v + v_i, \epsilon)$

    if $TFR(f(X + v), y) \geq \delta$ **then**

        return v

---

the end of the minute. The dataset is divided into a set for training the alpha models, a set for crafting TUAPs, and six test sets to evaluate the attack. The data between 11/9/2017-1/1/2018 is used to train the alpha models. To craft the TUAPs, 40 samples are uniformly sampled from each of the three trading days between 2/1/2018-4/1/2018 (a total of 120 samples). The data between 5/1/2018-15/2/2018 (five trading days per week) are used to create six test sets: $T_1, ..., T_6$. For each week, we build a corresponding test set by uniformly sampling 100 samples that represent an increase of the stock price and an additional 100 that represent a decrease of the stock price. For $1 \leq i \leq 6$, T_i denotes the test set of the i'th week (i.e., we use the first week for T_1, etc.). This sampling method helps to ensure that imbalances in the data do not influence our evaluation process.

5.2   Feature Extraction

Before feeding the input into the models, we perform preprocessing on the raw data based on [1]. However, while [1] only uses the closing price of each minute, we aggregate five groups of five consecutive minutes, and for each group, we extract the following features: the trend's indicator, standard deviation of the price, and average price. The trend indicator is set to be the linear coefficient among the closing prices of five consecutive minutes. The features extracted from the sliding window of 25 min of the raw data are used to build one input sample for our alpha model. Each sample is a vector of the following features: the last five pseudo-log returns, the last five standard deviations of price, the last five trend indicators, the last minute, and the last hour. The pseudo-log return is calculated based on the average price of each five-minute group $AVGp_1, ..., AVGp_5$ and defined as $log(\frac{AVGp_i}{AVGp_{i-1}})$. Thus, the preprocessing takes a sliding window of 25 min of the raw data and creates an input sample with 17 features.

5.3 Models

We use TensorFlow and Keras to implement three supervised alpha models which, for each processed sample, predict the stock's price movement at the end of the next five minutes. The models differ in terms of their architecture: The DNN is a deep neural network with five hidden dense layers and a softmax layer; the CNN has a 1D convolution layer, two dense layers, and a softmax layer; and the RNN has two LSTM layers, a dense layer, and a softmax layer. Since a model with high directional accuracy (DA) allows the user to develop a profitable investment strategy, the models are trained on the same data to maximize the DA. The models achieve 66.6%–67.2% and 65.6%–68.3% DA on the training and test sets respectively, promising results when compared to the results of other HFT alpha models [1,6,11]. Since the models perform binary classification, a DA above 50% can be used to build a profitable trading strategy.

5.4 Evaluation

For simplicity, we create TUAPs that force the three alpha models to predict that the stock price will increase. For each model, we evaluate the TUAPs' performance using the six test sets $(T_1 - T_6)$ with the following measurements: targeted fooling rate (TFR), untargeted fooling rate (UFR), and perturbation size. The TFR denotes the percentage of input samples that are classified as the target label and reflects the attacker's ability to control the AT system's decision regardless of the stock's state. Although technical analysis is common in HFT, to the best of our knowledge, there are no known attacks against HFT AT systems that use technical indicators. Therefore, to demonstrate the attack's added value, we compare the attack to random perturbations of the same size. However, measuring random perturbations with the TFR fails to reflect the unwanted prediction flips caused by random noise. Thus, we measure the UFR of the perturbations, which is defined as the percentage of input samples that are misclassified. It is important to note that the goal of the TUAP is to cause all samples to be classified as the adversary's target, regardless of the true label. Therefore, a successful attack is measured with TFR, while UFR measures the randomness effect of the perturbation on the prediction result. The perturbation size is the average percentage of change in the stock's closing price, ensuring that the perturbation remains undetected for each stock. A TUAP of a dollar size is small for a stock that is $2000 a share, yet dramatic for a penny stock. The relative size is also helpful for comparing the effects of different perturbations on different stocks. Therefore, in this study, all of the perturbations are relative to the target stock price: 0.02% of the price. Our code is available at https:// github.com/nehemya/Algo-Trade-Adversarial-Examples.

6 White-Box Attack

In this experiment, we examine five stocks: Google (GOOG), Amazon (AMZN), BlackRock (BLK), IBM, and Apple (AAPL). For each stock, we use

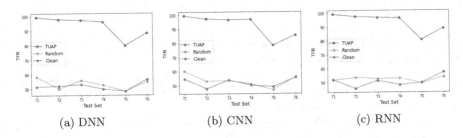

(a) DNN   (b) CNN   (c) RNN

Fig. 3. The mean TFR (percentage) of five stocks for the TUAP, random perturbation, and clean data. The TFR is presented for each of the six test sets and the three models.

Algorithm 1 to craft three TUAPs, one for each alpha model, and randomly sample three perturbations that are the same size as the TUAPs (i.e., 0.02% of the stock's price). Then, we evaluate the attack performance on the six test sets $T_1 - T_6$. Since the perturbations are trained on data from one point in time and evaluated on six unknown test sets from later periods of time, we expect that the performance of the TUAPs will gradually degrade as we move away in time from the time period of the training set; hence, the TUAP will achieve the highest TFR and UFR for T_1, and the lowest for T_6. Nevertheless, the random perturbations are not expected to show any predictable behavior, and their effect on the classification result will not correlate to the time that has elapsed from the training set time.

We examine the TFR for the TUAP and random perturbation for each of the three alpha models and compare them to the clean (original) results. As shown in Fig. 3, the random noise does not have a major impact on any of the models On average, the random perturbations cause changes in the TFR that do not exceed 2%, and thus the alpha models' prediction is not largely affected by them. However, the TUAP creates dramatic changes in all alpha models' classification results, and the average TFR scores obtained by the TUAP are greater than 92%. The results support the hypothesis that the attacker can use the TUAP to control the alpha model's prediction. To improve our understanding of the effect of the random perturbation, we also examine the UFR (see Fig. 4). The results suggest that the TUAP causes a higher UFR than the random perturbation. However, Fig. 3 suggests that the classification flips caused by the TUAP are the result of input samples that have been pushed to be classified as the target label. Such effects are not demonstrated by the random perturbation.

As expected, while the effects of the random perturbations do not follow a certain pattern, the TUAP's TFR is highest for the earlier test sets (e.g., T_1) and gradually decreases for the later test sets. However, an exception is found for T_5, which represents data of 2/2/2018-8/2/2018 and demonstrates poorer performance than any other test set, including the later test set T_6. This exception may stem from several massive drops in the market that occurred during this time period [17,26]. Although our datasets are balanced, each sample is based on 25 min of market data which reflect the drop in the market. Thus,

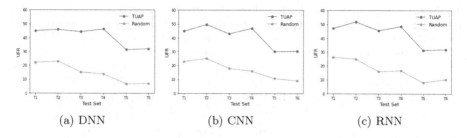

Fig. 4. The mean UFR (percentage) of five stocks for the TUAP and random perturbation. The UFR is presented for each of the six test sets and the three models.

fooling an alpha model to predict an increase in a stock value in this week is a challenging task for a TUAP trained on normal market data.

Additionally, due to the heavy monitoring of the stock market, an attacker should consider the TUAP's size: a larger perturbation is more likely to fool the alpha model, but also has a higher risk of being detected. Therefore, we examine how the perturbation size affects the fooling rate. Since we can achieve a high TFR by using TUAPs with a small size relative to the stock's price (i.e., 0.02%), we now examine the attack's effect on stocks in different price ranges, thus inspecting perturbations from similar absolute sizes (i.e., the number of dollars). To do so, we define three price categories and randomly choose five stocks from each category:

- High ($900+): GOOG, GOOGL, AMZN, ISRG, and PCLN.
- Medium ($400 − −$650): BLK, REGN, EQIX, AZO, and MTD.
- Low ($100 − −$200): ADP, UPS, IBM, AAPL, and AON.

As shown in Table 1, the TUAPs fool the alpha models for stock data from all price categories examined, with a TFR greater than 89.5%. While the relative perturbation size is similar, the TUAPs affected each category differently; the effect on low-priced stocks is the greatest, but the medium-priced stocks are less affected by the attack. The results regarding the untargeted fooling rate support the findings from our previous experiment. We note that we examine the low-priced stocks in data from the S&P 500 index, which contains only large companies. Since the results indicate that targeting the low-priced stocks is the safer option for the attacker, we believe that future work should examine stocks with a price lower than 100$.

7   Black-Box Attack

Assuming the attacker has full knowledge of the target system is unrealistic in the real world, where traders conceal this information. Therefore, we evaluate the attack under black-box settings, where the attacker only has access to the model's input. Since the attacker can manipulate the market stream, he/she can utilize the TUAP's transferability property to attack AT systems with an

Table 1. Comparison of the TUAP and random perturbation effect on stocks at three price levels, including the average stock price and average absolute perturbation price. Each category is evaluated using the directional accuracy on clean data, the TFR and UFR on data with the TUAP, and the UFR on data with the random perturbation.

Stock price category	Average stock price	Average TUAP size	Clean DA	TFR TUAP	UFR TUAP	UFR random
High	$1100	$0.266	66.65	91.35	41.41	15.64
Medium	$545	$0.152	68.01	89.55	39.58	15.96
Low	$141	$0.036	67.26	93.93	43.93	18.08

Table 2. The transferability (TFR) of the TUAP between the three alpha models on (a) IBM and (b) Apple data. The rows are the source (surrogate) models, the columns define the target (unknown) model, and the size denotes the relative TUAP size.

Target	DNN	CNN	RNN	Size
DNN	-	95.04	95.00	0.027
CNN	94.45	-	94.75	0.028
RNN	94.25	95.00	-	0.026

(a) IBM

Target	DNN	CNN	RNN	Size
DNN	-	93.7	93.66	0.024
CNN	93.16	-	93.41	0.022
RNN	93.95	94.62	-	0.024

(b) AAPL

unknown alpha model architecture. Thus, the broker sends compromised market data targeting one AT system, which could affect other bots and, in turn, potentially influence the entire market. Since traders are protective of their AT systems' architecture, there is a lack of open-source AT implementations, and thus inexperienced traders often use alpha models with similar architecture; this increases the risk of a transferable perturbation.

In this experiment, we craft a TUAP for each alpha model and transfer it to the other two models. The results in Table 2 show that all of the TUAPs are highly transferable and sometimes achieved a TFR similar to that of the attacked model. This likely stems from the models' preprocessing; although the alpha models have different learning model architectures, they share the same code and vulnerability. However, our results indicate that an attack from a malicious or compromised broker targeting a popular open-source AT system implementation could affect other bots using that software. The presence of multiple compromised AT systems could cause a misrepresentation of the market's supply and demand, which might affect the behavior of AT systems that do not share that vulnerability.

8   Mitigation

While technology is advancing at a rapid pace, government regulation and enforcement systems are largely unaware of the risks that such advancement poses (e.g., the threat of adversarial examples). Unlike known cyber attacks on the stock market, which perform notable transactions (e.g., hack, pump and dump [20]), our attack performs small perturbations that can be considered a common error in the data. Combining an imperceptible attack and the lack of knowledge about this threat allows attackers to exploit the market with minimal risk. Therefore, we call on the finance community to raise awareness of the risks associated with using machine learning models in AT. Since the traders using the AT systems will be the first entity to suffer from our attack, we examine several mitigation methods that can be used to protect AT bots. In this section, we assume that the TUAP, its training set, and the percentage of perturbed samples in the test sets are known to the defender, and the attacker cannot tweak the attack to bypass the defense, as shown in various domains [3]. Although it is an unrealistic assumption that gives a significant edge to the defender, it allows us to discuss the challenges of protecting against adversarial perturbations in AT.

A common mitigation approach involves the use of a detector to identify perturbed data and filter it out. Due to the defender's unrealistic advantage, we can use the TUAP to build two simple classifiers, with k-nearest neighbors (kNN) and ANN architectures, to identify perturbed data. We trained the detectors on the same training set used to craft the TUAP, but added the perturbation to 10% of the data. Then, we created $T'_1, ..., T'_6$ test sets, such that T'_i is a combination of 10% perturbed data (i.e., T_i) and 90% benign data that was sampled from ith week. Figure 5 shows that while the kNN detector failed to detect the perturbed data, the ANN detector identified more samples but obtained a high false positive rate, which makes it unreliable. A possible explanation for the results is that identifying adversarial perturbations requires the detector to model and predict the normal behavior of the market, a challenging task that the entire AT system tries to perform. Moreover, the performance of both detectors decreases as time passes; thus, the defender will have to retrain a new detector every few weeks. This is not feasible since in real life the defender would have to build the detector for unseen TUAPs without knowing their distribution in the market data. Additionally, a complex detector adds computational overhead to the AT system, which can make it irrelevant in HFT. Therefore, some traders might prefer to risk being attacked in order to maintain an effective AT system.

An alternative approach is to train the model to correctly classifying both benign and perturbed data samples, which can be achieved by performing adversarial retraining [13]: After training the alpha model, the defender creates perturbed data, which is labeled as the benign samples and then used to retrain the model. By doing so, the defender avoids the computational overhead associated with an additional component to the AT system. We used the attack's TUAP to perform adversarial retraining on the alpha model. As shown in Fig. 6, the alpha model loses its ability to predict the market when the percentage of adversarial examples used for retraining increases. When adversarial examples are 40% of the retraining data, the TFR decreases from more than 90% to around 70%, and the directional accuracy drops from almost 70% to less than 60%, which indicates that the defense reduces the alpha model's ability to learn from the

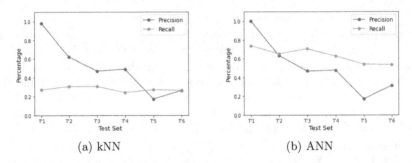

Fig. 5. The precision (blue) and recall (orange) of supervised detectors trained on the TUAP training set, with 10% perturbed data: (a) kNN and (b) neural networks. (Color figure online)

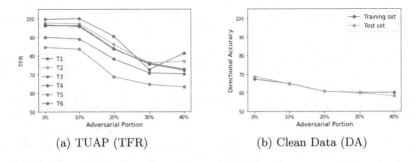

Fig. 6. The effects of adversarial retraining for different portions of adversarial examples in the retraining set on (a) the perturbed evaluation sets (TFR), and (b) on the model's ability to predict the market for clean data (DA).

training set. Therefore, improving the model's robustness to adversarial examples is unsuitable for this domain.

Finally, we suggest a simple solution in which the trader collects the market data from several brokers, compares it and filters out mismatches. While the solution is trivial, it might be expensive for an individual trader who must pay multiple brokers for the market data. Additionally, in HFT, the data might contain inaccuracies due to technical issues or mismatches due to time differences between brokers operating around the world. As a result, traders may prefer to risk an attack over losing money or decreasing the AT system's performance. However, regulatory authorities are not limited by the challenges discussed. They can perform offline analysis, compare the data from many brokers, and utilize complex detectors. Even if those methods are not used routinely, they can be applied when unexplained abnormal behavior is seen in the market. Although securing the stock market may be challenging and no comprehensive solution currently exists, the war may already have begun, and efforts to defend against adversarial examples should start with increasing the finance community's awareness of the risks of using learning models in the stock market.

9 Conclusions

In this study, we demonstrate how adding a TUAP to the market data stream in real time, allows an attacker to influence the alpha model's predictions, thus controlling the entire AT system. Our results show that HFT systems are highly susceptible to adversarial inputs. The use of a TUAP ensures that the attack can be performed in real life, where attackers cannot predict the market's behavior. Adversarial perturbations are much stealthier than known manipulations against the stock market. Since the size of our TUAPs is 0.02% of the stock price, the attack might not be flagged as such by monitoring systems and instead be viewed as a common error in the data. Our experiments also showed that TUAPs are transferable to different AT systems and that a perturbation targeting one alpha model can also fool another model. Since the manipulated data in this study is sent by the broker, a TUAP added to the market data can change the behavior of multiple AT bots, and their actions may start a cascade effect, influencing other invulnerable systems and possibly the entire market. Given the lack of diversity in open-source bot implementations online, inexperienced traders often use alpha models with similar architecture, a situation in which transferable perturbations can increase the potential damage, as shown in our study. Finally, we demonstrated potential mitigation methods against adversarial perturbations and discussed the concerning findings. Since many regulatory authorities and traders are unfamiliar with adversarial perturbation, we strongly suggest that the finance community examine this risk and take the steps required to protect financial markets from such threats.

References

1. Arévalo, A., Niño, J., Hernández, G., Sandoval, J.: High-frequency trading strategy based on deep neural networks. In: Huang, D.-S., Han, K., Hussain, A. (eds.) ICIC 2016. LNCS (LNAI), vol. 9773, pp. 424–436. Springer, Cham (2016). https://doi.org/10.1007/978-3-319-42297-8_40
2. Arnoldi, J.: Computer algorithms, market manipulation and the institutionalization of high frequency trading. Theory Cult. Soc. **33**(1), 29–52 (2016)
3. Athalye, A., Carlini, N., Wagner, D.: Obfuscated gradients give a false sense of security: circumventing defenses to adversarial examples. In: International Conference on Machine Learning, pp. 274–283. PMLR (2018)
4. Bianchi, D., Tosun, O.K.: Cyber attacks and stock market activity. SSRN (2019)
5. Bigiotti, A., Navarra, A.: Optimizing automated trading systems. In: Antipova, T., Rocha, A. (eds.) DSIC18 2018. AISC, vol. 850, pp. 254–261. Springer, Cham (2019). https://doi.org/10.1007/978-3-030-02351-5_30
6. Chen, G., Chen, Y., Fushimi, T.: Application of deep learning to algorithmic trading. Stanford. https://stanford.io/3dllsMC. Accessed June 2021
7. Chong, E., Han, C., Park, F.C.: Deep learning networks for stock market analysis and prediction: methodology, data representations, and case studies. Expert Syst. Appl. **83**, 187–205 (2017)
8. Coutts, J.A., Cheung, K.C.: Trading rules and stock returns: some preliminary short run evidence from the Hang Seng 1985–1997. Appl. Financ. Econ. **10**(6), 579–586 (2000)

9. Domm, P.: False rumor of explosion at white house causes stocks to briefly plunge. CNBC (2013). https://cnb.cx/35SVKKU. Accessed June 2021

10. Fisher, M.: Syrian hackers claim AP hack that tipped stock market by \$136 billion. Is it terrorism? Washington Post 23 (2013)

11. Giacomel, F., Galante, R., Pereira, A.: An algorithmic trading agent based on a neural network ensemble: a case of study in North American and Brazilian stock markets. In: 2015 IEEE/WIC/ACM International Conference on Web Intelligence and Intelligent Agent Technology (WI-IAT), vol. 2, pp. 230–233. IEEE (2015)

12. Goldblum, M., Schwarzschild, A., Cohen, N., Balch, T., Patel, A.B., Goldstein, T.: Adversarial attacks on machine learning systems for high-frequency trading. arXiv:2002.09565 (2020)

13. Goodfellow, I.J., Shlens, J., Szegedy, C.: Explaining and harnessing adversarial examples. arXiv:1412.6572 (2014)

14. Gunning, D.: Explainable artificial intelligence (XAI). Defense Advanced Research Projects Agency (DARPA), nd Web 2, 2 (2017)

15. Kumar, G., Jain, S., Singh, U.P.: Stock market forecasting using computational intelligence: a survey. Arch. Comput. Methods Eng. **28**(3), 1069–1101 (2020). https://doi.org/10.1007/s11831-020-09413-5

16. Madry, A., Makelov, A., Schmidt, L., Tsipras, D., Vladu, A.: Towards deep learning models resistant to adversarial attacks. arXiv:1706.06083 (2017)

17. Matt, E.: February was an insane month for the stock market. CNN (2018). https://cnn.it/3j8Q7Ah. Accessed June 2021

18. Mitchell, C.: Erroneous trade. Investopedia (2021). https://bit.ly/2SxaU5C. Accessed June 2021

19. Moosavi-Dezfooli, S.M., Fawzi, A., Fawzi, O., Frossard, P.: Universal adversarial perturbations. In: Proceedings of the IEEE Conference on Computer Vision and Pattern Recognition, pp. 1765–1773 (2017)

20. Nakashima, E.: Hack, pump and dump. The Washington Post (2007). https://wapo.st/3vSsIWs. Accessed June 2021

21. Neyret, A.: Stock market cybercrime. Autorité des Marchés Financiers (2020). https://bit.ly/3xPE0wg. Accessed June 2021

22. Nickdl: S&P 500 intraday data. Kaggle (2018). https://bit.ly/3gRJgJV. Accessed June 2021

23. Pang, X., Zhou, Y., Wang, P., Lin, W., Chang, V.: An innovative neural network approach for stock market prediction. J. Supercomput. **76**(3), 2098–2118 (2018). https://doi.org/10.1007/s11227-017-2228-y

24. Rooney, K., Khorram, Y.: Hackers look to buy brokerage log-ins on the dark web with Robinhood fetching highest prices. CNBC (2020). https://cnb.cx/3zX9an1. Accessed June 2021

25. Smith, T.: Broker. Investopedia (2020). https://bit.ly/2SVpWCC. Accessed June 2021

26. Stacey, B.C., Bar-Yam, Y.: The stock market has grown unstable since February 2018. arXiv:1806.00529 (2018)

27. Szegedy, C., et al.: Intriguing properties of neural networks. arXiv:1312.6199 (2013)

28. Treleaven, P., Galas, M., Lalchand, V.: Algorithmic trading review. Commun. ACM **56**(11), 76–85 (2013)

Continuous-Action Reinforcement Learning for Portfolio Allocation of a Life Insurance Company

Carlo Abrate[1], Alessio Angius[1], Gianmarco De Francisci Morales[1],
Stefano Cozzini[2], Francesca Iadanza[2], Laura Li Puma[3], Simone Pavanelli[2],
Alan Perotti[1(✉)], Stefano Pignataro[2], and Silvia Ronchiadin[3]

[1] ISI Foundation, Turin, Italy
alan.perotti@isi.it
[2] Intesa Sanpaolo Vita, Turin, Italy
[3] Intesa Sanpaolo Innovation Center, Turin, Italy

Abstract. The asset management of an insurance company is more complex than traditional portfolio management due to the presence of obligations that the insurance company must fulfill toward the clients. These obligations, commonly referred to as *liabilities*, are payments whose magnitude and occurrence are a byproduct of insurance contracts with the clients, and of portfolio performances.

In particular, while clients must be refunded in case of adverse events, such as car accidents or death, they also contribute to a common financial portfolio to earn annual returns. Customer withdrawals might increase whenever these returns are too low or, in the presence of an annual minimum guaranteed, the company might have to integrate the difference. Hence, in this context, any investment strategy cannot omit the interdependency between financial assets and liabilities.

To deal with this problem, we present a stochastic model that combines portfolio returns with the liabilities generated by the insurance products offered by the company. Furthermore, we propose a risk-adjusted optimization problem to maximize the capital of the company over a pre-determined time horizon.

Since traditional financial tools are inadequate for such a setting, we develop the model as a Markov Decision Process. In this way, we can use Reinforcement Learning algorithms to solve the underlying optimization problem. Finally, we provide experiments that show how the optimal asset allocation can be found by training an agent with the algorithm Deep Deterministic Policy Gradient.

Keywords: Reinforcement learning · Portfolio allocation

1 Introduction

Portfolio management is a core activity in finance, whereby an entity, such as a fund manager or an insurance company, oversees the investments of its clients

© Springer Nature Switzerland AG 2021
Y. Dong et al. (Eds.): ECML PKDD 2021, LNAI 12978, pp. 237–252, 2021.
https://doi.org/10.1007/978-3-030-86514-6_15

to meet some agreed-upon financial objectives. In the context of an insurance company (henceforth simply referred to as 'company'), the clients not only contribute premiums to a common fund to buy assets, but also acquire the right to be paid in case of certain events (e.g., death in the case of a life insurance policy). Therefore, the company has to manage not only the assets, but also the liabilities deriving from the insurance. This combination of asset-liability management, and their inter-dependency, is one of the reasons why the insurance case is more complex than traditional portfolio management.

In this paper, we consider the problem of a company that handles insurance products for its clients, and wishes to optimize the risk-adjusted returns of the investment portfolio, while at the same time ensuring that its future liabilities are covered despite possible market fluctuations. These liabilities can be stochastic, and are usually correlated to some of the assets available to the company. In this scenario, one cannot just optimize for the risk-adjusted return, rather the investment portfolio has also to match the liabilities, and in particular their due dates. Finally, in a life insurance setting, the time horizon of the problem is relatively long (e.g., 30 years), and the portfolio gets rebalanced sporadically.

Commonly used financial tools for asset allocation such as Modern Portfolio Theory (MPT) [17] are inadequate for the considered setting. First, Markowitz's theory does not take into account liabilities and the future negative cash flows they generate. Second, it assumes a single decision point where the portfolio is optimized. While the methodology can be repeatedly applied at each decision point, it fails to take account for the path dependency of the problem: previous choices affect later ones. For instance, the decision to buy a risky asset early on in the lifetime of the fund might affect the ability to face negative cash flows later on, and thus inform a more conservative strategy. Clearly, an optimal strategy needs to take into account the whole decision space of the problem, i.e., the whole *sequence* of decisions (asset allocations) that lead to the final outcome.

Given the stochastic nature of markets and the multi-period decision nature of the problem, it is only natural to use a Markov Decision Process (MDP) as a model. An MDP is an extension of a Markov chain (a stochastic model of a sequence of events) that allows for account possible actions so that the stochastic outcomes are partly under the control of a 'decision maker'. The system moves in discrete steps from a state s to a new state s' according to some transition probability $P_a(s, s')$, which also depends on the action a taken. The transition generates a reward $R_a(s, s')$, and the goal is to find an optimal *policy*, i.e., a (stochastic) mapping of states to actions, such that the expected reward is maximized.

While there are several possible ways to solve an MDP, such as linear and dynamic programming [5], for large systems Reinforcement Learning (RL) is the de-facto standard tool to tackle the problem [26].

The contributions of this paper can be summarized as follows:

- We describe, formalize, and implement a realistic model of the asset-liability management process for an insurance company as a Markov Decision Process. The action space of the model is particularly challenging to explore, as each action can be sampled from a continuous $k-1$ simplex (where k is the number of available assets).

- We adapt a well-known algorithm for deep reinforcement learning for continuous action spaces (DDPG [14]) to our problem. To do so, we employ several techniques that are necessary for a quick and stable convergence: a warm-up stage to pre-train the critic network, a modification to the exploration policy to maintain important structural constraints of the problem, and a careful crafting of the reward function to implement domain-specific, parametric asset allocation constraints.
- We show experimentally that our solution is able to outperform a traditional mean-variance optimization baseline computed via Monte-Carlo sampling.

2   Problem Definition

This section provides a detailed description of the inner workings of a life-insurance company. We begin with a description of the mathematical model underlying the financial evolution of the company. Then, we provide a brief description of the implementation in terms of components and their interaction. Finally, we formalize the optimization problem. The Appendix includes further details about the components described in this Section.

The problem consists in optimizing the investments of an insurance company in order to maximize the profits. On the one side, the company manages a segregated fund that handles a portfolio of *assets* of different nature (equity, bonds, cash). On the other side, the company sells insurance products that differ from each other in their client characterization (in terms of age, behavioral properties such as the probability to pay premiums), and the percentage of the profits owed to the client from the returns generated by the segregated fund during the year. Irrespective of the profits generated by the portfolio, policies usually stipulate a guaranteed minimum return on investment for the clients. This minimum, referred to as *Minimum Annual Yield* (MAY) and denoted with κ, is particularly important because the insurance company must integrate the amount whenever the returns of the segregated fund are not able to meet the MAY. Conversely, the insurance company is allowed to take part of the *Surplus* (SP), by retaining a fixed spread over the surplus, or a fraction of it.

The profit of the company consists of the residual surplus once all the cash flows of the policies have been paid off. These payments, referred to as *liabilities*, are a consequence of several factors such as: insurance claims, and integration to reach the MAY. Liabilities depend on the type of insurance policy, but are also connected to the profits generated during the year for the client. For instance, the probability of client withdrawal may be affected by the amount of profits generated by the fund. To cover the liabilities, every insurance product is associated with *reserves*, which represent the value of the outstanding liabilities. Unused reserves contribute to the profits of the company.

2.1   Formalization

Our goal is to optimize the asset-liability management of the fund given an *economic scenario*, over a finite time horizon in $[0, T]$ divided into discrete slots of one year. This scenario is a stochastic process which describes the financial market, based on existing models whose parameters are calibrated by using historical data. The model which generates the scenario is a black box from the point of view of the optimization, and can only be queried to generate a new realization from the process. Each realization from the process provides the information necessary to characterize the financial assets along the considered time interval. These random variables describe *Key Financial Indicators*(KFI) such as equity indexes, interest rates, and market spreads. Therefore:

Definition 1. *An* Economy *is a realization of KFIs from the stochastic process $\mathcal{E}$ which defines the economic scenario.*

We assume a set of financial asset classes, denoted with $\mathcal{C}$ and indexed from 1 to $|\mathcal{C}|$, that can be exchanged during the considered time horizon. Assets of each class are created at every time unit by combining a set of basic properties specific of the asset class with their corresponding KFIs. The creation of an asset corresponds to the definition of the minimal set of terms that allow for its accounting.

Definition 2. *An asset is a tuple composed of seven terms* $Y = \langle c, t^0, p^0, t^p, m, r, \overline{\chi} \rangle$:

- $c \in \mathcal{C}$ *the class of the asset;*
- $t^0 \in [-\infty, T]$ *the issue time (can be arbitrarily back in time);*
- $p^0 \in \mathbb{R}$ *the issue price, the market price of the asset at the moment of creation;*
- $t^p \in [-\infty, T]$ *the purchase time (can be arbitrarily back in time);*
- $m \in [0, M]$ *the remaining maturity of the asset;*
- $r \in \mathbb{R}$ *the redeem value of the asset;*
- $\overline{\chi} \in \mathbb{R}^M$ *a vector of coupons paid every year by the asset up to maturity (maximum maturity M).*

The accounting of any single asset Y at a given time t requires four basic functions: market value $f_{MV}(t, Y)$, book value $f_{BV}(t, Y)$, cash-flow $f_{CF}(t, Y)$, and generated income $f_{GI}(t, Y)$. The collection of assets owned by the fund at time t is the *portfolio*.

Definition 3. *The portfolio is a multiset* $\mathcal{P}(t) = \{Y_1 : n_1, Y_2 : n_2, \dots\}$ *where every Y_i is an asset that has not been sold yet and has $t_i^p \leq t < t_i^p + m_i$ (purchased before t and not expired yet), and $n_i \in \mathbb{R}$ is its nominal amount, i.e., how many units of that asset the portfolio contains.*

The accounting functions listed above apply to the portfolio as the sum of the function applied to each asset weighted by its nominal amount. To disambiguate the notation, we use the letter g to denote the functions applied to the portfolio while we keep the letter f for the functions applied to a single asset. As an example, the market value applied to the portfolio corresponds to $g_{MV}(t)$.

The contribution of a single asset class c to the portfolio value is calculated as follows:

$$A_c(t) = \frac{\sum_{Y_i \in \mathcal{P}(t) | c_i = c} n_i \cdot f_{MV}(t, Y_i)}{g_{MV}(t)}. \tag{1}$$

Definition 4. *We define the asset allocation at time t as a vector* $\overline{A}(t) = \langle A_1(t), A_2(t), \ldots, A_{|\mathcal{C}|}(t)\rangle$.

The portfolio is modified by means of selling and buying functions that take in input the current portfolio $\mathcal{P}(t)$ and a target asset allocation $\overline{X}_t = \langle X_1, X_2, \ldots, X_{|\mathcal{C}|}\rangle$.

Selling is performed first in order to free resources to buy new assets. Selling is guided by a projection function $g_{sell}(\mathcal{P}(t), \overline{X}_t)$ that returns in output a multiset $S = \{Y_1 : s_1, Y_2 : s_2, \ldots\}$ which contain the nominal amount of each asset in the portfolio that has to be sold in order to move the asset allocation toward $\overline{X}$. Thus, after the selling actions, the nominal amount of every asset $Y_i \in \mathcal{P}(t)$ is equal to $n_i - s_i$. The purchase of new assets is done in a similar way by using a projection function $g_{buy}(\mathcal{P}(t), \overline{X}_t)$ that provides a multiset of new assets $\{\tilde{Y}_1 : n_1^b, \tilde{Y}_2 : n_1^b, \ldots, \tilde{Y}_k : n_k^b\}$ bought from the market where n_i^b is the nominal amount of the asset to be added to the portfolio.

Putting all together, we can derive the portfolio at the next time step as:

$$\mathcal{P}(t+1) = (\mathcal{P}(t) \setminus g_{sell}(\mathcal{P}(t), \overline{X}_t)) \cup g_{buy}(\mathcal{P}(t), \overline{X}_t). \tag{2}$$

In order to complete the functions necessary to describe the segregated fund, let us define the capital gain of the portfolio at time t as follows:

$$g_{CG}(t, S) = \sum_{Y_i \in \mathcal{P}(t)} s_i \cdot (f_{MV}(t, Y_i) - f_{BV}(t, Y_i)), \tag{3}$$

and the portfolio return as $g_{PR}(t, S) = \frac{g_{GI}(t) + g_{CG}(t,S)}{1/2(g_{BV}(t-1) + g_{BV}(t))}$. The insurance company has to face liabilities in the form of insurance claims due to deaths and client withdrawal from the contract (surrender). Each insurance product guarantees different benefits to the clients. Hence, its liabilities affect the profits of the company differently from those of another product. For this reason, we assume that the ith insurance product is completely described in terms of the negative cash flow generated by the product.

Definition 5. *The i-th insurance product is a function* $q_{NF}(\mathcal{Z}_i, \mathcal{R}(t))$ *which determines the negative cash flow generated by the product as function of a set of parameters* $\mathcal{Z}_i$ *and the set of portfolio returns* $\mathcal{R}(t)$ *for time* $t \in [1, T]$.

The market value of the portfolio is monitored yearly and adjusted every time it moves outside a certain range in comparison with a projection of the (discounted) liabilities in the future, denoted by $q_{DL}(t)$.

Adjustments are capital injections/ejections that corresponds to loans. Let $g_{CI}(t)$ be the function that determines the amount of cash that is paid or earned at time t by applying the interest rate ϕ_t^{inj} to the open loans plus an additional penalty ϵ for cash injections. Finally, we can define the return on capital at time t as $g_R(t) = \frac{g_{CA}(t) - g_{CA}(t-1)}{g_{CA}(t-1)}$ where $g_{CA}(t) = g_{MV}(t) - q_{DL}(t) - (g_{MV}(0) - q_{DL}(0)) + g_{IJ}(t)$ is the fund capital gain, net of the overall discounted liabilities and the total injection $g_{IJ}(t)$ which corresponds to of the sum all the capital adjustments (injections and ejections).

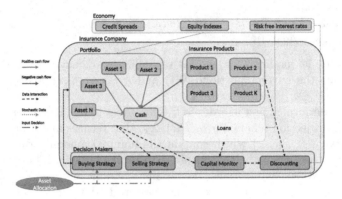

Fig. 1. Diagram describing the main components and interactions of the Insurance Company Model.

2.2   Implementation Details

Figure 1 provides a graphical description of the model, its components, and their interactions. Components have been realized as black boxes, so that they can be implemented with the desired level of detail and substituted without affecting the soundness of the model as a whole.

At the top of the figure, we observe the *Economy* which provides three different classes of KFIs. The current implementation is based on a combination of Cox-Ingersoll-Ross models [3] but the underlying process can be changed transparently.

At the bottom we find the block *Decision Maker* which is composed of: *Buying* and *Selling strategy* which correspond to the the functions $g_{sell}(\mathcal{P}(t), \overline{X})$, and $g_{buy}(\mathcal{P}(t), \overline{X})$, respectively; the *Discounting* which perform the projection of the liabilities in the future and discounts them according to a discount curve given by the Economy; finally, the component named *Capital Monitor* implements capital injection/ejection mechanism.

The component labelled as *Loans* manages the state of the loans and computes the costs at every time unit. Costs are computed by using an interest curve taken from the Economy. *Insurance Products* is a collection of insurance products where each entry stores the state of the reserves and calculates the negative cash flow generated by the product. Finally, the component *Portfolio* contains all the assets that have been bought and have not reached their maturity. The asset referring to *Cash* is unique and always present because it interacts with other components.

To exemplify the temporal dynamic of the interactions, Algorithm 1 shows the pseudo-code of the routine required to move the Company one year forward in the future. This function constitutes the cornerstone for building the environment of our RL framework.

The first observation is that the time update does not occur at the end of the function but in the middle. This is because, in principle, this routine describes

---

Algorithm 1. Step forward in the evolution of the segregated fund in time

---

```
function STEP(X̄)
    costLoans = loans.g_CI(t)
    discounting = disc.q_DL(t)insuranceProds
    inj = capitalMonitor.verify(portfolio.g_MV(t), discounting)
    if inj ≠ 0 then
        loans.insert(inj)
    sells ← g_sell(portfolio, X̄)
    new ← g_buy(portfolio, X̄)
    portfolio = (portfolio\sells) ∪ new
    returns = returns ∪ portfolio.getReturn(sells)
    t = t + 1
    ncashflow = insuranceProds.q_NF(returns)
    pcashflow = portfolio.g_CF(t)
    portfolio.updateCash(pcashflow, ncashflow, costLoans)
    return portfolio.g_CA(t)
```

---

what happens between the end of the current year and the beginning of the next. The operations performed at the end of the year are: the computation of the costs of the loans which can be either positive or negative and will be subtracted from the cash in the next year; the capital injection/ejection if needed; finally, the selling and buying operations as well as the computation of the capital gain of the year. Then, the time counter is increased and the cash is updated by considering negative and positive cash flow together with the costs of the loans. Finally, the routine ends by returning the current capital. Let us remark that the capital does not change only because of the cash flow, but also as a consequence of the changes of the KFIs that are embedded in the assets composing the portfolio.

2.3 Optimization Problem

Our goal is to optimize the average final return on capital, adjusted for its volatility. Specifically, we measure volatility as the standard deviation of the return on capital over the time horizon, given an asset allocation strategy and an economic scenario.

The volatility provides an estimation of the yearly oscillations of the returns within each simulation run. The idea behind its use is to penalize portfolios that lead to large oscillations of the returns during the considered time interval, which are a hindrance to the payment of the liabilities. Let $\mu = \frac{1}{T}\sum_{t=1}^{T} g_R(t)$ be the average of the return within the same realization, and let $\sigma = \sqrt{\frac{1}{T}\sum_{t=1}^{T}(g_R(t) - \mu)^2}$ be the standard deviation. The objective function can be written as follows:

$$\underset{\overline{X}_0,...,\overline{X}_{T-1}}{\operatorname{argmax}} = \underset{\mathcal{E}}{\mathbb{E}}\left[\mu - \lambda \cdot \sigma\right] \tag{4}$$

where $\overline{X}_0, \ldots, \overline{X}_{T-1}$ are the asset allocations at any point in time and λ is a *risk aversion* factor representing the weight of the volatility over the return on capital, and the expectation is over the possible realizations of the economy $\mathcal{E}$.

We define the problem in such a way that the objective function in Eq. (4) can be guided by two different classes of constraints. The first class (*Type 1*) is necessary to maintain the problem sound from a theoretical point of view:

$X_{t,i} \geq 0 \ \forall t,i;\ \ |\overline{X}_t| = 1 \ \ \forall t$, which verifies that each target asset allocation is long-only and properly defined on a simplex. The second class (*Type 2*) includes constraints depending on external parameters that are used to restrict the domain of the asset allocation; for example, we might want to set boundaries for the allocation of a subset of the asset classes (e.g., no more than 60% allocation on all bonds). By denoting the subset with $\mathcal{Q} \subset \mathcal{C}$, we can formalize this type of constraint as $\check{\beta} \leq \sum_{q \in \mathcal{Q}} A_c(t)q \leq \hat{\beta}, \ \forall t$.

3   Solution

We use DDPG [14] as a starting point for the implementation of our Reinforcement Learning agent. DDPG, or Deep Deterministic Policy Gradient, is an actor-critic, off-policy, model-free algorithm based on deterministic policy gradient, and that can operate over continuous action spaces. DDPG belong to the set of actor-critic agents, whose high-level architecture is depicted in Fig. 2.

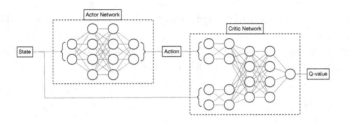

Fig. 2. Actor-Critic agent architecture

The *critic* network learns to approximate the temporally discounted cumulative reward of an action on a given state, exploiting the Bellman equation as in Q-learning. The *actor* network, given a state, learns to produce actions that maximize the Q-value estimated by the critic. It is worth observing that the actor receives no direct feedback from the environment: the back-propagated error used to train the actor flows through the critic first. During the experimental phase, which will be described in the next section, we observed that, thanks to the off-policy property of the algorithm, pre-training the critic on randomly sampled actions (and the respective environment-generated rewards) had a strong positive impact on the performance of the RL agent. We therefore systematically perform a critic *warm-up* phase before undergoing the standard actor-critic training loop.

3.1   Structural and Parametric Constraints

In our specific settings, actions are asset allocations, and are therefore modeled as a point on a simplex. Within our Reinforcement Learning agent, the actions are produced by the actor, and ensuring that these actions are on a simplex can be easily achieved by setting the last actor activation function as a softmax. We call these requirements **structural constraints**. However, DDPG implements RL-exploration by means of a *perturbation policy* that adds to the action noise produced by an Ornstein-Uhlenbeck process [6]. Clearly, a noisy action would likely violate the structural constraints, thus producing non-admissible actions. In order to maintain action admissibility, we modified the standard DDPG approach by moving the perturbation upstream with respect to the activation function. We have adopted the recently-proposed *parameter perturbation* approach, where in order to perform explorative actions we add noise to the actor weights [23]. By doing so we are sure to produce exploratory actions that satisfy the structural constraints, as the action is produced by the final softmax activation function of the actor. The weights are then reverted to their previous values before proceeding with the training.

Our specific setting might impose additional, domain-related constraints, such as upper or lower bounds on specific assets, for instance: *the Equity asset shall not surpass 20% of the total asset allocation*. Since these values vary from one scenario to another, we have implemented them in a parametric fashion, where the threshold values are read from external configuration files, and we call them **parametric constraints**. Unlike the structural constraints, there is no straightforward way to design an actor network so that all proposed actions are compliant with the parametric constraints. Instead of structurally preventing the actor from expressing actions that violate the parametric constraints, we elected to teach the agent, as a whole, that such actions are undesirable. We have therefore added a regularization term to the environment reward that penalizes the action by an amount proportional to the excess threshold violation, by using a hinge loss function. With this approach, the actor can quickly learn that the simplest way to obtain higher rewards is to propose admissible actions. At the same time, this approach allows for high flexibility, since the parametric constraints are set in the environment, and thus decoupled from the agent architecture.

4   Experimental Evaluation

Before presenting the results obtained by using the reinforcement learning framework to solve the asset allocation problem, we describe those settings that are shared by all the experiments presented in this section. We assume an initial asset allocation composed of cash only. The initial amount of cash is equal to 1050, while the reserves amount to 1000, which implies an initial capital of 50. The interest rate on loans is set to the interest rate of the "Italian BTP" bond with one year maturity, and the penalty ϵ is set to 2%. Similarly, the discounting interest rate is set to the 30% of "Italian BTP" bonds. A single insurance product is considered. The product guarantees a minimum yield of 0.5% per annum, and uses a uniform distribution over time of the payments for surrender or death.

In order to have a baseline to compare our RL framework to, we evaluate it on a simplified scenario on which the traditional Markowitz/Black-Litterman [1,17] approach can be applied. In particular, we consider a scenario in which:

- a single asset allocation is decided at time zero;
- rebalancing aims only to replenish negative amounts of cash by selling the other assets "pro quota" at every time $t > 0$.

These assumptions lead to a "fire and forget" scenario in which a single decision taken at the beginning determines the overall quality of the investments. Hence, $\overline{X}_0$ is the only decisional variable, and the entries of asset allocations $\overline{X}_{t>0}$ are determined directly the from state of the portfolio according to the formula:

$$X_{t,i} = \begin{cases} max(0, A_i(t)) & i = \text{Cash} \\ \frac{A_i(t)}{max(0,A_C(t))+\sum_{i \neq C} A_i(t)} & \text{otherwise.} \end{cases} \quad (5)$$

The use of a single decisional variable allows the comparison of the policy found by the agent with the results obtained by performing a gird search on the action space combined with Monte-Carlo sampling. The grid search is performed by exploring the action space simplex with a fixed step size in $\{0.20, 0.10, 0.05, 0.02, 0.01\}$. Each action is evaluated by averaging the obtained reward over 500 realizations of the economy. To avoid stochastic effects from affecting the comparison, these realizations are drawn in advance and fixed for all the actions of the search, and are used in round-robin during the training of the agent. The number of realization is sufficiently large that the probability of an agent exploring all them on a given small section of the action space is negligible.

4.1 Three Assets Scenario.

In the first experiment we focus on a scenario with three assets: cash, equity, and bond. We include a parametric constraint that sets 0.17 as an upper bound for the equity asset, and set the λ risk-aversion coefficient to 0.2. In order to create a controlled experimental environment, we run a set of simulations with 0.01 grid step – corresponding in this scenario to 5151 simulations. From this fine-grained set of experiments we can obviously extract coarser subsets by increasing the grid step size, as shown in Table 1.

We use the coarsest grid (step = 0.20) for the warm-up phase of the Critic, while keeping the more fine-grained best actions and rewards aside in order to use them to evaluate the Actor's performance during and after training. The warm-up phase is a standard fully supervised learning task, and we report the Critic loss (computed as mean absolute percentage error) during training in Fig. 3a. We then store the pre-trained critic weights and re-load them in subsequent experiments.

The core learning task for all our experiments is the training of our custom DDPG agent, and this process involves several hyper-parameters. These

Table 1. Parameters and results for the grid-search based simulations: respectively, step size for the grid, number of different actions explored, best action found with the given grid, corresponding average reward estimated on the 500 fixed realizations of the economy.

Step	# actions	Best action	Best reward
0.20	21	[0.0, 0.20, 0.80]	2.552
0.10	66	[0.0, 0.10, 0.90]	2.707
0.05	231	[0.0, 0.15, 0.85]	2.790
0.02	1326	[0.0, 0.16, 0.84]	2.799
0.01	5151	[0.0, 0.17, 0.83]	2.811

include structural details for the Actor neural network (number of neurons per layer, weight initialization parameters), training details (learning rate and decay for both the Actor and Critic), memory buffer parameters (capacity, batch size), and a noise parameter governing the weight perturbation process used for exploration. We therefore carried out a hyper-parameter optimization, where we observed that our system is rather sensitive to hyperparameter setting, with the Actor prone to converge on one-hot actions – most commonly assigning everything to bonds. The first hyper-parameter search rounds were used to define an 'admissibility subspace' of hyper-parameters that did not cause the agent to spiral into such states, while subsequent iterations (such as the one visualized in Fig. 3b) allowed to progressively approximate the known optimal scores. To obtain these results we trained a batch of 32 agents with different configurations of hyper-parameters and, every 100 iterations, measured their average score on the set of 500 pre-computed realizations. In Fig. 3b we show the cross-agent average score and, as shaded area, its 99% confidence interval; we also show the known best scores for grids with increasing granularity (as reported in Table 1) as horizontal lines, with the black line corresponding to the .20 step used for the Critic warm-up.

Figure 3c shows the learning curve of the optimal agent, able to match and even surpass the best known action, corresponding to the 0.01-step grid. Figure 3d also reports the actions played by the optimal Actor during the training phase. It clearly shows that the agent learns to assign the Equity asset (which gives the highest reward) to the highest possible value that would not incur a penalty (horizontal black line, corresponding to the set parametric constraint of .17).

We remark that we use this three assets scenario as a sandbox where it is still feasible to exhaustively explore the action space with non-trivial grid steps in order to compute the best action and reward; with an increasing number of assets this procedure quickly becomes computationally too expensive, as the number of actions to explore grows exponentially.

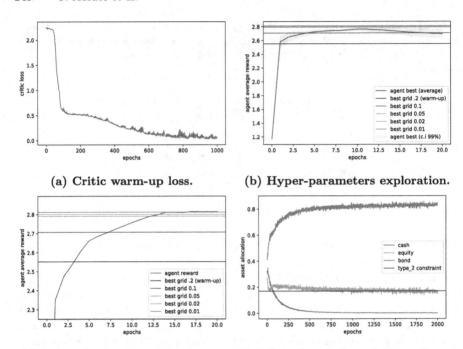

(a) **Critic warm-up loss.**   (b) **Hyper-parameters exploration.**

(c) **Selected agent's training score.**   (d) **Selected agent's training actions.**

Fig. 3. Training agents on a three assets scenario.

4.2   Six Assets Scenario

The second experiment aims to show that a near optimal solution can still be found when actions have larger dimensionality. In particular, we test the case in which the portfolio is composed only of cash, and Italian BTP Bonds with 3, 5, 10, 20, and 30 years tenors. No constraints have been considered; hence, any portion of the action space might contain candidates for the optimum. Furthermore, the risk-aversion factor λ has been set to a high value of 4 in order to avoid that the optimal solution comprises solely of the most profitable and most risky asset, i.e., the 30-years bond. In this setting, we perform 15 trainings of the agent by using only 21 actions for the warm-up. This number of actions corresponds to an exhaustive search on a grid with step size equal to 0.5. Only two actions used for the warm-up were able to provide a positive reward. The largest average reward included in the warm-up was equal to 0.0607 and was obtained by investing equally in BTP with 5 and 30 years tenors.

All the experiments provided an improvement from the initial warm-up from a minimum of 3.9% (reward 0.0631) to a maximum of 21.7% (0.0739). Figure 4 provides a summary of the experiments by showing the evolution of the best action found by the agent, both in terms of asset allocation[1] and reward over

---

[1] The other three assets are omitted as they go to zero very quickly.

the training epochs. In order to provide a further comparison, we provide also the best action found with an exhaustive search performed with a step size 0.1. In this setting, the testing of a single action for all the 500 economies requires around one minute, and the grid contains 3003 actions; hence, whole computation required more than 2 days. In spite of this, the obtained reward is still quite far from the best found by the agent, whose training requires only two hours. The rationale behind this gap can be explained by observing the evolution of the best asset allocation in Fig. 4b where we can notice that a near optimal solution can be found only at precision below 1%. In particular, the best reward found was generated by an action representing an asset allocation where only BTP at 5,10, and 30 years had non-zero weights equal to 0.19, 0.361, and 0.449, respectively.

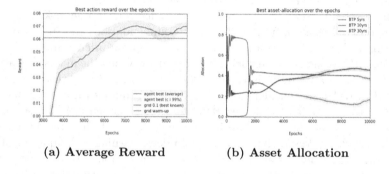

(a) **Average Reward**   (b) **Asset Allocation**

Fig. 4. Training agents on a six assets scenario

5   Related Work

The excellent results obtained in games [18,25] and robotics [13,22] have put the spotlight on the ability of RL to find near optimal solutions in large multi-stage, high-dimensional problems. And as such, they have drawn the attention of the financial sector since modern portfolio theory deals with similar settings.

Modern portfolio theory, initiated by Nobel-prize-winner Markowitz [17] and improved by Black and Litterman [1], consists in finding the optimal financial allocation over a single time horizon by using mean-variance asset allocation models. These models heavily rely on Markov processes to characterize the stochastic nature of the economy. Hence, they naturally suggests the coupling of Markov Decision Process (MDP) with Reinforcement Learning (RL) as a framework to solve these problems [26]. It is thus not surprising that the literature on RL methods for asset allocation problems is growing year by year [24].

For example, Wang and Zhou [27] present a framework, called exploratory-mean-variance (EMV), for continuous portfolio selection (action) in continuous time and continuous wealth (state) spaces. Q-learning methods are also common. Halperin [8] provides an example of a data-driven and model-free methods for optimal pricing and hedging of options with RL by constructing a risk-adjusted MDP for a discrete-time version of the classical Black-Scholes-Merton model. Nevmyvaka et al. [21] use Q-learning for large scale optimal order execution.

Direct policy search for portfolio allocation is instead presented by Moody et al. [19,20], and a tree-search approach that integrates the advantages in solving continuous action bandit problem with sample-based rollout methods is introduced by Mansley et al. [15]. The algorithm, named Hierarchical Optimistic Optimization applied to Tree (HOOT), adaptively partitions the action space, thus enabling it to avoid the pitfalls encountered in algorithms that use a fixed action discretization.

De Asis et al. [4] explore fixed-horizon temporal difference (TD) reinforcement learning algorithms for a new kind of value function that predicts the sum of rewards over a fixed number of future time steps. Jangmin et al. [9] perform dynamic asset allocation with a reinforcement-learning framework which uses the temporal information from both stock recommendations and the ratio of the stock fund over the asset. Buhler et al. [2] tackle option pricing and hedging by using deep RL methods. [10] explains how to handle When the model available to the agent is estimated from data, Since the seventies, portfolio theory has been extended in order to consider liabilities. Notable examples are *Asset-Liability Management* (ALM) and *dedicated portfolio theory* models [12]. These models were considered intractable before it was suggested that they can be handled with an underlying Markovian structure and deep learning techniques [2,11]. In this direction, Fontoura et al. [7] consider the optimization of investment portfolios where investments have to match (or outperform) a future flow of liabilities within a time constraint. They address an ALM problem with a variation of Deep Deterministic Policy Gradient algorithm (DDPG). In spite of the fast growing literature, only one work [7], takes in consideration a multi-stage setting that takes into account both asset-allocation and liabilities by still allowing the use of off-the-shelf RL methods. However, liabilities are far from the level of detail of those presented in the current work, since their description is limited to simple phenomena such as inflation. To the best of our knowledge, our work is the first RL framework able to describe a strong correlation between asset allocation and liabilities.

6   Conclusions

This paper presented a framework for the asset management of a life insurance company which differs from traditional portfolio management due to the strong dependency between the profits of the portfolio and the liabilities generated by the obligations toward the clients. The framework has been developed as a Reinforcement Learning environment by maintaining flexibility in many aspects of the problem. The most important are: (*i*) not being bound to any specific set of assets; (*ii*) having user-defined buying/selling strategies; (*iii*) the modeling of the liabilities directly from the parameters of the insurance products that generate them; (*iv*) general strategies for capital control and leverage.

We defined a risk-adjusted optimization problem to maximize the capital over a finite time horizon by choosing the asset-allocations at possibly any time unit. We validated the framework by means of a set of experiments performed on a simplified scenario where a single asset allocation must be chosen at time zero. Despite the smaller setting, experiments demonstrate how fast the problem grows in complexity by pointing at RL as the only viable solution for the problem.

Testing our proposed framework in a proper multi-stage setting is the future work with the highest priority, although proper baselines for this case need to be devised. However, the generality of the framework suggests many other problems. For example, the compounding effect on the capital is currently not addressed but should be taken into account as well as the definition of different measures for the control of the risk. In addition, while our framework defines the objective function in line with modern portfolio theory for comparison purposes, the literature on risk-adjusted MDPs [16] might provide a more robust grounding for our portfolio allocation problem. On the experimental side, since the results so far have shown marked oscillations when the agent is close to a near optimal policy, early stopping strategies should be explored. Finally, the design of more advanced buying and selling strategies is an orthogonal but nevertheless interesting future direction.

Acknowledgements. The research was conducted under a cooperative agreement between ISI Foundation, Intesa Sanpaolo Innovation Center, and Intesa Sanpaolo Vita. The authors would like to thank Lauretta Filangieri, Antonino Galatà, Giuseppe Loforese, Pietro Materozzi and Luigi Ruggerone for their useful comments.

References

1. Black, F., Litterman, R.: Global portfolio optimization. Financ. Anal. J. **48**(5), 28–43 (1992)
2. Buhler, H., Gonon, L., Teichmann, J., Wood, B.: Deep hedging (2018)
3. Cox, J.C., Ingersoll, J.E., Ross, S.A.: A theory of the term structure of interest rates. Econometrica **53**(2), 385–407 (1985). ISSN 00129682, 14680262
4. De Asis, K., Chan, A., Pitis, S., Sutton, R.S., Graves, D.: Fixed-horizon temporal difference methods for stable reinforcement learning. arXiv preprint arXiv:1909.03906 (2019)
5. Denardo, E.V.: On linear programming in a Markov decision problem. Manag. Sci. **16**(5), 281–288 (1970)
6. Doob, J.L.: The Brownian movement and stochastic equations. Ann. Math. 351–369 (1942)
7. Fontoura, A., Haddad, D., Bezerra, E.: A deep reinforcement learning approach to asset-liability management. In: 2019 8th Brazilian Conference on Intelligent Systems (BRACIS), pp. 216–221. IEEE (2019)
8. Halperin, I.: QLBS: Q-learner in the Black-Scholes(-Merton) worlds. arXiv preprint arXiv:1712.04609 (2017)
9. Jangmin, O., Lee, J., Lee, J.W., Zhang, B.T.: Adaptive stock trading with dynamic asset allocation using reinforcement learning. Inf. Sci. **176**(15), 2121–2147 (2006)

10. Jiang, N., Kulesza, A., Singh, S., Lewis, R.: The dependence of effective planning horizon on model accuracy. In: Proceedings of the 2015 International Conference on Autonomous Agents and Multiagent Systems, AAMAS 2015, Richland, SC, pp. 1181–1189. International Foundation for Autonomous Agents and Multiagent Systems (2015). ISBN 9781450334136

11. Krabichler, T., Teichmann, J.: Deep replication of a runoff portfolio (2020)

12. Leibowitz, M., Fabozzi, F.J., Sharpe, W.: Investing: The Collected Works of Martin L. Leibowitz. Probus Professional Pub (1992)

13. Levine, S., Finn, C., Darrell, T., Abbeel, P.: End-to-end training of deep visuomotor policies. J. Mach. Learn. Res. **17**(39), 1–40 (2016)

14. Lillicrap, T.P., et al.: Continuous control with deep reinforcement learning. arXiv preprint arXiv:1509.02971 (2015)

15. Mansley, C., Weinstein, A., Littman, M.: Sample-based planning for continuous action Markov decision processes. In: Twenty-First International Conference on Automated Planning and Scheduling (2011)

16. Marcus, S.I., Fernández-Gaucherand, E., Hernández-Hernandez, D., Coraluppi, S., Fard, P.: Risk sensitive Markov decision processes. In: Byrnes, C.I., Datta, B.N., Martin, C.F., Gilliam, D.S. (eds.) Systems and Control in the Twenty-First Century. PSCT, vol. 22, pp. 263–279. Springer, Heidelberg (1997). https://doi.org/10.1007/978-1-4612-4120-1_14

17. Markowitz, H.: Portfolio selection. J. Financ. **7**(1), 77–91 (1952)

18. Mnih, V., et al.: Human-level control through deep reinforcement learning. Nature **518**(7540), 529–533 (2015). ISSN 00280836

19. Moody, J., Saffell, M.: Learning to trade via direct reinforcement. IEEE Trans. Neural Netw. **12**(4), 875–89 (2001)

20. Moody, J., Wu, L., Liao, Y., Saffell, M.: Performance functions and reinforcement learning for trading systems and portfolios. J. Forecast. **17**(5–6), 441–470 (1998)

21. Nevmyvaka, Y., Feng, Y., Kearns, M.: Reinforcement learning for optimized trade execution. In: Proceedings of the 23rd International Conference on Machine Learning, ICML 2006, pp. 673–680. Association for Computing Machinery, New York (2006)

22. Peters, J., Vijayakumar, S., Schaal, S.: Reinforcement learning for humanoid robotics. In: IEEE-RAS International Conference on Humanoid Robots (Humanoids2003), Karlsruhe, Germany, 29–30 September (2003). CLMC

23. Plappert, M., et al.: Parameter space noise for exploration. arXiv preprint arXiv:1706.01905 (2017)

24. de Prado, M.L.: Advances in Financial Machine Learning, 1st edn. Wiley, Hoboken (2018)

25. Silver, D., Hassabis, D.: Mastering the game of go with deep neural networks and tree search. Nature **529**, 484–503 (2016)

26. Sutton, R.S., Barto, A.G.: Reinforcement Learning: An Introduction. MIT Press, Cambridge (2018)

27. Wang, H., Zhou, X.Y.: Continuous-time mean-variance portfolio selection: a reinforcement learning framework. Math. Financ. **30**(4), 1273–1308 (2020)

XRR: Explainable Risk Ranking
for Financial Reports

Ting-Wei Lin[1], Ruei-Yao Sun[1], Hsuan-Ling Chang[2], Chuan-Ju Wang[3],
and Ming-Feng Tsai[1(✉)]

[1] Department of Computer Science, National Chengchi University,
Taipei City, Taiwan
mftsai@nccu.edu.tw
[2] Department of Finance, National Taiwan University,
Taipei City, Taiwan
D05723004@ntu.edu.tw
[3] Research Center for Information Technology Innovation, Academia Sinica,
Taipei City, Taiwan
cjwang@citi.sinica.edu.tw

Abstract. We propose an eXplainable Risk Ranking (XRR) model that
uses multilevel encoders and attention mechanisms to analyze financial
risks among companies. In specific, the proposed method utilizes the
textual information in financial reports to rank the relative risks among
companies and locate top high-risk companies; moreover, via attention
mechanisms, XRR enables to highlight the critical words and sentences
within financial reports that are most likely to influence financial risk
and thus boasts better model explainability. Experimental results evaluated on 10-K financial reports show that XRR significantly outperforms
several baselines, yielding up to 7.4% improvement in terms of ranking
correlation metrics. Furthermore, in our experiments, the model explainability is evaluated by using finance-specific sentiment lexicons at word
level and a newly-provided annotated reference list at the sentence level
to examine the learned attention models.

Keywords: Financial risk ranking · Finance text mining · Financial
sentiment analysis

1 Introduction

Most finance literature on risk analysis has focused on quantitative approaches [1,
9,23]. One of the most important works [9] discovered that the size of a company
and its book-to-market ratio are the key factors to financial risk; outside of
these two key factors, other factors that may as well affect financial risk are still
uncertain. With the progress in text analytics, there have been many studies
trying to uncover other potential risk factors by exploiting alternative textual
information (e.g., news, reviews, and financial reports) to analyze financial risk [7,
14,19,21,24].

© Springer Nature Switzerland AG 2021
Y. Dong et al. (Eds.): ECML PKDD 2021, LNAI 12978, pp. 253–268, 2021.
https://doi.org/10.1007/978-3-030-86514-6_16

Due to the noise within finance documents and the information gap between texts and financial numerical measures, it is difficult to predict the exact finance quantities (e.g., stock return and volatility) and to extract useful information and relations directly by using textual information. Thus, the work in [24] proposes using ranking-based methods for analyzing financial risk with the use of textual information and shows that ranking-based methods are more suitable than regression-based methods for such an analytic task. However, the work in [24] and other pioneering studies such as [14, 22] mainly use simple and hand-crafted features to describe financial documents, like bags-of-words, noun phrases, and named entities. Thus, these approaches are difficult to model complex structures or semantics in texts, which limits their potential and usage scenarios.

In recent years, deep neural networks such as CNN [15], GRU [5], and BERT [6] have demonstrated promising results across NLP tasks such as document classification and sentiment analysis [2, 8]. The advancements are due to the superiority of these techniques in learning semantically meaningful representations. Although such deep learning approaches can extract the latent features from texts, most of these models are not explainable, which is however a vital ingredient in models for finance applications. To some extent, attention mechanisms alleviate the explainability problem [26], since attention layers explicitly weight the components' representations; thus, it can be said that attention mechanisms are in some way capable of identifying meaningful information as a post-hoc justification of the model prediction.

To advance the state of the art, we propose an eXplainable Risk Ranking model (XRR) to capture key information from financial reports and investigate related financial risks. Specifically, XRR is a deep neural network model incorporating multilevel explainable structures and learning to rank techniques for ranking relative risks defined by post-event return volatility [16] among companies. To build the XRR model, we first design a multilevel explainable structure to model the complex structures within financial texts by using sequence encoders based on bidirectional gated recurrent units (GRUs) at both the word and sentence levels. At each level, the attention mechanism is leveraged to make the model explainable. Moreover, unlike many previous hierarchical deep neural network architectures, which are mainly on classification tasks [7, 17], XRR ranks the relative risks among companies and locates top high-risk companies. To enable this, we propose a pairwise ranking loss based on a siamese network with two parallel multilevel explainable structures. In addition, instead of adopting naive stock return volatility, we propose using the post-event return volatility as the proxy of financial risk because it excludes the effect of several important macro-economic factors and is thus more effective for monitoring the event effect on the change of stock prices than the stock return volatility [16, 25].

We conduct comprehensive experiments using a large collection of 10-K financial reports from 1996 to 2013, consisting of 39,083 reports in total. The results show that the proposed XRR significantly outperforms other baselines in terms of all evaluation metrics. For robustness, we also conduct a comparison on different financial risk proxies and conduct several financial analyses to verify

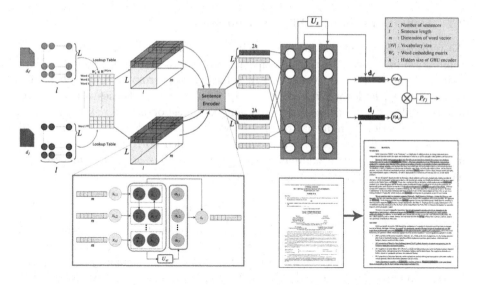

Fig. 1. XRR network structure

our results. Moreover, we conduct evaluation and discussion by using external finance-specific sentiment lexicons and an annotated reference list at the sentence level to examine the learned financial sentiment texts with high attention scores and the corresponding financial risks. In this evaluation, XRR exhibits a stronger retrieval power compared to the baselines and provides more insightful understanding into the impact of the financial texts on companies' future risks. In summary, XRR advances the state of the art in the following three dimensions.

1. (Model) We propose a multilevel explainable network architecture for risk ranking with financial reports, allowing for modeling financial texts with more complex structures and highlighting crucial information at both the word and sentence levels.
2. (Risk measure) We propose using the post-event return volatility as a risk proxy for such text analytic tasks, and our experiments also attest the appropriateness of the proxy for the tasks.
3. (Resource) We provide a high quality sentence-level risk-annotated list and use the list to evaluate the attention weights for sentences and examine the explainability of our model.

2   Methodology

We first formulate the risk ranking problem, and then provide a brief description of the post-event return volatility. Finally, we describe the proposed XRR model in detail.

2.1   Definitions and Problem Formulation

We rank the companies along with their relative financial risks with the use of companies' associated textual information via a pairwise ranking model. Note that we here use the post-event return volatility as a proxy of financial risk for each company. Following the work in [24], we slot the volatilities within a year into several risk levels; thus, each company c_i corresponds to a risk level $v_i \in \mathbb{Z}$. Given a collection of financial reports $\mathcal{D}$, we generate a set of pairs of financial reports $\{(d_\ell, d_j)|d_\ell, d_j \in \mathcal{D}\}$, each element in which corresponds to a pair of financial reports for two companies c_ℓ and c_j. We thus have the pairwise risk model $f : \mathbb{R}^p \to \mathbb{R}$ for comparison between companies c_ℓ and c_j such that

$$E(d_\ell, d_j) = \mathbb{1}_{\{v_\ell > v_j\}}, \tag{1}$$

where v_i denotes the risk level of company c_i and p denotes the dimension of the representation of a report d_i. Note that the rank order of the set of companies is specified by the real score that the model f takes. In particular, $f(\mathbf{d}_\ell) > f(\mathbf{d}_j)$ is taken to mean that the model asserts that $c_\ell \succ c_j$, where $\mathbf{d}_i \in \mathbb{R}^p$ denotes the representation of report d_i and $c_\ell \succ c_j$ means that c_ℓ is ranked higher than c_j; that is, the company c_ℓ is riskier than c_j.

2.2   Post-event Return Volatility

Post-event volatility has been widely used as a proxy of financial risk in finance research, especially in the case of event study [13]. In contrast to the naive stock return volatility, which is defined as the standard deviation of the daily stock returns over a certain period, post-event volatility calculation takes into account macro-economic factors; thus, such a measure excludes the effect of these macro-economic factors and is effective for monitoring the event's effect on the change of stock prices. As a result, for event study, it is considered a more suitable risk proxy than the naive stock return volatility, though many data mining works adopt the naive stock return volatility to conduct the analysis. Note that in the above context, "event" refers to the filing of a financial report.

Following the definition in [16,25], we define the post-event return volatility as the root-mean-square error from a Fama and French three-factor model [9] for days [6, 252] after the event and at least 60 daily observations. Then, we focus on modeling the effect on the post-event return volatility of a company after its report filing. For comparison purposes, we also include the results of naive stock return volatility in the Experiments section.

2.3   Multilevel Explanation Structure

Inspired by several hierarchical language networks [7,12,27], we construct XRR, our pairwise risk ranking model, using a multilevel structure to represent pairs of financial reports. The structure is mainly made of a word-level embedding matrix and two major components at both word and sentence levels: the GRU sequence encoder and the multilevel attention mechanism (see Fig. 1).

Embedding Matrix. Given the set of word vocabulary $\mathcal{W}$, we embed each word $w \in \mathcal{W}$ into a real-valued vector x through a embedding matrix $W_e \in \mathbb{R}^{|\mathcal{W}| \times m}$, where m is the dimension of word vectors.

GRU Sequence Encoder. Given a report $d \in \mathcal{D}$ with L sentences $\{s_1, s_2, \dots s_L\}$, s_t denotes the embedded representation of the t-th sentence. In each report, the t-th sentence consists of l words $\{w_{t1}, w_{t2}, \dots, w_{tl}\}$, where $w_{ti} \in \mathcal{W}$. To encode both sentences and documents, we adopt bidirectional GRUs at both the word and sentence level, respectively, which leverage past and future information to better utilize contextual finance information. Generally speaking, in the sentence encoder, for the ℓ-th word in the t-th sentence, $w_{t\ell}$, with its corresponding word embedding $x_{t\ell}$ from W_e, the word can be depicted by concatenating the forward hidden state $\overrightarrow{h}_{t\ell}$ and the backward one $\overleftarrow{h}_{t\ell}$ of the GRU encoders; that is, the annotation of the ℓ-th word in the t-th sentence becomes

$$h_{t\ell} = \overrightarrow{h}_{t\ell} \oplus \overleftarrow{h}_{t\ell} = \overrightarrow{\mathrm{GRU}}(x_{t\ell}) \oplus \overleftarrow{\mathrm{GRU}}(x_{t\ell}),$$

for $\ell = 1, 2, \dots l$, where $\overrightarrow{h}_{t\ell}, \overleftarrow{h}_{t\ell} \in \mathbb{R}^h$, $\oplus$ denotes the concatenation operator, and h refers to the hidden size of a GRU encoder. Then, we have $h_{t\ell} \in \mathbb{R}^{2h}$ and $H_w = (h_{t1}, \cdots, h_{tl}) \in \mathbb{R}^{l \times 2h}$.

Following the same process, in the document encoder, the t-th sentence is represented by concatenating the forward hidden state $\overrightarrow{h}_t$ and the backward one $\overleftarrow{h}_t$, i.e.,

$$h_t = \overrightarrow{h}_t \oplus \overleftarrow{h}_t = \overrightarrow{\mathrm{GRU}}(s_t) \oplus \overleftarrow{\mathrm{GRU}}(s_t),$$

Then we have $h_t \in \mathbb{R}^{2h}$ and $H_s = (h_1, \cdots, h_L) \in \mathbb{R}^{L \times 2h}$.

Multilevel Attention Mechanism. To provide fine-grained explainable results, the proposed XRR involves one level of attention at the word level and one at the sentence level; these pay more or less attention to individual words and sentences and capture influential texts in financial reports with respect to financial risks. Specifically, for the t-th sentence, we feed each word annotation $h_{t\ell}$ through a fully-connected layer to yield $u_{t\ell}$ as the hidden representation of $h_{t\ell}$, after which the attention mechanism measures the importance of the hidden representation $u_{t\ell}$ with a word level context vector U_w and obtains a normalized importance weight $\alpha_{t\ell}$ through a softmax function. After that, we compute the sentence vector s_t as a weighted sum of the word annotations. Mathematically speaking, we have

$$u_{t\ell} = \tanh\left(W_w h_{t\ell} + b_w\right), \ \ell = 1, 2, \dots l,$$

$$\alpha_{t\ell} = \frac{\exp(u_{t\ell}^\top U_w)}{\sum_{i=1}^{l} \exp(u_{ti}^\top U_w)}, \ \ell = 1, 2, \dots l,$$

$$s_t = \sum_{\ell=1}^{l} \alpha_{t\ell} h_{t\ell},$$

where $W_w \in \mathbb{R}^{a \times 2h}$, $b_w \in \mathbb{R}^a$, and $U_w \in \mathbb{R}^a$.

Similar to the above procedure, we feed the hidden representation of each sentence annotation h_t by using a single-layer perceptron to get u_t, which is associated with a normalized importance weight α_t via a sentence level context vector U_s, i.e.,

$$u_t = \tanh\left(W_s h_t + b_s\right), \ t = 1, 2, \ldots L,$$

$$\alpha_t = \frac{\exp(u_t^\top U_s)}{\sum_{i=1}^{L} \exp(u_i^\top U_s)}, \ t = 1, 2, \ldots L,$$

where $W_s \in \mathbb{R}^{a \times 2h}$, $b_w \in \mathbb{R}^a$, and $U_s \in \mathbb{R}^a$.

Finally, with the weight vector α_t for $t = 1, \cdots, L$, the representation of each report $d_i \in \mathcal{D}$, $\mathbf{d}_i$, is computed as a weighted sum of the sentence annotations as

$$\mathbf{d}_i = \sum_{t=1}^{L} \alpha_t h_t. \tag{2}$$

2.4 Pairwise Deep Ranking

We use a pairwise approach to rank the financial reports according to their financial risk levels. To this end, we build a pair of multilevel structures described in the previous subsection, with the weights shared across both sides of the structures, as illustrated in Fig. 1. Given a pair of financial reports (d_ℓ, d_j), where the company associated with d_ℓ is riskier than that with d_j according to their risk levels, the goal of the ranking model $f(\cdot)$ is to generate a higher score for d_ℓ. Denote $\Psi = \left\{(d_\ell, d_j) \mid E(d_\ell, d_j) = 1\right\}$ as the set of all "positive" pairs, each element in which is fed into two separate but identical hierarchical structures. Our goal is to learn a score function $f(\cdot)$ that satisfies

$$f(\mathbf{d}_\ell) > f(\mathbf{d}_j), \forall (d_\ell, d_j) \in \Psi, \tag{3}$$

where $\mathbf{d}_i$ denotes the dense representation of report d_i obtained from Eq. (2). Note that in practice, we implement a siamese network for $f(\cdot)$ that adopts the same weights while working in tandem on two different input vectors to compute comparable output vectors. To obtain an overall risk ranking for all companies (reports), we adopt a standard RankNet [4] loss layer to learn a posterior probability distribution $P_{\ell j}$ that is close to the target probability $E(d_\ell, d_j)$ defined in Eq. (1) for each pair (d_ℓ, d_j), where

$$P_{\ell j} = \frac{\exp\left(f(\mathbf{d}_\ell) - f(\mathbf{d}_j)\right)}{1 + \exp\left(f(\mathbf{d}_\ell) - f(\mathbf{d}_j)\right)}. \tag{4}$$

A natural choice for measuring the closeness between two probability distributions is binary cross-entropy; thus we have the objective function to be minimized as

$$\min - \sum_{(d_\ell, d_j) \in \Psi} \left(E(d_\ell, d_j) \log P_{\ell j} + (1 - E(d_\ell, d_j)) \log\left(1 - P_{\ell j}\right)\right). \tag{5}$$

3 Experiments

3.1 Data Description

We conducted experiments on a large collection of 10-K reports from year 1996 to year 2013 provided by [25], which are annual reports required by the Securities and Exchange Commission (SEC) providing comprehensive overviews of companies' business and financial conditions and which include audited financial statements. Specifically, following previous studies in [3,14,24,25], we used only Item 7 "Management's Discussion and Analysis of Financial Conditions and Results of Operations" (MD&A) in the experiments as it contains the most important forward-looking statements for companies. Moreover, the post-event volatilities corresponding to each report is also provided by [25].

3.2 Experimental Settings

We first split the post-event return volatilities of companies within a year into five different risk levels[1] and generated a set of pairs of financial reports based on the relative difference of levels among the companies. Due to the huge numbers of document pairs, we sampled 3,000 pairs to train the model in each epoch; moreover, we differentiated the pair sampling probabilities based on their degree of proximity to the testing year; that is, pairs closer to the testing year were given a higher sampling probability. In addition, the dimension of the word vector, m, depended on the pre-trained word embedding models used, the hidden size of the GRU (h) was set to 100, and the attention size (a) was set to 100. The maximum number of words in sentences (l) and that of sentences in documents (L) were set to 150 and 70, respectively. The values of the model hyperparameters for the compared method were decided using a grid search over different settings; we used the combination that led to the best performance.

3.3 Pre-trained Word Embedding

We evaluated different word embedding models to construct the pre-trained word embedding matrix W_e.

1. **Fin-Word2Vec** [25] denotes vectors pre-trained via Word2Vec with a skip-gram model trained on the 10-K Corpus (39083 reports from 18 years); each word is represented as a 300-dimensional vector.
2. **BERT-Large, Uncased** [6] contains 24-layer, 1024-hidden, 16 heads, and 340M parameters; each word in a document is represented by a 1024-dimensional vector, and only the word embedding is used in our model.[2]

---

[1] We here split the volatilities based on 30-th, 60-th, 80-th, and 90-th percentiles, yielding the average numbers of the five categories per year as 702, 702, 467, 234, and 234, respectively.

[2] Note that in BERT models, words in different sentences (or documents) are associated with different representations; to reflect this, we treat words in different documents as different words.

Table 1. Performance comparison

Metric	Method	Model	Test year								
			2001	2002	2003	...	2010	2011	2012	2013	Average
τ	Classification	Fasttext	0.475	0.388	0.401	...	0.449	0.460	0.452	0.463	0.426
		HAN	0.527	0.474	0.582	...	0.557	0.569	0.590	0.593	0.535
	Ranking	RankSVM	0.549	0.521	0.525	...	0.589	0.592	0.593	0.591	0.547
		XRR (G)	0.536	0.501	0.502	...	0.580	0.607	0.623	0.607	0.547
		XRR (B)	0.541	0.525	0.518	...	0.591	0.616	0.632	0.625	0.559
		XRR (F)	**0.570**	**0.541**	**0.553**	...	**0.605**	**0.616**	**0.637**	**0.629**	**0.573**[*]
ρ	Classification	Fasttext	0.589	0.493	0.506	...	0.573	0.583	0.568	0.585	0.540
		HAN	0.648	0.587	0.599	...	0.690	0.702	0.720	0.727	0.661
	Ranking	RankSVM	0.685	0.657	0.661	...	0.733	0.733	0.731	0.732	0.686
		XRR (G)	0.671	0.632	0.636	...	0.720	0.750	0.762	0.748	0.684
		XRR (B)	0.675	0.659	0.657	...	0.732	0.756	0.772	0.766	0.697
		XRR (F)	**0.702**	**0.675**	**0.691**	...	**0.749**	**0.760**	**0.773**	**0.768**	**0.711**[*]

Notation * denotes significance compared to the best baseline under a permutation test with $p < 0.05$.

3. **GloVe** [20] representations are 300-dimensional word vectors[3] trained on 840 billion tokens of Common Crawl data.

In the following experiments, we denote each word embedding model with the first character of its name (i.e., F, B, G) with parentheses, e.g., XRR (B) for XRR with BERT-Large. For fair comparison, the original word embeddings are all fine-tuned in both our proposed XRR and the baseline HAN in the following experiments.

3.4 Compared Methods

We compare XRR with several baseline models including a ranking-based and two multi-class classification models.

1. **TFIDF-Rank**[4] uses TF-IDF as reports' representations plus pairwise deep ranking.
2. **FastText** is proposed by [11], a simple and efficient baseline for document classification.
3. **HAN** is proposed by [27], adopting hierarchical networks with attention mechanisms for document classification. We here used GloVe as the pre-trained word embedding and sorted the companies using the probabilities of the high-risk class in the softmax layer.

3.5 Experimental Results

To evaluate the performance of our model, we adopted Spearman's Rho (ρ) [18] and Kendall's Tau (τ) [10] as our rank correlation metric. Table 1 tabulates the

---

[3] https://nlp.stanford.edu/projects/glove/.
[4] We also adopt RankSVM with TF-IDF as features by following [24], the results of which are close to the ones of TFIDF-Rank.

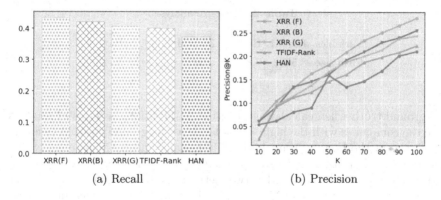

(a) Recall   (b) Precision

Fig. 2. Evaluation on high-risk companies

experimental results, in which all reports from the five-year period preceding the testing year are used as the training data. For example, the reports from 1996 to 2000 constitute the training data, and the trained model is tested on the reports of year 2001. The boldface number in the table denotes the best result among all methods per test year. As shown in the table, the proposed XRR reveals the strong correlations between the predicted financial risk levels and the actual levels. We attribute the superior performance of XRR to the following observations: 1) The TFIDF-Rank and XRR ranking-based methods successfully identify relative risks between each financial document pair and yield better performance than the two classification models; 2) XRR models a much more complex structure of representations of financial texts than the traditional bag-of-words model, yielding better performance than TFIDF-Rank.

In addition, we compare the proposed XRR using different pre-trained word embeddings. The results show that XRR (F), the model with Fin-Word2Vec, yields consistently better performance than those with GloVe or BERT. A closer look at the results shows that although XRR with BERT yields better results than that with GloVe, the model using a domain-specific word embedding, i.e., XRR (F), still achieves the best performance among the three. This demonstrates that a high-quality, domain-specific word embedding is also an important factor for such a task.[5] On the other hand, while correctly ranking all reports along with their financial risk is important, financial scholars and practitioners may care more about locating the most risky companies. To examine this type of performance,[6] we further use the concepts of precision@K and recall in information retrieval as our evaluation metrics, where we use the realized post-event volatilities to rank the companies in each year and treat the top-K companies as

---

[5] Due to resource limitations, we could not train a domain-specific BERT model; however, we speculate that using a domain-specific BERT would yield further improvements.

[6] We omit the comparison to Fasttext here as its performance in Table 1 distances it from the other three models.

Table 2. Firm size analysis

Variables	Rank 1	Rank 2	Rank 3	Rank 4	Rank 5
Firm size	8.5052	7.8410	6.9821	6.1892	5.7281

our ground truth when calculating precision. In addition, in terms of recall, we take the companies with the highest risk levels as the ground truth. As shown in Fig. 2, our method outperforms both TFIDF-Rank and HAN in terms of these two metrics, indicating that the proposed XRR is more effective at locating high-risk companies than the other two methods. Note that in the following subsections, we use the results of XRR (F), the best model, for further analyses and explainability discussion. We also omit the notation denoting the pre-trained word embedding, i.e., "(F)", to simplify the notation.

3.6 Fine-Grained Analysis

We here conduct a fined-grained analysis to further investigate the performance of companies associated with different risk levels. To do so, we first equally split the companies within a year into five different risk levels according to their realized post-event return volatilities; we then calculate the ρ and τ correlation metrics for companies in each rank. As shown in the heat map in Fig. 3, where the color denotes the correlation, the proposed model yields better performance for companies with higher financial risk, which shows that the model effectively locates high-risk companies, thus making our approach useful in practice. Also, we investigate the relation between the predicted risk levels and the average firm size[7] of the companies at each risk level. According to [9], smaller firms are typically associated with higher financial risk than larger ones. To examine the rationality of our prediction, we equally split the firms based on our predicted scores in each year into five risk levels and calculate the average firm size separately in each of the five groups. Table 2 shows that the predicted high-risk companies (Rank 5) are on average small in terms of their firm size, which indicates that our model learned from textual information from financial reports yields findings consistent with the literature in finance.

3.7 Different Risk Measure Analysis

To demonstrate the suitability of using post-event return volatility as our risk proxy, we compare its performance with the naive stock volatility in Fig. 4. The definition of the naive stock volatility is the standard deviation of stock returns[8] over a certain period. Following the setting in [25], we choose daily stock returns

---

[7] The firm size is defined as the logarithm of the sum of all current and long-term assets held by a company (in million dollars).

[8] The stock return is the appreciation in the price plus any dividends paid, divided by the original price of the stock.

for 12 months after the report filing date to calculate the naive stock return volatility. In Fig. 4 we observe that the correlations between the predicted risk scores and post-event volatilities are much higher than those between the predicted scores and the naive stock return volatility. This is because the naive stock return volatility is a noisy risk proxy for pure textual analysis, as it does not exclude other macro-economic or human behavior risk, making it difficult for models to capture the relation between text and risk. One obvious case in year 2008, the well-known financial crisis, shows that the naive stock return volatility was drastically affected by the market, causing its lowest correlation of the whole sample period.

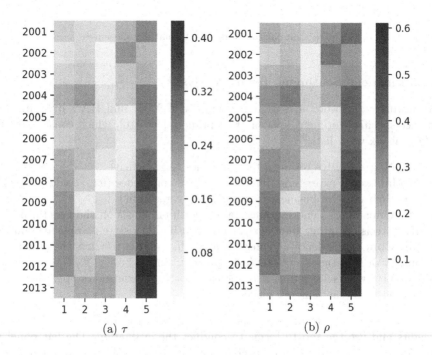

Fig. 3. Fine-grained correlation analysis

4   Discussions on Explainability

In financial practice, instead of directly making final decisions, machine learning models usually play roles in assisting financial professionals; thus, model explainability is vital in many finance application scenarios. To make our model applicable in practice, we here conduct post-hoc justifications to examine the expainability of our model.

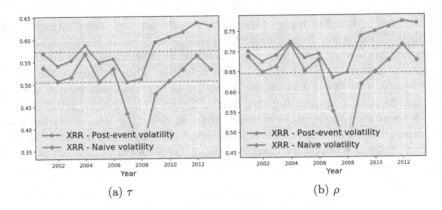

Fig. 4. Comparison of different volatility measures

4.1 Financial Sentiment Terms Analysis

We evaluate the word attention mechanism of XRR and HAN by using the finance-specific sentiment lexicon (FL) proposed by [16], which consists of the following six word lists:[9]

1. **Fin-Neg:** negative business terminologies (e.g., deficit)
2. **Modal:** words expressing different levels of confidence (e.g., could, might).
3. **Fin-Pos:** positive business terminologies (e.g., profit)
4. **Fin-Unc:** words denoting uncertainty, with emphasis on the general notion of imprecision rather than exclusively focusing on risk (e.g., appear, doubt).
5. **Fin-Con:** words denoting constraining, a factor that restricts the amount or quality of investment options (e.g., prevent, limit).
6. **Fin-Lit:** words reflecting a propensity for legal contest or, per our label, litigiousness (e.g., amend, forbear).

We first rank the terms in each sentence according to their learned attention weights and use the top-10 terms to conduct the evaluation. The left panel in Fig. 5 plots the precision@10 for each method, for which the terms in the union of the six word lists are considered as the ground truth. Observe that compared to the other two methods, XRR captures more terms listed in the lexicon; note that Random denotes the methods that randomly select 10 terms from each sentence. In addition, in the right panel of Fig. 5, we conduct a finer analysis by treating the words in each word list as the ground truth. An interesting finding is that XRR locates more negative words in **Fin-Neg** than the other two methods. Moreover, our XRR gains the top-3 performance increment compared with HAN for the word lists **Fin-Lit** (15.3%), **Fin-Unc** (14.7%) and **Fin-Neg** (14.6%). Previous literature shows that negative and litigious terms are usually highly correlated with financial risk [16,24]. For instance, *deficit* usually means "an excess of liabilities over assets, of losses over profits, or of expenditure over income in

---

[9] https://sraf.nd.edu/textual-analysis/resources/.

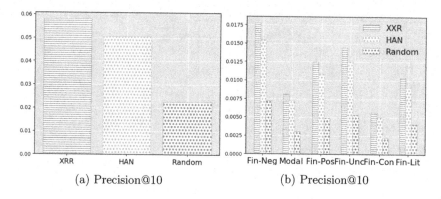

(a) Precision@10   (b) Precision@10

Fig. 5. Sentence attention analysis

finance"; it is clear that a company's report that is highly associated with *deficit* usually implies higher future risk. This finding shows that the proposed model is consistent with many previous findings and highlights negative financial words more than other models.

4.2 Financial Sentiment Sentences Analysis

We further use an annotated list at the sentence level to analyze the results of sentence-level attention mechanisms in XRR. The reference list contains 2,432 sentences labeled as risk-related ones. In particular, there are 1,539 high risk-related sentences and 896 low risk-related ones, each of which is selected from the MD&A sections of the used 10-K dataset.[10] For evaluation, we treat the 1,539 high risk-related sentences in financial reports as our ground truth. In each financial report containing at least one high-risk labeled sentence, we rank all of the sentences according to their learned attention weights and use the top-10 sentences to conduct the evaluation in terms of precision and recall. As shown in Fig. 6, the XRR model is generally capable of highlighting more risky sentences in terms of both metrics; note that the dotted lines in the figure denote the average performance over different years. These results again demonstrate that the sentence-level attention weights of XRR reveal a stronger and a more straightforward relation between texts and financial risk than other models.

Furthermore, we provide two example sentences that are associated with high attention scores in Fig. 7, where that in (a) is in the annotated list and its attention weight is four times the average attention weight of sentences in the reports associated with the highest risk level. Also, our model also identifies a non-labeled sentence (b) as a high weighted sentence in which the terms "redeem" and "loss" are both associated with negative effects for the company and might bring uncertainty and risk in the future. Such results demonstrate that the XRR model effectively finds the important parts within a document regarding financial

---

[10] The list will be publicly available upon publication.

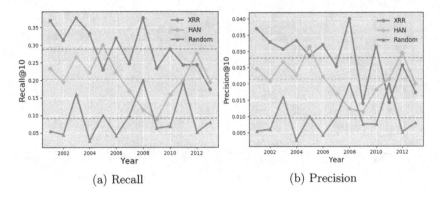

Fig. 6. Sentence attention analysis

risk. Therefore, considering financial scholars and practitioners' concerns about risky information in financial reports, these examples indicate that our model spotlights texts that are highly correlated to high risk in financial reports and effectively provides the important parts within a document as a brief summary thereof.

	From Chromcraft Revington, Inc., From 10-K
(a)	Forward-looking statements are not guarantees of performance or outcomes and are subject to certain risks and uncertainties that could cause actual results or outcomes to differ materially from those reported, expected or anticipated as of the day of this report.
	From Timberland BanCorp, Inc., 2008 Form 10-K
(b)	In June 2008, the Company redeemed its $ 29.1 million investment in the AMF family of mutual funds for the underlying securities and cash, and recorded a loss of $2.8 million.

Fig. 7. Examples of sentence attention

5   Conclusion

We propose XRR to rank companies to keep them in line with their relative risk levels specified by their post-event volatilities, in which the textual information in financial reports is leveraged to make the prediction. Experimental results on a large-scale financial report dataset demonstrate that our approach exhibits a stronger ranking power compared to the baselines. Also, the evaluation on explainability attests the effectiveness of our model for providing explainable results.

Reproducibility

To facilitate reproducibility of the results in this paper, we are sharing the code at https://github.com/cnclabs/codes.fin.attention.git.

References

1. Aikman, D., et al.: Funding liquidity risk in a quantitative model of systemic stability. Cent. Bank. Anal. Econ. Policies Book Ser. **15**, 371–410 (2011)
2. Akhtar, M.S., Kumar, A., Ghosal, D., Ekbal, A., Bhattacharyya, P.: A multilayer perceptron based ensemble technique for fine-grained financial sentiment analysis. In: Proceedings of EMNLP, pp. 540–546 (2017)
3. Buehlmaier, M.M., Whited, T.M.: Are financial constraints priced? Evidence from textual analysis. Rev. Financ. Stud. **31**(7), 2693–2728 (2018)
4. Burges, C., et al.: Learning to rank using gradient descent. In: Proceedings of ICML, pp. 89–96 (2005)
5. Chung, J., Gulcehre, C., Cho, K., Bengio, Y.: Empirical evaluation of gated recurrent neural networks on sequence modeling. arXiv preprint arXiv:1412.3555 (2014)
6. Devlin, J., Chang, M.W., Lee, K., Toutanova, K.: BERT: pre-training of deep bidirectional transformers for language understanding. In: Proceedings of NAACL-HLT, pp. 4171–4186 (2018)
7. Ding, X., Zhang, Y., Liu, T., Duan, J.: Deep learning for event-driven stock prediction. In: Proceedings of IJCAI, pp. 2327–2333 (2015)
8. Dos Santos, C., Gatti, M.: Deep convolutional neural networks for sentiment analysis of short texts. In: Proceedings of COLING, pp. 69–78 (2014)
9. Fama, E.F., French, K.R.: Common risk factors in the returns on stocks and bonds. J. Financ. Econ. **33**(1), 3–56 (1993)
10. Kendall, M.G.: A new measure of rank correlation. Biometrika **30**(1/2), 81–93 (1938)
11. Grave, E., Mikolov, T., Joulin, A., Bojanowski, P.: Bag of tricks for efficient text classification. In: Proceedings of EACL, pp. 427–431 (2017)
12. Hu, Z., Liu, W., Bian, J., Liu, X., Liu, T.Y.: Listening to chaotic whispers: a deep learning framework for news-oriented stock trend prediction. In: Proceedings of WSDM, pp. 261–269 (2018)
13. Ito, T., Lyons, R.K., Melvin, M.T.: Is there private information in the FX market? the Tokyo experiment. J. Financ. **53**(3), 1111–1130 (1998)
14. Kogan, S., Levin, D., Routledge, B.R., Sagi, J.S., Smith, N.A.: Predicting risk from financial reports with regression. In: Proceedings of NAACL, pp. 272–280 (2009)
15. LeCun, Y., Bottou, L., Bengio, Y., Haffner, P., et al.: Gradient-based learning applied to document recognition. Proc. IEEE **86**(11), 2278–2324 (1998)
16. Loughran, T., McDonald, B.: When is a liability not a liability? Textual analysis, dictionaries, and 10-Ks. J. Financ. **30**(1), 81–93 (2011)
17. Luo, L., et al.: Beyond polarity: interpretable financial sentiment analysis with hierarchical query-driven attention. In: Proceedings of IJCAI, pp. 4244–4250 (2018)
18. Myers, J.L., Well, A., Lorch, R.F.: Research Design and Statistical Analysis, vol. 30. Lawrence Erlbaum (2003)
19. Nopp, C., Hanbury, A.: Detecting risks in the banking system by sentiment analysis. In: Proceedings of EMNLP, pp. 591–600 (2015)

20. Pennington, J., Socher, R., Manning, C.D.: GloVe: global vectors for word representation. In: Proceedings of EMNLP, pp. 1532–1543 (2014). http://www.aclweb.org/anthology/D14-1162
21. Rekabsaz, N., Lupu, M., Baklanov, A., Hanbury, A., Dür, A., Anderson, L.: Volatility prediction using financial disclosures sentiments with word embedding-based IR models. arXiv preprint arXiv:1702.01978 (2017)
22. Schumaker, R.P., Chen, H.: Textual analysis of stock market prediction using breaking financial news: the AZFin text system. ACM Trans. Inform. Syst. (TOIS) 27(2), 12 (2009)
23. Toma, A., Dedua, S.: Quantitative techniques for financial risk assessment: a comparative approach using different risk measures and estimation methods. Proc. Econ. Financ. 8, 712–719 (2014)
24. Tsai, M.F., Wang, C.J.: On the risk prediction and analysis of soft information in finance reports. Eur. J. Oper. Res. 257(1), 243–250 (2016)
25. Tsai, M.F., Wang, C.J., Chien, P.C.: Discovering finance keywords via continuous-space language models. ACM Trans. Manage. Inform. Syst. (TMIS) 7(3), 7 (2016)
26. Wiegreffe, S., Pinter, Y.: Attention is not not explanation. arXiv preprint arXiv:1908.04626 (2019)
27. Yang, Z., Yang, D., Dyer, C., He, X., Smola, A., Hovy, E.: Hierarchical attention networks for document classification. In: Proceedings of NAACL, pp. 1480–1489 (2016)

Healthcare and Medical Applications (including Covid)

Healthcare and Medical Applications
Machine Care

Self-disclosure on Twitter During the COVID-19 Pandemic: A Network Perspective

Prasanna Umar, Chandan Akiti, Anna Squicciarini[(✉)], and Sarah Rajtmajer

College of Information Sciences and Technology, Pennsylvania State University,
University Park, State College, PA 16802, USA
{pxu3,cra5302,acs20,smr48}@psu.edu

Abstract. Amidst social distancing, quarantines, and everyday disruptions caused by the COVID-19 pandemic, users' heightened activity on online social media has provided enhanced opportunities for self-disclosure. We study the incidence and the evolution of self-disclosure temporally as important events unfold throughout the pandemic's timeline. Using a BERT-based supervised learning approach, we label a dataset of over 31 million COVID-19 related tweets for self-disclosure. We map users' self-disclosure patterns, characterize personal revelations, and examine users' disclosures within evolving reply networks. We employ natural language processing models and social network analyses to investigate self-disclosure patterns in users' interaction networks as they seek social connectedness and focused conversations during COVID-19 pandemic. Our analyses show heightened self-disclosure levels in tweets following the World Health Organization's declaration of pandemic worldwide on March 11, 2020. We disentangle network-level patterns of self-disclosure and show how self-disclosure characterizes temporally persistent social connections. We argue that in pursuit of social rewards users intentionally self-disclose and associate with similarly disclosing users. Finally, our work illustrates that in this pursuit users may disclose intimate personal health information such as personal ailments and underlying conditions which pose privacy risks.

Keywords: Self-disclosure · Twitter · Privacy

1 Introduction

The COVID-19 pandemic has impacted a majority of the world population. As of March 2021, more than 117 million people worldwide have been infected by the coronavirus and more than 2.59 million have died. Much of the world has been living with lockdowns and quarantines since the early months of 2020. Amidst these circumstances, people have resorted to online resources to stay connected in their personal and professional lives. As a result, there has been an unprecedented surge in online activity. Social media usage has increased by

© Springer Nature Switzerland AG 2021
Y. Dong et al. (Eds.): ECML PKDD 2021, LNAI 12978, pp. 271–286, 2021.
https://doi.org/10.1007/978-3-030-86514-6_17

61% as people converge to these online platforms to support their social inter-actions [25]. Twitter, a popular microblogging site, has seen substantial increase in number of active users during the pandemic [2].

The convergence of people to social media, particularly micro-blogging sites like Twitter, is an evident phenomenon during natural disasters (e.g., earth-quakes, hurricanes, floods) and social change events (e.g., black lives matter, occupy wall street) [28,31]. Amidst the heightened online activity, users can dis-close sensitive and private information. In fact, existing literature on social media use during disasters has maintained that a significant portion of user messaging is of a personal nature [27,42]. Some informational and emotional disclosures are relevant to raising situational awareness during these events and helping in response (e.g., location, life and property loss, mental states) [27]. But, instances of personal disclosures not directly relevant to disaster response have also been observed [27]. Therefore, it is yet unknown how this behavior is different from usual sharing practices. Further, it is unclear how to characterize self-disclosure in health-related crises.

Notably, the COVID-19 pandemic as a health crisis is different than other types of disasters given the scale of the crisis and the global restrictions on move-ment it has brought for such an extended period of time. Amidst concerns of financial security, health risks and social isolation [35], social media provides an avenue for "collective coping" wherein users seek and receive emotional, infor-mational and instrumental support [28]. Individuals find a sense of community online and feel supported through sharing with others co-experiencing similar problems. Online sharing serves therapeutic functions [18] and enables sense-making in stressful crisis situations [28]. In addition, stressful life events have been shown to mitigate privacy concerns linked to self-disclosure in online social networks [48,49]. Accordingly, we suggest that users curate their social connec-tions and disclose intentionally to reap social benefits during difficult times.

In this work, we seek to detect levels of self-disclosure in users' public tweets related to the COVID-19 pandemic and characterize these disclosures. We categorize self-disclosure in tweets along several dimensions, namely, infor-mation, thoughts, feelings, intimacy and relationships. Leveraging a BERT-based automated labelling scheme trained on human annotations, we assess levels of self-disclosure and its dimensions in more than 31 million tweets. We analyze the labelled data to characterize the phenomenon of self-disclosure during the COVID-19 pandemic. Our work is guided by the following research questions.

- RQ1: What sharing patterns characterize the interaction networks in Twitter and how do these patterns evolve temporally?
- RQ2: Does self-disclosure aid in fostering persistent and focused social inter-actions?
- RQ3: What content characterizes health-related disclosures among temporally persistent user interactions during the pandemic?

Our findings support the role of self-disclosure in soliciting social connect-edness and curating support networks during the pandemic. Our analyses pro-vide several important insights that lead to the following observations. First, we observe heightened self-disclosure levels in tweets following the World Health Organization's March 11 2020 pandemic declaration, signaling a shift in users' sharing patterns in step with heightened awareness and anxiety around the crisis. Second, we find that self-disclosure levels remain consistently high many months into the pandemic. Our analyses of users' reply networks yield novel insights into the temporal evolution of user groups in terms of self-disclosure levels and topical conformity. Specifically, users' interactions within reply networks show more frequent and more intimate self-disclosures temporally. Further, users tend to connect with other users with similar self-disclosure levels, i.e., users show assortative [34] behavior in terms of sharing patterns. Self-disclosures appear to foster more focused and on-topic conversations. Finally, health-related conversations among users include disclosures of personal ailments and health conditions signaling shifts in users' risk perceptions towards sensitive personal health information (PHI) and engagement in such disclosures for potential social rewards.

2   Dataset

The dataset used in our analyses is a subset of a recently collected COVID-specific Twitter repository [14]. The original repository consisted of about 508 million tweet IDs. These tweet IDs corresponded to tweets that were collected using a specific set of keywords (e.g., Coronavirus, CDC, COVID-19, pandemic, SocialDistancing, quarentinelife, etc.) and by following a set of accounts focused on COVID-19 (e.g., CoronaVirusInfo, V2019N, CDCemergency, CDCgov, WHO, etc.). Around June 6th, there was a significant increase in volume of the tweets collected because of changes in collection infrastructure. The transition, however, did not result in any gaps within the timeline of the collected tweets (See [14] for details). Using Python's Twarc package, we re-hydrated the tweets from the tweet IDs. We considered only the original content (English) posted by users i.e., replies and filtered all retweets and quotes. It has been noted that users with high number of followers do not necessarily reciprocate interactions from other users [29]. Highly followed users, by this measure, are not necessarily the most important in the network. Hence, we also removed all tweets from verified accounts. Direct replies to tweets from verified accounts were also removed to exclude the mostly non-reciprocated and one-way interactions within the Twitter network. Similarly, we found majority of user mentions to be targeted towards verified accounts and were not reciprocated. Therefore, we removed user mentions. Our resulting corpus contained just over 31 million tweets, collected from 1/21/2020 till 8/28/2020. We grouped the tweets temporally into three phases. Division into phases was done to test temporal changes in self-disclosing trends that occurred as a result of real-world events related to the pandemic. Specifically, we considered the World Health Organization's declaration of the global pandemic on March 11, 2020 as a "starting" point for the pandemic [41]. Similarly, we selected July 1, 2020 as the beginning of Phase III in our data to reflect the relative easing of strict quarantine and travel restrictions [1]. Accordingly, Phases I (Jan 21 - Mar 11), II (Mar 12 - Jun 30), and III (Jul 1 - Aug 28) comprised of over 4.18 million, 11.83 million, and 15 million tweets respectively.

3   Self-disclosure Measurements

3.1   Measurement Scale

We adopted an existing self-disclosure scale [46] to measure level of personal disclosure in tweets[1]. Self-disclosure is operationalized per this measurement scale as a composite value of five items, each measured on an integer scale between 1 (not at all) and 7 (completely), where 1 represents no disclosure and 7 is the highest level of self-disclosure. Individual items within this framework measure disclosure of: personal information; personal thoughts; personal feelings and emotions; importance/intimacy of the disclosure; and, disclosure of close relationships (See Fig. 1 for details).

3.2   Manual Annotations

We labelled a sample of 5000 tweets for self-disclosure using the survey in [46]. The labelling survey was deployed on Amazon Mechanical Turk where each tweet was labelled by three crowd-sourced raters. The labeling task was conducted under the protocol 14947 approved by the Pennsylvania State University's Institutional Review Board (IRB). To ensure quality labels, we provided detailed instructions and examples in the survey. Raters were asked to label each tweet along the five dimensions of self-disclosure considering only the text of the tweet. We, therefore, replaced the weblinks in the tweets with a token :URL: and replaced any emoticon with its textual version. We authorized workers only in United States with at least 98% of their past submissions and at least 100 submissions accepted. Further, we discarded responses (about 1% of total submissions) from workers who failed to answer an attention check question within the survey.

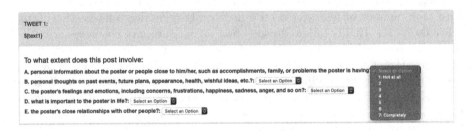

Fig. 1. Labelling survey for a tweet showing five questions that represent five dimensions of self-disclosure.

The crowd-sourced workers rated each tweet on an integer scale from 1 (Not at all) to 7 (Completely) for presence of self-disclosure according to each of the five dimensions – namely information, thoughts, feelings, intimacy and relations (See Fig. 1). For each of these individual ratings, we calculated Gwet's AC2, a chance-corrected agreement statistic [24]. As the individual dimensions

---

[1] Authors of [46] reported a reliability of 0.72 (Cronbachś alpha) for the scale.

Table 1. Inter-rater agreement for self-disclosure dimensions.

Items	Gwetś AC2	95% CI	Percent agreement	Benchmark
Information	0.869	0.860–0.877	0.922	Almost perfect
Thought	0.258	0.240–0.276	0.797	Fair
Feeling	0.651	0.636–0.666	0.859	Substantial
Intimacy	0.849	0.842–0.856	0.905	Almost perfect
Relation	0.971	0.969–0.974	0.975	Almost perfect

of self-disclosure were measured on an ordinal scale, we used the weighted version (ordinal) of Gwet's AC2 statistic and interpreted the magnitude using a bench-marking procedure in [24]. Agreement between raters varied for individual dimensions ranging from fair agreement for thought to better agreement for other dimensions (See Table 1). Ratings for each dimension were calculated by averaging the ratings provided by three raters. A final self-disclosure rating was compiled as an average of ratings across the five individual dimensions.

3.3   Label Generation

We generated labels for an unlabelled tweet using labelled examples of tweets in each of the five dimensions of self-disclosure: information, thought, feeling, intimacy and relation. We built separate models for each dimension and aggregated the ratings for all five dimensions to get a self-disclosure rating.

We formulate the labeling process as a regression problem. Formally, we learn a model $h_\theta(x)$ from a set of $(N_u + N_l)$ training samples, where N_u and N_l are the number of unlabeled and labeled examples respectively. The labeled dataset $\mathcal{D}_l = \{(x_i, y_i)\}_{i=1}^{N_l}$ where $y_i \in [1, 7]$ is a small dataset of 5000 samples. We use few-shot learning method [16] to give the model the ability to label unseen samples with only a few labeled known samples. Our learning model is the transformer-based language model called BERT [16]. This learning model has state-of-the-art performance on several standard NLP tasks [44] that closely relate to our regression problem. Thus, BERT is extremely suitable for transferring the learnt knowledge θ to our regression problem.

Domain Fine-Tuning. Following [23], we fine-tuned the pre-trained BERT again on the huge unlabeled data $\mathcal{D}_u$. We use the Masked Language Modeling (MLM) and Next Sentence Prediction (NSP) objectives to fine-tune the BERT model. Fine-tuning the language model on target domain data improves performance of NLP tasks and we observe the same in our results in Table 2.

Training Method. In a standard supervised training method, we sample a batch of b samples $\mathcal{B}_r = \{(x_{r_i}, y_{r_i})\}_{i=1}^{b}$ sampled randomly from the N_l labeled samples. We then pass the training batch $\mathcal{B}$ to the model h_θ to obtain the outputs

Table 2. RMSE and accuracy (weighted) within ±0.5 and ±1 ranges of true labels.

Label	BERT-base			Fine-tuned			Few-Shot		
	rmse	±0.5	±1.0	rmse	±0.5	±1.0	rmse	±0.5	±1.0
Information	1.689	46.4	63.5	1.213	51.3	68.1	1.027	57.2	74.1
Thoughts	1.827	27.8	45.4	1.653	31.2	47.3	1.406	33.2	54.9
Feelings	1.522	47.8	59.1	1.454	46.9	58.7	1.339	49.6	64.0
Intimacy	0.903	59.8	88.9	0.855	67.2	90.1	0.921	87.6	88.8
Relation	0.639	88.3	94.7	0.632	88.1	94.9	0.586	94.8	95.7

$\{\hat{y}_{r_i}\}_{i=1}^{b}$. The parameters θ are trained with the loss $\frac{1}{b}\sum_{i=1}^{b}(y_{r_i} - \hat{y}_{r_i})$. As the data-imbalances add huge bias to the model, we re-sample the training samples to balance the samples for each class or ranges.

The few-shot learning method [8] learns to predict labels using a support sample set as knowledge. This learning paradigm works well in low-resource settings. We sample episodes instead of batches, where each episode has a support batch $\mathcal{B}_s = \{(x_{s_i}, y_{s_i})\}_{i=1}^{b}$ and query batch $\mathcal{B}_q = \{(x_{q_i}, y_{q_i})\}_{i=1}^{b}$. Every batch we sample has nearly equal representation from all label classes/ranges. The regression layer $\theta_R \subset \theta$ is removed in this model. Instead, θ_R is inferred from the sentence representations of support set samples. In each episode θ_R is learned with respect to $\mathcal{B}_s$ and then used to predict the labels on $\mathcal{B}_q$. The regression loss is calculated similarly to the supervised learning method and model parameters θ are updated using back-propagation.

We set batch size b to 50, as a lower batch size leads to instability in solving for θ_R. The BERT model outputs sentence representations of dimension 768. We train the model for 3 epochs. Our batch sampling strategy ensures equal number of samples in the six range spans for labels in [1.0–7.0] that are – [1.0–1.5], [1.5, 2.5), [2.5, 3.5), [3.5, 4.5), [4.5, 5.5), [5.5, 7.0].

Evaluation. We use two baseline models to evaluate the performance of our method – namely a standard pre-trained *bert-base* model and a *bert-base* model fine-tuned on the unlabeled dataset. Both baselines are trained with batch size of 32 with a learning rate of $5e-4$ and for 2 epochs. For each sample, we assign an appropriate range/class based on the true label (e.g., [1.5, 2.5) is the range for true label 2.3). Then, the sample prediction is evaluated for this range as a true positive if it falls within margins of ±0.5 (and ±1.0) of the selected range. The results shown in Table 2 indicate that average performance of our method is better than the baseline models.

4   Analysis

In this section, we describe our methodology to understand patterns of self-disclosure during the Covid-19 pandemic, and present our findings. We construct both directed and undirected reply-based graphs wherein users are represented as vertices and pairwise reply interactions between users are represented as edges. We posit that for our study of predominantly conversation-oriented behaviors such as self-disclosure a suitable representation of the system is a network that captures reply-based interactions between users. While studies often characterize Twitter as a static network [6,29], it has been acknowledged that such networks can be misleading [22,26]. The follower/following relationships are mostly not reciprocated and follower/following-based networks do not give actual representations of users' active reciprocated interactions [26].

4.1 Self-disclosure Assortativity in Twitter Reply Networks

In order to understand the self-disclosure patterns that characterize the Twitter interaction network (RQ1), we examine if users' sharing patterns are similar to their social connections. That is, we peruse the assorativity of users' interaction networks in terms of self-disclosure patterns.

Reciprocal-Reply Network. We create reciprocal-reply networks [11] to explore the assortative mixing of users according to their patterns of self-disclosure. Particularly, we define an undirected graph $G(V, E)$ with a set of vertices, V and a set of edges pairwise amongst them, E. For users $v_j \in V$ and $v_k \in V$, an edge e_{jk} represents a reciprocal reply relationship between them, i.e., existence of replies by both users to each other. Each edge is assigned a weight w_{jk} calculated as the sum of number of interactions (replies) between two users v_j and v_k. Three reciprocal-reply networks were created to represent each temporal Phase in the dataset. Here, mean self-disclosure characterizes each node as an attribute and it is calculated as the average of self-disclosure levels across all tweets posted by the user (node) within the particular phase. Essentially, two nodes v_j and v_k connected by an undirected edge e_i had attributes j_i and k_i. We calculate assortativity based on average self-disclosure using a weighted version of the continuous assortativity coefficient in [21]. Specifically, assortativity coefficient is defined using the Eq. 1 where W is the sum of all edge weights. The values for assortativity coefficient range from -1 to 1. Positive values of this coefficient means similarities among connected nodes and dissimilarities results in negative values.

$$r_c^w = \frac{\sum_i w_i j_i k_i - W^{-1} \sum_i w_i j_i \sum_{i'} w_{i'} k_{i'}}{\sqrt{[\sum_i w_i j_i^2 - W^{-1} \sum_i w_i j_i^2][\sum_i w_i k_i^2 - W^{-1} \sum_i w_i k_i^2]}} \quad (1)$$

Results. We found evidences of assortativity for mean self-disclosure among users (See Table 3). For the first Phase, the network had negligible but positive assortativity coefficient (0.003) which increased for Phase II (0.239) and Phase III (0.218). While there are no formal guidelines for interpreting assortative coefficient, we follow the most recent study that re-purposes correlation coefficient ranges to classify networks into levels of assortativity [30]. Accordingly, the

Table 3. Assortative coefficient for reciprocal reply networks.

Phase	#Nodes	#Edges	SD	Information	Thought	Feeling	Intimacy	Relation
Phase I	9474	5479	0.003	0.165	−0.001	−0.002	−0.014	−0.005
Phase II	8201	4334	0.239	0.245	0.313	0.259	0.147	0.156
Phase III	25372	14216	0.218	0.263	0.280	0.248	0.116	0.148

first Phase network is interpreted as neutral (i.e., neither assortative nor disassortative) and the networks in subsequent phases are considered to be weakly assortative. Along the dimensions of self-disclosure, similar increasing patterns were observed. However, the reciprocal-reply networks in all three phases are neutral for feeling and intimacy dimensions of self-disclosure.

4.2 Persistent Groups and Self-disclosure

In order to understand how the occurrences of self-disclosure characterize and aid in the persistent and focused social interactions (RQ2), we examine the temporally persistent social groups. For these groups of users, we peruse temporal evolution of self-disclosure and the relationships with topical conformity.

Directed Reply Networks. We use directed sub-networks to extract self-disclosure patterns and the relationships between self-disclosure and the topical conformity (divergence) within the social connections that temporally persistent groups of users maintain. Specifically, we define a graph $G(V, E)$ on vertex set V and edge set E. For a user $v_i \in V$, edge e_{ij} represents a reply by user v_i to user v_j. Each directed edge e_{ij} is assigned a weight w_{ij} representing the number of these replies. Three such graphs were created, one for each temporal Phase in the data and each graph consisted of all reply interactions between all interacting users within that Phase. We then detect communities in the graphs associated with each Phase using a directed Louvain community detection algorithm optimized for directed modularity [17]. Higher values closer to 1 for modularity indicates stronger community structure and as such, the directed modularity scores for three phases in our study were 0.93, 0.98 and 0.94 respectively. We identify persistent groups of (at least 2) users which interact within same communities across three phases. That is, a persistent group represents a set of users which is a part of a larger community in Phase I and persisted as a group within common communities across subsequent phases, although the group as a whole can be a part of different communities in subsequent phases as communities evolve. In total, we pulled out 549 persistent groups totalling 13469 users. Figure 2 shows an example of a persistent group across three phases of the pandemic timeline. For these persistent groups, we examined self-disclosing behaviors across three phases. Additionally, we disentangled the relationship between self-disclosure and the tightness of conversational content posted by the set of users in the persistent group as measured by topical divergence.

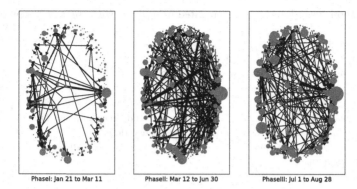

Phase I: Jan 21 to Mar 11   Phase II: Mar 12 to Jun 30   Phase III: Jul 1 to Aug 28

Fig. 2. Directed reply networks for an exemplarly persistent group across phases. Node size is proportional to activity of the user and edge width is proportional to number of replies. Average self-disclosures per phase are 1.18, 1.30, and 1.27 respectively.

Topical Divergence. We perform topical modeling (using Latent Dirichlet Allocation (LDA) [10]) of the tweets from all users in all the persistent groups in order to understand if there is a relationship between self-disclosure in temporally persistent groups and topical conformity in their conversations. We removed hashtags, user mentions, weblinks, and emoticons. We also removed words that appeared in over 90% of the tweets and those that appeared in less than 20 tweets. Multiple topic models were created for a corpus of pre-processed tweets with number of topics varying from 1 to 20. We used coherence score [38] as a measure of quality and interpretability of the topic models. Our extracted best topic model included 17 topics and a coherence score of 0.50 (See Table 4). According to this 17-topic model, we assigned a latent topic distribution vector for each tweet representing probabilities corresponding to each of the topics.

For persistent groups across phases, we measure conformity or lack thereof in conversational content across group members by means of topical divergence. Specifically, we computed the Jensen-Shannon divergence (JSD) for each persistent group across the three phases using the following formulation [37]:

$$JS(g^s) = H(\beta_g^s) - \frac{\sum_{t \in T_g^s} H(\beta_t)}{|T_g^s|} \tag{2}$$

where $\beta_g^s(i) = \frac{\sum_{t \in T_g^s} \beta_t(i)}{|T_g^s|}, \forall i = 1, ..., n$ for n the number of topics is the mean topic distribution of group g at Phase s over all its users' tweets (T_g^s). Here, β_t is the latent topic distribution of tweet t and H is the Shannon-entropy function (logarithmic base 2). The divergence score ranges from 0 to 1 with 1 being totally conforming conversation.

Results. Here, we present our findings on temporal evolution of self-disclosure for persistent groups. Also, we report on the relationship between self-disclosure and topical conformity in the content by the users within these groups.

Table 4. Top keywords for topics generated using LDA with coherence score of 0.50.

1	Home, reopen, close, open, stay	10	Health, outbreak, warn, spread, travel
2	Mask, wear, face, people, social_distancing	11	News, live, update, late, australia
3	Cdc, government, control, datum, expert	12	School, child, family, student, kid
4	Test, positive, testing, result, symptom	13	Like, look, good, time, day
5	People, know, bad, think, die	14	Trump, president, response, white_house, election
6	Death, case, number, rate, toll	15	Vaccine, study, scientist, new, drug
7	Crisis, million, business, pay, government	16	Fight, india, th, june, july
8	Case, new, report, death, total	17	Market, economy, fear, hit, amid
9	Patient, hospital, die, doctor, care		

Disclosure Patterns. For 549 persistent user groups across three phases, there was a significant difference in self-disclosure rating ($\chi^2(2) = 469.93, p < 0.001, W = 0.428$). Post-hoc analysis with Friedman-Conover tests and Holm-Bonferroni correction revealed significant differences across all phase pairs ($p < 0.001$). Mean values of self-disclosure for three phases were 1.19, 1.38 and 1.35 respectively. It is in line with the overall trend in self-disclosing behavior across all tweets in the dataset through three phases (See Fig. 3).

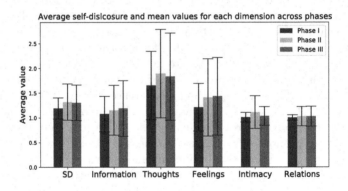

Fig. 3. Average values of SD and its dimensions across phases.

Topical Divergence. We find significant negative correlation between topical divergence and self-disclosure in Phase II and Phase III . Correlations for consecutive phases were -0.11 ($p < 0.05$), -0.55 ($p < 0.001$) and -0.49 ($p < 0.001$) respectively. These findings show that as self-disclosure increases, conversations are more focused and on-topic.

4.3   Characterizing Sensitive Disclosures in Temporally Persistent Social Connections

As users maintained social connections through the pandemic with parallel increases in sharing behavior, we delve further into the content of the disclosures.

COVID-19 being a health related crises, we seek to answer RQ3 and characterize the sensitive health disclosures within the persistent social connections.

Sensitive Health-Related Disclosure. We analysed tweets for specific types of health-related disclosure, namely, disclosure of symptoms and diseases. We looked for these specific revelations within the tweets of persistent group members that were classified as having some level (>1) of informational self-disclosure. To extract these fine-grained utterances, we created a supervised learning model to classify health related tweets. We used an existing manually annotated Twitter dataset [36] with labels specifying health-related content for training purposes. The dataset contained 5128 tweet IDs corresponding to tweets that were labeled according one of five categories: sick, health, unrelated, not English, and ambigous. Excluding the tweets that could not be retrieved, non-English and ambiguous tweets, we compiled 2419 tweets. We binarized the dataset into 987 health-related tweets (sick, health) and 1432 non-health related tweets. We use our first baseline BERT based model to train on this dataset and we infer a binary health-related vs non-health related label for all the tweets from all persistent groups. We use the same hyperparameters used in our labeling baseline. The model trained with 5-fold cross-validation yielded average (validation) precision, recall and F1-score of 78.8%, 84.4%, and 81.4% respectively.

We used a pre-trained model [40] to detect disclosures of symptoms and diseases in health-related tweets that were tagged as containing at least some (>1) levels of information disclosure. Authors of [40] trained and evaluated this model on a Twitter dataset and reported 72% F1-score for detection of medical entities. Using the trained model, we detected the sensitive disclosures of symptoms and diseases within the informational disclosures in the health-related tweets by the persistent groups.

Results. Topics of conversation within persistent groups highlighted health-related discussions. About 29% of all tweets within persistent groups were tagged as health-related and 83% of the persistent groups had at least some health-related tweets. Notably, 99.7% of these health related tweets belonged to the seven topics that featured health-related keywords (See topics 3–6, 8–9, 15 in Table 4). Zooming in on health-related tweets that had at least some informational disclosure (rating > 1), we detected disclosures of personal ailments and symptoms (see Table 5).

5 Discussion

Our analyses showed increased levels of self-disclosure in COVID-19 related tweets after March 11, 2020 when the WHO declared the outbreak a global pandemic (also observed in recent work [41]). This increase, registered both in terms of quantity and intimacy of self disclosure, coincided with acute temporal events in pandemic timeline and suggests that self-disclosure has served

Table 5. Examples of disclosures of personal ailments.

'Damn. 1. I have a cold. 2. I have not been to China. 3. I have travelled in the last week. Once to London. How worried should I be?'	'cold'
'Wondering if the sore throat I developed this afternoon is the coronavirus. I guess we shall soon see'	'sore throat', 'coronavirus'
'I though i will be fine at ome spend the dya sleeping yesterday and now woke up with a head ache again and diff breathing before going to see a cardiologist i need to pass a test to eliminate f* * *ing covid do not want to go too tired'	'head ache', 'breathing'
'I have very little positivity to share I am afraid today. My Son is visiting & we are going out with Dogs. I am concerned for him, he has the same Kidney Condition as I, he inherited before I knew I had from my Dad. My Girls & Grandchildren as is in'	'Kidney Condition'

an important role ameliorating social and emotional challenges linked with the crisis. Users have turned to online communities for support [13]. Recent work studying potential changes in individual perceptions of self-disclosure and privacy during the pandemic [33] supports this view.

Reciprocal-reply networks reveal assortative mixing of users based on self-disclosure behavior after March 11. Such self-organized mixing patterns in online social networks as a result of acute disaster has been observed in recent work [19]. Authors of [19] showed that (degree) assortative mixing patterns vary with evolution of disaster as critical events unfold and emergent social cohesion is intentional in pursuit of specific needs. We suggest that stresses of the pandemic may have likewise enabled selective mixing of users in terms of self-disclosure, following work on the role of self-disclosure in maintaining relationships and psychological coping [3]. Our results provide initial evidence of users' curation of social connections and strategic self-disclosure in pursuit of social rewards.

We have also shown that self-disclosure by users within temporally persistent social groups supports focused, on-topic conversations, highlighting the role of self-disclosure in maintaining stable support structure. Further studies could delve deeper into these effects in emergent support-oriented communities, particularly in crisis.

Amongst users within persistent social groups, we found disclosure of sensitive personal health information (PHI) such as physical ailments, symptoms and underlying health conditions. While observed in dedicated online health communities (OHC) [47], such sensitive voluntary disclosures in Twitter during crises is relatively under-studied. Studies on OHC show that pursuit of informational and emotional support motivates PHI disclosures [50]. We speculate that users in our dataset similarly disclosed sensitive PHI to garner support from their Twitter community. As noted by [33], the pandemic may have changed privacy perceptions towards sensitive PHI. Additional work in this area could shed light on the motivations for and differences in PHI disclosures in user engagements during crises vs normal times.

6   Related Work

Since 2020, a body of literature has emerged studying activity in Twitter to understand user sentiment [39], explore prevalence and prevention of misinformation [45], and analyze hate speech [20] during the pandemic. Often, these studies perform raw tweets collection, conduct content analyses, and build models to answer specific research questions related to trends in online social behavior. As a result, over the past year several Twitter datasets [7,15] and computational models [32,51] have been released. Yet, studies to date have not focused on analyses of the extant network in which these trends occur. Further, we are not aware of any study that looks into network effects on self-disclosure during the pandemic. We attempt to fill these gaps.

Outside the domain of crisis informatics, self-disclosure has been studied as an intentional and influenced behavior which has both intrinsic and extrinsic rewards [3]. Intrinsically, it has therapeutic benefits that can help in psychological well-being [43] and extrinsically, it plays a role in building relationships, social connectedness, and maintaining relationships [4]. Increasingly, studies have perused self-disclosure in social networking sites where users look to interact with others for both intrinsic and extrinsic benefits. However, we find differing approaches for operationalization and measurement of self-disclosure throughout the literature [3]. Of interest for observational studies, [9] proposed a 3-item scale (levels of information, thoughts and feelings) to measure self-disclosure in online posts. However, we follow a more recent work [46] that modified this scale to include the intimacy of disclosure.

Similar to [46], most studies create automated models to scale self-disclosure labels in small manually annotated data to larger samples [5,12]. Such models employ highly curated dictionaries and extensive feature engineering which limit the inference process and performance on unseen data. Here, we use transfer-learning techniques on NLP models for labeling of our self-disclosure text.

7   Conclusion

Our study sheds light on the increase in users' self-disclosure during the pandemic and the role of self-disclosure in persistent and transient online groups. We have suggested that users share personal information in their online communities to garner social support. Reinforcing this argument, our results showed that as users maintained social connections temporally, self-disclosure increased as did topical conformity within conversations. Disclosures of users within persistent groups revealed sensitive personal health information. As such, our study points toward shifts in users' privacy perceptions in the wake of the COVID-19 pandemic.

As our findings are empirical in nature, a limitation of our work relates to the data we rely on. Although the dataset captures tweets in the important timeline of the pandemic, it is a sample of COVID-19 related conversations on Twitter. Hence, the results of this study need to be interpreted accounting for the effects of missing data in the sample.

Acknowledgements. Work from all the authors was supported in part by the National Science Foundation under Grant 2027757.

References

1. Coronavirus: How lockdown is being lifted across Europe. Accessed 08 Mar 2021
2. Twitter sees record number of users during pandemic, but advertising sales slow. Accessed 08 Mar 2021
3. Abramova, O., Wagner, A., Krasnova, H., Buxmann, P.: Understanding self-disclosure on social networking sites - a literature review. In: AMCIS 2017 Proceedings, pp. 1–10, no. August (2017)
4. Aharony, N.: Relationships among attachment theory, social capital perspective, personality characteristics, and Facebook self-disclosure. Aslib J. Inf. Manag. (2016)
5. Bak, J., Lin, C.Y., Oh, A.: Self-disclosure topic model for classifying and analyzing Twitter conversations. In: 2014 Conference on Empirical Methods in Natural Language Processing (EMNLP), Doha, Qatar, pp. 1986–1996. Association for Computational Linguistics, October 2014
6. Bakshy, E., Hofman, J.M., Mason, W.A., Watts, D.J.: Everyone's an influencer: quantifying influence on Twitter. In: Proceedings of the Fourth ACM International Conference on Web Search and Data Mining, pp. 65–74 (2011)
7. Banda, J.M., et al.: A large-scale Covid-19 Twitter chatter dataset for open scientific research-an international collaboration. arXiv preprint arXiv:2004.03688 (2020)
8. Bao, Y., Wu, M., Chang, S., Barzilay, R.: Few-shot text classification with distributional signatures (2020)
9. Barak, A., Gluck-Ofri, O.: Degree and reciprocity of self-disclosure in online forums. CyberPsychol. Behav. **10**(3), 407–417 (2007)
10. Blei, D.M., Ng, A.Y., Jordan, M.I.: Latent Dirichlet allocation. J. Mach. Learn. Res. **3**, 993–1022 (2003)
11. Bliss, C.A., Kloumann, I.M., Harris, K.D., Danforth, C.M., Dodds, P.S.: Twitter reciprocal reply networks exhibit assortativity with respect to happiness. J. Comput. Sci. **3**(5), 388–397 (2012)
12. Caliskan Islam, A., Walsh, J., Greenstadt, R.: Privacy detective: detecting private information and collective privacy behavior in a large social network. In: 13th Workshop on Privacy in the Electronic Society, pp. 35–46. ACM (2014)
13. Chakraborty, T., Kumar, A., Upadhyay, P., Dwivedi, Y.K.: Link between social distancing, cognitive dissonance, and social networking site usage intensity: a country-level study during the Covid-19 outbreak. Internet Research (2020)
14. Chen, E., Lerman, K., Ferrara, E.: COVID-19: the first public coronavirus Twitter dataset. arXiv e-prints arXiv:2003.07372, March 2020
15. Chen, E., Lerman, K., Ferrara, E.: Tracking social media discourse about the Covid-19 pandemic: development of a public coronavirus Twitter data set. JMIR Public Health Surveill. **6**(2), e19273 (2020)

16. Devlin, J., Chang, M.W., Lee, K., Toutanova, K.: BERT: pre-training of deep bidirectional transformers for language understanding (2019)
17. Dugué, N., Perez, A.: Directed Louvain: maximizing modularity in directed networks. Ph.D. thesis, Université d'Orléans (2015)
18. Ernala, S.K., Rizvi, A.F., Birnbaum, M.L., Kane, J.M., De Choudhury, M.: Linguistic markers indicating therapeutic outcomes of social media disclosures of schizophrenia. Proc. ACM Hum.-Comput. Interact. 1(CSCW), 1–27 (2017)
19. Fan, C., Jiang, Y., Mostafavi, A.: Emergent social cohesion for coping with community disruptions in disasters. J. R. Soc. Interface 17(164), 20190778 (2020)
20. Fan, L., Yu, H., Yin, Z.: Stigmatization in social media: documenting and analyzing hate speech for Covid-19 on Twitter. Proc. Assoc. Inf. Sci. Technol. 57(1), e313 (2020)
21. Farine, D.: Measuring phenotypic assortment in animal social networks: weighted associations are more robust than binary edges. Anim. Behav. 89, 141–153 (2014)
22. Gonçalves, B., Perra, N., Vespignani, A.: Modeling users' activity on Twitter networks: validation of Dunbar's number. PloS One 6(8), e22656 (2011)
23. Gururangan, S., et al.: Don't stop pretraining: adapt language models to domains and tasks (2020)
24. Gwet, K.L.: Handbook of inter-rater reliability: the definitive guide to measuring the extent of agreement among raters. Advanced Analytics, LLC (2014)
25. Holmes, R.: Is Covid-19 social media's levelling up moment? Forbes 24 (2020)
26. Huberman, B.A., Romero, D.M., Wu, F.: Social networks that matter: Twitter under the microscope. arXiv preprint arXiv:0812.1045 (2008)
27. Imran, M., Elbassuoni, S., Castillo, C., Diaz, F., Meier, P.: Extracting information nuggets from disaster-related messages in social media. In: ISCRAM (2013)
28. Jurgens, M., Helsloot, I.: The effect of social media on the dynamics of (self) resilience during disasters: a literature review. J. Contingencies Crisis Manag. 26(1), 79–88 (2018)
29. Kwak, H., Lee, C., Park, H., Moon, S.: What is Twitter, a social network or a news media? In: Proceedings of the 19th International Conference on World Wide Web, pp. 591–600 (2010)
30. Meghanathan, N.: Assortativity analysis of real-world network graphs based on centrality metrics. Comput. Inf. Sci. 9(3), 7–25 (2016)
31. Miyabe, M., Miura, A., Aramaki, E.: Use trend analysis of Twitter after the great east Japan earthquake. In: ACM 2012 Conference on Computer Supported Cooperative Work Companion, pp. 175–178 (2012)
32. Müller, M., Salathé, M., Kummervold, P.E.: Covid-Twitter-BERT: a natural language processing model to analyse Covid-19 content on Twitter. arXiv preprint arXiv:2005.07503 (2020)
33. Nabity-Grover, T., Cheung, C.M., Thatcher, J.B.: Inside out and outside in: how the Covid-19 pandemic affects self-disclosure on social media. Int. J. Inf. Manag. 55, 102188 (2020)
34. Noldus, R., Van Mieghem, P.: Assortativity in complex networks. J. Complex Netw. 3(4), 507–542 (2015)
35. Ognyanova, K., et al.: The state of the nation: a 50-state Covid-19 survey report #4 (2020)
36. Paul, M., Dredze, M.: You are what you tweet: analyzing Twitter for public health. In: International AAAI Conference on Web and Social Media, vol. 5 (2011)
37. Purohit, H., Ruan, Y., Fuhry, D., Parthasarathy, S., Sheth, A.: On understanding the divergence of online social group discussion. In: International AAAI Conference on Web and Social Media, vol. 8 (2014)

38. Röder, M., Both, A., Hinneburg, A.: Exploring the space of topic coherence measures. In: Eighth ACM International Conference on Web Search and Data Mining, pp. 399–408. ACM (2015)

39. Sanders, A.C., et al.: Unmasking the conversation on masks: natural language processing for topical sentiment analysis of Covid-19 Twitter discourse. medRxiv, pp. 2020–08 (2021)

40. Scepanovic, S., Martin-Lopez, E., Quercia, D., Baykaner, K.: Extracting medical entities from social media. In: ACM Conference on Health, Inference, and Learning, pp. 170–181 (2020)

41. Squicciarini, A., Raitmaier, S., Umar, P., Blose, T.: A tipping point? Heightened self-disclosure during the coronavirus pandemic. In: IEEE Second International Conference on Cognitive Machine Intelligence (CogMI), pp. 141–146. IEEE (2020)

42. Takahashi, B., Tandoc, E.C., Jr., Carmichael, C.: Communicating on Twitter during a disaster: an analysis of tweets during typhoon Haiyan in the Philippines. Comput. Hum. Behav. **50**, 392–398 (2015)

43. Tamir, D.I., Mitchell, J.P.: Disclosing information about the self is intrinsically rewarding. Proc. Natl. Acad. Sci. **109**(21), 8038–8043 (2012)

44. Wang, A., Singh, A., Michael, J., Hill, F., Levy, O., Bowman, S.R.: Glue: a multi-task benchmark and analysis platform for natural language understanding (2019)

45. Wang, Y., Gao, S., Gao, W.: Can predominant credible information suppress misinformation in crises? Empirical studies of tweets related to prevention measures during Covid-19. arXiv preprint arXiv:2102.00976 (2021)

46. Wang, Y.C., Burke, M., Kraut, R.: Modeling self-disclosure in social networking sites. In: 19th ACM Conference on Computer-Supported Cooperative Work & Social Computing, CSCW 2016, pp. 74–85. ACM (2016)

47. Yuchao, W., Ying, Z., Liao, Z.: Health privacy information self-disclosure in online health community. Front. Public Health **8**, 1023 (2020)

48. Zhang, R.: The stress-buffering effect of self-disclosure on Facebook: an examination of stressful life events, social support, and mental health among college students. Comput. Hum. Behav. **75**, 527–537 (2017)

49. Zhang, R., Fu, J.S.: Privacy management and self-disclosure on social network sites: the moderating effects of stress and gender. J. Comput.-Mediat. Commun. **25**(3), 236–251 (2020)

50. Zhang, X., Liu, S., Chen, X., Wang, L., Gao, B., Zhu, Q.: Health information privacy concerns, antecedents, and information disclosure intention in online health communities. Inf. Manag. **55**(4), 482–493 (2018)

51. Zong, S., Baheti, A., Xu, W., Ritter, A.: Extracting Covid-19 events from Twitter. arXiv preprint arXiv:2006.02567 (2020)

COVID Edge-Net: Automated COVID-19 Lung Lesion Edge Detection in Chest CT Images

Kang Wang$^{(\boxtimes)}$, Yang Zhao, Yong Dou, Dong Wen, and Zikai Gao

National Laboratory for Parallel and Distributed Processing, School of Computer,
National University of Defense Technology, Changsha, Hunan, China
{wangkang,zhaoyang10,yongdou,wendong19,gaozk18}@nudt.edu.cn

Abstract. Coronavirus Disease 2019 (COVID-19) has been spreading rapidly, threatening global health. Computer-aided screening on chest computed tomography (CT) images using deep learning, especially, lesion segmentation, is an effective complement for COVID-19 diagnosis. Although edge detection highly benefits lesion segmentation, an independent COVID-19 edge detection task in CT scans has been unprecedented and faces several difficulties, e.g., ambiguous boundaries, noises and diverse edge shapes. To this end, we propose the first COVID-19 lesion edge detection model: COVID Edge-Net, containing one edge detection backbone and two new modules: the multi-scale residual dual attention (MSRDA) module and the Canny operator module. MSRDA module helps capture richer contextual relationships for obtaining better deep learning features, which are fused with Canny features from Canny operator module to extract more accurate, refined, clearer and sharper edges. Our approach achieves the state-of-the-art performance and can be a benchmark for COVID-19 edge detection. Code related to this paper is available at: https://github.com/Elephant-123/COVID-Edge-Net.

Keywords: COVID-19 · Edge detection · Canny operator · Multi-scale residual dual attention · Computed tomography (CT) images

1 Introduction

As one of the most serious pandemics, Coronavirus Disease 2019 (COVID-19) [1–3] has been spreading violently around the world since December 2019, causing a devastating effect on global public health and economy. Because it has fast progression and infectious ability [4], it is necessary to develop effective tools or methods to accurately diagnose and evaluate COVID-19. Although the reverse transcription polymerase chain reaction (RT-PCR) [7,8] becomes the gold standard for COVID-19 screening, it is time-consuming and suffers from high false

Supported by the National Key Research and Development Program of China (Grant No. 2018YFB0204301).

Y. Dong et al. (Eds.): ECML PKDD 2021, LNAI 12978, pp. 287–301, 2021.
https://doi.org/10.1007/978-3-030-86514-6_18

negative rates [5,6]. Computed tomography (CT) technique [9] is widely preferred due to its non-invasive imaging and three-dimensional view of the lung, which is regarded as a significant complement to RT-PCR tests.

Recently, deep learning-based applications on COVID-19 CT images have demonstrated quite promising results in lesion segmentation [13,15–19] and COVID-19 diagnosis [10,11], particularly, COVID-19 segmentation is an essential step for COVID-19 follow-up assessment. Several COVID-19 segmentation works [13,15–19] in CT scans have appeared, among which the Inf-Net model [13] achieves the state-of-the-art performance. Different from other segmentation approaches, Inf-Net utilizes the edge attention to model infection boundaries for better feature representations, effectively illustrating edges benefit segmentation performance. However, Inf-Net mainly exploits low-level features to represent edges and its edge extraction is a part of segmentation, thus, edge detection is insufficient. Moreover, there is no independent COVID-19 edge detection task currently. Based on above inspirations, we propose a new task of independent COVID-19 edge detection.

Up to now, to improve edge detection performance, some edge detection works [12,14] using deep learning methods have existed in many applications, where [12] presents a dynamic feature fusion (DFF) model to produce weighted fusion features, acquiring excellent performance in semantic edge detection. However, DFF model is unable to enjoy same superiority in COVID-19 edge detection due to COVID-19 CT scans's characteristics: (1) ambiguous boundaries caused by the low contrast between infected regions and normal tissues, (2) noises (e.g., blood vessels in lungs), (3) the high variation in shapes, sizes and positions of infected edges. Furthermore, DFF model ignores capturing richer contextual relationships from original images in the initial feature extraction stage and merely considers deep learning features as edge features, which leads to limited COVID-19 edge representations.

To alleviate above problems, we come up with the first COVID-19 lung lesion edge detection model named COVID Edge-Net. Our COVID Edge-Net consists of the edge detection backbone, an effective multi-scale residual dual attention (MSRDA) module and the Canny operator module. The edge detection backbone is capable of detecting basic but coarse COVID-19 edges by extracting discriminative deep learning features. The MSRDA module added in the backbone mainly focuses on semantic features (i.e., edge shapes, sizes and positions), helping to capture richer contextual relationships from CT slices and boost edge identification with better deep feature representations. The Canny edge detection operator can highlight and locate thinner, more continuous and more refined boundaries, which is combined with the deep learning method to further enrich edge information. In a nutshell, our contributions in this paper are fourfold:

- It is the first time to propose a COVID-19 infection lesion edge detection model called COVID Edge-Net, which has the following clinical implications: (1) Due blurred edges of lesions make it difficult for doctors to identify boundaries accurately, this work can assist doctors to locate boundaries of lesions more intuitively and provide appropriate clinical guidance. (2) It is also able to raise COVID-19 infected segmentation performance in CT scans.

- An effective multi-scale residual dual attention (MSRDA) module is designed to help capture richer semantic relationships from multiple scales for detecting more accurate and clearer edges.
- The traditional Canny operator is considered and combined with the deep learning method to enhance feature representations for extracting more refined, more continuous and sharper edges.
- Our proposed method is superior to existing models and advances the state-of-the-art performance, which can be regarded as a benchmark for COVID-19 infection lesion edge detection.

2   Related Works

2.1   COVID-19 Segmentation

Up to now, abundant COVID-19 segmentation researches have occurred. For instance, [17] exploited several preprocessing and data augmentation methods to generate random image patches for COVID-19 segmentation, reducing the over-fitting risk. Zhou et al. [18] incorporated spatial and channel attention strategies to the U-Net model and introduced the focal tversky loss to solve small lesion segmentation. Aggregated residual transformations and soft attention mechanism were used by Chen et al. [19] to improve the ability of distinguishing various COVID-19 symptoms. Although these approaches overcome some problems caused by limited data and diverse lesion shapes in COVID-19 segmentation tasks, they ignore another important information, i.e., lesion edge information, which has the potential to improve segmentation performance. Later, Fan et al. [13] put forward the Inf-Net model, which achieves the state-of-the-art result in COVID-19 segmentation. It exploits a parallel partial decoder to aggregate high-level features and uses the reverse attention to enhance feature representations. Furthermore, the edge attention is utilized to model COVID-19 boundaries, providing more plentiful feature descriptions for the segmentation. Different from other works, Fan et al. considered COVID-19 edge information, which benefits COVID-19 segmentation. However, Inf-Net's edge extraction is merely used as a submodule of the segmentation task, and mainly low-level features are used as edge features, all of which lead to insufficient edge detection. Currently, there does not exist the sole edge detection task of COVID-19 infected regions. To this end, we propose an independent COVID-19 lesion edge detection task rather than as a submodule for the first time.

2.2   Edge Detection

Several semantic edge detection works achieve fantastic results in other applications, such as natural scenes. Yu et al. proposed the CASENet model [14], which is a novel end-to-end deep semantic edge detection architecture via ResNet. In CASENet model, category-wise edge activations from the top layer are fused with the same set of bottom layer features. Its multi-scale feature fusion method greatly benefits the semantic edge detection task, however, it adopts a fixed weight fusion strategy that forces images with different semantics to share the same weights. To better consider the heterogeneity in contributions made by different locations of feature maps, a new dynamic feature fusion (DFF) strategy was proposed by Hu et al. [12]. They designed a weight learner to assign different fusion weights for different feature maps and locations adaptively. Although Hu et al.'s DFF method reaches superior performance in edge detection of natural scenes, it is not completely suitable for COVID-19 edge detection due COVID-19 CT scans have their own traits (e.g., unclear infected edges, diverse lesion shapes of the same disease, noises) compared with natural images. Meanwhile, DFF's multi-layer features extracted from ResNet are directly applied to the feature fusion layer, ignoring capturing richer contextual relationships from original images. Merely deep learning features are considered in DFF, which are still unable to depict edge information fully. To solve above issues, we propose two new modules, where the multi-scale residual dual attention (MSRDA) module is designed to capture richer contextual features from original images and the Canny operator module is used to extract more edges and emphasize edge information.

3   Methodology

3.1   Task Definition

COVID-19 infection lesion edge detection task aims to outline specific contours of infected areas. Particularly, given an one-channel grayscale input image X, the task outputs an edge map $\hat{Y}$ with single channel, which has the same size as X. Each value in $\hat{Y}$ is denoted as $\hat{Y}(p|X, W) \in [0, 1]$, indicating the computed COVID-19 edge probability at pixel p, where W stands for edge detection network's parameters, and $p \in \{1, 2 \cdots, |X|\}$.

3.2   Overview of COVID Edge-Net

To extract more accurate, more continuous and sharper edges, we address COVID Edge-Net model for COVID-19 edge detection (shown in Fig. 1). The input image is fed to residual blocks to generate multi-scale basic features. Then an effective multi-scale residual dual attention (MSRDA) module is used to generate semantically enhanced features, which are processed by feature normalization blocks and a concatenation operation. Later, the adaptive weight fusion block produces weighted deep learning features, which are combined with traditional Canny features from the Canny operator module to further highlight edge features. In the end, one 1×1 convolution operation and the sigmoid function follow to obtain predicted edges. The backbone consisting of residual blocks, feature normalization blocks and the adaptive weight fusion block is described in Sect. 3.3. The MSRDA module and the Canny operator module are specifically introduced in Sect. 3.4 and Sect. 3.5, respectively. And global loss function is displayed in Sect. 3.6.

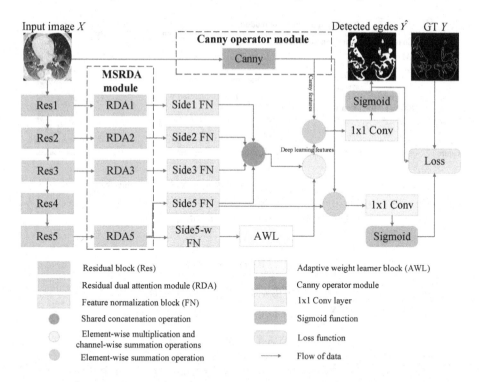

Fig. 1. Overall architecture of our COVID Edge-Net model.

3.3 The Edge Detection Backbone

Our edge detection backbone adopts a dynamic feature fusion (DFF) model [12] via ResNet [21]. In detail, the input image X is transmitted into residual blocks to generate a set of features with different scales. The first three and the fifth stack of residual blocks are directly followed by feature normalization blocks, producing one-channel and K-channel response maps with original image size for Side1-3 and Side5 respectively. K is the number of categories of objects, and $K = 1$ in our task. These response maps are concatenated into a $4K$-channel feature map F_{cat} by shared concatenation, which replicates three one-channel response maps of Side1-3 for K times to separately concatenate with each map of the K-channel response maps in Side5. Another feature normalization block (Side5-w) is connected to the fifth stack of the residual block to generate a $4K$-channel feature map, which goes into the adaptive weight learner to predict dynamic fusion weights W_l. The final output $\hat{Y}_D$ of DFF is computed as $\hat{Y}_D = \sigma(f(F_{cat}, W_l))$, where f represents element-wise multiplication and channel-wise summation operations, σ is the sigmoid function.

Loss Function. The backbone's loss function L is disassembled to two losses:

$$L = w_1 L_{fuse} + w_2 L_{side},$$

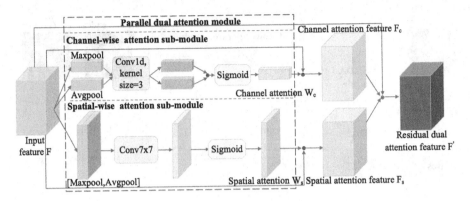

Fig. 2. Residual dual attention module.

$$L_{fuse} = \sum_p \{-\alpha Y(p) log \hat{Y}_D(p|X, W_D) - (1 - \alpha)$$
$$(1 - Y(p)) log(1 - \hat{Y}_D(p|X, W_D))\},$$
$$L_{side} = \sum_p \{-\alpha Y(p) log \hat{Y}_{D\_s}(p|X, W_D) - (1 - \alpha)$$
$$(1 - Y(p)) log(1 - \hat{Y}_{D\_s}(p|X, W_D))\}, \qquad (1)$$

where L_{fuse}, L_{side} denote its loss function for final output and Side5 output, respectively. w_1, w_2 are corresponding weighting factors to balance two losses. L_{fuse} and L_{side} adopt class-balanced cross-entropy loss function for balancing the loss between positive and negative classes. α is a class-balancing weight, $\alpha = |Y_{edge}|/|Y|$, $|Y_{edge}|$ expresses the size of the edge ground truth (GT) label set. $Y(p) \in \{0, 1\}$, $\hat{Y}_D(p|X, W_D) \in [0, 1]$ and $\hat{Y}_{D\_s}(p|X, W_D) \in [0, 1]$ are the GT, the predicted final edge probability and the edge probability from Side5 output at pixel $p \in \{1, 2 \cdots, |X|\}$, respectively. W_D stands for the backbone's parameters.

3.4 Multi-scale Residual Dual Attention (MSRDA) Module

To strengthen semantic information in captured features, we design a novel parallel dual attention module as shown in Fig. 2, including channel-wise and spatial-wise attention sub-modules.

In the channel attention sub-module, the input feature F is processed by max pooling and average pooling operations to aggregate each feature map's spatial information, respectively. Then a fast and shared $1D$ convolution with kernel size 3 rather than MLP [29] follows to capture non-linear dependencies across all channels, due that the dimensionality reduction in MLP may have a negative impact on the final accuracy performance [30]. In the end, the channel-wise attention feature F_c is expressed as:

$$F_c = F \otimes \sigma(1Dconv(AvgPool(F)) \oplus 1Dconv(MaxPool(F))), \qquad (2)$$

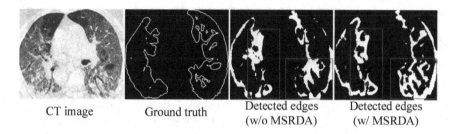

CT image   Ground truth   Detected edges   Detected edges
                                         (w/o MSRDA)   (w/ MSRDA)

Fig. 3. Visualization of the edge detection with (w/) and without (w/o) the MSRDA module.

where $\oplus$ denotes the element-wise summation; σ is the sigmoid function; $\otimes$ stands for the element-wise multiplication. In the spatial attention sub-module, max pooling and average pooling operations are performed along the channel axis, respectively. Two produced feature maps are concatenated and forwarded to a standard convolution with kernel size 7, generating the spatial attention map. The spatial-wise attention feature F_s is computed as:

$$F_s = F \otimes \sigma(Conv7 \times 7([AvgPool(F); MaxPool(F)])). \tag{3}$$

To make full use of more features and enrich context information, we propose the residual structure to combine original features with attention features. The residual dual attention feature F' is represented as:

$$F' = F_c \oplus F_s \oplus F, \tag{4}$$

where $\oplus$ is the element-wise summation operation. Then the residual dual attention mechanism is used for multiple basic descriptors generated by residual blocks to enhance feature representations, forming the multi-scale residual dual attention (MSRDA) module as shown in Fig. 1. Visualized results in Fig. 3 clarify that the MSRDA module helps detect more accurate and complex edges, which is beneficial to COVID-19 edge detection.

3.5 Canny Operator Module

Canny operator [28] is considered as one of the most classical algorithms for image edge detection. It is simple and its specific steps are as follows:

Step1: Use Gaussian filter to smooth the image.
Step2: Calculate the amplitude and direction of the image gradient after filtering.
Step3: Perform the non-maximum suppression for gradient amplitude to obtain thinner edges.
Step4: Select two thresholds T1 and T2 and connect edges. A pixel can be regarded as a strong edge point, weak edge point, or non-edge point when its gradient is beyond T1, between T1 and T2, or lower than T2. When strong

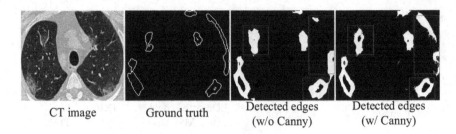

| CT image | Ground truth | Detected edges (w/o Canny) | Detected edges (w/ Canny) |

Fig. 4. Visualization of the edge detection with (w/) and without (w/o) the Canny module.

edge points appear in the 8 neighborhoods around the weak edge point, the weak edge point is changed into a strong edge point to augment the strong edge set.

The Canny feature F_{Canny} of the input image X is obtained through Canny operator, and then combined with weighted deep learning feature F_w. The final fusion feature F_{f_fuse} is represented as:

$$F_{f\_fuse} = Conv1 \times 1(F_{Canny} \oplus F_w), \tag{5}$$

where $\oplus$ is the element-wise summation operation. The visualization in Fig. 4 demonstrates that our Canny module helps detect thinner, clearer and sharper edges, contributing to COVID-19 infection edge detection.

3.6 Global Loss Function

Based on the final fusion features F_{f_fuse}, our final prediction $\hat{Y}$ is computed as:

$$\hat{Y} = \sigma(F_{f\_fuse}), \tag{6}$$

where σ is the sigmoid function. Our COVID Edge-Net adopts the same loss function as the backbone (Sect. 3.3), considering two losses. However, $\hat{Y}_D(p|X, W_D) \in [0,1]$ in backbone's L_{fuse} is replaced by $\hat{Y}(p|X, W) \in [0,1]$, which is our final predicted edge probability at pixel p. $\hat{Y}_{D\_s}(p|X, W_D) \in [0,1]$ in backbone's L_{side} is changed into $\hat{Y}_s(p|X, W) \in [0,1]$ that is our Side5 output's edge probability in Fig. 1, where Canny features are incorporated.

4   Experiments and Discussions

4.1   Experimental Settings

The Experimental Dataset and Augmentations. Our experiments rely on two COVID-19 CT datasets [20]: COVID-19 CT segmentation dataset and Segmentation dataset nr.2 (13th April), which are publicly available. COVID-19

CT segmentation dataset [20] contains 100 CT images from different COVID-19 patients and is collected by the Italian Society of Medical and Interventional Radiology. We randomly select 50 CT images as training samples and the remaining 50 images for testing, whose GT edges are generated via their segmentation labels. The larger Segmentation dataset nr.2 (13th April) released later consists of 829 slices (373 infected slices and 456 non-infected slices) extracted from 9 CT volumes of real COVID-19 patients, where 373 infected CT images are used as our experimental data for COVID-19 lung lesion edge detection. Among them, 186 randomly selected slices are regarded as the training set and the rest as the test set, whose GT edges are also produced based on segmentation marks given by radiologists. These experimental datasets suffer from a small sample size, thus, we augment training samples in each dataset by resizing each CT image with scaling factors {0.5, 0.75, 1, 1.25, 1.5} referring to [12] and employing random mirroring and cropping during the training process. In the test phase, each CT slice in COVID-19 CT segmentation dataset is resized to 512 × 512, and Segmentation dataset nr.2 (13th April)'s each CT image is cropped into 576 × 576.

Training Settings. Our model is based on ResNet18 [21] pre-trained on ImageNet [22]. K in Sect. 3.3 is set as one, and weighting factors in loss function are set as $w_1 = w_2 = 1$. Two thresholds T1 and T2 we used in the Canny operator are set to 200 and 100, respectively. We use SGD optimization, the learning rate is initialized to 0.05 and the "poly" policy is used for its decay. The crop size, batch size, training epoch, momentum, weight decay, and seed are set as 352 × 352, 16, 50, 0.9, 1e−4, 1, respectively. Our experiments depend on PyTorch and one NVIDIA 2080 Ti GPU. For fair comparisons, all edge detection experiments use the same training settings.

Evaluation Metrics. Following [12], Maximum F-measure (MF) at optimal dataset scale (ODS) with different matching distance tolerances is used as a common metric for edge detection performance, where F-measure is the harmonic average of precision and recall as shown in Eq. (7) and ODS means each image in the dataset uses the same threshold to evaluate image edges and achieve the entire dataset's maximum F-measure.

$$F - measure = \frac{2 \cdot precision \cdot recall}{precision + recall}. \tag{7}$$

We also consider two cases of MF (ODS) metric under one matching distance tolerance: with morphological thinning (w/ MT) and without morphological thinning (w/o MT).

4.2 Comparison with State-of-the-Arts

We compare the performance of our COVID Edge-Net model with state-of-the-art edge detection methods [12,14,28] on COVID-19 CT segmentation dataset and Segmentation dataset nr.2 (13th April), and evaluate MF(ODS) with different matching distance tolerances that are set as 0.02, 0.06, 0.10, respectively.

Table 1. Performance comparison of edge detection on COVID-19 CT segmentation dataset

Edge detection methods	MF(0.02)		MF(0.06)		MF(0.10)	
	w/ MT	w/o MT	w/ MT	w/o MT	w/ MT	w/o MT
Canny [28]	32.20%	45.15%	32.55%	46.77%	32.55%	46.77%
CASENet [14]	60.38%	42.87%	84.37%	56.71%	90.73%	66.78%
DFF [12]	**84.14%**	54.53%	90.83%	72.02%	93.45%	72.89%
Ours	83.58%	**63.80%**	**94.70%**	**85.30%**	**95.94%**	**91.57%**

Table 2. Performance comparison of edge detection on Segmentation dataset nr.2 (13th April)

Edge detection methods	MF(0.02)		MF(0.06)		MF(0.10)	
	w/ MT	w/o MT	w/ MT	w/o MT	w/ MT	w/o MT
Canny [28]	3.46%	5.76%	3.46%	5.76%	3.46%	5.76%
CASENet [14]	79.67%	74.74%	89.92%	**98.96%**	89.92%	**98.96%**
DFF [12]	75.38%	64.31%	90.77%	98.62%	90.77%	98.62%
Ours	**92.54%**	**78.29%**	**94.03%**	96.05%	**94.03%**	96.05%

On the COVID-19 CT segmentation dataset, Table 1 shows that ours exceeds the DFF method in almost all cases, and is completely superior to Canny and CASENet methods. When the matching distance tolerance is 0.10, ours achieves state-of-the-art results that are 95.94% MF(ODS) with MT and 91.57% MF(ODS) without MT. Specifically, our method surpasses DFF with 2.49% and 18.68% under 0.10 matching distance tolerance, respectively. As the matching distance tolerance is stricter, our approach is 3.87% and 13.28% better than the DFF under 0.06 matching distance tolerance, respectively. Under the strictest matching distance tolerance (0.02), our approach is 9.27% higher than DFF when ignoring MT, 23.20% and 20.93% better than CASENet with and without MT, 51.38% and 18.65% higher than Canny with and without MT. We also present performance comparison results of COVID-19 lung lesion edge detection on the larger Segmentation dataset nr.2 (13th April) in Table 2. It is evident that our proposed approach is far better than Canny method in all cases. Meanwhile, when the matching distance tolerance is the strictest 0.02, ours is obviously superior to other competing approaches. Specifically, ours achieves promising results that are 92.54% MF(ODS) with MT and 78.29% MF(ODS) without MT, which are 17.16% and 13.98% better than DFF considering MT and ignoring MT, 12.87% and 3.55% higher than CASENet with and without MT, respectively. Under 0.06 and 0.10 matching distance tolerances, our proposed approach has 94.03% MF(ODS) with MT, which is beyond DFF 3.26% and 4.11% higher than CASENet method; however, DFF and CASENet have slightly better MF(ODS) leaving the MT out of consideration. In the case of higher matching distance

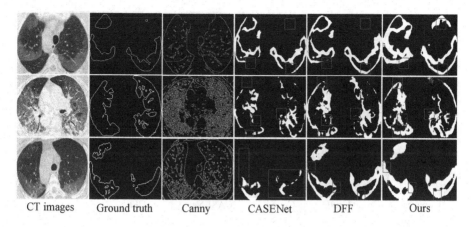

CT images   Ground truth   Canny   CASENet   DFF   Ours

Fig. 5. Qualitative comparison of edge detection on COVID-19 CT segmentation dataset.

tolerance, COVID-19 lung lesion edges produced by CASENet and DFF are more accurate without MT; our proposed method is able to get more promising results after MT. In general, our proposed method outperforms other state-of-the-arts in most cases. In addition, qualitative comparisons are also provided by visualizing some edge detection results in Fig. 5 and Fig. 6. On two datasets, we observe that Canny detects excessive useless edges because of the low contrast between infected regions and non-infected regions. Compared with other deep learning methods: CASENet and DFF, results in red boxes demonstrate that our COVID Edge-Net method has the capability of predicting more accurate, more continuous, sharper and clearer object edges, having higher edge detection performance by taking full advantage of multi-scale semantic information and fused features.

4.3 Ablation Study

In this subsection, we conduct ablation experiments to validate the performance of each newly proposed module in our COVID Edge-Net, taking COVID-19 CT segmentation dataset as an example, results of which are displayed in Table 3. DFF via ResNet18 is our baseline model. The comparison of Baseline (DFF) and Baseline+Canny clearly shows that Canny operator boosts performance without MT. Thus, the Canny operator module has the ability of refining and enhancing edges in COVID-19 CT images. Baseline (DFF) and Baseline+MSRDA demonstrate that the MSRDA module increases the baseline performance with MT. MSRDA strategy enables a model to identify much more edges that cannot be detected by the baseline. With these two complementary modules, the performance of our model is significantly enhanced no matter whether MT is considered or not considered. Furthermore, our MSRDA module is compared with multi-scale residual convolutional block attention module (MSRCBAM), where convolutional block attention module (CBAM) is proposed in [29]. It can be shown that

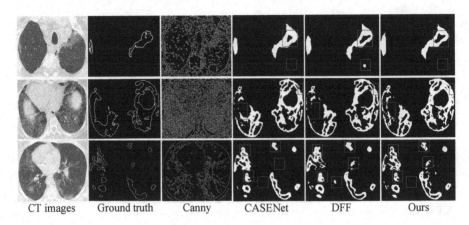

| CT images | Ground truth | Canny | CASENet | DFF | Ours |

Fig. 6. Qualitative comparison of edge detection on Segmentation dataset nr.2 (13th April).

Table 3. Ablation study of our COVID Edge-Net on COVID-19 CT segmentation dataset

Edge detection methods	MF(0.02)		MF(0.06)		MF(0.10)	
	w/ MT	w/o MT	w/ MT	w/o MT	w/ MT	w/o MT
Baseline (DFF)	84.14%	54.53%	90.83%	72.02%	93.45%	72.89%
Baseline+Canny	73.41%	55.67%	90.36%	74.31%	93.64%	83.11%
Baseline+MSRCBAM	72.67%	44.59%	87.45%	63.59%	92.89%	78.12%
Baseline+MSRDA	**84.85%**	44.58%	94.70%	60.61%	95.71%	66.49%
Baseline+MSRCBAM+Canny	79.57%	60.57%	93.39%	80.16%	93.52%	85.56%
Ours	83.58%	**63.80%**	**94.70%**	**85.30%**	95.94%	**91.57%**

Baseline+MSRDA is superior to Baseline+MSRCBAM with MT, and the whole method we proposed completely outperforms Baseline+MSRCBAM+Canny. Above all demonstrate the effectiveness of the integration of the two modules (i.e., MSRDA and Canny modules) into the Baseline (DFF).

4.4   Additional Experiments

We conduct COVID-19 segmentation experiments to further verify the performance of our algorithm on two COVID-19 segmentation datasets. The one-channel edge feature map from each edge detection model (e.g., our model, Canny, DFF) is replicated into a 64-channel map and then replaces Inf-Net's 64-channel edge feature [13]. We introduce GT edges via same operation as well. To make fair comparisons, we use the same training parameters and evaluated metrics as Inf-Net, and comparisons are shown in Table 4 and Table 5. The segmentation effect with the best edge features (GT edges) is far beyond original Inf-Net in Table 4 and Table 5, which reflects that better edges benefit segmentation. Furthermore, on the COVID-19 CT segmentation dataset, we observe

Table 4. Performance comparison of segmentation on COVID-19 CT segmentation dataset

Segmentation methods	Dice	Sen.	Spec.	S_α	$E_\emptyset^{mean}$	MAE
U-Net [23]*	0.439	0.534	0.858	0.622	0.625	0.186
Dense-UNet [26]*	0.515	0.594	0.840	0.655	0.662	0.184
Attention-UNet [25]*	0.583	0.637	0.921	0.744	0.739	0.112
U-Net++ [24]*	0.581	0.672	0.902	0.722	0.720	0.120
Gated-UNet [27]*	0.623	0.658	0.926	0.725	0.814	0.102
Inf-Net [13]*	0.682	0.692	0.943	0.781	0.838	0.082
Inf-Net(with Canny's edges)	**0.722**	**0.823**	0.920	0.773	0.865	0.083
Inf-Net(with DFF's edges)	0.713	0.732	0.946	**0.798**	0.870	0.075
Inf-Net(with our edges)	0.718	0.736	**0.948**	**0.798**	**0.872**	**0.074**
Inf-Net(with GT edges)	**0.780**	**0.821**	**0.952**	**0.861**	**0.888**	**0.059**

Note: Dice: Dice similarity coefficient, Sen.: Sensitivity, Spec.: Specificity, S_α: Structure Measure, $E_\emptyset^{mean}$: Enhance-alignment Measure, MAE: Mean Absolute Error.
*: All experiment data here refer to [13].

Table 5. Performance comparison of segmentation on Segmentation dataset nr.2 (13th April)

Segmentation methods	Dice	Sen	Spec	S_α	$E_\emptyset^{mean}$	MAE
Inf-Net [13]	0.802	0.831	0.961	0.861	0.938	0.020
Inf-Net(with Canny's edges)	0.808	**0.855**	0.964	0.861	**0.945**	0.019
Inf-Net(with DFF's edges)	0.812	0.849	0.963	0.867	0.942	**0.018**
Inf-Net(with our edges)	**0.814**	0.850	**0.967**	**0.868**	0.943	**0.018**
Inf-Net(with GT edges)	**0.894**	**0.904**	**0.988**	**0.930**	**0.965**	**0.012**

Note: Dice: Dice similarity coefficient, Sen.: Sensitivity, Spec.: Specificity, S_α: Structure Measure, $E_\emptyset^{mean}$: Enhance-alignment Measure, MAE: Mean Absolute Error.

that Inf-Net(with our edges) outperforms other excellent segmentation models [13] (e.g., U-Net-based models [23–27] and Inf-Net) for all metrics and exceeds Canny and DFF methods in segmentation for most metrics from Table 4. Similarly, Table 5 describes that Inf-Net(with our edges) absolutely defeats Inf-Net and outperforms Canny and DFF approaches in segmentation under most evaluation metrics on the Segmentation dataset nr.2 (13th April). Obviously, COVID Edge-Net is able to extract more accurate and richer edges than Inf-Net's edge extraction submodule, further enhancing segmentation performance.

5 Conclusions

In this paper, we present the first COVID Edge-Net for automatic COVID-19 lung lesion edge detection. On the one hand, an effective MSRDA module is designed and combined with edge detection backbone to extract more distinguishable deep learning features by capturing richer contextual relationships from CT scans. On the other hand, our network leverages Canny features to further enrich edge information by multi-feature fusion. Our proposed method achieves state-of-the-art COVID-19 edge detection performance compared to other competing approaches, and significantly benefits segmentation performance. It has the potential to be developed as a clinical tool for COVID-19 CT images analysis. Code related to this paper is available at: https://github.com/Elephant-123/COVID-Edge-Net.

References

1. Zhu, N., et al.: A novel coronavirus from patients with pneumonia in China, 2019. N. Engl. J. Med. **382**(8) (2020)
2. Wang, C., Horby, P.W., Hayden, F.G., Gao, G.F.: A novel coronavirus outbreak of global health concern. Lancet **395**(10223), 470–473 (2020)
3. Oudkerk, M., Büller, H.R., Kuijpers, D., et al.: Diagnosis, prevention, and treatment of thromboembolic complications in COVID-19: report of the national institute for public health of the Netherlands. Radiology **297**(1), E216–E222 (2020)
4. Coronavirus COVID-19 global cases by the center for systems science and engineering at johns Hopkins university. https://coronavirus.jhu.edu/map.html. Accessed 24 November 2020
5. Liang, T., et al.: Handbook of COVID-19 prevention and treatment. The first affiliated hospital, Zhejiang university school of medicine. Compil. Accord. Clin. Exp. **68** (2020)
6. Shan, F., et al.: Lung infection quantification of COVID-19 in CT images with deep learning. arXiv preprint arXiv:2003.04655 (2020)
7. Fang, Y., et al.: Sensitivity of chest CT for COVID-19: comparison to RT-PCR. Radiology **296**(2), E115–E117 (2020)
8. Ai, T., et al.: Correlation of chest CT and RT-PCR testing for coronavirus disease 2019 (COVID-19) in china: a report of 1014 cases. Radiology **296**(2), E32–E40 (2020)
9. Ng, M.Y., et al.: Imaging profile of the COVID-19 infection: radiologic findings and literature review. Radiol. Cardiothorac. Imaging **2**(1), e200034 (2020)
10. Kang, H., et al.: Diagnosis of coronavirus disease 2019 (COVID-19) with structured latent multi-view representation learning. IEEE Trans. Med. Imaging **39**(8), 2606–2614 (2020)
11. Wang, J., et al.: Prior-attention residual learning for more discriminative COVID-19 screening in CT images. IEEE Trans. Med. Imaging **39**(8), 2572–2583 (2020)
12. Hu, Y., Chen, Y., Li, X., Feng, J.: Dynamic feature fusion for semantic edge detection. arXiv preprint arXiv:1902.09104 (2019)
13. Fan, D.P., et al.: Inf-net: automatic COVID-19 lung infection segmentation from CT images. IEEE Trans. Med. Imaging **39**(8), 2626–2637 (2020)
14. Yu, Z., Feng, C., Liu, M.Y., Ramalingam, S.: CASENet: deep category-aware semantic edge detection. In: Proceedings of the IEEE Conference on Computer Vision and Pattern Recognition, pp. 5964–5973 (2017). https://doi.org/10.1109/CVPR.2017.191
15. Qiu, Y., Liu, Y., Xu, J.: Miniseg: An extremely minimum network for efficient covid-19 segmentation. arXiv preprint arXiv:2004.09750 (2020)

16. Wang, Y., et al.: Does non-COVID19 lung lesion help? investigating transferability in COVID-19 CT image segmentation. arXiv preprint arXiv:2006.13877 (2020)
17. Müller, D., Rey, I.S., Kramer, F.: Automated chest CT image segmentation of COVID-19 lung infection based on 3d u-net. arXiv preprint arXiv:2007.04774 (2020)
18. Zhou, T., Canu, S., Ruan, S.: An automatic COVID-19 CT segmentation network using spatial and channel attention mechanism. arXiv preprint arXiv:2004.06673 (2020)
19. Chen, X., Yao, L., Zhang, Y.: Residual attention u-net for automated multi-class segmentation of COVID-19 chest CT images. arXiv preprint arXiv:2004.05645 (2020)
20. COVID-19 CT segmentation dataset. https://medicalsegmentation.com/covid19/
21. He, K., Zhang, X., Ren, S., Sun, J.: Deep residual learning for image recognition. In: Proceedings of the IEEE Conference on Computer Vision and Pattern Recognition, pp. 770–778 (2016). https://doi.org/10.1109/CVPR.2016.90
22. Deng, J., Dong, W., Socher, R., Li, L.J., Li, K., Fei-Fei, L.: ImageNet: a large-scale hierarchical image database. In: 2009 IEEE Conference on Computer Vision and Pattern Recognition, pp. 248–255. IEEE (2009). https://doi.org/10.1109/CVPR.2009.5206848
23. Ronneberger, O.: Invited talk: u-net convolutional networks for biomedical image segmentation. In: Bildverarbeitung für die Medizin 2017. I, pp. 3–3. Springer, Heidelberg (2017). https://doi.org/10.1007/978-3-662-54345-0_3
24. Zhou, Z., Rahman Siddiquee, M.M., Tajbakhsh, N., Liang, J.: UNet++: a nested u-net architecture for medical image segmentation. In: Stoyanov, D., et al. (eds.) DLMIA/ML-CDS -2018. LNCS, vol. 11045, pp. 3–11. Springer, Cham (2018). https://doi.org/10.1007/978-3-030-00889-5_1
25. Oktay, O., et al.: Attention u-net: Learning where to look for the pancreas. arXiv preprint arXiv:1804.03999 (2018)
26. Li, X., Chen, H., Qi, X., Dou, Q., Fu, C.W., Heng, P.A.: H-DenseUNet: hybrid densely connected UNet for liver and tumor segmentation from CT volumes. IEEE Trans. Med. Imaging 37(12), 2663–2674 (2018)
27. Schlemper, J., et al.: Attention gated networks: learning to leverage salient regions in medical images. Med. Image Anal. 53, 197–207 (2019)
28. Canny, J.: A computational approach to edge detection. IEEE Trans. Pattern Anal. Mach. Intell. PAMI 8(6), 679–698 (1986)
29. Woo, S., Park, J., Lee, J.Y., So Kweon, I.: CBAM: convolutional block attention module. In: Proceedings of the European Conference on Computer Vision (ECCV), pp. 3–19 (2018). https://doi.org/10.1007/978-3-030-01234-2_1
30. Wang, Q., Wu, B., Zhu, P., Li, P., Zuo, W., Hu, Q.: ECA-Net: efficient channel attention for deep convolutional neural networks. In: Proceedings of the IEEE/CVF Conference on Computer Vision and Pattern Recognition, pp. 11534–11542 (2020)

Improving Ambulance Dispatching with Machine Learning and Simulation

Nikki Theeuwes, Geert-Jan van Houtum⬤, and Yingqian Zhang$^{(\boxtimes)}$⬤

Eindhoven University of Technology, 5612 AZ Eindhoven, The Netherlands
{G.J.v.Houtum,yqzhang}@tue.nl

Abstract. As an industry where performance improvements can save lives, but resources are often scarce, emergency medical services (EMS) providers continuously look for ways to deploy available resources more efficiently. In this paper, we report a case study executed at a Dutch EMS region to improve ambulance dispatching. We first capture the way in which dispatch human agents currently make decisions on which ambulance to dispatch to a request. We build a decision tree based on historical data to learn human agents' dispatch decisions. Then, insights from the fitted decision tree are used to enrich the commonly assumed closest-idle dispatch policy. Subsequently, we use the captured dispatch policy as input to a discrete event simulation to investigate two enhancements to current practices and evaluate their performance relative to the current policy. Our results show that complementing the current dispatch policy with redispatching and reevaluation policies yields an improvement of the on-time performance of highly urgent ambulance requests of 0.77% points. The performance gain is significant, which is equivalent to adding additional seven weekly ambulance shifts.

Keywords: Ambulance dispatching · Machine learning · Decision trees · Discrete event simulation · Logistics

1 Introduction

Emergency medical services (EMS) providers continuously look for ways to deploy limited available resources more efficiently. In the Netherlands, the fraction of highly urgent ambulance requests (A1 requests) with a response time of fewer than 15 min has been consistently below the national target of 95% throughout the past years, with a performance of 92.4% in 2017. Advances in ambulance logistics will contribute to the provision of sufficient emergency medical care, given the available resources.

The operational problems in EMS literature include both ambulance dispatching and relocation in order to maximize the fraction of ambulance requests with a *response time* below a certain threshold time, or the *on-time performance*. Response time is defined as the time between the moment an ambulance request arrives at a dispatch center and the moment the ambulance arrives at the

© Springer Nature Switzerland AG 2021
Y. Dong et al. (Eds.): ECML PKDD 2021, LNAI 12978, pp. 302–318, 2021.
https://doi.org/10.1007/978-3-030-86514-6_19

request location. It is predominantly assumed that ambulances are dispatched according to a 'closest-idle' policy (e.g. [10,13]). Alternative dispatch policies are often modifications of this policy (e.g. [7,8]). However, not only does this policy neglect practical considerations (e.g. the distinction between urgency levels or shift ends), it is also known to be suboptimal when maximizing the on-time performance [4]. Therefore, it can be expected that in practice dispatch agents tend to deviate from this commonly assumed dispatch policy, jeopardizing the relevance of alternative policies developed with the closest-idle policy at its foundation.

Knowledge obtained by dispatch agents in practice can be very useful in the development of improved dispatching policies [1]. In this paper, we formally capture this knowledge, or expertise, in the form of the current dispatch policy for the Dutch EMS region of Brabant Zuid-Oost (BZO). Capturing the current dispatch policy has three main benefits: (1) *Creating transparency*: Insights can be deducted that can help create awareness among dispatch agents, which might improve consistency and fairness of the process. (2) *Improving process*: Insights from the captured dispatch policy also give rise to opportunities for improvement. The captured dispatch policy provides a basis to improve upon by extending it with a number of additional or adapted decision rules. Contrary to developing an improved dispatch policy from scratch, our approach complements, rather than replaces, current dispatch practices. This ensures both the incorporation of practical considerations in the resulting policy and that it is in line with the way in which dispatch agents currently work, which are expected to foster adoption in practice; (3) *Evaluating fairly*: the captured dispatch policy can be used as input to a simulation of an EMS region. Such a simulation can also be used to fairly evaluate potential improvements of the dispatch process by comparing its performance to that of the current dispatch policy. The use of a benchmark that resembles current practices allows for more accurate conclusions regarding the potential of the evaluated alternative policy in practice.

Decision makers are often not completely aware of the reasoning behind their expert judgments, making it hard for them to verbally express their decision process [6]. However, mental decision models can be formally approximated through machine learning models. We select *decision tree induction* to capture the current dispatch policy of the BZO region, since this method results in a policy representation that is both transparent and interpretable. In the BZO region the fraction of A1 requests has been consistently below the nationally-set target of 95% (i.e., 91.7% in 2017), while the fraction of moderately urgent (A2) requests with a response time of less than 30 min has consistently exceeded its target of 95%. Therefore, the on-time performance for A1 requests is generally regarded as the main performance measure in EMS management.

Our work contributes to the field of EMS management as well as to that of applying machine learning to capture expert decisions:

- We are the first to formally capture current ambulance dispatch practices using machine learning. We apply decision tree induction to obtain a transparent representation of the current dispatch decision process in the BZO region (see Sect. 4.1).

- We apply a unique post-processing phase which combines knowledge from both practice and literature with the learned decision tree to further improve the quality of the learned model in terms of accuracy and conciseness. The resulting model enriches the commonly assumed closest-idle dispatch policy through the use of penalty values that reflect the risk associated with certain ambulance characteristics (Sect. 4.2).
- We illustrate an application of the captured current dispatch policy by proposing two enhancements to it and evaluating these in a simulation using the captured policy as a practically relevant benchmark (Sect. 5).

Before making these contributions in Sect. 4 and Sect. 5, we discuss related literature in Sect. 2 and the collection of data in Sect. 3. We conclude this paper in Sect. 6.

2   Related Work

The existing studies in EMS management generally evaluate the proposed dispatch policies through a simulation in which many simplifying modelling choices and assumptions are made. For example, Lee [7] simulated a hypothetical square grid of 25 vertices with a fixed driving time for all edges. He did not distinguish between urgency levels and assumed a general distribution for transfer times and a static number of ambulances. Jagtenberg et al. [4] simulated the actual EMS region of Utrecht, but assumed a static relocation policy, static request arrivals, and static ambulance capacity, treatment and transfer times.

The existing, limited number of studies applying machine learning to model expert decisions generally seems to have the captured expert knowledge as the ultimate goal of their efforts, mostly to automate decision making. Maghrebi et al. [9] conducted a feasibility study of automating the process of determining the order of concrete deliveries. They employ machine learning to match expert decisions with the objective of decreasing dependency on human resources. Lafond et al. [5] compare three machine learning techniques in capturing human classification behavior using a simulated naval air defense task. However, capturing expert decisions with the objective to support future decisions implicitly assumes that the captured expert knowledge is optimal, or at least neglects the fact that insight into current practices provides a good opportunity for the identification and evaluation of improvement of the decision making process. In Lafond et al. [6], a learning technique is applied to functionally mirror expert mental models. Their objective is to improve decision quality by recognizing when a decision maker is deviating from his usual decision patterns, since this might indicate probable errors. It still assumes the captured policy to be the correct, or desired one, which was a limitation as acknowledged by the authors. Donnot et al. [3] first apply a deep neural network to historic decision data to mimic human decisions in the prevention of violating power flow limits in a power plant, and then use simple simulation to evaluate the effect of each action proposed by the captured decision model before suggesting it to the decision maker. While this approach does not actually improve on the captured decisions, it does distinguish between bad and good decisions and only uses the good ones to support future decision making.

To the best of our knowledge, there are no studies which have captured expert decisions with the objective to use the resulting policy as a basis to improve upon or as input for fair evaluation of alternative policies. Moreover, most of the studies did not derive decisions from real data, but rather generated this data by presenting experts with an artificial (simulated) task. In comparison, we expect decisions derived from historic data resemble actual decisions more closely. In addition, in capturing ambulance dispatch decisions, we apply a post-processing phase which combines knowledge from both the domain and literature with the learned model to further improve the quality the resulting model.

3 The Data Set: Historic Dispatch Decisions

We approached the induction of the current dispatch policy as a classification problem. We gathered data on historic dispatch decisions made by BZO's dispatch agents. The data set has been compiled such that it reflects all information available to the agent at the decision moment, which might have affected the decision. We have structured the decision to be captured around the *dispatch proposal*. In the Netherlands, upon being presented with an ambulance request, a dispatch agent uses the national dispatch system to generate such a dispatch proposal. A dispatch proposal is an ordered list of all ambulances available for dispatch to the concerned request, based on an increasing driving time to the request location. By structuring the decision to be captured around such a dispatch proposal, we have implicitly assumed that, for any dispatch decision to be made, a dispatch proposal is generated and one of the ambulances in the proposal is dispatched. The set of ambulances available for dispatch depends on the request's urgency. Regardless of the request's urgency this set includes all idle ambulances, i.e. those driving to, or waiting at, a station. Besides idle ambulances, this set includes ambulances which have already been dispatched to a less urgent request, but did not arrive at that request's location yet, and ambulances that have arrived at a hospital and are busy transferring a patient. While these ambulances are not idle (yet), they might be redispatched or requested to accelerate the transfer process respectively. Lastly, since dispatch agents have the possibility to request assistance from neighbouring EMS regions, these ambulances are also included in the dispatch proposal. Summarizing, the objective of our formalization effort was to determine which ambulance is dispatched to a request, given the corresponding dispatch proposal, and why a dispatch agent might decide to deviate from dispatching the closest-idle ambulance. This implies that the *class* of each *instance* is the rank of the ambulance that was actually dispatched in the corresponding dispatch proposal.

Table 1. Features with $i \in \{1, 2, 3, 4, 5\}$ being dispatch proposal options

No.	Feature	Symbol	Data type
0	Rank of i in dispatch proposal (class)	C	Nominal: $\{1, 2, 3, 4, 5+\}$
1	Urgency	U	Ordinal: $\{A1, A2\}$
2	Passed time	P	Numeric (minutes)
3–7	Driving time of i	D_i	Numeric (minutes)
8–12	Status of i	S_i	Nominal: $\{1, 2, 3, 6\}$
13–17	Idle status indicator of i	SI_i	Binary
18–22	Status time of i	ST_i	Numeric (minutes)
23–27	Remaining shift time of i	RS_i	Numeric (minutes)
28–32	Own ambulance indicator of i	$Rown_i$	Binary
33–37	Region BZO & BNO indicator of i	Rbo_i	Binary
38	Number of idle ambulances	I	Numeric
39	Single coverage	Cov	Numeric (%)
40–44	Percentual coverage reduction of i	PCR_i	Numeric (%)
45–49	Absolute coverage reduction of i	ACR_i	Numeric (%)
50–53	Driving time diff. i and $i+1$	ΔD_i	Numeric (Min.)
54–57	Perc. coverage reduction diff. i and $i+1$	ΔPCR_i	Numeric (%)
58–61	Abs. coverage reduction diff. i and $i+1$	ΔACR_i	Numeric (%)
62–66	Expected response time of i	E_i	Numeric (Min.)

3.1 Feature Engineering

Upon making a dispatch decision, a dispatch agent has multiple screens at his/her disposal which show information regarding the concerned ambulance request, the ambulance options included in the generated dispatch proposal, and a map of the region displaying all on-duty ambulance locations and statuses. Since dispatch agents are dedicated to making dispatch decisions, which happens under time pressure, we assume that all information presented to a dispatch agent is considered to be relevant to the dispatch decision. We transformed such domain knowledge by the process of feature engineering. Data was obtained for September and October 2018 from GMS. Only data on ambulance requests (dispatches) within the BZO region were used. This led to a total of 4506 instances to fit BZO's current dispatch policy on. Table 1 shows the features for which values were obtained from the available data for each of the instances. For a more detailed description of data collection and (pre-)processing, we refer to [12].

    The first two features relate to the ambulance request which requires a dispatch decision. The urgency (U) of this request is relevant since it determines the response time target. 95% of highly urgent ($A1$) requests should have a response time less than fifteen minutes, while 95% of moderately urgent ($A2$) requests should have a response time less than thirty minutes. Since the response time of a request starts at the moment the corresponding call arrives at the dispatch center, the time that has passed since call arrival (P) is also relevant.

Features three to thirty-seven concern pieces of information listed for each of the ambulance options in the generated dispatch proposal, with i referring to the ith option in a dispatch proposal, $i \in \{1, 2, 3, 4, 5\}$. Note that for each instance only features referring to properties of the first five options in the concerned proposal are included. This choice was made since the class distribution in our instance set is particularly unbalanced, with the higher ranked dispatch options being represented more strongly. Recall that ambulances in a dispatch proposal are ordered based on their driving time to the concerned incident and the main performance measure depends strongly on this driving time, which leads to a natural preference for higher ranked options. To ensure a sufficient number of samples of each class to be available, classes five and up were combined to form one class. Furthermore, we were especially interested in an agent's reasons for deviating from sending the closest idle ambulance, which were expected to become apparent by distinguishing between the first few options of a dispatch proposal. The resulting class distribution is: 67% (class 1), 20% (class 2), 7% (class 3), 3% (class 4), 3% (class 5). Since the importance of the classes is ordered, it is more important that the higher ranked classes are predicted correctly. Hence we do not balance the dataset but let the decision tree algorithm favour the more important classes during learning.

The status of each dispatch option i (S_i) may either be idle (driving towards or waiting at a station) or busy but available for dispatch (on its way to a less urgent request or transferring a patient at a hospital). The idle status indicator of dispatch option i (SI_i) indicates whether S_i is idle. Furthermore, the status time of option i (ST_i) is equal to the time since the status of each dispatch option last changed, while the time until the end of each dispatch option's eight hour shift, which may be negative in case of overtime, is reflected by feature RS_i. The dispatch proposal shows for each option to which region it belongs, and thus by which region it is controlled. We captured this information in binary features $Rown_i$ and Rbo_i, where the first reflects whether option i belongs to the own region (BZO), and the second indicates whether option i belongs to either the own region or the adjacent BNO region, where dispatch agents operate from the same dispatch center as BZO's dispatch agent.

Features thirty-eight through forty-nine reflect the information that the dispatch agent might deduct from the map of the region displaying all on-duty ambulance locations and statuses. The number of idle ambulances (I) and the single coverage (Cov) reflect the extent to which the region is prepared for future requests. Based on discussions with BZO's dispatch agents, I includes both idle ambulances and ambulances that are busy transferring a patient at a hospital, since these are expected to become idle in the very near future and may even be requested to accelerate the transfer process if necessary. The single coverage feature refers to the fraction of the BZO region (in terms of 4-digit postal code areas) that can be reached within a response time of fifteen minutes by at least one ambulance [2]. Additionally, we introduced two features that relate to the reduction in preparedness, i.e. single coverage, of the region that would be caused by dispatching option i. ACR_i does so in absolute terms, while PCR_i relates the coverage reduction to the current single coverage (Cov).

A dispatch agent might infer relevant information based on the relation between feature values. Features fifty through sixty-six were constructed by performing logical operations on our initial list of features and selecting meaningful ones. These additional features include the difference between subsequent dispatch options in driving time (ΔD_i), percentual and absolute coverage reduction (ΔPCR_i and ΔACR_i), and the expected response time of each dispatch option i (E_i). Here, the expected response time of option i is made up of the time that passed since arrival of the call (P), its driving time to the request's location (D_i), and one minute that is expected to be required for making the dispatch decision and for an ambulance to start driving after being dispatched.

4 Capturing the Dispatch Policy with a Decision Tree

We use a decision tree to learn the current dispatch process, due to its transparent nature. Its interpretability allows us to gain insight into the current dispatch routine, which can be leveraged both as a basis to improve the current dispatch process and as a benchmark in the evaluation of potential improvements.

We split the data into a training set (70% of instances) and a test set (remaining 30% of instances). We use the implementation of CART (Classification and Regression Trees) in scikit-learn [11]. We tune the parameters, i.e. feature selection method, maximum tree depth, and the minimum number of instances at a leaf node, by applying stratified 10-fold cross-validation on the training set. Then the final decision tree has been trained on the complete training set. Subsequently, the resulting decision tree has been evaluated using the test set.

Since our objective of capturing the current dispatch process is to identify which ambulance is actually dispatched, the larger sized classes are of greater interest than the smaller ones. By definition, this relative interest in correctly predicting each class is reflected in the class distribution. Hence, we do not balance the training set but let the algorithm favour the more important classes. In addition, we choose the weighted F1-score, where the F1-score of each class is weighted by its sample size, as the main performance measure.

4.1 Performance Analysis of the Learned Decision Tree and Policy

Additionally, we define the *Weighted Mean Error* performance measure. For the problem at hand, if the actual dispatch decision was to dispatch the first option, predicting dispatch of the third option is actually more wrong than predicting dispatch of the second option. Therefore, we defined the following additional performance measure:

$$WME = \frac{\sum_{d=0}^{k-1} d \sum_{i,j \in \{1,2,...,k\}:|i-j|=d} m_{i,j}}{\sum_{i,j \in \{1,2,...,k\}} m_{i,j}},$$

where k equals the number of possible classes, in our case $k = 5$, and the $m_{i,j}$ are cells in the confusion matrix, where rows and columns are indicated by i and j respectively. Naturally, while we strive towards a dispatch prediction model with a weighted F1-score that is as high as possible, we prefer the mean distance to the actual class to be as low as possible.

To place the performance of the resulting decision tree into perspective, its performance has been compared to the dispatch policy that is commonly assumed in literature, the *closest-idle policy*. Notice that in literature this policy generally does not include the additional dispatch options that are available to BZO's dispatch agents, namely ambulances that are not completely idle but nevertheless available to (certain) incidents and external ambulances that belong to other regions. Therefore, we have defined two dispatch policies to which the performance of our fitted dispatch policy have been compared: *(1) The limited closest-idle policy*: corresponding to the policy that is commonly assumed in literature, i.e. dispatching the highest ranked ambulance in the dispatch proposal that is completely idle (on the road or at station) and belongs to the own region. *(2) The extended closest-idle policy*: corresponding to the commonly assumed policy but adapted to include the additional available dispatch options, i.e. always dispatching option one in the dispatch proposal.

Figure 1 depicts the learned decision tree. Figures 2a, b, and c show the confusion matrices and performance measures for the learned dispatch policy, the limited closest-idle policy and the extended closest-idle policy respectively. Figure 2 shows that the learned dispatch model outperforms both interpretations of the closest-idle policy, in terms of the weighted F1-score, as well as the weighted mean error. However, while the difference in performance between the learned model (a) and the extended closest-idle policy (c) is quite significant, the improvement in predictive performance of the learned model (a) relative to the basic, limited closest-idle policy (b) is less apparent. This observation leads us to believe that BZO's dispatch agents generally make limited use of the additional dispatch options available to them.

This insight is confirmed by studying the learned decision tree, depicted in Fig. 1a, in more detail. There are several clear 'decision paths', which have been highlighted in Fig. 1b. These highlighted decision paths indicate the dominant dispatch decision. Note that some of these paths, and the insights derived from them, can be regarded as more important than others due to the larger number of samples following that path. The weight of each path indicates the number of samples following that path.

The main reasons that might lead a dispatch agent to deviate from dispatching the highest ranking dispatch option (i.e. option 1) quickly become clear from the splits on the most dominant path (leading to [A]). These main reasons include this highest ranking ambulance:

- **Not being immediately available for dispatch:** due to its status. For example, the ambulance is transferring a patient at a hospital, meaning that it might require some time to be relieved from its current request and redispatched to the new request.

- **Not belonging to the own region:** meaning that the concerned dispatch center needs to be requested, which takes time, and the dispatch request might be denied.
- **Nearing the end of its shift:** causing a risk of overtime if it is dispatched.

The first two of these reasons confirm that dispatch agents make limited use of the additional dispatch options available to them. Possibly, this is the case because these issues add a potential delay to the indicated driving time. Such a potential delay adds a degree of uncertainty to the ambulance's expected driving time, which gives the dispatch agent good reasons to deviate from this option. Naturally, the potential delay is only relevant if the difference between the driving time of that option and the subsequent option is less than this expected delay. This is reflected by the node at the top of node group [A] in Fig. 1b, as well as at several other nodes in the tree.

It can be deducted that, if there are enough reasons to deviate from the highest ranking ambulance option, the subsequent option is considered. However, the same reasons to deviate seem to hold for this option, e.g. see the path in Fig. 1b leading to node [B], where option 3 is considered due to the status of option 2, and that same path eventually leading to leaf node [C], where option 4 is considered due to the status of option 3.

However, subsequent options cannot be considered indefinitely, since the driving time to the request increases with each option. Naturally, despite the dispatch agents being risk averse and preferring subsequent options if there is a potential delay for the closest option, the selected option should still be able to arrive on-time. Since the driving time increases with each option, the driving time, or expected response time, of the furthest option we consider, option 5, is a good indication of whether previous options are able to arrive on-time. This is why multiple nodes testing for the closeness of option 5 to the incident are present in the decision tree, see nodes [D] and [E]. It can be seen that if the closeness of option 5 is sufficiently small, generally lower ranked options are selected for dispatch than when this is not the case.

This is also why the learned model performs significantly better than the limited closest-idle policy in terms of its weighted mean error. In case of sufficient available capacity, dispatch agents clearly prefer risk averse dispatch options. However, while the learned model recognizes that in case of scarcity the dispatch agent is required to choose an ambulance to be dispatched among risky options, the limited closest-idle policy keeps considering subsequent options until a risk-free (completely idle and own region) option is found. In other words, while the performance of the fitted model is similar to the limited closest-idle policy for the majority of dispatch decisions to be made, i.e. in case of sufficient capacity, it strongly outperforms this commonly assumed policy in case of scarce capacity. This ability of the fitted model is especially relevant since dispatch decisions made under scarce capacity are precisely where the expertise and human judgment of the dispatch agents can make a difference.

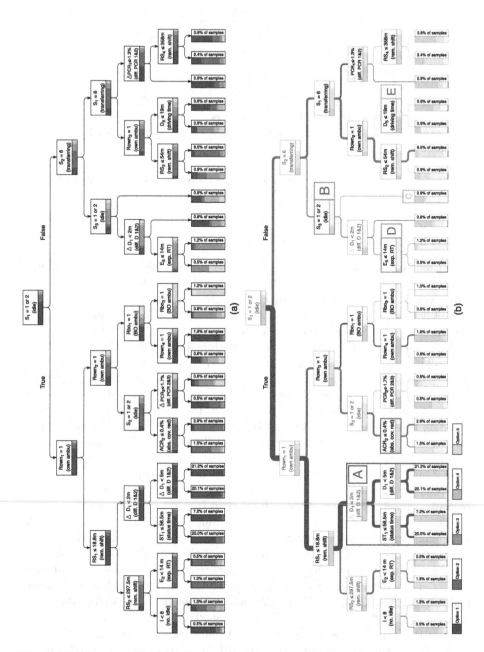

Fig. 1. Visualization of learned dispatch decision model with colors indicating the class distribution of the instances reaching each node: (a) complete model and (b) model including highlighted decision paths indicating its dominant dispatch decision

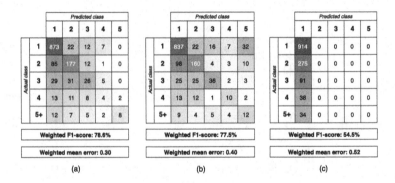

Fig. 2. Confusion matrices and performance measures for (a) the learned dispatch policy, (b) the limited closest-idle policy, and (c) the extended closest-idle policy

4.2   The Penalty-Based Closest-Idle Policy

The fitted dispatch policy is quite complex. Combined with the fact that a simple model such as the limited closest-idle policy is able to predict dispatch decisions quite well in case of sufficient ambulance capacity, but performs very bad in case of limited capacity due to its inability to consider risky options, leads us to propose a concise, penalty-based policy to represent the dispatch decisions made by BZO's dispatch agents. In line with the three main reasons to deviate from dispatching an ambulance that were deducted from the learned decision tree, penalty terms are defined based on an ambulance's status, region and time until the end of its shift to reflect the potential delay or risk associated with the value of these features. For each ambulance option, its total time penalty is determined based on its status, region and remaining shift time, after which it is added to its driving time. Then, the dispatch option with the lowest driving time plus total penalty is dispatched. In other words, this policy can be called the *penalty-based closest-idle (PBCI) policy*. This approach reflects dispatching agents' preference for a completely idle ambulance from the own region, but ensures that in case of scarce capacity still one of the risky options is selected for dispatch.

These penalty terms are fitted on the training data, such that they result in a maximum weighted F1-score. This is done through an exhaustive search of integer penalty values. The performance of the resulting penalty model is evaluated on the test data. Figure 3 shows the fitted penalty values, the confusion matrix and performance measures. It is shown that both the weighted F1-score and the weighted mean error have improved even further compared to the fitted decision tree. Algorithm 1 shows the resulting PBCI dispatch policy.

The PBCI policy has been presented to and validated by BZO's dispatch agents. Not only did they confirm that the PBCI policy makes sense and is likely to resemble the majority of their dispatch decisions, it also started a constructive discussion on how to improve upon their current decisions. In conclusion, insights from our learned dispatch decision prediction model were used to enrich the commonly assumed closest-idle dispatch policy using penalty values reflecting the

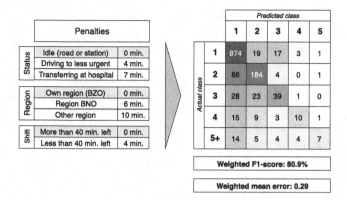

Fig. 3. Fitted penalty values (on train data) and performance (on test data) of PBCI

Algorithm 1. Algorithm of the PBCI dispatching policy

1: **for** each dispatch option in the dispatch proposal i **do**
2:    $penalty_i = 0$
3:    **if** ambulance is transferring a patient at a hospital **then**
4:       $penalty_i = penalty_i + 7$ (min.)
5:    **else if** ambulance is on its way to a less urgent request **then**
6:       $penalty_i = penalty_i + 4$ (min.)
7:    **if** ambulance is of BNO region **then**
8:       $penalty_i = penalty_i + 6$ (min.)
9:    **else if** ambulance is of neither BZO nor BNO region **then**
10:       $penalty_i = penalty_i + 10$ (min.)
11:    **if** shift of ambulance ends within 40 minutes **then**
12:       $penalty_i = penalty_i + 4$ (min.)
13:    Penalized driving time of i = driving time of ambulance i + $penalty_i$
14: Dispatch ambulance with smallest penalized driving time

---

risk associated with certain ambulance characteristics. The result of this post-processing phase is a concise policy that has significantly greater resemblance to the actual dispatch decisions made by BZO's dispatch agents compared to the policy that is generally assumed in literature.

5   Current Policy as a Basis for Improvement

The captured dispatch policy provides insight into current practices and gives rise to opportunity for improvement. The PBCI policy provides a basis to improve upon, as well as a benchmark that is close to current practices. To illustrate a possible application of the PBCI policy, we have defined two potential enhancements to current practices and evaluated their potential using a realistic simulation. These enhancements were defined to complement, rather than replace, the current dispatch decision process. Using the PBCI policy as a basis for improvements ensures that practically relevant considerations are included in the improved decision process, fostering adoption. The two potential enhancements to the current dispatch process we propose are (1) *consistently*

314   N. Theeuwes et al.

redispatching ambulances that are on their way to a less urgent request to a more urgent request if this leads to a response time improvement and (2) *reevaluation of active dispatch decisions* upon service completion of an ambulance.

Consistent Redispatching. From the captured current dispatching process, it can be seen that a dispatch option that is not completely free (on the road or at a station) is considered to be risky due to a potential delay. While a potential delay is difficult to avoid if the ambulance is busy transferring a patient at a hospital, it might be avoided in case of redispatching an ambulance that is currently on its way to a less urgent request. The consistent redispatching policy always dispatch an ambulance that is currently on its way to a less or non-urgent request if this is the best dispatch option for a highly urgent (A1) request. The enhancement is similar to 'reroute-enabled dispatching' as proposed by [8], who evaluated this policy for a hypothetical EMS region consisting of a 16 × 16 grid, deterministic environment. It is interesting to evaluate the potential performance improvement of consistently redispatching an ambulance whenever it is the best dispatch option, since the performance improvement might outweigh the disadvantages.

Reevaluation of Dispatch Decision. Currently dispatch decisions are only made upon arrival of a new request. A dispatch decision is made by selecting the best option from those ambulances that are available at that moment. However, the system of ambulances is very dynamic and during the time the dispatched ambulance is driving towards the request, another ambulance may complete serving another request. This other ambulance may in fact be a better dispatch decision than the ambulance that is already on its way. Reevaluation of the dispatch decision might contribute towards improving performance. Contrary to the 'Parallelism' dispatch policy of [7], the consideration of a busy ambulance only after it has completed service, prevents dependency on the realization of highly variable treatment times. Furthermore, to prevent reevaluated dispatch decisions resulting in only a marginal difference in response time, as is the case for the 'free ambulance exploitation' policy of [8], in our case a reevaluated dispatch decision will only lead to the recently freed ambulance being dispatched instead of the current one if this leads to a response time improvement of at least one minute for highly urgent (A1) requests, or a direct improvement of the on-time performance for less urgent (A2) requests.

5.1 Evaluating Potential Enhancements Using Simulation

These two potential enhancements to the current dispatch policy have been evaluated using a realistic simulation that accurately captures the complex dynamics of a real-life size ambulance system within a reasonable computation time. We developed a discrete-event simulation in which the BZO region is aggregated into 138 subregions, corresponding to 4-digit postal codes. Locations of ambulance stations, hospitals, and requests are mapped onto the centroid of its postal code. While our focus is on the performance of urgent (i.e. A1 and A2) requests, we

Table 2. Realized and simulated performance under current dispatch policy

	A1 requests		A2 requests	
	On-time (%)	Mean RT (min:sec)	On-time (%)	Mean RT (min:sec)
Realized	92.13	9:33	97.10	14:32
Simulated	93.63	9:02	97.07	13:38

Table 3. Resulting performance for potential dispatch enhancements

(1) Redispatching	(2) Reevaluating	A1 requests		A2 requests		Redispatches/yr.	Reevaluations/yr.
		On-time (%)	Mean RT (min:sec)	On-time (%)	Mean RT (min:sec)		
Base		93.63 (+/-0.05)	9:02 (+/-0:00)	97.07 (+/-0.05)	13:38 (+/-0:01)	1425	
x		94.06 (+/-0.05)	8:55 (+/-0:00)	96.15 (+/-0.05)	14:04 (+/-0:01)	3293	
	x	94.04 (+/-0.04)	8:56 (+/-0:01)	97.50 (+/-0.05)	13:34 (+/-0:01)	1413	823
x	x	94.40 (+/-0.05)	8:50 (+/-0:00)	96.73 (+/-0.05)	13:58 (+/-0:02)	3269	772

also simulate non-urgent patient transports to capture all dynamics in the utilization of the available ambulance capacity. Furthermore, driving times between each pair of postal codes are assumed to be deterministic, but dynamic, as supplied by the *driving time model* of the RIVM (non-public). The simulation is able to accurately deal with the dynamic arrival of ambulance requests of multiple urgency levels, dynamic ambulance capacity, realistic relocation decisions and a wide range of practical considerations. Furthermore, the captured current dispatch process allowed us to be the first to evaluate alternative dispatch policies by comparing the simulated performance to that of a practically relevant benchmark. The interaction with neighbouring EMS regions was excluded from the simulation due to its complexity. Its effect on the extent to which the simulation resembles reality is expected to be limited due to the fact that external ambulances are rarely dispatched (<2% of requests).

Table 2 shows that simulating current practices, represented by the PBCI policy, results in a slightly better performance for highly urgent A1 requests and similar performance for moderately urgent A2 requests compared to realized values in the practice of the BZO region. The simulation slightly outperforms reality because the simulation decisions are made consistently, while in practice variations in dispatch decisions occur due to human judgment and differences between dispatch agents. Because we have only a small difference between the realized and simulated performance, we can conclude that our simulation model, with the use of the PBCI policy, is representative for the BZO region.

5.2   Performance of the Improved Policy

Table 3 shows the resulting performance measures for the two potential enhancements. Besides the main performance measures relating to the response time of urgent requests, the last two columns provide further insight into the effect of both enhancements from which conclusions regarding the effect on ambulance crew disturbance can be deducted. From the effects on performance caused by each dispatch enhancement individually, it can be concluded that both *consistent redispatching* and *reevaluation* of active dispatch decisions upon service completion of an ambulance lead to a significant improvement of the fraction of A1 requests that is served on-time, namely 0.43 and 0.41% points (pp) respectively. However, while *consistent redispatching* is quite detrimental for the on-time performance of A2 requests, the *reevaluation* enhancement even improved this measure with 0.43 pp. This detrimental effect of the *consistent redispatching* enhancement on the A2 on-time performance is mostly caused by the fact that an ambulance is redispatched regardless of whether an alternative ambulance is available for dispatch to the original request, and whether this ambulance is able to arrive on-time. While under the current dispatch policy on average 3.9 redispatches are initiated each day, this number increases to a little over 9 redispatches per day in case of consistent redispatching. Given the number of shifts on an average day, this implies that an ambulance crew is only redispatched once every four shifts, which does not seem excessive. From the number of *reevaluations* leading to the recently freed ambulance being dispatched, and thus for the currently dispatched ambulance to be redirected, it can be deducted that such a decision is made on average 2.3 times per day. The disturbance to the ambulance crew of this number of redirections is likely to be quite limited.

We also simulated the combination of enhancements. Adding both the *consistent redispatch* and *reevaluation* enhancement yields an even larger performance gain, improving the A1 on-time performance by 0.77 pp. The performance gain of both of these enhancements individually is quite complementary, as combining these enhancements leads to an A1 on-time performance gain of almost the sum of the individuals performance gains. Further, the fact that the *reevaluation* enhancement is beneficial to the performance of A2 requests mitigates part of the detrimental effect of the *consistent redispatch* enhancement, leading only to a reduction of 0.33 pp. Combining these two enhancements, however, also leads to a larger number of redirections (resulting from either being redispatched or from a reevaluated dispatch decision), which may cause disturbance to ambulance crews. Yet with an average of approximately eleven redirections per day, or an ambulance being redirected once every three eight-hour shifts, this disturbance is likely to be outweighed by the resulting performance gain.

To place the performance gain into perspective, we added additional weekly shifts to the shift roster. The performance gain from our approach is equivalent to adding more than seven weekly ambulance shifts, while our approach does not require additional available resources (see [12] for more details).

6   Conclusion

We captured the way in which dispatch agents currently make decisions on which ambulance to dispatch to a request. Insights from the fitted decision tree were used to enrich the commonly assumed closest-idle dispatch policy, using penalty values reflecting the risk associated with ambulance characteristics. Subsequently, we illustrated an application of the captured dispatch policy by defining two enhancements to current practices and evaluating their performance in a simulation. The proposed approach can be applied to other EMS regions to improve ambulance dispatching.

Dispatch agents in the EMS region Brabant-Zuidoost have indicated to be very happy about the potential of these enhancements to the current dispatch policy in their attempt to push the on-time performance of highly urgent A1 requests to 95%. These process adaptations are essentially free and instantaneous measures to improve performance without increasing the available ambulance capacity. As future research, it is interesting to conduct a field experiment to confirm the potential of the proposed enhancements in practice.

Acknowledgements. We would like to thank GGD Brabant-Zuidoost for providing us dispatch data and the overall collaboration. We would like to thank Marko Boon for his help with the development of our simulation model.

References

1. Aringhieri, R., Bruni, M.E., Khodaparasti, S., Van Essen, J.: Emergency medical services and beyond: addressing new challenges through a wide literature review. Comput. Oper. Res. **78**, 349–368 (2017)
2. Bélanger, V., Ruiz, A., Soriano, P.: Recent optimization models and trends in location, relocation, and dispatching of emergency medical vehicles. Eur. J. Oper. Res. **272**(1), 1–23 (2019)
3. Donnot, B., Guyon, I., Schoenauer, M., Panciatici, P., Marot, A.: Introducing machine learning for power system operation support. arXiv preprint arXiv:1709.09527 (2017)
4. Jagtenberg, C.J., Bhulai, S., van der Mei, R.D.: Dynamic ambulance dispatching: is the closest-idle policy always optimal? Health Care Manage. Sci. **20**(4), 517–531 (2016). https://doi.org/10.1007/s10729-016-9368-0
5. Lafond, D., Roberge-Vallières, B., Vachon, F., Tremblay, S.: Judgment analysis in a dynamic multitask environment: capturing nonlinear policies using decision trees. J. Cogn. Eng. Decis. Making **11**(2), 122–135 (2017)
6. Lafond, D., Tremblay, S., Banbury, S.: Cognitive shadow: a policy capturing tool to support naturalistic decision making. In: 2013 IEEE International Multi-Disciplinary Conference on Cognitive Methods in Situation Awareness and Decision Support (CogSIMA), pp. 139–142. IEEE (2013)

7. Lee, S.: Role of parallelism in ambulance dispatching. IEEE Trans. Syst. Man Cybern.: Syst. **44**(8), 1113–1122 (2014)
8. Lim, C.S., Mamat, R., Braunl, T.: Impact of ambulance dispatch policies on performance of emergency medical services. IEEE Trans. Intell. Transp. Syst. **12**(2), 624–632 (2011)
9. Maghrebi, M., Sammut, C., Waller, S.T.: Feasibility study of automatically performing the concrete delivery dispatching through machine learning techniques. Eng. Constr. Archit. Manage. **22**(5), 573–590 (2015)
10. Maxwell, M.S., Restrepo, M., Henderson, S.G., Topaloglu, H.: Approximate dynamic programming for ambulance redeployment. INFORMS J. Comput. **22**(2), 266–281 (2010)
11. Pedregosa, F., et al.: Scikit-learn: machine learning in Python. J. Mach. Learn. Res. **12**, 2825–2830 (2011)
12. Theeuwes, N.: Formalization and improvement of ambulance dispatching in Brabant-Zuidoost. Master's thesis, Eindhoven University of Technology (2019)
13. Van Barneveld, T.: The minimum expected penalty relocation problem for the computation of compliance tables for ambulance vehicles. INFORMS J. Comput. **28**(2), 370–384 (2016)

Countrywide Origin-Destination Matrix Prediction and Its Application for COVID-19

Renhe Jiang[1,4], Zhaonan Wang[1], Zekun Cai[1], Chuang Yang[1], Zipei Fan[1,4],
Tianqi Xia[2], Go Matsubara[2], Hiroto Mizuseki[3], Xuan Song[1,4(✉)],
and Ryosuke Shibasaki[1]

[1] The University of Tokyo, Tokyo, Japan
{jiangrh,znwang,songxuan}@csis.u-tokyo.ac.jp
[2] LocationMind Inc., Tokyo, Japan
[3] BlogWatcher Inc., Tokyo, Japan
[4] Southern University of Science and Technology, Shenzhen, China

Abstract. Modeling and predicting human mobility are of great significance to various application scenarios such as intelligent transportation system, crowd management, and disaster response. In particular, in a severe pandemic situation like COVID-19, human movements among different regions are taken as the most important point for understanding and forecasting the epidemic spread in a country. Thus, in this study, we collect big human GPS trajectory data covering the total 47 prefectures of Japan and model the daily human movements between each pair of prefectures with time-series Origin-Destination (OD) matrix. Then, given the historical observations from past days, we predict the countrywide OD matrices for the future one or more weeks by proposing a novel deep learning model called Origin-Destination Convolutional Recurrent Network (ODCRN). It integrates the recurrent and 2-dimensional graph convolutional components to deal with the highly complex spatiotemporal dependencies in sequential OD matrices. Experiment results over the entire COVID-19 period demonstrate the superiority of our proposed methodology over existing OD prediction models. Last, we apply the predicted countrywide OD matrices to the SEIR model, one of the most classic and widely used epidemic simulation model, to forecast the COVID-19 infection numbers for the entire Japan. The simulation results also demonstrate the high reliability and applicability of our countrywide OD prediction model for a pandemic scenario like COVID-19.

Keywords: Human mobility · Origin-destination · OD matrix · Graph convolutional network · Deep learning · COVID-19

1 Introduction

Nowadays big human mobility data are being collected from various sources such as smart phone apps, car navigation systems, WiFi access points, and laser

---

R. Jiang and Z. Wang—Equal contribution.

© Springer Nature Switzerland AG 2021
Y. Dong et al. (Eds.): ECML PKDD 2021, LNAI 12978, pp. 319–334, 2021.
https://doi.org/10.1007/978-3-030-86514-6_20

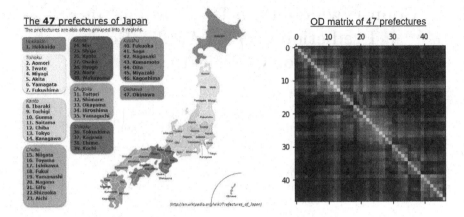

Fig. 1. Illustration of the total 47 prefectures of Japan (left) and the OD matrix among the 47 prefectures on 2020/01/01 (right).

sensors, with which modeling and predicting crowd flow [16,20,39,40] and taxi/bike demand [13,25,31,35] become possible and essential for smart-city application scenarios. On the other hand, the coronavirus disease 2019 (COVID-19) outbreak has swept more than 180 countries and territories since late January 2020, which has caused significant losses to public health as well as the economy at a worldwide scale. Against this background, human mobility data are also utilized to understand and forecast the epidemic spread situation in city, country, or all over the world, as human movements are taken as the most important factor for highly contagious diseases with human-to-human transmission. In this study, to model and predict the COVID-19 spread over the entire Japan, we collect big human GPS trajectory data covering the total 47 prefectures of Japan and model the daily human movements between each pair of prefectures with time-series Origin-Destination (OD) matrix. With the daily OD matrix, we can easily know how many people move from one prefecture to another, and further apply the SEIR model, one of the most fundamental compartmental models in epidemiology, to simulate the COVID-19 infection number for each prefecture of Japan by taking the effects of human movements among prefectures into account.

To this end, we aim to predict the countrywide OD matrices of Japan as illustrated in Fig. 1. However, it is a non-trivial and quite unique task in the following aspects. (1) Each prefecture is in an irregular polygon shape, which forms together as a non-euclidean space. Normal convolution neural network (CNN) [22] is difficult to be directly applied to capture the spatial dependencies among the prefectures. Therefore, some grid-based state-of-the-arts for OD matrix prediction including GEML [32] and CSTN [26] can't perform well on our prefecture-level OD matrix prediction task, neither for some CNN-based deep models for crowd flow prediction tasks [20,25,35,39,40,42]. (2) The spatial dependencies simultaneously exist along both Origin axis and Destination axis in OD matrix. Taking the capital city Tokyo as an example, people from other prefectures transit to Tokyo, meanwhile Tokyo people leave Tokyo for other prefectures. (3) It is necessary to predict multiple days of OD matrix like one week or more for COVID-19 application scenario, so that experts and officials can correspondingly make and publish the intervention policies for the following period of time. However, previous OD matrix models (i.e., GEML [32], CSTN [26], and MPGCN [29]) are only able to do next-one-step forecast, where each step is merely half an hour or one hour.

To tackle these challenges, we present Origin-Destination Convolutional Recurrent Network (ODCRN) for multi-step Origin-Destination matrix prediction. Specifically, ODCRN consists of two types of graph convolution units: one takes in a pre-defined static graph (*e.g.* adjacency matrix) as auxiliary input, while the other utilizes Dynamic Graph Constructor (DGC) to dynamically generate an OD graph pair based on the current observation. Each unit recurrently performs OD convolution (OD-Conv) to simultaneously capture the two-sided spatial dependency in Origin-Destination matrix and the temporal dependency in observational sequence. In addition, ODCRN has an encoder-decoder structure to firstly encode a sequence of OD matrices into hidden tensors, then step-wise decode them to make a sequence of predictions. In summary, our work has the following contributions:

- We collect big human GPS trajectory data for the total 47 prefectures of Japan that cover the entire COVID-19 period from 2020/01/01 to 2021/02/28.
- We propose a novel deep model for countrywide OD matrix prediction that utilizes the graph convolution network and the recurrent neural network to capture the complex spatial and temporal dependencies in the countrywide OD matrix sequence.
- We implement a classic epidemic simulation model (SEIR model) to forecast the COVID-19 infection number for the entire Japan by taking the human movements among prefectures into account.
- We further collect the reported COVID-19 infection number of each prefecture in Japan. With the ground-truth infection data and the epidemic simulation model, we validate the applicability of our predicted OD matrices for long-term countrywide COVID-19 infection forecast.

The remainder of this paper is organized as follows. In Sect. 2, we introduce the related works about the crowd/traffic flow prediction and mobility-based COVID-19 prediction. In Sect. 3, we describe our problem definition. In Sect. 4, we propose a deep learning model for countrywide OD matrix prediction. In Sect. 5, we implement an OD matrix-based epidemic simulation model. In Sect. 6, we present the evaluation results about OD matrix prediction and COVID-19 prediction. In Sect. 7, we give our conclusion.

2   Related Work

2.1   Crowd and Traffic Flow Prediction

Trajectory-based deep learning models [10,11,18,19,27] have been proposed to predict each individual's movement by utilizing the recurrent neural networks

(RNNs). However, due to the limitation of scalability, it is difficult to apply the trajectory-based models to a country-level prediction task as there are just too many trajectories to learn. On the other hand, by meshing a city map into several grid-regions and aggregating the trajectories for each grid-region, crowd and traffic flow information can be obtained [16]. Following this strategy, a series of spatiotemporal models [25,31,35,36,39,42] were proposed to predict the demand, inflow and outflow of taxi/bike/crowd for each grid-region. Thanks to the euclidean property of the grid space, these approaches can employ normal convolution neural networks (CNNs) to capture the spatial dependency in an analogous way with the image/video prediction task. In parallel with the grid-based modeling strategy, graph is used as a more general solution for modeling the crowd/traffic demand or flow among irregular regions with arbitrary polygon shapes [3,13,30]. Also, some graph-based models like STGCN [37], AST-GCN [14], DCRNN [24], and GraphWaveNet [33] are proposed to predict the traffic volume recorded by the roadway sensors. To learn the spatial correlations among nodes, all of these models employ graph convolution network (GCN) that can work in a non-euclidean space.

However, no matter based on grid or graph, the inflow and outflow models can only indicate how many people will flow into or out from a region over a period of time. They can't answer how many of these people or cars come from or transit to which regions. To address this, [20,40] are proposed to model the grid-based crowd transition which depicts how a crowd of people transit among the entire mesh-grids. In particular, GEML [32], CSTN [26], and MPGCN [29] are specially designed for OD matrix prediction task. But still they are not ideal or well-validated solutions for our COVID-19 application scenario due to the following reasons. (1) [26,29,32] are tailored for single-step OD prediction, while our task requires a multi-step prediction. Because forecasting the COVID-19 infection numbers for the next one or more weeks rather than only one day is more meaningful and useful for experts and policy makers. Correspondingly, the OD matrices must be predicted for multiple days. (2) [26,32] are based on mesh-grids, while our OD matrix is based on prefectures that have irregular shapes. (3) The OD prediction of [26,29,32] is conducted at a citywide and level in short term (1 h), while our task needs to do the OD prediction at a countrywide level with relatively longer term (one or more weeks).

2.2   Mobility-Based COVID-19 Simulation

Since the outbreak of COVID-19, mobility data has been widely used to model the disease's spatial propagation and shown great potential [1,4,6–8,12,21,23]. For example, [7] utilizes the Baidu Migration Data [1] and the airline transportation data to simulate the spread of COVID-19 on both national and international levels, [23] infers the undocumented infection rate of COVID-19 and its substantial impact in conjunction with mobility data.

Accurately capture the inter-regional mobility patterns is essential for modeling and predicting disease spread. The mobility patterns used in current studies mainly derived from three aspects: (a) Official Trip Census Data [4,8,12]. (b)

Mobilephone Location Data [6,7,23]. (c) Transportation Flux Data (e.g., Airline, Railway) [7,8]. Based on data sources' spatial scale, propagation simulations with different spatial resolutions have been proposed, e.g., [4] models the spread of COVID-19 in Italy at the province level with the official published commuter data among cities. Besides, some works predicted the future propagations to validate the model's efficiency [6,21], e.g., [6] did out-of-sample prediction of daily confirmed cases for the Chicago metro area. However, none of these works consider possible mobility changes in the future. Instead, they used historical mobility directly when predicting, which is our work trying to address.

3   Problem Definition

Given big human GPS trajectory data, Origin-Destination (OD) matrix prediction can be performed through the following definitions.

Definition 1 (Trajectory and Trip Segmentation): Typically, a user's trajectory is a sequence of timestamp-location pairs denoted as $[(t_1, l_1), (t_2, l_2), ..., (t_n, l_n)]$, where each location l is represented by a longitude-latitude coordinate. Then we do trip segmentation for each user's trajectory and obtain the origin and destination of each trip as follows:

$$[(t_1, l_1), (t_2, l_2), ..., (t_n, l_n)] \xrightarrow{segmentation} [(o_1, d_1), (o_2, d_2), ..., (o_m, d_m)], \quad (1)$$

where the original trajectory is segmented into m trips, i.e. m OD pairs, $o.l$ and $d.l$ are the origin and destination location, $o.t$ is the departure time leaving from origin o, and $d.t$ is the arrival time for destination. The origin and destination locations are essentially a series of stay points among any consecutive two of which people move from one to another by different means of transportation such as TRAIN, BUS, WALK, BIKE, and etc. We let $\mathcal{T}$ denote all of the trip-segmented trajectories.

Definition 2 (Origin-Destination Matrix): Given a spatial area divided into N non-overlapping regions $\{r_1, r_2, ..., r_N\}$ and a temporal range equally divided into T consecutive and non-overlapping timeslots $\{\tau_1, \tau_2, ..., \tau_T\}$, Origin-Destination (OD) matrix $\Omega \in \mathbb{R}^{N \times N}$ can be aggregated from the trip-segmented trajectories $\mathcal{T}$. OD transition number Ω_τ^{ij} between each two regions r_i, r_j with respect to timeslot τ is defined as follows:

$$\Omega_\tau^{ij} = |\{(o, d) \in \mathcal{T} \mid o.l \in r_i \wedge d.l \in r_j \wedge o.t \in \tau \wedge d.t \in \tau\}|, \quad (2)$$

where $|\cdot|$ denotes the cardinality of a set. In our study, we take the entire Japan as the spatial area, total 47 prefectures as the non-overlapping 47 regions, and set each timeslot τ as one day. Since the main application scenario of our study is COVID-19, we collect the GPS trajectory data from the beginning of COVID-19 pandemic to the very latest, i.e., 2020/01/01~2021/02/28, 425 days in total.

Definition 3 (Origin-Destination Matrix Prediction): Given historical a steps of OD matrices $X_\tau \in \mathbb{R}^{\alpha \times N \times N} = [\Omega_{\tau-\alpha+1}, ..., \Omega_{\tau-1}, \Omega_\tau]$ from timeslot τ-$(\alpha-1)$ to to τ, predicting the next β steps of OD matrices $Y_\tau \in \mathbb{R}^{\beta \times N \times N} = [\Omega_{\tau+1}, \Omega_{\tau+2}, ..., \Omega_{\tau+\beta}]$ from timeslot τ to $\tau+\beta$ is to build a model f as follows:

$$X_\tau = [\Omega_{\tau-\alpha+1}, ..., \Omega_{\tau-1}, \Omega_\tau] \xrightarrow[\theta]{f(\cdot)} Y_\tau = [\Omega_{\tau+1}, \Omega_{\tau+2}, ..., \Omega_{\tau+\beta}] \quad (3)$$

4 OD Matrix Prediction Model

4.1 Overview

We present Origin-Destination Convolutional Recurrent Network (ODCRN), demonstrated in Fig. 2, for multi-step Origin-Destination matrix prediction. To be specific, ODCRN consists of two types of computational units: one type of Origin-Destination Convolutional Recurrent Unit (ODCRU) takes in a pre-defined static graph (*e.g.* adjacency matrix) as auxiliary input, while the other ODCRU utilizes Dynamic Graph Constructor (DGC) to dynamically generate an OD graph pair based on the current observation. Each ODCRU cell recurrently performs OD convolution (OD-Conv) to simultaneously capture the two-sided spatial dependency (i.e., along Origin axis and Destination axis) in OD matrix and the temporal dependency in observational sequence. In addition, ODCRN has an encoder-decoder structure to firstly encode a sequence of OD matrices into hidden tensors, then stepwise decode them to make a sequence of predictions.

4.2 Origin-Destination Convolution (OD-Conv)

In Origin-Destination matrix, one can observe both local and global spatial correlations which entangle and exist on both sides of the origin and destination. In reality, this two-sided dependency does not necessarily hold equivalent on the origin side and destination side. It is quite straightforward that the correlation between prefectures being origins depends on the similarity of their residential functionality, while the correlation between prefectures being destinations is mostly decided by the similarity of their commercial or entertaining functionality. To capture this special two-sided dependency, one intuitive solution is to treat an OD matrix as an image (of one channel) and filter it with regular convolutional kernel. However, this approach is in fact inappropriate as it not only loses the global view but regards submatrices in an OD matrix as equivalent, in which most OD transitions actually happen close to the diagonal. Keeping the big picture in mind, we adopt MGCNN [28], which is an extended bidimensional form of GCN based on the two-dimensional discrete Fourier transform (2D-DFT), and propose an Origin-Destination Convolution (OD-Conv) to solve the problem, which is formulated as:

$$\underline{H} = \sigma(\Theta \star_{(P_{(O)}, P_{(D)})} \underline{\Omega}) = \sigma\left(\sum_{k_o, k_d=0}^{K} \underline{\Omega} \times_1 \tilde{P}_{(O)}^{k_o} \times_2 \tilde{P}_{(D)}^{k_d} \times_3 W_{k_o, k_d} \right) \quad (4)$$

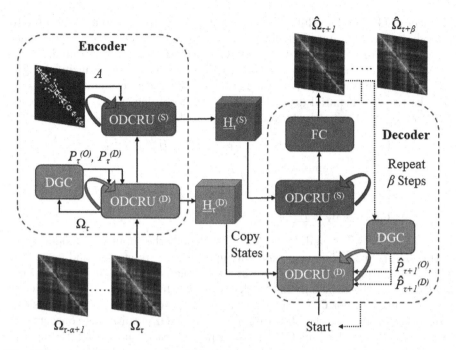

Fig. 2. Proposed Origin-Destination Convolutional Recurrent Network (ODCRN) for multi-step OD matrix prediction. ODCRN consists of two types of computational units (ODCRU): one takes in pre-defined static graph as auxiliary input, the other dynamically generates od graph pair based on the current observation.

In the equation, $\underline{\Omega} \in \mathbb{R}^{N \times N \times \nu}$ and $\underline{H} \in \mathbb{R}^{N \times N \times \mu}$ are the input and hidden state of an OD-Conv operation, which is denoted by $\Theta \star_{(P_{(O)}, P_{(D)})}$, where Θ or W stands for learnable parameters given an OD graph pair $(P_{(O)}, P_{(D)})$ representing the correlations of prefectures being origins and being destinations, respectively. It is noteworthy that MPGCN [29] also employs Eq. 4 to handle the two-sided dependency in OD matrices and further utilizes LSTM and pre-defines a rule for deriving momentary correlation graphs to model temporal dynamics in OD matrices. However, we find these two additions are in fact suboptimal and propose ODCRU with DGC for finer temporal dynamic modelling.

4.3   Origin-Destination Convolutional Recurrent Unit (ODCRU)

Convolutional Recurrent Unit (CRU) is a class of computational methods that utilizes convolution to replace matrix multiplication as the basic operation in a recurrent cell (*e.g.* GRU to ConvGRU). Such substitution equips the unit with extra capability to capture localized spatial dependency, with the natural advantage of handling sequential dependency by the recurrent structure. As a result, CRU has been widely adopted in not only video tasks [34], but also general spatio-temporal prediction problems [20,26,38,42]. Moreover, the recent advances in Graph Convolution Networks (GCN) [5,15,28] prompt attempts to generalize CRU to Graph Convolutional Recurrent Unit (GCRU) [17,24] so that the global, non-Euclidean spatial dependency could be further captured.

In a similar fashion, we extend CRU to ODCRU by utilizing Origin-Destination Convolution (OD-Conv) in each recurrent cell to simultaneously capture the two-sided spatial dependency and temporal dependency in a sequence of OD matrices. Taking the form of GRU, we define ODCRU as:

$$
\begin{cases}
\mathbf{u}_\tau = sigmoid(\Theta_\mathbf{u} \star_{(P_{(O)},P_{(D)})} [\underline{\Omega}_\tau^{(l)}, \ \underline{H}_{\tau-1}^{(l)}] + b_\mathbf{u}) \\
\mathbf{r}_\tau = sigmoid(\Theta_\mathbf{r} \star_{(P_{(O)},P_{(D)})} [\underline{\Omega}_\tau^{(l)}, \ \underline{H}_{\tau-1}^{(l)}] + b_\mathbf{r}) \\
\underline{C}_\tau = tanh(\Theta_C \star_{(P_{(O)},P_{(D)})} [\underline{\Omega}_\tau^{(l)}, \ (\mathbf{r}_\tau \odot \underline{H}_{\tau-1}^{(l)})] + b_C \\
\underline{H}_\tau^{(l)} = \mathbf{u}_\tau \odot \underline{H}_{\tau-1}^{(l)} + (1 - \mathbf{u}_\tau) \odot \underline{C}_\tau
\end{cases}
\tag{5}
$$

where $\underline{\Omega}_\tau \in \mathbb{R}^{N \times N \times \nu}$ and $\underline{H}_\tau \in \mathbb{R}^{N \times N \times \mu}$ denote the input and hidden state at timeslot τ; $\mathbf{u}_\tau$, $\mathbf{r}_\tau$ and $\underline{C}_\tau$ represent update gate, reset gate and candidate state, respectively; and $\Theta_\mathbf{u}$, $\Theta_\mathbf{r}$, Θ_C are learnable parameters in corresponding OD-Convs. As the basic building block of ODCRN framework, ODCRU requires auxiliary inputs of an OD graph pair $(P_{(O)}, P_{(D)})$ to account for the two-sided dependency. Based on the observation that most OD transitions concentrated around the diagonal of an OD matrix, one can easily infer that the spatial closeness plays an important role in OD matrix prediction. In practice, we adopt the definition of adjacency matrix to represent this spatial locality, formally:

$$
A_{i,j} = \begin{cases} 1, & \text{if prefecture } i \text{ and } j \text{ are geographically adjacent} \\ 0, & \text{otherwise} \end{cases}
\tag{6}
$$

Then, letting $(P_{(O)}, P_{(D)}) = (A, A^\mathsf{T})$ gives the most straightforward assignment for the input OD graph pair. However, solely relying on this definition is not enough for three reasons: (1) global view is absent; (2) two-sided dependency is not really handled because adjacency matrix is symmetric; (3) dynamic spatial correlation is overlooked since A is time-invariant. The dynamicity of spatial correlation manifests itself in the cases where people commute across-prefecture for work in workdays and go out on weekends.

4.4   Dynamic Graph Constructor (DGC)

To solve the aforementioned three problems, we propose a Dynamic Graph Constructor (DGC) to dynamically generate an observation-dependent OD graph pair at each timeslot. This idea is rooted in the field of graph signal processing where an important task is to learn a reasonable graph structure based on observational data [9,14,41]. In our case, we aim to learn a pair of time-variant graphs to represent the dynamic two-sided dependency in prefectures. Specifically, we propose the learning schema below to satisfy our needs:

$$
\begin{cases}
P_\tau^{(O)} = softmax(relu(\Omega_\tau W_O \Omega_\tau^\mathsf{T})) \\
P_\tau^{(D)} = softmax(relu(\Omega_\tau^\mathsf{T} W_D \Omega_\tau))
\end{cases}
\tag{7}
$$

where $\Omega_\tau \in \mathbb{R}^{N \times N}$ is the input of OD matrix observation at timeslot τ; $W_O \in \mathbb{R}^{N \times N}$ and $W_D \in \mathbb{R}^{N \times N}$ are two learnable parameter matrices, used for discovering hidden patterns under destinations and origins, respectively; *relu* rectifies the core term to be non-negative and *softmax* normalizes each row. The learnt OD graph pair $(P_\tau^{(O)}, P_\tau^{(D)})$ has good properties to represent the time-variant, two-sided, entangled local and global dependencies on a scale of 0 to 1.

5   OD Matrix Based Epidemic Simulation Model

SIR is seen as one of the most fundamental compartmental models in epidemiology, widely used for modeling and predicting the spread of infectious diseases such as measles, mumps and rubella [2]. SEIR, as a variant of SIR, consists of four compartments: S for the number of susceptible, E for the number of exposed, which means the individuals in an incubation period but not yet infectious, I for the number of infectious, and R for the number of recovered or deceased (or immune) individuals. To represent the number of susceptible, infected and recovered individuals varying over time, SEIR model is formally expressed by the following set of ordinary differential equations:

$$\frac{dS}{dt} = \mu N - \beta S \frac{I}{N} - \mu S$$
$$\frac{dE}{dt} = \beta S \frac{I}{N} - \varepsilon E - \mu E$$
$$\frac{dI}{dt} = \varepsilon E - \gamma I - \mu I \tag{8}$$
$$\frac{dR}{dt} = \gamma I - \mu R$$

where N = S + E + I + R, β is the effective contact rate of infected individual[1], ε is the progression rate to infectious state, γ and μ are the rates of recovery and mortality, respectively. In our implementation, we ignore μ and only use β, ε, γ to construct the model.

However, the classic SIR and SEIR model can only simulate the infection number varying over time for single region. Thus, in this study, we extend it to a multi-region SEIR model that can simultaneously simulate the time-varying infection numbers for multiple regions and take the OD transitions among regions into account. To this end, we introduce an SEIR matrix $\Psi \in \mathbb{R}^{N \times 4}$ to denote the S, E, I, R numbers of N regions. Note that according to the population density and the intervention policy, the effective contact rate β varies from region to region also from time to time, so we introduce a vector $\mathcal{B}_t \in \mathbb{R}^N$ to denote the different β values for N regions at time t. Meanwhile, ε and γ prove to be decided by the intrinsic property of specific infectious disease, therefore, regions share the same time-constant value under COVID-19 scenario.

$$\Psi_t^{i,:} = [S_t^{(i)}, E_t^{(i)}, I_t^{(i)}, R_t^{(i)}] \xrightarrow[\mathcal{B}_t^{(i)}, \varepsilon, \gamma]{Eq.\ (8)} \Psi_t'^{i,:} = [S_t'^{(i)}, E_t'^{(i)}, I_t'^{(i)}, R_t'^{(i)}], \forall i \in N \tag{9}$$

---

[1] β here different with Definition 3 is a widely used notation for epidemic parameter.

$$+ \Delta \Psi_t = [\overline{\Omega_t}]^T \cdot \Psi_t \tag{10}$$

$$- \Delta \Psi_t = [\overline{\Omega_t}]^\Sigma \odot \Psi_t \tag{11}$$

$$\Psi_{t+1} = \Psi_t' + \sigma(+\Delta\Psi_t - \Delta\Psi_t) \tag{12}$$

Then the OD matrix-based SEIR algorithm is proposed as follows: (1) Initialize the SEIR matrix Ψ with the population data and infection data of each prefecture; (2) Given $\mathcal{B}_t^{(i)}$ and ε, γ, the S, E, I, R numbers for each region r_i can be updated as Eq. (9); (3) Normalize the OD transition matrix by row to get the transition probability from origin-region r_i to destination-region r_j, and further set the diagonal value to zero to eliminate the self-transition value; (4) We denote the normalized OD matrix with zero diagonal value as $\overline{\Omega}$. Using $\overline{\Omega}$, the inflow of S, E, I, R coming from other regions (i.e., $+\Delta\Psi$) can be calculated with Eq. (10), where $[]^T$ denotes matrix transpose and $\cdot$ denotes matrix multiplication; (5) To derive the outflow of S, E, I, R (leaving SEIR) of each region (i.e., $-\Delta\Psi$), we sum $\overline{\Omega}$ by row to get the total outside transition probability of each origin-region, and let S, E, I, R people in each origin-region share the same transition value. These two operations are together denoted as $[]^\Sigma$. As shown by Eq. (11), $-\Delta\Psi$ can be calculated through element-wise product $\odot$ between $[\overline{\Omega}]^\Sigma \in \mathbb{R}^{N \times 4}$ and $\Psi \in \mathbb{R}^{N \times 4}$; (6) Ψ can be updated from t to $t+1$ by adding up the three parts, namely intra-region SEIR, inflow SEIR, and outflow SEIR as Eq. (12). σ is a new introduced parameter that denotes the actual inter-region transition rate under epidemic control policies such as self-quarantine and work-from-home.

In our study, ε, γ, and σ are empirically tuned and set to 0.2, 0.1, 0.1, respectively. By using the daily OD matrices $[\Omega_1, \Omega_2, ..., \Omega_T]$ and reported COVID-19 infection number of each prefecture $[I_1^{1:N}, I_2^{1:N}, ..., I_T^{1:N}]$, we employ Particle Swarm Optimization (PSO) algorithm to estimate the time-varying and region-varying $\mathcal{B}$ through Eq. (9)–(12). Finally, using the optimized $\mathcal{B}$ and the predicted OD matrices $[\hat{\Omega}_{T+1}, \hat{\Omega}_{T+2}, ..., \hat{\Omega}_{T+7}]$, we can forecast the COVID-19 infection numbers $[\hat{I}_{T+1}^{1:N}, \hat{I}_{T+2}^{1:N}, ..., \hat{I}_{T+7}^{1:N}]$ for the future one week via Eq. (9)–(12).

6 Experiment

6.1 Data

We collaborate with Blogwatcher Inc. to get big human GPS trajectory data that cover 5 million people in the 47 prefectures of Japan. The location data are collected through smartphone apps that have a built-in module provided by Blogwatcher Inc. under user's consent. Any personally identifiable information were not collected. Data attributes are anonymized ID, timestamp, longitude, latitude, accuracy, OS type. The raw data file of one month is approximately 1TB in csv format, and contains around 180 GPS records per day per user. After data cleaning and trip segmentation, each ID has average 10 GPS records corresponding to either origin location or destination location. We select 2020/1/1/–2021/2/28 (425 days) as the target time period. Correspondingly, we collect COVID-19 infection number of each prefecture in the same time period. To check the representativeness of our GPS data, we further compare the population proportion of each prefecture with Census data and obtain $\mathbb{R}^2 \geq 0.8$. According to Definition 1–3, OD transition data among 47 prefectures are stored as a (425, 47, 47) tensor and COVID19 infection data are stored as a (425, 47) tensor.

6.2 Setting

We make natural logarithm of the original OD tensor to have a relatively neat distribution. We split the data with ratio 6.4:1.6:2 to get train/validation/test datasets respectively. Adam is employed as the optimizer, where the batch size set to 16 and the learning rate to 0.0001. The training algorithm would either be early-stopped if the validation error converged within 20 epochs or be stopped after 200 epochs. The observation step α and prediction step β are both set to 7, which means we use the past one week of observations to do the next one week prediction. PyTorch was used to implement our proposed model. The experiments are performed on a GPU server with four 1080Ti graphics cards. Two layers of ODCRU are respectively used to construct the encoder and decoder of our proposed ODCRN. In each ODCRU, the size of the hidden state is set to 32. Finally, we evaluate the overall performance on the multi-step OD matrix prediction using three metrics: *MSE* (Mean Square Error), *RMSE* (Root Mean Square Error), *MAE* (Mean Absolute Error).

6.3 Evaluation on OD Matrix Prediction

We implement four classes of baselines to compare and evaluate our proposed model on the OD matrix prediction task, including:

Naive Forecasting Methods: (1) MonthlyAverage. We take the average of past 28 days of OD matrices as the prediction. **(2) CopyLastWeek.** We directly copy the OD matrix from last week (recent 7 days) as the prediction.

Video-Like Predictive Models: (3) ST-ResNet [39]. ST-ResNet is proposed to predict crowd flow of each region in a city. This model merges the time and flow dimensions together and uses three branches of CNN network to extract the seasonality of the data. **(4) PCRN** [42]. PCRN is built based on ConvGRU to take both recent observations and periodic weekly/daily patterns into account.

Graph-based Spatio-Temporal Models: (5) ST-GCN [37]. ST-GCN is one of the earliest models that integrate temporal convolution (TCN) and graph convolution (GCN) to do spatiotemporal modeling. **(6) DCRNN** [24]. DCRNN developed a new type of GCN called diffusion convolution and embedded it into GRU to perform recurrent graph convolution. **(7) Graph WaveNet** [33]. Graph WaveNet is also based on TCN and GCN, but it proposes an adaptive/learnable graph to replace the static adjacency graph.

OD Matrix Prediction Models: (8) GEML [32]. The origin-destination matrix prediction model is a state-of-the-art graph-based transition prediction model that utilizes graph embedding and periodic-skip LSTM to predict the OD matrix. **(9) CSTN** [26]. CSTN is a grid-based model for taxi OD matrix

Table 1. Comparison of overall performance between four classes of baselines and proposed ODCRN on multi-step origin-destination matrix prediction task in power on natural exponential function

Model	MSE	RMSE	MAE
MonthlyAverage	0.1915	0.4376	0.3000
CopyLastWeek	0.2630	0.5128	0.3191
STResNet [39]	0.1648	0.4060	0.2822
PCRN [42]	0.1636	0.4044	0.2864
STGCN [37]	0.1656	0.4070	0.2910
DCRNN [24]	0.1682	0.4102	0.2954
Graph WaveNet [33]	0.1632	0.4040	0.2887
GEML [32]	0.1606	0.4008	0.2806
CSTN [26]	0.1608	0.4010	0.2857
MPGCN [29]	0.1609	0.4011	0.2859
ODCRN (w/o DGC)	0.1585	0.3982	0.2820
ODCRN	**0.1558**	**0.3947**	**0.2802**

prediction, where the OD matrix and DO matrix are respectively modeled by two branches of euclidean CNNs and then fused together. **(10) MPGCN** [29]. MPGCN applied 2DGCN to multiple graphs including adjacency graph, POI similarity graph, and correlation graph to predict the OD matrix.

Overall Performance: In Table 1, we compare the overall performance between the adopted four classes of baselines and proposed ODCRN on the multi-step OD matrix prediction task. Overall, deep learning based approaches as a group

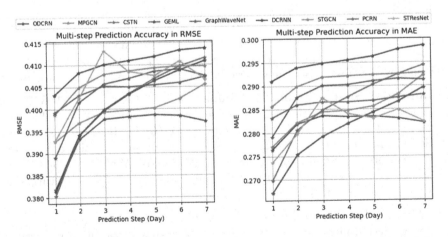

Fig. 3. Comparison of stepwise performance between deep learning based models on multi-step origin-destination matrix prediction task

outperforms two naive forecasting methods to a great extent. The experimental results also show that the difference between video-like and graph-based predictive models are not significant. This phenomenon might be explained by the way we define the static graph, for which we employ adjacency matrix that only accounts for local dependency. In addition, OD matrix prediction oriented models demonstrate superior performance compared with regular graph-based methods. Our proposed ODCRN model, by simultaneously capturing the dynamic two-sided spatial and temporal dependency, reaches the best performance in all metrics. Besides, Fig. 3 illustrates the comparison of stepwise performance between all deep learning based models. Generally, the prediction accuracy drops as the forecasting horizon increases. Compared with other models, ODCRN turns out to be less prone to extreme values and more stable and consistent throughout the whole-week prediction period.

6.4   Evaluation on COVID-19 Simulation

With the predicted OD matrices, we use the OD matrix based SEIR model Eq. (9)–(12) to forecast the COVID-19 infection numbers from 2020/12/12 to 2021/1/6 (four weeks). The epidemic parameter $\mathcal{B}$ is estimated with the COVID-19 data from 2020/11/12 to 2020/12/11. We demonstrate the performance over two metropolitan areas as shown in Fig. 4. Kanto metropolitan area (Fig. 4-Left) consists of four prefectures, Tokyo, Chiba, Kanagawa, and Saitama. Kansai metropolitan area (Fig. 4-Right) consists of three prefectures, Osaka, Kyoto, and Hyogo. These two areas respectively containing the biggest two cities of Japan, namely Tokyo and Osaka, have extremely high population density, that results in a severe epidemic situation during COVID-19. Japanese government specially lifted The State of Emergency for these two areas. We plot the time-series ground-truth and prediction number with solid line and dotted line respectively as Fig. 4, through which we can see that our model generally achieves a satisfactory performance and behaves rather robust for the first three weeks. However, since the

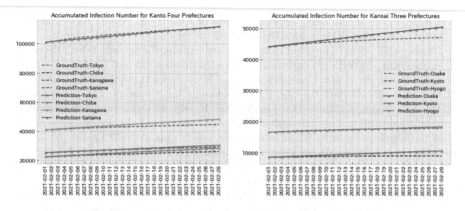

Fig. 4. OD matrix based COVID-19 prediction for Kanto and Kansai area.

epidemic situation in both Kanto and Kansai area was changing very rapidly, the pre-estimated time-varying $\mathcal{B}$ could not remain effective for the fourth week.

7   Conclusion

In the worldwide COVID-19 emergency, human mobility has been taken as a significant factor for the epidemic spread. In this study, we model countrywide human mobility with origin-destination transition matrix and apply it to forecast the COVID-19 infection numbers for all of the prefectures in Japan. For multi-step Origin-Destination matrix prediction, we present a novel deep learning model called Origin-Destination Convolutional Recurrent Network (ODCRN) with encoder-decoder structure. It can perform graph convolution along the Origin axis and the Destination axis to simultaneously capture the two-sided spatial dependency in Origin-Destination matrix. Then we extend the classic SEIR model to OD matrix based epidemic model to do the multi-region infection prediction. The evaluation results demonstrate the high reliability and applicability of our model for COVID-19 scenario. The code of our model has been uploaded to github https://github.com/deepkashiwa20/ODCRN.git.

References

1. https://qianxi.baidu.com/
2. https://en.wikipedia.org/wiki/Compartmental_models_in_epidemiology/The_SIR_model
3. Bai, L., Yao, L., Kanhere, S., Wang, X., Sheng, Q., et al.: STG2Seq: spatial-temporal graph to sequence model for multi-step passenger demand forecasting. In: IJCAI, pp. 1981–1987 (2019)
4. Bertuzzo, E., et al.: The geography of COVID-19 spread in Italy and implications for the relaxation of confinement measures. Nat. Commun. **11**(1), 1–11 (2020)
5. Bruna, J., Zaremba, W., Szlam, A., Lecun, Y.: Spectral networks and locally connected networks on graphs. In: International Conference on Learning Representations (2014)
6. Chang, S., et al.: Mobility network models of COVID-19 explain inequities and inform reopening. Nature **589**(7840), 82–87 (2021)
7. Chinazzi, M., et al.: The effect of travel restrictions on the spread of the 2019 novel coronavirus (COVID-19) outbreak. Science **368**(6489), 395–400 (2020)
8. Della Rossa, F., et al.: A network model of Italy shows that intermittent regional strategies can alleviate the COVID-19 epidemic. Nat. Commun. **11**(1), 1–9 (2020)
9. Diao, Z., Wang, X., Zhang, D., Liu, Y., Xie, K., He, S.: Dynamic spatial-temporal graph convolutional neural networks for traffic forecasting. In: Proceedings of the AAAI Conference on Artificial Intelligence, vol. 33, pp. 890–897 (2019)
10. Feng, J., et al.: DeepMove: predicting human mobility with attentional recurrent networks. In: Proceedings of the 2018 World Wide Web Conference, pp. 1459–1468. International World Wide Web Conferences Steering Committee (2018)
11. Gao, Q., Zhou, F., Trajcevski, G., Zhang, K., Zhong, T., Zhang, F.: Predicting human mobility via variational attention. In: The World Wide Web Conference, pp. 2750–2756. ACM (2019)

12. Gatto, M., et al.: Spread and dynamics of the COVID-19 epidemic in Italy: effects of emergency containment measures. Proc. Natl. Acad. Sci. **117**(19), 10484–10491 (2020)
13. Geng, X., et al.: Spatiotemporal multi-graph convolution network for ride-hailing demand forecasting. In: 2019 AAAI Conference on Artificial Intelligence (AAAI 2019) (2019)
14. Guo, S., Lin, Y., Feng, N., Song, C., Wan, H.: Attention based spatial-temporal graph convolutional networks for traffic flow forecasting. In: Proceedings of the AAAI Conference on Artificial Intelligence, vol. 33, pp. 922–929 (2019)
15. Hamilton, W., Ying, Z., Leskovec, J.: Inductive representation learning on large graphs. In: Advances in Neural Information Processing Systems, pp. 1024–1034 (2017)
16. Hoang, M.X., Zheng, Y., Singh, A.K.: FCCF: forecasting citywide crowd flows based on big data. In: Proceedings of the 24th ACM SIGSPATIAL International Conference on Advances in Geographic Information Systems, pp. 1–10 (2016)
17. Hu, J., Yang, B., Guo, C., Jensen, C.S., Xiong, H.: Stochastic origin-destination matrix forecasting using dual-stage graph convolutional, recurrent neural networks. In: 2020 IEEE 36th International Conference on Data Engineering (ICDE), pp. 1417–1428. IEEE (2020)
18. Jiang, R., et al.: Deep ROI-based modeling for urban human mobility prediction. Proc. ACM Interact. Mob. Wearable Ubiquit. Technol. **2**(1), 1–29 (2018)
19. Jiang, R., et al.: DeepUrbanMomentum: an online deep-learning system for short-term urban mobility prediction. In: AAAI, pp. 784–791 (2018)
20. Jiang, R., et al.: DeepUrbanEvent: a system for predicting citywide crowd dynamics at big events. In: Proceedings of the 25th ACM SIGKDD International Conference on Knowledge Discovery & Data Mining, pp. 2114–2122. ACM (2019)
21. Kraemer, M.U., et al.: The effect of human mobility and control measures on the COVID-19 epidemic in china. Science **368**(6490), 493–497 (2020)
22. LeCun, Y., Bottou, L., Bengio, Y., Haffner, P.: Gradient-based learning applied to document recognition. Proc. IEEE **86**(11), 2278–2324 (1998)
23. Li, R., et al.: Substantial undocumented infection facilitates the rapid dissemination of novel coronavirus (SARS-CoV-2). Science **368**(6490), 489–493 (2020)
24. Li, Y., Yu, R., Shahabi, C., Liu, Y.: Diffusion convolutional recurrent neural network: data-driven traffic forecasting. In: International Conference on Learning Representations (2018)
25. Lin, Z., Feng, J., Lu, Z., Li, Y., Jin, D.: DeepSTN+: context-aware spatial-temporal neural network for crowd flow prediction in metropolis. In: Proceedings of the AAAI Conference on Artificial Intelligence, vol. 33, pp. 1020–1027 (2019)
26. Liu, L., Qiu, Z., Li, G., Wang, Q., Ouyang, W., Lin, L.: Contextualized spatial-temporal network for taxi origin-destination demand prediction. IEEE Trans. Intell. Transp. Syst. **20**(10), 3875–3887 (2019)
27. Liu, Q., Wu, S., Wang, L., Tan, T.: Predicting the next location: a recurrent model with spatial and temporal contexts. In: Proceedings of the AAAI Conference on Artificial Intelligence, vol. 30 (2016)
28. Monti, F., Bronstein, M., Bresson, X.: Geometric matrix completion with recurrent multi-graph neural networks. In: Advances in Neural Information Processing Systems, pp. 3697–3707 (2017)
29. Shi, H., et al.: Predicting origin-destination flow via multi-perspective graph convolutional network. In: 2020 IEEE 36th International Conference on Data Engineering (ICDE), pp. 1818–1821. IEEE (2020)

30. Sun, J., Zhang, J., Li, Q., Yi, X., Liang, Y., Zheng, Y.: Predicting citywide crowd flows in irregular regions using multi-view graph convolutional networks. IEEE Trans. Knowl. Data Eng. (2020)

31. Wang, D., Cao, W., Li, J., Ye, J.: DeepSD: supply-demand prediction for online car-hailing services using deep neural networks. In: 2017 IEEE 33rd International Conference on Data Engineering (ICDE), pp. 243–254. IEEE (2017)

32. Wang, Y., Yin, H., Chen, H., Wo, T., Xu, J., Zheng, K.: Origin-destination matrix prediction via graph convolution: a new perspective of passenger demand modeling. In: Proceedings of the 25th ACM SIGKDD International Conference on Knowledge Discovery & Data Mining, pp. 1227–1235 (2019)

33. Wu, Z., Pan, S., Long, G., Jiang, J., Zhang, C.: Graph WaveNet for deep spatial-temporal graph modeling. In: IJCAI, pp. 1907–1913 (2019)

34. Xingjian, S., Chen, Z., Wang, H., Yeung, D.Y., Wong, W.K., Woo, W.C.: Convolutional LSTM network: a machine learning approach for precipitation nowcasting. In: Advances in Neural Information Processing Systems, pp. 802–810 (2015)

35. Yao, H., et al.: Deep multi-view spatial-temporal network for taxi demand prediction. In: Proceedings of the AAAI Conference on Artificial Intelligence, vol. 32 (2018)

36. Ye, J., Sun, L., Du, B., Fu, Y., Tong, X., Xiong, H.: Co-prediction of multiple transportation demands based on deep spatio-temporal neural network. In: Proceedings of the 25th ACM SIGKDD International Conference on Knowledge Discovery & Data Mining, pp. 305–313 (2019)

37. Yu, B., Yin, H., Zhu, Z.: Spatio-temporal graph convolutional networks: a deep learning framework for traffic forecasting. In: Proceedings of the 27th International Joint Conference on Artificial Intelligence, pp. 3634–3640. AAAI Press (2018)

38. Yuan, Z., Zhou, X., Yang, T.: Hetero-ConvLSTM: a deep learning approach to traffic accident prediction on heterogeneous spatio-temporal data. In: Proceedings of the 24th ACM SIGKDD International Conference on Knowledge Discovery & Data Mining, pp. 984–992. ACM (2018)

39. Zhang, J., Zheng, Y., Qi, D.: Deep spatio-temporal residual networks for citywide crowd flows prediction. In: Proceedings of the AAAI Conference on Artificial Intelligence, vol. 31 (2017)

40. Zhang, J., Zheng, Y., Sun, J., Qi, D.: Flow prediction in spatio-temporal networks based on multitask deep learning. IEEE Trans. Knowl. Data Eng. **32**(3), 468–478 (2019)

41. Zhang, Q., Chang, J., Meng, G., Xiang, S., Pan, C.: Spatio-temporal graph structure learning for traffic forecasting. In: Proceedings of the AAAI Conference on Artificial Intelligence, vol. 34, pp. 1177–1185 (2020)

42. Zonoozi, A., Kim, J.J., Li, X.L., Cong, G.: Periodic-CRN: a convolutional recurrent model for crowd density prediction with recurring periodic patterns. In: IJCAI, pp. 3732–3738 (2018)

Single Model for Influenza Forecasting of Multiple Countries by Multi-task Learning

Taichi Murayama[✉][iD], Shoko Wakamiya[iD], and Eiji Aramaki[iD]

Nara Institute of Science and Technology (NAIST), Ikoma, Japan
{taichi.murayama.mk1,wakamiya,aramaki}@is.naist.jp

Abstract. The accurate forecasting of infectious epidemic diseases such as influenza is a crucial task undertaken by medical institutions. Although numerous flu forecasting methods and models based mainly on historical flu activity data and online user-generated contents have been proposed in previous studies, no flu forecasting model targeting multiple countries using two types of data exists at present. Our paper leverages multi-task learning to tackle the challenge of building one flu forecasting model targeting multiple countries; each country as each task. Also, to develop the flu prediction model with higher performance, we solved two issues; finding suitable search queries, which are part of the user-generated contents, and how to leverage search queries efficiently in the model creation. For the first issue, we propose the transfer approaches from English to other languages. For the second issue, we propose a novel flu forecasting model that takes advantage of search queries using an attention mechanism and extend the model to a multi-task model for multiple countries' flu forecasts. Experiments on forecasting flu epidemics in five countries demonstrate that our model significantly improved the performance by leveraging the search queries and multi-task learning compared to the baselines.

Keywords: Infectious disease · Influenza · User-generated content · Time-series prediction · Attention · Multi-task learning

1 Introduction

The control of infectious diseases is an important task for public health authorities as well as all industry stakeholders worldwide. Various infectious diseases in addition to COVID-19, which has recently attracted global attention, have had a significant impact on global health and the economy. The forecasting of infectious disease epidemics is necessary to execute appropriate measures for their control. In particular, influenza epidemics, a representative class of severe infectious diseases, leads to 290,000 to 650,000 deaths annually [25]. Such instances have motivated public health authorities to forecast the consequences of influenza in different countries.

© Springer Nature Switzerland AG 2021
Y. Dong et al. (Eds.): ECML PKDD 2021, LNAI 12978, pp. 335–350, 2021.
https://doi.org/10.1007/978-3-030-86514-6_21

Many studies relating to flu forecasting models have been conducted for a long time. In recent years, besides models by leveraging historical flu activity, several models have been proposed to forecast the flu volume by exploiting online user-generated contents (UGCs) such as search query data and social media posts to capture human movements as social sensors [4, 10, 22]. The majority of existing flu forecasting models by leveraging UGCs and historical flu activity data focus on one country or each area in one country. However, we assume that it is feasible to create a single flu forecasting model targeting multiple countries because the flu time series in each country exhibit strong seasonality and therefore, hold strong similarity. For example, Pearson correlations of the flu time series in the five countries (US, JP, UK, AU and FR) with different cultures, locations, and languages have a moderate correlation with one another (almost all correlations are over 0.6, refer to Appendix A.[1].) Moreover, in terms of search queries, which are a representative resource, it has been reported that the user search behaviors for health themes in different countries are similar [3, 18, 29]; for example, similar search queries are used when looking for a specific disease. Thus, it is possible that a single model can achieve sufficient flu forecasting for different countries. Also, the training of a single model using various flu-related data can capture the nature of flu epidemics in each country by escaping from overfitting, which is caused by a lesser degree of historical data in one country for training [14, 15].

Our study challenges flu forecasting for various countries with one model as a multi-task problem, which enables two or more tasks to be learned jointly and shares information between the respective tasks. In other words, we treat each country as each task within the framework of multi-task learning. Besides, for the development of a flu prediction model with higher performance, we solve two issues; how to find suitable search queries and how to leverage the search queries in the model construction. We address these issues in the following parts of the paper.

The first issue is how to select queries and keywords in search engines as a resource for flu forecasting. Many methods using UGCs for forecasting the flu volume have been developed since the emergence of Google Flu [10], which demonstrated that the number of search queries capturing human behaviors was a good resource for forecasting. Certain studies [12, 27, 28, 32] have depended on "Google Correlate," which returns English search queries that are the most highly correlated to an input time series, for the selection of suitable search queries. However, this approach cannot be used in many areas (non-English-speaking areas) and it has already been unavailable since December 2019. Therefore, we discuss a method for selecting search queries in languages other than English to create a flu forecasting model for multiple countries. In particular, we examine two transfer methods of search queries from English to other languages (Japanese and French): the translation-based method and the combination method of word alignment and time-series correlation (Sect. 3).

---

[1] Our appendix file is uploaded to https://hkefka385.github.io/project/file/PKDD 2021_Appendix.pdf.

The second issue is how to effectively incorporate search queries into a flu forecasting model. Two types of data have been applied extensively: historical flu activity data involving the previous year's data (known as "historical ILI data") [23,24,26] and online UGC data [4,31,32], which mainly consist of search query data. A representative example of simultaneous inputs is the ARGO model [27], which is based on linear regression using the input data of the Google search time series and the historical ILI data. The ARGO has exhibited superior results for flu forecasting in the US [17]. However, it has recently been reported that the effect of the search query data in a forecast model is small, and historical ILI data is sufficient as input [1]. According to these reports, there remains room for considering how to effectively integrate the search query data, whereas these data have improved the forecasting performance in certain cases. That is, the simple methods of handling these two resources are insufficient for improving forecasting models. Furthermore, the overall mutual effect between the historical ILI data and search query data is difficult to capture effectively using existing models, which makes it difficult to extract this effect and apply it to tasks. To tackle this issue, we propose a model that combines inputs by considering the characteristics of input data. This approach is based on two aspects: the flu time series exhibits strong seasonality and search query data are useful features for forecasting non-seasonal parts. Specifically, the search query data are used to forecast the deseasonalized component of flu data by leveraging the attention mechanism [5], which is useful for considering the feature importance (Sect. 4.2). Subsequently, we use the model addressing the task as a base and extend it to the flu forecasting model for multiple countries (Sect. 4.3).

Similar to ours, Zou et al. [31] proposed a multi-task model based on linear and Gaussian regression to forecast the flu volume in the following two problem settings: several states in the US, and two countries, namely the US and England. Our multi-task model further develops the above in two aspects: we tackle flu forecasting in five countries, each of which differs in terms of the area or language, and we apply not a simple model such as a statistical model, but our novel neural network-based model for multi-task learning to achieve higher accuracy and long-term forecasting. Other related studies are discussed in detail in Appendix B.

In summary, we aim to construct a flu forecasting model targeting multiple countries by leveraging multi-task learning while solving two issues as below. First, to find suitable search queries, we examine the transfer methods of the search queries from English to other languages. Second, we effectively incorporate the search query data into the model, and propose a novel forecasting model that considers the characteristics of the input data, historical ILI data, and search query data. The experiments demonstrate that the proposed models and methods achieve the best accuracy among comparative models for forecasting flu epidemics in five countries.

2   Datasets

ILI Rates from Health Agencies. We obtained weekly ILI rates, representing the number of ILI cases per 100,000 people in a population, as a measure of ILI activity for the US, Japan, Australia, England, and France from their established syndromic surveillance systems, namely the Centers for Disease Control and Prevention[2], the National Institute of Infectious Diseases[3], Australian Sentinel Practices Research Network[4], Public Health England[5], and GPs Sentinelles Network[6], respectively. The England data span from 2013/41st week to 2020/29th week, whereas the others span from 2013/26th week to 2020/29th week. We denote these countries using the corresponding country codes, namely US, JP, AU, FR, and UK.

Search Query Data. Time series of weekly search query frequencies were retrieved through Google Trends[7] as the UGC data. The frequency represents the weekly search activity of the queries within a specific region. The two methods for selecting search queries are described in Sect. 3. The time series of the Google Trends data in the training period were normalized to have a minimum value of zero and maximum value of one (min-max normalization). The data span was the same as that of the ILI rate data.

3   Methods for Finding Search Queries

We proposed two transfer methods, namely the translation-based and word-alignment and temporal correlation based (WT-based) methods, to explore multilingual search queries using a list of English search queries, which were created in previous research [31] and placed in a URL[8]. As input for the proposed model, we selected the top L English search queries for the US, AU, and UK based on the list, and selected each search query in JP and FR corresponding to the English search query based on these one-to-one query mapping methods. The usefulness of mapping from English to other languages is described in [18,29,32]. These studies pointed out that the volume movement in the search queries is similar among countries with certain health conditions.

Translation-Based Method: This is the simplest transfer method for the conversion of English into other languages. To select other languages' queries, we translated English search queries into those of the target language. We used Google Translate[9] for the translation-based method. For Japanese morphemes, which are not separated by spaces, we divided each morpheme and inserted spaces between them.

---

[2] https://www.cdc.gov/.
[3] https://www.niid.go.jp/niid/ja/.
[4] https://aspren.dmac.adelaide.edu.au/.
[5] https://www.gov.uk/government/organisations/public-health-england.
[6] https://www.sentiweb.fr/.
[7] https://trends.google.com.
[8] https://github.com/binzou-ucl/google-flu-mtl.
[9] https://translate.google.com.

WT-Based Method: It is possible that the translation-based approach, which simply maps the queries to the target language, will not capture suitable queries. For example, in Japanese, the abbreviation of influenza, "flu," is translated into "I-N-FU-LU-E-N-ZA" and is not translated into the Japanese abbreviation of influenza, "I-N-FU-LU." Moreover, it is difficult to select the suitable orthographical variant, the three categories of which used by the three Japanese writing scripts are applied (kanji-script, hiragana-script, and katakana-script). We solved these problems using the combination WT-based method, which considers the semantic similarity to the English search queries and temporal similarity to the historical ILI data.

Word alignment is one method that is used for creating cross-lingual word embeddings to compute word similarities in different languages, and is trained using sources of monolingual text with a smaller cross-lingual corpus of aligned text [19]. This approach can solve the above problems. For the word alignment, we used the method to learn cross-lingual word embeddings proposed by Zhou et al. [30]. We needed to prepare word embeddings based on the monolingual text for English and the target languages (Japanese and French). For this purpose, we obtained the word embedding dataset [11] learned by fasttext from Wikipedia corpora [7]. Thereafter, we applied these word embeddings to the word alignment method. To search for words with similar meanings, we used cosine similarity to map each word in the search query, except for prepositions and articles, to the k most similar words in other languages using the common word embedding space created by the word alignment. The similarity score was represented by Θ_w.

Temporal correlation is a method for finding a better search query based on the similarity of the time series of the search queries to the time series of the historical ILI data for the forecast. It was calculated by the Pearson correlation between the time series of the search query, for which candidates were provided by the word alignment, and the time series of the historical ILI in each country. The score was represented by Θ_t.

The WT-based method selects the search query with the best score in the equation $\Theta_w + \Theta_t$ corresponding to an English search query. This is inspired by [32], which used a similar method of selecting search queries for creating a transfer model of flu forecasts. Our research differs from the previous research in terms of the motivation whereby we discuss how to find better search queries for flu forecasts.

4   Building a Flu Forecasting Model for Multiple Countries

4.1   Problem Formulation

Our aim is to forecast the future ILI rates in various countries. We formulate this problem as a supervised machine learning task. Let $\mathbf{X} = \{x_{t-N+1}, ..., x_{t-1}, x_t\} \in \mathbb{R}^N$ be a time series of historical ILI data containing N weekly data points. Let $\mathbf{Q} = \{q_{t-N+1}, ..., q_{t-1}, q_t\} \in \mathbb{R}^{N \times L}$ be the search query data containing N

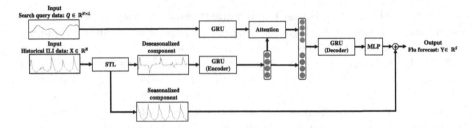

Fig. 1. Architecture of proposed model. Historical ILI data are divided into seasonalized and deseasonalized components. We apply the deseasonalized part to the encoder—decoder model comprising GRUs with an attention mechanism considering search queries.

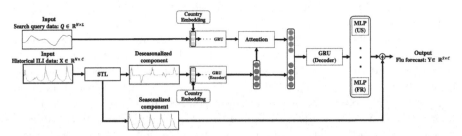

Fig. 2. Architecture of proposed model expanded to multi-task learning. The red boxes indicate the share of different parameters in the model for each country. The blue boxes indicate the same parameters. Furthermore, country embedding is introduced as the initial latent state of the GRUs. (Color figure online)

weekly data points and L queries. Our model forecasts the true S-step-ahead values $\mathbf{Y} = \{x_{t+1}, ..., x_{t+S}\} \in \mathbb{R}^S$. We learn a function $f : \{\mathbf{X}, \mathbf{Q}\} \to \mathbf{Y}$ that maximizes the prediction accuracy in each country.

4.2 Model Structure

Our model is motivated by the idea that search query data are useful features for forecasting non-seasonal parts of flu data. This concept originates from a previous study [20], which reported that the flu forecasting accuracy is improved by splitting the forecasting part from the historical ILI data and search query data. The model architecture is presented in Fig. 1. For the data preparation, we divide the historical ILI data into the seasonalized and deseasonalized components. Under the assumption that the seasonalized component has a constant frequency in the future, we forecast the deseasonalized component in the future. For the forecasting, we apply the encoder—decoder model considering the search query data using an attention mechanism [5].

Flu Decomposition: We use the seasonal-trend decomposition using LOESS (STL) method [9], which considers the following time-series model with the trend and seasonality: $y_t = \tau_t + s_t + r_t, t = 1, 2, ..., N$, where y_t denotes the historical ILI data at time t, τ_t is the trend in the time series, s_t is the seasonal signal with period T, and r_t is the reminder signal. The seasonal signal describes the repeated patterns in the specified period T, which remain constant over time. The trend describes the continuous increase or decrease. The detailed decomposition algorithm is outlined in [9].

In our method, the historical ILI data are divided into seasonalized and deseasonalized components. The deseasonalized component $\mathbf{X}^\tau$ represents the residual that is obtained by subtracting the seasonalized part $\mathbf{X}^s$ from the historical ILI data $\mathbf{X}$; $\mathbf{X}^\tau = \mathbf{X} - \mathbf{X}^s$. Our neural network-based architecture is developed to forecast the future value of a deseasonalized component. It is assumed that the seasonalized component $\mathbf{X}^s$ exhibits a constant pattern in the future. Subsequently, the flu forecast value $\mathbf{Y}$ is output by simply adding the value based on the pattern of the seasonalized component to the forecast value of the deseasonalized component using our model.

Encoder–decoder Model of Deseasonalized Component: Our model employs an encoder—decoder architecture to forecast more than two weeks ahead. This architecture is composed of gated recurrent units (GRUs) [8], representing a simple and powerful variant of the RNN, and an attention mechanism, which indicates that the neural network pays close attention to parts of the data when performing tasks. The GRUs are used to capture the hidden representations of the deseasonalized component of the historical ILI data $\mathbf{X}^\tau$ and search query data $\mathbf{Q}$, and the attention is used to help our model to focus on salient changes in the time series in each query regarding the historical ILI data. The attention mechanism computes the importance of each query with respect to the forecast and aids in making our model transparent and interpretable.

To capture the hidden representation of the deseasonalized component of the historical ILI data $\mathbf{X}^\tau$ as the encoder, the GRUs use the input data $\mathbf{X}_t^\tau$ and previous hidden representation $\mathbf{H}_{t-1}$, as follows:

$$\mathbf{r}_t = \sigma\left(U_r \mathbf{X}_t^\tau + W_r \mathbf{H}_{t-1}\right), \quad \mathbf{f}_t = tanh\left(U_h \mathbf{X}_t^\tau + \mathbf{H}_{t-1} \odot W_h \mathbf{r}_t\right),$$
$$\mathbf{z}_t = \sigma\left(U_z \mathbf{X}_t^\tau + W_z \mathbf{H}_{t-1}\right), \quad \mathbf{H}_t = (1 - \mathbf{z}_t) \odot \mathbf{H}_{t-1} + \mathbf{z}_t \odot \mathbf{f}_t, \tag{1}$$

where $\mathbf{z}_t$ and $\mathbf{r}_t$ represent the reset and update gates at time t, respectively. In this case, $U_z, U_r, U_h \in \mathbb{R}^{1 \times M}$, and $W_z, W_r, W_h \in \mathbb{R}^{M \times M}$ are parameters for the respective gates, whereas M is the GRU output dimension. We combine Eq. (1) as follows:

$$\mathbf{H}_i^\tau = GRU\left(\mathbf{X}_i^\tau\right), \quad i \in \{t - N + 1, ..., t\}, \tag{2}$$

where $\mathbf{H}_t^\tau \in \mathbb{R}^{1 \times M}$, which is the last GRU hidden state, is used as the hidden representation. The search query data also leverage the GRU, as is the case with the historical ILI data.

$$\mathbf{H}_{i,j}^q = GRU\left(\mathbf{Q}_{i,j}\right), \quad i \in \{t - N + 1, ..., t\}, \quad j \in \{1, ..., L\}, \tag{3}$$

where $\mathbf{H}_t^q \in \mathbb{R}^{L \times M}$, which is the last GRU hidden state, is used as the hidden representation and L is the number of queries.

The combination representation by the attention mechanism is obtained from the hidden representations $\mathbf{H}_t^{\tau}$ and $\mathbf{H}_t^q$. In general, an attention mechanism can be defined as mapping a query q and a set of key–value pairs $\{k, v\}$ to an output o. For each position i, we compute the attention weighting as the inner product between the query q_i and key k_i at every position. For the application of our model, we treat the hidden representation of the deseasonalized component $\mathbf{H}_t^{\tau}$ as the query, and the hidden representation of the search queries $\mathbf{H}_t^q$ as the key and value. Position i indicates the location of each search query representation ($i \in \{1, ..., L\}$). The query, key, and value representations are calculated from each representation through linear projection, as follows:

$$\mathbf{S}_q = \mathbf{W}^q \mathbf{H}_t^{\tau}, \qquad \mathbf{S}_k = \mathbf{W}^k \mathbf{H}_t^q, \qquad \mathbf{S}_v = \mathbf{W}^v \mathbf{H}_t^q, \qquad (4)$$

where $\mathbf{S}_q \in \mathbb{R}^{1 \times M}$ indicates the query representation, and $\mathbf{S}_k, \mathbf{S}_v \in \mathbb{R}^{L \times M}$ indicate the key and value representations, respectively. Following the linear projection, the dot-product attention computes the importance of each query representation and the attention representation $\mathbf{H}^{\tau q}$; $\mathbf{H}^{\tau q} = \text{Softmax}(\mathbf{S}_q \mathbf{S}_k) \mathbf{S}_v$, where $\text{Softmax}(\mathbf{S}_q \mathbf{S}_k)$ represents the importance of each query and the dimension of $\mathbf{H}^{\tau q}$ is M. Thereafter, we apply the feature, concatenating the attention representation $\mathbf{H}^{\tau q}$ and hidden representation of the deseasonalized component $\mathbf{H}_t^{\tau}$, to a multi-layer perceptron (MLP); $\mathbf{H}^{enc} = \text{MLP}([\mathbf{H}_t^{\tau} \cdot \mathbf{H}^{\tau q}])$, where the dimension of $\mathbf{H}^{enc}$ is M.

For the inference of the deseasonalized value of the flu data in the forecast $\{t + 1, ..., t + S\}$, we apply $\mathbf{H}^{enc}$ to the GRU as the decoder and MLP, which constitute two layers.

$$\begin{cases} \mathbf{H}_i^{dec} = GRU\left(\mathbf{X}_t^{\tau}, \mathbf{H}^{enc}\right), & i = t + 1 \\ \mathbf{H}_i^{dec} = GRU\left(\mathbf{O}_{i-1}^{schedule}\right), & i \in \{t + 2, ..., t + S\} \end{cases} \qquad (5)$$

$$\hat{\mathbf{O}}_i = MLP(\mathbf{H}_i^{dec}), \quad i \in \{t + 1, ..., t + S\}, \qquad (6)$$

where $\hat{\mathbf{O}}_i$, which is the decoder output, represents the forecast of the deseasonalized value at time i. Moreover, $\mathbf{O}_{i-1}^{schedule}$ refers to the value to be applied the scheduled sampling [6], which is a system of feeding the model with either ground truth values with a probability of ϵ or forecasts from the model with a probability of $1 - \epsilon$. This resolves the problem that the discrepancy between the input distributions of the training and testing can lead to poor performance, as the ground truth values are replaced by forecast values generated by the model.

Finally, we can calculate the forecast of the flu volume $\hat{\mathbf{Y}}_i$ at time i by simply adding the forecast of the deseasonalized value $\hat{\mathbf{O}}_i$ to the seasonalized value $\mathbf{X}_i^s$; $\hat{\mathbf{Y}}_i = \hat{\mathbf{O}}_i + \mathbf{X}_i^s, i \in \{t + 1, ..., t + S\}$.

Training: For the model training, we need to determine the true value of the deseasonalized component $\mathbf{O}_i$. This is achieved by a simple method, namely subtracting the seasonal part $\mathbf{X}_i^s$ that is assumed to have a constant frequency in the future season from the true flu volume $\mathbf{Y}_i$. We use the mean squared error (MSE) loss between the true value of the deseasonalized component $\mathbf{O}$ and the forecast value $\hat{\mathbf{O}}$.

4.3 Extension to Multi-task Model

We extend the proposed model to possess the capability of multi-task learning for flu forecasting in various countries. Our model aims to improve the expressive ability by means of multi-task learning, which shares part of the learning representations. The architecture of our multi-task model is presented in Fig. 2. In Fig. 2, the components surrounded by blue share all the parameters of the hidden features, whereas those surrounded by red have different parameters set depending on the country. The GRUs in our model use the same parameters for each task; in particular, parameters of Eqs. (1), (2), (3), and (5) are the same. The attention and MLP for the final output are set as country-specific; parameters of Eqs. (4) and (6) differ for each country.

Furthermore, we propose "country embedding" as the initial latent representation of two GRUs regarding the time series of the search queries and deseasonalized component for the multi-task learning of the flu forecasting. The proposal is based on the possibility of flexible modeling even in the shared representations by changing the initial latent state depending on the forecast target. The country embedding is calculated as follows: $\mathbf{H}^{country} = \text{MLP}(\text{Country\_id})$, where $\mathbf{H}^{country} \in \mathbb{R}^M$ indicates the initial hidden representation of the GRUs as the input of Eqs. (2) and (3), and "Country_id" is the value assigned according to the country (e.g., the "Country_id" of US is 1 and that of JP is 2). At each step in the training process of the multi-task learning, we randomly select a country, followed by a random training batch $\{\mathbf{X}^{country\_id}, \mathbf{Q}^{country\_id}, \mathbf{Y}^{country\_id}\}$; that is, we set one batch containing only the data of one country at a time. Our experimental code is public in https://github.com/hkefka385/single-model-for-influenza-forecasting

5 Experiments and Results

5.1 Experimental Settings

We forecasted the ILI rates in the five countries (US, JP, AU, FR, and UK) using the proposed model. To validate the forecasting model, the proposed model and other comparative models forecasted the ILI rates from weeks 1 to 5. We assessed the forecasting performance using three year-long datasets including three flu terms (2017/30th to 2018/29th weeks, 2018/30th to 2019/29th weeks, and 2019/30th to 2020/29th weeks). We set 52 weeks (one year) as the validation period before the testing period, and we set more than three years from the initial week of the ILI data to before the validation period as the training period. We decided to use the WT-based method to identify search queries with all of the models, because the WT-based method is a better approach than translation-based method. (Note that the comparison between the WT-based and translation-based methods is examined in Sect. 6.3.) We set 52 weeks as N and 5 weeks as S, which indicated the number of weeks ahead for the forecast. Furthermore, we set 10 as L, which indicated the number of search queries in the English list as input, and set 100 as k, which indicated the parameter of the WT-based method. We subsequently selected the learning rate and hidden layer sizes of GRU M as (0.001, 0.01, 0.1, 1.0) and (8, 16, 32, 64), respectively, in the validation period. During training, all model parameters were updated in a gradient-based manner following the Adam update rule [13]. We set the number of epochs to 300 with early stopping.

We validated the proposed model in the experiments.

- **Proposed w/o sq**: The proposed model was trained using only the historical ILI data of a target country.
- **Proposed_single**: The proposed model was trained using the data of a target country. The model was the same as that introduced in Sect. 4.2.
- **Proposed_multi2**: The proposed model was trained using the data of two target countries, namely the US and JP, for multi-task learning, as in the model introduced in Sect. 4.3.
- **Proposed_multi5**: The proposed model was trained using the data of five target countries for multi-task learning.

5.2   Comparative Models

- **GRU:**   The GRU model, one of the recurrent-based models, captures the temporal dependencies in the data and preserves the back-propagated error through the time and layers, referring to Eq. (1). It has been used successfully in influenza forecasting [16]. We employed an encoder—decoder architecture based on the GRU for the multi-step-ahead forecast. Two variations of the GRU were used in the experiments: "GRU w/o sq" had only historical ILI data, and "GRU" had historical ILI and search query data.
- **ARGO:**   The ARGO model [27] is an autoregressive (AR) model with Google search queries as exogenous variables. The simple architecture of this model enables one-step-ahead forecast of the flu volume [2,17,21]. The model fails to produce a multi-step-ahead forecast because it requires search query data in advance of the week that we wish to forecast. The parameters and input data are the same as those of the proposed model.
- **Transformer:**   The Transformer is one of the most successful models in the NLP. Thus far, the Transformer-based flu forecasting model has achieved the highest accuracy [32].
- **Two-stage:**   The Two-stage model [20], composed of long short-term model and AR model, was developed inspired by a similar idea to ours, in that the usefulness of the input data differs; historical ILI data and search query data are useful for forecasting the seasonality and trend, respectively. For the multi-step-ahead forecast, we extended the two-stage model to the encoder—decoder architecture.

- **Multi-task Elastic Net (MTEN):** The MTEN [31] was proposed as a multi-task model for flu forecasting of US regional areas from search query data. This model extends the standard elastic net model to a multi-task version. We used the same search queries as those of the proposed model as input. The model outputs a one-step-ahead forecast for the same reason as that of the ARGO model.
- **GRU_multi:** For the simple comparative method for multi-task, we make one unified model on GRUs, which is trained on the aggregated data of five countries. The model is the same setting as GRU, which is one of the comparative methods.

To compare the forecast performance levels of each model, we use two evaluation metrics: the coefficient of determination R^2 with a higher value indicating better performance, and root mean squared error RMSE with a lower value indicating better performance.

5.3 Results

The experimental results for US are presented in Table 1. (We examine the experimental results of the other countries in Sect. 6.1, and the experimental results for JP in detail are presented in Appendix C.) This result indicates that the proposed model (particularly our multi-task model) outperformed most baseline methods, confirming the benefits of the model architecture and multi-task learning. **GRU w/o sq** and **GRU** were superior baseline models and achieved approximately 0.8 to 0.9 for R^2 in the one-week-ahead forecasts for each country by capturing the temporal dependencies with the RNN architecture. **Transformer**, a state-of-the-art flu forecasting method, and **Two-stage** achieved relatively better scores in the near-ahead forecasts (from 1-week to 3-week) than the GRU-based models, but had almost the same scores in the far-ahead forecasts (from 4-week to 5-week). These results indicate that it is not easy to improve the accuracy of far-ahead forecasts. In contrast, the statistical model **ARGO** achieved relatively lower accuracy than the deep learning models. We assume that the deep learning-based models were more suitable for flu forecasting in terms of obtaining far-ahead forecast architecture with ease and exhibiting relatively higher accuracy than the statistical-based models, although the calculation cost was high. Likewise, **MTEN** based on the statistical model and multi-task learning had the same characteristics. It tended to exhibit lower accuracy than the other models because its input was only search query data. **GRU_multi**, a comparative method for the validation of multi-task, had lower accuracy. It shows the difficulty of forecasting with a single model without devising model architecture and learning.

Compared to these models, the proposed models (**Proposed_single, Proposed_multi2**, and **Proposed_multi5**) achieved the best scores with respect to the terms, metrics, and any-ahead forecasts. These results reveal that the architecture in the proposed model is useful for flu forecasting. **Proposed_single** achieved the best score among the models without multi-task learning in almost

Table 1. Model forecasting performances for US.

Term	Model	Multi	Input		1-week		2-week		3-week		4-week		5-week	
			Historical	Query	RMSE	R²	RMSE	R²	RMSE	R²	RMSE	R²	RMSE	R²
	GRU w/o sq		✓		0.797	0.841	0.925	0.787	1.033	0.734	1.103	0.697	1.150	0.671
	Transformer		✓		0.509	0.917	0.673	0.860	0.903	0.811	1.005	0.744	1.221	0.641
	*Proposed w/o sq		✓		0.392	0.961	0.599	0.905	0.819	0.832	0.984	0.758	1.109	0.695
	GRU		✓	✓	0.783	0.849	0.905	0.791	1.025	0.741	1.097	0.705	1.138	0.654
2017/30th	ARGO		✓	✓	0.405	0.954	—	—	—	—	—	—	—	—
–	Two-stage		✓	✓	0.450	0.938	0.667	0.879	0.849	0.825	0.977	0.752	1.405	0.527
2018/29th	*Proposed_single		✓	✓	0.323	0.973	0.558	0.922	0.770	0.849	0.947	0.776	1.078	0.711
	MTEN	✓		✓	0.450	0.934	—	—	—	—	—	—	—	—
	GRU_multi	✓	✓	✓	0.284	0.956	0.665	0.863	0.826	0.695	1.078	0.595	1.233	0.651
	*Proposed_multi2	✓	✓	✓	0.276	0.981	0.550	0.924	0.768	0.853	0.925	0.787	1.038	0.732
	*Proposed_multi5	✓	✓	✓	**0.237**	**0.986**	**0.498**	**0.941**	**0.692**	**0.837**	**0.805**	**0.832**	**0.942**	**0.770**
	GRU w/o sq		✓		0.305	0.945	0.400	0.906	0.451	0.880	0.496	0.855	0.546	0.811
	Transformer		✓		0.263	0.942	0.359	0.917	0.403	0.904	0.451	0.873	0.511	0.843
	*Proposed w/o sq		✓		0.248	0.961	0.323	0.937	0.391	0.909	0.454	0.878	0.525	0.838
	GRU		✓	✓	0.283	0.940	0.371	0.915	0.439	0.887	0.472	0.865	0.528	0.838
2018/30th	ARGO		✓	✓	0.467	0.875	—	—	—	—	—	—	—	—
–	Two-stage		✓	✓	0.308	0.947	0.417	0.891	0.481	0.854	0.517	0.857	0.541	0.810
2019/29th	*Proposed_single		✓	✓	**0.201**	**0.976**	0.302	0.946	0.378	0.916	0.439	0.886	0.494	0.855
	MTEN	✓		✓	0.429	0.915	—	—	—	—	—	—	—	—
	GRU_multi	✓	✓	✓	0.383	0.910	0.448	0.888	0.603	0.725	0.739	0.689	0.820	0.644
	*Proposed_multi2	✓	✓	✓	0.232	0.968	**0.268**	**0.957**	**0.323**	**0.938**	**0.388**	**0.888**	**0.454**	**0.856**
	*Proposed_multi5	✓	✓	✓	0.255	0.963	0.296	0.941	0.369	0.915	0.404	0.877	0.499	0.843
	GRU w/o sq		✓		0.698	0.882	0.910	0.807	1.096	0.713	1.153	0.683	1.167	0.648
	Transformer		✓		0.659	0.892	0.919	0.807	1.099	0.712	1.154	0.680	1.218	0.652
	*Proposed w/o sq		✓		0.538	0.932	0.838	0.837	1.084	0.725	1.171	0.683	1.241	0.605
	GRU		✓	✓	0.705	0.870	0.925	0.791	1.108	0.702	1.165	0.681	1.176	0.620
2019/30th	ARGO		✓	✓	0.984	0.758	—	—	—	—	—	—	—	—
–	Two-stage		✓	✓	0.602	0.918	0.924	0.817	1.081	0.726	1.231	0.609	1.224	0.590
2020/29th	*Proposed_single		✓	✓	0.469	0.949	0.694	0.881	0.809	0.846	0.863	0.824	0.918	0.799
	MTEN	✓		✓	0.992	0.760	—	—	—	—	—	—	—	—
	GRU_multi	✓	✓	✓	0.724	0.889	0.980	0.740	1.185	0.635	1.304	0.589	1.305	0.590
	*Proposed_multi2	✓	✓	✓	0.409	0.961	0.641	0.904	0.770	0.861	0.840	0.833	0.910	0.802
	*Proposed_multi5	✓	✓	✓	**0.370**	**0.971**	**0.605**	**0.920**	**0.696**	**0.878**	**0.787**	**0.853**	**0.831**	**0.841**

* indicates the variation in the proposed model. Bold indicates the best score in each metric and each term.

all terms, in which it exhibited the best score in the near-ahead forecast, whereas it had a lower score in the far-ahead forecast than the GRU-based models.

The high degree of the score improvement in **Proposed_multi2** and **Proposed_multi5** compared to Proposed_single demonstrated the usefulness of the multi-task learning. In the near-ahead forecast, the multi-task learning effects were sometimes not observed, whereas the scores of these models in the far-ahead forecast were significantly improved. For example, in the term 2017 to 2018 in US, the five-week-ahead forecast by Proposed_multi5 achieved an improvement of 0.136 points in the RMSE and 0.059 points in the R^2 compared to Proposed_single. Using data from different countries for simultaneous training, the model obtained the latent features of the time series of the ILI rates, thereby improving the forecasting performance. The difference in the accuracy of the model trained using the data of two countries (Proposed_multi2) and that trained using the data of five countries (Proposed_multi5) was not large.

Table 2. Forecasting performances of each model for ILI rates in JP, UK, AU, and FR from 2017/30th week to 2018/29th week.

Country	Model	1-week		2-week		3-week		4-week		5-week	
		RMSE	R^2	RMSE	R^2	RMSE	R^2	RMSE	R^2	RMSE	R^2
JP	GRU	3.412	0.939	4.019	0.923	5.223	0.915	5.982	0.826	6.164	0.813
	Proposed_single	2.517	0.964	3.218	0.944	3.688	0.934	4.898	0.884	5.822	0.836
	GRU_multi	3.261	0.944	3.901	0.882	5.072	0.820	6.552	0.776	6.752	0.756
	Proposed_multi5	**2.429**	**0.970**	**2.878**	**0.951**	**3.411**	**0.941**	**4.057**	**0.920**	**4.423**	**0.905**
UK	GRU	1.900	0.910	2.639	0.809	2.738	0.794	2.783	**0.787**	3.185	0.722
	Proposed_single	1.794	0.912	2.591	0.816	2.959	0.770	2.901	0.741	3.100	0.729
	GRU_multi	6.080	0.757	8.751	0.629	9.764	0.538	10.546	0.461	10.797	0.435
	Proposed_multi5	**1.510**	**0.935**	**2.199**	**0.873**	**2.675**	**0.808**	**2.709**	0.783	**2.992**	**0.745**
AU	GRU	1.754	0.939	2.085	0.914	2.430	0.884	2.739	0.852	3.122	0.807
	Proposed_single	1.764	0.938	2.131	0.922	2.480	0.883	2.683	0.859	3.058	0.816
	GRU_multi	2.458	0.933	3.099	0.876	4.080	0.821	4.674	0.765	5.018	0.728
	Proposed_multi5	**1.650**	**0.942**	**1.999**	**0.928**	**2.391**	**0.899**	**2.592**	**0.879**	**2.794**	**0.849**
FR	GRU	0.283	0.868	0.427	0.675	0.521	0.517	0.565	0.434	0.587	0.391
	Proposed_single	0.266	0.874	0.413	0.696	0.507	0.542	0.551	0.461	0.560	0.443
	GRU_multi	0.377	0.883	0.500	0.601	0.791	0.333	0.945	0.170	1.180	0.067
	Proposed_multi5	**0.234**	**0.904**	**0.375**	**0.751**	**0.452**	**0.611**	**0.527**	**0.511**	**0.552**	**0.466**

Table 3. Comparison of forecasting performances of translation-based and WT-based methods using Proposed_single model in JP and FR from 2017/30th week to 2018/29th week.

Country	Method	1-week		2-week		3-week		4-week		5-week	
		RMSE	R^2	RMSE	R^2	RMSE	R^2	RMSE	R^2	RMSE	R^2
JP	Translation-based	**2.492**	**0.964**	3.307	0.939	3.770	0.929	**4.800**	0.880	5.976	0.828
	WT-based	2.517	**0.964**	**3.218**	**0.944**	**3.688**	**0.934**	4.898	**0.884**	**5.822**	**0.836**
FR	Translation-based	0.278	0.856	0.432	0.661	0.531	0.491	0.592	0.407	0.594	0.405
	WT-based	**0.266**	**0.874**	**0.413**	**0.696**	**0.507**	**0.542**	**0.551**	**0.461**	**0.560**	**0.443**

6   Discussions

6.1   Multi-model Performance for Other Countries

Table 2 displays the forecast performances of four models (GRU, Proposed_single, GRU_multi, and Proposed_multi5) for the ILI rates in JP, UK, AU, and FR from 2017/30th week to 2018/29th week. These results suggest that the multi-task learning model Proposed_multi5 achieved the best score in almost all ahead forecasts, as well as the flu forecasting result in US. Multi-task learning is not limited to a number of countries, but can be applied to various countries with different languages and environments, and the experimental results revealed that the multi-task method improved the forecasting performance.

6.2   Comparison of Models Without and with Search Queries

Recent research relating to flu forecasts [1] claimed that the effect of search queries is small. To tackle this problem, our research presents a model with an attention mechanism that effectively considers search queries. To examine the search queries' effectiveness, we validated the degree of improvement of the two variation models, namely the GRU-based (GRU w/o sq and GRU) and proposed (Proposed w/o sq and Proposed_single) models, without and with search queries.

The experimental results for the flu forecast in US (Table 1) indicate that the change from GRU w/o sq to GRU resulted in an average improvement of 0.007 points in the RMSE, and of 0.001 points in the R^2. However, the change from Proposed w/o sq to Propose_single resulted in an average improvement of 0.091 points in the RMSE, and of 0.017 points in the R^2. This suggests that the search query data resulted in the GRU-based models, which simply used the search query data as input, exhibits low improvement scores by adding them. However, the proposed model, with a well-crafted architecture for the search query data input, achieved a significantly improved score. These results confirm that it is difficult to treat search queries as input for flu forecasting, and it is necessary to contribute to the score improvement by considering the model devices, such as the introduction of an attention mechanism.

6.3   Analysis of the Methods to Find Search Queries

We compared the translation-based and WT-based methods for the selection of search queries. For comparison, we experimented with the flu forecast from 2017/30th week to 2018/29th week in JP and FR using the Proposed_single model with the translation-based and WT-based methods.

The results in Table 3 demonstrate that the WT-based method achieved better scores than the translation-based method in all experimental metrics in FR and most experimental metrics in JP. However, the degree of improvement in the accuracy was not large. For example, for R^2, the two-week-ahead forecast for JP exhibited only a 0.005 point improvement, and that for FR exhibited only a 0.035 point improvement. Our model based on a neural network can consider a small number of search queries as input for efficient calculation, compared to the multi-task model [31] based on a statistical method that can consider many search queries. We assume that the architecture of our model, which does not involve a large number of search queries as input, is insignificantly affected by the selection of search queries. Although the results demonstrated that the WT-based method was superior as the selection method for our flu forecasting model, substantial room for consideration remains, such as which method is better for models dealing with a large number of search queries.

7   Conclusions

In this study, we attempted to construct a flu forecasting model targeting multiple countries by leveraging multi-task framework. Also, we addressed two tasks: finding suitable search queries in languages other than English and leveraging the search query data as input for the forecasting model. We revealed that the WT-based method is a better approach for the exploration of search queries.

Moreover, we proposed a novel forecasting model considering the characteristics of the input data, historical ILI data and search query data, and demonstrated the usefulness of the model architecture. Throughout the flu forecasting experiments in multiple countries, the proposed model achieved the highest performance by acquiring the latent features in the flu time series and by treating the task as multi-task learning.

Our experiments demonstrated the feasibility of constructing a flu forecasting model targeting multiple countries and the usefulness of search query data as input for the proposed model. However, the method of searching for suitable search queries remains a major challenge, which our research has not yet solved. Although we used the list of English search queries, a method for identifying appropriate search queries without relying on external resources is required. Moreover, it is necessary to examine a method to apply the proposed flu forecasting model to new infectious diseases from short period data, such as COVID-19, for dealing with a pandemic.

References

1. Aiken, E.L., Nguyen, A.T., Santillana, M.: Towards the use of neural networks for influenza prediction at multiple spatial resolutions. arXiv preprint arXiv:1911.02673 (2019)
2. Aiken, E.L., et al.: Real-time estimation of disease activity in emerging outbreaks using internet search information. PLoS Comput. Biol. **16**(8), e1008117 (2020)
3. Andreassen, H.K., et al.: European citizens' use of e-health services: a study of seven countries. BMC Public Health **7**(53) (2007)
4. Aramaki, E., Maskawa, S., Morita, M.: Twitter catches the flu: detecting influenza epidemics using Twitter. In: Proceedings of EMNLP, pp. 1568–1576 (2011)
5. Bahdanau, D., Cho, K., Bengio, Y.: Neural machine translation by jointly learning to align and translate. arXiv preprint arXiv:1409.0473 (2014)
6. Bengio, S., et al.: Scheduled sampling for sequence prediction with recurrent neural networks. In: Proceedings of NIPS, pp. 1171–1179 (2015)
7. Bojanowski, P., et al.: Enriching word vectors with subword information. Trans. Assoc. Comput. Linguist. **5**, 135–146 (2017)
8. Chung, J., et al.: Empirical evaluation of gated recurrent neural networks on sequence modeling. arXiv preprint arXiv:1412.3555 (2014)
9. Cleveland, R.B., et al.: STL: a seasonal-trend decomposition. J. Off. Stat. **6**(1), 3–73 (1990)
10. Ginsberg, J., et al.: Detecting influenza epidemics using search engine query data. Nature **457**(7232), 1012–1014 (2009)
11. Grave, E., et al.: Learning word vectors for 157 languages. In: Proceedings of LREC (2018)
12. Hansen, D., et al.: Seasonal web search query selection for influenza-like illness (ILI) estimation. In: Proceedings of SIGIR, pp. 1197–1200 (2017)
13. Kingma, D.P., Ba, J.: Adam: a method for stochastic optimization. arXiv preprint arXiv:1412.6980 (2014)
14. Lampos, V., Zou, B., Cox, I.J.: Enhancing feature selection using word embeddings: the case of flu surveillance. In: Proceedings of Web Conference, pp. 695–704 (2017)

15. Lazer, D., et al.: The parable of Google flu: traps in big data analysis. Science **343**(6176), 1203–1205 (2014)
16. Liu, L., Han, M., Zhou, Y., Wang, Y.: LSTM recurrent neural networks for influenza trends prediction. In: Zhang, F., Cai, Z., Skums, P., Zhang, S. (eds.) ISBRA 2018. LNCS, vol. 10847, pp. 259–264. Springer, Cham (2018). https://doi.org/10.1007/978-3-319-94968-0_25
17. Lu, F.S., et al.: Improved state-level influenza nowcasting in the United States leveraging internet-based data and network approaches. Nat. Commun. **10**(1), 1–10 (2019)
18. Mavragani, A., Ochoa, G., Tsagarakis, K.P.: Assessing the methods, tools, and statistical approaches in google trends research: systematic review. JMIR **20**(11), e270 (2018)
19. Mogadala, A., Rettinger, A.: Bilingual word embeddings from parallel and non-parallel corpora for cross-language text classification. In: Proceedings of NAACL, pp. 692–702 (2016)
20. Murayama, T., et al.: Robust two-stage influenza prediction model considering regular and irregular trends. PloS One **15**(5), e0233126 (2020)
21. Ning, S., Yang, S., Kou, S.: Accurate regional influenza epidemics tracking using internet search data. Sci. Rep. **9**(1), 1–8 (2019)
22. Polgreen, P.M., et al.: Using internet searches for influenza surveillance. Clin. Infect. Dis. **47**(11), 1443–1448 (2008)
23. Venna, S.R., et al.: A novel data-driven model for real-time influenza forecasting. IEEE Access **7**, 7691–7701 (2019)
24. Wang, L., Chen, J., Marathe, M.: DEFSI: deep learning based epidemic forecasting with synthetic information. In: Proceedings of AAAI, vol. 33, pp. 9607–9612 (2019)
25. W.H.O. website: Influenza (seasonal) (2018). http://www.who.int/news-room/fact-sheets/detail/influenza-(seasonal)
26. Wu, Y., et al.: Deep learning for epidemiological predictions. In: Proceedings of SIGIR, pp. 1085–1088 (2018)
27. Yang, S., Santillana, M., Kou, S.C.: Accurate estimation of influenza epidemics using Google search data via ARGO. PNAS **112**(47), 14473–14478 (2015)
28. Yang, S., et al.: Using electronic health records and internet search information for accurate influenza forecasting. BMC Infect. Dis. **17**(1), 332 (2017)
29. Ybarra, M., Suman, M.: Reasons, assessments and actions taken: sex and age differences in uses of internet health information. Health Educ. Res. **23**(3), 512–521 (2008)
30. Zhou, C., et al.: Density matching for bilingual word embedding. In: Proceedings of NAACL, pp. 1588–1598 (2019)
31. Zou, B., Lampos, V., Cox, I.: Multi-task learning improves disease models from web search. In: Proceedings of Web Conference, pp. 87–96 (2018)
32. Zou, B., Lampos, V., Cox, I.: Transfer learning for unsupervised influenza-like illness models from online search data. In: Proceedings of Web Conference, pp. 2505–2516 (2019)

Automatic Acoustic Mosquito Tagging with Bayesian Neural Networks

Ivan Kiskin[1]([✉]) [iD], Adam D. Cobb[3] [iD], Marianne Sinka[2] [iD], Kathy Willis[2] [iD],
and Stephen J. Roberts[1] [iD]

[1] Department of Engineering, University of Oxford, Oxford OX1 3PJ, UK
{ikiskin,sjrob}@robots.ox.ac.uk
[2] Department of Zoology, University of Oxford, Oxford OX1 3SZ, UK
{marianne.sinka,kathy.willis}@zoo.ox.ac.uk
[3] SRI International, Washington, D.C., VA 22209, USA
adam.cobb@sri.com

Abstract. Deep learning models are now widely used in decision-making applications. These models must be robust to noise and carefully map to the underlying uncertainty in the data. Standard deterministic neural networks are well known to be poor at providing reliable estimates of uncertainty and often lack the robustness that is required for real-world deployment. In this paper, we work with an application that requires accurate uncertainty estimates in addition to good predictive performance. In particular, we consider the task of detecting a mosquito from its acoustic signature. We use Bayesian neural networks (BNNs) to infer predictive distributions over outputs and incorporate this uncertainty as part of an automatic labelling process. We demonstrate the utility of BNNs by performing the first fully automated data collection procedure to identify acoustic mosquito data on over 1,500 h of unlabelled field data collected with low-cost smartphones in Tanzania. We use uncertainty metrics such as predictive entropy and mutual information to help with the labelling process. We show how to bridge the gap between theory and practice by describing our pipeline from data preprocessing to model output visualisation. Additionally, we supply all of our data and code. The successful autonomous detection of mosquitoes allows us to perform analysis which is critical to the project goals of tackling mosquito-borne diseases such as malaria and dengue fever.

Keywords: Acoustic machine learning · Bayesian deep learning · Audio event detection

1 Introduction

Vector-borne diseases are responsible for over 700,000 deaths annually [42]. *Vectors* are living organisms that can transmit infectious pathogens between humans, or from animals to humans. Dengue, yellow fever and malaria are examples of such mosquito-borne diseases, with malaria constituting one of the most

© Springer Nature Switzerland AG 2021
Y. Dong et al. (Eds.): ECML PKDD 2021, LNAI 12978, pp. 351–366, 2021.
https://doi.org/10.1007/978-3-030-86514-6_22

severe public health problems in the developing world. While there are many challenges associated with tackling these diseases, one important task is in information gathering. In order to respond to large outbreaks quickly and even predict future ones, it is vital that we develop models that are able to reliably detect and identify mosquitoes.

As part of this work, we demonstrate a novel application of Bayesian deep learning for labelling large amounts of acoustic mosquito data that has been collected in an unsupervised manner. We showcase that incorporating Bayesian methods into the tagging process can be extremely beneficial to domain experts who must eventually check and label data for themselves. As part of the HumBug project, we have developed an end-to-end pipeline to autonomously record, detect and archive mosquito sound. Our pipeline utilises conventional microphones that are found in low-cost mobile phones, and simple adaptions to bednets already commonly used in malaria-endemic areas [38]. This allows broad participation, and the possibility of providing a method for widespread detection in people's homes. Our work is part of an emerging field where image and acoustic data is used for building solutions to mosquito control [10,11,18,29]. In order to assist research in methods utilising the acoustics of mosquitoes, we describe our open-source research contributions as follows:

- **Code:** https://github.com/HumBug-Mosquito/MozzBNN. A Bayesian convolutional neural network (BCNN) pipeline for mosquito acoustic event detection. The model achieves 89% sensitivity and 97% specificity on out-of-sample test data. We demonstrate how to apply this model to difficult, raw, unlabelled field data through filtering predictions by uncertainty metrics intrinsic to probabilistic models. In carefully setting the thresholds of the uncertainty metrics, we avoid the need to manually filter through hundreds of hours of data that mostly consists of noise.
- **Data:** http://doi.org/10.5281/zenodo.4904800. We provide the output of our prediction pipeline applied to a diverse set of acoustic mosquito recordings of over 1,500 h of uncurated field data. We also supply all the data used for training, validating, and testing this model. In total, this forms 20 h of mosquito audio recordings expertly labelled with tags precise in time, of which 18 h are annotated with 36 different mosquito species.

The remainder of the paper is structured as follows. In Sect. 2.1 we describe previous mosquito detection efforts, and the context for our contributions. In Sect. 2.2 we review related work in acoustic machine learning and Bayesian deep learning. Section 3.1 describes our full pipeline, breaking down the function of each component. In Sect. 3.2, we formally introduce BNNs and the uncertainty metrics which we use for autonomous data collection. Section 4 showcases our BCNN, detailing the exact architecture, and its parameterisation. In Sect. 5.1 we show how our model performs on out-of-sample database data, and discuss our expectation of real-world performance from these results. Section 5.2 shows how we use uncertainty metrics to evaluate performance of our algorithm over large-scale, real-world, unlabelled data. In Sect. 6 we identify future directions and summarise our findings.

2   Background

2.1   Mosquito Control Efforts

Mosquitoes are unique in the way they fly. They have a particularly short, truncated wingbeat allowing them to flap their wings faster than any other insect of equivalent size – up to 1,000 beats per second [2,37]. This produces their very distinct and identifiable flight tone and has led many researchers to try and use their sound to attract, trap or kill them [11,15,16,30,33].

There are over 100 genera of mosquito in the world containing over 3,500 species [14]. Only one genus (*Anopheles*) contains species capable of transmitting the parasites responsible for human malaria. It contains over 475 formally recognised species of which, approximately 75 are vectors of human malaria and around 40 are considered truly dangerous [39]. These 40 species are inadvertently responsible for more human deaths than any other creature. In 2019, for example, malaria caused around 229 million cases of disease across more than 100 countries resulting in an estimated 409,000 deaths [42]. Mosquito surveys are used to establish vector species' composition and abundance, human biting rates and thus their potential to transmit pathogens. Traditional survey methods, such as human landing catches, which collect mosquitoes as they land on the exposed skin of a collector, can be time consuming, expensive and are limited in the number of sites they can survey. They can also be subject to collector bias, either due to variability in the skill or experience of the collector, or in their inherent attractiveness to local mosquito fauna. These surveys can also expose collectors to disease. Moreover, once the mosquitoes are collected, the specimens still need to undergo post-sampling processing for accurate species identification. Consequently, an affordable automated survey method that detects, identifies and counts mosquitoes could generate unprecedented levels of high-quality occurrence and abundance data.

2.2   Acoustic Machine Learning

Detecting the presence of a mosquito in audio data falls within the broader area of audio event detection. Within speech recognition, where audio applications were most common, previous work in applying machine learning techniques has seen approaches evolve from using Hidden Markov models for making classifications on phenomes or Mel-frequency cepstral coefficients (MFCCs) [19], to using convolutional neural networks (CNNs) for end-to-end learning [35]. Similarly to computer vision, audio event recognition has undergone a paradigm shift from hand-crafted representations to models which also learn end to end [9]. Recently, much of the success in this area has been seen from applying CNNs [34,36], where the task is to classify signals in the spectral feature space (such as short-time Fourier and log-mel transforms). Examples of successful applications in audio event and scene classification tasks can be found in the Detection and Classification of Acoustic Scenes and Events (DCASE) challenges of the years 2018 to 2020 [7,8]. For an event detection tagging-based task in 2018, the top five submissions were found to commonly utilise the log-mel feature space. Across a range of tasks in 2020, log-mel energies were overwhelmingly the most commonly used feature transform in high-ranking submissions [8]. Other feature spaces such as wavelets [25] have shown potential in acoustic insect classification. However, more work is to be done before finding computationally viable continuous wavelet transforms for real-time use. We therefore also utilise log-mel features in our work. We also use a model similar to the supplied baseline in 2018 Task 2, with elements of the top-performing models [7], as we would like to deploy a well-tested architecture for robust model performance in the field.

The vast majority of acoustic ML works have focused on deterministic approaches to classification, where uncertainty over predictions is not factored in (and is not encouraged due to the scoring function of typical ML challenges [7,8,20]). While deep learning has become an important tool for machine learning practitioners, the ability to generalise this tool to a wide range of scientific challenges is still in its infancy. In particular, we stress the importance of quantifying the uncertainty associated with the outputs of these models, through the use of BNNs. It is for this reason that our approach is to use current state-of-the-art methods to signal classification and place them in a Bayesian framework. The use of BNNs has not become widespread in audio classification, though recent applications have emerged [4], and BNNs are growing in interest in parallel application domains [5,12]. As a final point, we will also highlight the option to use the framework of Bayesian decision theory with Bayesian neural networks to estimate the risk associated with certain classifications [3]. This is especially important for mosquito detection, as asymmetrical cost functions for making classifications are often encountered [26].

3   Methods

3.1   HumBug Pipeline

To showcase our application, we show a schematic of our pipeline in Fig. 1. In the following paragraphs we break down the system by each component.

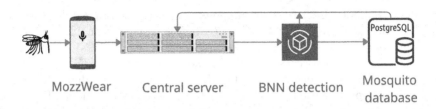

MozzWear   Central server   BNN detection   Mosquito database

Fig. 1. Project workflow. Our MozzWear app is used to record audio. The app synchronises to a central server. Audio input to BNN(s). Successful detections are used to create a curated PostgreSQL database. Information feeds back to improve the model.

Capturing Mosquito Acoustic Data on a Smartphone. Mosquitoes are small insects and the physical movement of air caused by their beating wings, responsible for the high-pitched whine of their flight tone, can easily be lost within even moderate background noise. Thus, to ensure our smartphones record data of high enough quality we needed to complete two steps. First, to develop an app (MozzWear) to detect and record the mosquito's flight tone using the in-built microphone on a smartphone. For the app, we use 16-bit mono PCM wave audio sampled at 8,000 Hz. These parameters are chosen as a result of prior work on acoustic low-cost smartphone recording solutions for mosquitoes [22,25,27].[1]

Secondly, we require a means to ensure that a mosquito flies close enough to the smartphone microphone to capture its flight tone (the adapted bednet). We have developed an adapted bednet that uses the inherent behaviour of host-seeking mosquitoes to make them fly close enough to the phone's internal microphone to passively record flight tone (Fig. 2). Its design is based on traditional rectangular bednets found across the malaria-endemic world. The bednet is adapted by the addition of a second outer canopy and a detachable pocket [38]. The pocket is placed at the highest point of the outer canopy above the occupant's head and holds a budget smartphone running the MozzWear app (Fig. 2b). The occupant switches on the app as they enter the bednet at night. Host-seeking mosquitoes are attracted to the CO_2 in the breath of the occupant and become trapped within the second canopy of the bednet. Here they naturally migrate to the highest point of the net where their flight tone is recorded. This design targets night-active mosquito species with a predilection to feed on humans. These characteristics are common amongst the dominant malaria vectors in Sub-Saharan Africa.

(a) Bednet with four smartphones positioned to trial the best location for recording mosquitoes.

(b) Bednet pockets to hold smartphones.

Fig. 2. Deployment in Tanzania (Oct 2020) to trial the effectiveness of acoustic mosquito detection with low-cost non-invasive measures.

---

[1] Due to bandwidth requirements in rural areas, our latest version uses 32 kbps AAC.

(a) Sample cups used to record   (b) Low-budget Itel A16 smartphones used
wild captured mosquitoes.   for data collection of bednet data.

Fig. 3. Equipment used in the recording process for curated and field data.

Central Server. Following app recording, the audio is synchronised by the user to a central server, which performs voice activity detection for removing speech to preserve privacy. The data then enters the classification engine, in its current iteration a Bayesian convolutional neural network (BCNN), which we describe in Sects. 3.2 and 4. Positive predictions are then filtered and screened, and stored in a curated database (Sect. 5.2). The data is then fed back to the server to update the model. We note that our database and algorithms are constantly undergoing improvement thanks to the feedback loop in our workflow. Please visit [24] or the links from Sect. 1 for the latest models and data.

Mosquito Database. There are a number of variables that influence mosquito flight tone including the size of the mosquito [41], its age [32] and the air temperature [40]. Thus, in order to develop an algorithm to discern different mosquito species from their flight tone, a training dataset is needed that captures the natural variation within a population. We therefore built a database of flight tones recorded from both laboratory grown and wild captured mosquitoes. Details of the dataset and a full breakdown of all available metadata, including time of recording, method of capture, recording device, species, and more are given in [24]. In summary, live mosquitoes were captured and recorded in Thailand, and South East Tanzania. To record the mosquito sounds, each captured mosquito was placed into a sample cup large enough for free flight (Fig. 3a) and their flight tone was recorded using a high specification field microphone (Telinga EM-23) or a selection of locally available smartphones (Fig. 3b) running our MozzWear app.

We also included in this database flight tone data of multiple species recorded from laboratory cultures (either free flying in culture cages, or free flying around bednets as in Fig. 2a). These included recordings from the Ifakara Health Institute, Tanzania, the United States Army Medical Research Unit in Kenya (USAMRU-K), the Center for Disease Control (CDC) Atlanta, the London School of Tropical Medicine and Hygiene (LSTMH), and the department of Zoology at the University of Oxford.

3.2   Bayesian Neural Networks

To provide principled uncertainty estimation for our described pipeline, we require a model that can provide distributions for each section of audio data. Bayesian neural networks offer a probabilistic alternative to neural networks by specifying prior distributions over the weights [28,31]. The placement of a prior $p(\omega_i)$ over each weight ω_i leads to a distribution over a parametric set of functions. The motivation for working with BNNs comes from the availability of uncertainty in its function approximation, $\mathbf{f}^\omega(\mathbf{x})$. When training on a dataset $\{\mathbf{X}, \mathbf{Y}\}$ we want to infer the posterior $p(\omega|\mathbf{X}, \mathbf{Y})$ over the weights:

$$p(\omega|\mathbf{X}, \mathbf{Y}) = \frac{p(\mathbf{Y}|\omega, \mathbf{X})p(\omega)}{p(\mathbf{Y}|\mathbf{X})}. \tag{1}$$

We define the prior $p(\omega)$ for each layer $l \in L$ as a product of multivariate normal distributions $\prod_{l=1}^{L} \mathcal{N}(\mathbf{0}, \lambda_l^{-1}\mathbf{I})$ (where λ_l is the prior length-scale) and the likelihood $p(\mathbf{y}|\omega, \mathbf{x})$ as a softmax for multi-class (c_i) classification:

$$p(\mathbf{y} = c_i|\omega, \mathbf{x}) = \frac{\exp\{\mathbf{f}_{c_i}^\omega(\mathbf{x})\}}{\sum_{c_j} \exp\{\mathbf{f}_{c_j}^\omega(\mathbf{x})\}}. \tag{2}$$

In testing, the posterior is then required for calculating the predictive distribution $p(\mathbf{y}^*|\mathbf{x}^*, \mathbf{X}, \mathbf{Y})$ for a given test point $\mathbf{x}^*$. At test time, techniques involving variational inference (VI) [17] replace the posterior over the weights with a variational distribution $q_\theta(\omega)$, where we have defined our distribution to depend on the variational parameters $\boldsymbol{\theta}$. Dropping weights during test time is known as Monte Carlo (MC) dropout [12] and acts as a test-time approximation for calculating the predictive distribution. We opt for MC dropout for our models, as MC dropout provides a cheap approximation of the predictive distribution without requiring the storage of any additional variational parameters or large ensembles of network samples.

Having trained a BNN, we have a collection of model weights $\{\omega\}_{s=1}^{S}$ for our MC inference scheme of S dropout samples, but only a single model for a regular deterministic network. We want the output of our model $\mathbf{y}^*$ to display its confidence in a label. For example, for binary detection, the least confident prediction would be a vector of $[0.5, 0.5]$. This vector corresponds to the maximum entropy prediction, which indicates a high level of uncertainty. On the other hand, a minimum entropy prediction would be a vector of $[1.0, 0.0]$ or $[0.0, 1.0]$, which corresponds to the highest confidence possible. For a model displaying any degree of confidence, we would like to verify to which degree this is consistent, and correct [4]. Therefore, the predictive entropy is a useful way to navigate from the softmax output to a single value that can indicate the confidence of a model in its prediction. For a deterministic network this is simply $-\sum_c p_c \log p_c$ for a single test input $\mathbf{x}^*$, where p_c is the probability of each class (i.e. each element in the vector). For the MC approach there are multiple outputs, where each output corresponds to a different weight sample, $\omega^{(s)}$. There are different ways to work with the entropy formulation, but we start with the standard solution which is to average over the outputs and then work with the expected value of the output. This forms the posterior predictive entropy $\tilde{\mathcal{H}}$:

$$\tilde{\mathcal{H}} = -\sum_c \tilde{p}_c \log \tilde{p}_c, \quad \text{where} \quad \tilde{p}_c = 1/S \sum_s p_c^{(s)}. \tag{3}$$

This does not take into account the origin of the uncertainty (i.e. is it the model that is unsure, or is the data simply noisy), but for practical purposes it is a useful tool as it will tell us how much to trust the prediction. However, there are other ways that we can decompose the uncertainty to distinguish the model uncertainty from the data uncertainty. For example, it would be helpful to distinguish between two scenarios that $\tilde{\mathcal{H}}$ cannot capture:

A: All samples equally uncertain, e.g. $S = 2$, $\mathbf{y}^* = \{[0.5, 0.5], [0.5, 0.5]\}$
B: All samples are certain, yet fully disagree, e.g. $\mathbf{y}^* = \{[1.0, 0.0], [0.0, 1.0]\}$

It might be the case that all the MC samples for the same input result in multiple predictions, with all having the same exact maximum entropy distribution, $[0.5, 0.5]$. The $\tilde{\mathcal{H}}$ resulting from this scenario would, however, be the same as sampling two Monte Carlo predictions, where each prediction assigns a 1.0 to a different class. To distinguish between the two cases, we first introduce the expectation over the entropy with respect to the parameters $\mathbb{E}[\mathcal{H}]$:

$$\mathbb{E}[\mathcal{H}] = 1/S \sum_s h(\boldsymbol{\omega}_s), \quad \text{where} \quad h(\boldsymbol{\omega}) = -\sum_c p_c(\boldsymbol{\omega}) \log p_c(\boldsymbol{\omega}). \tag{4}$$

Now, if we go back to scenario A, $\tilde{\mathcal{H}} = \log 2$, $\mathbb{E}[\mathcal{H}] = 0$. Let us compare to scenario B, where $\tilde{\mathcal{H}} = \log 2$, but now $\mathbb{E}[\mathcal{H}] = \log 2$ (see Appendix A). As the prediction is independent of the samples drawn, the expectation of the entropy with respect to the weights here is equal to the posterior predictive entropy, and hence despite sharing the same posterior predictive entropy, the expectations are not equal. This allows us to determine whether the uncertainty in our model is due to high disagreement between samples, which could be due to an out of distribution test point, or whether the model is familiar with the data regime but correctly shows a higher entropy prediction due to the presence of noise.

The mutual information (MI) [13], $I(\mathbf{y}^*, \boldsymbol{\omega})$ between the prediction $\mathbf{y}^*$ and the model posterior over $\boldsymbol{\omega}$ can then be written as:

$$I(\mathbf{y}^*, \boldsymbol{\omega}) = \tilde{\mathcal{H}} - \mathbb{E}[\mathcal{H}]. \tag{5}$$

The MI will measure how much one variable, say $\boldsymbol{\omega}$, tells us about the other random variable, say $\mathbf{y}^*$ (or vice-versa). If $I(\mathbf{y}^*, \boldsymbol{\omega}) = 0$, then that tells us that $\boldsymbol{\omega}$ and $\mathbf{y}^*$ are independent, given the data. In the scenario where the predictions completely disagree with each other for a given $\mathbf{x}^*$, for each $\boldsymbol{\omega}_s$ drawn from the posterior, we get very different predictions. This informs us that $\mathbf{y}^*$ is very dependent on the posterior draw and thus $I(\mathbf{y}^*, \boldsymbol{\omega}) = \log 2 - 0 = \log 2$. However, if $\mathbf{y}^* = [0.5, 0.5]$ for all $\boldsymbol{\omega}_s \sim p(\boldsymbol{\omega}|\mathbf{Y}, \mathbf{X})$, then the different draws from the posterior distribution have no effect on the predictive distribution and therefore the mutual information between the two distributions is zero, as $\mathbb{E}[\mathcal{H}] = h(\boldsymbol{\omega}) = \tilde{\mathcal{H}}$ (they are independent). We therefore use the MI to threshold incoming predictions to help autonomously label our field data in Sect. 5.2.

4   Model Configuration

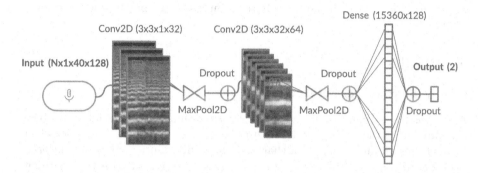

Fig. 4. BCNN architecture with tensor dimensions. Log-mel spectrograms are input with $w = 40, h = 128$, and passed into two convolutional layers, with 32, and 64, (3×3) kernels of stride 1. Following repeated pooling and dropout, the feature maps are flattened and fully connected to a dense layer of 128 units, before a final dropout and softmax output layer. All activation functions are ReLUs, omitted here for clarity.

We utilise log-mel spectrogram features for our model input (illustrated in Fig. 4 for a particularly loud mosquito sample). It is important to consider how to parameterise the feature transform, based on trading off frequency and time resolution, which is a direct result of the Heisenberg uncertainty principle [6]. A crucial related design decision is the selection of the number of feature windows that are used to represent a sample, $\mathbf{x} \in \mathbb{R}^{h \times w}$, where h is the height of the two-dimensional matrix, and w is the width. The longer the window, w, the better potential the network has of learning appropriate dynamics, but the smaller the resulting dataset in number of samples. It may also be more difficult to learn the salient parts of the sample that are responsible for the signal, resulting in a weak labelling problem [21]. Early mosquito detection efforts have used small windows due to a restriction in dataset size. For example, [11] supplies a rich database of audio, however the samples are limited to just under a second. However, despite the mosquito's simple harmonic structure, its characteristic sound also derives from the temporal variations. We suspect this flight behaviour tone is better captured over longer windows, since we achieved more robust results with $w = 40, h = 128$, corresponding to 40 frames per window, each of 64 ms duration for a total audio slice of 2.56 s per sample (hop length of 512 samples and NFFT of 2048). We use a BCNN with the architecture as shown in Fig. 4. This model structure is directly based on previous work in mosquito detection. In [25], the authors demonstrated mosquito detection capability better than that of human domain experts, when trained on held out recordings within a controlled experiment. In [22] they also compared a range of 1-D feature vector classifiers (Support Vector Machines, Random Forests, etc.) and showed that the neural network model gave the best performance. Therefore we use the same proven model but incorporate MC dropout at test time. We further increased the size of a training input, and added an additional convolution and pooling layer due to the greater availability of data compared to the model used in [23]. The utilisation of dropout layers in both training and testing produces estimates of uncertainty.

5   Results

5.1   Validation Performance

An important assumption in modelling is that training and test data have been generated from the same underlying distribution. We aim to train a model which learns to discriminate classes of that underlying distribution. However, in practice, due to the myriad of variables that can change for an acoustic recording, such as the environmental conditions, we find this assumption to not hold true. As an example, the statistics of noise are varying throughout time by the introduction of novel environments, resulting in non-stationary dynamics. In particular, consider our binary model of detecting a mosquito signal, and detecting the absence of signal, i.e. noise. We require a noise class which is representative of the deployment scenario, which is not known in advance. There are several sources of noise which we need to address, e.g. the noise profile of the recording devices themselves, as well as the non-stationary environments in which the devices are deployed. We have attempted to mitigate this by collecting data from a wide range of devices in varying conditions as described in Sect. 3.1.

We would like to both maximise the data available for training, but also reserve sufficient data for rigorous evaluation. As of April 2021, our dataset contains data from 7 experimental setups, and 5 input devices. One strategy is to hold out entire recordings from each experiment to produce a training dataset that has sources from each experimental setup. However, training the model on signal and noise sources for those experiments will allow memorisation of the signal and noise characteristics. As the samples seen during test time will very closely approximate those seen in training [25], the model will report results that will not be representative of its true predictive power. Instead, if we have sufficient data to split training and testing into three experiments used for training, and one held out for testing, we can use a K-fold cross-validation that withholds entire experiments. We also note that in practice, these experiments will all contain varying quantities (and quality) of samples per class, which further complicates issues. We believe there is no one-size-fits-all approach, and emphasise it is important to understand the sources of data when designing a model. We opt to hold out two experiments for testing purposes, and cross-validate our model on the remaining five experiments.

	Duration (h)	Class acc. (%)
Signal **A**	2.8	89.27 ± 0.07
Noise **A**	1.3	94.05 ± 0.11
Noise **B**	3.0	97.99 ± 0.05

(a) Signal **A**: collation of laboratory mosquito recording; Noise **A**: corresponding background. Noise **B**: Environmental background noise near bednets.

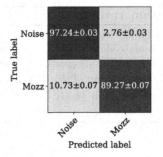

(b) Confusion matrix of (a).

Fig. 5. Out-of-sample performance on held-out test data, estimated with $S = 10$ MC dropout samples (mean ± standard deviation).

We collate the test data experiments into the sources of Fig. 5 and achieve a mean classification accuracy of 97% for the noise class (over 4.3 h of data), and 89% on the mosquito class (over 2.8 h of data). The standard deviation is given across 10 MC dropout samples drawn at test time. These class accuracies would be highly desirable for a model deployed in the field. However, it is important to consider the process of data labelling. In forming samples for the BNN input, any audio clip which is shorter than the window length of 2.56 s is discarded, and thus the resulting test data only consists of sections that contain either signal or noise for the entire duration. It is therefore expected to encounter lower classification accuracy when generalising to new incoming data, as we do not have guarantees on performance over shorter mosquito events, or if the sample contains partially noise, and partially mosquito. This can be in part mitigated by stepping through incoming data, and aggregating neighbouring predictions to provide resolution at a finer time scale.

5.2 Automatically Labelling Field Data with Uncertainty Metrics

In this section we tackle the challenge of analysing model performance from data collected at large scale in field studies. To do so, we make use of the open-source audio editor Audacity [1] to produce an audio-visual output. This serves as a useful tool for researchers from a range of communities to easily disseminate results. In the field trial we conducted in Tanzania in November 2020 we gathered 1,500 h of recordings from 16 mobile phones (Fig. 3b). As is common in biological applications, manually labelling such a dataset is near impossible due to its size. Algorithm 1 summarises the process by which we pass incoming audio data through the BNN and then import the audio and predicted labels to screen detections in Audacity. Figure 6 illustrates the automatic tagging process for one particular section of recording from the field trial. The upper graphic shows the spectrogram, and the label track is generated by the BCNN.

Our probabilistic model allows us to both estimate the presence of a mosquito, as well as quantify how certain our model is in its predictions. To

Algorithm 1: BCNN detection

---

for *audio file* **do**

  Calculate sliding window log-mel (40×128 frames, each frame 64 ms);

  Calculate BCNN predictions with S MC dropout samples;

  Calculate mean of $\bar{p}_c$, $\mathcal{H}$, $I(\mathbf{y}^*, \boldsymbol{\omega})$ per section with $\bar{p}_{\text{mosquito}} > p_{\text{threshold}}$;

  Write labels as $\{t_{\text{start}}, t_{\text{end}}, \hat{p}_c, \hat{\mathcal{H}}, \hat{I}(\mathbf{y}^*, \boldsymbol{\omega})\}$;

end

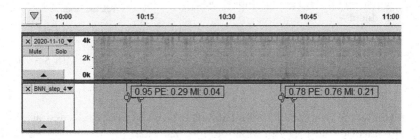

Fig. 6. BCNN predictions on unlabelled field data (Nov 2020) in Audacity in the form: $\{\hat{p}_{\text{mosquito}}, \hat{\mathcal{H}}, \hat{I}\}$. Two windows with mosquito present were correctly identified in this section of audio, recorded with the arrangement of Fig. 2.

showcase its effectiveness on field data collected from South East Tanzania, we vary the threshold of uncertainty and study the performance metrics that result from them. We fix the model probability and predictive entropy threshold, and threshold by the MI, which best captures model confidence, as discussed in Sect. 3.2. We vary the MI threshold from its maximum value of 1.0 ($\log_2(2)$, Appendix A for max MI calculation) through a series of discrete steps as given in Table 1. We calculate the quantity of positives that the model produces for those values, and estimate the precision and negative predictive value, NPV (which can be thought of as the precision for the negative class), by manually screening

Table 1. Effect of mutual information thresholding on the precision and the negative predictive value (NPV). Positives: duration of audio which was predicted as positive. Mosquito recovered: duration of the mosquito audio recovered from all the data.

$p_{\text{threshold}}$	$I_{\text{threshold}}(\mathbf{y}^*, \boldsymbol{\omega})$	NPV	Positives	Precision	Mosquito recovered
0.7	1.0	$\gtrsim 98\%$	18 h 1 m	12%	2 h
0.7	0.1	$\gtrsim 99\%$	5 h 30 m	30%	1 h 39 m
0.7	0.05	$\gtrsim 99\%$	1 h 39 m	54%	53 m
0.7	0.02	$\gtrsim 99\%$	38 m	58%	22 m
0.7	0.01	$\gtrsim 99.9\%$	20 m	60%	12 m
0.7	0.005	$\gtrsim 99.99\%$	5 m	99%	5 m

the detections. Our key result is that the model has well-calibrated uncertainty, as the precision increases from 12% to 99% with the tightening of the mutual information threshold from 1.0 to 0.005. It also illustrates the problems an equivalent deterministic neural network would have, as a probability threshold of 0.7 on its own is not sufficient to provide a useful detector, despite showing strong performance in previous tasks. At the extreme end of confidence, we approach 100% precision and negative predictive value, which is a remarkable result from an input of 1,500 h of novel data. The trade-off this comes with is a prediction of a very small quantity of data (low recall). In practice, we would choose a point on the MI operating curve which balances an acceptable precision and recall of the model. Following further tweaking based on the results of Table 1, we screened the predictions with thresholds of $p = 0.8, \mathcal{H} = 0.5, I = 0.09$. The results of this process have been uploaded to our database in [24], and can be accessed with the metadata country: Tanzania, location_type: field.

6 Conclusion

In this paper we demonstrated how to successfully deploy Bayesian convolutional neural networks for the automatic identification and labelling of mosquitoes. We used BCNNs to lessen the burden of manually labelling the rare mosquito events. The automatic identification of likely mosquitoes reduced the size of the data required for labelling from 1,500 h to 18 h, or less, depending on the uncertainty threshold. As a result, the challenge of tagging extremely rare mosquito events was made easier by using the model to correctly identify likely mosquito events and remove large proportions of the noise.

Key to the success of our implementation was the use of uncertainty metrics. We used the mutual information to filter through the real-world data and verified that the model's precision increased as the mutual information threshold was reduced. We highlight that the use of the mutual information was only possible because we used a BNN. Standard neural networks do not provide stochastic output and therefore do not allow for meaningful measurements of the mutual information. As a result, the analysis shown in Sect. 5.2 would not be possible with deterministic networks.

In conclusion, we are the first to apply Bayesian neural networks in the context of mosquito detection and highlight the utility of estimating the uncertainty as part of the labelling process. In future work we will continue to explore further inference schemes for neural networks as well as incorporate Bayesian decision theory. We also hope to use our pipeline for automatically tagging mosquitoes to build larger labelled datasets that can then be used to build more sophisticated models for future real-world field experiments.

Acknowledgements. This work was funded by the Bill and Melinda Gates Foundation (OPP1209888). We would like to thank Dr. Emanuel Kaindoa, Dickson Msaky (IHI Tanzania), Paul I Howell and Dustin Miller (CDC, Atlanta), Dr. Sheila Ogoma (USAMRU-K), Dr. Vanessa Chen-Hussey, James Pearce (LSHTM), Prof. Theeraphap, Dr. Rungarun Tisgratog and Jirod Nararak (Kasesart University, Bangkok). We also thank NVIDIA for the grant of a Titan Xp GPU.

A Appendix

Scenario B (samples are certain, yet fully disagree), $\mathbf{y}^* = \{[1.0, 0.0], [0.0, 1.0]\}$:

$$\tilde{p}_1 = \frac{1}{2}\sum_s p_1^{(s)} = \frac{1}{2}(1+0) = \frac{1}{2}, \quad \tilde{p}_2 = \frac{1}{2}\sum_s p_2^{(s)} = \frac{1}{2}(0+1) = \frac{1}{2}, \quad (6)$$

$$\tilde{\mathcal{H}} = -(\frac{1}{2}\log\frac{1}{2} + \frac{1}{2}\log\frac{1}{2}) = \log 2, \quad (7)$$

$$h^{(1)} = -((0)\log 0 + (1)\log 1) = 0, \quad h^{(2)} = -((1)\log 1 + (0)\log 0) = 0, \quad (8)$$

$$\mathbb{E}[\mathcal{H}] = \frac{1}{2}(0+0) = 0, \quad (9)$$

$$I(\mathbf{y}^*, \boldsymbol{\omega}) = \tilde{\mathcal{H}} - \mathbb{E}[\mathcal{H}] = \log 2. \quad (10)$$

Scenario A (all samples equally uncertain), $\mathbf{y}^* = \{[0.5, 0.5], [0.5, 0.5]\}$:

$$\tilde{p}_1 = \frac{1}{2}\sum_s p_1^{(s)} = \frac{1}{2}(\frac{1}{2}+\frac{1}{2}) = \frac{1}{2}, \quad \tilde{p}_2 = \frac{1}{2}\sum_s p_2^{(s)} = \frac{1}{2}(\frac{1}{2}+\frac{1}{2}) = \frac{1}{2}, \quad (11)$$

$$\tilde{\mathcal{H}} = -(\frac{1}{2}\log\frac{1}{2} + \frac{1}{2}\log\frac{1}{2}) = \log 2, \quad (12)$$

$$\mathbb{E}[\mathcal{H}] = h(\boldsymbol{\omega}) = \tilde{\mathcal{H}} = \log 2, \quad (13)$$

$$I(\mathbf{y}^*, \boldsymbol{\omega}) = \tilde{\mathcal{H}} - \mathbb{E}[\mathcal{H}] = 0. \quad (14)$$

References

1. Audacity: Audacity(R): Free audio editor and recorder [computer application] (2018). https://audacityteam.org/. version 2.2.2. Accessed 21 Jan 2021
2. Bomphrey, R.J., Nakata, T., Phillips, N., Walker, S.M.: Smart wing rotation and trailing-edge vortices enable high frequency mosquito flight. Nature **544**(7648), 92–95 (2017)
3. Cobb, A.D.: The practicalities of scaling Bayesian neural networks to real-world applications. Ph.D. thesis, University of Oxford (2020)
4. Cobb, A.D., Jalaian, B.: Scaling Hamiltonian Monte Carlo inference for Bayesian neural networks with symmetric splitting. arXiv preprint arXiv:2010.06772 (2020)
5. Cobb, A.D., Roberts, S.J., Gal, Y.: Loss-calibrated approximate inference in Bayesian neural networks. arXiv preprint arXiv:1805.03901 (2018)
6. De Bruijn, N.: Uncertainty principles in Fourier analysis. Inequalities **2**(1), 57–71 (1967)
7. Detection and Classification of Acoustic Scenes and Events 2018: 2018 results (2018). http://dcase.community/challenge2018/task-general-purpose-audio-tagging-results. Accessed 04 Apr 2021
8. Detection and Classification of Acoustic Scenes and Events 2020: 2020 results (2020). http://dcase.community/challenge2020/task-acoustic-scene-classification-results-a. Accessed 04 Apr 2021

9. Dieleman, S., Schrauwen, B.: End-to-end learning for music audio. In: IEEE International Conference on Acoustics, Speech and Signal Processing (ICASSP), pp. 6964–6968 (2014)
10. Dou, Z., et al.: Acoustotactic response of mosquitoes in untethered flight to incidental sound. Sci. Rep. **11**(1), 1–9 (2021)
11. Fanioudakis, E., Geismar, M., Potamitis, I.: Mosquito wingbeat analysis and classification using deep learning. In: 2018 26th European Signal Processing Conference (EUSIPCO), pp. 2410–2414 (2018)
12. Gal, Y., Ghahramani, Z.: Dropout as a Bayesian approximation: representing model uncertainty in deep learning. In: International Conference on Machine Learning, pp. 1050–1059 (2016)
13. Gal, Y., Islam, R., Ghahramani, Z.: Deep Bayesian active learning with image data. In: International Conference on Machine Learning, pp. 1183–1192. PMLR (2017)
14. Greenwalt, Y.S., Siljeström, S.M., Rose, T., Harbach, R.E.: Hemoglobin-derived porphyrins preserved in a middle Eocene blood-engorged mosquito. Proc. Natl. Acad. Sci. **110**(46), 18496–18500 (2013)
15. Jakhete, S., Allan, S., Mankin, R.: Wingbeat frequency-sweep and visual stimuli for trapping male Aedes aegypti (Diptera: Culicidae). J. Med. Entomol. **54**(5), 1415–1419 (2017)
16. Johnson, B.J., Ritchie, S.A.: The siren's song: exploitation of female flight tones to passively capture male Aedes aegypti (Diptera: Culicidae). J. Med. Entomol. **53**(1), 245–248 (2016)
17. Jordan, M.I., Ghahramani, Z., Jaakkola, T.S., et al.: An introduction to variational methods for graphical models. In: Jordan, M.I. (ed.) Learning in Graphical Models, pp. 105–161. Springer, Heidelberg (1998). https://doi.org/10.1007/978-94-011-5014-9_5
18. Joshi, A., Miller, C.: Review of machine learning techniques for mosquito control in urban environments. Ecol. Inform. 101241 (2021)
19. Juang, B.H., Rabiner, L.R.: Automatic speech recognition - a brief history of the technology development. Georgia Institute of Technology and the University of California **1**, 67 (2005)
20. Kaggle: BirdCLEF 2021 - Birdcall Identification (2021). https://www.kaggle.com/c/birdclef-2021/leaderboards. Accessed 01 Apr 2021
21. Kiskin, I., Meepegama, U., Roberts, S.: Super-resolution of time-series labels for bootstrapped event detection. In: Time-series Workshop at the International Conference on Machine Learning (2019)
22. Kiskin, I., et al.: Mosquito detection with neural networks: the buzz of deep learning. arXiv preprint arXiv:1705.05180 (2017)
23. Kiskin, I., Wang, L., Cobb, A., et al.: Humbug Zooniverse: a crowd-sourced acoustic mosquito dataset. In: International Conference on Acoustics, Speech, and Signal Processing 2020, NeurIPS Machine Learning for the Developing World Workshop 2019 (2019, 2020)
24. Kiskin, I., et al.: HumBugDB: a large-scale acoustic mosquito dataset. Zenodo (2021). https://doi.org/10.5281/zenodo.4904800
25. Kiskin, I., Zilli, D., Li, Y., Sinka, M., Willis, K., Roberts, S.: Bioacoustic detection with wavelet-conditioned convolutional neural networks. Neural Comput. Appl. **32**(4), 915–927 (2018). https://doi.org/10.1007/s00521-018-3626-7
26. Li, Y., et al.: Cost-sensitive detection with variational autoencoders for environmental acoustic sensing. In: NeurIPS Workshop on Machine Learning for Audio Signal Processing (2017)

27. Li, Y., et al.: Mosquito detection with low-cost smartphones: data acquisition for malaria research. In NeurIPS Workshop on Machine Learning for the Developing World (2017)
28. MacKay, D.J.: A practical Bayesian framework for backpropagation networks. Neural Comput. **4**(3), 448–472 (1992)
29. Minakshi, M., Bharti, P., Chellappan, S.: Identifying mosquito species using smartphone cameras. In: 2017 European Conference on Networks and Communications (EuCNC), pp. 1–6. IEEE (2017)
30. Mukundarajan, H., Hol, F.J.H., Castillo, E.A., Newby, C., Prakash, M.: Using mobile phones as acoustic sensors for high-throughput mosquito surveillance. elife **6**, e27854 (2017)
31. Neal, R.M.: Bayesian Learning for Neural Networks. Lecture Notes in Statistics, vol. 118. Springer, Heidelberg (2012). https://doi.org/10.1007/978-1-4612-0745-0
32. Ogawa, K., Kanda, T.: Wingbeat frequencies of some anopheline mosquitoes of East Asia (Diptera: Culicidae). Appl. Entomol. Zool. **21**(3), 430–435 (1986)
33. Perevozkin, V.P., Bondarchuk, S.S.: Species specificity of acoustic signals of malarial mosquitoes of anopheles maculipennis complex. Int. J. Mosq. Res. **2**(3), 150–155 (2015)
34. Piczak, K.J.: Environmental sound classification with convolutional neural networks. In: 2015 IEEE 25th International Workshop on Machine Learning for Signal Processing (MLSP). IEEE (2015)
35. Sainath, T.N., et al.: Deep convolutional neural networks for large-scale speech tasks. Neural Netw. **64**, 39–48 (2015)
36. Salamon, J., Bello, J.P.: Deep convolutional neural networks and data augmentation for environmental sound classification. IEEE Signal Process. Lett. **24**(3), 279–283 (2017)
37. Simões, P.M., Ingham, R.A., Gibson, G., Russell, I.J.: A role for acoustic distortion in novel rapid frequency modulation behaviour in free-flying male mosquitoes. J. Exp. Biol. **219**(13), 2039–2047 (2016)
38. Sinka, M.E., et al.: HumBug – an acoustic mosquito monitoring tool for use on budget smartphones. Methods in Ecology and Evolution (2021). https://doi.org/10.1111/2041-210X.13663
39. Sinka, M.E.: A global map of dominant malaria vectors. Parasites Vectors **5**(1), 1–11 (2012)
40. Unwin, D., Corbet, S.A.: Wingbeat frequency, temperature and body size in bees and flies. Physiol. Entomol. **9**(1), 115–121 (1984)
41. Villarreal, S.M., Winokur, O., Harrington, L.: The impact of temperature and body size on fundamental flight tone variation in the mosquito vector Aedes aegypti (diptera: Culicidae): implications for acoustic lures. J. Med. Entomol. **54**(5), 1116–1121 (2017)
42. World Health Organization: Fact Sheet (2020). https://www.who.int/news-room/fact-sheets/detail/vector-borne-diseases. Accessed 26 Jan 2020

Multitask Recalibrated Aggregation Network for Medical Code Prediction

Wei Sun[1] ⓘ, Shaoxiong Ji[1](✉) ⓘ, Erik Cambria[2] ⓘ, and Pekka Marttinen[1] ⓘ

[1] Aalto University, 02150 Espoo, Finland
{wei.sun,shaoxiong.ji,pekka.marttinen}@aalto.fi
[2] Nanyang Technological University, Singapore 639798, Singapore
cambria@ntu.edu.sg

Abstract. Medical coding translates professionally written medical reports into standardized codes, which is an essential part of medical information systems and health insurance reimbursement. Manual coding by trained human coders is time-consuming and error-prone. Thus, automated coding algorithms have been developed, building especially on the recent advances in machine learning and deep neural networks. To solve the challenges of encoding lengthy and noisy clinical documents and capturing code associations, we propose a multitask recalibrated aggregation network. In particular, multitask learning shares information across different coding schemes and captures the dependencies between different medical codes. Feature recalibration and aggregation in shared modules enhance representation learning for lengthy notes. Experiments with a real-world MIMIC-III dataset show significantly improved predictive performance.

Keywords: Medical code prediction · Multitask learning · Recalibrated aggregation network

1 Introduction

Clinical notes generated by clinicians contain rich information about patients' diagnoses and treatment procedures. Healthcare institutions digitized these clinical texts into Electronic Health Records (EHRs), together with other structural medical and treatment histories of patients, for clinical data management, health condition tracking and automation. To facilitate information management, clinical notes are usually annotated with standardized statistical codes. Different diagnosis classification systems utilize various medical coding systems. One of the most widely used coding systems is the International Classification of Diseases (ICD) maintained by the World Health Organization[1]. The ICD system is used to transform diseases, symptoms, signs, and treatment procedures into standard medical codes and has been widely used for clinical data analysis, automated medical decision support [8], and medical insurance reimbursement [24].

---

[1] https://www.who.int/standards/classifications/classification-of-diseases.

© The Author(s) 2021
Y. Dong et al. (Eds.): ECML PKDD 2021, LNAI 12978, pp. 367–383, 2021.
https://doi.org/10.1007/978-3-030-86514-6_23

The latest ICD version is ICD-11 that will become effective in 2022, while older versions such as ICD-9 and ICD-9-CM, ICD-10 are also concurrently used. Other popular medical condition classification tools include the Clinical Classifications Software (CCS) and Hierarchical Condition Category (HCC) coding.

This paper primarily studies ICD and CCS coding systems because of their individual characteristics of popularization and simplicity. CCS codes maintained by the Healthcare Cost and Utilization Project (HCUP[2]) provide medical workers, insurance companies, and researchers with an easy-to-understand coding scheme of diagnoses and processes. On the other hand, the ICD coding system provides a comprehensive classification tool for diseases and related health problems. Nonetheless, the CCS and ICD codes have a one-to-many relationship that enables the CCS software to convert ICD codes into CCS codes with a smaller label space at different levels. For instance, in Fig. 1, the ICD-CCS mapping scheme converts "921.3" ("Contusion of eyeball") and "918.1" ("Superficial injury of cornea") to the same CCS code "239", which represents the "Superficial injury; contusion". The CCS code "239" establishes a connection between two different ICD codes.

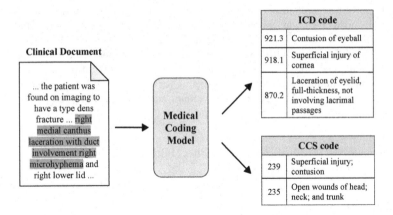

Fig. 1. An example of medical code prediction, where ICD and CCS codes are used as the coding systems. The second column of each tables shows the disease name corresponding to each medical code.

Medical codes concisely summarize useful information from vast amounts of inpatient discharge summaries, and have high medical and commercial value. They are consequently of interest for both medical institutions and health insurance companies. For example, major insurance companies use standard medical codes in their insurance claim business [4]. Professional coders do the medical coding task by annotating clinical texts with corresponding medical codes. Since manual coding is error-prone and labor-consuming [23], automated coding is needed. Taking the ICD coding as an example, many publications have

---

[2] www.hcup-us.ahrq.gov/toolssoftware/ccs/ccs.jsp.

proposed automated coding approaches, including feature engineering-based machine learning methods [15,25] and deep learning methods [5,17,22].

However, the automated medical coding task is still challenging as reflected in the following two aspects. Clinical notes contain noisy information, such as spelling errors, irrelevant information, and incorrect wording, which may have an adverse impact on representation learning, increasing the difficulty of medical coding. Also, it is a challenge to benefit from the relationship between different medical codes, especially when the label is high-dimensional. Existing automatic ICD coding models, such as CAML [22] and MultiResCNN [17], have limited performance because they do not consider the relationship between ICD codes. In the medical ontology, there exists certain connections between different concepts. For example, in the ICD coding system, "921.3" and "918.1", representing "Contusion of eyeball" and "Superficial injury of cornea", respectively, belong to "Superficial injury; contusion". Medical coding models may suffer from underperformance if they can not effectively capture the relationships between medical codes. For example in Fig. 1, the highlight area in a clinical document is converted into corresponding medical codes, including ICD codes and CCS codes.

In this paper, we propose a novel framework called MT-RAM, which combines MultiTask (MT) learning with a Recalibrated Aggregation Module (RAM) for medical code prediction. In particular, the RAM improves the quality of representation learning of clinical documents, by injecting rich contextual information and performing nested convolutions, thereby solving the challenge of encoding noisy and lengthy clinical notes. In multitask training, we consider the joint training on two tasks, ICD and CCS code prediction. MultiTask Learning (MTL) is inspired by human learning, where people often apply the knowledge from previous tasks to help with a new task [33]. It makes full use of the information contained in each task, shares information between related tasks through common parameters, and enhances training efficiency [6,30]. In addition, MTL reduces over-fitting to specific tasks by regularizing the learned representation to be generalizable across tasks [18]. In the context of the two medical coding systems, CCS coding can promote the training on the ICD codes; further, the CCS codes can inform about the relationship between the ICD codes, thereby improving model performance.

Our contributions fall into the following four aspects.

- To the best of our knowledge, this paper is the first to adopt multitask learning for medical code prediction and demonstrate the benefits of leveraging multiple coding schemes.
- We design a recalibrated aggregation module (RAM) to generate clinical document features with better quality and less noise.
- We propose a novel framework called MT-RAM, which combines multitask learning, bidirectional GRU, RAM and label-aware attention mechanism.
- Experimental results show competitive performance of our framework across different evaluation criteria on the standard real-world MIMIC-III database when compared with several strong baselines.

Our paper is organized as follows: Sect. 2 introduces related work; Sect. 3 describes the proposed model; Sect. 4 performs a series of comparison experiments, an ablation study and a detailed analysis of the properties of the RAM; finally, Sect. 5 provides concluding remarks.

2   Related Work

Automated Medical Coding. Automated medical coding is an essential and challenging task in medical information systems [25]. Healthcare institutes use different medical coding systems such as ICD, one of the most widely used coding schemes. The majority of early automated medical coding works use machine learning algorithms. Larkey and Croft [16] proposed a ICD code classifier with multiple models, including K-nearest neighbor, relevance feedback, and Bayesian independence classifiers. Perotte et al. [25] presented two ICD coding approaches: a flat and a hierarchy-based SVM classifier. The experiments showed that hierarchical SVM model outperforms flat SVM because it captures the hierarchical structure of ICD codes.

Neural networks have gained popularity for medical coding with the recent advances of deep learning techniques. Recurrent neural networks capture the sequential nature of medical text and have been applied by several studies such as the attention LSTM [26], the Hierarchical Attention Gated Recurrent Unit (HA-GRU) [2], and the multilayer attention-based bidirectional RNN [31]. Convolutional networks also play an important role in this field. Mullenbach et al. [22] proposed Convolutional Attention network for Multi-Label classification (CAML). Li and Yu [17] utilized a Multi-Filter Residual Convolutional Neural Network (MultiResCNN), and Ji et al. [11] developed a dilated convolutional network. Fine-tuning retrained language models as an emerging trend for NLP applications has been reported to have limits in medical coding by several initial studies [11,17] and a comprehensive analysis on the pretraining domain and fine-tuning architectures [12].

Multitask Learning. Multitask learning is a machine learning paradigm that jointly trains multiple related tasks to improve the performance of each task and the generalization of the model. Multitask learning is widely used in various medical applications such as drug action extraction [34], biological image analysis [32] and clinical information extraction [3,28]. In recent years, researchers have studied leveraging multitask learning strategies to better process medical notes. Malakouti et al. [20] jointly trained different diagnostic models to improve performance of each diagnostic task. This work implemented the parameter sharing between tasks by utilizing the bottom-up and top-down steps. This multitask learning framework improved the performance and the generalization ability of independently learned models. Si and Roberts [27] presented a CNN-based multitask learning network for inpatient mortality prediction task, which comprises some related tasks such as 0-day, 30-day, 1-year patient death prediction.

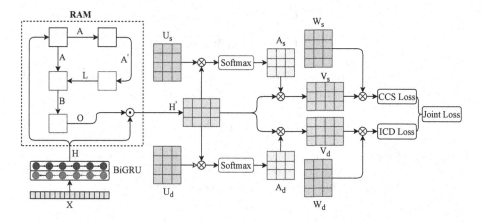

Fig. 2. Model architecture. In the Recalibrated Aggregation Module (RAM), "⊙" denotes as element-wise multiplication, "□" represent a *down node*; '▢' indicates a *lateral node*; "□" represents a *up node*; "⊗" is the matrix multiplication operation.

3   Method

This section describes the proposed Multi-Task Recalibrated Aggregation Network, referred as **MT-RAM**, as it combines the **M**ulti-**T**ask learning scheme and a **R**ecalibrated **A**ggregation **M**odule. The overall architecture of our MT-RAM network has five parts as shown in Fig. 2. We use word embeddings pretrained by the word2vec [21] as the input. Secondly, we use the bidirectional gated recurrent unit (BiGRU) [7] layer to extract document representation features capturing sequential dependencies in clinical notes. Next, a RAM module is used to improve the quality of the feature matrix and the efficiency of training for the multitask objective. Fourthly, the attention classification layers with two branches of ICD and CCS codes are composed of label-wise attention mechanism and linear classification layers. The last part combines the respective losses of the two classification heads and performs multitask training.

3.1   Input Layer

Denote a clinical document with n tokens as $w = \{w_1, w_2, \ldots, w_n\}$. We utilize word2vec [21] to pretrain each clinical document to obtain word embedding matrices. A word embedding matrix, referred to $\mathbf{X} = [\mathbf{x}_1, \mathbf{x}_2, \ldots, \mathbf{x}_n]^{\mathrm{T}}$, is the combination of each word vector $\mathbf{x}_n \in \mathbb{R}^{d_e}$, where d_e is the embedding dimension. Next, we feed word embedding matrix $\mathbf{X} \in \mathbb{R}^{n \times d_e}$ into the BiGRU layer to extract document representation features.

3.2   Bidirectional GRU Layer

We use a bidirectional GRU layer to extract the contextual information from the word embeddings $\mathbf{X}$ of the input documents. We calculate the latent states of GRUs on i-th tokenx_i:

$$\overrightarrow{\mathbf{h}_i} = \overrightarrow{\mathrm{GRU}}(\mathbf{x}_i, \overrightarrow{\mathbf{h}_{i-1}}) \tag{1}$$

$$\overleftarrow{\mathbf{h}_i} = \overleftarrow{\mathrm{GRU}}(\mathbf{x}_i, \overleftarrow{\mathbf{h}_{i+1}}) \tag{2}$$

where $\overrightarrow{\mathrm{GRU}}$ and $\overleftarrow{\mathrm{GRU}}$ represent forward and backward GRUs, respectively. Final operation is to concatenate the $\overrightarrow{\mathbf{h}_i}$ and then $\overleftarrow{\mathbf{h}_i}$ into hidden vector $\mathbf{h}_i$:

$$\mathbf{h}_i = \mathrm{Concat}(\overrightarrow{\mathbf{h}_i}, \overleftarrow{\mathbf{h}_i}) \tag{3}$$

Dimension of forward or backward GRU is set to d_r. Bidirectional hidden vectors $\mathbf{h}_i \in \mathbb{R}^{2d_r}$ are horizontally concatenated into a resulting hidden representation matrix $\mathbf{H} = [\mathbf{h}_1, \mathbf{h}_2, \ldots, \mathbf{h}_n]^T$, where the dimension of $\mathbf{H} \in \mathbb{R}^{n \times 2d_r}$.

3.3   Recalibrated Aggregation Module

We propose a **R**ecalibrated **A**ggregation **M**odule (RAM) that abstracts features learned by the BiGRU, recalibrates the abstraction, aggregates the abstraction and the recalibrated features, and eventually combines the new representation with the original one. This way, the RAM module can reduce the effect of noise in the clinical notes and lead to improved representations for medical code classification. In detail, the RAM leverages a nested convolution structure to extract and aggregate contextual information, which is used to recalibrate the noisy input features. In addition to this, through the convolutions, the RAM attains global receptive fields during feature extraction, which is complementary to the GRU-based recurrent structure described in Sect. 3.2. With these two characteristics, our RAM can improve the encoding of noisy and lengthy clinical notes. The RAM consists of feature aggregation and recalibration. The calculation flow of RAM is shown in Fig. 3 and described as below.

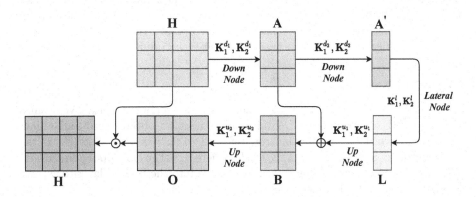

Fig. 3. The calculation flow of the RAM

Firstly, the hidden representation $\mathbf{H}$ from the BiGRU layer passes through two down nodes to obtain matrices $\mathbf{A}$ and $\mathbf{A}'$. This downsampling process can be denoted as:

$$\mathbf{A} = \bigwedge_{n=1}^{d_r} \left\{ \mathbf{K}_2^{d_1} \left[\tanh \left(\bigwedge_{m=1}^{d_r} \left(\mathbf{K}_1^{d_1} \mathbf{H} \right)_m \right) \right]_n \right\} \in \mathbb{R}^{n \times d_r}, \qquad (4)$$

where $\bigwedge_{m=1}^{d_r}$ represents dislocation addition, i.e., the second matrix is shifted by one unit to the right based on the position of the first matrix. The overlapped area is summed up. We repeat this operation until the last matrix and cut off unit vectors on both sides of the concatenated matrix. In Eq. 4, $\mathbf{K}_1^{d_1} \in \mathbb{R}^{2d_r \times k \times d_r}$ and $\mathbf{K}_2^{d_1} \in \mathbb{R}^{d_r \times k \times d_r}$ represent two convolutional kernel groups in the first down node and k is the kernel size. The second downsampled matrix $\mathbf{A}' \in \mathbb{R}^{n \times \frac{d_r}{2}}$ can also be obtained in a similar way with different convolutional kernel groups $\mathbf{K}_1^{d_2} \in \mathbb{R}^{d_r \times k \times \frac{d_r}{2}}$ and $\mathbf{K}_2^{d_2} \in \mathbb{R}^{\frac{d_r}{2} \times k \times \frac{d_r}{2}}$. Next, we use a lateral node with another two convolutional kernel groups $\mathbf{K}_1^{l} \in \mathbb{R}^{\frac{d_r}{2} \times k \times \frac{d_r}{2}}$ and $\mathbf{K}_2^{l} \in \mathbb{R}^{\frac{d_r}{2} \times k \times \frac{d_r}{2}}$, which have consistent in and out channel dimensions, to transform $\mathbf{A}'$ into lateral feature matrix $\mathbf{L} \in \mathbb{R}^{n \times \frac{d_r}{2}}$. We recover $\mathbf{L}$ with a up node and pair-wisely add the recovered signal with the first downsampled feature matrix $\mathbf{A}$ to obtain the primarily aggregated matrix $\mathbf{B} \in \mathbb{R}^{n \times d_r}$ as denoted in Eq. 5, where $\mathbf{K}_1^{u_1} \in \mathbb{R}^{\frac{d_r}{2} \times k \times d_r}$ and $\mathbf{K}_2^{u_1} \in \mathbb{R}^{d_r \times k \times d_r}$ represent deconvolutional kernel groups in the first up node.

$$\mathbf{B} = \mathbf{A} + \bigwedge_{n=1}^{d_r} \left\{ \mathbf{K}_2^{u_1} \left[\tanh \left(\bigwedge_{m=1}^{d_r} \left(\mathbf{K}_1^{u_1} \mathbf{L} \right)_m \right) \right]_n \right\} \qquad (5)$$

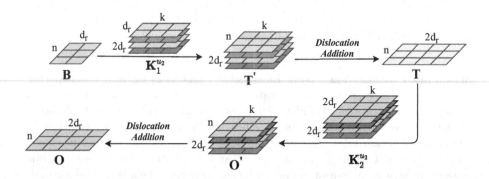

Fig. 4. Recover weight matrix $\mathbf{O}$ from the primary aggregation $\mathbf{B}$ in the RAM module. k is the kernel size, and d_r and $2d_r$ refer to the input and output feature dimensions in a up node.

Secondly, we perform upsampling operations on the aggregated feature matrix $\mathbf{B}$ to obtain weight matrix $\mathbf{O} \in \mathbb{R}^{n \times 2d_r}$ as illustrated in Fig. 4. Specifically, we leverage a deconvolution kernel group $\mathbf{K}_1^{u_2} \in \mathbb{R}^{d_r \times k \times 2d_r}$ to obtain the intermediate representation $\mathbf{T} \in \mathbb{R}^{n \times 2d_r}$. The different colors of $\mathbf{K}_1^{u_2}$ in Fig. 7 correspond to how the different parts of the matrix $\mathbf{T}' \in \mathbb{R}^{n \times k \times 2d_r}$ are calculated. This process is denoted as:

$$\mathbf{T} = \bigwedge_{m=1}^{2d_r} \mathbf{T}'_m = \bigwedge_{m=1}^{2d_r} (\mathbf{BK}_1^{u_2})_m. \tag{6}$$

We adopt a deconvolution operation on the intermediate representation $\mathbf{T}$ to get the weight matrix $\mathbf{O} \in \mathbb{R}^{n \times 2d_r}$, denoted as:

$$\mathbf{O} = \bigwedge_{n=1}^{2d_r} \mathbf{O}'_n = \bigwedge_{n=1}^{2d_r} (\tanh(\mathbf{T}) \mathbf{K}_2^{u_2})_n, \tag{7}$$

where $\mathbf{K}_2^{u_2}$ represents the deconvolution kernel group.

Finally, we employ the feature recalibration in a way similar to the attention mechanism, where the "attention" score is learned by an iterative procedure with convolutional feature abstraction (Eq. 4) and de-convolutional feature excitation (Eq. 7). Specifically, we multiply the input feature matrix $\mathbf{H}$ by the weight matrix $\mathbf{O}$ to obtain the recalibrated feature matrix $\mathbf{H}' \in \mathbb{R}^{n \times 2d_r}$, denoted as:

$$\mathbf{H}' = \tanh(\mathbf{O} \odot \mathbf{H}), \tag{8}$$

where "$\odot$" represents element-wise multiplication. The recalibration operation enhances the original features with contextual information injection through the weight matrix $\mathbf{O}$, which comprises rich semantic information that is consequently less sensitive to errors. It enables the RAM module to have improved generalization ability and, in the end, improved performance in medical coding.

3.4 Attention Classification Layers

Features extracted by lower layers in shared modules are label-agnostic. The Recalibrated Aggregation Module inherits the capacity of learning label-specific features from the Squeeze-and-Excitation block [10] to some extent. In order to make different positions of clinical notes correspond to different medical codes, we develop the label attention for classification layers to reorganize the characteristic information related to medical codes and enhance label specifications. Working together with the RAM module and label attention mechanism, our model can achieve label-aware representation learning, which is helpful for multitask heads as described in the next section (Sect. 3.5).

The attention classification layers are described as follows. We take a subscript d to denote a type of medical code. It can be generalized into different coding systems. Specifically, d represents the ICD code in our paper. For simplicity, the bias term is omitted. The attention scores of medical code $\mathbf{A}_d \in \mathbb{R}^{n \times m}$ can be calculated as:

$$\mathbf{A}_d = \text{Softmax}(\mathbf{H}' \mathbf{U}_d) \tag{9}$$

where $\mathbf{H}'$ is the document features extracted by the RAM block, $\mathbf{U}_d \in \mathbb{R}^{d_r \times m_d}$ represents the parameter matrix of query in the attention mechanism, and m_d denotes the number of target medical code. The attentive document features $\mathbf{V}_d \in \mathbb{R}^{d_r \times m_d}$ can be obtained by:

$$\mathbf{V}_d = \mathbf{A}_d^{\mathrm{T}} \mathbf{H}' \tag{10}$$

The label-wise attention mechanism captures the selective information contained in the document encoding $\mathbf{H}'$ and the query matrix $\mathbf{U}_d$ determines what information in the encoding matrix to prioritize.

Then, we use a fully-connected max pooling layer as a classifier, which affines the weight matrix to obtain the score vector $\mathbf{Y}_d \in \mathbb{R}^{m_d \times 1}$ denoted as:

$$\mathbf{Y}_d = \mathrm{Pooling}(\mathbf{W}_d \mathbf{V}_d^{\mathrm{T}}) \tag{11}$$

where $\mathbf{W}_d \in \mathbb{R}^{m_d \times m_d}$ represents the linear weight of the score vector. We use the Sigmoid activation function to produce the probability logits $\bar{\mathbf{y}}_d$ for final prediction.

3.5 Multitask Training

We introduce two self-contained tasks for multitask learning, i.e., ICD and CCS code prediction. The two medical coding branch tasks enter different coding processes and back-propagate the ICD code loss and CCS code loss, respectively. The structure of the two coding processing branches is similar. By passing the encoded features of clinical notes through the label attention module, we can get the weighted document features of the ICD code $\mathbf{V}_d \in \mathbb{R}^{d_r \times m_d}$ and the CCS code $\mathbf{V}_s \in \mathbb{R}^{d_r \times m_s}$, where m_d and m_s is the number of ICD and CCS codes respectively. With the linear classifier layer, the prediction probability of ICD and CCS codes are generated as $\bar{\mathbf{y}}_d$ and $\bar{\mathbf{y}}_s$.

The medical code assignment is a typical multi-label classification task. We use the binary cross entropy loss as the loss function of each sub-task in the multitask setting. The ICD coding loss and CCS coding loss are denoted as:

$$\mathcal{L}_d = \sum_{i=1}^{m_d} \left[-y_{d_i} \log(\bar{y}_{d_i}) - (1 - y_{d_i}) \log(1 - \bar{y}_{d_i}) \right] \tag{12}$$

$$\mathcal{L}_s = \sum_{i=1}^{m_s} \left[-y_{s_i} \log(\bar{y}_{s_i}) - (1 - y_{s_i}) \log(1 - \bar{y}_{s_i}) \right] \tag{13}$$

where $y_{d_i}, y_{s_i} \in \{0, 1\}$ are the target medical code labels. $\bar{y}_{d_i}$ and $\bar{y}_{s_i}$ represent prediction probability of ICD and CCS codes, and the number of ICD and CCS codes are denoted as m_d and m_s respectively. We adopt joint training for the two medical coding losses to facilitate multitask learning. The joint training loss is defined as

$$\mathcal{L}_M = \lambda_d \mathcal{L}_d + \lambda_s \mathcal{L}_s, \tag{14}$$

where λ_d and λ_s are scaling factors of ICD and CCS codes.

4 Experiments

We perform a series of experiments to validate the effectiveness of our proposed model on public real-world datasets. Source code is available at https://github.com/VRCMF/MT-RAM.

4.1 Datasets

MIMIC-III (ICD). The third version of Medical Information Mart for Intensive Care (MIMIC-III)[3] is a large, open-access dataset consists of clinical data associated with above 40,000 inpatients in critical care units of the Beth Israel Deaconess Medical Center between 2001 and 2012 [13]. Following Mullenbach et al. [22] and Li and Yu [17], we segment all discharge summaries documents based on the patient IDs, and generate 50 most frequent ICD codes for experiments. We refer MIMIC-III dataset with top 50 ICD codes as the MIMIC-III ICD dataset. There are 8,067 discharge summaries for training, and 1,574 and 1,730 documents for validation and testing, respectively.

MIMIC-III (CCS). We utilize the ICD-CCS mapping scheme, provided by the HCUP, to convert the ICD codes and obtain the dataset with CCS codes. The converted CCS dataset denotes as MIMIC-III CCS, which contains 38 frequent CCS labels. Because the MIMIC-III ICD dataset shares the discharge summary documents with the CCS dataset, the documents used for CCS code training, validation and testing are consistent with the ICD code documents. We change several conflicting mapping items so that ICD and CCS codes can achieve one-versus-one matching. The converted CCS codes are then used as the labels of discharge summaries.

4.2 Settings

Data Preprocessing. Following the processing flow of CAML [22], the non-alphabetic tokens, such as punctuation and numbers, are removed from clinical text. All tokens are transformed into lowercase format, and we replace low-frequency tokens (appearing in fewer than three documents) into the 'UNK' token. We train the word2vec [21] on all discharge summaries to obtain the word embeddings. The maximum length of each document is limited to 2,500, i.e., documents longer than this length are truncated. The kernel size of convolution layer in the RAM module is 3.

Evaluation Metrics. To evaluate the performance of models in CCS and ICD code (collectively called medical code) datasets, we follow the evaluation protocols of previous works [17,22]. We utilize micro-averaged and macro-averaged F1, micro-averaged and macro-averaged AUC (area under the receiver operating characteristic curve), precision at k as the evaluation methods. Precision

---

[3] https://mimic.physionet.org/gettingstarted/access/.

at k ('P@k' in shorthand) is the proportion of k highest scored labels in the ground truth labels. When calculating of micro-averaged scores, each clinical text and medical codes are treated as separate predictions. During the computing of macro-averaged metrics, we calculate the scores for each medical code and take the average of them. We run our model ten times and report the mean and standard deviation of all the metrics.

Hyper-parameter Tuning. We refer to the previous works [17,22] and apply some common hyper-parameter settings. Specifically, we set the word embedding dimension to 100, the maximum document length to 2500, dropout rate to 0.2, the batch size to 16, and the dimension of hidden units to 300. In the choice of learning rate, 0.008 is the optimal learning rate, which achieves good model performance and consumes moderate time to converge. We set the scaling factors λ_d and λ_s to 0.7 and 0.3 respectively. We use different optimizers to train our model, including Adam [14], AdamW [19] and SGD+momemtum [29]. Although the AdamW optimizer can shorten the training time, its predictive performance is not as good as the Adam. The performance of the SGD+momentum and the Adam are close, while Adam converges faster.

4.3   Baselines

CAML [22] comprises a single convolutional backbone and a label-wise attention mechanism, achieving high performance for ICD code prediction.
DR-CAML [22], i.e., the Description Regularized CAML, is an extension of CAML that incorporates the ICD description to regularize the CAML model.
HyperCore [5] uses the hyperbolic representation space to leverage the code hierarchy and utilize the graph convolutional network to capture the ICD code co-occurrence correlation.
MultiResCNN [17] adopts a multi-filter convolutional layer to capture various text patterns and a residual connection to enlarge the receptive field.

4.4   Results

MIMIC-III (ICD Codes). Table 1 shows that the results of our MT-RAM model performs better than all baseline models on all evaluation metrics. When compared with the state-of-the-art MultiResCNN [17], our model has improved the scores of macro-AUC, micro-AUC, macro-F1, micro-F1 and P@5 by 2.2%, 1.5% 4.5%, 3.6% and 2.3% respectively. Our model outperforms the CAML [22], which is the classical automated ICD coding model, by 4.6%, 3.4%, 11.9%, 9.2% and 5.5%. The improvement of our model in macro-F1 and micro-F1 is more significant than other metrics by comparing with HyperCore [5], specifically by 4.2% and 4.3% respectively. While other scores see moderate improvement by 1% ~ 3%. Recent pretrained language models such as BERT [9] and its domain-specific variants like ClinicalBERT [1] are omitted from the comparison because

Table 1. MIMIC-III results (ICD code). Results are shown in %. We set different random seeds for initialization to run our model for 10 times. Results of MT-RAM are demonstrated in *means ± standard deviation*

Models	AUC-ROC		F1		P@5
	Macro	Micro	Macro	Micro	
CNN	87.6	90.7	57.6	62.5	62.0
CAML	87.5	90.9	53.2	61.4	60.9
DR-CAML	88.4	91.6	57.6	63.3	61.8
HyperCore	89.5 ± 0.3	92.9 ± 0.2	60.9 ± 0.1	66.3 ± **0.1**	63.2 ± 0.2
MultiResCNN	89.9 ± 0.4	92.8 ± 0.2	60.6 ± 1.1	67.0 ± 0.3	64.1 ± **0.1**
MT-RAM (ours)	**92.1** ± **0.1**	**94.3** ± **0.1**	**65.2** ± **0.3**	**70.7** ± 0.2	**66.4** ± 0.2

these models are limited to process text with 512 tokens and have been reported with poor performance by two recent studies [12,17].

MIMIC-III (CCS Code). We evaluate the CAML, DR-CAML and the MultiResCNN on the MIMIC-III CCS dataset and record the results in Table 2. Since the Hypercore [5] does not provide the source code, we omit it from the comparison. Following the practice described in the section of hyper-parameter tuning, we set all the parameters of the CAML and the MultiResCNN to be consistent with the hyper-parameters of the original works except for the learning rate.

As shown in Table 2, we can see that our model obtains better results in the macro AUC, micro AUC, macro F1, micro F1, P@5, compared with the strong MultiResCNN baseline. The improvement of our model is 1.6% in both macro AUC and micro AUC, 4.2% in macro F1, 3.4% in micro F1, and 2.7% in P@5. DR-CAML uses the ICD code description to achieve performance improvement. DR-CAML uses the description of ICD codes to improve the performance of CAML. But on MIMIC-III (CCS) dataset, this description will cause interference to CAML, so the result of DR-CAML is worse. Our model improves the F1 macro metric by 5.5%, comparing with the CAML model.

Table 2. MIMIC-III results (CCS code). We run each model for 10 times and each time set different random seeds for initialization. Results of all models are demonstrated in *means ± standard deviation*

Models	AUC-ROC		F1		P@5
	Macro	Micro	Macro	Micro	
CAML	89.2 ± 0.3	92.2 ± 0.3	60.9 ± 0.9	67.5 ± 0.4	64.5 ± 0.4
DR-CAML	87.5 ± 0.4	90.5 ± 0.4	59.3 ± 1.0	65.6 ± 0.6	62.6 ± 0.5
MultiResCNN	89.2 ± 0.2	92.4 ± 0.2	62.9 ± 0.9	68.8 ± 0.6	64.6 ± 0.3
MT-RAM (ours)	**92.2** ± **0.1**	**94.6** ± **0.1**	**69.4** ± **0.1**	**74.4** ± 0.2	**68.4** ± **0.1**

4.5   Ablation Study

We examine the general usefulness of the two main components - multitask training (MTL) and RAM module, by conducting an ablation study, where we consider the performance of three representative ICD coding models: CAML, MultiResCNN, and the GRU-based model (our method), with and without the specific components.

Multitask Learning. We firstly investigate the effectiveness of the multitask learning (MTL) scheme. From Table 3, we can observe that CAML and BiGRU have been improved by a relatively large margin across all evaluation metrics with multitask training. The CAML with MTL achieves 7.6% and 5.2% improvement in macro and micro F1, respectively, and obtains increases by about 2% to 3% in other scores. Similarly, the BiGRU with MTL has achieved a good improvement in macro and micro F1, increased by 4.2% and 3.3% respectively. For the MultiResCNN model, the multitask learning also contributes to relatively good results, which is 2.3% improvement in the macro F1 score. The reason why multitask learning can improve the performance of the model is the information exchange between the two tasks. Intuitively, there exists a correlation relationship between ICD and CCS coding systems This leads to complementary benefits for both ICD and CCS code prediction tasks. CAML and MultiResCNN have achieved significant gains by incorporating the multitask learning aggregation framework as a whole, i.e., the multitask learning scheme and the RAM together. Therefore, the gain of the multitask learning aggregation framework is not limited to some special network structures, and it has strong generalization ability.

Table 3. Ablation study

Models	AUC-ROC		F1		P@5
	Macro	Micro	Macro	Micro	
CAML	87.5	90.9	53.2	61.4	60.9
CAML + RAM	91.3	93.5	61.4	67.4	65.1
CAML + MTL	90.8	93.2	60.8	66.6	64.0
CAML + MTL + RAM	**91.4**	**93.8**	**62.5**	**68.7**	**65.3**
MultiResCNN	89.9	92.8	60.6	67.0	64.1
MultiResCNN + RAM	91.2	93.4	62.4	68.1	64.7
MultiResCNN + MTL	90.8	93.2	62.9	67.8	64.3
MultiResCNN + MTL + RAM	**91.7**	**93.9**	**64.1**	**69.0**	**65.0**
BiGRU	91.0	93.4	60.4	66.6	64.4
BiGRU + RAM	91.7	93.6	63.5	69.1	65.0
BiGRU + MTL	91.8	94.1	64.6	69.9	66.2
BiGRU + MTL + RAM (MT-RAM)	**92.1**	**94.3**	**65.1**	**70.6**	**66.4**

Recalibrated Aggregation Module. The second part of ablation study if examines whether the proposed Recalibrated Aggregation Module (RAM) can learn useful features and consequently lead to better performance. In Table 3, the performance of the three models has been greatly improved after including the RAM module to the multitask BiGRU architecture. The micro F1 scores of CAML, MultiResCNN and MT-RAM have been improved by 2.1%, 1.2% and 0.8%, respectively. The RAM module helps the GRU-based model achieve greater improvement than convolution-based models.

4.6   A Detailed Analysis of the Properties of the RAM

We conduct an exploratory study to investigate the effectiveness of element-wise multiplication in the final feature weighting stage. We denote models applying the multitask learning and multiplicative to CAML and MultiResCNN as MT-CAML + RAM (Mult) and MT-MultiResCNN + RAM (Mult), respectively. The RAM (Add) means to replace the multiplication operation in RAM with an addition operation. From Table 4, we can observe that the model with RAM (Mult) outperforms models with RAM (Add) in most evaluation metrics. Although the results of MT-RAM (Add) in F1 macro, F1 micro and P@5 are slightly better than the results of MT-RAM (Mult), the gap is marginal. Considering the generalization ability and performance improvement of the two modules, the RAM with multiplication operation outperforms the RAM with addition operation.

Table 4. Analysis of RAM: multiplicative versus additive

Models	AUC-ROC		F1		P@5
	Macro	Micro	Macro	Micro	
MT-CAML + RAM (Add)	91.1	93.5	62.1	68.1	65.0
MT-CAML + RAM (Mult)	**91.4**	**93.8**	**62.5**	**68.7**	**65.3**
MT-MultiResCNN + RAM (Add)	91.1	93.3	62.4	67.7	64.1
MT-MultiResCNN+ RAM (Mult)	**91.7**	**93.9**	**64.1**	**69.0**	**65.0**
MT-RAM (Add)	92.0	94.1	**65.9**	**70.8**	**66.7**
MT-RAM (Mult)	**92.1**	**94.3**	65.1	70.6	66.4

Regarding to the position of RAM in the multitasking learning framework, we found that it is best to embed the RAM in the shared layers. Compared with putting RAM in the two branches of the framework, RAM module embedded in the shared layers helps two sub-tasks share more information. If RAM is embedded in two sub-branch networks, the depth of the sub-network will increase and the shared part will decrease. The deepening of the sub-network will interfere with the network convergence and make training more difficult. At the same time, reducing the shared part will reduce the amount of information exchange between sub-tasks, which will affect the improvement of the model by the multitask learning scheme.

5 Conclusion

In this paper, we proposed a novel multitask framework for the automated medical coding task, which improved feature learning for clinical documents and accounted for the dependencies between different medical coding systems. We designed a Recalibrated Aggregation Module (RAM) to enrich document features and reduce noisy information. Furthermore, we leveraged multitask learning to share information across different medical codes. We demonstrated that the combination of multitask learning and RAM improved automatic medical coding considerably. In addition, these components are generalizable and can be successfully integrated to other overall architectures. The experimental results on the real-world clinical MIMIC-III database showed that our framework outperformed previous strong baselines. Finally, we believe our framework can be beneficial not only in medical coding tasks, but also in other text label prediction tasks.

Acknowledgments. This work was supported by the Academy of Finland (grant 336033) and EU H2020 (grant 101016775). We acknowledge the computational resources provided by the Aalto Science-IT project. The authors wish to acknowledge CSC - IT Center for Science, Finland, for computational resources.

References

1. Alsentzer, E., et al.: Publicly available clinical BERT embeddings. In: Proceedings of the 2nd Clinical Natural Language Processing Workshop, pp. 72–78 (2019)
2. Baumel, T., Nassour-Kassis, J., Cohen, R., Elhadad, M., Elhadad, N.: Multi-label classification of patient notes a case study on ICD code assignment. arXiv preprint arXiv:1709.09587 (2017)
3. Bi, J., Xiong, T., Yu, S., Dundar, M., Rao, R.B.: An improved multi-task learning approach with applications in medical diagnosis. In: Daelemans, W., Goethals, B., Morik, K. (eds.) ECML PKDD 2008. LNCS (LNAI), vol. 5211, pp. 117–132. Springer, Heidelberg (2008). https://doi.org/10.1007/978-3-540-87479-9_26
4. Bottle, A., Aylin, P.: Intelligent information: a national system for monitoring clinical performance. Health Serv. Res. **43**(1p1), 10–31 (2008)
5. Cao, P., Chen, Y., Liu, K., Zhao, J., Liu, S., Chong, W.: HyperCore: hyperbolic and co-graph representation for automatic ICD coding. In: Proceedings of the 58th Annual Meeting of the Association for Computational Linguistics, pp. 3105–3114 (2020)
6. Chandra, R., Gupta, A., Ong, Y.-S., Goh, C.-K.: Evolutionary multi-task learning for modular training of feedforward neural networks. In: Hirose, A., Ozawa, S., Doya, K., Ikeda, K., Lee, M., Liu, D. (eds.) ICONIP 2016. LNCS, vol. 9948, pp. 37–46. Springer, Cham (2016). https://doi.org/10.1007/978-3-319-46672-9_5
7. Cho, K., et al.: Learning phrase representations using RNN encoder-decoder for statistical machine translation. arXiv preprint arXiv:1406.1078 (2014)
8. Choi, E., Bahadori, M.T., Schuetz, A., Stewart, W.F., Sun, J.: Doctor AI: predicting clinical events via recurrent neural networks. In: Machine Learning for Healthcare Conference, pp. 301–318. PMLR (2016)

9. Devlin, J., Chang, M.W., Lee, K., Toutanova, K.L.: BERT: pre-training of deep bidirectional transformers for language understanding. In: NAACL-HLT (2019)

10. Hu, J., Shen, L., Sun, G.: Squeeze-and-excitation networks. In: Proceedings of the IEEE Conference on Computer Vision And Pattern Recognition, pp. 7132–7141 (2018)

11. Ji, S., Cambria, E., Marttinen, P.: Dilated convolutional attention network for medical code assignment from clinical text. In: Proceedings of the 3rd Clinical Natural Language Processing Workshop at EMNLP, pp. 73–78 (2020)

12. Ji, S., Hölttä, M., Marttinen, P.: Does the magic of BERT apply to medical code assignment? A quantitative study. arXiv preprint arXiv:2103.06511 (2021)

13. Johnson, A.E.W., et al.: MIMIC-III, a freely accessible critical care database. Sci. Data **3**(1), 1–9 (2016)

14. Kingma, D.P., Ba, J.: Adam: a method for stochastic optimization. arXiv preprint arXiv:1412.6980 (2014)

15. Koopman, B., Zuccon, G., Nguyen, A., Bergheim, A., Grayson, N.: Automatic ICD-10 classification of cancers from free-text death certificates. Int. J. Med. Inform. **84**(11), 956–965 (2015)

16. Larkey, L.S., Croft, W.B.: Combining classifiers in text categorization. In: Proceedings of the 19th Annual International ACM SIGIR Conference on Research and Development in Information Retrieval, pp. 289–297 (1996)

17. Li, F., Hong, Y.: ICD coding from clinical text using multi-filter residual convolutional neural network. In: Proceedings of the AAAI Conference on Artificial Intelligence, vol. 34, pp. 8180–8187 (2020)

18. Liu, X., He, P., Chen, W., Gao, J.: Multi-task deep neural networks for natural language understanding. arXiv preprint arXiv:1901.11504 (2019)

19. Loshchilov, I., Hutter, F.: Decoupled weight decay regularization. arXiv preprint arXiv:1711.05101 (2017)

20. Malakouti, S., Hauskrecht, M.: Hierarchical adaptive multi-task learning framework for patient diagnoses and diagnostic category classification. In: 2019 IEEE International Conference on Bioinformatics and Biomedicine (BIBM), pp. 701–706. IEEE (2019)

21. Mikolov, T., Sutskever, I., Chen, K., Corrado, G.S., Dean, J.: Distributed representations of words and phrases and their compositionality. arXiv preprint arXiv:1310.4546 (2013)

22. Mullenbach, J., Wiegreffe, S., Duke, J., Sun, J., Eisenstein, J.: Explainable prediction of medical codes from clinical text. arXiv preprint arXiv:1802.05695 (2018)

23. O'malley, K.J., Cook, K.F., Price, M.D., Wildes, K.R., Hurdle, J.F., Ashton, C.M.: Measuring diagnoses: ICD code accuracy. Health Serv. Res. **40**(5p2), 1620–1639 (2005)

24. Park, J.-K., et al.: The accuracy of ICD codes for cerebrovascular diseases in medical insurance claims. J. Prev. Med. Public Health **33**(1), 76–82 (2000)

25. Perotte, A., Pivovarov, R., Natarajan, K., Weiskopf, N., Wood, F., Elhadad, N.: Diagnosis code assignment: models and evaluation metrics. J. Am. Med. Inform. Assoc. **21**(2), 231–237 (2014)

26. Shi, H., Xie, P., Hu, Z., Zhang, M., Xing, E.P.: Towards automated ICD coding using deep learning. arXiv preprint arXiv:1711.04075 (2017)

27. Si, Y., Roberts, K.: Deep patient representation of clinical notes via multi-task learning for mortality prediction. In: AMIA Summits on Translational Science Proceedings 2019, p. 779 (2019)

28. Suk, H.-I., Lee, S.-W., Shen, D.: Deep sparse multi-task learning for feature selection in Alzheimer's disease diagnosis. Brain Struct. Funct. **221**(5), 2569–2587 (2016). https://doi.org/10.1007/s00429-015-1059-y
29. Sutskever, I., Martens, J., Dahl, G., Hinton, G.: On the importance of initialization and momentum in deep learning. In: International Conference on Machine Learning, pp. 1139–1147. PMLR (2013)
30. Yosinski, J., Clune, J., Bengio, Y., Lipson, H.: How transferable are features in deep neural networks? arXiv preprint arXiv:1411.1792 (2014)
31. Yu, Y., Li, M., Liu, L., Fei, Z., Wu, F.X., Wang, J.: Automatic ICD code assignment of Chinese clinical notes based on multilayer attention BiRNN. J. Biomed. Inform. **91**, 103114 (2019)
32. Zhang, W., Li, R., Zeng, T., Sun, Q., Kumar, S., Ye, J., Ji, S.: Deep model based transfer and multi-task learning for biological image analysis. IEEE Trans. Big Data **6**(2), 322–333 (2016)
33. Zhang, Y., Yang, Q.: A survey on multi-task learning. arXiv preprint arXiv:1707.08114 (2017)
34. Zhou, D., Miao, L., He, Y.: Position-aware deep multi-task learning for drug-drug interaction extraction. Artif. Intell. Med. **87**, 1–8 (2018)

Open Data Science to Fight COVID-19: Winning the 500k XPRIZE Pandemic Response Challenge

Miguel Angel Lozano[1]([✉])(iD), Òscar Garibo i Orts[2](iD), Eloy Piñol[2](iD),
Miguel Rebollo[2](iD), Kristina Polotskaya[3](iD), Miguel Angel Garcia-March[2](iD),
J. Alberto Conejero[2](iD), Francisco Escolano[1](iD), and Nuria Oliver[4](iD)

[1] University of Alicante, Alicante, Spain
malozano@ua.es
[2] IUMPA and VRAIN, Universitat Politècnica de València, València, Spain
[3] University Miguel Hernández, Elche, Spain
[4] ELLIS (European Lab. for Learning and Intelligent Systems) Unit Alicante,
Alicante, Spain

Abstract. In this paper, we describe the deep learning-based COVID-19 cases predictor and the Pareto-optimal Non-Pharmaceutical Intervention (NPI) prescriptor developed by the winning team of the 500k XPRIZE Pandemic Response Challenge, a four-month global competition organized by the XPRIZE Foundation. The competition aimed at developing data-driven AI models to predict COVID-19 infection rates and to prescribe NPI Plans that governments, business leaders and organizations could implement to minimize harm when reopening their economies. In addition to the validation performed by XPRIZE with real data, the winning models were validated in a real-world scenario thanks to an ongoing collaboration with the Valencian Government in Spain. We believe that this experience contributes to the necessary transition to more evidence-driven policy-making, particularly during a pandemic.

Keywords: SARS-CoV-2 · Computational epidemiology · Data science for public health · Recurrent neural networks · Non-pharmaceutical interventions · Pareto-front optimization

1   Introduction

During a pandemic, predicting the number of infections under different circumstances is important to inform public health, health care and emergency system responses. Different approaches to predict the evolution of a pandemic have been proposed in the literature, including traditional compartmental meta-population models –such as SIR or SEIR [12], complex network [18], agent-based individual [9] and purely data-driven time series forecasting [23] models.

Given the exponential growth in the number of SARS-CoV-2 infections and the pressure in the health care systems, most countries in the world have implemented non-pharmaceutical interventions (NPIs) during the current coronavirus

© Springer Nature Switzerland AG 2021
Y. Dong et al. (Eds.): ECML PKDD 2021, LNAI 12978, pp. 384–399, 2021.
https://doi.org/10.1007/978-3-030-86514-6_24

pandemic, designed to reduce human mobility and limit human interactions to contain the spread of the virus. These NPIs range from closing schools and non-essential workplaces to requiring citizens to wear masks and limiting national and/or international travel. How to model the impact that the applied NPIs have on the progression of the pandemic is a non-trivial task, particularly for traditional meta-population approaches. Moreover, the social and economic costs of applying NPIs for a sustained period of time has led to the largest global recession in history, with more than a third of the global population under confinement during the first wave of the pandemic in March - April of 2020. The global GDP shrunk by nearly 22 trillion of US dollars as of January 2021, according to the IMF[1]. Beyond the economic cost, the social cost of the pandemic is also staggering, preventing children and teenagers from attending schools, cancelling cultural activities and forbidding people to visit their friends or relatives.

In view of these challenges, the XPRIZE foundation organized in November of 2020 a global competition called the 500K XPRIZE Pandemic Response Challenge sponsored by Cognizant [1]. This four-month challenge focused on the development of data-driven AI systems to *predict* COVID-19 infection rates and *prescribe* Non-pharmaceutical Intervention Plans that governments and communities could implement to minimize harm when reopening their economies.

In this paper, we describe the predictor and prescriptor models developed by ValenciaIA4COVID, the winning team of the competition. The paper is organized as follows: Sect. 2 provides an overview of the most relevant related work. The data used in the competition is described in Sect. 3. The predictor and the prescriptor models are presented in Sect. 4 and 5, respectively, followed by the experimental results in Sect. 6. The main conclusions of our work and our future lines of research are outlined in Sect. 7.

2   Related Work

We built a COVID-19 infections predictor based on Long Short Term Memory (LSTM) networks [13]. Here, we briefly provide an overview of the approaches that are the most similar to ours, *i.e.* based on recurrent neural networks. Comparative analyses with other methods can be found in *e.g.* [25].

Chatterjee et al. [7] applied stacked, bidirectional LSTMs and compared them with multilayer LSTMs. They obtained good accuracy in the prediction of the total number of cases and deaths in the world. Moreover, they did not find any statistical correlation between COVID-19 cases and temperature, sunshine, and precipitation, showing that the number of infections mostly depends on the behavior and density of the population. In [8], LSTMs were used to predict the evolution of the pandemic in Canada and compared it with the USA, Spain, and Italy. Prompt interventions were found to have a strong impact in minimizing the total number of infections, though the accuracy of their predictions was good only for a relatively short time period. Other examples of early works explored using LSTMs

---

[1]   https://www.dw.com/en/coronavirus-global-gdp-to-sink-by-22-trillion-over-covid-says-imf/a-56349323.

to predict COVID-19 cases and the effect of NPIs in India [3] and Iran [4], with accurate results within a prediction interval of one week up to a month.

Clustering algorithms have been used to improve the models' performance. In [19] the authors use an LSTM to predict cases in different states of Brazil. First, they cluster nations by their temporal series of infections and then assign each Brazilian state to the closest cluster. Global COVID-19 case data was also used in [14] to cluster countries according to their outcomes.

To the best of our knowledge, our work is the first to propose a bank of LSTMs to predict the evolution of the coronavirus pandemic in 236 countries and regions in the world, with good prediction results over a long time period (up to 180 days) and taking into consideration the NPIs applied in each country/region.

Regarding the prescriptor part of our work, there are very few related references. In [24] a multi-objective genetic algorithm was used to find optimal policies using data from Wuhan. Sameni presents an approach to find a balance between interventions and the number of cases with a core compartmental model. This approach requires evaluating the impact of the policy on the evolution of the disease [22]. Several works evaluated the effectiveness of NPIs: see [20,21] for studies in Italy, Taiwan and Malaysia or [6,10] for recent studies in Europe. Finally, Miikkulainen *et al.* propose a neuroevolution approach to identify a Pareto-optimal set of NPIs [17], that was recommended during the Challenge.

3   Data

The coronavirus is the first global pandemic for which there is extensive data captured and shared on a daily basis for most countries and regions in the world. The Challenge leveraged publicly available official COVID-19 case data together with the Oxford COVID-19 Government Response Tracker data set[2] as the main data sources to be used during the competition [11]. This data set provides information for 186 countries and state/region-level data for the US, UK, Canada, and Brazil. The Challenge considered 182 countries[3], the 50 US states and the 4 regions in the UK, yielding a total of 236 countries or regions. In the rest of the paper, we will use GEO to denote the countries/regions.

The available data sources can be split into *case*-related data, *i.e.* number of daily confirmed COVID-19 cases, and *action or NPI*-related data, *i.e.* the NPIs and their level of activation each day for each GEO. In the Challenge, we considered 12 NPIs of two types: *confinement-based* and *public health-based*, that are summarized with all their possible levels of activation in Table 1.

4   Predictors of COVID-19 Cases

This part of the Challenge required building a predictor of the number of confirmed COVID-19 cases in the 236 GEOs for up to 180 days into the future,

---

[2]   https://www.bsg.ox.ac.uk/research/research-projects/coronavirus-government-response-tracker.

[3]   Tonga, Malta, Turkmenistan and Virgin Islands- were not considered due to lack of reliable data.

Table 1. NPIs considered in the Challenge and their possible activation values. The predictor is trained with confinement interventions (C1 to C8). Both confinement and public health interventions (H1 to H3 and H6) are considered in the prescriptor.

NPI name	Values	NPI name	Values
C1. School closing	[0,1,2,3]	C7. Internal movement restrictions	[0,1,2]
C2. Workplace closing	[0,1,2,3]	C8. International travel controls	[0,1,2,3]
C3. Cancel public events	[0,1,2]	H1. Public information campaigns	[0,1,2]
C4. Restrictions on gatherings	[0,1,2,3]	H2. Testing policy	[0,1,2,3]
C5. Close public transport	[0,1,2]	H3. Contact tracing	[0,1,2]
C6. Stay at home requirements	[0,1,2,3]	H6. Facial coverings	[0,1,2,3,4]

and considering the different NPIs implemented in each GEO. Evidently, the NPIs should impact the transmission of the disease and hence the number of cases. Next, we summarize our notation, followed by a description of our deep learning-based predictive model.

4.1   Notation

In the following, we will use the following terms and notation:

1. GEO: We denote as GEO a country or a region (*e.g.* California). We use the index j to refer to each GEO.

2. Population (P^j): P^j denotes the total population of GEO j. We assume that each GEO's population is constant during the entire period of time.

3. NewCases (X_n^j): The daily number of new cases on day n and GEO j is denoted by X_n^j. The first day considered is March, 11th 2020.

4. ConfirmedCases (Y_n^j): The cumulative number of confirmed cases up to day n in GEO j is given by $Y_n^j = \sum_{i=1}^{n} X_i^j$.

5. SmoothedNewCases (Z_n^j): We compute the average number of new cases between days $n - K + 1$ and n in GEO j as $Z_n^j = \frac{1}{K} \sum_{i=0}^{K-1} X_{n-i}^j$. This prevents noise due to different imputation policies (some GEOs do not report cases on weekends, while others do). We use $K = 7$ to smooth over one week.

6. CaseRatio (C_n^j): The ratio of cases between two consecutive days is denoted by $C_n^j = Z_n^j / Z_{n-1}^j$. It indicates the growth/decrease in the number of cases.

7. Susceptible Population (S_n^j): The number of susceptible individuals to be infected with coronavirus on day n and for GEO j is denoted by S_n^j.

8. ScaledCaseRatio (R_n^j): It is the CaseRatio C_n^j divided by the proportion of susceptible individuals in GEO j, $R_n^j = C_n^j \frac{P^j}{S_n^j}$. It captures the effects of a finite population, as it depends on proportion of susceptible individuals in GEO j.

9. Action (A_n^j): The vector with the applied NPIs in GEO j on day n.

10. Stringency of A_n^j ($Str_{A_n}^j$): The stringency of an NPI applied in GEO j on day n is given by $Str_{A_n}^j = \sum_{i=C1}^{H6} a_n^j(i) \cdot Cost^j(i)$, where $Cost^j$ is the cost vector of each of the 12 different types of NPIs ([C1...C8,H1,H2,H3,H6]) in GEO j.

11. Intervention Policy (IP): The sequence of daily 12-dimensional NPI or action vectors applied over a time period T.

12. Stringency of an Intervention Policy: The sum of the stringencies of the NPIs or actions A_n^j applied each day n over the time period T.

We denote estimations with a $\widehat{\ }$ symbol, *e.g.* $\widehat{X}_n^j$ is the estimated number new cases and $\widehat{R}_n^j$ the estimated scaled case ratio, both for GEO j and day n.

4.2 SIR Epidemiological Model

The predictors model the dynamics of the epidemics in each GEO j using an underlying basic SIR compartmental meta-population model [2]. In this model, the population is divided into three different states: S (Susceptible), Z (Infected), and D (Removed, due to recovery or death). The dynamics of such an SIR model is included in the S.M.[4] The evolution of the number of infected individuals is given by $\frac{dZ^j}{dt} = \beta \frac{S^j}{P_j} Z^j - \mu Z^j$, where β is the infection rate which controls the probability of transition between the S and Z; and μ is the recovery or removal rate, controlling the probability of transition between the Z and D states. When discretizing $\frac{dZ^j}{dt}$ for two consecutive days, we obtain

$$Z_n^j = Z_{n-1}^j + \beta \frac{S_{n-1}^j}{P_j} Z_{n-1}^j - \mu Z_{n-1}^j = \left(1 + \beta \frac{S_{n-1}^j}{P_j} - \mu \right) Z_{n-1}^j. \qquad (1)$$

which yields

$$R_n^j = \frac{(1-\mu)P_j}{S_n^j} + \beta = \frac{Z_n^j}{Z_{n-1}^j} \frac{P^j}{S_n^j}. \qquad (2)$$

This equation links R_n^j with the parameters of the SIR model. The larger the R_n^j, the larger $\frac{Z_n^j}{Z_{n-1}^j}$ and hence the larger the growth in the number of cases. Given that μ is constant in (2), the larger the infection rate β, the larger the R_n^j. Moreover, the infection rate and thus R_n^j depend on the applied NPIs.

If we predict $\widehat{R}_n^j$, we can estimate the number of cases for day n at GEO j:

$$\widehat{X}_n^j = \left(\widehat{R}_n^j \frac{S_{n-1}^j}{P_j} - 1 \right) K Z_{n-1}^j + X_{n-K}^j. \qquad (3)$$

where $K = 7$ is the size of the temporal window used to compute Z_n. As previously explained, X_{n-K} is the reported new cases for day $n - K$; $\widehat{R}_n^j$ is the predicted R_n^j; P^j is the population of GEO j; and Z_{n-1}^j is the cumulative number of cases averaged over K days for day $n - 1$ in GEO j.

Thus, the goal of the predictors is to estimate $\widehat{R}_n^j$ given the data up to day $n - 1$. Since R_n^j depends on the transmission rate and the dependency of the transmission rate on the NPIs, the predictors consider the number of COVID-19 infections (*context*) and the applied NPIs (*actions*) each day in each GEO.

---

[4]   https://github.com/malozano/valencia-ia4covid-xprize/raw/master/docs/supplementary.pdf.

4.3   Baseline or Standard Predictor

The baseline or standard predictor was provided by the Challenge organizers
[17]. It consists of two parallel LSTMs, one to model the *context* – given by
the R_n^j – and the other to model the *actions* (A_n^j) applied on day n in GEO j.
Figure 1 (left) depicts the architecture of this baseline model. It uses the context
and action data to get predictions separately, joining both outputs via a lambda
merge layer.

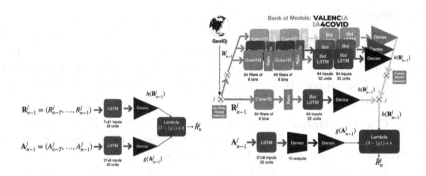

Fig. 1. Left: Baseline LSTM-based predictor; Right: ValenciaIA4COVID predictor.

The lambda layer combines the output of the context LSTM h (top) and
the output of the action LSTM g (down), represented in Fig. 1. The input to
the LSTM h is the vector of values of R_n in the previous T days in GEO j,
namely $\mathbf{R}_{n-1}^j = (R_{n-T}^j, \ldots, R_{n-1}^j)$. The input to the LSTM g is the matrix
of 12-dimensional NPIs (actions) taken during the previous T days in GEO j,
namely $\mathbf{A}_{n-1}^j = (A_{n-T}^j, \ldots, A_{n-1}^j)$.

In our experiments we set $T = 21$, similarly to [17]. Such time window mitigates the noise due to how different GEOs report cases (*e.g.* Spain does not
report confirmed cases during the weekends and holidays, France reports just
four days per week, etc.). Moreover, this temporal granularity enables the model
to consider the average period of 12–15 days between being exposed to the coronavirus, being detected and tested as a new confirmed case [15].

The output of the lambda layer for day n is the predicted $\widehat{R}_n^j$ given by

$$\widehat{R}_n^j = f(\mathbf{A}_{n-1}^j, \mathbf{R}_{n-1}^j) = (1 - g(\mathbf{A}_{n-1}^j))h(\mathbf{R}_{n-1}^j) \qquad (4)$$

with $g(\mathbf{A}_{n-1}^j) \in [0,1]$ and $h(\mathbf{R}_{n-1}^j) \geq 0$. More details about the baseline model
can be found in [17]. Note that when making predictions into the future, the
R_{n-i}^j values in the vector $\mathbf{R}_n^j$ are replaced by the estimations provided by the
predictor, namely $\widehat{R}_{n-i}^j$, for $n - i >$ current_day, $i = 1, \ldots, T$.

4.4   ValenciaIA4COVID (V4C) Predictor

Similarly to the baseline predictor, we implemented an architecture with 2 LSTM-based branches: a *context* branch, where we modeled the R_n time series and an *action* branch, where we modeled the time series of the eight confinement-based ([C1...C8]) Non-pharmaceutical Interventions. While we did not consider public health-based NPIs, we improved the baseline predictor in several ways. We denote this improved model as the ValenciaIA4COVID or V4C predictor.

4.4.1   Context Branch

We identified large variability in the time series of confirmed COVID-19 cases depending on the GEO, which made it difficult for a single LSTM *context* model to perform well everywhere. More precisely, the analysis of the weights of a single model trained on all the data showed that the LSTM matrices were full rank. Hence, we opted for a bank of LSTM context models, shown in Fig. 1 (right).

Bank of Context Models. We created the bank as follows: First, we clustered the GEOs via a K-means algorithm applied to the time series of reported number of COVID-19 cases per 100K inhabitants. We optimized the number of clusters using the Elbow method, obtaining 15 different clusters shown in the S.M.

Next, we trained a *reference* LSTM model with data from the 20 most-affected GEOs and 15 different *cluster* LSTM models using data from all the GEOs in each of the 15 clusters. In our experiments, we set March 11th, 2020 as the starting date for training the models. We then evaluated the reference and all the cluster models on our testing data for all the GEOs. Our testing period started on Nov. 1st for long-term evaluation and Dec. 1st for short-term evaluation, ending on Dec. 21st, 2020. We automatically selected the model with the lowest MAE per 100K inhabitants in each GEO, applying Occam's razor principle to minimize the number of models in our bank. Thus, we favored the *reference* model when it obtained a similar performance to the best of the cluster models. As a result of this process, we selected nine models: the *reference* model, applied in 135 GEOs; and eight *cluster* models applied in the remaining GEOs. A visualization of the cluster and model assignments can be found here[5].

LSTMs Architecture. In the context branch (h) we implemented two different LSTM-based architectures, as depicted in Fig. 1 (right): one for the *reference* model and the other for each of the eight *cluster* models. The *reference* model includes a convolutional layer with ReLu activation function and a bidirectional LSTM followed by a dense layer. Each convolutional layer has 64 filters of size 8. This reference model empirically generalized well for 135 GEOs.

The *cluster* models consist of a stacked version of the architecture of the reference model, with two convolutional layers and two stacked bidirectional LSTMs. Each convolutional layer also has 64 filters of size 8 with ReLu as the activation function and add a final dense layer. After the double $1D$ convolution spans the characterization of the input sequence, the first LSTM encodes such

---

[5] https://tinyurl.com/cjstz4yc.

a characterization in states of 64 dimensions (bidirectional) and feeds into the second LSTM, whose units can now operate at a different time scale. This added complexity enabled the models to perform well in the GEOs where the reference model did not. After model selection, we obtained a bank of eight different cluster models.

4.4.2   Action Branch

We used an LSTM followed by two dense layers to smooth the output and hence better capture non-linearities. Similarly to [17], we used a sigmoid activation function to guarantee that the action layer's output to be in [0,1]. Since increasing the activation or stringency of an NPI should not decrease its effectiveness, g is constrained to satisfy the condition: if $\min(A - A') \geq 0 \longrightarrow g(A) \geq g(A')$. This constraint is enforced by setting all trainable parameters of g to be non-negative (absolute value) after each parameter update. Note that convolution here is not considered in order to keep the raw NPI constraints. The V4C predictor only considers the confinement NPIs, so each A_n^j is an 8-dimensional vector with the level of activation of the eight confinement NPIs (see Table 1).

4.4.3   Merge Function

The two branches use the data from the last 21 days that are combined into a final dense layer to get the predicted $\widehat{R}_n$. The outputs of each branch (h and g) are merged by the lambda function defined in (4). Thus, the predicted $\widehat{R}_n$ provided by the *context* branch is modified by the output from the *action* branch. The stricter the NPIs, the larger the output from the action layer, thus reducing the context layer's output. Finally, once the model gives the predicted $\widehat{R}_n$, the predicted number of new infections for day n, $\widehat{X}_n$, is obtained using (3).

5   Prescriptor of Intervention Policies

The final phase of the XPRIZE competition required building a *prescriptor* which would recommend for each GEO and for any period of time, up to 10 different Intervention Policies (IP) with the best balance between their economic/social cost and the resulting number of COVID-19 cases.

Thus, it entailed solving a two-objective optimization problem by identifying the set of solutions that would be on the Pareto front [5, 16, 17]. On the one hand, there is the *stringency* of a certain IP which captured the sum of the costs of implementing such a policy. On the other hand, there is the number of COVID-19 cases per 100K inhabitants which would result from applying such IP. Given that this is a hypothetical scenario, the number of COVID-19 infections under the IPs was estimated by the *baseline* or standard predictor provided by the XPRIZE Challenge organizers. All the teams used the same predictor to enable the judges to compare the prescriptors from different teams properly.

Our goal in the Prescription phase of the competition was to develop an *interpretable*, data-driven and flexible prescription framework that would be

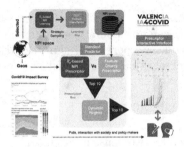

Fig. 2. V4C Prescriptor. The (offline) learning box (in blue) infers the convergence $\widehat{R}_n$ for the sampled NPIs, and the Gradient Boosted Trees identify the feature importance. The prescriptor relies on the standard XPRIZE predictor. The first set of NPIs is obtained by the NPI-$\widehat{R}_n$ mapping; the second set, using a feature importance-based greedy algorithm. These two sets compete and up to 10 non-dominated IPs are selected. (Color figure online)

usable by non machine-learning experts, such as citizens and policymakers in the Valencian Government. Our design principles were therefore driven by developing explainable and transparent models. The Challenge entailed finding the set of Pareto-optimal IPs with the best trade-off between their economic/social costs and their associated number of resulting COVID-19 cases. An intervention policy IP_1 *dominates* another intervention policy IP_2 if the stringency(IP_1) $\leq$ stringency(IP_2) and the resulting number of COVID-19 cases under IP_1 < than under IP_2. The goal was to find up to 10 IPs for each GEO, for any time period and any costs that would dominate the rest of possible IPs. As in the case of our predictor, we decided to combine complementary approaches to have a more robust solution, shown in Fig. 2.

5.1 Modeling the NPI - COVID-19 Cases Space

Before building the prescriptor, we performed an exploratory data analysis of the problem space. Our goal was to shed light on the relationship between the NPIs and the resulting number of COVID-19 cases. Considering all the possible values of each dimension of the NPI or action vector, there are 7,776,000 possible combinations of NPI vectors that could be applied at each time step.

Each NPI vector, when applied for a minimum amount of time, would lead to a reduction or increase in the number of COVID-19 cases in the GEO where it is applied (see Eq. 4). To better understand the impact that different NPI vectors have on the number of COVID-19 cases, we ran numerous experiments where we called the predictor with different values of the NPI vector over varying time periods of 30 to 90 days and on a sample of 21 representative GEOs from different continents[6], namely: United States, Brazil, India, Mexico, Italy, China, United Kingdom, France, England, Russia, Iran, Spain, Argentina, Colombia, New York State, Peru, Germany, Poland, South Africa, Texas and California. For each case, we obtained the resulting $\widehat{R}_n$ estimated by the predictor.

---

[6] We selected amongst the most affected countries and regions across the globe.

In our experiments, we observed that the **same NPI vector** would lead to the **same convergence** $\widehat{R}_n$ in **all the GEOs** and over **any time period** provided that the NPI was applied for long enough (see a justification in the S.M.). Moreover, we found that the convergence time of $\widehat{R}_n$ is inversely proportional to its value. As per Eq. (2), note that the larger the $\widehat{R}_n$, the larger the number of resulting COVID-19 cases. We refer to this finding as the R_n *synchronization principle*. Moreover, all countries underwent a transitory period of ≈ 21 days since the application of a certain NPI before their $\widehat{R}_n$ started converging towards its convergence value. Figure 3 illustrates the convergence of the $\widehat{R}_n$ for two different NPI vectors in the 21 selected GEOs.

5.2 Prescriptors

5.2.1 Prescriptor Method 1: R_n-based NPI Selection

Based on the R_n *synchronization principle*, one could easily obtain the Pareto-optimal front of intervention policies if the mapping between the 7.8 million of possible combinations of the NPI vector and their associated convergence $\widehat{R}_n$ were to be known. Unfortunately, generating such a mapping was not feasible in the time frame provided by the Challenge as it would require making millions of calls to the predict function. Hence, we opted for computing a sample of such a matrix (whose distribution is shown in the S.M.), obtained as (1) all the NPI vectors with stringencies [0 to 6] and [28 to 34]; (2) all NPI vectors with one and two non-zero entries; and (3) a random sample of 10,000 NPIs.

For each NPI in the sample, we computed the convergence $\widehat{R}_n$, and the resulting total number of COVID-19 cases in 20 and 60 days.

Using this NPI-$\widehat{R}_n$ matrix, we trained state-of-the-art machine-learning models to predict the $\widehat{R}_n$ for any given NPI vector. The best performing and explainable model were Gradient Boosted Trees, which obtained a MAE on the test set of 0.0003. While such MAE was still too large for us to be able to fill-in all the missing elements in the NPI-$\widehat{R}_n$ matrix, we carried out a feature importance analysis and discovered that the C2, C1, H2, C4 and C5 interventions are, in this order, the most important to predict their associated $\widehat{R}_n$ and hence the resulting number of COVID-19 cases (see S.M. for details).

Thus, we also included in our NPI-$\widehat{R}_n$ matrix all the NPI vectors with non-zero values in their C1, C2, C4, C5 and H2 interventions and zero in the rest of the dimensions. This led to a total of 54,652 NPI vectors.

As a result, we generated a matrix with the mapping between these different NPI vectors, their associated stringencies (at cost 1), the number of cases that they would lead to at 20 days and at 60 days, and their convergence $\widehat{R}_n$. We carried out all computations on the sample of 21 previously listed GEOs.

At run time, given an input cost vector, the prescriptor computes the stringency of each row in the NPI-$\widehat{R}_n$ matrix and identifies the NPI combinations that are on the Pareto front by selecting those that lead to the best trade-off between their stringencies, their associated number of cases at 20 and 60 days and their convergence $\widehat{R}_n$. More details are included in the S.M.

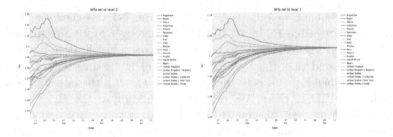

Fig. 3. $\hat{R}_n$ convergence for two different NPI vectors on 21 representative GEOs.

5.2.2   Prescriptor Method 2: Feature Greedy NPI Selection

As per the feature importance analysis described above and given a cost vector, we developed a greedy NPI prescriptor as follows: each dimension of the NPI vector is ranked by its *priority*, computed as its feature importance divided by its cost. This prescriptor consists of a greedy algorithm that consecutively activates to its maximum value each NPI dimension by order of its priority. This method is related to the greedy strategies developed to solve the knapsack problem[7].

5.2.3   Prescriptor Combination

Each of the methods above provides a set of NPI recommendations for each GEO for each day. From such a set, we select the 10 best NPIs that satisfy the following criteria: (1) they are not dominated by any other NPI; and (2) they contribute to having a diverse set of NPIs that cover the full range of possible stringency values. Additional details are included in the S.M.

5.3   Intervention Policy Definition

Finally, the prescriptor needs to provide a set of up to 10 Intervention Policies, *i.e. dynamic* regimes of applying the selected NPIs over the time period of interest. To do so, we compute all possible combinations of subsequently applying the selected NPIs in chunks of minimum 14 days (to enable the NPIs to act) and identify the Pareto-front set of combinations that would yield the optimal trade-off between stringency and number of cases. The total number of chunks is dynamically determined. From this set of combinations, we again select the 10 that (1) are not dominated by any other policy; (2) contribute to having a diverse set of policies along the stringency axis and (3) minimize the changes in NPIs, as every NPI change has a social cost from a practical perspective.

Two screenshots of the interactive visualization that we developed so policymakers could easily compare the prescribed IPs are shown in the S.M. and can be found here[8].

---

[7] See https://en.wikipedia.org/wiki/Knapsack_problem..

[8] https://public.tableau.com/app/profile/kristina.p8284/viz/PrescriptionsWeb/Visualize.

6   Experimental Results

In this Section, we report the results of quantitatively evaluating our predictor both in short and long-term prediction scenarios and qualitatively assessing the performance of our predictor and prescriptor in hypothetical scenarios. Our source code is publicly available[9].

6.1   Predictor

We evaluated the predictive performance of our COVID-19 cases predictor and compared it to the baseline model under different scenarios. We computed both the Mean Absolute Error (MAE) of the estimated number of COVID-19 cases per 100K inhabitants for each GEO in the Challenge and the Mean Rank of our model when compared to the baseline model.

All the models were trained with data from the Oxford COVID-19 Government Response Tracker dataset, from March 11th to December 17th 2020, for the 20 most affected countries in terms of confirmed cases.

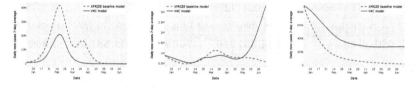

Fig. 4. Smoothed predicted daily new cases worldwide (7-day average) for three different future scenarios based on different values of the NPI vector: zero (left), frozen (center) and maximal (right) NPIs applied. Note how without any NPIs there is a large wave of infections, which is avoided when the NPIs set to their maximal values.

As the consistency of the model is an important characteristic to assess, we evaluated the models both in short-term and long-term predictions. Short-term evaluations consisted in generating predictions for 3 weeks ahead into the future for the time period between Dec 1st and Dec 21st, 2020. Long-term evaluations were two-fold: First, with historic data, we tested the predictions between Nov 1st and Dec 21st, 2020; Second, we ran the predictors under three different 180-day prediction scenarios: (i) a scenario where the NPIs were frozen as of their values in Dec 21st 2020; (ii) a scenario with all NPIs in all GEOs were set to their maximum levels; and (iii) a scenario where all NPIs in all GEOs were set to 0. The behavior of our model under these three conditions made intuitive sense, as depicted in Fig. 4.

Table 2 displays the MAE per 100K inhabitants and the Mean Rank of the proposed model when compared to the baseline model provided by the XPRIZE organizers. We also include the results of only using our *reference* context model

---

[9] https://github.com/malozano/valencia-ia4covid-xprize.

without the clusters. As seen on the Table, our model outperforms the baseline model in all evaluation scenarios in terms of MAE and Mean Rank. Moreover, during the predictor evaluation phase of the XPRIZE Challenge, our predictor ranked third in the world in Mean Rank amongst all the teams, first in Mean Rank in Asian and in European GEOs. As per our collaboration with the President of the Valencian Government in Spain, we were able to share the predictions of our predictor during the 3rd wave of the COVID-19 pandemic that started right after Christmas of 2020. Figure 5 shows the predictions of our model (blue) when compared to the baseline predictor (red) and the ground truth (yellow). As seen in the Figure, our predictor was very accurate in predicting the evolution of the pandemic while taking into account the different NPIs that were implemented at the time. It provided valuable input to the Government in their decision-making.

Table 2. Predictor results in short and long-term evaluations in the 236 GEOS.

Predictor	Short-term		Long-term	
	MAE	Mean Rank	MAE	Mean Rank
XPRIZE LSTM baseline	157.924142	2.106383	935.340780	2.297872
V4C (w/o clusters)	138.208982	2.144681	825.375377	**1.834043**
V4C with clusters	**126.331216**	**1.748936**	**803.587381**	1.868085

6.2   Speed and Resource Use

In terms of training, we used an Intel Core i7 with 256 Gb RAM and GPU. The training time of the *reference* model with 20 trials was 108 min and of the *cluster* models ranged between 24 min (largest cluster with 106 GEOs) and 44 s (smallest cluster with 2 GEOs).

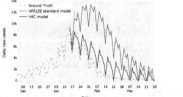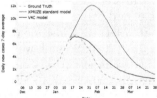

Fig. 5. Predictions vs ground truth for the Valencian region (Spain) during the third wave: daily new cases (left) and smoothed daily new cases (right).

We carried out our prediction experiments on an Intel Core i7, 4 cores, 2,7 Ghz, 16 GB 2133 MHz LPDDR3. Table 3 (Top) summarizes the times needed

Table 3. Top: Total time needed to generate predictions for all the GEOs. Bottom: Prescriptor results: # of dominating / # of dominated prescriptions for 5-day (from Aug 1st to Aug 5th, 2020), 31-day (from Jan 1st to Jan 31st, 2021) and 90-day (from Jan 1st to Mar 31st, 2021) time periods.

	Window size of prediction		
Predictor	**31-days**	**61-days**	**180-days**
Baseline	212 s	409 s	1,092 s
V4C	417 s	597 s	1,239 s
Prescriptor	**31-days**	**61-days**	**180-days**
Greedy	127/1814	130/1829	163/1839
Feature greedy	921/114	930/117	**986/163**
V4C prescriptor	**927/47**	**934/48**	**986/137**

to produce a prediction for all the GEOs by the baseline model and our proposed model for three different sizes of the prediction period. As seen on the Table, the computation needs of our model were well below the maximum time allowed in the XPRIZE competition (60 min). We favored simplicity in our design and aimed to minimize the energy consumption to be as planet-friendly as possible.

6.3 Prescriptor

Given the hypothetical nature of the prescriptor, we were not able to quantitatively evaluate its performance against ground truth. However, we did carry out domination tests between the IPs recommended by our model when compared to a greedy algorithm for the 236 GEOs in the Challenge and under both unitary and random costs policies for a time period of 60 days into the future. Figure 6 depicts the recommended IPs by our model (orange and green) when compared to a greedy prescriptor (blue).

Table 3 (bottom) shows the number of times the IPs recommended by our prescriptor dominated and were dominated by the IPs suggested by the greedy approach for all GEOs. Moreover, our prescriptor provided the IP recommendations in under 2 h for all GEOs in the Challenge, well below the maximum allowed limit of 6 h.

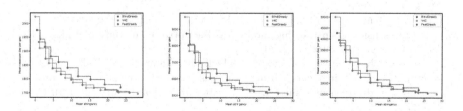

Fig. 6. Number of cases vs stringency obtained from prescriptions generated for 5 days (left), 31 days (center) and 90 days (right).

7   Conclusions and Future Work

In this paper, we have described the models developed by the winning team of the 500K XPRIZE Pandemic Response Challenge. The competition entailed first developing a model to predict the number of COVID-19 cases in 236 countries/regions in the world, for up to 180 days into the future and considering the Non-pharmaceutical Interventions deployed in each country/region. In this phase, we developed an LSTM-based bank of models which outperformed the baseline model provided by the Challenge organizers and yielded the third best Mean Rank amongst all the teams in the competition. The proposed model was successfully used by the President of the Valencian government in Spain during the third wave of COVID-19 infections in December - February 2021.

Next, the teams were asked to develop a prescription model that would recommend up to 10 Intervention Policies (IPs) in each of the 236 GEOs in the world for any time period and costs that would achieve the best trade-off between the total cost of the IP and the resulting number of coronavirus infections. Our winning solution leveraged the R_n *synchronization principle* to provide Pareto-optimal IPs that clearly dominated other approaches.

We believe that this work contributes to the necessary transition to more evidence-driven policy-making, particularly during a pandemic. Future lines of work include developing the intervention prescriptor within the Valencian Government, developing a theoretical proof of the R_n synchronization principle and including the impact of vaccinations in our model.

Acknowledgements. The authors have been partially supported by grants FONDOS SUPERA COVID-19 Santander-CRUE (CD4COVID19 2020–2021), Fundación BBVA for SARS-CoV-2 research (IA4COVID19 2020-2022) and the Valencian Government. We thank the University of Alicante's Institute for Computer Research for their support with computing resources, co-financed by the European Union and ERDF funds through IDIFEDER/2020/003. MAGM acknowledges funding from MEFP Beatriz Galindo program (BEAGAL18/00203).

References

1. 500k XPRIZE Pandemic Response Challenge, sponsored by Cognizant. https://www.xprize.org/challenge/pandemicresponse
2. Allen, L.: Some discrete-time SI, SIR, and SIS epidemic models. Math. Biosci. **124**(1), 83–105 (1994)
3. Arora, P., Kumar, H., Panigrahi, B.K.: Prediction and analysis of COVID-19 positive cases using deep learning models: a descriptive case study of India. Chaos Solit. Fractals **139**, 110017 (2020)
4. Ayyoubzadeh, S., Ayyoubzadeh, S., Zahedi, H., Ahmadi, M., Kalhori, S.: Predicting COVID-19 incidence through analysis of Google trends data in Iran: data mining and deep learning pilot study. JMIR Public Health Surveill. **6**(2), e18828 (2020)
5. Belakaria, S., Deshwal, A., Doppa, J.: Max-value entropy search for multi-objective bayesian optimization. In: Wallach, H., Larochelle, H., Beygelzimer, A., d'Alché-Buc, F., Fox, E., Garnett, R. (eds.) NeurIPS, vol. 32 (2019)

6. Brauner, J.M., et al.: Inferring the effectiveness of government interventions against COVID-19. Science **371**(6531) (2021)
7. Chatterjee, A., Gerdes, M., Martinez, S.: Statistical explorations and univariate timeseries analysis on COVID-19 datasets to understand the trend of disease spreading and death. Sensors **20**(11), 3089 (2020)
8. Chimmula, V.K.R., Zhang, L.: Time series forecasting of COVID-19 transmission in Canada using LSTM networks. Chaos Solit. Fractals **135**, 109864 (2020)
9. Ferguson, N., et al.: Strategies for containing an emerging influenza pandemic in Southeast Asia. Nature **437**(7056), 209–214 (2005)
10. Flaxman, S., et al.: Estimating the effects of non-pharmaceutical interventions on COVID-19 in Europe. Nature **584**, 257–261 (2020)
11. Hale, T., et al.: A global panel database of pandemic policies (Oxford COVID-19 Government Response Tracker). Nat. Hum. Behav. 1–10 (2021)
12. Hethcote, H.: The mathematics of infectious diseases. SIAM Rev. **42**(4), 599–653 (2000)
13. Hochreiter, S., Schmidhuber, J.: Long short-term memory. Neural Comput. **9**(8), 1735–1780 (1997)
14. Khan, M., Hossain, A.: Machine learning approaches reveal that the number of tests do not matter to the prediction of global confirmed COVID-19 cases. Front. Artif. Intell. Appl. **3**, 90 (2020)
15. Lauer, S., Grantz, K., Bi, Q., Jones, F., et al.: The incubation period of coronavirus disease 2019 (COVID-19) from publicly reported confirmed cases: estimation and application. Ann. Intern. Med. **172**(9), 577–582 (2020)
16. Lu, Z., et al.: NSGA-Net: neural architecture search using multi-objective genetic algorithm (extended abstract). In: Bessiere, C. (ed.) Proceedings of the 29th International Joint Conference on Artificial Intelligence (AI), IJCAI-20, pp. 4750–4754 (2020)
17. Miikkulainen, R., et al.: From prediction to prescription: evolutionary optimization of nonpharmaceutical interventions in the COVID-19 pandemic. IEEE Trans. Evol. Comput. **25**(2), 386–401 (2021)
18. Pastor-Satorras, R., Castellano, C., Van Mieghem, P., Vespignani, A.: Epidemic processes in complex networks. Rev. Mod. Phys. **87**, 925–979 (2015)
19. Pereira, I., et al.: Forecasting COVID-19 dynamics in Brazil: a data driven approach. Int. J. Environ. Res. Public Health **17**(14), 5115 (2020)
20. Rahman, M., et al.: Data-driven dynamic clustering framework for mitigating the adverse economic impact of COVID-19 lockdown practices. Sustain. Cities Soc. **62**, 102372 (2020)
21. Riccardi, A., Gemignani, J., Fernández-Navarro, F., Heffernan, A.: Optimisation of non-pharmaceutical measures in COVID-19 growth via neural networks. IEEE Trans. Emerg. Topics Comput. **5**(1), 79–91 (2021)
22. Sameni, R.: Model-based prediction and optimal control of pandemics by nonpharmaceutical interventions. arXiv preprint arXiv:2102.06609 (2021)
23. Tayarani, N., Mohammad, H.: Applications of artificial intelligence in battling against COVID-19: a literature review. Chaos Solit. Fractals 110338 (2020)
24. Yousefpour, A., Jahanshahi, H., Bekiros, S.: Optimal policies for control of the novel coronavirus disease outbreak. Chaos Solit. Fractals **136**, 1109883 (2020)
25. Zeroual, A., Harrou, F., Dairi, A., Sun, Y.: Deep learning methods for forecasting COVID-19 time-series data: a comparative study. Chaos Solit. Fractals **140**, 110121 (2020)

Mobility and Transportation

Getting Your Package to the Right Place: Supervised Machine Learning for Geolocation

George Forman[✉][ID]

Amazon, Bellevue, WA, USA
ghforman@amazon.com

Abstract. Amazon Last Mile strives to learn an accurate delivery point for each address by using the noisy GPS locations reported from past deliveries. Centroids and other center-finding methods do not serve well, because the noise is consistently biased. The problem calls for supervised machine learning, but how? We addressed it with a novel adaptation of *learning to rank* from the information retrieval domain. This also enabled information fusion from map layers. Offline experiments show outstanding reduction in error distance, and online experiments estimated millions in annualized savings.

Keywords: Learning to rank · Geospatial supervised learning

1 Introduction

Amazon Last Mile delivers millions of packages daily to homes and businesses all over the world. To do this efficiently requires myriad optimization technologies, most of which rely on accurate geocoding. The geolocation (latitude, longitude) of each address is needed for partitioning and optimizing routes among vehicles, and guiding drivers on the road and to the door. Here we focus on the geolocation

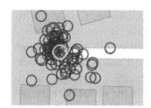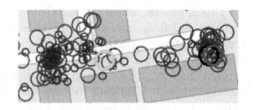

Fig. 1. (Left) The centroid (cyan) of the GPS fixes from past deliveries (blue) lies in the middle of the street, whereas GeoRank correctly identified the doorstep (red), which is neither a centroid nor a high density point. (Right) The centroid (cyan) lies at an unrelated building between GPS clusters near the apartment (east) and the leasing office (west). The doorstep (black) was correctly identified by the machine learning ranking model (red). (Color figure online)

© Springer Nature Switzerland AG 2021
Y. Dong et al. (Eds.): ECML PKDD 2021, LNAI 12978, pp. 403–419, 2021.
https://doi.org/10.1007/978-3-030-86514-6_25

problem of determining a precise *delivery point* (DP) geocode for each address, i.e. the location of the customer's doorstep, building entrance, or loading dock, as appropriate. Marking an accurate DP on the driver's map is especially useful and time-saving wherever house number signage is weak, missing, or obscured by trees. Inaccurate DPs lead to a bad driver experience, which may require walking around to find neighboring house numbers to deduce the correct delivery location. And this effort may get repeated each day by different drivers. Further, badly mislocated DPs can lead to inefficient route planning, sending packages on the wrong vehicles, and even misdeliveries or missed delivery time promises.

A strawman method for the DP would be to compute the *centroid* of GPS fixes from past deliveries.[1] Unfortunately, this can point drivers to the middle of the street (see the hypothetical example in Fig. 1 left) or to an unrelated building, depending on GPS noise and exactly when the driver marks the delivery complete. Centroids and mediods are prone to outliers (frequently miles away) and also make poor choices with multi-modal distributions, where they can fall on an unrelated building between popular delivery locations (Fig. 1 right). These examples also illustrate that selecting dense locations via clustering or Kernel Density Estimation (KDE) [18] does not quite suit, as the best point may have low density at the edge of the cloud.

The complexity of the geospatial inference problem clearly calls for some kind of supervised machine learning (ML) rather than a relatively simple geometric computation, but the research literature does not provide guidance. We need to train from a collection of situations where we have labeled the best point, and expect the system to learn to estimate the best point in new situations.

To do this, we have adapted *learning to rank* from the information retrieval domain, where, for example, if a user clicks on only the #3 search result, it implies a preference for #3 over #1 and over #2; these two implicitly labeled preference pairs can then be added to a training set to learn to rank more effectively for future searches. In our geospatial domain, when we manually label the best building entrance as the DP for an address, it can yield hundreds of labeled preference pairs between candidate locations based on distance. After training the ML ranking model on many labeled addresses, it can be applied to new situations to estimate the best DP.

This approach, which we call *GeoRank*, has several advantages: It is highly accurate and dominates other methods we have explored. It can deal with a variety of different situations simply by additional supervision. It is much easier to evaluate or label individual cases in this domain (with satellite map backgrounds) and, it is more objective than traditional information retrieval or ads ranking, where it is difficult to know that any given document or ad is truly not of interest to an anonymous user. Finally, it can leverage information from the underlying map while not requiring the map to be complete or even accurate.

---

[1] Before there is any delivery history for an address, the process is bootstrapped by other approximate geocoding methods to guide the driver. Third-party geocodes are not used in our geocode computations.

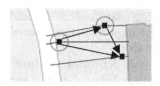

Fig. 2. Diagram representing rank comparisons between 3 candidate locations (black squares), the arrows indicating the winner of each pairwise comparison using feature vectors involving historical GPS point density (blue) and distances to roads and buildings (red or green lines), if present in the map. Given the three pairwise comparisons, it chooses the eastern point as the delivery point. (Color figure online)

The contributions of this paper include (1) a description of a valuable geospatial task not previously in the machine learning research literature, (2) two very large ranking datasets (387K;445K cases with 43M;49M candidates with precomputed feature vectors and loss labels) released publicly to enable others to research effective, scalable ranking methods in this domain, and (3) our novel, geospatial supervised learning method, and evaluations thereof. The following section describes the GeoRank method in more detail, including candidate generation, feature extraction, and other algorithmic issues. Section 3 shows the method is highly effective in experiments on the New York and Washington datasets. Section 4 discusses limitations of the model and a brief description of additional offline and online evaluations we conducted before deploying the method in Amazon Last Mile. Section 5 describes related work and Sect. 6 concludes with future work.

2   Supervised Geolocation by Ranking

The inference task for each address is to estimate the best delivery point (DP) given as input a set of noisy GPS fixes of past deliveries. We adapt supervised ranking for our geospatial task as follows: For each address, we determine a set of candidate DP points and make pairs thereof (Sect. 2.1). For each pair, we extract a feature vector (Sect. 2.2), which includes information drawn from the map, where available. During training, we use the measured loss from the ground-truth labeled DP point to establish the preference order of each pair. We frame the base learning task as binary classification of the preference order, as in *pairwise* ranking [14, ch. 3]. During inference, we simply apply the pairwise binary classifier to all pairs to predict the candidate point of minimum loss.

The loss for a candidate location is its distance to the ground-truth labeled DP point. Additionally, we add a +20 m penalty if that candidate lies atop a different building outline than the one attached to the label, if available. This is to train the system to prefer ambiguous locations outside buildings rather than show a pin on the wrong building. Note that some areas of the map have no building outlines available, and some may be missing or incorrect.

2.1   Candidate Filtering and Generation

Simply considering each past delivery location as a candidate naturally results in long $O(N^2)$ run times when there are thousands of past deliveries. We greatly improved scalability by filtering near-duplicate candidates on a virtual hash grid; this filter and other scalability improvements reduced several days of computing for the US to less than half a day.

When there are very few past deliveries, the best point available may not be particularly close to the building. Where building outlines are available, we also generate candidate points along the faces of nearby buildings (see the diagram in Fig. 2). This helps solve a troublesome problem with occasional tall buildings with multipath GPS reflections that exhibit a *consistent GPS bias* away from the building, not generally noted in the GPS literature. Even where all the past GPS fixes are on the wrong side of the street, the system can recover by considering candidates on building faces.

We are able to generate a class-balanced training set by randomly choosing whether to put the better candidate in the first or second position of each pair. For training, rather than generate all $\frac{N(N-1)}{2}$ pairs of candidates—which produces vastly more pairs for those addresses having more delivery history (or having more scattered points that get past deduplication)—we generate just $O(N)$ pairs, selecting the best vs. each of the others. Not only did training time improve, but it also led to improved model accuracy. This is akin to research in information retrieval ranking that shows selecting more pairs with the most relevant documents can lead to improved ranking, e.g. [4]. (We also limit the number of training pairs from any single address to 100, so that addresses with many deliveries do not dominate the learning.)

2.2   Feature Vectors

We compute three kinds of features from which the GeoRank model learns to do its ranking. Each feature is designed to be invariant to rotation and resilient to outliers or missing information in the map.

Features based on the GPS fixes from past deliveries

Our app gathers a GPS fix at various driver events, e.g. photo-on-delivery or when the driver marks a package as delivered, which may or may not be close to where the package was actually dropped off. Given a history of G GPS fixes for a particular address, we compute the following features for each candidate DP: the density of past GPS fixes nearby (e.g. using Gaussian KDE with a bandwidth of 25m), the distance to the GPS fix having maximum KDE, the mean distance to the K-nearest neighbors ($K = \sqrt{G}$), and the percentage of those K neighbors that were delivered to the office (mail room, receptionist, etc., rather than the customer or customer's doorstep, as noted by the driver). The intuition behind this last feature is to discriminate between the leasing office and separate apartment buildings. We intend the DP to identify the individual apartment building entrance, as it is comparatively trivial for the driver to find the shared leasing office. (For scalability we limit G to a random sample of ≤500 past deliveries. Here we cannot use the near-duplicate filter described previously, else we lose fine-grained information about density.)

Features drawn from the underlying map

The local map can provide useful geospatial context. For example, drivers often mark packages as delivered when they get back to their vehicle, but GPS fixes located on the street or in a parking lot are unlikely to be good customer DP locations compared to GPS fixes nearer building outlines. Thus, for each candidate DP, we compute: the distance to the nearest street, the distance to the nearest parking lot (zero inside the parking lot), the distance to the nearest building (zero inside), the distance to the building closest to most GPS fixes, etc. To compute these features efficiently, we build in-memory geospatial indices: a KD-tree for map points marked with an address, and Sort-Tile-Recursive R-trees [16] for streets, buildings, and parking lots.

We use a maximum feature distance of 1000m to cover the common situation where the map is incomplete, e.g. areas lacking parking lots or building outlines. This maximum value serves as an indicator to the ML model that the feature is locally missing.

Occasionally the map contains an explicitly marked address point. Where available, one can imagine using such information to bypass the ranking computation altogether, but any map error would cause DP errors. Instead, we include this information as an additional feature: the distance to the nearest building or point that is marked with the *sought* house number and street name, if available (else 1000m). This feature, which includes text address matching logic, enables the ranker to leverage the information but also to override it where there is sufficient evidence from past GPS data that disagree with the map. The discrepancy may be because of errors in the map (see Fig. 3 where house number 18 is recorded incorrectly) or because deliveries are actually around back or are redirected to another building.

Context features

For all candidate pairs, we compute these context features: the number of past deliveries, the number of building outlines nearby (some areas have none), the median and P10 distance between pairs of GPS fixes (indicating how dispersed the points are; we found the average or P75 very sensitive to a single outlier), the point density (number of GPS points ÷ median distance), the median GPS-reported accuracy of the fixes (worse in city canyons), and whether there is

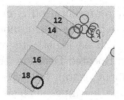

Fig. 3. Though the map marks house 18 at the south (black circle), the GPS evidence (blue) indicates it is actually at the north, which the GeoRank model correctly selected (red). Meanwhile the centroid (cyan; some data not shown) is near the street, which would leave ambiguity between the two northerly buildings for the driver. (Color figure online)

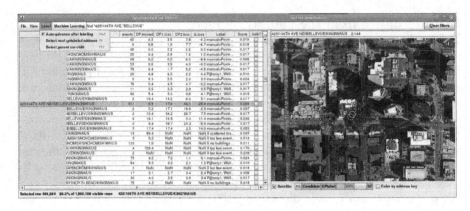

Fig. 4. Research GUI showing our Amazon building in Bellevue. Blue circles show past GPS fixes; square dots show candidate points to rank; dashed circles show DP choices by different methods. (Color figure online)

any nearby address in the map with an exact match. These context features can be leveraged across the whole training set to learn preferences in different situations. For example, the ranker could potentially learn different behavior where GPS accuracy tends to be weaker.

Pairwise ranking for a linear model f often uses the difference-vector $\mathbf{u} - \mathbf{v}$, where $\mathbf{u}$ and $\mathbf{v}$ are the feature vectors of the two candidates in the pair. (Proof sketch: the pairwise binary classifier $f(\mathbf{u}) \gtrless f(\mathbf{v}) \equiv \mathbf{w} \cdot \mathbf{u} \gtrless \mathbf{w} \cdot \mathbf{v} \equiv \mathbf{w} \cdot (\mathbf{u} - \mathbf{v}) \gtrless 0$, where $\mathbf{w}$ is the weight vector to be learned by the model.) Since pairs stem from the same address, context features have the same value for both candidates, rendering their difference useless to the classifier. Thus, we compute $\mathbf{u}$ and $\mathbf{v}$ from only the first two kinds of features above, and generate the composite feature vector of the pair as $(\mathbf{u} - \mathbf{v}, \mathbf{u}, \mathbf{v}, \mathbf{c})$, where $\mathbf{c}$ are the context features appended at the end. Evaluations of feature importance show that all four portions of the feature vector are used by the base classifiers.

2.3 Base Classifiers and Implementation

Although the difference-vector representation is motivated by linear classifiers, we found better performance with non-linear models. We experimented with a variety of base classifiers, such as logistic regression, SVM, decision trees, Random Forests and Gradient Boosted Decision Trees. The number of training pairs can be in the millions for a region, but with an efficient, thread-parallel implementation of decision tree learning, such as in the SMILE library [12], the base classifier usually trains in 1–10 minutes and exhibits 98–99% pairwise accuracy on a holdout set. Once the data is staged, separate regions are computed as *embarrassingly parallel* jobs on a fleet of AWS EC2 instances.

Figure 4 shows a screenshot of our custom Java Swing GUI tool, which was essential to research, develop, and debug the details of our GeoRank method.

Table 1. Datasets

	New York (NY)	Washington (WA)
cases	387,054	445,073
candidates	43,436,526	48,992,148
avg candidates/case	112.2 (2–500)	110.1 (2–500)
file size	6.1 GB	6.8 GB

We used it to inspect results, label DP locations, and sort & search a table with millions of addresses for informative cases to label, e.g. via active learning where multiple models disagree widely.

3 Experiments

We have done extensive offline and online experiments to develop, refine, and validate our geospatial supervised learning method. Here we describe a limited set of experiments to answer fundamental questions about its performance, which illustrate its effectiveness.

3.1 Datasets

The experiments are conducted on two labeled ranking datasets that we generated for New York state and Washington state, each containing many millions of candidate points (see Table 1). Although the ranking problem is fundamentally geospatial, in order to release the data for research and reproducibility, we have constructed it so that it does not contain any information about actual addresses or physical locations, and it is not a random sample of our actual cases. Nonetheless, it is a valuable resource for research: this domain has fundamentally different qualities than ranking datasets in information retrieval and ad ranking, where query sets are sparse, subjective, and discretized into a few levels. But for these datasets the average number of candidates to be ranked per case is over 100, and each is labeled with a non-negative scalar loss. When we split the dataset into folds for train and test sets, we partition based on a hash of the normalized address fields (excluding the apartment number, so an apartment complex will not be split across train and test). Only the randomized fold number is included in the dataset, which has 100 distinct folds, should others wish to perform consistent cross-validation splits and/or consider learning curves with fine granularity. These datasets have 18 features per candidate, plus 16 context features per case. Together they generate 70 features per pair, when expanded as described at the end of Sect. 2.2.

3.2 Loss vs. Business Objective

Recall that the loss is a measure of distance to the ground truth label, which represents a judgment of the best delivery point, penalized by +20m if the point falls on the wrong building. In this domain there are very many addresses that are relatively straightforward to process, e.g. where the GPS fixes are fairly close together and are near the best delivery point, such as the front door of a lone building. But it is the occasional large geolocation errors that cause the greatest expense: because of a stray geocode far away, we may place packages on the wrong delivery vehicle, and the driver may either have to drive far outside their planned route and time, or else return the package to the delivery station at the end of their route for a later redelivery attempt—running the risk of missing the delivery date promised to the customer. Thus, rather than focus on the mean loss, as most machine learning work, we focus on the P95 loss.

This objective is fundamentally different than optimizing the average loss or the mean squared error. Consider two Gedanken experiments to make this plain. First, suppose that 90% of the cases had 1m loss, and with a variant model we could reduce loss to exactly zero for only these cases. It would bring the average down, but the last meter of perfection would hardly make a difference to delivery drivers in the real world. If this variant model were also slightly worse in the tail, the performance objective should reflect this problem. Second, suppose that the P99.99 were either in the next state or else in another country. The difference between these two can have a large effect on the average or the mean squared error, but the business cost of these two problems would be about the same. Hence, we focus on the P95 loss as the objective to optimize in this paper (in practice we also use higher tails). Another advantage of using a percentile instead of a mean is that the metric is unaffected by small errors in labeling precision, such as when an auditor clicks a few pixels off from the ground truth point; this also speeds up labeling and greatly focuses label validation efforts on a small minority of points.

3.3 How Does It Perform Against Baselines?

We begin by framing the performance against several baselines: random selection, centroid/mediod, maximum KDE, and oracle selection. These illustrate the feasible range of performance, and the latter represents an unrealizable lower bound. Even the oracle cannot achieve zero loss in many cases, because no candidate has been generated that is exactly zero distance from the DP label, which may itself be imperfect.

Figure 5 shows, for each dataset, the loss of each method across the whole distribution from P01 to P99 (lower is better). Each point was determined by 20-fold cross-validation (CV), and the vertical width represents the 95% confidence

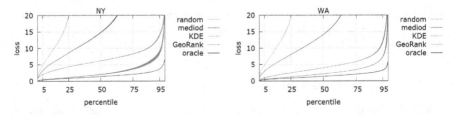

Fig. 5. Comparing methods across whole CDF loss distribution; each point shows 95% confidence interval from 20-fold CV.

interval of the value (using T-distribution with 19 degrees of freedom). Zoom to see the width, which is barely discernable in many cases.

Random: selects one of the candidate DP points at random. Its median loss (54 NY; 55 WA) and P95 loss (157; 138) are off the chart, literally. This oblivious method does nothing to avoid outlier points, and represents a kind of upper-bound just as a majority-voting baseline does in classification experiments.

Mediod: selects the candidate nearest the centroid. Its P95 loss is also off the chart (84; 78). Whenever there are multi-modal point distributions, e.g. between the leasing office and the customer's apartment building in a large multi-building community, it will tend to select a point between the two, usually an unrelated building. This would point drivers to the wrong building for delivery (as in Fig. 1 right). In situations such as large warehouses or malls with multiple entry points, the centroid will tend to point to the middle of the building. This is sufficient for most drivers, assuming the entrances are plain, but may not enable an optimized route plan.

Maximum KDE: selects the candidate in the densest cloud of GPS fixes. This can be quite competitive. If there are multiple clusters at different building entrances, it usually picks the more popular entry. These points tend to be somewhat away from the face of the building, however. Often the densest locations tend toward the parking location of the vehicle. All of these methods so far are oblivious to the real-world constraints, e.g. that building entrances do not lie inside parking lots (actually, there can be underground buildings on hillsides with rooftop parking—everything happens in this domain).

Oracle: selects the best available candidate point. It does this, of course, by cheating: it uses the hidden loss of the test case to make its choice, and as such is not a practical algorithm. It is useful here to understand the lower bound on loss, given the candidate DPs that are available from the practical generation algorithm described in Sect. 2.1. Its loss at P99 suggests future work in candidate generation.

GeoRank: supervised geolocation learning. Overall, this approach solves this geospatial problem very nicely: its loss distribution tightly hugs the oracle performance up until the tail of the distribution, and at P99 it rejoins the loss of the KDE method—but does not exceed it, as we shall see. If we subtract the oracle loss as the lower bound, GeoRank at P95 reduced the delta loss by 50–53% of the KDE algorithm.

   To complete the 20-fold CV in a timely manner, rather than train on all 95% of the dataset available for training, we trained each fold on only 20% of the dataset. (Thus, the confidence intervals are more accurate than if the models each trained on highly overlapped training sets.) This yielded 6–7M labeled pairs to train each model—plenty for an accurate pairwise classifier. The decision tree learning algorithm simply splits nodes best-first based on the Gini index,

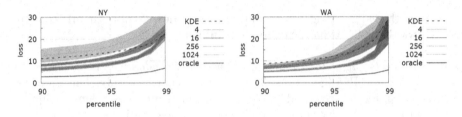

Fig. 6. Zooming on the tail of the loss distribution, as we vary model capacity: the number of leaves in the decision tree.

up to a maximum of 1024 leaf nodes, which it always used. Each fold trains in ~5 min in parallel on 16 Xeon 2.3 GHz CPUs; together they inference 13K addresses/second, even with the $O(N^2)$ pairwise comparisons used to determine which candidate has the most wins.

3.4 How Is the Tail Affected by Model Capacity?

In Fig. 6 we zoom in on the tail of the loss curve (P90–P99), as we vary the pairwise classifier's model capacity: the number of leaf nodes in the decision tree. When just 4 leaves are permitted, its performance was worse than KDE. With 16 leaves, it beat KDE except for the extreme tail of the distribution. With more model capacity, it always beat KDE. The 1024 curve represents our default for GeoRank.

3.5 Lesion Studies and RankNet Comparison

Finally, we perform a series of independent lesion studies on the method, in order to measure the relative importance of various component ideas. For these experiments, we want to have confidence intervals, so we again use 20-fold CV, but to reduce the computation load we train on just 5% of the data (which the previous experiment showed was sufficient, and it saves a great deal of time, esp. for the RankNet comparison, later).

Figure 7 shows the P95 loss of each variant under 20-fold cross-validation, and the whiskers extend to cover the 95% confidence interval. Just for reference, the vertical lines indicate the performance of the oracle and the KDE method. The baseline performance is the basic GeoRank method.

The second data point indicates the performance of using the classifier trained from the opposite state. In both cases the result was statistically significantly worse. This endorses the idea of having separate models trained for each region, as regional geometric patterns may vary. For example, we observed the setbacks from the road were often larger in Arizona.

The next comparison simply removes two components from the four-part composite feature vector; $\mathbf{u}$ and $\mathbf{v}$ are removed, reducing the total number of features from 70 to 34 (18 difference features $\mathbf{u} - \mathbf{v}$ and the 16 context features).

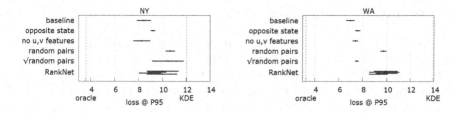

Fig. 7. Lesion studies on the GeoRank method and RankNet comparison.

Removing these features had a relatively smaller effect on performance, which was not statistically significant for NY.

The next two bars represent changes in how we generate training pairs. Recall that we pair the best candidate against each of the other candidates. A common approach is simply to generate random pairs, rather than all $O(N^2)$ pairs, which can overwhelm computing resources. For each candidate, we pick another at random to pair with it, producing $O(N)$ pairs, but the result is significantly and substantially worse.

The other variant, marked with the $\sqrt{}$ symbol, generates training pairs as follows: for each candidate $i = 2..n$ in the training list sorted by loss, we randomly select one of the first $\lfloor \sqrt{i} \rfloor$ candidates. The idea is to focus more attention on the better candidates, but not overly focus on the single best candidate. It worked better than random pairs on average for both states (though not significantly so for NY); it is nonetheless significantly worse than the 'best vs. rest' strategy employed by GeoRank.

Finally, we replaced our pairwise ranker with RankNet [7] from the RankLib research implementation [9]. The four variants represent efforts at parameter tuning, varying the number of training epochs and whether or not the context features were included (oddly, they often hurt RankNet's performance). In all cases and for both states it performed worse on average than the baseline, though not always statistically significantly. We considered running similar comparisons with other well-known information retrieval ranking algorithms such as LambdaMART, but adapting them to use our loss scale rather than discretized document relevance is beyond the scope of this paper—potential future work.

4   Discussion

We have done additional lesion studies that are beyond the scope of this paper. For example, we have demonstrated that if all building outlines are removed from the map when generating the features for the test cases, the quality of the geolocation degrades only a little. This is an important property, for there are whole regions of our world map that contain no building outlines yet. It would be complicated to have to train separate models for situations with and without building outlines, and then to correctly classify when to use each model. Better to have a single robust model that can cope with their absence.

4.1   Real-World Offline Evaluations

When we began to apply machine learning to this business problem, we ran into a hitch: For years our established way to measure the quality of our DPs was by their average distance to deliveries, as reported by the GPS fixes. And yet, by this objective metric, there would be no way to outperform the centroid, by definition. Thus, we had to drive the adoption of a different goal metric, which would rightly show improvement when we selected a good building entrance, even if it were away from the dense center of the point cloud. But we had no automated way to determine the true quality of a DP, otherwise we would already have solved the problem. In view of this, our internal Curated Ground Truth (CGT) program was born: a worldwide manual labeling effort, with various quality controls to ensure that we are grading ourselves against accurate points. Given this labeled dataset of thousands of randomly selected addresses, we were able to determine that the GeoRank method reduced the P95 error distance vs. the existing legacy system by ~18%. These CGT points were only used for evaluation of the final model, not for model training or hyper-parameter optimization. In fact, we need to maintain separation of the points used for training and model selection vs. those held-out points that are secreted away only for use in monitoring the health and quality of our systems. Because the majority of cases are straightforward and provide little incremental insight, the sampling of points for training and model selection are biased toward the tail by various means, including query-by-committee active learning. Given that the CGT points are randomly sampled in order to correctly identify the percentiles, we sought additional validation of the GeoRank model before risking its live deployment. We explored the tail in further offline testing. In some states we identified thousands of cases (excluding training cases) where GeoRank moved the DP by over 100m from what was previously vended. Though this was a only a small fraction of the whole dataset, they could prove to be costly if the software threw some points far astray, which would break customer delivery date promises and erode trust. We obtained a random sample of such points using the research GUI and were able to quickly label a good fraction of them, though some tail cases are quite difficult to understand. In this skewed sample, we determined that the median loss of the old points was ~16x the median loss of the GeoRank model. This was a strong endorsement indeed, though only for a small sample. We also performed some automated offline testing against a large number of OpenStreetMap addresses [1], which again showed strongly favorable results.

4.2   Real-World Online Evaluations

Once we believed that the GeoRank delivery points were superior in offline testing, we moved to online A/B testing, dialing up to 10% treatment across the US. The assignment of treatment and control groups was determined by a hash of the address, excluding any apartment number so that a complex would not fall into both groups, for greater statistical power. Analysis of the service time per package determined a substantial and statistically significant improvement, projecting millions of dollars saved annually. One aspect of owning the data quality of an upstream system is that your errors impact many downstream processes. Besides service time improvements, there were also savings because of improved planning, since the DPs were now more truthful.

4.3   Limitations

Several things have become clear after substantial labeling and domain experience. First, there is no way to do the job accurately without seeing the historical delivery data. Although you may identify the front door of a building address by three methods and even walk there yourself, it might be that deliveries are actually redirected around back to a loading dock or even to a distant campus-wide mail hub.

Second, having more delivery history helps both in labeling as well as in GeoRanking. However, a good fraction of customer addresses are new and have very little history to work from, especially in areas of rapidly growing demand, such as India. Thus, there is a natural labeling bias and research bias toward addresses with more delivery history. How can one accurately geocode given a single, possibly noisy delivery event in an area of the map that is yet uncharted?

Third, there can be more than one delivery location for a single address, and in different ways. From the event history, we may see multiple clusters, but only by deeper investigation (or machine learning) can we determining things like 'small packages are accepted at the office, but large packages must go to the loading dock.' Or that 'packages are accepted at the leasing office on Tuesday and Saturday mornings, but otherwise all packages must be driven to the individual apartments.' Though manual labeling for multiple delivery locations is harder, fortunately they can easily be represented in a ranking dataset: for each candidate, simply take the minimum loss compared to the alternative DP labels. If we wish to compute the alternate DP locations, we can re-run the ranking algorithm after removing candidates near the DP that was chosen on the first iteration. Though ranking is fast, we can avoid the $O(N^2)$ pairwise comparisons if we keep track of the matrix of pairwise wins. If the second run chooses a sufficiently distant point, then it identified an alternative; but sometimes it would

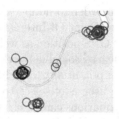

Fig. 8. Long driveway with locked gate. The model experienced high distance loss because it picked the gate (red) instead of the southern garage or the house (black label). (Color figure online)

simply pick the next closest candidate to the removed area. This is another area for future work. It can be difficult to decide whether multiple alternatives are warranted or not, given scattered data.

Fourth, labeling or locating the best building entrance or loading dock in the real world can be arbitrarily difficult. There are addresses that have large amounts of delivery history, and yet remain impossible to nail down, such as a complex hospital with multiple entrances, buildings, and delivery procedure complexity as well. Because of these biases and others, none of our labeled datasets fairly represent the full difficulty of the general problem. And regardless of labeling difficulty, it is unclear what the best distributed sample should be: Should it be weighted by package volume? Or by service time, so difficult addresses are worth more? Or by the frequency that *inexperienced* drivers visit an unfamiliar, complex location. We know that the cases with high loss do not always represent high business cost. For example, in the tail we see a plethora of cases where a customer has a locked gate across a long driveway (see Fig. 8). Though the best DP is at the house, it may be that nearly all packages are delivered near the locked gate. Though this results in high measured loss, it does not result in any real driver confusion or delays. And though we would like to label the apartment door as the correct DP, what about situations where 99% of deliveries go to the leasing office? Should we consider it a high loss case if the GeoRank model chooses the office?

5   Related Work

The task of *geocoding* is the process of mapping address text or an IP address to an (often coarse) geographic location, which requires geographic databases. Our *geolocation* problem is substantially different: given multiple noisy samples of a location, determine a (precise) geographic location for future deliveries; this can be done with the points alone by computing the centroid, or the argmax KDE point—or by the supervised GeoRank method we developed, which has the advantage that it can also leverage features from maps.

Note that our geolocation problem is not to be confused with research on 'geographic information retrieval,' which are traditional information retrieval (IR) applications that aim to improve the ranking of their search results by leveraging the user's location in order to adapt to regional preferences [2]. ML ranking has also been applied to Point-Of-Interest (POI) information retrieval, which leverages the user's noisy GPS position as well as features such as user history, popularity of venue, and nearby social network friends. The learned ranking model optimizes the short list of potential named locations (such as tourist sites or restaurants) from which the user may select to 'check-in,' i.e. confirm their location [13,20,22]. These confirmations can be used as a ground-truth POI label for testing or retraining the ranking model. Such IR applications measure their success by metrics on the ranked position of the correct answer(s) in the search results list; whereas our task measures loss in terms of meters away from the ground-truth location. Other related work includes the destination prediction problem popularized by the ECML/PKDD taxi trajectory prediction competition [3,6], although some have approached destination prediction by building models to score or rank a few candidates, such as home, work, or school (which is akin to classification models with a few classes) or a city's popular tourist destinations [5,11]. Finally, there is general geospatial work to re-identify delivery locations, such as by [17] which used centroids of past 'stay point' locations.

There has been a tremendous amount of research in learning to rank [14], esp. for information retrieval (IR) and, more profitably, for advertising. The field has benefited greatly from having research datasets available, such as the LETOR collection [15]. Similarly, we hope to launch research in supervised geolocation with the two datasets we provide; being orders of magnitude larger than LETOR, they are useful for more general ranking research, e.g. selective sampling or scalability research [19]. For confidentiality reasons, neither the address nor the actual locations can be reconstructed from the data; thus, we have also provided location-invariant feature vectors based on attributes from the map, etc. Should some future researcher be in a position to release data including latitude/longitude locations, many creative research avenues could be pursued involving features from maps.

As mentioned in Sect. 3.1, geo-ranking data is substantially different. First, each case has many labeled candidates, whereas traditional ranking datasets are much sparser. Second, relevance judgments for traditional datasets, which are hard to obtain objective truth for, often have a small ordinal ranking for each query, indicating the rough degree of document relevance, with a default of 'irrelevant' for most ungraded documents. Geo-ranking datasets have a continuous real-number for the loss, which provides a total ranking of all candidate points. Third, traditional datasets often have shared pool candidates, e.g. documents in a fixed collection searched by many different queries. In our datasets, candidate points are not shared across addresses; each has a distinct loss and feature vector dependent on the target address.

There have been a variety of algorithmic improvements in learning to rank, following a progression: (1) point-wise learns a regression for each point independently; (2) pair-wise learns to select the better of a pair of points; and (3) list-wise learns to return a list of the top-K points optimized by any list-scoring method. List-wise ranking is not necessary for our domain, as we only seek a single best location. A common methodology for low-latency situations is to train a model on pairwise examples with known or implicitly inferred user preferences, in order to learn a pointwise scoring function that can be run independently in $O(N)$ time (embarrassingly parallel) for thousands of candidate documents or ads selected by a traditional information retrieval system [8]. In our domain, we only have hundreds not thousands of candidates per address, so an $O(N^2)$ pairwise comparison is plenty fast and appears to be more accurate generally. There is algorithmic research to reduce the $O(N^2)$ pairwise comparisons to $O(N \log N)$, which may help scale other applications [10,21].

6   Conclusion and Future Work

We hypothesized that the learning to rank paradigm would adapt well for our geolocation problem. It proved able to efficiently and accurately place delivery points near building entrances. By showing an accurate point on the map in our app, we help drivers more quickly and accurately identify the correct delivery address. Online A/B tests showed that it resulted in time savings worth millions of dollars annualized.

It is fortunate that the method was effective with the existing data quality. This is faster and more frugal than efforts to try to obtain better input data, e.g. expensive GPS devices. The GeoRank method makes up for relatively poor GPS precision in big cities by leveraging map information, which also tends to be more complete in cities. And yet the method is not dependent on the map, for there are large regions with few building outlines and many missing roads. We have since applied ranking to other geolocation problems successfully, such as the parking location. It's always 'Day 1' at Amazon.

References

1. Open Street Map (OSM). www.openstreetmap.org
2. GIR'10: 6th Workshop on Geographic Information Retrieval. ACM (2010)
3. ECML/PKDD Competition: Taxi Trajectory Prediction (2015). https://www.kaggle.com/c/pkdd-15-predict-taxi-service-trajectory-i
4. Aslam, J.A., Kanoulas, E., Pavlu, V., Savev, S., Yilmaz, E.: Document selection methodologies for efficient and effective learning-to-rank. In: SIGIR'09 (2009)
5. Baraglia, R., Muntean, C.I., Nardini, F.M., Silvestri, F.: Learnext: learning to predict tourists movements. In: CIKM '13, pp. 751–756 (2013)
6. de Brébisson, A., Simon, É., Auvolat, A., Vincent, P., Bengio, Y.: Artificial neural networks applied to taxi destination prediction. arXiv:1508.00021 (2015)
7. Burges, C., et al.: Learning to rank using gradient descent. In: ICML '05, pp. 89–96 (2005)
8. Burges, C.J.: From RankNet to LambdaRank to LambdaMart: an overview. Technical report MSR-TR-2010-82, Microsoft Research (2010)
9. Dang, V.: The Lemur Project-RankLib. https://sourceforge.net/p/lemur/wiki/RankLib/
10. Hong, L.J., Luo, J., Zhong, Y.: Speeding up pairwise comparisons for large scale ranking and selection. In: IEEE WSC '16, pp. 749–757 (2016)
11. Lassoued, Y., Monteil, J., Gu, Y., Russo, G., Shorten, R., Mevissen, M.: A hidden Markov model for route and destination prediction. In: ITSC'17, pp. 1–6 (2017)
12. Li, H.: SMILE: statistical machine intelligence and learning engine. https://haifengl.github.io/
13. Lian, D., Xie, X.: Mining check-in history for personalized location naming. ACM Trans. Intell. Syst. Technol. 5(2), 1–25 (2014)
14. Liu, T.Y.: Learning to Rank for Information Retrieval. Springer, Heidelberg (2011). https://doi.org/10.1007/978-3-642-14267-3
15. Qin, T., Liu, T.Y., Xu, J., Li, H.: LETOR: a benchmark collection for research on learning to rank for information retrieval. Inf. Retrieval 13(4), 346–374 (2010). https://doi.org/10.1007/s10791-009-9123-y

16. Rigaux, P., Scholl, M., Voisard, A.: Spatial Databases with Application to GIS. Morgan Kaufmann, Boston (2002)
17. Ruan, S., et al.: Doing in one go: delivery time inference based on couriers' trajectories. In: KDD'20, pp. 2813–2821 (2020)
18. Scott, D.: Multivariate Density Estimation: Theory, Practice, and Visualization. Wiley, Hoboken (1992)
19. Sculley, D.: Large scale learning to rank. In: NIPS 2009 Workshop on Advances in Ranking (2009)
20. Shaw, B., Shea, J., Sinha, S., Hogue, A.: Learning to rank for spatiotemporal search. In: WSDM'13, pp. 717–726 (2013)
21. Wauthier, F., Jordan, M., Jojic, N.: Efficient ranking from pairwise comparisons. In: ICML'13, Atlanta, Georgia, USA, vol. 28, pp. 109–117 (2013)
22. Ying, J.J.C., Lu, E.H.C., Kuo, W.N., Tseng, V.S.: Urban point-of-interest recommendation by mining user check-in behaviors. In: UrbComp'12, pp. 63–70 (2012)

Machine Learning Guided Optimization for Demand Responsive Transport Systems

Louis Zigrand[1]([✉])(iD), Pegah Alizadeh[2](iD), Emiliano Traversi[1](iD),
and Roberto Wolfler Calvo[1,3](iD)

[1] LIPN (CNRS – UMR 7030), Université Sorbonne Paris Nord, Paris, France
{zigrand,traversi,wolfler}@lipn.univ-paris13.fr
[2] Léonard de Vinci Pôle Universitaire, Research Center, Paris La Défense, France
pegah.alizadeh@devinci.fr
[3] DIM, Università di Cagliari, Cagliari, Italy

Abstract. Most of the time, objective functions used for solving static combinatorial optimization problems cannot deal efficiently with their real-time counterparts. It is notably the case of Shared Mobility Systems where the dispatching framework must adapt itself dynamically to the demand. More precisely, in the context of Demand Responsive Transport (DRT) services, various objective functions have been proposed in the literature to optimize the vehicles routes. However, these objective functions are limited in practice because they discard the dynamic evolution of the demand. To overcome such a limitation, we propose a Machine Learning Guided Optimization methodology to build a new objective function based on simulations and historical data. This way, we are able to take the demand's dynamic evolution into account. We also present how to design the main components of the proposed framework to fit a DRT application: data generation and evaluation, training process and model optimization. We show the efficiency of our proposed methodology on real-world instances, obtained in a collaboration with Padam Mobility, an international company developing Shared Mobility Systems.

Keywords: Demand responsive transport · Surrogate modeling · Combinatorial optimization

1 Introduction

Shared Mobility Systems cover all means of transport that are shared between users, either sequentially or with grouping. In particular, Demand Responsive Transports (DRTs) are shared transport systems where the vehicles adapt their routes dynamically to the demand rather than using fixed routes and timetables. This growing mode of transport, unlike classic public transport, allows the users

---

Supported by Padam Mobility under CIFRE Convention 2019/1809 (to L. Z.).

Y. Dong et al. (Eds.): ECML PKDD 2021, LNAI 12978, pp. 420–436, 2021.
https://doi.org/10.1007/978-3-030-86514-6_26

to book a place in a vehicle by requesting in real time their departure and arrival points as well as their desired pick-up or drop-off time [3]. The motivation of using such hybrid models is twofold: they straddle conventional public transport and taxis, as their schedules and routes are quite flexible, and they constitute a viable alternative to individual transport due to a lower cost of use. Still, the management of a DRT system needs efficient decision tools to handle the users' requests, the routing of the vehicles as well as the quality of the service [14,28].

1.1 Context

This work is performed jointly with Padam Mobility, a well-established company that provides technological support to DRT services. Their production, which has been operational in around 50 territories for 5 years, generates a significant amount of data: each territory involves hundreds of service points and thousands of travel requests monthly. They operate as follows: at any time, a user can submit a new request to the system via an application. A request stands for a departure location, an arrival location and a desired time of pick-up or drop-off. If the request needs to be served on the same day, it is named an *online* request; otherwise, it is named an *offline* request (also called *in-advance* in the literature). Each night, Padam Mobility optimizes the initial vehicles' routes for the next day by giving the offline requests to an Offline Optimization Framework (OOF). The day after, the vehicles start following the routes scheduled by this offline planning. During the day, each time that an online request pops up, an insertion algorithm decides either to accept the request and suggest a trip proposition to the user, or to reject it immediately. Then, if a proposition is validated by the user, the algorithm updates the routes with regards to the accepted request.

1.2 Motivation

The optimization of the vehicles offline scheduling can be modeled as a Dial-a-Ride Problem (DaRP) [13]. A DaRP can be static or dynamic: in the first case, all requests are known in advance, while the system handles requests as they occur in the second case . Our work is on the Dynamic DaRP but the design of the offline planning can be viewed as a Static DaRP tackled with a scenario based optimization algorithm to take into account the future online requests. The vast majority of the algorithms present in the DaRP literature use objective functions related to the minimization of the time traveled [22]. As for Padam Mobility, it is the Total Duration of the Rides (TDR) i.e., the accumulated time on the road of all vehicles during the service that is being minimized.

We display in Fig. 1 a basic example of what motivated our work. Here, we describe six requests by their pick-up (P) and drop-off (D) locations. In each scheduled path, the first four, in blue, are offline requests while the last two, in red, are the online ones. The solid lines represent the offline planning of the vehicles while the dotted ones show the possibility to insert the online requests within those initial schedules.

In terms of operational cost, Fig. 1a shows an optimized offline planning regarding the offline requests and the TDR. However, this set of routes cannot

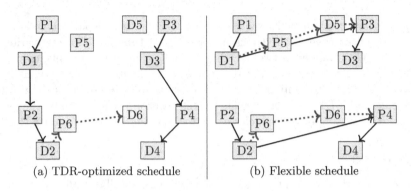

(a) TDR-optimized schedule   (b) Flexible schedule

Fig. 1. Visual comparison between two offline schedules

serve every online request due to the implied detour. On the other hand, the initial routes displayed in Fig. 1b are sub-optimal in terms of TDR but allow the system to serve all the online requests. This is a very simple but visual case where minimizing the TDR can lead to bad routes when online requests start to arrive. Since the online requests are unknown to our system, we are interested in studying the historical demand's data for a specific city. This will allow us to design more flexible offline schedules regarding the online requests, like the ones shown in Fig. 1b, and thus to increase their acceptance rate.

1.3   Contribution

In this work, we mainly focus on improving the algorithms used to optimize the offline planning of a DRT service, in order to increase its online requests acceptance rate. To the best of our knowledge, there exist only a few works that deal with the scheduling of routes without knowing all the requests ahead of time (see Sect. 2) and none of them considers such a procedure. Therefore, the main contributions of this work are the following:

- In Sect. 3, we propose to build a Machine Learning model able to estimate, for a given set of routes of vehicles, the expected number of online requests that such initial set of routes will be able to serve the day after. We then optimize the offline planning of a DRT service using this objective function.
- The data used to train the proposed model is produced via a Simulation Framework, based on the historical data of Padam Mobility. To analyse the challenging data with Machine Learning approaches, we propose in Sect. 4 a framework that models the data generation, the training process and the prediction phase with a generic approach.
- The results compared to the existing objective functions in Sect. 5 show the efficiency of our approach. We experimentally demonstrate that using traditional myopic approaches do not provide routes with the necessary flexibility to react to the arrival of online requests.

We stress the fact that the proposed methodology is not tailored only for Padam Mobility as it could be adapted to many DRT systems.

2   Related Work

Our methodology is at the frontiers of 3 computer science fields: Combinatorial Optimization, Simulation-based Optimization (SbO) and Machine Learning. The first provides the application, the DaRP, and the general techniques to solve it. Then, looking at the problem under the lenses of SbO allows us to view the problem in a new light with the definition of a new objective function. Finally, Machine Learning techniques applied to Surrogate Modeling provide a solution to computational limitations met with SbO, with means to learn a more suitable objective function. In the rest of this section, we present the literature related to each of the mentioned fields that are the most related to our approach.

Dial-a-Ride Problem. There is a large body of research directed at the Static DaRP in Combinatorial Optimization [13]. The exact approaches [7], which are mainly based on the Branch and Bound method, can guarantee the optimality of the solution but are expensive in terms of time and resources. Heuristic approaches [17] are far less expensive but can return sub-optimal solutions instead of globally optimized ones. Among them, the Adaptive Large Neighborhood Search (ALNS) method has been shown to perform well on several instances of the Static DaRP [11,28]. In all those approaches, the most classic objectives are either linked to operating costs or to the service quality, such as the number of unserved requests, the total duration of passenger transport, the total duration of the rides, the number of vehicles required, etc. [22]. The uncertainty related to the online requests in the dynamic version of the DaRP can be tackled by working on the algorithms in charge of the offline planning and the insertion of the online requests. Given the center of interest of this work, we solely focus on the first axis. One way to make space in the offline schedule is to add fake requests from a clustering of historical data to the set of in-advance requests and solve a Static DaRP [26] but this model proved too simple to improve the flexibility of the rides. Two-stage [6] and multi-stage [24] stochastic programming models have been proposed for the Dynamic and Stochastic Vehicle Routing Problem to optimize the offline schedule but these approaches provide limited enhancement due to the simplified models used within the recourse phase.

Simulation-Based Optimization. SbO designs a subfield of Operations Research where the evaluation of a solution is not computed with an explicit mathematical formula but by the means of simulations [2]. Such models can provide a better description of real-world situations than simplified procedures, if any exists, but at the price of needing bigger computation resources. Hence, SbO often goes with Surrogate-based Optimization [4]. To the best of our knowledge, there has been no research on using SbO to handle the offline planning of DRT services.

Surrogate Modeling. Also known as Metamodeling, it forms a subfield of Machine Learning that consists in representing a complex model f with a simpler model $\hat{f}$ at the price of some approximation. The purpose of the latter can be, for instance, to enable a faster computation of new values of f. As simulations are usually expensive in both computer resources and time, this paradigm is often found in the context of SbO [2,4] and is one of many interactions between the Machine Learning and Combinatorial Optimization fields [5]. In particular, how to obtain simple but accurate models in the fewest possible simulations has been studied in various works, such as for non-differentiable objective functions [9], complex multi-objective optimization [20] or large-scale problems [21]. For a more in-depth analysis of Surrogate Modeling, we refer the reader to [1].

Machine Learning Techniques. As the resulting model should be able to discriminate between good and bad solutions, we face here a ranking problem. This kind of problem is well known and can be tackled with various "Learning to Rank" techniques [18]. In our case, as the output of a simulation is not deterministic (see Sect. 4.3), we do not have a reliable ground truth of the ranking between the solutions. Consequently, we cannot apply conventional pairwise nor listwise algorithms to handle our problem. Thus, our objective is to learn a pointwise ranking function where the diversity of the training set will allow us to statistically describe the best solutions. To do so, the most common Supervised Machine Learning techniques in the literature are Gaussian Process Regressions (GPRs), Artificial Neural Networks (ANNs) and Radial Basis Functions (RBFs). A GPR model, also known as Kriging method, is based on the idea of considering the function f as a Bayesian model [25]. These models have been used in various applications, such as the optimization of the gait for quadrupedal and bipedal robots [19] or the optimization of hydrofoil shape design [23]. An ANN is a set of connected processing units that receive, transform and transfer information from one to another. They have been shown to outperform classic regression models (see for example [16]). General guidelines about how to model a stochastic simulator with ANNs are discussed in [10] and applied to a job shop problem. Recently, Convolutional Neural Networks (CNNs) have notably proven to be effective in modeling fluid dynamics applications [12,31]. RBFs follow the idea that the value of an entry depends solely on its distance to predefined reference points [15]. A particular variant, Radial Basis Function Networks (RBFNs), designs a kind of neural network where RBFs are used in place of activation functions and has shown promising results [30].

3   Machine Learning Guided Optimization

To better illustrate the generality of our methodology, namely Machine Learning Guided Optimization (MLGO) framework, we keep this section as general as possible. Ideally, we would like to solve the following optimization problem:

$$\max_{x \in X} f(x) \tag{1}$$

where X represents the domain of the variables x and f is a generic objective function defined over the domain X.

However, the evaluation of f can only be done through simulations and such a process is too time consuming to be used in practice in an optimization algorithm where thousands of calls to f would be made. To overcome this drawback, we propose to use a surrogate model $\hat{f}$ of f. A key aspect in our method is therefore to ensure that the obtained model is sufficiently accurate and simple.

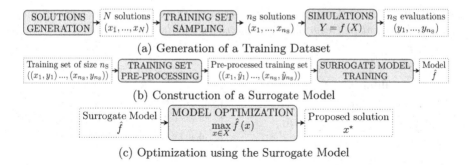

(a) Generation of a Training Dataset

(b) Construction of a Surrogate Model

(c) Optimization using the Surrogate Model

Fig. 2. Overview of the MLGO Framework

We present in Fig. 2 an overview of the MLGO approach in 3 steps:

- Fig. 2a – *Training Dataset.* The goal of this step is to create the dataset required to train the model. It starts by generating a pool of solutions of our problem from which a set of n_S distinct solutions $(x_1, \ldots, x_{n_S})$ is sampled (see Sect. 4.2). Then, those solutions are evaluated with f (see Sect. 4.3) to obtain their realized values $(y_1 = f(x_1), \ldots, y_{n_S} = f(x_{n_S}))$.
- Fig. 2b – *Model Training.* This second step takes the training dataset from the previous step, $((x_1, y_1), \ldots, (x_{n_S}, y_{n_S}))$, pre-processes it and computes the surrogate model $\hat{f}$ through a training phase (see Sect. 4.4).
- Fig. 2c – *Optimization.* Finally, $\hat{f}$ is defined as the objective function within an optimizer (see Sect. 4.5) to obtain a solution to the problem.

4   MLGO Applied to DRT Systems

We describe in this section how the main components of the MLGO framework are developed to fit a DRT application and ours in particular.

4.1   Model and Notations

Before going into detail, we present some notations and definitions that will be used in the rest of the paper. We note V the set of n_V vehicles available, $B = [\text{lat}_{\min}, \text{lat}_{\max}] \times [\text{long}_{\min}, \text{long}_{\max}]$ a bounding box defining the considered territory and $D \in B$ the coordinates of the vehicles depot. The time horizon T is discretized into a sequence of n_T regular time steps $(t_1 \ldots t_{n_T})$.

Definition 1. *An online request is represented by a pick-up time $t_p \in T$ and place $(lat_p, long_p) \in B$, a drop-off time $t_d \in T$ and place $(lat_d, long_d) \in B$, and an arrival time $t_a \in T$. An offline request has the same elements, except for the absence of a t_a as the user's request arrived in the past and is already served.*

Definition 2. *An online (resp. offline) scenario is a set of online (resp. offline) requests that want to (resp. must) be served by the fleet V of vehicles.*

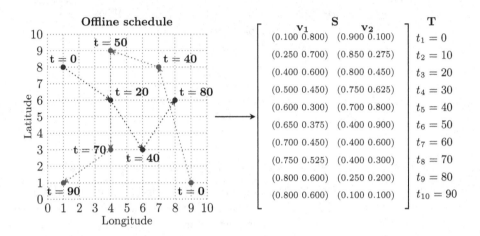

Fig. 3. Modeling of the offline schedule of two vehicles as a tensor

Definition 3. *A solution x corresponds to a set of routes for the n_V vehicles, leaving from D after t_1 and returning to D before t_{n_T}. A solution is formally modeled by a tensor $\mathbf{S} \in \mathbb{R}^{V \times T \times 2}$ where, $\forall (v, t) \in V \times T$, $\mathbf{S}_{v,t}$ is the normalized position (with respect to B) of the vehicle v at time step t. A solution is said feasible for a given offline scenario if its planning can serve all its offline requests.*

Definition 3 implies that, in general, a randomly chosen tensor $\mathbf{S} \in \mathbb{R}^{V \times T \times 2}$ does not represent a feasible solution. It is therefore not an easy task to obtain a set of diversified solutions (see Sect. 4.2 for more details). We provide in Fig. 3 a simple but visual example of the tensor representation of a solution.

We recall that, in this work, we suppose the offline scenario to be given and the online scenario to be uncertain, which matches the situation where the OOF is executed each night for the next service. This implies that the generation of solutions and the optimization (see Fig. 2) take as input the same offline scenario: in both cases, we need to produce one or more feasible solutions while the feasibility of a solution only depends on the offline scenario considered.

Also, the objective function f used in Equation (1) and Fig. 2 is the expected rate of accepted online requests returned by a simulator, being in our case the one developed by Padam Mobility (see Sect. 4.3).

4.2   Generation of Feasible Solutions

In the literature, most of the works on surrogate modeling consider problems where generating a sample of the space of solutions can easily be done with techniques such as Latin Hypercube Sampling [15] or Full Factorial Sampling [23]. Nonetheless, such methods can be used only if no restriction holds on the solutions. In our case, the high number of constraints defining the feasible region of the underlying DaRP (see Definition 3) requires the use of more sophisticated techniques to generate a solution.

To generate a diversified set of feasible solutions, we chose to launch the Adaptive Large Neighborhood Search (ALNS) developed by Padam Mobility (see Sect. 4.5) on the considered offline scenario without any objective function for a few minutes and save each new schedule found during the search. Once a large enough number of solutions has been obtained by this procedure, we use a stratified sampling strategy based on the KMeans clustering algorithm, the tensor representation of the solutions (see Definition 3) and the Euclidean distance to cover the solution space as homogeneously as possible. In practice, this procedure allowed us to produce diversified training sets of 1800 samples, validation sets of 200 samples and testing sets of 1000 samples for all our instances.

4.3   Simulation Framework

The Simulation Framework must take as input a feasible solution x and return the expected number of accepted online requests $f(x, s)$ for an online scenario s.

Any procedure that does this job can be used. In our case, Padam Mobility has its own simulator that provides a good enough representation of how a DRT service behaves through a working day. In particular, it induces some randomness in the behaviour of the virtual users when they are facing equivalent propositions for their requests to be served. As a change of a few minutes on a serving time can have an impact on future requests and considering practical experiments, we will then consider the output of a simulation as stochastic but stable. More precisely, ~ 10 runs of a solution through the simulator is enough to fully evaluate it.

The set of online requests that will actually arrive along the day can be viewed as a random variable. In this work, we make the hypothesis that we have at our disposal a stochastic model to generate plausible scenarios of online requests for a given day. Recent works, such as [27] or [29], sustain this assumption.

We therefore decide to design a new objective function by first selecting n_σ online scenarios from a given pool of online scenarios (see Sect. 5). Then, we simulate once the working day for each of the selected online scenario, starting from a given offline scenario, and we return the average percentage of accepted online requests over the n_σ online scenarios.

4.4   Surrogate Model

The Surrogate Model must be a model $\hat{f}$ that imitates the original and unknown objective function f: for a feasible solution x and a set of online scenarios S, $\hat{f}(x) \sim f(x, S)$. In principle, any supervised approach can be used to obtain $\hat{f}$.

In our case, we present in Sect. 5.1 the various Machine Learning models considered within this study as well as the methodology used to decide which one should be used for the optimization. Nonetheless, the design choices of $\hat{f}$ should follow two main principles: firstly, it must be a relatively minimalist and compact model so that the training phase is not significantly time consuming. Secondly, it must scale well with the size of the instances without losing in quality.

In terms of data pre-processing, the input values are the tensor representation of the schedules (see Definition 3) while the output values of the training set are standardized. Then, as we experimentally observed that our instances present Gaussian-like distributions of values over their generated pool of offline schedules, the weights of the Weighted Mean Square Error loss function used to train the models are designed so that each value has a similar impact on the loss.

4.5 Offline Optimization Framework

The Offline Optimization Framework (OOF) must consider an offline scenario s_{Off} and return an optimized schedule $x = \text{OOF}(s_{Off}, \mathcal{O})$ for an objective $\mathcal{O}$.

In this work, we used a version of ALNS [11,28] modified by Padam Mobility to handle their own application, in order to respect their customized constraints. The ALNS method is a Local Search metaheuristic. This variety of algorithms explores the search space of feasible solutions by applying local changes until no improvement can be found and therefore a (locally) optimal solution is identified.

In our context, the advantage of this method is that we can keep the structure of the in-house ALNS and change only the part related to the evaluation of a solution by using the surrogate model presented in Sect. 4.4 in place of the currently used objective function, based on the minimization of the TDR.

5 Experiments

To assess the quality of our framework, we consider 25 challenging instances provided by our industrial partner. In Table 1, we display the following information relative to the selected instances: the identifier of each *Instance*, used in later references, the service *Duration* i.e., the time length during which users' requests can be served, the number of *Vehicles*, the number of historical *Offline requests* and the number of historical *Online requests*. Regardless of the service duration, the discrete time horizon T for the proposed instances is always of size 100.

Table 1. Presentation of the considered instances

Instance	A	B	C	D	E	F	G	H	I	J	K	L	M	N	O	P	Q	R	S	T	U	V	W	X	Y
Vehicles	2	2	3	2	2	3	3	2	2	2	12	12	5	6	12	11	12	9	8	13	11	11	9	12	11
Duration (in h)	7	7	7	7	7	7	7	7	7	7	12	15	13	13	15	15	15	13	13	15	15	13	15	15
Surface (in km)	46	46	46	46	46	46	46	46	46	46	197	197	144	144	197	197	197	197	144	144	197	197	144	197	197
Offline requests	30	41	35	30	41	48	45	42	44	52	41	49	45	58	62	45	51	63	91	86	82	92	109	86	86
Online requests	32	24	32	41	36	31	42	50	54	60	74	68	79	85	92	109	104	107	80	88	156	154	179	204	204

We note **I** the set of instances. Regarding the Simulation Framework presented in Sect. 4.3, we consider two sets of scenarios of online requests:

- *Historical Configuration (HC)*
  This option represents the optimistic point of view, where the online requests are perfectly known in-advance. Hence, we use $n_\sigma = 1$ scenario made of the historical online requests that occurred during the actual service.
- *Robust Configuration (RC)*
  This option represents a noisy forecast of the upcoming online requests. We generate $n_\sigma = 5$ scenarios based on the historical set of online requests with a randomized order of arrival. Furthermore, the departure and destination positions are moved randomly in a 500 meters radius as well as the requested time in a 30 minutes time window. This manually added noise represents the generation of scenarios based on a forecasted Origin-Destination matrix with areas of 1 km^2 and time steps of 30 minutes [29].

5.1   Choice of a Machine Learning Model for the Optimization

In this section, we first describe the Machine Learning techniques that we have implemented and tested to approximate the Simulation Framework. Then, we present the methodology used to evaluate the different models in order to choose which one should be used within the optimization process.

Presentation of the Surrogate Models

Radial Basis Function Network (RBFN). We implement the variant of this model where the centers of the Radial Basis Functions are computed based on a clustering technique, using the *KMeans* method of the scikit-learn Python package[1], before being fed to an ANN, using the TensorFlow Python package[2].

Gaussian Process Regression (GPR). We use the model provided by the scikit-learn Python package (See footnote 1) named *GaussianProcessRegressor*.

Feedforward Neural Network (FNN). Our FNN structure consists of a first layer to flatten the tensors provided in input as vectors of size $200 \times n_V$, 4 hidden layers with 1024 neurons, and a final layer with a single neuron to compute the output of the model. All nodes of the FNN have a linear activation function. The hyperparameters used for the training phase are: 5000 epochs, a batch size equal to the Training Set size, and an Adam optimizer with a learning rate of 1E-5. We implemented this model with the TensorFlow Python package (See footnote 2) .

---

[1] See https://scikit-learn.org/ for more information..

[2] See https://www.tensorflow.org/ for more information..

Convolutional Neural Network (CNN). Our architecture consists of 5 successive Convolutional Layers with a Kernel size of (1, 3), a Stride of (1, 2), a Dropout rate of 0.5 and a Rectified Linear Unit (ReLU) as activation function. The size of the tensor after each layer is respectively: $n_V \times 49 \times 32$, $n_V \times 24 \times 64$, $n_V \times 11 \times 128$, $n_V \times 5 \times 256$ and $n_V \times 1 \times 512$. The output of the last Convolutional Layer is then flattened as a vector of size $512 \times n_V$ and fed to a Fully Connected Layer of the same size with a linear activation function. Finally, the last layer is the Output Layer with a single neuron and a linear activation function to compute the output of the model. The hyperparameters used for the training of the CNN are: 10000 epochs, a batch size equal to the Training Set size, and an Adam optimizer with a learning rate of 1E-4. We implement this model with TensorFlow (See footnote 2).

Ensemble Learning Model (ELM). We define this model as a weighted sum of the previously cited models: as each Machine Learning technique learns differently through its learning phase, such model can take the best of them [8]. In practice, we used the following combination as it proved to be the most stable one, in terms of noise reduction: $\text{ELM} = 0.5 \times \text{FNN} + 0.35 \times \text{CNN} + 0.15 \times \text{GPR}$.

For the sake of fairness, the hyperparameters of each model have been optimized to obtain the highest possible accuracy, while maintaining a size that allows to train the methods in a reasonable amount of time.

Evaluation of the Surrogate Models

Notations. For each instance $I \in \mathbf{I}$, we note Train_I the training set and Test_I the test set generated for I. We note $\mathbf{M}$ the set of considered surrogate models.

Methodology. In order to evaluate the generalization capacity of the different surrogate models, we use the following process:

– For each instance $I \in \mathbf{I}$, we define $\text{Train}_I^{10\%}$ the subset of Train_I that contains the solutions with a value in the top 10% values of the set:

$$\text{Train}_I^{10\%} = \left\{ (x; y) \in \text{Train}_I \ \Big| \ y \geq 0.9 \times \left(\max_{(x';y') \in \text{Train}_I} y' \right) + 0.1 \times \left(\min_{(x';y') \in \text{Train}_I} y' \right) \right\}$$

– For each surrogate model $M \in \mathbf{M}$, we train M on $\text{Train}_I \setminus \text{Train}_I^{10\%}$ and evaluate the extended test set $\text{Test}_I \cup \text{Train}_I^{10\%}$ with the obtained model. Then, we note $\left(y_{I,k}^M \right)_{1 \leq k \leq K}$ the full evaluation by the Simulation Framework of the top K solutions of the extended test set of I according to M for a given $K \in \mathbf{N}^\star$. If more than one solution can be fully evaluated at the end of the optimization, this K represents some tolerance on the model forecast.

- Finally, $\forall\ I \in \mathbf{I}$, $\forall\ M \in \mathbf{M}$, we define $g_{I,K}^{M}$ the Relative Difference to the

  Best Solution of order $K \in \mathbf{N}^{\star}$ as follows: $g_{I,K}^{M} = \dfrac{y_{I,K}^{\mathrm{Best}} - \left(\max\limits_{1 \leq k \leq K} y_{I,k}^{M}\right)}{y_{I,K}^{\mathrm{Best}}}$, where

  $y_{I,K}^{\mathrm{Best}} = \max\limits_{\substack{M' \in \mathbf{M} \\ 1 \leq k \leq K}}\ y_{I,k}^{M'}$. The idea behind $g_{I,K}^{M}$ is to measure how well each model

  has learned what made a solution a good one in comparison to the others,
  up to a given tolerance, defined by the number of solutions considered K.

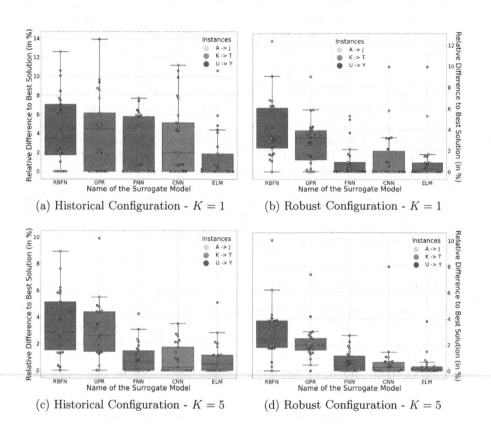

Fig. 4. Evaluation of the surrogate models

Results. We present in Fig. 4 the aggregated results of the previously cited surrogate models over the 25 considered instances. In both Fig. 4a and Fig. 4d, we can see that the ELM clearly provides the best results overall, in spite of a few outliers. In Fig. 4c and Fig. 4b, the situation is slightly more contrasted with similar performances of the FNN, CNN and ELM models. On the other hand, ELM clearly provides the best results in Fig. 4d, which is the most robust case, where we use the Robust Configuration, paired with a tolerance of 5 instances.

Therefore, as the ELM model provides the most stable results overall, we decide to use it within the OOF. We note ELM (HC) (resp. ELM (RC)) the ELM trained with the Historical (resp. Robust) Configuration.

5.2 Computational Results

The experiments were led on a computer equipped with an AMD Ryzen 7 3700x for CPU, allowing us to parallelize the evaluation through the simulator of the training set, a GeForce RTX 2060 SUPER for GPU, making the training of our ANNs be quick, and 16 Go of RAM while running on Ubuntu 20.04 LTS. Based on this configuration, we can evaluate the computational gain of our surrogate model in contrast with using the actual simulator within the OOF:

- Instances A to J: it takes a few seconds to run a simulation while it takes ~ 15 min to build our model then ~ 20 ms to make an evaluation. Thus, hours of computation time are saved after a thousand iterations of the optimizer.
- Instances K to Y: it takes more than ten seconds to run a single simulation while it takes ~ 30 min to build our model then ~ 40 ms to evaluate a solution afterwards. Hence, the time saved during the optimization phase becomes sizable even faster than for smaller instances.

To sum up, the design of our framework is a time-saver in contrast with a SbO design, notably by letting our model learn the stochastic behaviour of the Simulation Framework through the diversification of the training set and by making use of the parallelization capacity of modern computers.

5.3 Optimization Results

In this section, we compare the performances of the schedules obtained using the ELM with the ones that we obtain using the objective functions present in the literature: the Total Duration of the Rides (TDR), the Total Detour Time (TDT), the Forward Slack Time (FST), the Onboard Time (OT) and the Onboard Deviation (OD), all detailed in Table 2 (see [22,28] for more details).

Table 2. Classic objective functions from the literature

Name	Direction	Formula
TDR	Min	$\sum_{vehicle} [\text{Total Travel Time}]_{vehicle}$
TDT	Min	$\sum_{user} \left[\frac{\text{Actual Travel Time}}{\text{Direct Travel Time}}\right]_{user}$
FST	Max	$\sum_{s \in stops^a} [\text{Maximal Arrival Time}]_s - [\text{Arrival Time}]_s$
OT	Min	$\sum_{user} [\text{Actual Travel Time}]_{user}$
OD	Min	$\sum_{s \in segments^b} [\text{Passengers Onboard}]_s \times [\text{Travel Time}]_s$

a A stop is a location and time where a vehicle handles a request.
b A segment is a trip of a vehicle between two consecutive stops.

For each instance $I \in \mathbf{I}$, we run the OOF on its offline scenario with the objectives shown in Table 2 and with our fully trained ELM (HC) and ELM (RC) models. We set a time limit of 30 min for the optimizer to run and, to limit the impact of randomness, each combination of instance and objective function is solved 10 times with different random seeds. Then, for each objective $\mathcal{O}$, we note $x_I^{\mathcal{O}}$ the best solution found according to $\mathcal{O}$ for instance I and we evaluate it with 25 runs of the Simulation Framework for both configurations of online scenarios. Finally, for $C \in \{\mathrm{HC}, \mathrm{RC}\}$, we note $y_{I,C}^{\mathcal{O}}$ the full evaluation with the Simulation Framework of $x_I^{\mathcal{O}}$ for the set of online scenarios defined in C.

To analyze the performance of the objective functions in both configurations $C \in \{\mathrm{HC}, \mathrm{RC}\}$, we define $y_{I,C}^{\star} = y_{I,C}^{\mathrm{ELM\,(C)}}$ as a reference value: our ELM models have been designed to maximize it. Then, we define $g_{I,C}^{\mathcal{O}}$ the Relative Difference to Best Solution of objective $\mathcal{O}$ in configuration C as $g_{I,C}^{\mathcal{O}} = \frac{y_{I,C}^{\star} - y_{I,C}^{\mathcal{O}}}{y_{I,C}^{\star}}$.

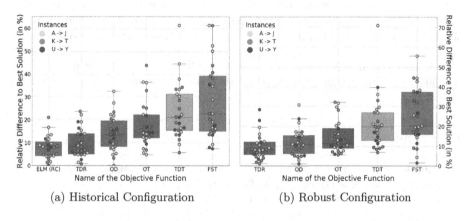

(a) Historical Configuration   (b) Robust Configuration

Fig. 5. Evaluation of the objective functions

We present in Fig. 5 the aggregated results of our study over all instances. Figure 5a presents how the solutions associated to each objective function would have performed in the reality. In the case of our ELM (RC) model, the observed gap can be interpreted as the cost of robustness. In spite of this, we can see that our model is more stable and provides better results than the traditional objectives overall. On the other side, Fig. 5b shows how much the newly proposed objective function performs better in comparison to the more classic objectives present in the literature in an uncertain scenario. More precisely, the ELM (RC) model is on average 9.5% better than TDR, its closest competitor, in such a context. The gap that we can find for most objectives and instances shows the lack of robustness of these functions and the place for improvement that we aim at filling with our method. Therefore, this study proves that the classic objective functions seem to be particularly unfit for the Dynamic DaRP.

6   Conclusion

In this paper, we present a new approach to model and optimize the offline planning of a Demand Responsive Transport (DRT) system, namely Machine Learning Guided Optimization. The idea of this framework is to train a Surrogate Model to estimate the expected number of online requests that a given offline schedule will be able to serve. Integrated within an optimizer, this model can then be used as an objective function to optimize the offline planning, in order to maximize the expected number of accepted online requests in the day after. We apply this methodology to a real DRT case study in collaboration with Padam Mobility, an international company specialized in Shared Mobility Systems. To obtain an effective algorithm, several aspects need to be considered: the definition of a proper dataset, an ad-hoc predictive model, and an optimisation algorithm. In this work, we show how to take care of each aspect. The experimental section of the paper clearly proves that the traditional approaches in the literature are outclassed by our framework, which provides the best performances overall. We hope that the presented work could motivate other researchers to investigate similar paradigms for other applications related to transportation problems.

Acknowledgement. We thank Anh-Dung NGUYEN and Samir NAIM from Padam Mobility for all the useful discussions and their continuous support throughout this project.

References

1. Alizadeh, R., Allen, J.K., Mistree, F.: Managing computational complexity using surrogate models: a critical review. Res. Eng. Des. **31**(3), 275–298 (2020)
2. Amaran, S., Sahinidis, N.V., Sharda, B., Bury, S.J.: Simulation optimization: a review of algorithms and applications. Ann. Oper. Res. **240**(1), 351–380 (2016)
3. Ambrosino, G., Nelson, J., Romanazzo, M.: Demand responsive transport services: towards the flexible mobility agency. ENEA (2004)
4. Barton, R.R., Meckesheimer, M.: Metamodel-based simulation optimization. Handb. Oper. Res. Manag. Sci. **13**, 535–574 (2006)
5. Bengio, Y., Lodi, A., Prouvost, A.: Machine learning for combinatorial optimization: a methodological tour d'horizon. Eur. J. Oper. Res. (2020). https://doi.org/10.1016/j.ejor.2020.07.063
6. Bernardo, M., Pannek, J.: Robust solution approach for the dynamic and stochastic vehicle routing problem. J. Adv. Transp. **2018** (2018). https://doi.org/10.1155/2018/9848104
7. Cordeau, J.F.: A branch-and-cut algorithm for the dial-a-ride problem. Oper. Res. **54**(3), 573–586 (2006)
8. Dietterich, T.G.: Ensemble methods in machine learning. In: Kittler, J., Roli, F. (eds.) MCS 2000. LNCS, vol. 1857, pp. 1–15. Springer, Heidelberg (2000). https://doi.org/10.1007/3-540-45014-9_1
9. Engilberge, M., Chevallier, L., Pérez, P., Cord, M.: Sodeep: a sorting deep net to learn ranking loss surrogates. In: Proceedings of the IEEE/CVF Conference on Computer Vision and Pattern Recognition, pp. 10792–10801 (2019)

10. Fonseca, D.J., Navaresse, D.O., Moynihan, G.P.: Simulation metamodeling through artificial neural networks. Eng. Appl. Artif. Intell. **16**(3), 177–183 (2003)
11. Gschwind, T., Drexl, M.: Adaptive large neighborhood search with a constant-time feasibility test for the dial-a-ride problem. Transp. Sci. **53**(2), 480–491 (2019)
12. Guo, X., Li, W., Iorio, F.: Convolutional neural networks for steady flow approximation. In: Proceedings of the 22nd ACM SIGKDD International Conference on Knowledge Discovery and Data Mining, pp. 481–490 (2016)
13. Ho, S.C., Szeto, W.Y., Kuo, Y.H., Leung, J.M., Petering, M., Tou, T.W.: A survey of dial-a-ride problems: literature review and recent developments. Transp. Res. Part B Methodol. **111**, 395–421 (2018)
14. Huang, A., Dou, Z., Qi, L., Wang, L.: Flexible route optimization for demand-responsive public transit service. J. Transp. Eng. Part A Syst. **146**(12), 04020132 (2020)
15. Ilievski, I., Akhtar, T., Feng, J., Shoemaker, C.: Efficient hyperparameter optimization for deep learning algorithms using deterministic RBF surrogates. In: Proceedings of the AAAI Conference on Artificial Intelligence (2017)
16. Johnson, V.M., Rogers, L.L.: Accuracy of neural network approximators in simulation-optimization. J. Water Resour. Plan. Manag. - ASCE **126**(2), 48–56 (2000)
17. Kirchler, D., Wolfler Calvo, R.: A granular tabu search algorithm for the dial-a-ride problem. Transp. Res. Part B Methodol. **56**, 120–135 (2013)
18. Liu, T.Y.: Learning to Rank for Information Retrieval. Springer, Heidelberg (2011)
19. Lizotte, D.J., Wang, T., Bowling, M.H., Schuurmans, D.: Automatic gait optimization with gaussian process regression. In: IJCAI, vol. 7, pp. 944–949 (2007)
20. Lv, Z., Wang, L., Han, Z., Zhao, J., Wang, W.: Surrogate-assisted particle swarm optimization algorithm with pareto active learning for expensive multi-objective optimization. IEEE/CAA J. Autom. Sinica **6**(3), 838–849 (2019)
21. Mairal, J.: Optimization with first-order surrogate functions. In: International Conference on Machine Learning, pp. 783–791. PMLR (2013)
22. Parragh, S.N., Doerner, K.F., Hartl, R.F.: A survey on pickup and delivery problems. J. für Betriebswirtschaft **58**(2), 81–117 (2008)
23. Ploé, P.: Surrogate-based optimization of hydrofoil shapes using RANS simulations. Ph.D. thesis, École centrale de Nantes (2018)
24. Saint-Guillain, M., Deville, Y., Solnon, C.: A multistage stochastic programming approach to the dynamic and stochastic VRPTW. In: Michel, L. (ed.) CPAIOR 2015. LNCS, vol. 9075, pp. 357–374. Springer, Cham (2015). https://doi.org/10.1007/978-3-319-18008-3_25
25. Snoek, J., Larochelle, H., Adams, R.P.: Practical Bayesian optimization of machine learning algorithms. In: Bartlett, P.L., Pereira, F.C.N., Burges, C.J.C., Bottou, L. (eds.) Advances in Neural Information Processing Systems 25: 26th Annual Conference on Neural Information Processing Systems 2012. Proceedings of a meeting held December 3-6, 2012, Lake Tahoe, Nevada, United States, pp. 2960–2968 (2012). https://proceedings.neurips.cc/paper/2012/hash/05311655a15b75fab86956663e1819cd-Abstract.html
26. Tensen, I.: Stochastic optimization of the dial-a-ride problem. Dealing with variable travel times and irregular arrival of requests in the planning of special transport services. Master's thesis, University of Twente (2015)
27. Toqué, F., Côme, E., El Mahrsi, M.K., Oukhellou, L.: Forecasting dynamic public transport origin-destination matrices with long-short term memory recurrent neural networks. In: 2016 IEEE 19th ITSC, pp. 1071–1076. IEEE (2016)

28. Vallée, S., Oulamara, A., Cherif-Khettaf, W.R.: Maximizing the number of served requests in an online shared transport system by solving a dynamic DARP. In: ICCL 2017. LNCS, vol. 10572, pp. 64–78. Springer, Cham (2017). https://doi.org/10.1007/978-3-319-68496-3_5

29. Wang, Y., Yin, H., Chen, H., Wo, T., Xu, J., Zheng, K.: Origin-destination matrix prediction via graph convolution: a new perspective of passenger demand modeling. In: Proceedings of the 25th ACM SIGKDD, pp. 1227–1235 (2019)

30. Yao, W., Chen, X., Huang, Y., van Tooren, M.: A surrogate-based optimization method with RBF neural network enhanced by linear interpolation and hybrid infill strategy. Optim. Methods Softw. **29**(2), 406–429 (2014)

31. Zhang, Y., Sung, W.J., Mavris, D.N.: Application of convolutional neural network to predict airfoil lift coefficient. In: AIAA/ASCE/AHS/ASC Conference (2018)

OBELISC: Oscillator-Based Modelling and Control Using Efficient Neural Learning for Intelligent Road Traffic Signal Calculation

Cristian Axenie[1], Rongye Shi[2(✉)], Daniele Foroni[1], Alexander Wieder[1],
Mohamad Al Hajj Hassan[1], Paolo Sottovia[1], Margherita Grossi[1],
Stefano Bortoli[1], and Götz Brasche[1]

[1] Intelligent Cloud Technologies Lab, Huawei Munich Research Center,
Riesstrasse 25, 80992 Munich, Germany
`cristian.axenie@huawei.com`
[2] EI Intelligence Twins Program, Huawei Cloud BU, Shenzhen, China
`shirongye@huawei.com`

Abstract. Traffic congestion poses serious challenges to urban infrastructures through the unpredictable dynamical loading of their vehicular arteries. Despite the advances in traffic light control systems, the problem of optimal traffic signal timing is still resistant to straightforward solutions. Fundamentally nonlinear, traffic flows exhibit both locally periodic dynamics and globally coupled correlations under deep uncertainty. This paper introduces Oscillator-Based modelling and control using Efficient neural Learning for Intelligent road traffic Signal Calculation (OBELISC), an end-to-end system capable of modelling the cyclic dynamics of traffic flow and robustly compensate for uncertainty while still keeping the system feasible for real-world deployments. To achieve this goal, the system employs an efficient representation of the traffic flows and their dynamics in populations of spiking neural networks. Such a computation and learning framework enables OBELISC to model and control the complex dynamics of traffic flows in order to dynamically adapt the green light phase. In order to emphasize the advantages of the proposed system, an extensive experimental evaluation on real-world data completes the study.

Keywords: Traffic control · Oscillator model · Spiking neural networks

1 Introduction

Road traffic congestion poses serious challenges to urban infrastructures and impacts both the social and the economic lives of people. Such fundamental

C. Axenie, R. Shi, D. Foroni, A. Wieder, M. A. H. Hassan, P. Sottovia, M. Grossi and S. Bortoli—Authors contributed equally to this research.

Y. Dong et al. (Eds.): ECML PKDD 2021, LNAI 12978, pp. 437–452, 2021.
https://doi.org/10.1007/978-3-030-86514-6_27

reason motivated large amounts of research and systems developed to analyze, model, and control road traffic towards avoiding congestion [17]. Looking at actual technology instantiations, such as SCOOT [9], SCATS [12], PRODYN [7], or LISA [6], adaptive traffic signal control systems detect vehicles as they approach a signalized cross well in advance of the stop line. This detection, from multiple crosses, is subsequently fed into a central system, which models the flow of traffic in the area. The traffic model is then used to adapt the phasing of the traffic light signals in accordance with the flow of traffic, thus minimizing unnecessary green phases and allowing the traffic to flow most efficiently. Despite the increasing complexity of such end-to-end solutions, research on optimization is still going on. Basically, one of the differentiating aspects among the existing systems is the traffic model they use, in other words, those aspects of the physics of traffic they capture. For instance, based on large amounts of high-resolution field traffic data, work in [8] used the conditional distribution of the green start times and traffic demand scenarios for improved performance. However, high amounts of high-resolution traffic data are expensive to acquire at scale and doesn't exploit the temporal periodicity at the local level of adjacent traffic lights. Using a relatively simple model to predict arrivals at coordinated signal approaches, the work of [3] assumes nearest-neighbor interactions between signals and uses a linear superposition of distributions to optimize traffic lights phase duration. Despite finding the optimal coordination, the algorithm couldn't handle unpredictable changes to platoon shapes (i.e. occasionally caused by platoon splitting and merging) or prediction during saturated conditions (i.e. traffic jams, accidents). Hence its rather limited adaptation capabilities to disruptions that can propagate in time and space in the system.

The main goal of this study is to introduce Oscillator-Based modelling and control using Efficient neural Learning for Intelligent road traffic Signal Calculation (OBELISC), a new methodology and system for jointly modelling, learning, and controlling the dynamics of traffic flows for effective phase duration calculation. In a very good review and perspective, the study of [2], introduced the formalism of oscillator-based traffic modelling and control. Despite the good mathematical grounding, the proposed approach was static, in that it removed all convergence and self-organization dynamics of the oscillators, by replacing it with the steady-state solution. Such an approach has benefits at the single intersection level, as also the authors claim, but will fail in large-scale heterogeneous road networks (i.e. non-uniform road geometry, disrupted traffic patterns, etc.). The approach of OBELISC introduces a novel type of nonlinear coupled oscillators model based on [15], along with a nonlinear control mechanism that allows it to capture complex flow patterns and unpredictable variations [16] in large road networks. This ensures a robust control of the oscillator-based model under dynamical demand changes based on measurement of local traffic data. A similar oscillator approach was used in [13] and later in [5] as area-wide signal control of an urban traffic network. Yet, due to their complex-valued dynamics and optimization, the systems could not capture both the spatial and temporal correlations under a realistic computational cost for real-world deployment.

Additionally, we are contributing with the release of a multi-cross urban traffic dataset, which contains 59 d of real urban road traffic data from 8 crosses in a city in China. Targeting a real-world deployment and superior run-time performance under real traffic flows, OBELISC is:

- using an efficient implementation in spiking neural networks [4],
- is avoiding optimization routines and operates in real-time,
- it excels in minimizing typical traffic key performance indices when the phase duration is calculated depending on the real-time demand measurements.

2 Materials and Methods

The dynamics of a traffic signal is periodic, with a phase of green - yellow - red light in one cycle, and is defined by three control parameters: a cycle length (i.e. sum of phases), a (phase) offset, and a split. The scope of our study, the phase duration calculation, is described for adjacent crosses signals in Fig. 1. Typically, for a responsive traffic signal control system, adjusting the phase duration is equivalent to optimizing a given objective function (e.g. such as minimizing travel time, waiting time, or stops) in real-time, based upon perceived traffic conditions. In this section, we introduce OBELISC, as a methodology and system for jointly modelling, learning, and controlling phase calculation that exploits the periodic (i.e. oscillatory) dynamics of traffic.[1]

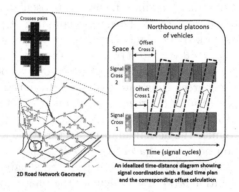

Fig. 1. Traffic light signal calculations: phase duration, offset, and cycles.

2.1 Oscillator-Based Modelling of Traffic Dynamics

Traffic has a strong periodic behavior. This motivates us to describe traffic light phasing phenomenon as a repeated collective synchronization problem, in which a large network of oscillators, each representing a traffic light controlling a possible movement direction in a cross, spontaneously locks to a common operation

---

[1] Codebase available at: https://github.com/omlstreaming/ecml2021.

phase. Subsequently, the phase duration adjustment factor is computed as a function of the oscillator time to synchronization. The intuition is the following: 1) each of the oscillators is injected with external traffic flow data impacting its local dynamics, and 2) the oscillator network converges to a steady state used to extract adaptive factor to adjust the traffic light phases. Despite the inevitable differences in the natural oscillation frequencies and injected data of each oscillator the network ensures that each of the coupled oscillators repeatedly locks phase. We extend the basic Kuramoto oscillator [10] with additional components to account for spatial as well as temporal interactions among the oscillators and an external perturbation model as described in Eq. 1.

$$\frac{d\theta_i(t)}{dt} = \omega_i(t) + k_i(t) \sum_{j=1}^{N} A_{ij} sin(\theta_j(t) - \theta_i(t)) + F_i sin(\theta^*(t) - \theta_i(t)) \qquad (1)$$

where:

θ_i - the amount of green time of traffic light i
ω_i - the frequency of traffic light i oscillator
k_i - the flow of cars passing through the direction controlled by oscillator i
A_{ij} - the static spatial adjacency coupling between oscillator i and oscillator j
F_i - the coupling of external perturbations (e.g. maximum cycle time per phase)
θ^* - the external perturbation (e.g. traffic signal limits imposed by law)

The model underlying OBELISC assumes that the change in allocated green time θ_i for a certain traffic light i, for a certain direction, depends on the: 1) the internal frequency of the corresponding (traffic light) oscillator ω; 2) the current flow of cars k_i in that direction; 3) the spatial coupling A_{ij} of the oscillators through the street network that weights the impact of a nonlinear periodic coupling of the oscillators $sin(\theta_j(t) - \theta_i(t))$; and 4) the external perturbation θ^* with weight F_i which ensures, for instance, that the output of the system stays in the bounds of realistic green time values imposed from the traffic laws. Given the known topological layout of the road network and the computed green times of each of the oscillators, when the dynamics converge (i.e. the solution of the differential Eq. 1), we infer the actual adaptive factor to be applied to the traffic light phase duration between adjacent (coupled) oscillators corresponding to adjacent moving directions. More precisely, given the steady state value of the green time (i.e. the solution $\theta_i(t_f)$), we calculate the phase duration as the time to synchronization of each oscillator relative to the ones coupled to it. From the dynamics synchronization matrix ρ at each time t the phase duration update is calculated as $\arg\max_t\{\rho(t) > \tau\}$ where $\rho_{ij}(t) = cos(\theta_i(t) - \theta_j(t))$ and $0 < \tau < 1$.

In order to ground the analytic formulation, we describe a simple, regular 5×5 lattice composed of $N = 25$ oscillators. For simplicity, in this example, each oscillator is responsible for an entire cross (i.e. the 4 adjacent directions: N, S, W, E) and the spatial coupling A_{ij} is given by the topology of the lattice, as shown in Fig. 2 a. Here, each oscillator i dynamics is described by the superposition of its natural oscillation frequency ω_i and the cumulative impact of neighboring (coupled through A_{ij}) oscillators weighted by the flow of cars k_i through the cross

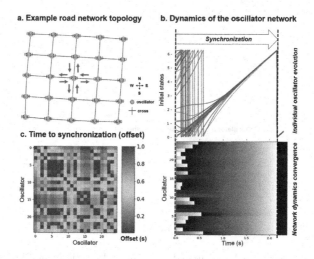

a. Example road network topology

b. Dynamics of the oscillator network

c. Time to synchronization (offset)

Fig. 2. Oscillator-based dynamics.

controlled by oscillator i. The external perturbation term $F_i sin(\theta^*(t) - \theta_i(t))$ is neglected for simplicity. Figure 2 b describes the internal dynamics of such a network model for traffic control where given the different initial conditions of each oscillator, the coupling dynamics enforces consensus after some time (i.e. 2.1s). The steady state is then used to extract the actual phase duration by simply calculating the time to synchronization $\arg\max_x\{\rho(t) > \tau\}$, as a per oscillator relative time difference, from the ρ matrix in Fig. 2 c. Here, the choice of τ determines how fast a suitable steady state is reached.

2.2 Robust Control of the Oscillator-Based Networked Dynamics

The network dynamics of OBELISC (Eq. 1), is judiciously parametrized to cope with the normal daily traffic profile. This can be visible in Fig. 3 where the model is able to keep the lost time through a single cross to an acceptable value, around 70s (see Fig. 3 b). In the case of traffic disruptions (e.g. accident, sport events, or adverse weather conditions), the system cannot capture the fast changing dynamics (i.e. steep derivatives) of the traffic flow (see Fig. 3 a) and, hence, performs poorly, for instance in preserving an acceptable time loss (i.e. difference in the duration of a trip in the traffic free vs. full traffic) over rush-hour (see Fig. 3b around 18:00). The example in Fig. 3 illustrates a limitation of such dynamic networked models, namely robustness to uncertainty. Be it structured uncertainty (e.g. sub-optimal choice of the internal oscillator frequency ω or a sudden time varying topological coupling A_{ij} through trajectory re-routing) or unstructured uncertainty (e.g. unmodelled dynamics through the single use of $\dot{\theta}(t)$ and neglecting rate of change given by the Laplace operator $\ddot{\theta}(t)$), the system in Eq. 1 is unable to converge to a satisfactory solution given input k and coupling constraints.

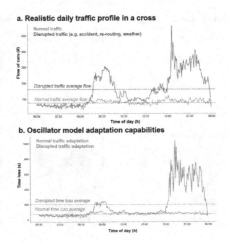

Fig. 3. Oscillator-based model dynamics adaptation capabilities.

To address this challenge, we extend Eq. 1 with a robust control law. We chose to systematically maintain stability of the oscillatory dynamics by using a robust control approach which ensures consistent performance in the face of uncertainties. Sliding mode control [16] is a well established control engineering method to compensate for uncertainty and handle highly nonlinear problems. At its core it captures and controls the impact of higher-order motion (i.e. second derivative) through a high-frequency switching of the control law towards synchronization. Such a discontinuous robust control "drives", through a regularizing control law term $u(t)$, the coupled dynamics of the oscillators towards a desired dynamics (i.e. sliding surface).

$$\frac{d\theta_i(t)}{dt} = \omega_i(t) + k_i(t)\sum_{j=1}^{N} A_{ij}sin(\theta_j(t) - \theta_i(t)) + F_i sin(\theta^*(t) - \theta_i(t)) + u_i(t) \quad (2)$$

with

$$u_i(t) = \epsilon_1 \int_0^t \hat{s}_i(\tau)d\tau$$

$$\frac{d\hat{s}_i(t)}{dt} = \epsilon_2(\sum_{i,j}(\hat{s}_j(t) - \hat{s}_i(t)) + s_i(t))$$

$$\frac{ds_i(t)}{dt} = \epsilon_3\sum_j(s_j(t) - \frac{d\hat{s}_i(t)}{dt}) - sign(\hat{s}_i(t))\frac{d^2\theta_i(t)}{dt^2}$$

$$0 < \epsilon_1 < \epsilon_2 < \epsilon_3 < 1$$

(3)

where:
$s_i(t)$ - the surplus energy of traffic light i oscillator
$\hat{s}_i(t)$ - the estimated surplus energy of traffic light i oscillator

The goal of the regularizing sliding mode control law u_i is to "push" the network of coupled oscillators, with a step size of ϵ, towards a dynamics which accommodates the disruptions in the flow of cars k (i.e. captured by $\ddot{\theta}_i(t)$). Intuitively, this assumes that the controller captures the second-order motion (i.e. $\ddot{\theta}_i(t)$) of the oscillator and compensates for it asymptotically until the surface is reached. This assumes, in first instance, choosing an appropriate sliding surface that minimizes the energy surplus $s_i(t)$ as illustrated in Fig. 4 c. Following Eq. 3, the regularizing control law $u_i(t)$ applied to oscillator i is the area under the curve (i.e. the integral) of the estimated energy surplus, depicted in Fig. 4 c. Interestingly, the (estimated) surplus energy, which keeps oscillator i away from the desired robust dynamics $\hat{s}_i(t)$ depends on the local oscillators interaction $\sum_{i,j}(\hat{s}_j(t) - \hat{s}_i(t))$ and the actual surplus energy. The change in surplus energy is the actual dynamics of convergence to the sliding surface and is based on the cumulative impact of neighboring oscillators $\sum_j s_j(t)$ and the Laplacean of the green time $\ddot{\theta}_i(t)$ weighted by the direction of the convergence $sign(\hat{s}_i(t))$. The property of insensitivity of sliding surface in Eq. 2 to the oscillatory dynamics[2] is utilized to control the reaction of the network of coupled oscillators to uncertainty. We realized this practically by adding the regularizing term $u_i(t)$ in the local dynamics of each oscillator described by Eq. 1. To get a better understanding of Eq. 2, we now exemplify, in Fig. 4, the impact the sliding mode controller has upon the dynamics of a road network when facing traffic disruptions from a real scenario (details about the data is provided in the Experiments and Results section). We consider a region composed of 8 crosses and $N = 29$ oscillators as described in Fig. 4 a.

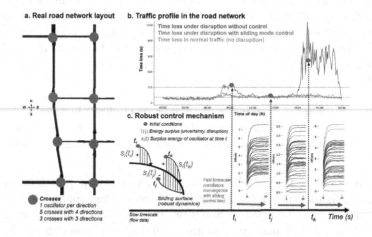

Fig. 4. Sliding Mode Control for oscillator-based model dynamics adaptation.

In our case, the network of coupled oscillators is a system with discontinuous control (i.e. the control law $u_i(t)$ uses the sign of the energy surplus to drive the

---

[2] For a thorough analysis of sliding modes invariance see [16].

system towards the robust dynamics). Basically, as shown in Fig. 4 b, c, given each sample of flow data $k_i(t_i...t_j...t_k)$ (from the road sensors) there is a fast convergence time-scale which allows the oscillators to reach steady state. This state is reached under sliding mode control by compensating for the disruptions in the traffic flow modelled by the second-order motion $\ddot{\theta}_i(t)$. The stationary state is subsequently probed for the actual phase duration, relative to each coupled oscillator by solving $\arg\max_x\{\rho(t) > \tau\}$ where $\rho_{ij}(t) = cos(\theta_i(t) - \theta_j(t))$ and $0 < \tau < 1$. Due to the fast changes, occurring during disruptions (see Fig. 4 b - rush hour around 18h00), in the slow time-scale of traffic flow (i.e. sensory data), the network of coupled oscillators benefits from the sliding mode control law to compensate for the abrupt changes and to reach consensus, as shown in Fig. 4 c - right panel. This consensus state describes the point when the system dynamics reached the sliding surface, in other words when the magnitude of the surplus energy decayed at a finite rate over the finite time interval (i.e. fast timescale in Fig. 4 c - left panel). The regularization approach we propose has a simple physical interpretation. Uncertainty in the system behavior in the face of disruptions appears because the motion equations of the dynamics in Eq. 1 are an ideal system model. Non-ideal factors such as unmodelled dynamics and sub-optimal parameter selection are neglected in the ideal model. But, incorporating them into the system model eliminates ambiguity in the system behavior which "slides" to a robust dynamics.

2.3   Representation, Learning, and Dynamics in Neural Networks

The notion of phase allows for a direct identification of the system's state in terms of a one-dimensional variable, described in Eq. 1. This facilitates an analytic approach to robustly control such dynamics, as shown in Eq. 3. Yet, such complex analytical description of networked dynamics is not tractable for large real-world deployments. In order to deploy an efficient traffic signal phase optimization with OBELISC, the data representation, the oscillatory network dynamics, and the robust controller, are implemented in the Neural Engineering Framework (NEF) [4]. NEF offers a systematic method of "compiling" high-level dynamics, such as ordinary differential equations (ODEs), into synaptic connection weights between populations of spiking neurons with efficient learning capabilities.

Representation of Traffic Flow Data. In NEF, neural populations represent time-varying signals, such as traffic flow data, through their spiking activity. Such signals drive neural populations based on each neuron's tuning curve, which describes how much a particular neuron will fire as a function of the input signal (see Fig. 5 - Encoding Neural Population, upper panel). The role of the representation (i.e. complemented by a pair of operations for encoding/decoding) is to provide a distributed version of the real-valued input signal. Basically, using this representation, we can estimate the input signal originally encoded by decoding the pattern of spikes (see Fig. 5 - Encoding Neural Population). The decoding weights are determined by minimizing the squared difference between the decoded estimate and the actual input signal and accounts for the weights learning process[3].

Learning Arbitrary Functions of Flow Data. Encoding and decoding operations on NEF neural populations representations allow us to encode traffic flow signals over time, and decode transformations (i.e. mathematical functions) of those signals. In fact, NEF allows us to decode arbitrary transformations of the input signal. In our case the right-hand side of Eq. 1 contains a non-linear combination of terms, out of which, for instance, the sinus of the relative phase difference $sin(\theta_j(t) - \theta_i(t))$ is decoded as a sinus transformation from a population encoding the phase difference $\theta_j(t) - \theta_i(t)$. The same principle applies to the robust controlled dynamics in Eq. 2 and is depicted in Fig. 5. This process determines how we can decode spike trains to compute linear and nonlinear transformations of the various signals encoded in a population of neurons. Essentially, this provides the means of learning the neural connection weights to compute the function between populations (e.g. product between the population encoding the spatial adjacency coupling A_{ij} and the population encoding the sinus transformation of the phase difference $\theta_j(t) - \theta_i(t)$).

Dynamics of Traffic Oscillator Network in Neural Networks Fundamentally, NEF automatically translates from standard dynamical systems descriptions to descriptions consistent with neural dynamics. Using the distributed neural representation of the traffic data and learning arbitrary functions of traffic data, we can now describe the combined dynamics implementation of the network of oscillators and the sliding mode controller. Figure 5 introduces the high-level implementation details. The neural implementation in Fig. 5 is bound to each oscillator i in the network. Each oscillator is fed with traffic flow data $k_i(t)$ corresponding to the direction it controls. The real-valued data is then encoded in a distributed pattern in the Encoding Neural Population. This encoding process is visible in the Spiking Activity and Neural Activation panels of Fig. 5, where each neuron encodes the input data in a frequency modulated train of spikes (Spiking Activity). The temporal activation of each of the encoding neurons relative to each other is illustrated in the Neural Activation panel. As one can see, in Fig. 5 - left and low-left panels, the decoded flow if cars is a noisy version of the actual input (intuitively, more neurons will provide a better reconstruction but more computational cost). The encoded traffic flow data is then fed to the actual combined dynamics (i.e. oscillator network and sliding mode controller) in the Robust Controller OBELISC Population. This neural population has a recurrent connection that implements the dynamics of the right-hand side of Eq. 2. More precisely, this population splits the Eq. 2 in terms and realizes each multiplication, nonlinear function, and summation in separate connected populations. Basically, the population encoding the oscillation frequency ω_i will be connected through a sum function to the population encoding the

---

[3] For a thorough overview of practical Neural Engineering Framework (NEF) see [4].

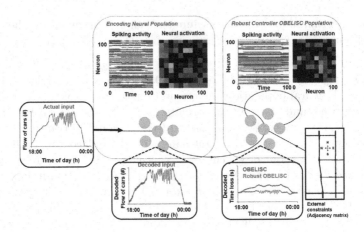

Fig. 5. Representation, Learning, and Dynamics of Robust Oscillator Network

sum of the external constraints (e.g. A_{ij} and F_i) weighting the phase differences $\theta_j(t) - \theta_i(t)$, both decoded from separate neural populations implementing the product and sinus functions. These operations implemented in neurons correspond to $A_{ij}sin(\theta_j(t) - \theta_i(t)) + F_isin(\theta^*(t) - \theta_i(t))$. In order to visualize the benefit of the sliding mode control in the overall dynamics, we also compute the time loss, as a simple metric, in the Robust Controller OBELISC Population. As previously mentioned, the sliding mode controller makes a trade-off between performance and control activity (i.e. better performance in terms of time loss under faster switches of the control law). Basically, this is visible in Fig. 5 - low right panel, between 18:00 and 24:00, where the OBELISC oscillator network dynamics performs smoother but worst in optimizing the time loss, whereas the Robust OBELISC (i.e. dynamics containing the sliding mode regularization) improves the time loss with the price of high-frequency low-amplitude oscillations.

3   Experiments and Results

The experiments and evaluation use the SUMMER-MUSTARD (Summer season Multi-cross Urban Signalized Traffic Aggregated Region Dataset) real-world dataset, which contains 59 d of real urban road traffic data from 8 crosses in a city in China[4]. The road network layout underlying is depicted in Fig. 4 a. In order to perform experiments and evaluate the system, we used the real-world traffic flows in the Simulator for Urban Mobility (SUMO) [11]. This realistic vehicular simulator generates routes, vehicles, and traffic light signals that reproduce the real car flows in the dataset.

In our experiments, we comparatively evaluated the adaptive behavior of OBELISC and relevant state-of-the-art approaches, against the static traffic

---

[4] We release the SUMMER-MUSTARD real-world dataset used in OBELISC experiments at: http://doi.org/10.5281/zenodo.5025264.

planning (i.e. police parametrized phases), used as baseline. We performed an extensive battery of experiments starting from the real-world traffic flows recorded over the 8 crosses in the SUMMER-MUSTARD dataset. In order to evaluate the adaptation capabilities, we systematically introduced progressive magnitude disruptions over the initial 59 d of traffic flow data. Disruptions, such as accidents and adverse weather determine a decrease in the velocity which might create jams. Additionally, special activities such as sport events or beginning/end of holidays increase the flow magnitude. Such degenerated traffic conditions might happen due to non-recurrent events such as accidents, adverse weather or special events, such as football matches. Using the real-world flow and SUMO, we reproduce the traffic flow behavior when disruption occurs starting from normal traffic flow data by reflecting the disruption effect on vehicles speed and/or network capacity and demand. We sweep the disruption magnitude from normal traffic up to 5 levels of disruption reflected over all the 8 crosses over the entire day.

The evaluated systems are the following:

- BASELINE - is a optimized static traffic planning that uses pre-stored timing plans computed offline using historic data in the real-world.
- MILP - a Mixed-Integer Linear Programming phase plan optimization implementation inspired from [14].
- OSCILLATOR - A basic implementation of a network of Kuramoto oscillators [15] for each direction in the road network cross.
- OBELISC - uses the core Kuramoto oscillator model from [15] and considers an external reference for cycle time F, flow modulation k, and a spatial topology weight A. We used two implementations, one using an underlying ODE solver (OBELISC ODE) and the second one using NEF spiking neural networks (OBELISC NEF).
- Robust OBELISC - extends the basic OBELISC with the regularizing sliding mode control law u. The Robust OBELISC, similar to OBELISC, has two versions, Robust OBELISC ODE and Robust OBELISC NEF, respectively.

Evaluation of the Phase Calculation Accuracy. For the evaluation of the different approaches for phase duration computation (i.e. BASELINE, MILP, OSCILLATOR, OBELISC, and Robust OBELISC), we followed the next procedure:

- Read relevant data from simulation experiment (without disruptions and with 5 levels of progressive disruptions) for each of the systems.
- Compute relevant traffic aggregation metrics (i.e. average time loss, average speed, and average waiting time).
- Rank experiments depending on performance.
- Perform statistical tests (i.e. a combination of omnibus ANOVA and posthoc pairwise T-test with a significance $p = 0.05$) and adjust ranking depending on significance.
- Evaluate best algorithms depending on ranking for subsets of relevant metrics (i.e. the metrics with significant difference).

Table 1. Performance evaluation for the different phase duration calculation methods.

System/Disruption level	Normal flow	1.1	1.2	1.3	1.4	1.5
Average time loss(s)						
BASELINE	102.535	114.600	136.229	241.383	197.399	202.113
MILP	151.281	153.781	203.301	309.671	223.017	257.464
OSCILLATOR	131.468	161.871	203.301	309.671	199.797	497.124
OBELISC (ODE)	131.825	270.167	131.077	151.281	309.671	134.257
OBELISC (NEF)	135.355	155.782	153.524	200.265	199.357	216.919
Robust OBELISC (ODE)	133.524	143.904	147.524	153.524	200.265	220.008
Robust OBELISC (NEF)	85.726	88.326	89.726	84.165	89.889	84.291
Average speed*						
BASELINE	5.81	5.67	5.46	5.02	4.94	4.75
MILP	5.97	5.87	5.46	5.03	4.92	4.61
OSCILLATOR	5.94	5.81	5.46	5.02	5.29	4.54
OBELISC (ODE)	5.97	4.75	5.14	5.22	5.04	5.11
OBELISC (NEF)	5.89	5.91	5.90	5.29	5.31	5.10
Robust OBELISC (ODE)	5.98	5.91	5.80	5.97	5.30	5.04
Robust OBELISC (NEF)	5.98	5.97	5.94	5.18	5.07	5.15
Waiting time(s)						
BASELINE	164.5	185.3	222.8	294.5	325.9	351.3
MILP	148.7	148.7	212.8	234.5	293.2	372.9
OSCILLATOR	115.7	142.2	215.8	286.5	208.5	418.3
OBELISC (ODE)	160.3	351.3	158.7	148.7	294.5	161.2
OBELISC (NEF)	137.1	137.6	139.4	216.0	204.2	236.3
Robust OBELISC (ODE)	139.4	141.4	149.4	169.8	216.8	252.5
Robust OBELISC (NEF)	128.7	145.7	148.8	159.2	162.4	158.7

* Average speed calculated as the ratio between distance traveled and time of travel.

Our evaluation results are given in Table 1 where each of the approaches is ranked across the disruption magnitude scale (no disruption to maximum disruption) over the specific metrics (i.e. average time loss, and average speed, and waiting time, respectively). For flow magnitude disruptions, the level of disruption (i.e. 1.1 ... 1.5) is a factor used to adjust the number of vehicles or the speed of vehicles (i.e. for adverse weather) during the disruption. The evaluation was performed on the entire dataset containing recorded traffic flows over 59 d from 8 crosses. The exhaustive experiments and evaluation in Table 1 demonstrate where our approach excels and where it fails to provide the best phase duration calculation. The chosen evaluation metrics reflect the overall performance (i.e. over multiple days) with respect to the most significant traffic metrics given the phase duration value computed by each of the systems.

The previous analysis is supported by the normalized ranking over the entire SUMMER-MUSTARD dataset in Fig. 6, where we provide a condensed visual representation of each system's performance. Here, we can see that if we consider the average time loss the BASELINE performs worst due to its pre-defined

timings and inability to adapt to unexpected disruptions during the daily traffic profile. At the other end of the ranking, both implementations of Robust
OBELISC provide minimal waiting time capturing the fast and steep changes in
the disrupted flows. Due to their similar core modelling and dynamics, OBELISC
systems and OSCILLATOR tend to provide similar performance, with a relative improvement on the OBELISC side in terms of duration, waiting time, and
speed metrics. This is due to its spatio-temporal extension beyond the basic
oscillator model that can capture also the spatial contributions of adjacent flows
beyond their temporal regularities when computing the phase duration. Looking at the various implementations of OBELISC, from the computational point
of view, the NEF spiking neural networks excel in performance over the ODE
versions due to their inherent learning and adaptation capabilities coupled with
the distributed representations when solving the dynamics. Finally, the Robust
OBELISC system provides overall superior performance through its discontinuous sliding mode control law that captures the deviation of the dynamics in
the presence of disruptions and compensates robustly for their impact on the
oscillator convergence (see Fig. 5).

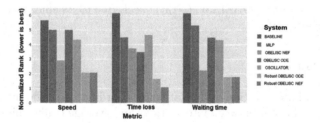

Fig. 6. Phase Duration Calculation System Ranking on All Metrics and Entire Dataset
(8 crosses over 59 d).

Evaluation of the Run-Time. In terms of run-time, the adaptive methods
provide different levels of performance, mainly due to the modelling and optimization types they use. The BASELINE is excluded as it is just the static
optimized plans allocation for the real traffic setting in SUMMER-MUSTARD,
basically, a simple value recall from a look-up-table. We measured the time
needed by each of the evaluated adaptive systems to provide a phase duration
estimate after a sensory sample (i.e. one sensory reading of traffic flow data).
As mentioned, each system uses a different computational approach: the MILP
uses a solver that implements an LP-based branch-and-bound algorithm, the
OSCILLATOR uses a Runge-Kutta 45 ODE solver, whereas OBELISC can be
implemented using Runge-Kutta 45 ODE solver or connected populations of
NEF spiking neural networks. The evaluation is given in Table 2 where the average value over the entire range of traffic conditions (normal and disruptions) is
considered. The experimental setup for our experiments used 3 machines, each
with 24 CPU cores and 132 GB RAM, and Apache Flink for stream processing

Table 2. Adaptive phase duration calculation run-time evaluation.

Model	Single cross	Region (8 crosses)
MILP	0.0510	0.3930
OSCILLATOR	0.0568	0.4544
Robust OBELISC ODE	0.0489	0.4534
Robust OBELISC NEF	**0.0071**	**0.0426**

and cluster management. As expected, at the level of a single intersection optimization, ODE solver approaches (i.e. MILP, OSCILLATOR, and OBELISC (ODE)) lie in the same range, providing a new phase duration value after 50 ms. At the region level, considering all 8 crosses, the run-time increases with an order of magnitude, with MILP overtaking the OSCILLATOR and OBELISC (ODE) due to MILP's constraint optimization efficiency at scale and the similar computations of OSCILLATOR and OBELISC (ODE). The fastest approach, both as single cross and regions level, is the NEF neural implementation of OBELISC. With more than 80% run-time improvement both at single cross-level and regional-level, OBELISC (NEF) excels due to its efficient computation and learning substrate.

4   Discussion

Traditionally, phase duration optimization for coordinated traffic signals is based on average travel times between intersections and average traffic volumes at each intersection.

Modelling. Our study introduces an end-to-end modelling, control, and learning system for road traffic phase duration optimization applicable to any road traffic layout, scale, and architecture (i.e. number of lanes per direction etc.). More precisely, using an oscillator-based model [15] of the traffic flow dynamics in large signalized road networks, the system exploits the periodic nature of the traffic signal circular phasing similar to [1,5] - termed OSCILLATOR in our experiments. OBELISC goes beyond OSCILLATOR by considering a weighted external perturbation (e.g. cycle time reference weight F), flow modulation k, and a spatial topology weight A. Such a modelling approach adapts to unpredictable disruptions in traffic flows (e.g. accidents, re-routing, adverse weather conditions) up to a certain extent, where the dynamics of the disruption doesn't perturb the self-organization of the coupled oscillators.

Robust Control. In reality, the "steep derivatives" of traffic flows do not allow OBELISC and OSCILLATOR to converge to the best phase duration value. In order to achieve high performance (i.e. minimizing metrics such as time loss or maximizing average speed), we complemented OBELISC with a sliding mode controller. Such a robust controller "pushes" the perturbed dynamics under disruptions towards a dynamics that "drive" the coupled oscillators network towards the optimal phase. This way, the Robust OBELISC system is capable to solve local and global traffic dynamics by exploiting the coupling among different oscillators describing traffic periodicity under disruptions. The proposed system in [14] - termed MILP in our experiments - used exact mathematical programming techniques (i.e. mixed-integer linear programming) for optimizing the control of traffic signals and has shown only limited adaptation capabilities.

Computation and Learning. Under real-world constraints of traffic control, OBELISC and Robust OBELISC cannot be implemented by simply integrating ODEs. To alleviate the typical convergence, stability, and robustness problems of ODE integration, we implemented OBELISC in efficient spiking neural networks using NEF. Basically, using distributed representations of traffic flow data, learning arbitrary functions from the data, and "compiling" the ODEs in neural populations, we gained efficient and flexible implementations of OBELISC (i.e. OBELISC NEF and Robust OBELISC NEF). Such a choice provided a clear advantage over the MILP implementation of [14] which formulated phase optimization into a continuous optimization problem without integer variables by modeling traffic flow as sinusoidal. The system solved a convex relaxation of the non-convex problem using a tree decomposition reduction and randomized rounding to recover a near-global solution. Given the complexity in expressing the system dynamics MILP performed well in simulations, yet the capability to adapt to sudden changes in the traffic situation are lacking (see the ranking in time loss, speed and waiting time in Fig. 6).

5   Conclusions

Traffic control is a multi-dimensional problem to be optimized under deep uncertainty. Modelling traffic dynamics is fundamental for traffic control. Aiming at capturing the periodic nature of traffic, we propose OBELISC, a system using a network of oscillators capturing the spatial and temporal interactions among different crosses in a traffic network. In order to adaptively cope with unexpected traffic flow disruptions OBELISC is extended with a sliding mode controller that strengthens its adaptation capabilities towards global consensus under high-magnitude disruptions. The system is implemented as a lightweight learning system that exploits the coupling interactions among different controlled oscillators. Our extensive evaluation of the system on real-world data and against state-of-the-art methods, demonstrates the advantages OBELISC brings. From capturing the periodic dynamics of traffic phasing, to embedding the spatial correlation among traffic flow along its temporal dimensions, and up to robustly adapting to unexpected traffic disruptions, OBELISC stands out as a flexible solution for phase duration calculation. Finally, benefiting from efficient learning and computation in spiking neural networks, OBELISC is a strong candidate for actual real-world deployment.

References

1. Akbas, A., Ergun, M.: Dynamic traffic signal control using a nonlinear coupled oscillators approach. Can. J. Civ. Eng. **32**(2), 430–441 (2005)
2. Chedjou, J.C., Kyamakya, K.: A review of traffic light control systems and introduction of a control concept based on coupled nonlinear oscillators. In: Kyamakya, K., Mathis, W., Stoop, R., Chedjou, J.C., Li, Z. (eds.) Recent Advances in Nonlinear Dynamics and Synchronization. SSDC, vol. 109, pp. 113–149. Springer, Cham (2018). https://doi.org/10.1007/978-3-319-58996-1_6
3. Day, C.M., Bullock, D.M.: Optimization of traffic signal offsets with high resolution event data. J. Transp. Eng. Part A Syst. **146**(3), 04019076 (2020)
4. Eliasmith, C., Anderson, C.H.: Neural Engineering: Computation, Representation, and Dynamics in Neurobiological Systems. MIT press, Cambridge (2003)
5. Fang, F., Xu, W., Lin, K., Alam, F., Potgieter, J.: Matsuoka neuronal oscillator for traffic signal control using agent-based simulation. Procedia Comput. Sci. **19**, 389–395 (2013)
6. GmbH, S.W.: LISA+ traffic-planning software lisa (2021). https://www.schlothauer.de/en/references/
7. Henry, J.J., Farges, J.L., Tuffal, J.: The prodyn real time traffic algorithm. In: Control in Transportation Systems, pp. 305–310. Elsevier (1984)
8. Hu, H., Liu, H.X.: Arterial offset optimization using archived high-resolution traffic signal data. Transp. Res. Part C Emerg. Technol. **37**, 131–144 (2013)
9. Hunt, P., Robertson, D., Bretherton, R., Royle, M.C.: The scoot on-line traffic signal optimisation technique. Traffic Eng. Control **23**(4) (1982)
10. Kuramoto, F., Nishikawa, I.: Onset of collective rhythms in large populations of coupled oscillators. In: Takayama, H. (eds.) Cooperative Dynamics in Complex Physical Systems. Springer Series in Synergetics, vol. 43, pp. 300–306. Springer, Berlin, Heidelberg (1989). https://doi.org/10.1007/978-3-642-74554-6_76
11. Lopez, P.A., et al.: Microscopic traffic simulation using sumo. In: The 21st IEEE International Conference on Intelligent Transportation Systems. IEEE (2018). https://elib.dlr.de/124092/
12. Lowrie, P.: Scats, sydney co-ordinated adaptive traffic system: a traffic responsive method of controlling urban traffic. Roads and Traffic Authority NSW, Traffic Control Section (1990)
13. Nishikawa, I., Kuroe, Y.: Dynamics of complex-valued neural networks and its relation to a phase oscillator system. In: Pal, N.R., Kasabov, N., Mudi, R.K., Pal, S., Parui, S.K. (eds.) ICONIP 2004. LNCS, vol. 3316, pp. 122–129. Springer, Heidelberg (2004). https://doi.org/10.1007/978-3-540-30499-9_18
14. Ouyang, Y., et al.: Large-scale traffic signal offset optimization. IEEE Trans. Control Netw. Syst. **7**(3), 1176–1187 (2020)
15. Strogatz, S.H.: From Kuramoto to Crawford: exploring the onset of synchronization in populations of coupled oscillators. Phys. D Nonlinear Phenom. **143**(1–4), 1–20 (2000)
16. Utkin, V.I.: Sliding mode control: mathematical tools, design and applications. In: Nistri, P., Stefani, G. (eds.) Nonlinear and Optimal Control Theory. Lecture Notes in Mathematics, vol. 1932, pp. 289–347. Springer, Berlin, Heidelberg (2008). https://doi.org/10.1007/978-3-540-77653-6_5
17. van Wageningen-Kessels, F., Van Lint, H., Vuik, K., Hoogendoorn, S.: Genealogy of traffic flow models. EURO J. Transp. Logist. **4**(4), 445–473 (2015)

VAMBC: A Variational Approach for Mobility Behavior Clustering

Mingxuan Yue$^{(\boxtimes)}$, Yao-Yi Chiang, and Cyrus Shahabi

University of Southern California, Los Angeles, USA
{mingxuay,yaoyic,shahabi}@usc.edu

Abstract. Many domains including policymaking, urban design, and geospatial intelligence benefit from understanding people's mobility behaviors (e.g., work commute, shopping), which can be achieved by clustering massive trajectories using the geo-context around the visiting locations (e.g., sequence of vectors, each describing the geographic environment near a visited location). However, existing clustering approaches on sequential data are not effective for clustering these context sequences based on the contexts' transition patterns. They either rely on traditional pre-defined similarities for specific application requirements or utilize a two-phase autoencoder-based deep learning process, which is not robust to training variations. Thus, we propose a variational approach named VAMBC for clustering context sequences that simultaneously learns the self-supervision and cluster assignments in a single phase to infer moving behaviors from context transitions in trajectories. Our experiments show that VAMBC significantly outperforms the state-of-the-art approaches in robustness and accuracy of clustering mobility behaviors in trajectories.

1 Introduction

Mobility behavior (of a trajectory) refers to the travel activity that describes a user's movements regardless of the spatial and temporal coverage of the movements. For example, the work-to-home commute is one such mobility behavior that is a sequence of visiting locations between one's home and working location. Understanding mobility behaviors has enormous values ranging from location recommendations, geo-advertisements to urban planning, public health, transportation policies and economic studies [7,17,36]. For example, in target advertising, a gas station owner can infer that the major mobility behavior of trajectories passing through their gas station is work commute, thus deciding to display financial ads on weekdays. For public health during a pandemic, policymakers could make a better decision on what types of businesses should be closed to reduce mobility more effectively in different neighborhoods. For instance, they may decide to close restaurants/pubs in a neighborhood where the majority of mobility behavior is for entertainment but not in a neighborhood where the main mobility behavior is for work commute. The former closure impacts entertainment but the latter will impact work. For economic studies, by labeling work

© Springer Nature Switzerland AG 2021
Y. Dong et al. (Eds.): ECML PKDD 2021, LNAI 12978, pp. 453–469, 2021.
https://doi.org/10.1007/978-3-030-86514-6_28

commutes, we can estimate the amount of jobs, or the amount of working people in the neighborhoods of a city. For transportation studies, when repairing (or constructing a new) bridge or a freeway segment, policymakers could better determine the dates and times for construction by considering the major mobility behavior passing through the area (e.g., weekend closure vs. weekdays).

Inferring the mobility behavior directly from a trajectory is difficult since the raw coordinates do not provide useful information about the surrounding environment of the visited locations. Instead, one promising approach is to first generate a "context sequence" for each trajectory from nearby geographic entities, e.g., Points-Of-Interest (POIs), and then infer mobility behaviors by clustering context sequences from large numbers of trajectories based on the context transitions (e.g., [35]). Here, a context sequence is an ordered list of real-value feature vectors, each describing the "context" of a visited location (e.g., sports, shopping, or dining venues) in a trajectory. Clustering context sequences based on their transition patterns (similar dependencies across different dimensions and positions in the sequences) is challenging. For example, a transition in the context sequence can be: rest (a place surrounded by many residential POIs)→ shopping (a place surrounded by many restaurants, theaters, and malls) → dating (a place surrounded by many scenic POIs). Such transitions are usually driven by the trajectory data and vary from one dataset to another. However, traditional time series clustering approaches are usually based on pre-defined similarity and alignments between sub-sequences and shapes [10, 26, 27]. Other typical sequence clustering approaches only handle discrete variables (e.g., [18, 31, 38]). Autoencoder-based clustering approaches using Recurrent Neural Networks (RNN) can convert sequences of real-value feature vectors into a fixed-length vector for clustering the dynamics in the sequences using a two-phase training process [23, 35]). The first phase learns an initial representation by self-supervision (i.e., reconstruction), and the second phase improves the representation and clustering performance by optimizing a customized clustering objective. However, the first phase's self-supervision objective highly depends on the initial parameters and could lead to a poor initial feature representation (i.e., irrelevant to the clustering objective), which cannot be refined in the second phase to improve the clustering performance. Consequently, clustering accuracy cannot be guaranteed across training variations [25].

This paper presents a novel Variational Approach for Mobility Behavior Clustering (VAMBC) that can robustly handle sequences of context vectors in a single training phase. VAMBC assumes the pre-existence of clusters in the latent space and jointly learns the hidden representation and cluster formation in an end-to-end process. Though variational clustering approaches are recently well developed for image data [11, 13, 20, 29], directly applying them to variable-length sequential data requires an RNN decoder, which is sensitive to small changes in the latent space [4], resulting in poor clustering accuracy and robustness. The main problem originates from having minimum involvement of cluster assignments when constructing the latent space from the input sequences. Hence, the model would generate poor clustering results like having only one or a few large clusters, leaving many clusters empty (called the "empty cluster" problem in the rest of the paper) or several similar clusters (called "trivial solution"). To address these challenges, VAMBC explicitly constructs two representations: one captures the unique information of a context sequence, and the other one captures the shared information within a cluster. We call the former the *individualized latent embedding* and the latter the *cluster latent embedding*. VAMBC makes the cluster latent embedding available to the cluster members during reconstruction and explicitly uses the embedding in constructing the latent space so that the final latent embedding is aware of the cluster assignments. VAMBC also encourages the cluster assignment to be flexible at early stages and become well separated as the model is trained adequately. Therefore, the model has sufficient involvement of the cluster membership in creating the embeddings and can avoid producing poor clustering results. We compare our approach with many baseline approaches, and the experimental results on real-world data show that VAMBC achieves a better clustering accuracy and robustness than all baselines.

The remainder of the paper is organized as follows. In Sect. 2, we review the related work. After introducing preliminaries in Sect. 3, we propose our model VAMBC in Sect. 4. Section 5 describes our experiments on real-world data and discussion of the ablation analysis followed by our conclusion in Sect. 6.

2 Related Work

Classical time series clustering approaches are widely developed for sequences indexed by regular time intervals, such as electrocardiogram (ECG) data. Researchers proposed various distance/similarity measurements (e.g., maximize the alignment) for time series and developed the corresponding clustering techniques (e.g., [10,26,27]). However, these pre-defined similarities designed for matching or aligning time series do not apply for context sequences on clustering the transition and dependencies. Researchers also study clustering other types of sequences like RNA and protein sequences [38], short text sequences [31,34], event and action sequences [18,28]. In these papers, the authors proposed various approaches using topic models, (Hidden) Markov models, graph transformations, etc. for specific problems. However, most of these approaches apply only to sequences of discrete variables and are limited to domain-specific objectives.

Recently deep-learning-based clustering approaches are widely investigated. One major group of these studies are based on various autoencoders and clustering neural network layers [16,23,32,35]. A few approaches in this group are designed for sequential data, such as [23,35], by using RNN layers for sequence modeling. However, these autoencoder-based approaches usually employ a two-phase training. The two-phase training performance highly relies on the result of its first phase (self-supervision), which does not always align with the clustering objective thus is not robust to training variations.

On the other hand, recent variational approaches can jointly learn the self-supervision and clustering structure from the beginning using various variational assumptions about the hidden space. For example, Dupont [13] proposed to use both a continuous latent space and a discrete latent space and concatenate the layers for reconstruction. Dilokthanakul et al. [11], Jiang et al. [20] and Rui et al. [29] proposed variational autoencoder models with a Gaussian Mixture assumption in the latent space for capturing the manifolds. However, most of these approaches studied image data, and it would bring more challenges mentioned in Sect. 1 when applying those to variable-length feature sequences that we study. In contrast, our proposed VAMBC approach explicitly solves the problems and produces robust and accurate clustering on the context sequences.

3   Preprocessing and Problem Definition

In this paper, we consider the mobility behavior clustering problem proposed in [35]. The goal is to cluster trajectories into groups that have similar mobility behaviors. Since raw trajectory data have various temporal and spatial scales and do not have any contextual information, we prepare our input data by applying the preprocessing steps in [35].

Here we briefly summarize the preprocessing procedure that transforms the raw trajectories into **context sequences**. Figure 1 shows the procedure of the preprocessing. First, the Stay Point Detection (SPD) step will extract important stay points (large colored points) from a raw trajectory (small grey points). Then the POIs (small colored points) surrounding each stay point will be grouped, counted, and transformed into context vectors (stacked squares at the bottom). The goal is to cluster these sequences of context vectors into different groups that have a similar transition of visit patterns. Formally, in the remainder of this paper, we study the following problem: Given a set of context sequences $X = \{x_i\}$ where $x_i = \{\vec{x}_{i,1}, \vec{x}_{i,2}, \ldots, \vec{x}_{i,L_i}\}$ is a variant-length sequence (i.e., L_i is the length of sequence x_i and is not fixed) of POI context vectors represented by $\vec{x}_{i,l} \in \mathbb{R}^D$ (where D is the number of POI types). Each element of the vector represents the likelihood of visiting the corresponding POI type (e.g., residence). The goal is to cluster the set of sequences X into K (a predefined hyper-parameter) groups, s.t., within each group the sequences are of similar context transitions.

4   The VAMBCModel

This section introduces our model VAMBC. Specifically, we first introduce our novel idea of decomposing the hidden variables to improve the involvement of cluster hidden variable y. Then we explain the derived training objectives with well-designed layers of the model and discuss their roles. Finally, we describe the network structure of VAMBC followed by a discussion comparing the mechanisms of VAMBC and other variational models for clustering.

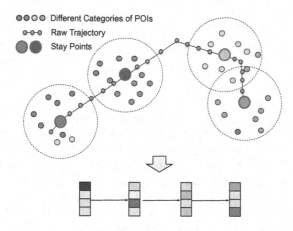

Fig. 1. Preprocess the raw trajectories

4.1   Decomposing Hidden Variables

The goal of the variational clustering model is maximizing the likelihood of the training data $\{x_i\}_{i=1}^N$ while learning a parametric latent embedding z_i representing the hidden information of each input sequence x_i and a latent variable y_i describing the cluster membership (i.e., the mobility behavior). In the following paragraphs, we hide the subscript i for simplicity.

To increase the involvement of cluster assignments (i.e., y) in constructing the latent embedding z, we decompose the hidden variable z into two independent parts: cluster latent information (z^c) and individualized latent information (z^b). Intuitively, each input can be represented using its cluster information (the cluster center) plus its individual (bias) information (the relative position to the cluster center). The cluster latent information is modeled as variable z^c that fully depends on the discrete variable y and, s.t., z^c is a learnable deterministic mapping from y, $z^c = f_c(y)$. Since the cluster latent information summarizes the latent characteristics of a cluster, we explicitly let z^c be the center of the cluster in the latent space that could be shared across x within individual clusters. In other words, for a given cluster k, $\mathbb{E}(Z_k)$ is the expectation of $Z_k = \{z_i | x_i \in \text{cluster } k\}$, s.t., $\mathbb{E}(Z_k) = z^c_{(y=k)} = f_c(y_k)$. We model the individualized latent representation as a continuous variable z^b that describes the bias to the cluster center, s.t., the distribution of z^b centers at 0 ($\mathbb{E}(z^b) = 0$). The overall latent representation z is modeled as the summation of the cluster latent representation and the individualized latent representation, i.e., $z = z^c + z^b$. In this way, the hidden space z still preserves the Gaussian-Mixture structure but can also be decomposed into two embeddings which can be supervised separately. Specifically, the generative process can be described in Eq. (1).

$$y \sim Cat(1/K), z^c = f(y; W) \tag{1}$$
$$z^b \sim \mathcal{N}(0, I)$$
$$z = z^c + z^b$$
$$x \sim \mathcal{N}(\mu_x(g(z; \theta)), \sigma_x^2(g(z; \theta))I)$$

In Eq. (1), y is a discrete variable that follows a categorical prior (denoted by $Cat(\cdot)$) and K is the predefined number of clusters. f is a deterministic function (implemented by a neural layer parameterized by W) of y that maps each cluster to a vector z^c. z^b is a continuous variable following a Gaussian prior $\mathcal{N}(0, I)$ and represents the individualized embedding. $g(z; \theta)$ denotes a neural network that decodes z to the input space parameterized by θ. $\mu_x(g(z; \theta))$ denotes the mean of the Gaussian likelihood distribution of x condition on z. We set $\sigma_x(g(z; \theta)) = 1$ which reduces the log likelihood to mean squared error following the common practice of VAE. We use $q(y, z|x)$ to approximate the posterior of $p(x, y, z)$. The problem can be reduced to maximizing the log-Evidence Lower Bound (ELBO). We refer the reader to [12, 21] for a detailed explanation of the derivation of ELBO. Thus the objective is minimizing the negative ELBO written as in Eq. (2).

$$-\mathcal{L}_{ELBO} = -\mathbb{E}_{y, z \sim q(y, z|x)} \log \frac{p(x, y, z)}{q(y, z|x)} \tag{2}$$

According to the proposed generative process, we can substitute $p(z) = p(z^b)p(z^c)$, $p(x, y, z) = p(y)p(z^b)p(z^c|y)p(x|y, z)$, $q(y, z|x) = q(y|x)q(z^b|x)q(z^c|y)$ into the ELBO. By ignoring $q(z^c|y)$ because it is deterministic, we can break down Eq. (2) and rewrite the (negative) ELBO as in Eq. (3).

$$-\mathcal{L}_{ELBO} \tag{3}$$
$$= -\mathbb{E}_{y, z \sim q(y, z|x)} (\log \frac{p(y)}{q(y|x)} + \log \frac{p(z^b)}{q(z^b|x)} + \log p(x|y, z))$$
$$= D_{KL}(q(y|x)||p(y)) + D_{KL}(q(z^b|x)||p(z^b))$$
$$- \mathbb{E}_{y \sim q(y|x), z^b \sim q(z^b|x), z^c = f(y; W)} \log p(x|y, z^b, z^c)$$

4.2   Training Objectives and Neural Layers

Now we expand all the Right-Hand-Side (RHS) terms in Eq. (3) and formulate the objectives.

The first RHS term $D_{KL}(q(y|x)||p(y))$ describes the KL distance between the posterior estimate $q(y|x)$ and its prior $p(y)$. Since the prior $p(y) \sim Cat(1/K)$ is a categorical distribution, we can expand this term as below.

$$D_{KL}(q(y|x)||p(y)) = \sum_y q(y|x) \log(q(y|x) \cdot K)$$
$$= - \text{Entropy}(y) + log(K), y \sim q(y|x)$$

The first RHS term turns out to be the negative entropy of y, where $y \sim q(y|x)$ (the constant $log(K)$ could be omitted). Intuitively, a small negative entropy indicates high randomness in $y \sim q(y|x)$, and a large negative entropy value indicates less randomness in $y \sim q(y|x)$. Minimizing the negative entropy could prevent the prediction of cluster probability $q(y|x)$ from being "overly-confident", i.e., always assigning the input to one cluster aggressively (output 0.99 as the probability of assignment). Therefore, the negative entropy term can prevent the model from having a result of empty clusters.

The posterior probability $q(y|x)$ is estimated using a Softmax activation after the encoder network. To enable sharing of cluster information, we need to sample the discrete variable y from $q(y|x)$, for which we employ the **Gumbel-Softmax layer**. Gumbel-Softmax can sample a pseudo one-hot vector (a real-value vector that is very similar to a one-hot vector) and propagates the parameter gradients backward to the previous Softmax layer [19]. Thus the output will be almost discrete (e.g., (1,0,0,0)) and multiple input sequences could share the same choice of y and hence the same cluster embedding z^c (e.g., $z_i^c = z_j^c = f_c(y_k)$ if x_i and x_j are both assigned to cluster k). In addition, Gumbel-Softmax is different from an Argmax operation on $q(y|x)$, which always chooses the cluster with the largest probability. Specifically, Gumbel-Softmax introduces randomness when sampling y according to the probability $q(y|x)$, so an input x assigned to cluster k_1 could "jump" to a different cluster k_2 in the next round if the likelihood of k_2 is similar to k_1. This avoids x being always assigned to the same cluster that is initially predicted.

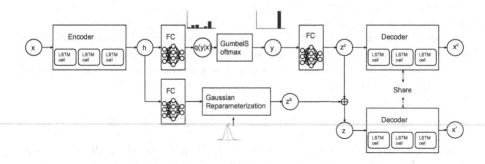

Fig. 2. VAMBC network structure.

The second RHS term $D_{KL}(q(z^b|x)||p(z^b))$ measures the Kullback–Leibler (KL) distance between the posterior $q(z^b|x)$ of the individualized latent embedding z^b and its prior $p(z^b) = N(0, I)$. Here we assume $q(z^b|x)$ is a Gaussian distribution with a learnable mean $\bar{z}_b$ and a constant variance following the constant-variance VAE (CV-VAE) which sacrifices a little capacity for robustness and mitigate the sensitivity in the decoder following [2,15]. Therefore, the KL term can be rewritten into the following form:

$$D_{KL}(q(z^b|x)||p(z^b)) = ||\bar{z}^b||_2^2 + constant \qquad (4)$$

The last RHS term $-\mathbb{E}_{y \sim q(y|x), z^b \sim q(z^b|x), z^c=f(y;W)} \log p(x|y, z^b, z^c)$, is the negative log likelihood of the observation x. Following the common practice of VAE, we can rewrite it to the mean square error (MSE) between the input data x and the reconstruction x'.

$$-\mathbb{E}_{y \sim q(y|x), z^b \sim q(z^b|x), z^c=f(y;W)} \log p(x|y, z^b, z^c)$$
$$= MSE(x, x')$$

In addition to the terms in $\mathcal{L}_{ELBO}$, we introduce a center loss regularizer $L_{center} = ||x - x^c||_2^2$. Here x^c is a sequence of the same dimension with input x (after padding), and is decoded from the center embedding z^c. The center loss could prevent the model from overly relying on the individualized embedding. Specifically, it generates a center sequence x^c from the cluster embedding z^c and minimizes the distance between x^c with all x assigned to this cluster. Therefore, the cluster embedding z^c is learned to be expressive to generate a sequence x^c similar to the sequences in the cluster. And $\mathcal{L}_{center}$ also improves the compactness and discrimination of clusters in the embedding space.

Finally, we can write the loss function of VAMBC in Eq. (5).

$$\mathcal{L} = MSE(x, x') + ||z^b||_2^2 - entropy(y) + ||x - x^c||_2^2$$
$$= \mathcal{L}_{recon} + \mathcal{L}_{KL} + \mathcal{L}_{NE} + \mathcal{L}_{center} \tag{5}$$

4.3   Network Design

Based on the loss function, we design our network structure by modeling the probabilities $q(y|x), q(z^b|x), p(x|y, z^b, z^c)$ with neural layers. Figure 2 shows our network structure. On the left side, we use (stacked) LSTM (Long Short-Term Memory, an advanced RNN) layers and Fully Connected (FC) layers with the softmax and nonlinear activation to model the posterior $q(y|x), q(z^b|x)$. Then in the middle of the network, the discrete variable y is sampled through a Gumbel-Softmax layer and mapped to the cluster embedding z^c. The continuous individualized embedding z^b is sampled via the Guassian reparameterization [21]. After obtaining z^c and z^b, the embedding z of input x is computed by adding z^c and z^b in the addition layer denoted by $\oplus$. Finally, on the right side of the network, LSTM layers (decoder) are used to decode the hidden embedding z into a reconstructed sequence, x'. The shared decoder also generates the cluster sequence x^c from z_c for computing the center loss.

As explained in Sect. 4.2, the network is supervised by the RHS terms to balance the self-supervision and clustering structure. The network also employs the Gumbel-Softmax and center loss to prevent early/local convergence and preserve the involvement of cluster memberships.

4.4   Relationship to VAE and Gaussian-Mixture VAE

Here we briefly describe the basic concepts of the Variational AutoEncoder (VAE), its extension to the clustering scenario and the differences between

VAMBC and the existing MoG-based VAEs. The goal of VAE is to learn a parametric latent embedding z and a generative model to maximize the marginal
likelihood of the training data $\{x_i\}_{i=1}^N$. Its objective in Eq. (6) is derived by
approximating the intractable posterior $p_\theta(z|x)$ with $q_\phi(z|x)$ and maximizing
the ELBO. In general, the ELBO includes two terms, one for the reconstruction
and the other for regularizing the hidden space to a Gaussian prior.

$$\mathcal{L}_{\text{VAE}} = \mathbb{E}_{\hat{p}(x)}[\mathbb{E}_{q_\phi(z|x)}[-log(p_\theta(x|z)] + D_{\text{KL}}(q_\phi(z|x)||p(z))] \qquad (6)$$

For clustering purposes, the VAE can be extended to learn the clustering
priors [3] driven by the data. The Gaussian prior in the hidden layer of VAE,
$p(z) = \mathcal{N}(0,1)$, in this case, is replaced with the Mixtures of Gaussians (MoG)
such as in [11,20,29]. The generative process could be described in Eq. (7).
Here y is a discrete hidden variable representing the cluster assignments, and z
is a continuous hidden variable that x is mapped to/conditional on. K is the
predefined number of clusters and $Cat(.)$ is the categorical distribution.

$$y \sim Cat(1/K), z \sim \mathcal{N}(\mu_y, \sigma_y^2 I) \qquad (7)$$
$$x \sim \mathcal{N}(\mu_x(z), \sigma_x^2(z)I)$$

The objective in Eq. (6) is then rewritten as:

$$\mathcal{L}_{\text{VAE}_{GM}} = \mathbb{E}_{\hat{p}(x)}[\mathbb{E}_{q_\phi(z,y|x)}[-log(p_\theta(x|z)] \qquad (8)$$
$$+ D_{\text{KL}}(q_\phi(z,y|x)||p(z,y))]$$

However when we use RNN to encode and decode the variant-length context
sequences (e.g., for learning the transition patterns of context vectors), the model
above would fall into local optimum and produce undesired clustering results.
Specifically, when applying the variational models to sensitive decoders, such as
RNNs, for sequence modeling, the model might initially learn to ignore the hidden variable z or y and go after the low hanging fruit, producing a decoder that
is easy to optimize [4]. Ignoring y could collapse the joint probability $q_\phi(z,y|x)$
to $q_\phi(z, y = 1|x)$ by assigning all data to one cluster $y = 1$ in the extreme case.
This would cause the problem of empty clusters. It is also possible to learn a trivial parameterization for $p(z,c)$ to collapse to $p(z) = N(0,1)$ by generating the
same Gaussian components in the MoG, i.e., $\mu_{y=1} = \mu_{y=2} = ... \mu_{y=K}$. Therefore
the model will be reduced to a general VAE without the clustering ability. The
reason causing the ignorance or the little supervision over y is that the model
requires z to include the information that can reconstruct x and to decide the
cluster assignment y from their conditional relationship. Especially when the
decoder is a sensitive RNN structure, there will not be enough capacity for z to
provide enough supervision on y. Instead, z will focus more on the reconstruction
thus makes the model inaccurate in clustering the context sequences.

On the contrary, VAMBC can avoid these problems by separating z into two
embeddings z_c and z_b, emphasizing on clustering and reconstruction, respectively. As shown in Fig. 3, we replace the conditional dependency between z and

y with a joint relationship and add self-supervision on y with a center loss with x_c. For the proposed modeling of the latent variables z_c, z_b and y, we carefully derived the objectives and delicately designed networks to fulfill the assumptions and prevent practical problems.

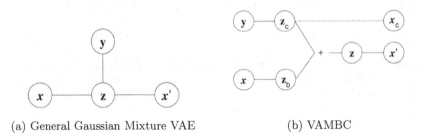

(a) General Gaussian Mixture VAE   (b) VAMBC

Fig. 3. Compare the graphic notations of a GMVAE and VAMBC

5   Experiments

In this section, we quantitatively evaluate the clustering performance of VAMBC by comparing it with the state-of-the-art approaches in Sect. 5.2. We also analyze variants of VAMBC to understand the role of each component in Sect. 5.3.

5.1   Environment and Experiment Settings

Datasets. Following [35], we utilize the GeoLife dataset [37] and DMCL dataset [8] produced by real human trajectories for the evaluation of our proposed approach. The POI information of the two datasets are from Open-StreetMap (OSM) [14] and the PKU Open Research Data [6], respectively. The experiments are evaluated based on the labeled moving behavior samples of the GeoLife and DMCL datasets reported in [35]. For GeoLife, six labels were provided as the ground-truth classes: "campus activities", "hangouts", "dining activities", "healthcare activities", "working commutes", "studying commutes". Four clusters were labeled in DMCL dataset: "studying commutes", "residential activities", "campus activities", "hangouts".

Baseline Approaches. We compare our approaches with the state-of-the-art clustering approaches from four categories:

- For classical time series clustering approaches, we include **KM-DTW** (KMeans with Dynamic Time Warping distance) [27], **KM-GAK** (KMeans with Global Assignment Kernel) [10], **k-Shape** [26] and **DB-LCSS** (DBSCAN with Longest Common Sub-Sequence distance) [24].

- For discrete sequence clustering approaches, we include **SGT** [28] and **MHMM** (Mixed Hidden Marcov Model) [30]. Since they work for discrete sequences, we transform the context sequences into discrete sequences by mapping the real-value vectors to discrete categories via pre-clustering all context vectors;
- For AutoEncoder based deep clustering approaches, we include **DTC** [23], **DETECT** [35], and adapted **IDEC*** [16] and **DCN*** [32] by replacing the encoder and decoder with LSTM layers to work with context sequences.
- For variational deep clustering approaches, we adapted **GMVAE*** [11,29], **VaDE*** [20] and **JointVAE*** [13] in the same way mentioned above. Here we also add KL Annealing [4] to GMVAE* to solve its KL vanishing problem. The approaches adapted from image researches are marked with "*" after their names.

Environment and Parameters. We implemented our approaches on a computing node with a 36 core Intel i9 Extreme processor, 128 GB RAM and 2 RTX2080Ti / Titan RTX GPUs. We implemented the KM-DBA, KM-GAK and kShape using tslearn[1]. DBSCAN clustering uses ScikitLearn[2] with LCSS distance[3]. We set the common sequence threshold as 0.15 for LCSS, and $\epsilon = 0.03$ and $minPts = 18$ as the neighborhood thresholds in DBSCAN. The proposed model VAMBC was built using Keras [9] with Tensorflow [1]. The discrete sequence clustering approach Mixed-HMM was implemented using the R package seqHMM.[4] The adapted baselines were revised for context sequences based on their public code on Github.[5, 6, 7] Both VAMBC and adapted baselines are using LSTM layers with 128 units in the encoder and decoder. The dimension of hidden variable z was set to 64.

5.2 Quantitative Analysis

Evaluation Metrics. We use three clustering metrics that are widely used in the clustering community [16,20,23,32]: Normalized Mutual Information (NMI) [5], Adjusted Rand Index (ARI) [33], and Clustering Accuracy (ACC) [5]. These metrics have different emphasis on evaluating the clustering quality; therefore, we believe a side-by-side comparison could indicate the overall clustering performances of the models. All of the three metrics reach 1 if the clustering result is fully consistent with ground truth. NMI and ACC have minimums of 0, and ARI has -1 as the minimum for the worst clustering result.

Evaluation Results. We conducted the experiments ten times following the practice in [16,20] and reported the clustering performance of the best/worst

---

[1] https://github.com/rtavenar/tslearn.
[2] https://scikit-learn.org/stable.
[3] https://github.com/maikol-solis/trajectory_distance.
[4] https://cran.r-project.org/web/packages/seqHMM/index.html.
[5] https://github.com/XifengGuo/IDEC.
[6] https://github.com/sarsbug/DCN_keras.
[7] https://github.com/slim1017/VaDE.

run and the average metrics with standard deviations (the numbers after ±) (Table 1). DB-LCSS always produces the same results, so we did not include its standard deviation in the table. We believe the average performance is important because in real-world use cases one would not be able to tell which run is better without knowing the ground truth. We compare the performance of VAMBC with the baselines in Table 1. We observe that VAMBC outperforms all the baselines on both the worst run and the average metrics in both datasets. In addition, the standard deviation of the metrics produced by VAMBC is extremely low, i.e., 1/3-1/8, as compared with the baselines for GeoLife. This result indicates VAMBC is robust and can produce accurate results regardless of repeating training. It is interesting to see the adapted DCN got the highest best NMI in GeoLife. But its variance across different experiments is high, and the average NMI is not as good which means it does not guarantee it produces a good result every time. This is because its first-phase training varies from one time to another and does not always produce a good initial representation for clustering.

5.3 Ablation Study

In this section, we demonstrate how different components of VAMBC work under the hood through ablation experiments. Specifically, we create three ablated variants of VAMBC by removing one component. We compare these variants by looking at different measurements during their training processes. In Fig. 4, we plot the curves of these measurements versus the training epoch. Figure 4a shows the curves of accuracy. Figure 4b shows the curves of negative entropy and Fig. 4c shows the curves of reconstruction errors. We plot the first 300 epochs and discard the rest of the curves, which already converge.

Removal of Negative Entropy. The negative entropy term in the loss penalizes the model if the clustering prediction is overly confident. In Fig. 4a, we can observe that the model without using negative entropy (green line) stays at a low accuracy after some fluctuations and climbs up but fails to converge to high accuracy. The low accuracy period is because this variant model aggressively assigns all data to two or three clusters and does not split more clusters. This can also be observed in Fig. 4b that during the same period (from epoch 100 to epoch 150), the negative entropy increases sharply. Although the accuracy increases again after this period (possibly start to split some clusters due to the randomness in the Gumbel-softmax component), it cannot fully escape from the overconfidence problem. In contrast, in Fig. 4b, the curve of VAMBC also increases but in a relatively restrained pace. This means the VAMBC becomes confident gradually about the cluster assignment because of the restrain from negative entropy. This way, using negative entropy in the model prevents the model from being dominated by one or a few clusters. We can also observe this phenomenon in Fig. 4c. The reconstruction loss of VAMBC drops relatively slowly during the first 100 epochs to let the model working on the cluster embedding and assignments. Therefore, we observe the VAMBC would eventually converge to a much

Table 1. Clustering performance comparison

Dataset	Method	NMI (aver)	NMI (best)	NMI (worst)	ARI (aver)	ARI (best)	ARI (worst)	ACC (aver)	ACC (best)	ACC (worst)
GeoLife	KM-DTW	0.610±0.021	0.645	0.579	0.635±0.019	0.656	0.617	0.742±0.031	0.763	0.655
	KM-GAK	0.591±0.057	0.657	0.507	0.505±0.076	0.573	0.392	0.737±0.033	0.770	0.688
	K-Shape	0.229±0.033	0.272	0.174	0.220±0.046	0.271	0.102	0.522±0.015	0.551	0.495
	DB-LCSS	0.547	0.547	0.547	0.412	0.412	0.412	0.697	0.697	0.697
	SGT	0.419±0.024	0.454	0.371	0.216±0.036	0.277	0.149	0.628±0.029	0.694	0.579
	MHMM	0.530±0.047	0.611	0.486	0.403±0.057	0.495	0.344	0.627±0.017	0.649	0.607
	IDEC*	0.605±0.035	0.673	0.572	0.465±0.097	0.664	0.404	0.67±0.08	0.819	0.596
	DCN*	0.646±0.051	**0.725**	0.594	0.635±0.065	0.693	0.503	0.782±0.061	0.840	0.624
	DTC	0.500±0.027	0.550	0.474	0.483±0.028	0.512	0.451	0.682±0.032	0.737	0.655
	DETECT	0.644±0.037	0.691	0.589	0.646±0.044	0.688	0.582	0.8±0.013	0.822	0.780
	GMVAE*	0.447±0.083	0.598	0.364	0.353±0.074	0.480	0.274	0.530±0.052	0.617	0.479
	VaDE*	0.631±0.053	0.669	0.502	0.603±0.078	0.658	0.440	0.783±0.037	0.822	0.720
	JointVAE*	0.459±0.056	0.556	0.408	0.227±0.123	0.442	0.161	0.519±0.062	0.597	0.473
	VAMBC	**0.697±0.015**	0.699	**0.692**	**0.7±0.019**	**0.719**	**0.682**	**0.825±0.01**	**0.842**	**0.810**
DMCL	KM-DTW	0.366±0.023	0.415	0.355	0.211±0.008	0.229	0.208	0.582±0.009	0.600	0.578
	KM-GAK	0.323±0.019	0.345	0.277	0.161±0.04	0.270	0.120	0.579±0.056	0.733	0.556
	K-Shape	0.409±0.055	0.531	0.344	0.241±0.06	0.396	0.183	0.616±0.08	**0.811**	0.522
	DB-LCSS	0.365	0.365	0.365	0.158	0.158	0.158	0.511	0.511	0.511
	SGT	0.458±0.012	0.466	0.440	0.256±0.009	0.262	0.242	0.763±0.005	0.766	0.755
	HMM	0.326±0.055	0.392	0.208	0.126±0.096	0.339	0.011	0.648±0.064	0.756	0.567
	IDEC*	0.442±0.012	0.448	0.409	0.333±0.006	0.338	0.318	0.776±0.005	0.778	0.767
	DCN*	0.447±0.02	0.479	0.413	0.343±0.014	0.375	0.328	0.781±0.011	0.800	0.767
	DTC	0.427±0.081	0.487	0.222	0.304±0.101	0.368	0.083	0.733±0.089	0.800	0.522
	DETECT	0.486±0.022	0.527	0.448	0.378±0.047	0.398	0.247	0.779±0.063	0.800	0.600
	GMVAE*	0.319±0.063	0.476	0.251	0.127±0.056	0.256	0.082	0.566±0.026	0.622	0.544
	VaDE*	0.456±0.02	0.493	0.446	0.341±0.007	0.355	0.338	0.778±0	0.778	0.778
	JointVAE*	0.12±0.123	0.263	0.000	0.044±0.048	0.104	0.000	0.524±0.016	0.544	0.511
	VAMBC	**0.512±0.02**	0.527	**0.475**	**0.384±0.013**	**0.398**	0.351	**0.799±0.004**	0.800	**0.789**

higher accuracy than the ablated variants because VAMBC can escape from the sub-optimums.

Removal of Gumbel-softmax. The Gumbel-softmax layer enables some randomness in the discrete variable. Such randomness enables an input to "jump" to a similar cluster if the model is not confident enough about their assignments. Without the Gumbel-softmax layer, the model would stay in a sub-optimal assignment and prevent other losses from directing the model to learn a better representation. As we can see in Fig. 4a, the curve (red line) without Gumbel-Softmax quickly goes up and stay at a certain accuracy until convergence.

Removal of Center Loss. The center loss regularizer is very important in preventing the model from ignoring the discrete variable and cluster latent embedding. As we can see in Fig. 4a, the curve (orange line) without the center loss quickly drops to a low accuracy after a spike. This indicates that the model will soon rely less on the cluster embedding to minimize the reconstruction, which is not ideal. In Fig. 4b, its negative entropy stays low, which also indicates that the model is reluctant to differentiate clusters and chooses to rely on the individualized embedding only.

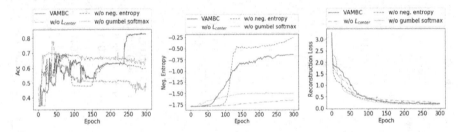

(a) Accuracy v.s. training epochs
(b) Negative Entropy v.s. training epochs
(c) Recon. Loss v.s. training epochs

Fig. 4. Changes of metrics by variants over their training epochs (Color figure online)

5.4 The Training Progress of VAMBC

To understand the change of the latent embedding and the cluster embedding in VAMBC, we visualize the learned embeddings at different epochs in Fig. 5 using t-SNE [22]. The red points denote the latent embeddings of the context sequences, and the black points represent the cluster embeddings z^c for each cluster. At the initial stages (epoch = 1 and 60), the model learns giant clusters (where many nearby black points locate) that can roughly reconstruct the data. Subsequently, the negative entropy and the reparameterization by Gumbel-Softmax encourage the model to split more clusters and finally (epoch = 400) the clusters are well separated and the cluster embeddings are well-distributed at the centers of each cluster.

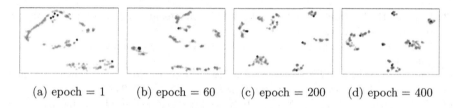

(a) epoch = 1   (b) epoch = 60   (c) epoch = 200   (d) epoch = 400

Fig. 5. Visualization of the training progress

6   Conclusion

In this paper, we proposed a novel deep learning framework VAMBC that can accurately and robustly cluster the context sequences of ordered real-value feature vectors based on their transition patterns to infer mobility behaviors. The framework explicitly decomposes the cluster latent representation and individualized latent representation via two reparameterization layers. Such decomposition and the finely designed network enable the model to learn the self-supervision and cluster structure jointly without collapsing to trivial solutions. The results evaluated on real-world data show that the proposed approach is more robust and accurate than a variety of baseline approaches.

References

1. Abadi, M., et al.: Tensorflow: large-scale machine learning on heterogeneous distributed systems. In: OSDI (2016)
2. Ballé, J., Laparra, V., Simoncelli, E.P.: End-to-end optimized image compression. In: ICLR (2017)
3. Bengio, Y., Courville, A., Vincent, P.: Representation learning: a review and new perspectives. TPAMI **35**(8), 1798–1828 (2013)
4. Bowman, S., Vilnis, L., Vinyals, O., Dai, A., Jozefowicz, R., Bengio, S.: Generating sentences from a continuous space. In: SIGNLL, pp. 10–21 (2016)
5. Cai, D., He, X., Han, J.: Locally consistent concept factorization for document clustering. IEEE TKDE **23**(6), 902–913 (2010)
6. Center, S.I.: Map poi (point of interest) data. Peking University Open Research Data Platform (2017)
7. Chang, B., Park, Y., Park, D., Kim, S., Kang, J.: Content-aware hierarchical point-of-interest embedding model for successive poi recommendation. In: IJCAI, pp. 3301–3307 (2018)
8. D.U. of Illinois at Chicago: Real trajectory data (2006). https://www.cs.uic.edu/~boxu/mp2p/gps_data.html
9. Chollet, F., et al.: Keras (2015). https://github.com/fchollet/keras
10. Cuturi, M.: Fast global alignment kernels. In: ICML, pp. 929–936 (2011)
11. Dilokthanakul, N., et al.: Deep unsupervised clustering with gaussian mixture variational autoencoders. arXiv preprint arXiv:1611.02648 (2016)
12. Doersch, C.: Tutorial on variational autoencoders. arXiv preprint arXiv:1606.05908 (2016)

13. Dupont, E.: Learning disentangled joint continuous and discrete representations. In: NIPS, pp. 710–720 (2018)
14. Foundation, O.: Openstreetmap data (2018). http://download.geofabrik.de/north-america.html
15. Ghosh, P., Sajjadi, M.S., Vergari, A., Black, M., Schölkopf, B.: From variational to deterministic autoencoders. arXiv preprint arXiv:1903.12436 (2019)
16. Guo, X., Gao, L., Liu, X., Yin, J.: Improved deep embedded clustering with local structure preservation. In: IJCAI (2017)
17. He, J., Li, X., Liao, L., Song, D., Cheung, W.K.: Inferring a personalized next point-of-interest recommendation model with latent behavior patterns. In: AAAI (2016)
18. Helske, S., Helske, J.: Mixture hidden markov models for sequence data: The seqhmm package in r. arXiv preprint: arXiv:1704.00543 (2017)
19. Jang, E., Gu, S., Poole, B.: Categorical reparameterization with gumbel-softmax. arXiv preprint arXiv:1611.01144 (2016)
20. Jiang, Z., Zheng, Y., Tan, H., Tang, B., Zhou, H.: Variational deep embedding: an unsupervised and generative approach to clustering. In: IJCAI (2017)
21. Kingma, D.P., Welling, M.: Auto-encoding variational bayes. arXiv preprint arXiv:1312.6114 (2013)
22. Van der Maaten, L., Hinton, G.: Visualizing data using t-SNE. JMLR 9(11) (2008)
23. Madiraju, N.S., Sadat, S.M., Fisher, D., Karimabadi, H.: Deep temporal clustering: fully unsupervised learning of time-domain features. arXiv preprint arXiv:1802.01059 (2018)
24. Morris, B., Trivedi, M.: Learning trajectory patterns by clustering: experimental studies and comparative evaluation. In: CVPR (2009)
25. Mrabah, N., Bouguessa, M., Ksantini, R.: Adversarial deep embedded clustering: on a better trade-off between feature randomness and feature drift. arXiv preprint arXiv:1909.11832 (2019)
26. Paparrizos, J., Gravano, L.: k-Shape: efficient and accurate clustering of time series. In: SIGMOD, pp. 1855–1870 (2015)
27. Petitjean, F., Ketterlin, A., Gançarski, P.: A global averaging method for dynamic time warping, with applications to clustering. Pattern Recogn. 44(3), 678–693 (2011)
28. Ranjan, C., Ebrahimi, S., Paynabar, K.: Sequence graph transform (sgt): A feature extraction function for sequence data mining (extended version). arXiv preprint arXiv:1608.03533 (2016)
29. Shu, R., Brofos, J., Langlotz, C.: A note on deep variational models for unsupervised clustering (2017)
30. Smyth, P.: Clustering sequences with hidden markov models. In: NIPS, pp. 648–654 (1997)
31. Xu, J., Xu, B., Wang, P., Zheng, S., Tian, G., Zhao, J.: Self-taught convolutional neural networks for short text clustering. Neural Netw. 88, 22–31 (2017)
32. Yang, B., Fu, X., Sidiropoulos, N.D., Hong, M.: Towards k-means-friendly spaces: simultaneous deep learning and clustering. In: ICML, pp. 3861–3870. JMLR (2017)
33. Yeung, K.Y., Ruzzo, W.L.: Details of the adjusted rand index and clustering algorithms, supplement to the paper an empirical study on principal component analysis for clustering gene expression data. Bioinformatics 17(9), 763–774 (2001)
34. Yin, J., Wang, J.: A dirichlet multinomial mixture model-based approach for short text clustering. In: SIGKDD, pp. 233–242 (2014)

35. Yue, M., Li, Y., Yang, H., Ahuja, R., Chiang, Y.Y., Shahabi, C.: Detect: deep trajectory clustering for mobility-behavior analysis. In: IEEE Big Data, pp. 988–997. IEEE (2019)
36. Zheng, Y.: Trajectory data mining: an overview. ACM TIST **6**(3), 1–41 (2015)
37. Zheng, Y., Zhang, L., Xie, X., Ma, W.Y.: Mining interesting locations and travel sequences from gps trajectories. In: WWW (2009)
38. Zou, Q., Lin, G., Jiang, X., Liu, X., Zeng, X.: Sequence clustering in bioinformatics: an empirical study. Brief. Bioinform. **21**(1), 1–10 (2020)

Multi-agent Deep Reinforcement Learning with Spatio-Temporal Feature Fusion for Traffic Signal Control

Xin Du, Jiahai Wang$^{(\boxtimes)}$, Siyuan Chen, and Zhiyue Liu

School of Computer Science and Engineering, Sun Yat-sen University,
Guangzhou, China
{duxin23,chensy47,liuzhy93}@mail2.sysu.edu.cn,
wangjiah@mail.sysu.edu.cn

Abstract. Traffic signal control (TSC) plays an important role in intelligent transportation system. It is helpful to improve the efficiency of urban transportation by controlling the traffic signal intelligently. Recently, various deep reinforcement learning methods have been proposed to solve TSC. However, most of these methods ignore the fusion of spatial and temporal features in traffic roadnets. Besides, these methods pay no attention to the correlations of the intersections in several local areas. This paper proposes a novel multi-agent deep reinforcement learning method with spatio-temporal feature fusion to solve TSC. The proposed method firstly calculates the correlations among different time steps to capture their temporal dependencies. Secondly, the proposed method constructs connected subnetworks to capture interactive relations among intersections in the subnetwork. Experimental results demonstrate that our method achieves state-of-the-art performance on synthetic and real-world datasets.

Keywords: Traffic signal control · Multi-agent deep reinforcement learning · Spatio-temporal feature fusion

1 Introduction

Along with the rapid urbanization process, a large number of crowd are gathering towards cities constantly. It leads to the increasing number of private cars and pedestrians. A series of traffic problems are following such as traffic congestions, greenhouse gas emissions, and road accidents. To address these problems, it is necessary to control traffic signals intelligently to regulate traffic order and reduce road accidents. The application of traffic signal control (TSC) to Hangzhou city brain v2.0 [10] is a good example. This city brain made dramatic achievements in TSC. Up to this year, this city brain controls more than 50% of the traffic signals on elevated road ramps in Hangzhou. It increases total traffic efficiency by 15.3%. Therefore, TSC plays an important role in relieving traffic congestions and increasing traffic efficiency.

© Springer Nature Switzerland AG 2021
Y. Dong et al. (Eds.): ECML PKDD 2021, LNAI 12978, pp. 470–485, 2021.
https://doi.org/10.1007/978-3-030-86514-6_29

Traditional methods use manually designed rules to control traffic signals. However, These rules can not adapt to complex traffic flows in modern society. In recent years, some reinforcement learning (RL) based methods [12,18,24,29] have emerged to make real-time decisions to solve TSC. These methods can adjust strategies online according to the feedback of the environment. Moreover, some multi-agent RL methods [18,29] handle each intersection as a single agent. These methods use graph neural networks to learn the interactions among agents. However, these methods only construct spatial dependency and ignore temporal dependency. Temporal dependency is fundamentally important in TSC. For example, the traffic conditions on Monday are similar to those on Mondays in history. This phenomenon reflects the periodic variation of traffic flows. Therefore, it is necessary to capture temporal dependency in TSC. Besides, these multi-agent RL methods only pay attention to the interactions of adjacent intersections, but traffic conditions are usually similar in a local area, which includes multiple intersections. These intersections may form a sequence, a square, or other shapes. For example, traffic congestions may happen in continuous road sections. To relieve traffic congestions, the intersections in the continuous road sections need to share vehicle flow information, but existing methods can not associate these intersections with each other. To tackle these shortcomings, this paper proposes a multi-agent deep reinforcement learning method with spatio-temporal feature fusion (MADRL-STFF) to solve TSC. The proposed method includes three modules. In the first module, the raw data of initial observations are inputted into an embedding layer. This layer can encode the raw data into initial feature representations. In the second module, spatio-temporal feature fusion components are designed to extract and fuse spatio-temporal features from the initial feature representations. These components help the agents to cooperate by exchanging their information to make decisions comprehensively. In the final module, a Q-value prediction layer is constructed to predict Q-values of the actions for each agent. The main contributions of this paper are threefold:

- An end-to-end multi-agent deep reinforcement learning method with spatio-temporal feature fusion, named MADRL-STFF, is proposed to solve TSC. To achieve the multi-agent cooperation, the proposed method uses graph neural network to make the neighbor agents and the agents in the same subnetwork share their observations and state representations. MADRL-STFF is evaluated on two synthetic datasets and three real-world datasets. The experimental results show the superiority of MADRL-STFF.
- MADRL-STFF captures spatio-temporal dependencies of related traffic signals by attention mechanism.
- MADRL-STFF constructs connected subnetworks to learn the interaction of vehicle flows in each local area. These connected subnetworks can share information among the intersections where traffic conditions are similar.

2   Related Works

For solving TSC task, conventional methods usually design fixed phase change rules of traffic signals. Some methods are still widely used in today's traffic signal control system, such as SCOOT and SCATS. These methods design a set of rules and select the best one according to the current traffic flow situation. Some other methods like [13] define fixed cycle-based phase sequence to control traffic signals. [22] proposes a method named max pressure control (MaxPressure) to maximizes traffic output volume by changing signal phases. Some methods use optimization methodologies to solve TSC such as [6,8]. These conventional methods are proposed based on their assumptions about the traffic model, but these assumptions can not adaptive enough to the real-time traffic patterns of modern complex traffic flows [27,34].

To address the shortcomings of conventional methods, recently RL technology is proposed to learn traffic signal control strategies online without prior knowledge. RL based methods can be divided into two types: single agent RL methods and multi-agent RL methods [9,23].

For single agent RL methods, [14] uses deep stacked autoencoder to approximate the Q-function for a single intersection. [4] proposes a deep recurrent Q-network to solve TSC. It uses long short-term memory (LSTM) to model sequential data of traffic signal phases. [17] combines two RL algorithms: policy gradient and value function based method. It can predict the best traffic signal phase by the two algorithms. [7] proposes an end-to-end TSC system to collect raw image data of real-time traffic flows. This system uses convolutional neural network (CNN) to learn the visual features from the raw image data. These visual features can be used in configuring TSC policies. [28] proposes a deep Q-network (DQN) [16] based model, called IntelliLight. IntelliLight consists of two parts: offline part and online part. The offline part uses the fix-time method like [13] to initialize the parameters of the model. The online part uses DQN to optimize the model. [15] combines double DQN and prioritized experience replay [20] to solve TSC. The common point of these single RL methods is that these methods are limited to control traffic signals in a single intersection. Besides, the complexities of these methods become increasingly higher as the scale of TSC grows. They can not adapt to multi-intersection TSC. Therefore, multi-agent RL methods are proposed to tackle this problem recent years.

For multi-agent RL methods, [19] first proposes a multi-agent RL method to solve TSC. It applies DQN and a coordination tool to multiple traffic signals. Besides, it also designs a new reward function to evaluate the real-time traffic condition properly. [18] uses graph convolutional networks (GCN) to coordinate multiple intersections. Similar to [18], [29] uses graph attention network (GAT) and evaluates it on their open-source traffic simulator CityFlow[1] [32]. [21] proposes a decentralized-to-centralized architecture. This architecture divides the traffic roadnet into multiple local regions. Each region is controlled by a single RL agent. These local agents are coordinated by a global agent to achieve the aim of centralized control. [5] proposes an advantage actor-critic based multi-agent RL method. It uses fingerprints of neighboring agents and a spatial discount factor to ensure the stable convergence of the method. [24] proposes a cooperative double Q-learning (Co-DQL) method. Co-DQL uses upper confidence bound [1] to

---

[1] http://cityflow-project.github.io.

balance exploitation and exploration during selecting actions. Besides, Co-DQL uses mean-field theory to learn a better coordinated strategies among agents. [12] proposes a two-stage hierarchical framework to combine RL with schedule-driven traffic control. This framework adopts decentralized training method and cooperate the agents by exchanging schedule information and traffic statistics. [3] proposes a decentralized network level method called MPLight to solve TSC.

It is worth noting that these multi-agent RL methods only capture spatial dependency without temporal dependency. Recently, [25] proposes a method called spatio-temporal multi-agent reinforcement learning method (STMARL). STMARL uses LSTM to extract temporal features and uses GAT to extract spatial features. However, STMARL pays no attention to the correlation of each couple of time steps. Besides, STMARL only fuses the features of neighbor agents. It pays no attention to the correlations of the intersections in several local areas. Therefore, to address these problems, this paper proposes MADRL-STFF to solve TSC. MADRL-STFF firstly uses attention mechanism to capture temporal dependencies among different time steps. Secondly, MADRL-STFF proposes two spatial feature fusion components: feature fusion of neighbor agents and feature fusion in connected subnetworks. These components can share information among the intersections in several local areas.

3   Problem Definition

Definition 1. (Traffic signal phase): Traffic signal phases indicate the directions allowing vehicles moving. There are four usually used phases [5] in TSC as shown in Fig. 1. These phases are going straight from west and east, turning left from west and east, going straight from north and south, turning left from north and south, respectively.

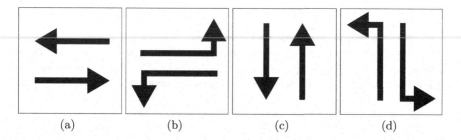

Fig. 1. Traffic signal phases. (a) Going straight from west and east. (b) Turning left from west and east. (c) Going straight from north and south. (d) Turning left from north and south.

Definition 2. (Traffic signal control problem): TSC can be casted as a Markov decision problem. This problem can be defined by the tuple $(\mathcal{S}, \mathcal{A}, \mathcal{P}, \mathcal{R}, \gamma)$:

- **State** $\mathcal{S}$: $\mathcal{S}$ is the state space of agents. Each agent controls the traffic signals of one intersection. The state of each agent at time t is denoted as $s_i^t \in \mathcal{S}$, where i is the index of agents. s_i^t consists of the traffic signal phase and vehicle queue length of the lanes connected with the intersection.
- **Action** $\mathcal{A}$: $\mathcal{A}$ is the action space of agents. The agent i can decide the action $a_i^t \in \mathcal{A}$ at time t every Δt period of time. The action a_i^t can be defined as traffic signal phase. Each agent can select actions from predefined four kinds of traffic signal phases.
- **Transition Function** $\mathcal{P}$: $\mathcal{P}$ is the transition function. This function maps the state-action pair at time t to the next state at time $t+1$. Formally, given the state s_i^t and the corresponding action a_i^t for agent i at time t, the next state s_i^{t+1} can be arrived with the transition probability $\mathcal{P}(s_i^{t+1}|s_i^t, a_i^t)$.
- **Reward** $\mathcal{R}$: $\mathcal{R}_i^t$ represents the immediate reward of agent i after taking the action a_i^t at time t. The reward should reflect the condition of traffic congestion. When there is a serious traffic congestion, the vehicle queue length is longer than ordinary times. Therefore, vehicle queue length can be used in representing the reward $\mathcal{R}$. $\mathcal{R}_i^t$ can be defined as $\mathcal{R}_i^t = -\sum_l L_{i,l}^t$, where $L_{i,l}^t$ represents the vehicle queue length at lane l. However, vehicle queue length only reflects the degree of the traffic congestion for one intersection. Therefore, travel time is usually adopted as the ultimate objective to quantify the efficiency of vehicle movements in traffic roadnets, but travel time is not proper as reward. The reason is that travel time as reward would be delayed and invalid in presenting the correctness of the action, because traffic signals and vehicle movements would influence the travel time of a vehicle [27].
- **Discount Factor** γ: $\gamma \in [0, 1]$ is the discount factor. It can balance the immediate reward and the future reward.

By the defined tuple above, TSC aims to maximize the reward of each agent by Q-learning. The optimization objective of TSC is defined as follows:

$$\text{Minimize} \quad \mathbb{E}[r_i^t + \gamma \max_{a_i^{t+1}} Q'(s_i^{t+1}, a_i^{t+1}) - Q(s_i^t, a_i^t)], \tag{1}$$

where r_i^t is the immediate reward of agent i at time t; γ is the discount factor; s_i^t and a_i^t is the state-action pair at time t; s_i^{t+1} and a_i^{t+1} is the state-action pair at time $t+1$; $Q(s,a)$ and $Q'(s,a)$ are current Q-network and target Q-network, respectively.

4   Method

This paper proposes MADRL-STFF to solve TSC. The framework of MADRL-STFF is presented in Fig. 2. This method includes three modules. The first module is spatio-temporal input embedding. This module encodes spatio-temporal input data into initial spatio-temporal feature representations. The second module is spatio-temporal feature fusion. This module includes temporal feature

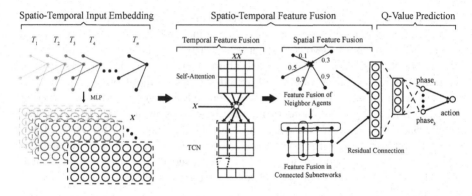

Fig. 2. The framework of MADRL-STFF. The first module is spatio-temporal input embedding. This module encodes spatio-temporal input data into initial spatio-temporal feature representations. The second module is spatio-temporal feature fusion. This module includes temporal feature fusion and spatial feature fusion. In temporal feature fusion, attention mechanism is used to capture the correlations and fuse the temporal features among different time steps. Then, TCN is used to capture temporal dependencies at regular intervals. In spatial feature fusion, the spatial structure features are fused in neighbor agents and constructed connected subnetworks. The final module predicts Q-values of the actions for each agent.

fusion and spatial feature fusion. In temporal feature fusion, attention mechanism is used to capture the correlations and fuse the temporal features among different time steps. Then, temporal convolutional network (TCN) [2] is used to capture temporal dependencies at regular intervals. In spatial feature extraction, the spatial structure features are fused in neighbor agents and connected subnetowrks. The final module predicts Q-values of the actions for each agent. The details of the framework are given as follows.

4.1 Spatio-Temporal Input Embedding

This module aims to encode spatio-temporal input data into initial spatio-temporal feature representations. Given the state $s_i^t \in \mathbb{R}^k$ of agent i at time t, s_i^t can be embedded into the initial feature representation $x_i^t \in \mathbb{R}^d$, where k is the state dimension; d is the embedding dimension. Here, the embedding layer is defined as a multi-layer perceptron (MLP). The embedding process is presented as follows:

$$x_i^t = \sigma(s_i^t W_e + b_e), \tag{2}$$

where $x_i^t \in X$; $X \in \mathbb{R}^{T \times N \times k}$ is the spatio-temporal feature matrix; T is the number of time steps; N is the number of agents; σ is the activation function ReLU; $W_e \in \mathbb{R}^{k \times d}$ and $b_e \in \mathbb{R}^d$ are weight parameters and bias vector, respectively.

4.2 Spatio-Temporal Feature Fusion

This module includes temporal feature fusion and spatial feature fusion.

Temporal Feature Fusion. Temporal feature fusion aims to capture temporal dependencies and fuse temporal features in different time steps. Temporal feature fusion consists of two components: self-attention layer and temporal convolutional network layer. At the self-attention layer, the correlation between two different time steps can be calculated by self-attention operation. Then, the new representation for each time step can be generated. The generation method combines the initial representations of all the time steps with their corresponding correlations. At the temporal convolutional network layer, a three-layer CNN with different dilation rates is proposed to capture temporal dependencies in different time steps. Then, a standard CNN is used to fuse the sequential features. The details of each component are described as follows.

– **Self-Attention**: Since the traffic conditions are correlated among different time steps, this component aims to capture these correlations and fuse the temporal features in different time steps. Formally, given two feature representation vectors $x_i^{t_1}$ and $x_i^{t_2}$ at time t_1 and t_2, respectively, the calculation process is presented as follows:

$$e_{t_1,t_2} = (x_i^{t_1})^T \cdot x_i^{t_2}, \qquad (3)$$

where $t_1, t_2 \in \{1, ..., T\}$; e_{t_1,t_2} is the attention weight between $x_i^{t_1}$ and $x_i^{t_2}$. Then, the feature representation for each time step can be updated as follows:

$$\alpha_{t_1,t_2} = \frac{exp(e_{t_1,t_2})}{\sum_{a=1}^{T} exp(e_{t_1,a})}, \qquad (4)$$

$$u_i^{t_1} = \sigma(W_u \cdot \sum_{a=1}^{T} \alpha_{t_1,a} \cdot x_i^a + b_u), \qquad (5)$$

where, α_{t_1,t_2} is the attention weight after normalization by softmax function; $W_u \in \mathbb{R}^{d \times d}$ and $b_u \in \mathbb{R}^d$ are learnable parameters; $u_i^{t_1} \in \mathbb{R}^d$ is the new representation of agent i at time t.

– **Temporal Convolutional Network**: In TSC, the evolution tendency of traffic flows should be learned by each agent to make better decisions. To achieve this target, the temporal dependencies, which are the correlations of the vehicle volumes at regular intervals should be captured. Temporal convolutional network (TCN) is adopted to capture these correlations in different time scales via different dilation rates. Since TCN can learn long sequence information in a non-recursive manner, TCN can solve sequence modeling problem more efficient than RNNs [31]. Therefore, a three-layer CNN with different dilation rates is proposed to fuse temporal features. Then, a standard CNN is used to merge the features at all the time steps. The feature fusion process is presented as follows:

$$(u_i^t)^{(r)} = \Theta^{(r)} *_{T^c} ([(u_i^1)^{(r-1)}, ..., (u_i^t)^{(r-1)}])$$

$$= \sum_{m=0}^{M-1} w_m^{(r)} \cdot (u_i^{t-cm})^{(r-1)}, \qquad (6)$$

$$y_i = \Theta' * ([(u_i^1)^{(3)}, ..., (u_i^T)^{(3)}]) = \sum_{t=0}^{T-1} w'_t \cdot (u_i^{t+1})^{(3)}, \tag{7}$$

where r is the index of CNN layers; $c = 2^{r-1}$ is the dilation rate; $\Theta^{(r)} = [w_0^{(r)}, ..., w_{M-1}^{(r)}] \in \mathbb{R}^M$ is the parameters of the r-th layer convolutional kernel; M is the length of the convolutional kernel; $*_{r^c}$ is the dilated causal operator [2] with dilation rate c; $\Theta' = [w'_0, ..., w'_{T-1}] \in \mathbb{R}^T$ is the convolutional kernel of the standard CNN; $y_i \in \mathbb{R}^d$ is the output feature representation of agent i. Besides, Zero padding strategy is used to keep the output length the same as the input length.

Spatial Feature Fusion. Spatial feature fusion aims to fuse spatial structure features among different traffic intersections in the roadnet. The roadnet is modeled as a simple graph. This section proposes two feature fusion components to fuse spatial features in this graph: feature fusion of neighbor agents (NeiFusion) and feature fusion in connected subnetworks (ConFusion). In NeiFusion, GAT is used to share the information of the neighbor agents with the target agent i. In ConFusion, connected subnetworks are constructed and the features of agents in the same connected subnetwork are fused by attention mechanism. Each component is described in detail as follows.

- **Feature Fusion of Neighbor Agents**: The states and strategies of neighbor agents support the target agent to make coordinative decisions. Therefore, this component uses GAT to fuse the features of the neighbor agents. Given the neighbor agents $\mathcal{N}_i$ of agent i, the correlations between $\mathcal{N}_i$ and agent i are calculated by attention mechanism. Then, the new feature representation of agent i can be generated by combining the representations of $\mathcal{N}_i$ with their corresponding correlations. The process is presented as follows:

$$e'_{i,j} = (W_t y_i)^T \cdot (W_s y_j), \tag{8}$$

$$\beta_{i,j} = \frac{exp(e'_{i,j})}{\sum_{a \in \mathcal{N}_i} exp(e'_{i,a})}, \tag{9}$$

$$g_i = \sigma(W_g \cdot \sum_{j \in \mathcal{N}_i} \beta_{i,j} \cdot y_i + b_g), \tag{10}$$

where $e'_{i,j}$ is the attention weight between y_i and y_j; $\beta_{i,j}$ is the attention weight after normalization by softmax function; $W_t, W_s, W_g \in \mathbb{R}^{d \times d}$ and $b_g \in \mathbb{R}^d$ are learnable parameters; $g_i \in \mathbb{R}^d$ is the output feature representation.
- **Feature Fusion in Connected Subnetworks**: The traffic conditions are usually highly correlated in connected intersections. These intersections can be included into a subnetwork to share their information. Therefore, this component aims to construct connected subnetworks and fuse the features of agents in the same connected subnetwork. To achieve this target, firstly, connected subnetworks are constructed by collecting the agents with the nearest

vehicle queue lengths. Secondly, each connected subnetwork can be represented by fusing agent features in this subnetwork. Thirdly, the correlations between the target agent i and the connected subnetworks of including agent i are evaluated by attention mechanism. Finally, the representations of these connected subnetworks are combined with their correlations to generate the new feature representation of agent i. The details of the process are given as follows.

Firstly, connected subnetworks are constructed by collecting the agents of having the nearest vehicle queue lengths. The construction algorithm is shown in supplementary material[2]. Formally, the connected subnetwork cs_i can be constructed initially by adding agent i. Then, at each iteration step, cs_i collects the nearest agent from the neighbor agents NS_i of cs_i by comparing their vehicle queue lengths. At last, there are N constructed connected subnetworks corresponding to N agents, respectively.

Secondly, each connected subnetwork can be represented by fusing agent features in this subnetwork. Given the agents in cs_i, a standard CNN is used to fuse the features of the agents in cs_i. The feature fusion process is presented as follows:

$$p_i = \Theta'' * (cs_i) = \sum_{j=1}^{|cs_i|} w''_{j-1} \cdot g_j^i, \tag{11}$$

where p_i is the feature representation of cs_i; $\Theta'' = [w''_0, ..., w''_{|cs_i|-1}] \in \mathbb{R}^{|cs_i|}$ is the convolutional kernel of the standard CNN; $g_j^i \in cs_i$.

Thirdly, to evaluate the importance of agent i in the connected subnetworks of including agent i, the correlations between the target agent i and these connected subnetworks are calculated by attention mechanism. The calculation process is presented as follows:

$$e''_{i,j} = (W'_t g_i)^T \cdot (W'_s p_j) \quad i \in cs_j, \tag{12}$$

where $e''_{i,j}$ is the attention weight between g_i and p_j; $W'_t, W'_s \in \mathbb{R}^{d \times d}$ are learnable parameters.

Finally, the new feature representation of agent i can be generated by the connected subnetworks of including agent i. The generation method is combining the feature representations of these connected subnetworks with their correlations. The calculation process is presented as follows:

$$\eta_{i,j} = \frac{exp(e''_{i,j})}{\sum_{i \in cs_a} exp(e''_{i,a})}, \tag{13}$$

$$f_i = \sigma(W_f \sum_{i \in cs_j} \eta_{i,j} \cdot p_j + b_f), \tag{14}$$

where $\eta_{i,j}$ is the attention weight after normalization by softmax function; $W_f \in \mathbb{R}^{d \times d}$ and $b_f \in \mathbb{R}^d$ are learnable parameters; $f_i \in \mathbb{R}^d$ is the output feature representation of this component.

---

[2] https://github.com/08doudou/MADRL-STFF-Appendix.

4.3   Q-Value Prediction

This module aims to predict Q-values of the actions for each agent. MLP is used in the calculation process as follows:

$$h_i = [g_i, f_i], \tag{15}$$

$$o_i = \sigma(h_i W_h + b_h), \tag{16}$$

where h_i is the residual connection of g_i and f_i; o_i is the predicted Q-value of agent i; $W_h \in \mathbb{R}^{d \times |\mathcal{A}|}$ and $b_h \in \mathbb{R}^{|\mathcal{A}|}$ are weight parameters and bias, respectively.

The pseudo code of MADRL-STFF is shown in supplementary material. To achieve the multi-agent cooperation, the proposed method uses graph neural network to make the neighbor agents share their observations and state representations in the learning process. Besides, connected subnetworks are constructed to share information among the agents in each subnetwork.

5   Experiment

5.1   Datasets

Following the previous works, our method is evaluated on two synthetic datasets and three real-world datasets[3] [26,29,34]. The two synthetic datasets are 6×6 uni-direction traffic roadnet ($Unidirec_{6 \times 6}$) and 6×6 bi-direction traffic roadnet ($Bidirec_{6 \times 6}$). The three real-world datasets are 3×4 traffic roadnet in Jinan (D_{Jinan}), 4×4 traffic roadnet in Hangzhou ($D_{Hangzhou}$) and 28×7 traffic roadnet in New York ($D_{NewYork}$). These datasets are deployed on an open-source traffic simulator CityFlow [32]. The details of these datasets are described as follows:

- $Unidirec_{6 \times 6}$: An uni-direction 6×6 traffic roadnet. The traffic flow in this roadnet is generated every 12 s in simulator from west to east and north to south.
- $Bidirec_{6 \times 6}$: A bi-direction 6×6 traffic roadnet. The traffic flow in this roadnet is generated every 40 s in simulator in both west-east and north-south directions.
- D_{Jinan}: There are 12 intersections in Dongfeng Sub-district, Jinan, China. The traffic data of these intersections are collected by roadside surveillance cameras. By these cameras, the time of entering the roadnet and the trajectory for each vehicle are recorded.
- $D_{Hangzhou}$: This dataset is generated by roadside surveillance cameras near 16 intersections in Gudang Sub-district, Hangzhou, China.
- $D_{NewYork}$: This dataset includes 196 intersections of Manhattan in New York. It is collected from open source taxi data.

---

[3] https://traffic-signal-control.github.io/.

5.2   Baseline Methods

Our method MADRL-STFF is evaluated with two categories of methods: traditional transportation methods and RL methods. The details of traditional transportation methods are described as follows:

- **Fixed-Time Control (Fixed-Time)** [13]: Fixed-Time uses pre-defined cycle-based phase sequence to control traffic signals.
- **Max Pressure Control (MaxPressure)** [22]: MaxPressure is a state-of-the-art network-level method for TSC. It can maximize traffic output volume by selecting the phase corresponding to the maximum pressure.

The details of RL methods are described as follows:

- **Light-IntellighT (LIT)** [33]: LIT is an individual deep RL method without considering neighbor agent information. It uses DQN to select the action with new designed state and reward.
- **PressLight** [30]: PressLight combines RL technology and MaxPressure method. It adds max pressure value into the reward to essentially evaluate the real-time traffic condition.
- **Graph Convolutional Network (GCN)** [18]: This method uses GCN to fuse neighbor information with the same attention weights.
- **CoLight** [29]: CoLight uses GAT to extract and fuse traffic features by combining neighbor information with their corresponding correlations.
- **Spatio-Temporal Multi-Agent Reinforcement Learning (STMARL)** [25]: STMARL learns spatio-temporal dependencies among multiple traffic signals. It uses LSTM to extract temporal features and uses GAT to extract spatial features.

Besides, to verify the effects of the spatio-temporal feature fusion components in MADRL-STFF, some variants of MADRL-STFF are proposed as follows:

- **MADRL-Temporal**: A variant of our method only using temporal feature fusion components.
- **MADRL-Spatial**: A variant of our method only using spatial feature fusion components.
- **MADRL w/o Att**: A variant of our method without self-attention component.
- **MADRL w/o TCN**: A variant of our method without temporal convolutional network component.
- **MADRL w/o NeiFusion**: A variant of our method without considering the feature fusion of neighbor agents (NeiFusion).
- **MADRL w/o ConFusion**: A variant of our method without considering the feature fusion in connected subnetworks (ConFusion).

Table 1. Performance comparison on synthetic datasets and real-world datasets w.r.t average travel time (the lower the better). * indicates the results of this method are obtained directly from the original paper. Note that the average travel time for LIT is missing, because LIT cannot be trained and updated simultaneously due to the limitation of CPU and memory on New York dataset.

	$Unidirec_{6\times6}$	$Bidirec_{6\times6}$	D_{Jinan}	$D_{Hangzhou}$	$D_{NewYork}$
Fixed-Time [13]	210.94	210.94	814.11	718.29	1830.07
MaxPressure [22]	186.56	195.49	343.90	407.17	1611.08
LIT [33]	261.87	257.52	299.08	299.53	–
PressLight [30]	183.09	175.69	692.72	885.55	1951.47
GCN [18]	208.43	207.65	570.30	481.30	1649.01
CoLight [29]	169.07	176.37	292.12	293.95	1460.86
STMARL* [25]	205.34	180.31	–	319.14	–
MADRL-STFF	**166.79**	**171.41**	**276.90**	**285.18**	**1318.55**

5.3 Performance Metrics and Parameter Settings

Following the existing methods [29,30], average travel time is used as the performance metric to evaluate the performances of different methods. After each training episode, the performances of these methods are tested by calculating the average travel time of all the vehicles spent in the roadnet (in seconds). The average of the last 10 episodes of testing is reported as the final result.

For all RL methods, the number of episodes is set to 200; the learning rate is set to 0.001; The discount factor γ is set to 0.8; The dimensions of all hidden layers in these methods are set to 20; The batch size is set to 20. Specifically for MADRL-STFF, the number of agents N_{cs} in a connected subnetwork is set to 4 on all the datasets.

The pseudo codes of MADRL-STFF and connected subnetworks construction algorithm, the sensitivity of N_{cs}, algorithm complexity and convergence analysis, attention visualization are shown in supplementary material.

5.4 Comparison with Baseline Methods

This section compares MADRL-STFF with baseline methods on two synthetic datasets and three real-world datasets. Most of baseline methods are evaluated by running their source codes on CityFlow platform, but the code of STMARL is not open-source. Therefore, the results of STMARL are obtained directly from the original paper. The source code of MADRL-STFF is available on request. The experimental results are shown in Table 1. Several observations can be found as follows:

- MADRL-STFF outperforms traditional transportation methods on synthetic datasets and real-world datasets in terms of average travel time. On synthetic datasets, MADRL-STFF outperforms Fixed-Time and MaxPressure by

Table 2. Ablation study of spatio-temporal feature fusion components w.r.t average travel time (the lower the better).

	$Unidirec_{6 \times 6}$	$Bidirec_{6 \times 6}$	D_{Jinan}	$D_{Hangzhou}$	$D_{NewYork}$
MADRL-Spatial	168.98	180.02	290.65	299.85	1417.59
MADRL-Temporal	168.31	179.40	289.64	295.44	1381.33
MADRL w/o Att	168.65	179.74	289.60	295.15	1366.01
MADRL w/o TCN	167.56	175.04	279.22	286.26	1344.45
MADRL w/o NeiFusion	167.47	179.31	279.26	289.52	1352.83
MADRL w/o ConFusion	166.87	176.73	285.83	292.40	1364.51
MADRL-STFF	**166.79**	**171.41**	**276.90**	**285.18**	**1318.55**

19.84% and 11.46% on average, respectively. On real-world datasets, MADRL-STFF outperforms Fixed-Time and MaxPressure by 51.42% and 22.53% on average, respectively. These traditional transportation methods control traffic signals by designing fixed rules and depending on prior knowledge. However, MADRL-STFF uses the RL technology to update the TSC strategies by the feedback of the environment. Therefore, MADRL-STFF can adapt to the dynamics of complex traffic scenarios more than traditional transportation methods.

– MADRL-STFF outperforms other RL baseline methods on synthetic datasets and real-world datasets by 14.64% and 26.09% on average, respectively. For these RL baseline methods, LIT is only applied to single intersection scenario. PressLight uses a simple DQN network to solve multi-intersection TSC, but PressLight pays no attention to the interactions among these intersections. GCN and CoLight capture spatial dependencies among multiple intersections, but they ignore temporal dependencies. STMARL uses LSTM to extract temporal features and uses GAT to extract spatial features. However, STMARL pays no attention to the correlation of each couple of time steps. Besides, STMARL only fuses the features of neighbor agents. It pays no attention to the correlations of the intersections in several local areas. Compared with these RL baseline methods, MADRL-STFF not only captures spatio-temporal dependencies to solve multi-intersection TSC, but also constructs connected subnetworks to share information among the intersections in several local areas. Therefore, MADRL-STFF achieves the better results than these RL baseline methods.

5.5   Effect of Spatio-Temporal Feature Fusion Components

To compare the effectiveness of spatio-temporal feature fusion components, the experiments are conducted by removing each feature fusion component from MADRL-STFF. The experimental results are shown in Table 2. The results demonstrate that MADRL-STFF outperforms all the variants on synthetic datasets and real-world datasets by 2.30% and 3.18% on average, respectively. It indicates the effectiveness of our feature fusion components. Besides, there are several observations as follows:

- Temporal feature fusion components (MADRL-Temporal) are more effective than spatial feature fusion components (MADRL-Spatial) on all the datasets. As shown in Table 2, in terms of average travel time, the increases of MADRL-Spatial are more than those of MADRL-Temporal on all the datasets. Maybe temporal feature fusion components can learn more features about variation tendency of traffic flows in history than spatial feature fusion components. These features can be used to make better decisions to reduce traffic congestions.
- In temporal feature fusion, self-attention is more effective than TCN. As shown in Table 2, in terms of average travel time, the increases of MADRL w/o Att are more than those of MADRL w/o TCN on all the datasets. The reason may be that self-attention can capture the correlation of each couple of time steps, but TCN only pays attention to the time steps at regular intervals. Therefore, self-attention can capture more temporal dependencies than TCN.
- In spatial feature fusion, the feature fusion of neighbor agents (NeiFusion) is more effective than that in connected subnetworks (ConFusion) on synthetic datasets. In contrast, ConFusion is more effective than NeiFusion on real-world datasets. As shown in Table 2, in terms of average travel time, the increases of MADRL w/o NeiFusion are more than those of MADRL w/o ConFusion on synthetic datasets. on real-world datasets, the increases of MADRL w/o ConFusion are more than those of MADRL w/o NeiFusion. On real-world datasets, the vehicle trajectories are more complicated than that on synthetic datasets. It may lead to the severe traffic congestions in several connected intersections, which are not limited to neighbor intersections. These connected intersections can be correlated by ConFusion. Therefore, ConFusion outperforms NeiFusion on real-world datasets. However, on synthetic datasets, there are only straight trajectories. In this scenario, neighbor intersections have direct impacts on the target intersection. Therefore, NeiFusion outperforms ConFusion on synthetic datasets.

6   Conclusion

This paper proposes a multi-agent deep reinforcement learning method with spatio-temporal feature fusion (MADRL-STFF) to solve TSC. The proposed method includes three modules. In the first module, the raw data of initial observations are inputted into an embedding layer. This layer can encode the raw data into initial feature representations. In the second module, spatio-temporal features are extracted and fused from the initial feature representations. For temporal feature fusion, the correlations among different time steps are captured by attention mechanism. For spatial feature fusion, feature fusion of neighbor agents and feature fusion in connected subnetworks are proposed to fuse spatial features. In the final module, a Q-value prediction layer is constructed to predict Q-values of the actions for each agent. The results of extensive experiments on synthetic datasets and real-world datasets validate the superiority of our method.

In the future, the proposed method will be extended to large-scale traffic roadnets [3]. Besides, some traditional transportation methods [6,22] and schedule-driven methods [11] can be used to learn the reward function and the dynamic lengths of phases in reinforcement learning, respectively.

Acknowledgements. This work is supported by the National Key R&D Program of China (2018AAA0101203), and the National Natural Science Foundation of China (62072483).

References

1. Auer, P., Cesa-Bianchi, N., Fischer, P.: Finite-time analysis of the multiarmed bandit problem. Mach. Learn. **47**(2–3), 235–256 (2002). https://doi.org/10.1023/A:1013689704352
2. Bai, S., Kolter, J.Z., Koltun, V.: An empirical evaluation of generic convolutional and recurrent networks for sequence modeling. arXiv preprint arXiv:1803.01271 (2018)
3. Chen, C., et al.: Toward a thousand lights: decentralized deep reinforcement learning for large-scale traffic signal control. In: AAAI 2020, vol. 34, no. 4, pp. 3414–3421 (2020)
4. Choe, C., Baek, S., Woon, B., Kong, S.H.: Deep Q learning with LSTM for traffic light control. In: 2018 24th Asia-Pacific Conference on Communications (APCC), pp. 331–336 (2018)
5. Chu, T., Wang, J., Codec, L., Li, Z.: Multi-agent deep reinforcement learning for large-scale traffic signal control. IEEE Trans. Intell. Transp. Syst. **21**(3), 1086–1095 (2020)
6. Gao, K., et al.: Solving traffic signal scheduling problems in heterogeneous traffic network by using meta-heuristics. IEEE Trans. Intell. Transp. Syst. **20**(9), 3272–3282 (2019)
7. Garg, D., Chli, M., Vogiatzis, G.: Deep reinforcement learning for autonomous traffic light control. In: 2018 3rd IEEE International Conference on Intelligent Transportation Engineering (ICITE), pp. 214–218 (2018)
8. Gottlich, S., Herty, M., Ziegler, U.: Modeling and optimizing traffic light settings in road networks. Comput. Oper. Res. **55**, 36–51 (2015)
9. Haydari, A., Yilmaz, Y.: Deep reinforcement learning for intelligent transportation systems: a survey. IEEE Trans. Intell. Transp. Syst., 1–22 (2020, in press). https://doi.org/10.1109/TITS.2020.3008612
10. Hsu, J.: Alibaba cloud launched 'ET City Brain 2.0' in Hangzhou (2018)
11. Hu, H.C., Smith, S.F., Goldstein, R.: Cooperative schedule-driven intersection control with connected and autonomous vehicles. In: IROS 2019, pp. 1668–1673 (2019)
12. Hu, H.C., Smith, S.F.: Learning model parameters for decentralized schedule-driven traffic control. In: ICAPS 2020, pp. 531–539 (2020)
13. Koonce, P., Rodegerdts, L.: Traffic signal timing manual. Technical report, United States. Federal Highway Administration (2008)
14. Li, L., Lv, Y., Wang, F.: Traffic signal timing via deep reinforcement learning. IEEE/CAA J. Autom. Sin. **3**(3), 247–254 (2016)

15. Liang, X., Du, X., Wang, G., Han, Z.: A deep reinforcement learning network for traffic light cycle control. IEEE Trans. Veh. Technol. **68**(2), 1243–1253 (2019)
16. Mnih, V., et al.: Human-level control through deep reinforcement learning. Nature **518**(7540), 529–533 (2015)
17. Mousavi, S.S., Schukat, M., Howley, E.: Traffic light control using deep policy-gradient and value-function-based reinforcement learning. IET Intell. Transp. Syst. **11**(7), 417–423 (2017)
18. Nishi, T., Otaki, K., Hayakawa, K., Yoshimura, T.: Traffic signal control based on reinforcement learning with graph convolutional neural nets. In: 2018 21st International Conference on Intelligent Transportation Systems, pp. 877–883 (2018)
19. Pol, E.V.D., Oliehoek, F.A.: Coordinated deep reinforcement learners for traffic light control. In: NeurIPS 2016 (2016)
20. Schaul, T., Quan, J., Antonoglou, I., Silver, D.: Prioritized experience replay. In: ICLR 2016 (2016)
21. Tan, T., et al.: Cooperative deep reinforcement learning for large-scale traffic grid signal control. IEEE Trans. Cybern. **50**(6), 2687–2700 (2020)
22. Varaiya, P.: The max-pressure controller for arbitrary networks of signalized intersections. In: Ukkusuri, S., Ozbay, K. (eds.) Advances in Dynamic Network Modeling in Complex Transportation Systems. Complex Networks and Dynamic Systems, vol. 2, pp. 27–66. Springer, New York (2013). https://doi.org/10.1007/978-1-4614-6243-9_2
23. Veres, M., Moussa, M.: Deep learning for intelligent transportation systems: A survey of emerging trends. IEEE Trans. Intell. Transp. Syst. **21**(8), 3152–3168 (2020)
24. Wang, X., Ke, L., Qiao, Z., Chai, X.: Large-scale traffic signal control using a novel multiagent reinforcement learning. IEEE Trans. Cybern. **21**(3), 1086–1095 (2020)
25. Wang, Y., et al.: STMARL: A spatio-temporal multi-agent reinforcement learning approach for cooperative traffic light control. IEEE Trans. Mob. Comput., 1–15 (2020, in press). https://doi.org/10.1109/TMC.2020.3033782
26. Wei, H., Zheng, G., Gayah, V., Li, Z.: A survey on traffic signal control methods. arXiv preprint arXiv:1904.08117 (2019)
27. Wei, H., Zheng, G., Gayah, V., Li, Z.: Recent advances in reinforcement learning for traffic signal control: A survey of models and evaluation. ACM SIGKDD Explor. Newsl. **22**(2), 12–18 (2020)
28. Wei, H., Zheng, G., Yao, H., Li, Z.: IntelliLight: A reinforcement learning approach for intelligent traffic light control. In: KDD 2018, pp. 2496–2505 (2018)
29. Wei, H., et al.: CoLight: Learning network-level cooperation for traffic signal control. In: CIKM 2019, pp. 1913–1922 (2019)
30. Wei, H., et al.: PressLight: Learning max pressure control to coordinate traffic signals in arterial network. In: KDD 2019, pp. 1290–1298 (2019)
31. Ye, J., Zhao, J., Ye, K., Xu, C.: How to build a graph-based deep learning architecture in traffic domain: A survey. IEEE Trans. Intell. Transp. Syst., 1–21 (2020, in press). https://doi.org/10.1109/TITS.2020.3043250
32. Zhang, H., et al.: CityFlow: A multi-agent reinforcement learning environment for large scale city traffic scenario. In: WWW 2019, pp. 3620–3624 (2019)
33. Zheng, G., et al.: Diagnosing reinforcement learning for traffic signal control. arXiv preprint arXiv:1905.04716 (2019)
34. Zheng, G., et al.: Learning phase competition for traffic signal control. In: CIKM 2019, pp. 1963–1972 (2019)

Monte Carlo Search Algorithms for Network Traffic Engineering

Chen Dang[1,2]([⊠]) [iD], Cristina Bazgan[2] [iD], Tristan Cazenave[2] [iD],
Morgan Chopin[1] [iD], and Pierre-Henri Wuillemin[3] [iD]

[1] Orange Labs, Châtillon, France
{chen.dang,morgan.chopin}@orange.com
[2] Université Paris-Dauphine, PSL Research University, CNRS, UMR 7243,
LAMSADE, 75016 Paris, France
{cristina.bazgan,tristan.cazenave}@dauphine.psl.eu
[3] Sorbonne Université, CNRS, UMR 7606, LIP6, 75005 Paris, France
pierre-henri.wuillemin@lip6.fr

Abstract. The aim of Traffic Engineering is to provide routing configurations in networks such that the used resources are minimized while maintaining a high level of quality of service (QoS). Among the optimization problems arising in this domain, we address in this paper the one related to setting weights in networks that are based on shortest path routing protocols (OSPF, IS-IS). Finding weights that induce efficient routing paths (e.g. that minimize the maximum congested link) is a computationally hard problem.

We propose to use Monte Carlo Search for the first time for this problem. More specifically we apply Nested Rollout Policy Adaptation (NRPA). We also extend NRPA with the *force_exploration* algorithm to improve the results. In comparison to other algorithms NRPA scales better with the size of the instance and can be easily extended to take into account additional constraints (cost utilization, delay, . . .) or linear/non-linear optimization criteria. For difficult instances the optimum is not known but a lower bound can be computed. NRPA gives results close to the lower bound on a standard dataset of telecommunication networks.

Keywords: Traffic engineering · Policy adaptation · Monte Carlo search

1 Introduction

Despite the emergence of new network routing technologies such as Segment Routing or MPLS (*MultiProtocol Label Switching*), many telecommunication networks still mostly rely on the computation of shortest paths for the transportation of packets, such as Open Shortest Path First (OSPF) or Intermediate System to Intermediate System (IS-IS). In such routing protocols, the network manager controls the data flow by simply supplying so-called administrative weights to the links of the networks. Then, every packet is routed from its origin

© Springer Nature Switzerland AG 2021
Y. Dong et al. (Eds.): ECML PKDD 2021, LNAI 12978, pp. 486–501, 2021.
https://doi.org/10.1007/978-3-030-86514-6_30

to its destination along the shortest paths induced by those weights. While this method has the advantage of being easy to manage, it lacks precise control over the paths that are elected to route the traffic because one can only modify those paths indirectly by changing the weights. As a consequence, the main challenge for a network manager is to find a set of weights that induce routing paths such that the load is minimized while maintaining a high level of QoS on operational networks. Unfortunately, this task turns out to be computationally hard to solve. In this paper, we are interested in one of the network optimization problems related to this issue: Given a bidirected graph and a set of demands, the task is to find a set of weights such that the demands routed along the induced shortest paths generate a minimum congestion *i.e.*, the maximum ratio value of the total traffic going through an edge over the edge's capacity is minimized. There are mainly two variants of this optimization problem studied in the literature namely the *splittable* and *unsplittable* versions. In the former, we allow each demand to be routed along several shortest paths while, in the latter, each demand is required to be routed on a unique shortest path between its origin and its destination.

Several authors proposed to solve this problem using integer programming models and meta-heuristics methods, the reader is referred to [6] for a complete overview of these approaches. Regarding the splittable variant of the problem, Fortz and Thorup [23] showed that it is NP-hard to approximate within a factor $\frac{3}{2} - \epsilon$ for all $\epsilon > 0$. Hence, to cope with the hardness of this problem, many different meta-heuristics approaches were investigated. Fortz and Thorup [23] first proposed a local search algorithm to solve the splittable variant which was latter implemented in the TOTEM library [27] and called IGP-WO. This approach was further extended to compute robust solutions against single link failures [24] or in the context of oblivious routing [2]. Genetic algorithms were also proposed to solve this problem [8,21]. The reader is referred to the surveys [1,22] for more details and references about the existing meta-heuristics approaches proposed to solve this splittable variant. Most of the previous meta-heuristics were tested on networks of small/moderate size and do not consider the unsplittable case or QoS constraints such as the delay. Regarding the unsplittable case, Bley [4] showed that this variant is NP-hard even on bidirected cycles and not $O(n^{1-o(1)})$-approximable unless $P = NP$ in the general case. In [5], the author proposed an exact algorithm using a two-phase approach: the problem is decomposed into a master problem that aims at finding an optimal shortest path routing, and a client problem which consists in finding a compatible set of weights for those shortest paths. This master problem is modeled using an integer linear program and solved using a branch-and-cut algorithm. In [3], further exact algorithms are proposed either based on a compact formulation of the problem or a dynamic programming algorithm using a tree decomposition of the input graph. Unfortunately, the current exact methods can only handle networks of moderate size (e.g. dozens of nodes) while real networks can have hundreds of routers and links. In this paper, we propose to use a Monte Carlo Search approach in order to get algorithms that (*i*) achieve a better scalability and (*ii*) can easily be extended to integrate operational constraints (unique shortest paths, delay, ...).

Monte Carlo Search algorithms have been successfully applied to many difficult problems but not yet to telecommunication networks optimization. We address in this paper the use of Monte-Carlo Search for this difficult problem. We compare UCT [26], Nested Monte Carlo Search (NMCS) [9] and Nested Rollout Policy Adaptation (NRPA) [32] which is an algorithm that learns a playout policy online on each instance. NMCS is an algorithm that works well for puzzles. It biases its playouts using lower level playouts. At level zero NMCS adopts a uniform random playout policy. Online learning of playout strategies combined with NMCS has given good results on optimization problems[31]. Other applications of NMCS include Single Player General Game Playing [28], Coding Theory [25], Cooperative Pathfinding [7], Software testing and heuristic Model-Checking [30], the Pancake problem, Games [13], Cryptography and the RNA inverse folding problem.

Online learning of a playout policy in the context of nested searches has been further developed for puzzles and optimization with Nested Rollout Policy Adaptation (NRPA) [32]. NRPA has found new world records in Morpion Solitaire and crosswords puzzles. Edelkamp, Cazenave and co-workers have applied the NRPA algorithm to multiple problems. They have optimized the algorithm for the Traveling Salesman with Time Windows (TSPTW) problem [15,16]. Other applications deal with 3D Packing with Object Orientation [18], the physical traveling salesman problem [19], the Multiple Sequence Alignment problem [20], Logistics [11,17], Graph Coloring [12] and Inverse Folding [10]. The principle of NRPA is to adapt the playout policy so as to learn the best sequence of moves found so far at each level.

The paper is organized as follows. Section 2 is devoted to the basic definitions and presentation of the optimization problem. Section 3 explains the application of Monte Carlo Search to the routing problem. Section 4 gives experimental results while concluding remarks and future research directions are given in Sect. 5.

2   Problem Formulation

In this paper we consider a bidirected graph that is a digraph where, for any arc uv, the reverse arc vu is also present. Given a bidirected graph $G = (V, A)$, every vertex $v \in V$ corresponds to a router while an arc uv corresponds to a link between routers u and v. Every arc uv is associated a capacity denoted by c_{uv}. Let K denote a set of demands or commodities to be routed in G. Each demand $k \in K$ is defined by a pair of vertices s^k and t^k representing the source and the target of k, a traffic volume D^k to be routed from s^k to t^k. Such a demand k will be denoted by the quadruplet (s^k, t^k, D^k). Given a metric $w \in Z_+^{|A|}$, each demand $k \in K$ is routed along the shortest paths between s^k and t^k. If there are more than one shortest paths joining the extremities of k, the traffic volume D^k is splitted evenly among those paths according to the so-called ECMP (Equal-Cost Multi-Path) rule. More precisely, the traffic volume that reaches a node $v \in V$ must be split equally among all arcs leaving v and belonging to the shortest paths toward destination t^k. We then define the *load* of an arc uv induced by w, denoted by $load(uv, w)$, as the amount of traffic traversing the arc uv over its capacity (see Fig. 1). The *congestion* $cong(w)$ of a given metric w is defined by $\max_{uv \in A} load(uv, w)$, that is the maximum load over all arcs.

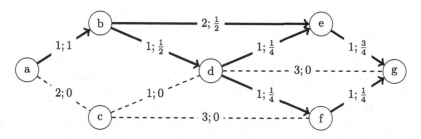

Fig. 1. Illustration of a shortest path routing with the ECMP rule. In this figure, we assume unit capacities and suppose that a demand k with traffic volume $D^k = 1$ must be routed from $s^k = a$ to $t^k = g$. A label $w_{uv}; load(uv, w)$ is associated to each arc $uv \in A$.

We are now in position to define the optimization problem studied in this paper. The MINIMUM CONGESTION SHORTEST PATH ROUTING (MIN-CON-SPR) problem is to find a metric $w \in Z_+^{|A|}$ and the routing paths induced by these weights such that the network congestion $cong(w)$ is minimum. The problem MIN-CON-SPR can be defined formally as follows:

MIN-CON-SPR

Input: A bidirected graph $G = (V, A)$, where each arc uv has a capacity $c_{uv} \geq 0$ and a set of communities K defined for each $k \in K$ by the quadruplet (s^k, t^k, D^k).

Output: A metric $w \in Z_+^{|A|}$ of minimum congestion $cong(w)$.

In this paper, we also consider the MIN-CON-SPR problem with some or all of the following additional constraints

> **Unicity:** In this constraint, we require that each demand is routed along a uniquely determined shortest path.
>
> **Delay:** This constraint requires that the routing paths have length at most the length of a shortest (s^k, t^k)-path (in terms of number of arcs) plus a constant $c \in N^+$.

From an operational point of view, the unicity constraint is sometimes required by the network manager to monitor the flow circulating in the system more easily. In addition to minimizing the congestion, the delay constraint ensure a certain level of QoS regarding the latency of answering the requests made by the clients.

It is worth noting that all of our results regarding the delay constraint can easily be extended to the more general case where each arc is associated with a latency value and each demand k has a delay value Δ^k and must be routed along shortest paths with total latency value less than Δ^k.

3   Monte Carlo Search on Routing Problem

Monte Carlo Search is a general optimization technique. We detail in this section how it can be used and improved for MIN-CON-SPR with or without the previous additional constraints.

3.1   Monte Carlo Search

In this section, we present three different Monte Carlo search-based approaches which are applicable to the target problem. The first approach is UCT (Upper Confidence Trees), which uses bandit ideas to guide Monte Carlo planning [26]. Assuming the state s, playouts will be completed in a certain amount of time and statistics about the states and the actions will be collected. Supposing the action space for state s is $\mathcal{A}(s)$, the action a is chosen such that the upper bound of the score is maximized:

$$a_s = \arg\max_{a \in \mathcal{A}(s)} \left(\bar{Q}_{s,a} + \tau \sqrt{\frac{\ln(N_s)}{N_{s,a}}} \right)$$

where $\bar{Q}_{s,a}$ is the estimated score of the action a at state s, N_s is the number of times state s was visited, $N_{s,a}$ is the number of times action a was selected at state s. τ is a constant value which controls the degree of exploration.

Another approach is NMCS (Nested Monte Carlo Search) [13]. By nesting the evaluation function inside another evaluation function, the ability of the traditional Monte Carlo is greatly improved. However this approach is more sensible to the size of the search space.

Algorithm 1: The playout algorithm

Function playout(*state, policy*):

    sequence ← []

    while *state is not terminal* **do**

        $z \leftarrow \sum_{a' \in \mathcal{A}(state)} e^{policy[code(state,a')]}$

        Draw a with probability $\frac{1}{z} e^{policy[code(state,a)]}$

        state ← play(*state, a*)

        append a to *sequence*

    end

    return (score(*state*), *sequence*)

NRPA (Nested Rollout Policy Adaptation) [32] is also used in our study. The NRPA can be decomposed into three principal functions: the playout function, the adapt function and the NRPA function. The Algorithms 1 and 2 show the three functions respectively. The NRPA use a domain specific code *code(state, a)* for the action a in the representation of the policy, where many actions may share the same code, and actions with different codes are searched separately. For each nesting level, NRPA recursively calls to the lower level, searching to improve its current best score. When it succeeds, the best score of the corresponding state *score(state)* is updated, and the current action sequence is recorded as the best sequence.

Algorithm 2: The adapt and NRPA algorithm

Function adapt (*policy, sequence, α*):

> *pol ← policy*
> *state ← root*
> **for** *a in sequence* **do**
>> $z \leftarrow \sum_{a' \in \mathcal{A}(state)} e^{policy[code(state,a')]}$
>> $\forall a' \in \mathcal{A}(state), pol[code(state, a')] \mathrel{-}= \alpha * \frac{1}{z} e^{policy[code(state,a')]}$
>> $pol[code(state, a)] \mathrel{+}= \alpha$
>> *state ←* play(*state, a*)
>
> **end**
> **return** *pol*

end

Function NRPA (*level, policy*):

> **if** *level* == 0 **then**
>> **return** playout(*root, policy*)
>
> **end**
> **else**
>> *bestScore ←* inf
>> **for** *N iterations* **do**
>>> *(result, new) ←* NRPA(*level − 1, policy*)
>>> **if** *result ≤ bestScore* **then**
>>>> *bestScore ← result*
>>>> *seq ← new*
>>>
>>> **end**
>>> *policy ←* adapt(*policy, seq*)
>>
>> **end**
>> **return** *(bestScore, seq)*
>
> **end**

end

3.2   Modeling with Monte Carlo Search

To model the MIN-CON-SPR problem with Monte Carlo Search algorithms, we suppose that a solution to the MIN-CON-SPR problem is represented by a point (i.e. the metric $w = \langle w_1, w_2, ..., w_{|A|} \rangle$) in the discrete space $[1, 65535]^{|A|}$. To reduce the search space, we set the value space of the metric as a subspace W of the original space $[1, 65535]$.

For each playout, the metric of the graph is assigned and the objective function is evaluated. In our case, $cong(w)$ is used as the score. After obtaining the congestion of the graph, an additional bias will be added in the case that the constraints are not fully satisfied, which will encourage the algorithm to explore the solutions with smaller congestion value which satisfies all the constraints. The final score for state s is then $Q_s = cong(w) + cost(\text{unchecked\_constraints})$.

Furthermore, we assume that the arcs of a graph have a default order, and the metric values corresponding to them are assigned sequentially. Thus, an action a is therefore a choice of metric values for an arc, and the state s is uniquely determined by the metric values already assigned to the arcs. For NRPA, the domain-specific code is uniquely determined by the node of the graph to which the metric is currently to be assigned.

3.3 Improvement

In order to improve the stability of the NRPA algorithm, a stabilized version of NRPA is proposed in [14] to encourage exploration before the adaptation of the policy. During the level 0 of NRPA, instead of running a single playout and use its result as the score, multiple playouts will be performed and only the best result will be used as the score. It improves the average scores for many problems. In our experiments, the stabilized NRPA also achieved better performance than the original NRPA. For brevity, we denote the stabilized NRPA with m playouts as NRPA(m).

We also found that, during the execution of the NRPA, for small and medium-sized graphs, the algorithm tends to prefer exploitation over exploration, which means that the same metric would be obtained many times without exploring new ones. To avoid or limit this behavior, we propose to (i) use a hashtable to record all explored metrics and their scores to avoid recalculation of the congestion and (ii) a *force_exploration* mechanism, which can be of independent interest for the NRPA algorithm. This mechanism works as follows: firstly, all explored metrics w are recorded with their hash codes. Instead of just proposing the metric based on the policy, if one metric has already been explored, a random metric value will be assigned to a random arc of the graph until the generated new metric have never been explored. This simple technique increases the exploration to the maximum, without changing the original NRPA's mechanic. We find that *force_exploration* greatly increases the performance of the NRPA and Stabilized NRPA.

For some graphs, it is difficult to find routing metrics that satisfy all constraints, especially unique path constraints. In such cases, using a unique metric for each arc can greatly increase the proportion of results that satisfy the constraints. However, this limits the number of metrics to be greater than or equal to the number of arcs. This will in many cases increase the proportion of valid solutions, *i.e.* solutions that satisfy the constraints. But as we will show later, in the absence of constraints, this restriction reduces the quality of the solution.

4   Experimental Results

The algorithms are implemented in C++ and the experiments are done on a server (64-core Intel(R) Xeon(R) Gold 5218 CPU), with 125 GB of memory. Only one core is used during the experiments.

4.1   Dataset

The experiments are done on several graphs from SNDlib [29] of different sizes. In addition to these instances, some random graphs are also generated using the same configuration as in [23]. The nodes are generated uniformly in a unit square, and the probability of having an arc between any two nodes is determined by a constant. The capacity of all arcs is set to 1000. We also used Waxman graphs [23] for our test. The probability of having an arc between two nodes is given by:

$$p(u,v) = \alpha e^{\frac{-d(u,v)}{\beta d_{\max}}}$$

where $d(u,v)$ is the Euclidean distance between u and v, $d_{\max}$ is the Maximum Euclidean distance between any two nodes, α and β are parameters which control the density of the graph. The capacities of the arcs are also set to 1000.

For the generated graphs, demands are generated the same way as [23], i.e., the traffic volume D^k for demand k between nodes s^k and t^k is:

$$D^k = \alpha S_{s^k} T_{t^k} C_{(s^k,t^k)} e^{\frac{-d(s^k,t^k)}{2d_{\max}}}$$

where $S_u, T_u \in [0,1]$ are two random numbers for node u, and $C_{(s,t)} \in [0,1]$ is a random number for couple (s,t). Every generated graph is verified to be connected. Table 1 shows the information of the graphs we used in our experiments. Each graph is pre-processed before the computation: all arcs connected to isolated nodes have a pre-determined metric, since their values do not affect the traffic and therefore are not considered again in the Monte Carlo computation.

Table 1. Information of networks: network name, number of nodes, number of arcs, number of demands, total demand, maximum demand

Name	$|V|$	$|A|$	$|K|$	$\sum D^k$	$\max(D^k)$	Name	$|V|$	$|A|$	$|K|$	$\sum D^k$	$\max(D^k)$
abilene	12	30	132	3000002	424969	rand50a	50	132	2450	81419	251
atlanta	15	44	210	136726	7275	rand50b	50	278	2450	86981	249
newyork	16	98	240	1774	42	rand100a	100	278	9900	269535	240
france	25	90	300	99830	1808	rand100b	100	534	9900	307699	228
norway	27	102	702	5348	14	wax50a	50	142	2450	85150	235
nobel-us	14	42	91	5420	324	wax50b	50	298	2450	82208	221
nobel-ger	17	52	121	660	50	wax100a	100	284	9900	331386	270
nobel-eu	28	82	378	1898	54	wax100b	100	492	9900	293799	243
brain	161	332	14311	12.3e9	69.1e6						

4.2   Comparison of the Monte Carlo Algorithms

With both unique path and delay constraints applied, the Monte Carlo search approaches are evaluated during a limited runtime.

During our experiments, we found that executing several different runs was generally better than executing only one long run, because different runs allows the policy to start over, thus avoiding the algorithm getting stuck at some local minimum. Table 2 shows the average score of each approach on 5 executions. Since for a limited period of time, UCT and NRPA can perform multiple runs of short duration or one long run, we kept both results for comparison. For NRPA and Stabilized NRPA, only force exploration is used.

Table 2. Comparison of the best scores of Monte Carlo Search Algorithms in limited runtime with all constraints. Format: average score of 5 executions (number of executions in which no valid solution was found). "–": no valid solution is found in all executions.

Class	Name	Runtime (min)	$|W|$	UCT		NMCS	NRPA		NRPA(10)
				Multiple	Single		Multiple	Single	
SNDlib	abilene	10	50	65.158	87.108	60.905	60.905	60.905	60.905
	atlanta	10	50	2.9608	4.3968	2.3626	2.318	2.318	2.318
	newyork	30	100	0.1255(1)	0.172(4)	0.0978	0.0636	0.062	0.0622
	france	30	100	3.983	–	3.20836	2.892	2.92	2.9268
	norway	60	150	–	–	0.508(2)	0.3054	0.295	0.3042
	nobel-us	10	50	29.48	35.04	25.68	25.2	25.2	25.2
	nobel-ger	10	100	4.44	6.06	4.4	4.4	4.4	4.4
	nobel-eu	30	100	12.08	14.6(3)	10.94	10.7	10.88	10.74
	brain	60	50	1.002	1.0513	0.9848	0.974	0.961	0.98

The table very clearly shows that NRPA and its variants outperform the other two MC methods. Moreover, the number of playouts of NRPA does not depend on the size of the graph or the size of the metric space, which makes it easier to scale the algorithm to larger graphs and search spaces. As for NMCS, it performs well with smaller graphs and small search spaces, but does not scale well to larger cases. Therefore, in the subsequent experiments, we will only consider the use of NRPA-based algorithms.

Since there are many variants for NRPA, we first investigated the effect of these techniques. Figure 2 shows the distribution of the scores on several SNDlib graphs with different techniques of NRPA. The more the distribution is concentrated around the low values, the higher the chance of getting lower congestion values, thus the better this configuration is.

The distribution clearly demonstrates the improvement of *force_exploration* for NRPA and stabilized NRPA, while stabilized NRPA greatly increases the ratio of valid solutions. However the effect of unique metrics is not as obvious, and this extra constraint can sometimes make it more difficult to find better results.

4.3   Impact of the Metric Space

Although in many previous studies of heuristics, the metric space is generally a continuous set of integers, in the course of our research, we found that the

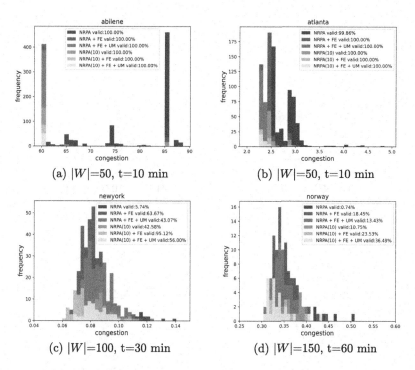

Fig. 2. Distribution of the congestion values with all constraints on SNDlib graphs

metric space has an important impact on the performance of the algorithm. For example, compared to a continuous set of integers or the set of prime numbers, a set of random numbers of the same size usually gives a much higher rate of valid solutions. Figure 3 shows an example of the distribution of scores obtained with different metric spaces of the same size. The random numbers are uniformly pre-generated in $[1, 65535]$, and remain the same during the experiment.

We also find out that for most graphs, when no constraints are applied, a smaller metric space helps the algorithm to converge better because the algorithm can better explore the search space. Figure 4 shows the convergence of different metric space sizes. However when unique path and delay constraints are applied, a small metric space can make it more difficult to find a metric that induces a valid solution. Therefore, increasing the search space can greatly increase the chance of obtaining a solution that satisfies all constraints. Figure 5 shows the influence of the metric space on the percentage of valid solutions.

4.4   Comparison

In this test, we compare the congestion value computed by our algorithm after a fixed amount of time with the congestion values obtained via other common approaches. The first approach for the problem, which is also the most basic approach is the UnitOSPF, which assigns all arcs the same unit metric value.

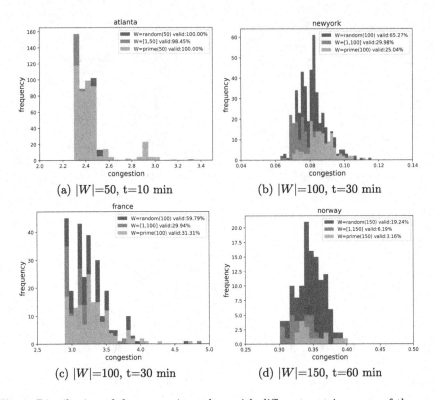

Fig. 3. Distribution of the congestion values with different metric spaces of the same size using NRPA with *force_exploration*

InvCapOSPF is another approach recommended by Cisco, which sets the metric inversely proportional to the arc's capacity. However, in many graphs the capacity on all arcs is the same, so in many cases this method will give the same results as UnitOSPF. We also compare our algorithm with the local search IGP-WO implemented in [27] and based on [23]. We slightly modify the objective function of IGP-WO to minimize the congestion and, when considering the unicity constraint, add a high penalty for solutions that violate that constraint. We did not further modify the algorithm to take into account the delay constraint as this would require deeper modifications and understanding of the implementation of IGP-WO.

In order to evaluate the quality of the heuristic solutions, we compare them with the optimal value obtained using the compact formulation of the MAXIMUM CONCURRENT FLOW (MCF) problem. It is not hard to see that any optimal solution for MCF is a lower bound for MIN-CON-SPR (denoted LPLB for Linear Programming Lower Bound). Indeed, a solution of a MCF instance defines routing paths for each demand that are not constrained to follow the ECMP rule or being induced by shortest paths w.r.t some metric.

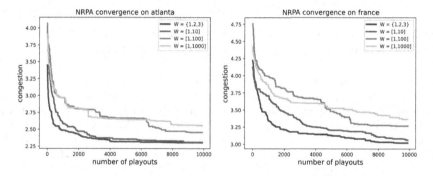

Fig. 4. Convergence of NRPA without constraints. The score is averaged on 10 runs.

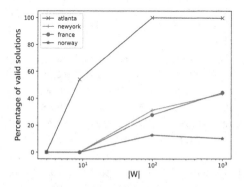

Fig. 5. Size of the metric space has a positive impact on the valid solution ratio when constraints are applied. The result is averaged on 1000 runs

Table 3 shows the comparison of the results. To keep the results consistent across configurations, for NRPA, the metric space size and computation time of each graph are consistent with those shown in Table 2 for the constrained cases. For all generated graphs, the metric space size is 250, and the computation time is 30 min for graphs of 50 nodes, 60 min for graphs of 100 nodes. However when no constraints are applied, the metric space for all graphs is set to $[1, 3]$ for better performance. The scores are averaged on 5 executions.

For random graphs and waxman graphs, the applied delay constraint is often too restrictive so that no valid solutions can be found. In this paper, we propose an automatic delay relaxation mechanism that allows the NRPA algorithm to relax the delay constraint when it is difficult to find a valid solution.

In the initial state, the delay constraint is actually defined as the length of the shortest path (in terms of arcs) plus one for each demand. We relax the constraint to shortest path plus c, where $c \in N^+$. Assuming that the computation has a target time or total number of runs T, we divide all the computations into different phases. At each stage, we count the total number of runned playouts, the number of valid solutions and the number of solutions that violate the delay constraint. After $T \times (1 - \frac{1}{2^c})$ time or iterations, if the percentage of valid solutions is less than 5% and the percentage of results that violate the delay constraint is greater than 10%, we move to the next stage, where all statistics are recalculated and $c = c + 1$, until c reaches a maximum provided value c_{max}.

Table 3. Maximum congestion value of state-of-the-art heuristics and our NRPA. For each constraint configuration ("Without constraints", "Unicity" and "All" *i.e.* both "Unicity" and "Delay") and each heuristic (if available for the given configuration), we show the congestion induced by the computed weights. This value is in bold if it is the best one among those returned by the other heuristics (w.r.t the configuration). In addition, a value is followed by * if equal to the lower bound LPLB (which is reported in the last column). Finally, an entry $c = i$ indicates the minimum value i of c for which we were able to find a solution when considering all constraints.

Name	Without constraints				Unicity		All	LPLB
	Unit OSPF	InvCap OSPF	IGP-WO [27]	NRPA	IGP-WO	NRPA	NRPA	
abilene	187.55	89.48	60.42	**60.412**	60.41	**60.41**	60.90	60.411
atlanta	3.26	3.37	**2.22**	**2.22**	**2.29**	**2.29**	2.32	2.18
newyork	0.076	0.076	**0.051**	0.053	**0.062**	0.065	0.064	0.045
france	4.12	4.12	**2.53**	2.56	**2.88**	**2.88**	2.89	2.41
norway	0.42	0.42	**0.28**	0.29	**0.29**	0.30	0.31	0.27
nobel-us	37.15	37.15	**24.4**	24.7	**24.7**	**24.7**	25.2	24.2
nobel-ger	5.54	5.54	3.9	**3.89**	4.4	**4.4**	4.4	3.87
nobel-eu	13.31	13.31	10.68	**10.67***	10.7	**10.7**	10.7	10.67
brain	1.415	1.415	0.962	**0.903***	0.972	**0.972**	0.974	0.903
rand50a	7.9	7.9	**5.55**	5.77	**5.84**	5.92	5.96(c = 2)	5.55
rand50b	**2.88***	**2.88***	**2.88***	**2.88***	–	**2.88**	2.88(c = 3)	2.88
rand100a	15.71	15.71	10.42	**9.59**	–	**10.35**	10.76(c = 4)	9.35
rand100b	4.15	4.15	4.38	**3.85**	–	**6.06**	5.94(c = 5)	3.76
wax50a	6.46	6.46	**4.63**	4.66	**4.665**	4.67	4.71(c = 2)	4.59
wax50b	**2.279***	**2.279***	2.284	**2.279***	–	**2.279**	2.279(c = 3)	2.279
wax100a	17.46	17.46	15.049	**15.048**	–	**15.049**	15.049(c = 4)	15.048
wax100b	5.51	5.51	4.14	**4.04**	–	**5.86**	5.91(c = 5)	3.44

The results show that NRPA performs very well for all three different constraint configurations on all sizes of graphs and is very close to the lower bound. Compared to local search, our algorithm gives better results in most cases. At the same time, only very little computational time and resources are used. The different runs can be computed in parallel, which substantially improves the running time of NRPA.

The proposed automatic delay relaxation mechanism is not the best way to solve the problem of minimizing the congestion of the graph while keeping the delay minimized. Nevertheless, we obtained rather encouraging results that show the strong adaptability of our approach and a promising potential for solving even more difficult variants of the problem (single-link failure, oblivious routing, capacity planning, . . .).

4.5 Random Dense Graphs

For dense networks, the number of potential routing paths increases rapidly, which makes the problem even harder to solve in particular with the unicity constraint, as observed in [5]. We show that NRPA can easily scale up to graphs with large amount of nodes and arcs. So we generated ten random graphs of different sizes with the same generation mechanism as described in Sect. 4.1, and the traffic between two nodes are generated with a probability of 0.1. The largest graph contains 1000 nodes and 99450 arcs.

Figure 6 shows the scores of the random graphs without constraints. The metric space is set to [1,3] for both local search and NRPA algorithms, and the scores of NRPA are averaged on 10 executions.

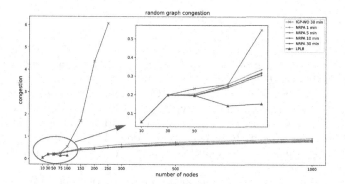

Fig. 6. Congestion with respect to the number of the nodes

Regarding the LPLB bound, with a compact formulation, we were not able to compute the lower bounds for instances larger than 100 nodes because the random graphs are more dense and thus the problem is too large to be solved. In future experiments, using a non-compact path formulation of the MCF may greatly improve the chances of obtaining lower bounds for larger graphs.

The results show that on large graphs, local search does not provide acceptable results within an execution time of 30 min. On the contrary, even on graphs with thousands of nodes, our method still gives reasonable results in a very short time.

5 Conclusion

In this work we applied for the first time the Monte Carlo Search approach in the context of setting efficient weights in IP networks, in particular for the MIN-CON-SPR problem. The principle of the Monte Carlo Search algorithm is to learn a policy online on each instance using nested levels of best solutions. We compare several Monte Carlo methods and propose the most appropriate to the target problem. Experiments show that for instances from the literature our approach is comparable with the existing ones. Nevertheless, for graphs of larger size, our approach outperforms the local search heuristics and gives results close to the lower bound. At the same time, this approach can be easily extended for problems with additional constraints and is not sensitive to the size of the graph or the size of the search space in particular the number of available weights, giving it a large range of applications. Furthermore, for the unsplittable case, this method may provide optimal solutions (or close to the optimal) for instances where exact approaches fail, especially for dense graphs [5]. For some instances where it is not possible to find a way to satisfy all the constraints, we also propose a mechanism for automatically relaxing the constraints. Another algorithm specifically aimed at optimizing congestion with the lowest possible delay constraint will be the direction of subsequent research.

References

1. Altin, A., Fortz, B., Thorup, M., Ümit, H.: Intra-domain traffic engineering with shortest path routing protocols. Ann. Oper. Res. **204**(1), 65–95 (2013). https://doi.org/10.1007/s10479-012-1270-7
2. Altin, A., Fortz, B., Ümit, H.: Oblivious OSPF routing with weight optimization under polyhedral demand uncertainty. Networks **60**(2), 132–139 (2012)
3. Benhamiche, A., Chopin, M.: Toward scalable algorithms for the unsplittable shortest path routing problem. Research report, Orange Labs (2020)
4. Bley, A.: Approximability of unsplittable shortest path routing problems. Networks **54**(1), 23–46 (2009)
5. Bley, A.: An integer programming algorithm for routing optimization in IP networks. Algorithmica **60**(1), 21–45 (2011)
6. Bley, A., Fortz, B., Gourdin, É., Holmberg, K., Klopfenstein, O., Pióro, M., Tomaszewski, A., Ümit, H.: Optimization of OSPF routing in IP networks. In: Koster, A., Muñoz, X. (eds.) Graphs and Algorithms in Communication Networks: Studies in Broadband, Optical, Wireless and Ad Hoc Networks. An EATCS Series, pp. 199–240. Springer, Heidelberg (2010). https://doi.org/10.1007/978-3-642-02250-0_8
7. Bouzy, B.: Monte-Carlo fork search for cooperative path-finding. In: Cazenave, T., Winands, M.H.M., Iida, H. (eds.) CGW 2013. CCIS, vol. 408, pp. 1–15. Springer, Cham (2014). https://doi.org/10.1007/978-3-319-05428-5_1
8. Buriol, L.S., Resende, M.G.C., Ribeiro, C.C., Thorup, M.: A hybrid genetic algorithm for the weight setting problem in OSPF/IS-IS routing. Networks **46**(1), 36–56 (2005)
9. Cazenave, T.: Nested Monte-Carlo search. In: Boutilier, C. (ed.) IJCAI, pp. 456–461 (2009)
10. Cazenave, T., Fournier, T.: Monte Carlo inverse folding. In: Monte Search at IJCAI (2020)
11. Cazenave, T., Lucas, J., Triboulet, T., Kim, H.: Policy adaptation for vehicle routing. Ai Commun. (2021)
12. Cazenave, T., Negrevergne, B., Sikora, F.: Monte Carlo graph coloring. In: Monte Search at IJCAI (2020)
13. Cazenave, T., Saffidine, A., Schofield, M.J., Thielscher, M.: Nested Monte Carlo search for two-player games. In: AAAI, pp. 687–693 (2016)

14. Cazenave, T., Sevestre, J.B., Toulemont, M.: Stabilized nested rollout policy adaptation. In: Monte Search at IJCAI (2020)
15. Cazenave, T., Teytaud, F.: Application of the nested rollout policy adaptation algorithm to the traveling salesman problem with time windows. In: Hamadi, Y., Schoenauer, M. (eds.) LION 2012. LNCS, pp. 42–54. Springer, Heidelberg (2012). https://doi.org/10.1007/978-3-642-34413-8_4
16. Edelkamp, S., Gath, M., Cazenave, T., Teytaud, F.: Algorithm and knowledge engineering for the TSPTW problem. In: 2013 IEEE Symposium on Computational Intelligence in Scheduling (SCIS), pp. 44–51. IEEE (2013)
17. Edelkamp, S., Gath, M., Greulich, C., Humann, M., Herzog, O., Lawo, M.: Monte-Carlo tree search for logistics. In: Clausen, U., Friedrich, H., Thaller, C., Geiger, C. (eds.) Commercial Transport. LNL, pp. 427–440. Springer, Cham (2016). https://doi.org/10.1007/978-3-319-21266-1_28
18. Edelkamp, S., Gath, M., Rohde, M.: Monte-Carlo tree search for 3D packing with object orientation. In: Lutz, C., Thielscher, M. (eds.) KI 2014. LNCS (LNAI), vol. 8736, pp. 285–296. Springer, Cham (2014). https://doi.org/10.1007/978-3-319-11206-0_28
19. Edelkamp, S., Greulich, C.: Solving physical traveling salesman problems with policy adaptation. In: 2014 IEEE Conference on Computational Intelligence and Games (CIG), pp. 1–8. IEEE (2014)
20. Edelkamp, S., Tang, Z.: Monte-Carlo tree search for the multiple sequence alignment problem. In: SOCS 2015, pp. 9–17. AAAI Press (2015)
21. Ericsson, M., Resende, M.G.C., Pardalos, P.M.: A genetic algorithm for the weight setting problem in OSPF routing. J. Comb. Optim. 6(3), 299–333 (2002). https://doi.org/10.1023/A:1014852026591
22. Fortz, B.: Applications of meta-heuristics to traffic engineering in IP networks. Int. Trans. Oper. Res. 18(2), 131–147 (2011)
23. Fortz, B., Thorup, M.: Increasing internet capacity using local search. Comput. Optim. Appl. 29, 13–48 (2000). https://doi.org/10.1023/B:COAP.0000039487.35027.02
24. Fortz, B., Thorup, M.: Robust optimization of OSPF/IS-IS weights. In: INOC, pp. 225–230 (2003)
25. Kinny, D.: A new approach to the snake-in-the-box problem. In: ECAI 2012, pp. 462–467. IOS Press (2012)
26. Kocsis, L., Szepesvári, C.: Bandit based Monte-Carlo planning. In: Fürnkranz, J., Scheffer, T., Spiliopoulou, M. (eds.) ECML 2006. LNCS (LNAI), vol. 4212, pp. 282–293. Springer, Heidelberg (2006). https://doi.org/10.1007/11871842_29
27. Leduc, G., et al.: An open source traffic engineering toolbox. Comput. Commun. 29(5), 593–610 (2006)
28. Méhat, J., Cazenave, T.: Combining UCT and Nested Monte Carlo search for single-player general game playing. IEEE TCIAIG 2(4), 271–277 (2010)
29. Orlowski, S., Pióro, M., Tomaszewski, A., Wessäly, R.: SNDlib 1.0-survivable network design library. Networks 55(3), 276–286 (2010)
30. Poulding, S.M., Feldt, R.: Heuristic model checking using a Monte-Carlo tree search algorithm. In: GECCO, pp. 1359–1366 (2015)
31. Rimmel, A., Teytaud, F., Cazenave, T.: Optimization of the Nested Monte-Carlo algorithm on the traveling salesman problem with time windows. In: Di Chio, C., et al. (eds.) EvoApplications 2011. LNCS, vol. 6625, pp. 501–510. Springer, Heidelberg (2011). https://doi.org/10.1007/978-3-642-20520-0_51
32. Rosin, C.D.: Nested rollout policy adaptation for Monte Carlo Tree search. In: IJCAI, pp. 649–654 (2011)

Energy and Emission Prediction for Mixed-Vehicle Transit Fleets Using Multi-task and Inductive Transfer Learning

Michael Wilbur[1]([✉]), Ayan Mukhopadhyay[1], Sayyed Vazirizade[1],
Philip Pugliese[2], Aron Laszka[3], and Abhishek Dubey[1]

[1] Vanderbilt University, Nashville, TN 37203, USA
michael.p.wilbur@vanderbilt.edu
[2] Chattanooga Area Regional Transportation Authority, Chattanooga, TN, USA
[3] University of Houston, Houston, TX, USA

Abstract. Public transit agencies are focused on making their fixed-line bus systems more energy efficient by introducing electric (EV) and hybrid (HV) vehicles to their fleets. However, because of the high upfront cost of these vehicles, most agencies are tasked with managing a mixed-fleet of internal combustion vehicles (ICEVs), EVs, and HVs. In managing mixed-fleets, agencies require accurate predictions of energy use for optimizing the assignment of vehicles to transit routes, scheduling charging, and ensuring that emission standards are met. The current state-of-the-art is to develop separate neural network models to predict energy consumption for each vehicle class. Although different vehicle classes' energy consumption depends on a varied set of covariates, we hypothesize that there are broader generalizable patterns that govern energy consumption and emissions. In this paper, we seek to extract these patterns to aid learning to address two problems faced by transit agencies. First, in the case of a transit agency which operates many ICEVs, HVs, and EVs, we use multi-task learning (MTL) to improve accuracy of forecasting energy consumption. Second, in the case where there is a significant variation in vehicles in each category, we use inductive transfer learning (ITL) to improve predictive accuracy for vehicle class models with insufficient data. As this work is to be deployed by our partner agency, we also provide an online pipeline for joining the various sensor streams for fixed-line transit energy prediction. We find that our approach outperforms vehicle-specific baselines in both the MTL and ITL settings.

Keywords: Energy prediction · Smart transit · Transfer learning · Multi-task learning

1 Introduction

Context: Public transit agencies are focused on finding ways to make their fixed-line bus systems more energy efficient by introducing electric vehicles (EVs)

© Springer Nature Switzerland AG 2021
Y. Dong et al. (Eds.): ECML PKDD 2021, LNAI 12978, pp. 502–517, 2021.
https://doi.org/10.1007/978-3-030-86514-6_31

and hybrid vehicles (HVs), which have reduced impacts on the environment in comparison to traditional vehicles with internal combustion engines (ICEVs). However, EVs and HVs are expensive and in practice, transit agencies have to manage a mixed-vehicle fleet, requiring complex scheduling and assignment procedures to maximize the overall energy efficiency [13,20,23] while satisfying the expectations of transit demand. This is turn requires the ability to estimate energy and emissions of vehicles on assigned routes and trips. Energy prediction models can be categorized based on their modeling scale. Microscopic models aim to estimate vehicle energy consumption at a high frequency [2]; however, this comes at the cost of reduced accuracy. For most system level optimization, macroscopic models that aim to predict energy consumption at an aggregated spatial or temporal span are sufficient [1,2].

State of the Art: There has been significant research on macroscopic models for EVs over recent years. For example, De Cauwer et al. used a cascade of ANN and linear regression models for energy consumption prediction for EVs using vehicle speed, voltage, current, SoC, road network characteristics, altitude, and weather [6]. Their model, however, did not use traffic data and the approach had a mean absolute error (MAE) of 12–14% of average trip consumption. Vepsäläinen et al. used a linear model using temperature, driver behavior, and roadway characteristics and found that EV energy consumption was 15% lower on suburban routes compared to city routes. A recent study by Pamula et al. used a DNN with stacked autoencoders and an multi-layer perceptron to predict energy consumption between stops. Their model used travel time, elevation change, and modeled weather as categorical variables [17]. However, most of the prior work relied on learning separate models for each vehicle class [1,3,17].

Challenges: There are several unresolved challenges for public transit operations teams. First, modern public bus fleets include not only a mix of vehicle classes (ICEV, HV, and EV), but also different vehicle models within each class. For example, out partner agency, Chattanooga Area Regional Transportation Authority (CARTA), manages a total of six ICEV models, two HV models, and two EV models. Training separate models for each type of vehicle ignores generalizable information that is not explicitly modeled in the feature space. For example, Ayman et al. modeled EVs and ICEVs without sharing model parameters between classes [1]. Second, the number of vehicles in each class varies greatly, which leads to an uneven distribution of data available for training the energy or emission prediction models. Third, and similar to the second problem in principle, when a new vehicle class is added to an existing fleet, the agency must deploy *some* vehicles, obtain data, and then learn a new predictive model from scratch.

Our Contributions: We address these challenges as multi-task learning (MTL) and inductive transfer learning (ITL) problems. Although different vehicle classes' energy consumption depends on a varied set of covariates through different nonlinear functions, we hypothesize that there are broader generalizable patterns that govern the consumption of energy and vehicle emission. That is, if an agency has access to *many* vehicles, and consequently data, from each vehicle class (ICEVs,

HVs, and EVs), we formulate emission (and energy) forecasting as an MTL problem. We show that this approach improves the predictive accuracy for all vehicle classes compared to a baseline where separate networks are trained to predict emissions (and energy) for each class. In a situation with imbalanced data or when an agency introduces a new model or class, we show that it is possible to learn a model for classes with sufficient data, and *transfer* the learned abstraction to improve the predictive accuracy for the class with insufficient data. The benefit of ITL is the ability to deploy the model earlier than the time required to collect enough samples to train a separate model for the new class. Finally, we highlight that real-world transit problems require collecting, cleaning, and joining data from various sources, formats, and precision. We provide a general online pipeline for joining the various sensor streams (vehicle telemetry and trajectory data with external data sources such as weather, traffic, and road infrastructure) for training and maintaining the fixed-line transit energy prediction models. We evaluate our MTL and ITL models using real-world data from our partner agency's mixed-fleet of EVs, HVs, and ICEVs. We show that in both the MTL and ITL settings, our approach outperforms state-of-the-art methods. The greatest improvements over baselines were in the ITL setting when the target vehicle class suffers from a lack of data. However, we also find that in some cases ITL does not work well, such as when transferring learned abstractions from EV to ICEV.

2 Model

2.1 Predicting Energy Consumed and Emissions

Transit agencies are concerned with reducing a) costs by limiting energy used, and b) the impact of their vehicles on the environment by reducing emissions. For ICEVs and HVs, energy expended by a vehicle is a function of the fuel consumed, measured in liters. On the other hand, the energy expended by an EV is a function of the dissipated charge of its battery, which is the change in its state-of-charge (SOC). This presents a problem since transit agencies primarily use prediction models to optimize the assignment of vehicles to trips. As a consequence, they require a common metric to compare across vehicle classes in their mixed-fleet for both energy consumed and emissions. For energy, we use kWh. For ICEVs and HVs, we convert liters of diesel fuel consumed to kWh using a conversion rate of 10.639 kWh/liter [7]. For EVs, we multiply the change in SOC and the capacity of the battery. We measure emissions as kg of CO_2. For ICEVs and HVs, fuel consumed in liters can be converted to emissions (kg CO_2) at a rate of 2.689 kg/liter [8]. For EVs, dissipation in charge can be converted to emissions (kg CO_2) at a rate of 0.707 kg/kWh [8]. As shown in Fig. 1, the function $g_i(\hat{Y}_i)$ represents the linear conversion between the predicted target (emission) and energy consumed for an arbitrary vehicle class denoted by the index i.

2.2 Preliminaries and Model Formulation

Our goal is to learn energy consumption and emissions in a mixed fleet of vehicles conditional on a set of relevant determinants (Fig. 1). We refer to learning

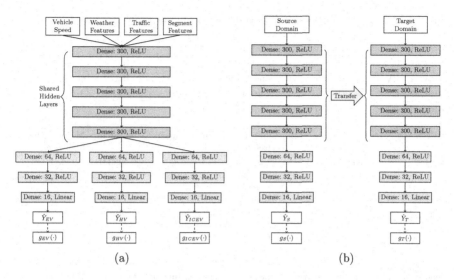

Fig. 1. (a) MTL Model: DNN with hard parameter sharing for predicting emissions (kg CO_2) of EVs ($\hat{Y}_{EV}$), HVs ($\hat{Y}_{HV}$) and ICEVs ($\hat{Y}_{ICEV}$). (b) ITL Model: shared-hidden layer parameters are frozen and transfered to the target model. Energy consumed (kWh) is a linear function $g_i(\cdot)$ for vehicle class i, separate of the neural network per the conversion discussed in Sect. 2.1.

prediction models as *tasks*, consistent with the terminology in the area of transfer learning [18]. We introduce the formalism for our problem next. We define a *domain* $\mathcal{D}$ as the combination of a feature space $\mathcal{X}$ and a probability distribution $P(X)$, where $X = \{x_1, x_2, \dots\} \in \mathcal{X}$. For example, $\mathcal{X}$ can include features like vehicle speed and weather. Given a specific domain, a *task* is then defined as $\mathcal{T} = \{\mathcal{Y}, f(\cdot)\}$ where $\mathcal{Y}$ is the space of output labels, and f is a predictive function over $y \in \mathcal{Y}$ conditional on x. Probabilistically, f denotes the probability of a realization of y given x ($P(y \mid x)$). For example, Y can denote the energy consumed by a vehicle, and subsequently, the function f can be used to denote a distribution on the energy consumed conditional on the determinants. Typically, f is unknown; instead, we assume access to observations (data) in the form of input-output pairs $\{(x_1, y_1), (x_2, y_2), \dots, (x_m, y_m)\}$. We deal with a scenario with multiple tasks (and associated domains). Specifically, there are three vehicle classes, and therefore three domains $\mathcal{D}_{EV}, \mathcal{D}_{HV}, \mathcal{D}_{ICEV}$ representing the domains of EVs, HVs and ICEVs, respectively. Similarly, we have three output label spaces $\mathcal{Y}_{EV}, \mathcal{Y}_{HV}$, and $\mathcal{Y}_{ICEV}$, and three predictive functions f_{EV}, f_{HV}, and f_{ICEV}, which need to be learned.

The functions f_{EV}, f_{HV}, and f_{ICEV} are parameterized by a set of parameters θ, that we seek to learn by minimizing a predefined loss function given the observed data. The input features for each of the vehicle class domains are derived from the characteristics of the road segments, weather, traffic features, and vehicle dynamics. Therefore, we can state that the feature spaces are equivalent, $X_{EV} = X_{HV} = X_{ICEV}$. Additionally, the marginal probability distributions over the features are independent of vehicle class and

Table 1. Data description; data collected from Jan 1 2020 to July 1 2020.

Data source	Description	Features	Frequency	Scope
ViriCiti - ICEVs	Vehicle telemetry	Fuel level, GPS	1 Hz	3 vehicles
ViriCiti - HVs	Vehicle telemetry	Fuel level, GPS	1 Hz	4 vehicles
ViriCiti - EVs	Vehicle telemetry	Current, voltage, GPS	1 Hz	3 vehicles
Clever Devices	Automated vehicle location	Trip ID, vehicle ID	0.1 Hz	All vehicles
HERE	Traffic (per TMC)	Jam factor, current speed, free flow speed	0.0166 Hz	Major roads, highways
DarkSky	Weather	Visibility, wind speed, precipitation intensity, humidity, wind gust, temperature	0.0033 Hz	Whole city
Static GTFS	Transit schedule	Routes, trip IDs, stop sequences, stop locations (latitude, longitude), schedule trip times, trip shape (GeoJSON)	Static	Whole city
GIC - Elevation	LiDAR elevation	Location, elevation (meters)	Static	Whole city
Trip Segments	Multiple sources	Segment length, time to travel, average speed, roadway type	Static	Whole city

therefore, the marginal probability distributions over the features are equivalent, $P(X_{EV}) = P(X_{HV}) = P(X_{ICEV})$. Finally, given that the feature spaces and marginal probability distributions are the same for all vehicle classes, we have that $\mathcal{D}_{EV} = \mathcal{D}_{HV} = \mathcal{D}_{ICEV}$.

As the energy consumed for ICEV and HV vehicles are measured in fuel (liters) consumed, the space of output labels $\mathcal{Y}$ is the set of positive real numbers $\mathbb{R}_+$. On the other hand, EV vehicles have regenerative braking, therefore the energy consumed can take negative values and the task space for EV vehicles is $\mathbb{R}$. Additionally, since the performance of the three vehicle classes varies greatly, we consider that the predictive functions for each vehicle class are different; as the conditional probability distributions are not equal and $P(Y_{EV}|X_{EV}) \neq P(Y_{HV}|X_{HV}) \neq P(Y_{ICEV}|X_{ICEV})$. Finally, we can generalize the problem to n classes of transit vehicles in the fleets (e.g. the classes can be categorized based on the model and year as well); such a generalization will focus on learning the tasks $\{\mathcal{T}_1 \neq \mathcal{T}_2, \cdots, \neq \mathcal{T}_n\} \in \mathcal{T}$, given the domains $\{\mathcal{D}_1 = \mathcal{D}_2, \cdots, = \mathcal{D}_n\} \in \mathcal{D}$.

3   Approach

We now discuss our approach to learning the energy prediction functions (f_{EV}, f_{HV}, and f_{ICEV}). In order to perform data-driven learning, we first need to accumulate data from various sources. In real-world problems pertaining to public transportation, creating a data pipeline is often an arduous task due to the variety of data sources, formats, recording precision, and data collection frequency. As a result, we begin by discussing the data sources (Table 1) and the data pipeline. We gather data from 3 ICEVs, 4 HVs, and 3 EVs from our partner agency for a period of six months from January 1, 2020 to July 1, 2020. Each vehicle has a telematics kit produced by ViriCiti LLC [22], that provides speed and GPS positioning at a minimum 1 Hz resolution. In addition, for ICEVs and HVs the sensors provide fuel consumed (liters) while for EVs we collect current and voltage levels which are used to calculate energy consumed as well as emissions. Each vehicle is equipped with a kit from Clever Devices [4]. The Clever Devices feed provides a unique vehicle ID corresponding to the vehicle ID in the ViriCiti feed, as well as the unique trip ID which maps to scheduled trips in the static General Transit Feed Specification (GTFS) [21].

We collect weather data from multiple weather stations within the transit region at 5-minute intervals using the DarkSky API [5], including temperature, humidity, wind speed, and precipitation. Traffic data was collected at 1-minute intervals using the HERE API [11], which provides speed recordings for segments of major roads. The traffic data is reported per *TMC* (Traffic Message Channel), which is a custom geographical mapping unit. We perform map matching similar to prior work [1] to obtain traffic data for each road segment of interest to us. Road network map data was collected from OpenStreetMaps [9]. Lastly, we collect static GIS elevation data from the state Geographic Information Council which provides high-resolution digital elevation models (DEMs) derived from LiDAR elevation imaging, with a vertical accuracy of approximately 10cm.

Fixed line transit vehicles travel at pre-determined times (trips) covering a sequence of stops along a route. The latitude and longitude of each stop and the geographical shape of the path (the route segment) that the vehicles travel by visiting each stop is specified using the static GTFS schedule published by CARTA. Using this information, it is straightforward to divide the path taken by a bus during a given trip into a sequence of segments $\langle SEG \rangle$, where each segment is marked by a start stop and an end stop. As the specific characteristics of segments are important, a unique segment is created for every spatial path that exists between a pair of stops. Note that effectively, each SEG_i is described using a discrete sequence of points (latitude and longitude), close enough to draw the shape of the road on the map. We use these segments as the fundamental spatial unit for which we predict emissions (or energy). This has two advantages: first, the generation of route segments for prediction can be derived directly from a transit agency's schedule, rather than relying on external infrastructure data such as OSM [1] or time intervals [3], and second, segments can be shared between trips thereby providing additional data for learning.

3.1 Mapping Vehicle Trajectories to Route Segments

To generate the joined data samples, we first map the vehicle trajectories to segments. By joining the ViriCiti and Clever Device feeds, we determine a set of GPS points that a vehicle traverses. We refer to this ordered sequence of points as a trajectory T consisting of spatial points $\{l_1, l_2, \dots\}$. Consider that the trajectory T serves the trip R. The goal of the mapping process is to label each location $l_i \in T$ to a corresponding segment $SEG_j \in R$, thereby representing the specific segment that each vehicle traverses at a specific point in time.

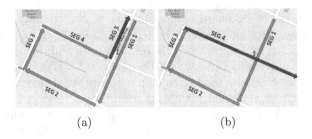

(a)   (b)

Fig. 2. (a) Overlapping segments. Segments 1 and 5 traverse the same section in opposite directions. (b) Intersecting segments. Vehicle locations near the intersection of segments 1 and 4 can lead to incorrect mapping. Stops not shown.

In principle, it is possible to perform an exhaustive search on the segments to identify the one that matches (or is the closest to) each point in a trajectory. However, such an approach does not work in practice with real-word trajectory feeds due to two reasons. <u>First</u>, routes often traverse segments between spatial points close to each other during trips. For example, consider the overlapping segments in Fig. 2a in which the vehicle passes through SEG_1 relatively early in the trip and through SEG_5 later. Due to noise in the measurement, a point early in the trip can erroneously get mapped to SEG_5, resulting in incorrect representation of the features that are induced by the segment. Similar problems arrise when segments cross each other as shown in Fig. 2b. Our exploratory analysis on the data obtained from our partner agency showed several examples of such incorrect mappings. <u>Second</u>, the mapping of trajectory data to segments is computationally challenging for transit agencies. As an example, consider our partner agency CARTA, which operates a total of 60 vehicles. The number for bigger cities is larger in orders of magnitude; for example, the New York Metropolitan Transit Authority (NY-MTA) operates more than 5000 buses [16]. Considering location data collected at the frequency 1 Hz for 3 years, the matching must be done for over 3.5×10^9 spatial locations, each of which could potentially be mapped to one out of hundreds of segments (for a larger city like New York, the number of matches is 3×10^{12}).

To alleviate these concerns, we propose an algorithm for mapping vehicle trajectories to route segments (Algorithm 1). The algorithm takes the trajectory T of the vehicle traversing the sequence of segments $\langle SEG \rangle$ of trip R. During matching, we maintain a lookahead window, denoted by W, that represents the number of segments to consider for the match. For example, if a location $l_i \in T$ is already matched to segment SEG_c in a route, then for matching the next location $l_{i+1} \in T$, we consider the set $\{SEG_c, \ldots, SEG_{c+W}\}$. By maintaining a short lookahead, we alleviate duplicate matches from segments further away in the route. Also, a shorter lookahead provides computational efficiency as opposed to an exhaustive search. We maintain a tolerance distance B for matching where a segment is matched to a location from a trajectory only if the distance between them is less than or equal to B. The function $dist(SEG_j, l_i)$ is used to calculate the minimum distance between segment SEG_j and GPS point l_i.

Algorithm 1: Mapping Trajectories to Route Segments

Input:
$R \leftarrow$ sequence of segments $\{SEG_0, \ldots, SEG_N\}$ for each trip
$T \leftarrow$ set of vehicle GPS locations l along the trip
$W \leftarrow$ number of segments to lookahead
$B \leftarrow$ max distance between segment and vehicle GPS
Output:
$TrajSegMap \rightarrow$ list of segments for each SEG in R
Initialization:
$c \leftarrow 1$, index of current segment
$TrajSegMap \leftarrow []$
for $i \in \{1, \ldots, |T|\}$ **do**
    $SegWindowDist \leftarrow []$
    for $j \in \{c, \ldots, c+W\}$ **do**
        if $j \leq |R|$ **then**
            $SegWindowDist.push(dist(SEG_j, l_i))$

    if $min(SegWindowDist) \leq B$ **then**
        $c \leftarrow c + argmin(SegWindowDist)$ $TrajSegMap[i] \leftarrow SEG_c$
    else
        $TrajSegMap[i] \leftarrow None$

3.2 Generating Samples

To generate the joined data samples, we split each of the trajectories T based on the locations mapped to trip segments. We create one data sample per continuous travel on a trip segment, providing average speed and the total fuel/energy consumption and emission on that segment. For ICEVs and HVs, the fuel consumed is provided in liters. While EVs provide state-of-charge (SOC) readings, the precision is too low to use for representing energy consumed. Therefore, we estimate the amount of energy from the battery current A and voltage V. The energy used between consecutive data points is given by $E_i = A_i \cdot V_i \cdot (TS_i - TS_{i-1})$, where E_i, A_i, and V_i are the consumed energy (Joule), current (Ampere), voltage (Volt) at time step i, respectively, and TS_i is the timestamp (in seconds) at time step i. To get the energy on a segment, the energy consumed between each sample is accumulated for all locations of the vehicle mapped to that segment.

Weather features for each sample are taken from the weather reading closest to the time at which the vehicle starts traversing a segment. For traffic features, we take the average jam factor (JF) and speed ratio (SR) of all TMCs mapped to the segment traversed by the vehicle when the vehicle enters a segment. Speed ratio is defined as the traffic speed divided by the free flow speed.

3.3 Learning

Recall that our goal is to address two specific problems. The first scenario is where a transit agency has access to *many* vehicles, and consequently data, from each vehicle class. In this case, our goal is to improve the predictive accuracy of f for all tasks. One method of addressing this problem is to learn a predictive model f over each vehicle class. However, we hypothesize that there are generalizable patterns between vehicle classes that can be leveraged to aid learning. Consequently, we formulate a MTL model as shown in Fig. 1a. We use hard parameter sharing to learn a common representation of the input features which enables us to extract generalizable patterns across the tasks. Additionally, each task (vehicle class) has a vehicle-specific set of hidden layers which outputs the predicted energy consumed/emissions for EVs ($\hat{Y}_{EV}$), HVs ($\hat{Y}_{HV}$), and ICEVs ($\hat{Y}_{ICEV}$) along route segments. At each training iteration, a batch of samples from EVs, HVs, and ICEVs is fed through the network and mean-squared error (MSE) loss is calculated between the predicted target and true target for each vehicle class. The gradient of the loss is then propagated back through the network.

The second problem we seek to address is where an agency has significant variation in the number of vehicles from each class. In such a case, while a common model can be learned using the MTL framework, the tasks with a significantly larger number of samples are likely to *dominate* learning. Also, learning a model solely for the task with few samples can result in overfitting. In this case, we seek to learn f for classes with sufficient data (source model) first, and *transfer* the learned abstraction to improve the predictive accuracy for the class with insufficient data (target model). Our ITL framework is shown in Fig. 1b. When training the target model, the transferred layers are frozen and only the vehicle-specific layers are updated during training.

4   Experiments and Results

Vehicle telemetry, weather, and traffic data is collected for a six-month period between January 1, 2020 and July 1, 2020 for 10 vehicles as shown in Table 2. We include two post-processing steps in generating the final datasets for each respective vehicle class. First, we remove partial trajectories by eliminating samples where the total distance traveled was less than 50% of the segment length and greater than 150% of the segment length. Second, to address outliers and potential errors in the mapping process, we remove samples with the target value (energy/emission) in the bottom 2% and top 2% quantiles. The final data size is shown in last column of Table 2.

The distributions of emissions (kg CO_2) and energy (kWh) consumption are shown in Fig. 3. As energy consumption for ICEVs and HVs is derived from liters of diesel fuel consumed, emissions must be greater than $0\,\text{kg}\,CO_2$ for these vehicle classes. The EVs in the fleet have regenerative braking, which allows for energy consumed, and thus emission, to be negative. We predict energy/emissions per route segment. The distributions over energy and emission for each of the vehicle classes has a long right tail and the average varies between vehicle classes. Therefore, the *task* of energy/emission prediction is also different, by virtue of having a different distribution over the space of output labels $\mathcal{Y}$.

Table 2. Data processing summary.

Class	Model year	Vehicles	Raw samples	Distance Filtering	Final samples
ICEV	2014	3	139,652	127,212	114,348
HV	2014	4	235,671	223,913	201,491
EV	2018	3	48,969	47,804	43,022

Table 3. Pearson's correlation coefficient of input features with emissions.

Class	Length segment	Time to travel	ΔElevation	Max ΔElevation	Speed ratio	Visibility	Wind speed	Precipitation	Humidity	Wind gust	Jam factor	Temperature	Avg speed
EV	0.860	0.752	0.523	0.222	0.038	0.008	−0.002	−0.003	−0.009	−0.012	−0.015	−0.037	−0.093
HV	0.916	0.838	0.505	0.135	0.038	0.006	0.004	−0.008	−0.008	−0.002	−0.026	0.013	−0.134
ICEV	0.886	0.865	0.539	0.103	0.028	0.004	0.011	−0.005	0.001	≈0	−0.016	−0.005	−0.262

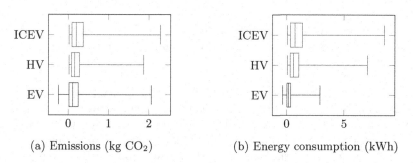

(a) Emissions (kg CO_2)   (b) Energy consumption (kWh)

Fig. 3. Distribution of (a) emissions (kg CO_2) and (b) energy (kWh) consumption per trip segment for each vehicle class.

The Pearson correlation coefficient between input features and emissions is provided in Table 3. Distance traveled and time to traverse the segment have a strong positive correlation with emissions. Δ Elevation, which is the change in elevation from the start to the end of the segment, also has a strong correlation with emissions for all vehicle types. Max Δ elevation, which is defined as the difference between the maximum and minimum elevation along the segment, has a relatively weaker correlation. Additionally, the average vehicle speed has a stronger negative correlation of −0.262 with emissions for ICEVs than with HVs (−0.134) and EVs (−0.093).

4.1 Hyperparameter Tuning and Baseline Models

We randomly select 43,022 samples from each vehicle class. For each vehicle class, we use 80% of the samples for training and 20% for testing. Of the training samples, 10% are withheld from training and used as a validation set to identify the best set of hyperparameters for the subsequent analyses. We perform the hyperparameter search using the model derived from the MTL formulation.

We tested shared hidden layer widths of {200, 300, 400} and shared hidden layer depths of {3, 4, 5}. We use 3 vehicle-specific layers and tested the configurations of {128, 64, 32} and {64, 32, 16}. Mean-squared error (MSE) is used for the loss function and the networks are optimized using the Adam algorithm [12].

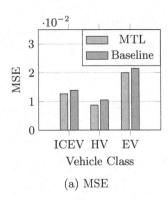 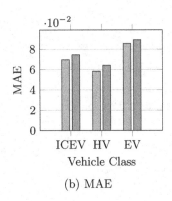

(a) MSE   (b) MAE

Fig. 4. (a) MSE and (b) MAE of MTL model compared to vehicle-specific neural network models (baseline) on testing set. Prediction target: emissions (kg CO_2).

We test learning rates of {0.01, 0.005, 0.001, 0.0005, 0.0001} and batch sizes of {64, 128, 256, 512}. The best performing configuration is shown in Fig. 1a, which consists of 5 shared hidden layers of 300 fully connected neurons with ReLU activation functions [15], and 3 vehicle-specific hidden layers of 64, 32, and 16 hidden neurons respectively. For the output layer we test using ReLU as well as linear activation functions for ICEVs and HVs and linear activation function for EVs, however we find that using a linear activation function as the output layer for all 3 vehicle classes provides the best performance. An early stopping strategy was performed, where we stopped training if MSE on the validation set did not improve for 10 epochs. The best performing learning rate was 0.0005 and the best batch size was 256.

In the baseline model no layers are shared between vehicle-classes resulting in a separate neural network for each vehicle class. The same grid search from the proposed models was used to find the hyperparameters of the baseline models. In all experiments, we use Kaiming initialization [10] to initialize the weights of the networks.

4.2   Multi-task Model Evaluation

First, we investigate the performance of the MTL model compared to vehicle-specific baseline models. To evaluate the robustness of the models, we train 10 MTL models (30 vehicle-specific models, 10 for each vehicle class) and present the average MSE and MAE in Fig. 4. Models are trained for up to 150 epochs. We find that for all vehicle classes, the MTL model outperforms the vehicle-specific baseline models. The mean percent improvement in MSE is 8.6%, 17.0%, and 7.0% for ICEVs, HVs, and EVs, respectively. The mean percent improvement in MAE is 6.4%, 9.0% and 4.0% for ICEVs, HVs, and EVs respectively.

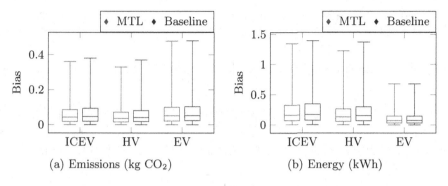

Fig. 5. Distribution of MTL and baseline model bias per sample for each vehicle class from bootstrap evaluation, 30 bootstrap iterations. Prediction target: (a) emissions and (b) energy.

Even with improved accuracy, it is important to investigate the bias and the variance of the proposed approaches. Therefore, we repeat the entire evaluation using 30 datasets creating through bootsrapping [19] from the original data. At each iteration, we sample a training set, with replacement, from the ICEV, HV, and EV datasets. The samples not selected for each training set are used as the testing set for that iteration. For each iteration, we train a single MTL model and vehicle-specific baseline models on the training set and evaluate on the testing set. The distribution of empirical bias per sample for the MTL and baseline models is presented in Fig. 5. We observe that the MTL model results in a lower bias for each vehicle class compared to the baseline models. The MTL model also results in lower median variance per sample.

4.3 Inductive Transfer Learning Evaluation

Next, we evaluate the performance of the ITL model formulated in Fig. 1b. To train the ITL models, we use data from all of the three vehicle classes, each of which contains 43,022 samples, as outlined in Sect. 4.1. For each pair of source and target task, we first train the source model, freeze the shared hidden layers, and transfer to the target model. Then, we optimize the target model's vehicle-specific layers. For each model, the available sample size to train the target model is varied from 2%, 5%, 10%, and 15% of the total number of available samples to investigate the influence of sample size in training of the target models. This is consistent with what transit agencies might face in practice; as a new vehicle is introduced, agencies gradually collect more data from it. We test our approach for all pairs of vehicle classes.

To compare the performance of the models, we train baseline models that only use the training data from the target domain. For example, while evaluating inductive transfer from EV to ICEV with 2% of the target data available, the baseline model is trained exclusively on the same amount data from ICEV class. In order to consider the randomness in training process, when evaluating

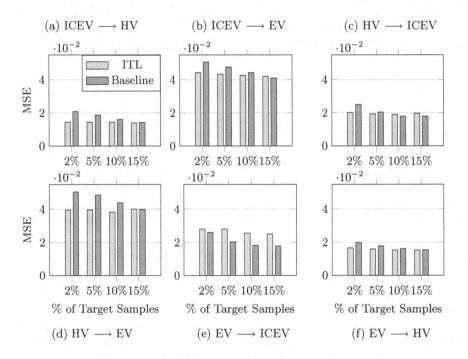

Fig. 6. ITL models compared to corresponding baselines. ITL model is trained on full dataset in the source vehicle class and is evaluated on the target vehicle class (source $\longrightarrow$ target). Average MSE compared to fraction of data samples used for training in the target vehicle class. Prediction target: emissions (kg CO_2).

the target and baseline models, we trained each model 10 times on 10 random samples from the target domain's dataset and 10 different initial values for the parameters using Kaiming initialization [10].

We provide the results of the proposed ITL approach in Fig. 6. We observe that in general, the proposed approach results in improved forecasting accuracy across the tested scenarios (except when EV is used as source and ICEV is used as target). We also observe that as the amount of data from the target domain increases, both the ITL and the baseline method show improved forecasting accuracy; however, the baseline methods shows relatively higher improvement, to the extent of outperforming the ITL framework in some cases (15% data from target domain in Fig. 6 b, c, e and f).

Additionally, we seek to understand the role of the shared-hidden layers in our proposed approach. Conceptually, the role of such layers in the target model is to extract generalizable patterns across the spectrum of tasks to aid learning in the target task. We use t-distributed stochastic neighbor embeddings (t-SNE) [14] to visualize the separation of multi-dimensional information in a two-dimensional space. In Fig. 7, we show t-SNE on the raw input features of the three vehicle classes color coded by emissions (kg CO_2). All three plots are very similar,

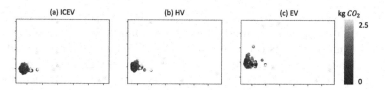

Fig. 7. t-SNE on raw input features for each data sample from the source domain. t-SNE parameters: number of components = 2, perplexity = 10, initialization = PCA, number of samples = 860 (2% of dataset)

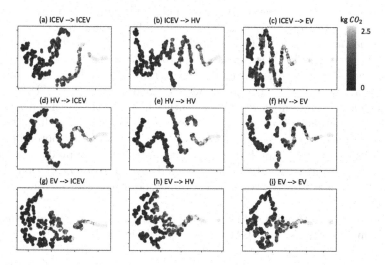

Fig. 8. t-SNE on the output of shared-hidden layers for each data sample from the target domain. t-SNE parameters same as Fig. 7.

thereby corroborating our assumption that the input features are similar across the tasks ($\mathcal{D}_{EV} = \mathcal{D}_{HV} = \mathcal{D}_{ICEV}$). We separately apply t-SNE on the output of the shared-hidden layers across all pairs of source and target tasks and show the results in Fig. 8. We observe that the ICEV source model and HV source model (plots (a) to (f) of Fig. 8) effectively discriminate the samples with high emissions and low emissions (increasing the distance between light points and dark points). On the other hand, EV source model (plots (g) to (i) in Fig. 8) shows poor discrimination, reflecting the negative transfer.

4.4 Discussion

We now present the key takeaways from the experiments. First, we observe that in general, both the MTL and the ITL framework outperform the baseline methods, thereby resulting in improved emission (and consequently energy) predictions for transit agencies that operate mixed-fleet vehicles. Second, we observe that the MTL, ITL, and baseline models are less accurate in predicting

EV emissions compared to HV and ICEV, most likely due to the complexity of the energy cycle in EV engines. Third, a key finding for practitioners is that the greatest improvements over baselines are seen when the target vehicle class suffers from lack of data. However, it is important to switch to standard models once sufficient data is collected for the class. The point at which such a switch should be made depends on the specific task and data at hand. In our work with CARTA, we implement a periodic check to facilitate such a switch. Fourth, we find that when the goal is to predict the emissions for ICEV class using a source model trained based on EV class dataset (this situation rarely arises in practice due to precedence of the ICEV class), ITL models underperformed baseline models, irrespective of the size of training data from the target domain. This indicates negative transfer between the EV domain and the ICEV domain.

Lastly, while this work is a general approach that can be used by cities to improve their energy prediction models there are a couple limitations agencies should be aware of. First, our models were trained on data from Chattanooga, TN, which is a mountainous city in the southern United States with a warm climate and limited snowfall or freezing temperatures. Therefore any direct transfer of our pre-trained models to other cities should take into account potential biases in these determinants. Second, like most macroscopic energy prediction models we do not take into account the impact of delays at stops or the number of passengers on the vehicles. We intend on incorporating these parameters into future work.

Code, data, and supplementary results of this study are available at https:// github.com/smarttransit-ai/ECML-energy-prediction-public

5   Conclusion

By framing emission (and energy) forecasting as an MTL problem, we showed that an agency with access to *many* vehicles can improve the predictive accuracy for EVs, HVs, and ICEVs over current state-of-the-art, vehicle-specific models. We also showed that in a situation with imbalanced data the predictive accuracy of classes with insufficient data can be improved by transferring a learned abstraction from vehicle classes with sufficient data through ITL. Lastly, we provided a general online pipeline for joining the various sensor streams for emission and energy prediction of mixed-vehicle transit fleets.

Acknowledgments. This material is based upon work supported by the National Science Foundation under grant 1952011 and Department of Energy, Office of Energy Efficiency and Renewable Energy (EERE), under Award Number DE-EE0008467. Any opinions, findings, and conclusions or recommendations expressed in this material are those of the author(s) and do not necessarily reflect the views of the National Science Foundation or the Department of Energy.

References

1. Ayman, A., Sivagnanam, A., Wilbur, M., Pugliese, P., Dubey, A., Laszka, A.: Data-driven prediction and optimization of energy use for transit fleets of electric and ICE vehicles. ACM Trans. Internet Technol. (2020)
2. Chen, Y., Wu, G., Sun, R., Dubey, A., Laszka, A., Pugliese, P.: A review and outlook of energy consumption estimation models for electric vehicles. Int. J. Sustain. Transp. Energy Environ. Pol. (2021)
3. Chen, Y., Zhu, L., Gonder, J., Young, S., Walkowicz, K.: Data-driven fuel consumption estimation: a multivariate adaptive regression spline approach. Transp. Res. Part C: Emerg. Technol. **83**, 134–145 (2017)
4. Clever Devices API documentation (2020). https://www.cleverdevices.com/
5. Dark Sky API documentation (2019). https://darksky.net/dev/docs
6. De Cauwer, C., Verbeke, W., Coosemans, T., Faid, S., Van Mierlo, J.: A data-driven method for energy consumption prediction and energy-efficient routing of electric vehicles in real-world conditions. Energies **10**(5), 608 (2017)
7. EIA energy conversion calculator (2021). https://www.eia.gov/energyexplained/units-and-calculators/energy-conversion-calculators.php
8. EPA greenhouse gases calculator (2021). https://www.epa.gov/energy/greenhouse-gases-equivalencies-calculator-calculations-and-references
9. Haklay, M., Weber, P.: OpenStreetMap: user-generated street maps. IEEE Pervasive Comput. **7**(4), 12–18 (2008)
10. He, K., Zhang, X., Ren, S., Sun, J.: Delving deep into rectifiers: surpassing human-level performance on ImageNet classification. In: Proceedings of the IEEE International Conference on Computer Vision, pp. 1026–1034 (2015)
11. HERE Api documentation (2019). https://developer.here.com/documentation
12. Kingma, D.P., Ba, J.: Adam: a method for stochastic optimization. arXiv preprint arXiv:1412.6980 (2014)
13. Lajunen, A.: Energy consumption and cost-benefit analysis of hybrid and electric city buses. Transp. Res. Part C **38**, 1–15 (2014)
14. Van der Maaten, L., Hinton, G.: Visualizing data using t-SNE. J. Mach. Learn. Res. **9**(86), 2579–2605 (2008)
15. Nair, V., Hinton, G.E.: Rectified linear units improve restricted Boltzmann machines. In: ICML (2010)
16. NY Mta subway and bus facts 2019 (2019). https://new.mta.info/agency/new-york-city-transit/subway-bus-facts-2019
17. Pamuła, T., Pamuła, W.: Estimation of the energy consumption of battery electric buses for public transport networks using real-world data and deep learning. Energies **13**(9), 2340 (2020)
18. Pan, S.J., Yang, Q.: A survey on transfer learning. IEEE Trans. Knowl. Data Eng. **22**(10), 1345–1359 (2009)
19. Parr, W.C.: A note on the jackknife, the bootstrap and the delta method estimators of bias and variance. Biometrika **70**(3), 719–722 (1983)
20. Sivagnanam, A., Ayman, A., Wilbur, M., Pugliese, P., Dubey, A., Laszka, A.: Minimizing energy use of mixed-fleet public transit for fixed-route service. In: Proceedings of the 35th AAAI Conference on Artificial Intelligence (AAAI-21) (2021)
21. Static GTFS reference (2021). https://developers.google.com/transit/gtfs/reference
22. ViriCiti SDK documentation (2020). https://sdk.viriciti.com/docs
23. Wu, X., Freese, D., Cabrera, A., Kitch, W.A.: Electric vehicles' energy consumption measurement and estimation. Transp. Res. Part D: Transp. Environ. **34**, 52–67 (2015)

CQNet: A Clustering-Based Quadruplet Network for Decentralized Application Classification via Encrypted Traffic

Yu Wang[1,2], Gang Xiong[1,2], Chang Liu[1,2], Zhen Li[1,2], Mingxin Cui[1,2], and Gaopeng Gou[1,2(✉)]

[1] Institute of Information Engineering, Chinese Academy of Sciences, Beijing, China
{wangyu1996,xionggang,liuchang,lizhen,uimingxin,
gougaopeng}@iie.ac.cn
[2] School of Cyber Security, University of Chinese Academy of Sciences, Beijing,
China

Abstract. Decentralized applications (DApps), along with the development of blockchain technology, are increasingly developed and deployed on blockchain platforms. DApps based on the same platform usually adopt similar traffic encryption settings and the same communication interface, leading to traffic less distinguishable. However, existing classification methods either require manual-design features or need lots of data to train the classifier, otherwise suffering from low accuracy. In this paper, we apply metric learning to DApps encrypted traffic classification problem and propose the clustering-based quadruplet network (CQNet). The CQNet can filter out useless samples to reduce the training dataset's redundancy data by utilizing the proposed algorithm, thereby improving the classifier's efficiency. Moreover, we adopt a quadruplet structure that can mine more restrictive relationships among quadruplets and provide rich information to the classifier. Our comprehensive experiments on the real-world dataset covering 60 DApps indicate that CQNet can achieve excellent performance with high efficiency and is superior to the state-of-the-art methods in terms of accuracy and efficiency.

Keywords: Encrypted traffic classification · Decentralized applications · Clustering · Quadruplet networks · Feature embedding · Metric learning

1 Introduction

With the surge in popularity and rapid development of blockchain, the volume of decentralized applications (DApps) rises sharply. That is attributed dramatically to DApps' resistance to censorship, making them more freedom. Until now, more than 3700 DApps are deployed on different blockchain platforms, such as Etherem (81.91%), Eos (8.97%), Steem (1.62%), etc. We focus on Ethereum [1] DApps in this paper, as it also has the most significant number of daily active

© Springer Nature Switzerland AG 2021
Y. Dong et al. (Eds.): ECML PKDD 2021, LNAI 12978, pp. 518–534, 2021.
https://doi.org/10.1007/978-3-030-86514-6_32

users, about one hundred thousand [2]. DApps are autonomously managed without the control of a single entity and blockchain technology can naturally provide anonymity to each user. These are the unique advantages of DApps that traditional applications cannot provide.

However, the problems faced by DApps and centralized applications are similar, i.e., how to manage the DApps network better and ensure a secure network environment. Network traffic classification naturally arises because it is a vital task for these two problems [10]. According to different priority strategies, DApps traffic should be classified for better network management. Malicious DApps traffic should also be identified for anomaly detection, thus guaranteeing the DApps network security. Traffic classification attracts many researchers and lots of methods have been proposed for website classification [3,14,15,19,20], mobile application classification [6,12,21,22,26] and user behavior classification [4,24], but few efforts have been made on DApps encrypted traffic classification.

While prior work has achieved good accuracy results, these methods designed the sophisticated network architecture combined with features extracted artificially from flows [9,10,15,18,20], which are based on professional knowledge, human effort and time-cost. Some studies use fewer or simpler features to achieve good results [4,5,11,21,24], which are unsatisfactory on DApps encrypted traffic classification. Some studies also resort to large dataset to improve performance (e.g., training on a large dataset contains 956 thousand flows [10]), which leads to the redundancy problem of dataset. All in all, the task of DApps encrypted traffic classification can be decomposed into two subtasks. The first is how to let the network automatically extract features and accurately classify DApps traffic. The second is how to improve the efficiency of training and testing.

In this paper, We propose a novel classification model using metric learning named clustering-based quadruplet network (CQNet) for DApps encrypted traffic classification. The CQNet aims to learn an embedding space, thereby mapping each encrypted traffic flow into the metric space to form an embedded vector. CQNet includes two mechanisms, filtration of easy dataset (FE-set) algorithm and quadruplet network. FE-set algorithm combines the three parts of mini-batch KMeans, Kuhn-Munkres algorithm and exploring centers of clusters to filter out easy samples from all flows. Hence, the original dataset can be split into the easy dataset and hard dataset. We construct quadruplets on the hard dataset as the quadruplet network's input, which can leverage more constraints among samples. FE-set algorithm and the quadruplet network are designed to solve DApps encrypted traffic classification efficiency and accuracy, respectively.

Contributions: Our contributions can be summarized as follows:

1) We explored the redundancy problem of DApps encrypted traffic dataset for the first time. FE-set algorithm can divide easy dataset and hard dataset, thereby improving the training efficiency.
2) We designed a quadruplet network, which can leverage more restrictive relationships among quadruplets and provide rich information to the classifier.

3) Our CQNet achieves outstanding results on the real-world network traffic data for the DApps encrypted traffic classification and outperforms the state-of-the-art methods.

Roadmap. Section 2 summarizes the related work. Section 3 describes the preliminaries. The detailed system architecture is proposed in Sect. 4. Section 5 shows the evaluation results. Finally, we conclude this paper in Sect. 6.

2   Related Work

Many conventional traffic classification methods are no longer suitable for current encryption scenarios, such as DPI (Deep Packet Inspection) and port-based methods. Here, we only introduce studies that are closely related to our work. Hence, prior work on encrypted traffic classification falls into three broad categories: (1) web application classification, (2) mobile application classification and (3) decentralized applications classification.

2.1   Web Application Classification

Panchenko et al. [13] presented a website fingerprinting method at Internet Scale. The accumulated sum of packet sizes was used to represent the progress of webpage loading. Hayes et al. [7] proposed a robust website fingerprinting technique based on Random Forest. The leaves of Random Forest are used to encode a new representation of the websites, thereby transforming 175 features into a different feature space, which are fed to a KNN classifier. Shi et al. [19] introduce an efficient feature optimization approach, based on a deep learning framework. It enhanced traffic classification performances by removing the redundant features. [20] designed convolutional Neural Networks (CNN) with sophisticated architecture. The model can have high accuracy for Tor websites identification by using only the packet direction sequence.

2.2   Mobile Application Classification

In [26], the authors used a suite of inference techniques to reveal a specific user action (i.e., send a tweet) on the Twitter app installed on an Android smartphone. Taylor et al. proposed a robust application identification method with the concept of the burst. They used statistical features of packet length with the Random Forest classifier to build the Appscanner [21], which can identify 110 applications with 96% accuracy. Condi et al. clustered the streams of each application user behavior by clustering methods [4], then they calculated the dynamic warping distance for each flow in terms of packet length. Several studies applied Markov models to identify smartphone applications [8,17].

2.3 Decentralized Applications Classification

DApps are emerging as a new service paradigm that relies on the underlying blockchain platform. Shen et al. generated high-dimensional features by fusing time series, packet length and burst sequence [18]. The accuracy of DApps traffic classification reached 90%. But the training and testing time of the method is much longer than other methods because of the large input vectors. Wang et al. [24] found that more than 60% of flows are short flows, leading to the burst feature's poor performance, so they only extracted time series and packet length to build a classifier using Random Forest. In this paper, we attempt to design a new deep learning network structure without needing professional knowledge and hand-crafted features.

3 Preliminaries

While prior work of encrypted traffic classification has obtained some insights, encrypted traffic classification in distributed DApps is still a considerable challenge. In this section, we provide DApps background, give the definition of DApps encrypted traffic classification problem and the limitation of existing methods.

3.1 DApps Background

DApps consist of frontend and backend, where the frontend implements user interfaces uniformly defined by blockchain platforms to present pages. Smart contracts acting as the backend connect to blockchain networks, utterly different from the backend of the web application. Smart contracts are the functionalities that determine the results of operations in DApp performed by users.

Most DApps provide browser plug-ins or websites so that users can easily access. When a user visits a DApp, the DApp client obtains the server's IP address equipped with the corresponding smart contract through **DNS** query and sends a request. Then, the smart contract determines the operation results and sends them to the **mempool**. All data records of these are packaged in the form of blocks by miners and stored on the distributed ledger. After these steps, the client obtains the updated information from blockchain to present pages through a new list of servers acquired from the smart contract server.

Ethereum DApps adopt the same communication interface, employ similar traffic encryption settings, store data and run smart contracts in the same blockchain platform, making the encrypted traffic of DApps more challenging to distinguish than the classification of traditional applications.

3.2 Problem Definition

The DApps encrypted traffic classification task is to classify flows into specific DApps with the raw traffic data as the only classification information. Assume that there are N samples and K classes of DApps in total. The z-th sample is defined as $f_z = \left[b_1^{(z)}, \ldots, b_{n_z}^{(z)} \right]$, where n_z is the length of f_z and $b_i^{(z)}$ stands for the size of packet $b_i^{(z)} \in [0, 1500)$ in bytes at time step i. The DApps label of f_z is denoted as L_z, $1 \le L_z \le K$. Our goal is to build a model to predict a label $\hat{L}_z$ that is exactly the real label L_z.

3.3   Limitation of Existing Methods

Existing encryption traffic classification methods face two challenges, efficiency (RQ1) and accuracy (RQ2).

Efficiency. To label dataset, the traffic classification is different from other research fields (i.e., **CV, NLP**). Traffic classification dataset can be automatically labeled by SNI (Server Name Indication) or process ID. Therefore, the dataset may contain many samples (e.g., nearly one million flows in [10]), including easy, semi-hard and hard samples [16]. Since the overly easy samples can satisfy the constraints well and produce almost zero loss, they do not contribute to the parameter update during back-propagation and consume a lot of time. So, how to filter out easy samples from the dataset to improve training efficiency? **(RQ1)**

Accuracy. As introduced in Sect. 2, the premise of good classification performance should be that no experts or a simple model to use.

We are inspired by the triplet network [16]. Flows could be placed in a common metric space and the explicit closeness could be measured by Euclidean distance. The function for each pair of flows interaction can be defined as:

$$d(f_a, f_p) = \left\| \alpha_{f_a} - \alpha_{f_p} \right\|_2^2 \qquad (1)$$

where $\| * \|_2$ denotes the L_2 - norm. α_f is the representation of traffic flow in the low dimensional space.

The triplet loss: Given a triple (f_a, f_p, f_n), $1 \le a, p, n \le N$, the label $L_a = L_p \ne L_n$. The loss guarantees the distance between anchor f_a and negative f_n is larger than that between f_a and positive f_p by a fixed margin:

$$d(f_a, f_p) + m \le d(f_a, f_n) \qquad (2)$$

The final objective function could be expressed as following:

$$\mathcal{L} = \sum_{L_a = L_p} \sum_{L_a \ne L_n} [d(f_a, f_p) - d(f_a, f_n) + m]_+ \qquad (3)$$

where $[x]_+ = max(x, 0)$ represents the hinge loss.

From a geometric perspective, the triplet loss only considers the relationship of two edges. The negative flow's position may be far from the same DApp's flow and close to another DApp's flow. This undoubtedly compromises the performance of the classifier. As shown in Fig. 1, the learning process will be stopped following the constraint of Eq. 2. We can observe that the sample with blue color is close to the yellow one and far from the other blue.

Fig. 1. An illustration of metric learning by using triplet network. The same color indicates that the samples belong to the same DApps. After training, the sample with blue color is close to the yellow one and far from the other blue. (Color figure online)

Due to the different distribution of flows for different DApps, the fixed margin for all DApps may not perform well. So, how to utilize more relationships among samples and adjust the margin to train the classifier? (**RQ2**)

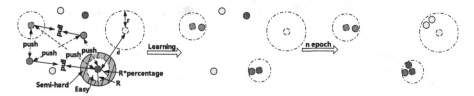

Fig. 2. An illustration of our proposed method CQNet. R represents each class's initial radius after clustering (including easy samples and semi-hard samples), R*percentage is the range that we finally selected as the easy dataset. And the semi-hard samples are classified into the hard dataset. The right of the figure represents the final situation after completed training.

4   CQNet

In this section, we will illustrate our clustering-based quadruplet network (CQNet) to circumvent the above two issues (RQ1 and RQ2). An illustration of CQNet is shown in Fig. 2. The CQNet aims to learn embeddings, such that flows generated from distinct DApps are embedded into a common metric space. Thus the embedded features favor discriminative between different DApps. The overall architecture of CQNet is shown in Fig. 3. We outline the underlying ideas of the work, including FE-set, the proposed quadruplet network.

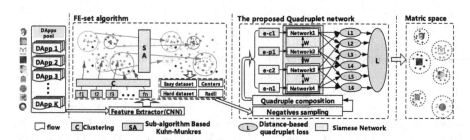

Fig. 3. The architecture overview of the CQNet. The FE-set algorithm aims to divide easy dataset and hard dataset, thus improving training efficiency. The quadruplet network aims to find constraints to improve classification accuracy.

4.1   FE-set (RQ1)

According to the problem definition in Sect. 3.2, given a sample f_z. In order to extract features automatically, we utilize the first n bytes (n = 64*64) to represent the flow, the raw data is $f_z = \left[b_1^{(z)}, \ldots, b_{m_z}^{(z)}\right]$, $\sum_{i=1}^{m_z} b_i^{(z)} = n$. For the whole dataset, $F = [f_1, \ldots, f_N]$. As shown in Fig. 4, F are converted to gray images for visualization [23]. By using the CNN architecture model pre-trained on the fashion-mnist, F is transformed into the embedded feature as the input to filter out easy samples, which are defined as $X = [x_1, \ldots, x_N]$.

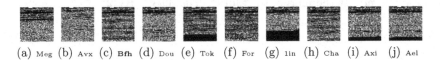

(a) Meg (b) Avx (c) Bfh (d) Dou (e) Tok (f) For (g) Iin (h) Cha (i) Axi (j) Ael

Fig. 4. Visualization of some classes of DApps traffic. It is obvious that DApps are different from each other and only a few images are similar.

The Proposed Algorithm. Considering the task of screening easy samples from N flows to form the easy dataset, $E = [EF_1, \ldots, EF_K]$, Where $EF_i = \left[F_1^{(i)}, \ldots, F_{l_i}^{(i)}\right]$, EF_{l_i} represents the easy samples belonging to the label i and l_i means the number of easy samples with label i, which may be zero. And the hard (including semi-hard and hard) dataset, $H = [HF_1, \ldots, HF_K]$. FE-set algorithm has the main idea: when samples belonging to the same class are also predicted to be the same class after using clustering, these samples are relatively close in the embedding space and form a cluster. In other words, these samples are easy to distinguish. So we choose a distance-based algorithm (mini-batch k-means) instead of other clustering algorithms (i.e., density-based methods). Next, we formally present the process, as exhibited in Algorithm 1.

FE-set algorithm considers the embedded features $X = [x_1, \ldots, x_N]$ as the input and starts with an initialization of the easy dataset E and hard dataset H. EX_i and HX_j represents the embedded features of each class. Then, it clusters X into K clusters through the mini-batch K-Means clustering algorithm. The number of cluster K is usually specified according to the category of DApps. Each flow in the dataset has a real label L_z and a predicted label $\hat{L}_z$. To correspond the real labels L and predicted labels $\hat{L}$ in the maximum number, we transform the task into a weighted bipartite graph maximum matching task, **Kuhn-Munkres** algorithm is used to solve this problem. We construct a matrix R as the input, the abscissa is the real label, the ordinate is the predicted label, the value in the matrix can be understood as the weight value and the number of samples that satisfy $R(i,j), L_{(i,j)} = i, \hat{L}_{(i,j)} = j$. The real label corresponds to the predicted label one-to-one after utilizing the **Kuhn-Munkres** algorithm. The samples that corresponded successfully are screened from the dataset and put into the easy dataset E. The remained samples are put into the hard dataset H.

Algorithm 1. Filtration of easy dataset (FE-set).

Input:
　　the embedded features $X = [x_1, \ldots, x_N]$, the real label $L = [l_1, \ldots, l_{N'14r}]$,
　　the raw data $F = [f_1, \ldots, f_N]$, the number of clusters K.
Output:
　　the easy dataset $E = [EF_1, \ldots, EF_K]$, the hard dataset $H = [HF_1, \ldots, HF_K]$,
　　the center set $CF = [cf_1, \ldots, cf_K]$, the radius set $Perc\_D = [perc\_d_1, \ldots, perc\_d_K]$.
1: Initialize E, H as empty sets
2: Predict clusters $\hat{L} = MiniBatchKMeans(X, K)$
3: Kuhn-Munkres($R = (L, \hat{L})$), obtain the corresponding relationship RE
4: Separate F into E and H according to RE
5: **for** $i \in [1, K]$ **do**
6: 　　**if** $len(EF_i) > 1$ **then**
7: 　　　　put i into a list YL
8: 　　**else**
9: 　　　　put i into a list NL
10: 　　**end if**
11: **end for**
12: **for** $i \in YL$ **do**
13: 　　put center $c_i = KMeans(EX_i, 1)$ into C, put f_{c_i} into CF
14: 　　**for** $X_{l_i}^i \in EX_i$ **do**
15: 　　　　put $d(X_{l_i}^i, c_i)$ into a list D
16: 　　**end for**
17: 　　Sort D, put the n percentile of D into $Perc\_D$
18: 　　Keep the ρ percentage closest samples in E. Put the others into H
19: **end for**
20: **for** $j \in NL$ **do**
21: 　　**for** $X_m^j \in HX_j$ **do**
22: 　　　　**for** $i \in YL$ **do**
23: 　　　　　　put $d_i(X_m^j, c_i)$ into a list $DC = [dc_1, \ldots, dc_K]$
24: 　　　　**end for**
25: 　　　　obtain $(index\_min, d\_min) = min(DC > 0)$, let $do_{index\_min} = d\_min$ for the list $DO = [do_1, \ldots, do_K]$
26: 　　**end for**
27: 　　obtain $(index, index\_min, d) = max(DO)$, put X_{index}^j into C, put f_{index}^j into CF, let $nl\_dj = d$ for the list NL_D
28: 　　calculate $perc\_d_j = (nl\_d_j - perc\_d_{index\_min}) * \rho$
29: **end for**
30: **return** $E, H, CF, Perc\_D$

Because we use the maximum matching, i.e., the amount of samples contained in the corresponding labels should be the largest, so the number of samples contained in a few correspondences between the true and predicted label may be 0 (i.e., $R(i,j) = 0$). These labels are added into NL and the remained labels are added into YL. Then, we directly use K-Means algorithm to obtain the center for each class in E and construct the center list $C = [c_1, \ldots, c_K]$, there may be $c_i = 0$. However, considering the samples at the edge of clusters cannot always be accurately predicted when clustering, we calculate the Euclidean distance D between each sample in the class to the center and sort D (The most prolonged d is R in Fig. 2). The percentage ρ closest samples to the center are selected as the real easy samples (i.e., r or R*percentage in Fig. 2). We record the n percentile of D as $perc\_d_i$ and use it as the radius of category i. The radius set is $Perc\_D = [perc\_d_1, \ldots, perc\_d_K]$. The rest of the samples can be regarded as semi-hard samples and transferred to H, so we obtain the two sets, E, H.

From the above, we get a set of centers C (the value of $c_i \neq 0$ if $L_i \in YL$). However, not all categories have a center in C ($L_j \in NL$), so we need to find the imaginary center of samples whose labels are in NL. For $L_j \in NL$, it calculates the Euclidean distance between each sample in category L_j and other existing centers $(c_i, i \in YL)$, takes the smallest value, then gets the sample with the maximum distance (denoted as $NL-D$) from the set formed by all the minimum values. This sample is used as the imaginary center of category L_j, and added into C. We can also obtain CF. The label of the nearest center and the distance are recorded as L_q and $nl\_d_{L_j}$, respectively. But there is no suitable radius to represent category L_j, thereby calculating $perc\_d_{L_j}$ as follows:

$$perc\_d_{L_j} = \left(nl\_d_{L_j} - perc\_d_{L_q}\right) * \rho \tag{4}$$

4.2   The Proposed Quadruplet Network (RQ2)

The triplet network has two constraints, the rationale is to favor distances between the anchor and negative sample while penalizing distances between the anchor and positive sample, which is also our network's goal.

Since each category's easy samples are around the corresponding center, the encryption traffic classification problem is turned into calculating the distance between the samples and the centers. After training the hard samples through the model, all samples should be close to each cluster's center. For testing, we can calculate the distance between the sample and each center and the category of the closest center is the class of the sample. In this subsection, we will introduce our proposed network, which leverages more information among samples to improve classification accuracy.

Quadruplet Composition. With Algorithm 1, we have filtered out easy samples, thereby reducing the network's training pressure. Inspired by the center loss [25], choosing the cluster center as the anchor for training is better and more efficient than randomly choosing two positive samples. However, only using the center loss often cannot achieve good results and it needs to be combined with other loss functions to obtain more feedback information.

We define a quadruplet, which adds a negative sample compared to the triplet. The illustration of CQNet is shown in Fig. 2. The positive and negative samples and the two anchors are embedded into the same metric space such that samples relevant to the two anchors form clusters around them. The main idea is to measure the six edges' relationships marked with 'Pull' and 'Push'. Given two different classes of center from CF as two anchors, $(cf_i, y_i), (cf_j, y_j)$ and two hard samples corresponding to respective center classes, $(f_i^{(y_i)}, y_i)$ (short for (f_i, y_i)), $(f_j^{(y_j)}, y_j)$ (short for (f_j, y_j)). Besides the two constraints from the triplet network, several constraints can be obtained from pairwise combinations within the quadruplet:

1) f_j should be close to cf_j.
2) f_i(or f_j) should be far away from cf_j(or cf_i).
3) cf_i should be far away from cf_j.

Negatives Sampling. As for the quadruplet, some classes of negative samples may be far away from the positive sample, random sampling from all classes may lead to many easy restrictive relationships. FE-set Algorithm 1 aims to filter out simple samples in positive samples, and the purpose of negatives sampling is to filter out easy negative samples.

For any two centers (c_i, c_j), we calculate the Euclidean distance $d(c_i, c_j)$, put it into the matrix CR, the abscissa and the ordinate both represent labels. After selecting f_i, we get the top τ ($\tau = 20$ in this paper) categories closest to y_i through the y_i-th row of CR and f_m is randomly selected from these categories to train the quadruplet network more effectively.

Network Structure. To accommodate the set of quadruplets, we propose a quadruplet network, which can transform f_i to z_i with a nonlinear mapping $Q_\theta : F \rightarrow Z$, θ is the set of weight parameters, F is the raw data of traffic flows. Since the quadruplet is from the same domain, the quadruplet network comprises two Siamese networks, the weights shared. We define $\phi(z_i, z_j) = d(z_i, z_j)$ as the similarity function between f_i and f_j.

Distance-Based Quadruplet Loss. The loss function often sets the margin to a fixed value such as 1 or 2. However, the flow distribution of each category is different. According to *Perc_D*, each cluster's radius is a different value in our dataset, $r \in (0.5, 3)$. And the distance between each center pair is also different. So the proposed distance-based quadruplet loss is improved based on Eq. 3.

As shown in Fig. 2, given outputs quadruplet features $\left[z_f^i, z_f^j, z_{cf}^i, z_{cf}^j\right]$, we can obtain six pairwise similarity value as $\left\{\phi\left(z_n^m, z_{n'}^{m'}\right)\right\}_{n,n'\in\{cf,f\}}^{m,m'\in\{y_i,y_j\}}$. For each pair, there are two states, pulling close or pushing away. However, there is a restrictive relationship, cf_i should be far away from cf_j, our overall method is related to the cluster center and radius so that we discard this restrictive relationship. Hence, the quadruplet loss with the fixed margin (i.e., m for pulling close and m' for pushing away) can be denoted as follows:

$$L_{m,m'} = \left[-d(z_f^i, z_f^j) + m'\right]_+ + \left[d(z_f^i, z_{cf}^i) - m\right]_+ + \left[d(z_f^j, z_{cf}^j) - m\right]_+ + \left[-d(z_f^i, z_{cf}^j) + m'\right]_+ + \left[-d(z_f^j, z_{cf}^i) + m'\right]_+ \tag{5}$$

We have obtained clusters' radii (i.e., *Perc_D*) through Algorithm 1 and the Euclidean distance between any two centers (i.e., CR). As shown in Fig. 2, $r \in Perc\_D$ and $d \in CR$. We adaptively set the margin threshold to make the network accommodate better to the distribution of different categories.

In order to limit the sample to the cluster, given $m(f_i, cf_i) = perc\_d_{y_i}$ and $m(f_j, cf_j) = perc\_d_{y_j}$. For the margin of sample and other centers, the negative sample f_j should be outside of the ball with $d(cf_i, cf_j) - r(y_j)$, so $m(f_i, cf_j) = CR(y_i, y_j) - perc\_d_{y_j}$ and $m(f_j, cf_i) = CR(y_i, y_j) - perc\_d_{y_i}$. For the margin of two samples with different classes, the distance between them should be larger than the distance between the closest samples of the two clusters, so $m(f_i, f_j) = CR(y_i, y_j) - perc\_d_{y_i} - perc\_d_{y_j}$.

5 Performance Evaluation

In this section, we first introduce the dataset and experimental settings. Then, we conduct extensive experiments to evaluate the effectiveness of CQNet, including hyperparameters selection, performance comparison and ablation studies.

5.1 Dataset Collection

We capture the traffic flows of DApps through the routers of a laboratory, meanwhile filter the non-SSL/TLS encrypted traffic. Due to **Chrome** is used as the designated browser by some DApps, so all visits use **Chrome**. The encrypted traffic is captured when users visit DApps through their PCs.

Table 1. The scale of DApps encrypted traffic dataset

Categories	DApps (Number of flows)
Exchanges	1inch(2703), SushiSwap(1508), dYdX(1641), Curve(1460), Matcha(6690), Nash(2023), Mirror(2649), Tokenlon(2356)
Development	Enigma(1543), Rocket Pool(3822), Aelf(999), MyContract(1573)
Finance	Tether(1032), MakerDAO(3863), Nexo(1016), AaveP(4513), Paxos(3495), Harvest(4589), Ampleforth(926), Synlev(1041), BarnBridge(3108)
Gambling	Dice2win(1551), FunFair(1062), Edgeless(2059), Kingtiger(1129)
Governance	Kleros(1510), Decentral Games(1536), Iotex(1026), Aragon(3574)
Marketplace	Knownorigin(2009), Ocean Market(6462), OpenSea(2099), Superrare(1306), District0x(1011), Cryptokitties(4722)
Media	AVXChange(46282), Refereum(1074), Megacryptopolis(13924)
Game	Axie Infinity(1049), BFH(3415), Evolution Land(1516), F1deltatime(6119), Nftegg(1006), Pooltogether(2353)
Property	Decentraland(3932), FOAM(6558)
Social	Livepeer(1337), Loom Network(1073), Catallax(1219), 2key(3705)
High risk	DoubleWay(1045), E2X(1054), Gandhiji(1143), Forsage(3501), Minereum(4557)
Security	Chainlink(1173), Quantstamp Security Network(3203)
Storage	Storj(1020), Numerai(2107)
Identity	LikeCoin(1021), SelfKey(1521)

To construct out DApps dataset, we select top-60 DApps on Ethereum with the most users [2]. The categories contain social, gambling, finance, marketplaces, etc. We collect 199,513 DApps traffic flows. The number of flows for each DApps is summarized in Tabel 1. The dataset is split into training and testing sets. And the validation set is constructed by random sampling from the training set (i.e., train : val : test = 7 : 1 : 2)

5.2   Experiments Settings

Baselines. To evaluate CQNet, we leverage the following six typical methods for comparison.

FFP [18], which fuses time series, packet length and burst features to the high-dimensional feature through a kernel function, which is fed to Random Forest classifier.

APPS (Appscanner) [21], which captures statistical features of packet length, such as mean, minimum, standard deviation of incoming, outgoing, and bi-directional flows. Then using Random Forest to identify mobile applications.

RF+LT [24], which extracts packet length sequence and time series. Then using Random Forest classifier to identify encrypted flows from 11 DApps.

DF+D (DeepFingerprinting) [20], which only uses the information of packet direction from flows, and sends it into a Convolutional Neural Networks to classify the encrypted flows of websites.

FS-net [10], which takes multi-layer bi-GRU encoder and decoder to learn features of flow sequence, which are utilized for classification of 18 applications.

DF+L, which uses the same Convolutional Neural Networks as DF+D, but the input is the packet length sequence.

Setting of the CQNet. We take the raw traffic data as the input of the CQNet. The feature extractor contains four layers. The first two are convolutional (i.e.,32 and 64 kernels of size of 5*5) and the others are fully-connected. As for the quadruplet network, it has four branches with shared weight, one of which has five layers. The first three are convolutional (i.e.,32 kernels of size of 9*9, 64 kernels of size of 5*5, and 128 kernels of size of 3*3) and we replace the output dimension of the final FC layer to be a common metric space without a softmax layer. The SGD optimizer with learning rate of 0.0005 is used and the batch size is 64.

5.3   Hyperparameters of CQNet

CQNet introduces two hyperparameters ρ and τ to control the easy dataset scale and the selection range of negative samples, respectively. We select 30 epochs to compare with other methods. When the epoch is larger than 30, the accuracy increment becomes trivial, less than 0.003, but the training time increases significantly. The setting of 30 epochs is also used in [20].

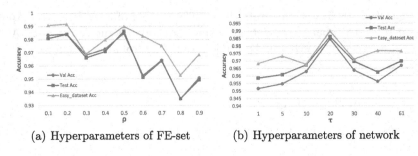

(a) Hyperparameters of FE-set   (b) Hyperparameters of network

Fig. 5. Performance of CQNet with respect to different value of ρ and τ.

First, we fix τ to 20 and train CQNet with different values of ρ (i.e., from 0.1 to 0.9, the interval is 0.1) and show the results in Fig. 5(a). The ρ represents the amount of data selected as the easy dataset after clustering. The smaller the value of ρ, the more samples are used to train the quadruplet network, the higher time-cost required. As such, we suggest setting ρ to 0.5.

Second, we fix ρ to 0.5. Different values of τ (i.e., 1, 5, 10, 20, 30, 40, 61) are set and the results are shown in Fig. 5(b). We find that the optimal value is around 20. Therefore, it is recommended to set τ with 20.

Table 2. Accuracy and time-cost comparisons on DApps traffic classification. The metrics of time-cost includes feature extraction time (FET), classifier training time (CTT), data testing time (DTT)

Method	FFP	APPS	RF+LT	DF+D	DF+L	FS-net	CQNet
Accuracy	0.9122	0.8437	0.8977	0.6502	0.7849	0.9611	0.9837
One epoch CTT	–	–	–	122.65	124.73	137.06	94.58
FET	2230.65	1895.19	1589.49	119.91	113.31	12.52	258.21
CTT	352.05	114.52	203.1	3724.96	3668.14	4184.28	2894.59
DTT	8.19	9.54	8.77	10.33	10.28	12.81	32.89
Total time	2590.89	2019.25	1801.36	3855.2	3791.73	4209.61	3185.69

5.4   Performance Comparison

We use **accuracy** and **time-cost** as the performance metrics, which is defined as the proportion of all DApps flows that are classified correctly. And the comparison results are shown in Table 2. We can make the following observations.

First, we can observe that CQNet outperforms the other methods, with the highest accuracy (0.9837 for hard dataset, 0.9897 for easy dataset), indicating that clustering-based metric learning is helpful to the task of DApps encrypted traffic classification. The confusion matrices of CQNet are shown in Fig. 6. Most of DApps can be accurately identified, while the classification accuracy of one

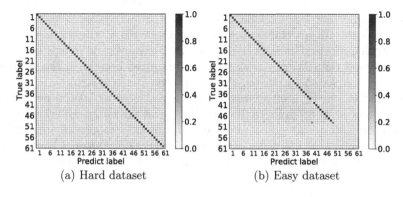

(a) Hard dataset   (b) Easy dataset

Fig. 6. Confusion Matrices of CQNet on hard dataset and easy datset.

DApp is lower than 0.8. To test the easy dataset similarity to all categories, we keep the centers of clusters which belong to NL, so there is no value in a row.

Second, machine learning and deep learning have different emphases on time-cost. The former requires manual extraction of more effective features, while the latter automatically learns more effective features, thus eliminating the need for many experts. The time-cost of our network is the lowest among all compared to deep learning methods. Therefore, it proves that our method can improve the overall efficiency of classification.

5.5 Ablation Studies

We evaluate the contribution of each of CQNet's components. The baseline is the quadruplet network with fixed loss and uses the original dataset to train and test (denoted as base). The other settings are baseline with distance-based quadruplet loss (denoted as base+d), baseline using the hard dataset (denoted as base+h), baseline with all CQNet's components (i.e., CQNet).

Table 3. Performances by different components

Accuracy	base	base+d	base+h	CQNet
Val Acc	0.9539	0.9691	0.9792	0.9837
Test Acc	0.9551	0.9714	0.9796	0.9842
Easy dataset Acc	–	–	0.9862	0.9897

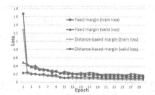

Fig. 7. Comparison results: fixed margin and distance-based margin.

The results are shown in Table 3. We can see that baseline performs the worst, but it still achieved 95.39% accuracy. Compared with the base model, the improvement of base+d indicates that the distance-based quadruplet loss is beneficial for DApps traffic classification. From Fig. 7, the proposed loss is smoother than the fixed margin loss. Besides, the improvement of base+h is more prominent and the efficiency is also greatly improved because of the reduction of training samples. As expected, CQNet achieves the best results.

To provide a more intuitive understanding of the cluster center, we visualize with four sets as shown in Fig. 8. It can be seen that the samples relevant to each anchor form a cluster around it and the radius of most categories are different, which also confirm the main idea of CQNet. Since not all categories have samples in the easy dataset, there is no sample around the few centers in Fig. 8(d).

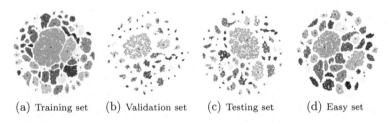

(a) Training set   (b) Validation set   (c) Testing set   (d) Easy set

Fig. 8. Visualization to show the performance of our CQNet on different sets by using t-SNE. The center of each category is denoted as a black dot.

6   Conclusion

In this paper, we proposed CQNet, an approach to filter out easy samples based on a clustering algorithm and classify DApps encrypted traffic through metric learning. The easy dataset and hard dataset are split by FE-set algorithm, which includes mini-batch KMeans algorithm, Kuhn-Munkres algorithm, etc. The hard dataset and center set of clusters are sent to the quadruplet network, which can leverage more restrictive relationships among samples. We validate the effectiveness of CQNet on the real-world network traffic, including above 60 DApps. The experimental results show that CQNet outperforms the state-of-the-art methods. Besides, using the trained classifier to test the easy dataset and its accuracy is higher than the testing set in the hard dataset.

Acknowledgements. This work is supported by The National Key Research and Development Program of China (No.2020YFB1006100, No.2020YFE0200500 and No.2018YFB1800200) and Key research and Development Program for Guangdong Province under grant No. 2019B010137003.

References

1. Ethereum. https://www.ethereum.org/. Accessed 21 June 2021
2. DApps store 2021. https://www.stateofthedapps.com/. Accessed 21 June 2021

3. Cai, X., Zhang, X.C., Joshi, B., Johnson, R.: Touching from a distance: website fingerprinting attacks and defenses. In: Proceedings of the ACM Conference on Computer and Communications Security, CCS, pp. 605–616 (2012)
4. Conti, M., Mancini, L.V., Spolaor, R., Verde, N.V.: Analyzing android encrypted network traffic to identify user actions. IEEE Trans. Inf. Forensics Secur. **11**(1), 114–125 (2016)
5. Feghhi, S., Leith, D.J.: A web traffic analysis attack using only timing information. IEEE Trans. Inf. Forensics Secur. **11**(8), 1747–1759 (2016)
6. Grolman, E., et al.: Transfer learning for user action identication in mobile apps via encrypted trafc analysis. IEEE Intell. Syst. **33**(2), 40–53 (2018)
7. Hayes, J., Danezis, G.: k-fingerprinting: a robust scalable website fingerprinting technique. In: 25th USENIX Security Symposium, pp. 1187–1203 (2016)
8. Korczynski, M., Duda, A.: Markov chain fingerprinting to classify encrypted traffic. In: INFOCOM, pp. 781–789 (2014)
9. Li, R., Xiao, X., Ni, S., Zheng, H.: Byte segment neural network for network traffic classification. In: International Symposium on Quality of Service, pp. 1–10 (2018)
10. Liu, C., He, L., Xiong, G., Cao, Z., Li, Z.: FS-Net: a flow sequence network for encrypted traffic classification. In: INFOCOM, pp. 1171–1179 (2019)
11. Liu, H., Wang, Z., Wang, Y.: Semi-supervised encrypted traffic classification using composite features set. J. Netw. **7**(8), 1195–1200 (2012)
12. Liu, J., Fu, Y., Ming, J., Ren, Y., Sun, L., Xiong, H.: Effective and real-time in-app activity analysis in encrypted internet traffic streams. In: International Conference on Knowledge Discovery and Data Mining, pp. 335–344 (2017)
13. Panchenko, A., et al.: Website fingerprinting at internet scale. In: 23rd Annual Network and Distributed System Security Symposium, NDSS (2016)
14. Rezaei, S., Liu, X.: Deep learning for encrypted traffic classification: an overview. IEEE Commun. Mag. **57**(5), 76–81 (2019)
15. Rimmer, V., Preuveneers, D., Juarez, M., van Goethem, T., Joosen, W.: Automated website fingerprinting through deep learning. In: 25th Annual Network and Distributed System Security Symposium, NDSS (2018)
16. Schroff, F., Kalenichenko, D., Philbin, J.: Facenet: a unified embedding for face recognition and clustering. In: IEEE Conference on Computer Vision and Pattern Recognition, CVPR, pp. 815–823 (2015)
17. Shen, M., Wei, M., Zhu, L., Wang, M.: Classification of encrypted traffic with second-order markov chains and application attribute bigrams. IEEE Trans. Inf. Forensics Secur. **12**(8), 1830–1843 (2017)
18. Shen, M., Zhang, J., Zhu, L., Xu, K., Du, X., Liu, Y.: Encrypted traffic classification of decentralized applications on Ethereum using feature fusion. In: Proceedings of the International Symposium on Quality of Service, IWQoS, pp. 18:1–18:10 (2019)
19. Shi, H., Li, H., Zhang, D., Cheng, C., Cao, X.: An efficient feature generation approach based on deep learning and feature selection techniques for traffic classification. Comput. Netw. **132**, 81–98 (2018)
20. Sirinam, P., Imani, M., Juarez, M., Wright, M.: Deep fingerprinting: undermining website fingerprinting defenses with deep learning. In: CCS, pp. 1928–1943 (2018)
21. Taylor, V.F., Spolaor, R., Conti, M., Martinovic, I.: Appscanner: automatic fingerprinting of smartphone apps from encrypted network traffic. In: IEEE European Symposium on Security and Privacy, EuroS&P, pp. 439–454 (2016)
22. Taylor, V.F., Spolaor, R., Conti, M., Martinovic, I.: Robust smartphone app identification via encrypted network traffic analysis. IEEE Trans. Inf. Forensics Secur. **13**(1), 63–78 (2017)

23. Wang, W., Zhu, M., Zeng, X., Ye, X., Sheng, Y.: Malware traffic classification using convolutional neural network for representation learning. In: 2017 International Conference on Information Networking, ICOIN, pp. 712–717 (2017)
24. Wang, Yu., Li, Z., Gou, G., Xiong, G., Wang, C., Li, Z.: Identifying DApps and user behaviors on Ethereum via encrypted traffic. In: Park, N., Sun, K., Foresti, S., Butler, K., Saxena, N. (eds.) SecureComm 2020. LNICST, vol. 336, pp. 62–83. Springer, Cham (2020). https://doi.org/10.1007/978-3-030-63095-9_4
25. Wen, Y., Zhang, K., Li, Z., Qiao, Y.: A discriminative feature learning approach for deep face recognition. In: Computer Vision - ECCV, pp. 499–515 (2016)
26. Zhou, X., Demetriou, S., He, D., Naveed, M.: Identity, location, disease and more: inferring your secrets from android public resources. In: CCS, pp. 1017–1028 (2013)

SPOT: A Framework for Selection of Prototypes Using Optimal Transport

Karthik S. Gurumoorthy[1]([✉]), Pratik Jawanpuria[2], and Bamdev Mishra[2]

[1] India Machine Learning, Amazon, Bangalore, India
gurumoor@amazon.com
[2] Microsoft, Hyderabad, India
{pratik.jawanpuria,bamdevm}@microsoft.com

Abstract. In this work, we develop an optimal transport (OT) based framework to select informative prototypical examples that best represent a given target dataset. Summarizing a given target dataset via representative examples is an important problem in several machine learning applications where human understanding of the learning models and underlying data distribution is essential for decision making. We model the prototype selection problem as learning a sparse (empirical) probability distribution having the minimum OT distance from the target distribution. The learned probability measure supported on the chosen prototypes directly corresponds to their importance in representing the target data. We show that our objective function enjoys a key property of submodularity and propose an efficient greedy method that is both computationally fast and possess deterministic approximation guarantees. Empirical results on several real world benchmarks illustrate the efficacy of our approach.

Keywords: Targeted prototype selection · Data subset selection · Optimal transport · Submodularity · Parallelizable Greedy method

1 Introduction

Extracting informative and influential samples that best represent the underlying data-distribution is a fundamental problem in machine learning [2,31,33,53,55]. As sizes of datasets have grown, summarizing a dataset with a collection of representative samples from it is of increasing importance to data scientists and domain-specialists [3]. Prototypical samples offer interpretative value in every sphere of humans decision making where machine learning models have become integral such as healthcare [5], information technology [26], and entertainment [42], to name a few. In addition, extracting such compact synopses play a pivotal tool in depicting the scope of a dataset, in detecting outliers [30], and for compressing and manipulating data distributions [43]. Going across domains to

---

K. S. Gurumoorthy, P. Jawanpuria and B. Mishra—Equal contribution.

Y. Dong et al. (Eds.): ECML PKDD 2021, LNAI 12978, pp. 535–551, 2021.
https://doi.org/10.1007/978-3-030-86514-6_33

identify representative examples from a source set that explains a different target set have recently been applied in model agnostic Positive-Unlabeled (PU) learning [13]. Existing works [52] have also studied the generalization properties of machine learning models trained on a prototypical subset of a large dataset.

Works such as [2,8,52,54] consider selecting representative elements (henceforth also referred to as *prototypes*) in the supervised setting, i.e., the selection algorithm has access to the label information of the data points. Recently [22,30] have also explored the problem of prototype selection in the unsupervised setting, in which the selection algorithm has access only to the feature representation of the data points. They view the given dataset Y and a candidate prototype set P (subset of a source dataset X) as empirical distributions q and p, respectively. The prototype selection problem, therefore, is modeled as searching for a distribution p (corresponding to a set $P \subset X$ of data points, typically with a small cardinality) that is a good approximation of the distribution q. For example, [22,30] employ the maximum mean discrepancy (MMD) distance [21] to measure the similarity between the two distributions.

It is well-known that the MMD induces the "flat" geometry of reproducing kernel Hilbert space (RKHS) on the space of probability distributions, as it measures the distance between the mean embeddings of distributions in the RKHS of a universal kernel [21,47]). The individuality of data points is also lost while computing distance between mean embeddings in the MMD setting. The optimal transport (OT) framework, on the other hand, provides a natural metric for comparing probability distributions while respecting the underlying geometry of the data [39,51]. Over the last few years, OT distances (also known as the Wasserstein distances) have found widespread use in several machine learning applications such as image retrieval [44], shape interpolation [48], domain adaptation [6,7,28,37], supervised learning [18,27], and generative model training [1], among others. The *transport plan*, learned while computing the OT distance between the source and target distributions, is the joint distribution between the source and the target distributions. Compared to the MMD, the OT distances enjoy several advantages such as being faithful to the ground metric (geometry over the space of probability distributions) and identifying correspondences at the fine grained level of individual data points via the transport plan.

In this paper, we focus on the unsupervised prototype selection problem and view it from the perspective of the optimal transport theory. To this end, we propose a novel framework for **S**election of **P**rototypes using the **O**ptimal **T**ransport theory or the **SPOT** framework for searching a subset P from a source dataset X (i.e., $P \subset X$) that best represents a target set Y. We employ the Wasserstein distance to estimate the closeness between the distribution representing a candidate set P and set Y. Unlike the typical OT setting, the source distribution (representing P) is unknown in SPOT and needs to be learned along with the transport plan. The prototype selection problem is modeled as learning an empirical source distribution p (representing set X) that has the minimal Wasserstein distance with the empirical target distribution (representing set Y). Additionally, we constrain p to have a small support set (which represents $P \subset X$).

The learned distribution p is also indicative of the relative importance of the prototypes in P in representing Y. Our main contributions are as follows.

- We propose a novel prototype selection framework, SPOT, based on the OT theory.
- We prove that the objective function of the proposed optimization problem in SPOT is submodular, which leads to a tight approximation guarantee of $\left(1 - e^{-1}\right)$ using greedy approximation algorithms [38]. The computations in the proposed greedy algorithm can be implemented efficiently.
- We explain the popular k-medoids clustering [43] formulation as a special case of SPOT formulation (when the source and the target datasets are the same). We are not aware of any prior work that describes such a connection though the relation between Wasserstein distance minimization and k-means is known [4,11].
- Our empirical results show that the proposed algorithm outperforms existing baselines on several real-world datasets. The optimal transport framework allows our approach to seamlessly work in settings where the source (X) and the target (Y) datasets are from different domains.

The outline of the paper is as follows. We provide a brief review of the optimal transport setting, the prototype selection setting, and key definitions in the submodular optimization literature in Sect. 2. The proposed SPOT framework and algorithms are presented in Sect. 3. We discuss how SPOT relates to existing works in Sect. 4. The empirical results are presented in Sect. 5. We conclude the paper in Sect. 6. The proofs and additional results on datasets are available in our extended version [23].

2   Background

2.1   Optimal Transport (OT)

Let $X:=\{\mathbf{x}_i\}_{i=1}^m$ and $Y:=\{\mathbf{y}_j\}_{j=1}^n$ be i.i.d. samples from the source and the target distributions p and q, respectively. In several applications, the true distributions are generally unknown. Their empirical estimates exist and can be employed as follows:

$$p:=\sum_{i=1}^m \mathbf{p}_i \delta_{\mathbf{x}_i}, \quad q:=\sum_{j=1}^n \mathbf{q}_j \delta_{\mathbf{y}_j}, \tag{1}$$

where the probability associated with samples $\mathbf{x}_i$ and $\mathbf{y}_j$ are $\mathbf{p}_i$ and $\mathbf{q}_j$, respectively, and δ is the Dirac delta function. The vectors $\mathbf{p}$ and $\mathbf{q}$ lie on simplices Δ_m and Δ_n, respectively, where $\Delta_k:=\{\mathbf{z} \in \mathbb{R}_+^k | \sum_i \mathbf{z}_i = 1\}$. The OT problem [29] aims at finding a transport plan γ (with the minimal transporting effort) as a solution to

$$\min_{\gamma \in \Gamma(\mathbf{p},\mathbf{q})} \langle \mathbf{C}, \gamma \rangle, \tag{2}$$

where $\Gamma(\mathbf{p},\mathbf{q}):=\{\gamma \in \mathbb{R}_+^{m \times n} | \gamma \mathbf{1} = \mathbf{p}; \gamma^\top \mathbf{1} = \mathbf{q}\}$ is the space of joint distribution between the source and the target marginals. Here, $\mathbf{C} \in \mathbb{R}_+^{m \times n}$ is the ground metric computed as $\mathbf{C}_{ij} = c(\mathbf{x}_i, \mathbf{y}_j)$ and the function $c : \mathcal{X} \times \mathcal{Y} \to \mathbb{R}_+ : (\mathbf{x}, \mathbf{y}) \to c(\mathbf{x}, \mathbf{y})$ represents the *cost* of transporting a unit mass from source $\mathbf{x} \in \mathcal{X}$ to target $\mathbf{y} \in \mathcal{Y}$.

The optimization problem (2) is a linear program. Recently, [10] proposed an efficient solution for learning entropy regularized transport plan γ in (2) using the Sinkhorn algorithm [32]. For a recent survey on OT, please refer to [39].

2.2   Prototype Selection

Selecting representative elements is often posed as identifying a subset P of size k from a set of items X (e.g., data points, features, etc.). The quality of selection is usually governed via a scoring function $f(P)$, which encodes the desirable properties of prototypical samples. For instance, in order to obtain a compact yet informative subset P, the scoring function should discourage redundancy. Recent works [22, 30] have posed prototype selection within the submodular optimization setting by maximizing a MMD based scoring function on the weights ($\mathbf{w}$) of the prototype elements:

$$l(\mathbf{w}) = \boldsymbol{\mu}^T \mathbf{w} - \frac{1}{2}\mathbf{w}^T \mathbf{K}\mathbf{w} \text{ s.t. } \|\mathbf{w}\|_0 \leq k. \tag{3}$$

Here, $\|\mathbf{w}\|_0$ is ℓ_0 norm of $\mathbf{w}$ representing the number of non-zero values, the entries of the vector $\boldsymbol{\mu}$ contains the mean of the inner product for every source point with the target data points computed in the kernel embedding space, and $\mathbf{K}$ is the Gram matrix of a universal kernel (e.g., Gaussian) corresponding to the source instances. The locations of non-zero values in $\mathbf{w}$, $supp(\mathbf{w}) = \{i : \mathbf{w}_i > 0\}$, known as its *support* correspond to the element indices that are chosen as prototypes, i.e. $P = supp(\mathbf{w})$. While the MMD-Critic method in [30] enforces that all non-zero entries in $\mathbf{w}$ equal to $1/k$, the ProtoDash algorithm in [22] imposes non-negativity constraints and learns $\mathbf{w}$ as part of the algorithm. Both propose greedy algorithms that effectively evaluate the *incremental* benefit of adding an element in the prototypical set P. In contrast to the MMD function in (3), to the best of our knowledge, ours is the first work which leverages the optimal transport (OT) framework to extract such compact representation. We prove that the proposed objective function is submodular, which ensures tight approximation guarantee using greedy approximate algorithms.

2.3   Submodularity

We briefly review the concept of submodular and weakly submodular functions, which we later use to prove key theoretical results.

Definition 1 (Submodularity and Monotonicity). *Consider any two sets* $A \subseteq B \subseteq [m]$. *A set function* $f(\cdot)$ *is submodular if and only if for any* $i \notin B$, $f(A \cup i) - f(A) \geq f(B \cup i) - f(B)$. *The function is called* monotone *when* $f(A) \leq f(B)$.

Submodularity implies diminishing returns where the incremental gain in adding a new element i to a set A is at least as high as adding to its superset B [19]. Another characterization of submodularity is via the submodularity ratio [12,16] defined as follows.

Definition 2 (Submodularity Ratio). *Given two disjoint sets L and S, and a set function $f(\cdot)$, the submodularity ratio of $f(\cdot)$ for the ordered pair (L, S) is given by:*

$$\alpha_{L,S} := \frac{\sum_{i \in S} [f(L \cup \{i\}) - f(L)]}{f(L \cup S) - f(L)}. \tag{4}$$

Submodularity ratio captures the increment in $f(\cdot)$ by adding the entire subset S to L, compared to summed gain of adding its elements individually to L. It is known that $f(\cdot)$ is submodular if and only if $\alpha_{L,S} \geq 1, \forall L, S$. In the case where $0 \leq \epsilon \leq \alpha_{L,S} < 1$ for an independent constant ϵ, $f(\cdot)$ is called *weakly submodular* [12].

We define submodularity ratio of a set P with respect to an integer s as follows:

$$\alpha_{P,s} := \max_{L,S:L \cap S = \emptyset, L \subseteq P, |S| \leq s} \alpha_{L,S}. \tag{5}$$

It should be emphasized that unlike the definition in [16, Equation 3], the above Eq. (5) involves the `max` operator instead of the `min`. This specific form is later used to produce approximation bounds for the proposed approach (presented in Algorithm 1). Both (strongly) submodular and weakly submodular functions enjoy provable performance bounds when the set elements are selected incrementally and greedily [16,22,38].

3 SPOT Framework

3.1 SPOT Problem Formulation

Let $X = \{\mathbf{x}_i\}_{i=1}^m$ be a set of m source points, $Y = \{\mathbf{y}_j\}_{j=1}^n$ be a target set of n data points, and $\mathbf{C} \in \mathbb{R}_+^{m \times n}$ represents the ground metric. Our aim is to select a small and weighted subset $P \subset X$ of size $k \ll m$ that best describes Y. To this end, we develop an optimal transport (OT) based framework for selection of prototypes. Traditionally, OT is defined as a minimization problem over the transport plan γ as in (2). In our setting, we pre-compute a *similarity* matrix $\mathbf{S} \in \mathbb{R}_+^{m \times n}$ from $\mathbf{C}$, for instance, as $\mathbf{S}_{ij} = \beta - \mathbf{C}_{ij}$ where $\beta > \|\mathbf{C}\|_\infty$. This allows to equivalently represent the OT problem (2) as a maximization problem with the objective function as $\langle \mathbf{S}, \gamma \rangle$. Treating it as a maximization problem enables to establish connection with submodularity and leverage standard greedy algorithms for its optimization [38].

We pose the problem of selecting a prototypical set as learning a sparse support empirical source distribution $w = \sum_{\mathbf{x}_i \in P} \mathbf{w}_i \delta_{\mathbf{x}_i}$ that has maximum closeness to the target distribution in terms of the optimal transport measure. Here, the weight $\mathbf{w} \in \Delta_m$, where $\Delta_m := \{\mathbf{z} \in \mathbb{R}_+^m | \sum_i \mathbf{z}_i = 1\}$. Consequently, $\mathbf{w}$ denotes the relative importance of the samples. Hence, the constraint $|P| \le k$ for the prototype set P translates to $|supp(\mathbf{w})| \le k$ where $supp(\mathbf{w}) \subseteq P$. We evaluate the suitability of a candidate prototype set $P \subset X$ with an OT based measure on sets. To elaborate, index the elements in X from 1 to m and let $[m] := \{1, 2, \dots, m\}$ denote the first m natural numbers. Given any index set of prototypes $P \subseteq [m]$, define a set function $f : 2^{[m]} \to \mathbb{R}_+$ as:

$$f(P) := \max_{\mathbf{w}:supp(\mathbf{w}) \subseteq P} \max_{\gamma \in \Gamma(\mathbf{w},\mathbf{q})} \langle \mathbf{S}, \gamma \rangle, \tag{6}$$

where $\mathbf{q} \in \Delta_n$ corresponds to the (given) weights of the target samples[1] in the empirical target distribution q as in (1). The learned transport plan γ in (6) is a joint distribution between the elements in P and Y, which may be useful in downstream applications requiring, e.g., barycentric mapping.

Our goal is to find that set P which maximizes $f(\cdot)$ subject to the cardinality constraint. To this end, the proposed SPOT problem is

$$P^* = \arg\max_{P \subseteq [m], |P| \le k} f(P), \tag{7}$$

where $f(P)$ is defined in (6). The entries of the optimal weight vector $\mathbf{w}^*$ corresponding to P^* in (7) indicate the importance of the prototypes in summarizing set Y. The SPOT (7) and the standard OT (2) settings are different as: (a) the source distribution w is learned as a part of the SPOT optimization problem formulation and (b) the source distribution w is enforced to have a sparse support of utmost size k so that the prototypes create a compact summary. In the next section, we analyze the objective function in the SPOT optimization problem (7), characterize it with a few desirable properties, and develop a computationally efficient greedy approximation algorithm.

3.2 Equivalent Reduced Representations of SPOT Objective

Though the definition of $f(\cdot)$ in (6) involves maximization over two coupled variables $\mathbf{w}$ and γ, it can be reduced to an equivalent optimization problem involving only γ (by eliminating $\mathbf{w}$ altogether). To this end, let $k = |P|$ and denote $\mathbf{S}_P$ a $k \times n$ sub-matrix of $\mathbf{S}$ containing only those rows indexed by P. We then have the following lemma:

Lemma 3. *The set function $f(\cdot)$ in (6) can be equivalently defined as an optimization problem only over the transport plan, i.e.,*

$$f(P) = \max_{\gamma \in \Gamma_P(\mathbf{q})} \langle \mathbf{S}_P, \gamma \rangle, \tag{8}$$

where $\Gamma_P(\mathbf{q}) := \{\gamma \in \mathbb{R}_+^{k \times n} | \gamma^\top \mathbf{1} = \mathbf{q}\}$. Let γ^* be an optimal solution of (8). Then, $(\mathbf{w}^*, \gamma^*)$ is an optimal solution of (6) where $\mathbf{w}^* = \gamma^* \mathbf{1}$.

---

[1] In the absence of domain knowledge, uniform weights $\mathbf{q} = 1/n$ can be a default choice.

A closer look into the set function in (8) reveals that the optimization for γ can be done in parallel over the n target points, and its solution assumes a closed-form expression. It is worth noting that the constraint $\gamma^T \mathbf{1} = \mathbf{q}$ as well as the objective $\langle \mathbf{S}_P, \gamma \rangle$ decouple over each column of γ. Hence, (8) can be solved across the columns of variable γ independently, thereby allowing parallelism over the target set. In other words,

$$f(P) = \sum_{j=1}^{n} \max_{\gamma^j \in \mathbb{R}_+^k} \left\langle \mathbf{S}_P^j, \gamma^j \right\rangle, \text{ s.t. } \mathbf{1}^T \gamma^j = \mathbf{q}_j \ \forall j, \tag{9}$$

where $\mathbf{S}_P^j$ and γ^j denote the jth column vectors of the matrices $\mathbf{S}_P$ and γ, respectively. Furthermore, if i_j denotes the location of the maximum value in the vector $\mathbf{S}_P^j$, then an optimal solution γ^* can be easily seen to inherit an extremely sparse structure with exactly one non-zero element in each column j at the row location i_j, i.e., $\gamma_{i_j,j}^* = \mathbf{q}_j, \forall j$ and 0 everywhere. So (9) can be reduced to

$$f(P) = \sum_{j=1}^{n} \mathbf{q}_j \max_{i \in P} \mathbf{S}_{ij}. \tag{10}$$

The above observation makes the computation $f(P)$ in (10) particularly suited when using GPUs. Further, due to this specific solution structure in (10), determining the function value for any incremental set is an inexpensive operation as shown below.

Lemma 4 (Fast incremental computation). *Given any set P and its function value $f(P)$, the value at the incremental selection $f(P \cup S)$ obtained by adding $s = |S|$ new elements to P, can be computed in $O(sn)$.*

Remark 5. By setting $P = \emptyset$ and $f(\emptyset) = 0$, $f(S)$ for any set S can be determined efficiently as discussed in Lemma 4.

3.3   SPOT Optimization Algorithms

As obtaining the global optimum subset P^* for the problem (7) is NP complete, we now present two approximation algorithms for SPOT: SPOTsimple and SPOTgreedy.

SPOTsimple: A Fast Heuristic Algorithm. SPOTsimple is an extremely fast heuristic that works as follows. For every source point $\mathbf{x}_i$, SPOTsimple determines the indices of target points $\mathcal{T}_i = \{j : \mathbf{S}_{ij} \geq \mathbf{S}_{\tilde{i}j} \text{ for all} \tilde{i} \neq i\}$ that have the highest similarity to $\mathbf{x}_i$ compared to other source points. In other words, it solves (10) with $P = [m]$, i.e., no cardinality constraint, to determine the initial transport plan γ where $\gamma_{ij} = \mathbf{q}_j$ if $j \in \mathcal{T}_i$ and 0 everywhere else. It then computes the source weights as $\mathbf{w} = \gamma \mathbf{1}$ with each entry $\mathbf{w}_i = \sum_{j \in \mathcal{T}_i} \mathbf{q}_j$. The top-$k$ source points based on the weights $\mathbf{w}$ are chosen as the prototype set P. The final transport plan γ_P is recomputed using (10) over P. The total computational cost incurred by SPOTsimple for selecting k prototypes is $O(mn)$.

Algorithm 1. SPOTgreedy

Input: sparsity level k or lower bound ϵ on increment in $f(\cdot)$, X, Y, s, and $\mathbf{q}$.
Initialize $P = \emptyset$
while $|P| \leq k$ or increment in objective $\geq \epsilon$. **do**
     Define vector $\boldsymbol{\beta}$ with entries $\boldsymbol{\beta}_i = f(P \cup \{i\}) - f(P)$, $\forall i \in [m] \setminus P$.
     S = Set of indices of top s largest elements in $\boldsymbol{\beta}$.
     $P = P \cup S$.
end while
$\gamma_P = \arg\max_{\gamma \in \Gamma_P(\mathbf{q})} \langle \mathbf{S}_P, \gamma \rangle$; $\mathbf{w}_P = \gamma_P \mathbf{1}$.
Return P, γ_P, $\mathbf{w}_P$.

SPOTgreedy: A Greedy and Incremental Prototype Selection Algorithm. As we discuss later in our experiments (Sect. 5), though SPOTsimple is computationally very efficient, its accuracy of prototype selection is sensitive to the skewness of class instances in the target distribution. When the samples from different classes are uniformly represented in the target set, SPOTsimple is indeed able to select prototypes from the source set that are representative of the target. However, when the target is skewed and the class distributions are no longer uniform, SPOTsimple primarily chooses from the dominant class leading to biased selection and poor performance (see Fig. 2(a)).

To this end, we present our method of choice SPOTgreedy, detailed in Algorithm 1, that leverages the following desirable properties of the function $f(\cdot)$ in (10) to *greedily and incrementally* build the prototype set P. For choosing k protototypes, SPOTgreedy costs $O(mnk/s)$. As most operations in SPOTgreedy involve basic matrix manipulations, the practical implementation cost of SPOTgreedy is considerably low.

Lemma 6 (Submodularity). *The set function $f(\cdot)$ defined in (10) is monotone and submodular* [36].

The submodularity of $f(\cdot)$ enables to provide provable approximation bounds for greedy element selections in SPOTgreedy. The algorithm begins by setting the current selection $P = \emptyset$. Without loss of generality, we assume $f(\emptyset) = 0$ as $f(\cdot)$ is monotonic. In each iteration, it determines those s elements from the remainder set $[m] \setminus P$, denoted by S, that when individually added to P result in maximum incremental gain. This can be implemented efficiently as discussed in Lemma 4. Here $s \geq 1$ is the user parameter that decides the number of elements chosen in each iteration. The set S is then added to P. The algorithm proceeds for $\lceil \frac{k}{s} \rceil$ iterations to select k prototypes. As function $f(\cdot)$ in (8) is both monotone and submodular, it has the characteristic of diminishing returns. Hence, an alternative stopping criterion could be the minimum expected increment ϵ in the function value at each iteration. The algorithm stops when the increment in the function value is below the specified threshold ϵ.

Approximation Guarantee for SPOTgreedy. We note the following result on the upper bound on the submodularity ratio (4). Let $s = |S|$. When $f(\cdot)$ is monotone, then

$$\alpha_{L,S} \leq \frac{\sum_{i \in S} [f(L \cup \{i\}) - f(L)]}{\max_{i \in S} [f(L \cup \{i\}) - f(L)]} \leq s \qquad (11)$$

and hence $\alpha_{P,s} \leq s$. In particular, $s = 1$ implies $\alpha_{P,1} = 1$, as for any $L \subseteq P$, $\alpha_{L,S} = 1$ when $|S| = 1$. Our next result provides the performance bound for the proposed SPOTgreedy algorithm.

Theorem 7 (Performance bounds for SPOTgreedy). *Let P be the final set returned by the SPOTgreedy method described in Algorithm 1. Let $\alpha = \alpha_{P,s}$ be the submodularity ratio of the set P w.r.t. s. If P^* is the optimal set of k elements that maximizes $f(\cdot)$ in the SPOT optimization problem (7), then*

$$f(P) \geq f(P^*) \left[1 - e^{-\frac{1}{\alpha}}\right] \geq f(P^*) \left[1 - e^{-\frac{1}{s}}\right]. \qquad (12)$$

When $s = 1$ we recover the known approximation guarantee of $\left(1 - e^{-1}\right)$ [38].

3.4   k-Medoids as a Special Case of SPOT

Consider the specific setting where the source and the target datasets are the same, i.e., $X = Y$. Let $n = |X|$ and $q_j = 1/n$ having uniform weights on the samples. Selecting a prototypical set $P \subset X$ is in fact a data summarization problem of choosing few representative exemplars from a given set of n data points, and can be thought as an output of a clustering method where P contains the cluster centers. A popular clustering method is the k-medoids algorithm that ensures the cluster centers are exemplars chosen from actual data points [43]. As shown in [36], the objective function for the k-medoids problem is

$$g(P) = \frac{1}{n} \sum_{j=1}^{n} \max_{\mathbf{z} \in P} l(\mathbf{z}, \mathbf{x}_j),$$

where $l(\mathbf{x}_i, \mathbf{x}_j) = \mathbf{S}_{ij}$ defines the similarity between the respective data points. Comparing it against (10) gives a surprising connection that the *k-medoids algorithm is a special case of learning an optimal transport plan with a sparse support in the setting where the source and target distributions are the same*. Though the relation between OT and k-means is discussed in [4,11], we are not cognizant of any prior works that explains k-medoids from the lens of optimal transport. However, the notion of *transport* loses its relevance as there is no distinct target distribution to which the source points need to be transported. It should be emphasized that the connection with k-medoids is only in the limited case where the source and target distributions are the same. Hence, the popular algorithms that solve the k-medoids problem [46] like PAM, CLARA, and CLARANS cannot be applied in the general setting when the distributions are *different*.

4 Related Works and Discussion

As discussed earlier, recent works [22, 30] view the unsupervised prototype selection problem as searching for a set $P \subset X$ whose underlying distribution is similar to the one corresponding to the target dataset Y. However, instead of the true source and target distributions, only samples from them are available. In such a setting, φ-divergences [9] e.g., the total variation distance and KL-divergence, among others require density estimation or space-partitioning/bias-correction techniques [47], which can be computationally prohibitive in higher dimensions. Moreover, they may be agnostic to the natural geometry of the ground metric. The maximum mean discrepancy (MMD) metric (3) employed by [22, 30], on the other hand, can be computed efficiently but does not faithfully lift the ground metric of the samples [17].

We propose an optimal transport (OT) based prototype selection approach. OT framework respects the intrinsic geometry of the space of the distributions. Moreover, there is an additional flexibility in the choice of the ground metric, e.g., ℓ_1-norm distance, which need not be a (universal) kernel induced function sans which the distribution approximation guarantees of MMD may no longer be applicable [21]. Solving the classical OT problem (2) is known to be computationally more expensive than computing MMD. However, our setting differs from the classical OT setup, as the source distribution is also learned in (6). As shown in Lemmas 3 & 4, the joint learning of the source distribution and the optimal transport plan has an equivalent but computationally efficient reformulation (8).

Using OT is also favorable from a theoretical standpoint. Though the MMD function in [30] is proven to be submodular, it is only under restricted conditions like the choice of kernel matrix and equal weighting of prototypes. The work in [22] extends [30] by allowing for unequal weights and eliminating any additional conditions on the kernel, but forgoes submodularity as the resultant MMD objective (3) is only weakly submodular. In this backdrop, the SPOT objective function (7) is submodular without requiring any further assumptions. It is worth noting that submodularity leads to a tighter approximation guarantee of $\left(1 - e^{-1}\right)$ using greedy approximation algorithms [38], whereas the best greedy based approximation for weak submodular functions (submodularity ratio of $\alpha < 1$) is only $(1 - e^{-\alpha})$ [16]. A better theoretical approximation of the OT based subset selection encourages the selection of better quality prototypes.

5 Experiments

We evaluate the generalization performance and computational efficiency of our algorithms against state-of-the-art on several real-world datasets. The codes are available at https://pratikjawanpuria.com. The following methods are compared.

- **MMD-Critic** [30]: it uses a maximum mean discrepancy (MMD) based scoring function. All the samples are weighted equally in the scoring function.
- **ProtoDash** [22]: it uses a *weighted* MMD based scoring function. The learned weights indicate the importance of the samples.

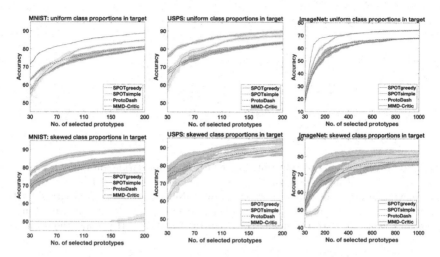

Fig. 1. Performance of different prototype selection algorithms. The standard deviation for every k is represented as a lighter shaded band around the mean curve corresponding to each method. [Top row] all the classes have uniform representation in the target set. [Bottom row] the challenging skewed setting where a randomly chosen class represents 50% of the target set (while the remaining classes together uniformly represent the rest).

- **SPOTsimple**: our fast heuristic algorithm described in Sect. 3.3.
- **SPOTgreedy**: our greedy and incremental algorithm (Algorithm 1).

Following [2,22,30], we validate of the quality of the representative samples selected by different prototype selection algorithms via the performance of the corresponding *nearest prototype classifier*. Let X and Y represent source and target datasets containing different class distributions and let $P \subseteq X$ be a candidate representative set of the target Y. The quality of P is evaluated by classifying the target set instances with 1-nearest neighbour (1-NN) classifier parameterized by the elements in P. The class information of the samples in P is made available during this evaluation stage. Such classifiers can achieve better generalization performance than the standard 1-NN classifier due to reduction of noise overfitting [8] and have been found useful for large scale classification problems [50,54].

5.1 Prototype Selection Within Same Domain

We consider the following benchmark datasets.

- **ImageNet** [45]: we use the popular subset corresponding to ILSVRC 2012–2017 competition. The images have 2048 dimensional deep features [24].

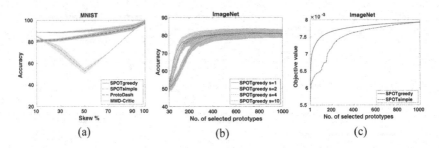

Fig. 2. (a) Comparisons of different algorithms in representing targets with varying skew percentage of a MNIST digit; (b) Performance of our SPOTgreedy algorithm with varying subset selection size s on the ImageNet dataset; (c) Comparison of the objective value (7) obtained by the proposed algorithms SPOTgreedy and SPOTsimple for various values of k. SPOTgreedy consistently obtains a better approximation.

- **MNIST** [34] is a handwritten digit dataset consisting of greyscale images of digits $\{0,\ldots,9\}$. The images are of 28×28 pixels.
- **USPS** dataset [25] consists of handwritten greyscale images of $\{0,\ldots,9\}$ digits represented as 16×16 pixels.
- **Letter** dataset [15] consists of images of twenty-six capital letters of the English alphabets. Each letter is represented as a 16 dimensional feature vector.
- **Flickr** [49] is the Yahoo/Flickr Creative Commons multi-label dataset consisting of descriptive tags of various real-world outdoor/indoor images.

Results on the Letter and Flickr datasets are discussed in the extended version [23].

Experimental Setup. In the first set of experiments, all the classes are equally represented in the target set. In second set of experiments, the target sets are skewed towards a randomly chosen class, whose instances (digit/letter) form $z\%$ of the target set and the instances from the other classes uniformly constitute the remaining $(100 - z)\%$. For a given dataset, the source set is same for all the experiments and uniformly represents all the classes. Results are averaged over ten randomized runs. More details on the experimental set up are given in the extended version [23].

Results. Figure 1 (top row) shows the results of the first set of experiments on MNIST, USPS, and ImageNet. We plot the test set accuracy for a range of top-k prototypes selected. We observe that the proposed SPOTgreedy outperforms ProtoDash and MMD-Critic over the whole range of k. Figure 1 (bottom row) shows the results when samples of a (randomly chosen) class constitutes 50% of the target set. SPOTgreedy again dominates in this challenging setting. We observe that in several instances, SPOTgreedy opens up a significant performance gap even with only a few selected prototypes. The average running time on CPU of algorithms on the ImageNet dataset are: 55.0 s (SPOTgreedy), 0.06 s (SPOTsimple), 911.4 s (ProtoDash), and 710.5 s (MMD-Critic). We observe that

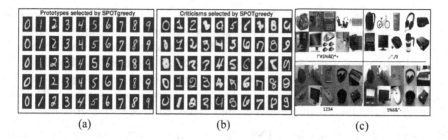

(a)   (b)   (c)

Fig. 3. (a) Prototypes selected by SPOTgreedy for the dataset containing one of the ten MNIST digits (column-wise); (b) Criticisms chosen by SPOTgreedy for the dataset containing one of the ten MNIST digits (column-wise); (c) Example images representing the ten classes in the four domains of the Office-Caltech dataset [20].

Table 1. Accuracy obtained on the Office-Caltech dataset.

Task	MMD-Critic	MMD-Critic+OT	ProtoDash	ProtoDash+OT	SPOTsimple	SPOTgreedy
$A \rightarrow C$	73.98	78.16	70.23	72.28	82.62	**83.60**
$A \rightarrow D$	75.16	72.61	77.71	71.97	80.25	**82.80**
$A \rightarrow W$	51.53	62.71	48.81	58.64	62.37	**75.59**
$C \rightarrow A$	83.71	86.17	83.82	87.25	71.92	**90.03**
$C \rightarrow D$	70.06	75.16	71.34	70.70	75.80	**89.17**
$C \rightarrow W$	49.83	54.92	46.44	53.56	70.85	**82.03**
$D \rightarrow A$	82.85	85.21	83.39	83.82	**91.00**	90.89
$D \rightarrow C$	78.25	78.34	75.40	79.41	85.38	**86.27**
$D \rightarrow W$	80.00	84.41	85.08	86.10	75.59	**92.20**
$W \rightarrow A$	71.60	78.56	68.38	74.71	**87.03**	84.99
$W \rightarrow C$	67.20	75.76	65.86	74.60	74.06	**83.12**
$W \rightarrow D$	92.36	**96.18**	88.54	89.81	86.62	94.90
Average	73.04	77.35	72.08	75.24	78.36	**86.30**

both our algorithms, SPOTgreedy and SPOTsimple, are much faster than both ProtoDash and MMD-Critic.

Figure 2(a) shows that SPOTgreedy achieves the best performance on different skewed versions of the MNIST dataset (with $k = 200$). Interestingly, in cases where the target distribution is either uniform or heavily skewed, our heuristic non-incremental algorithm SPOTsimple can select prototypes that match the target distribution well. However, in the harder setting when skewness of class instances in the target dataset varies from 20% to 80%, SPOTsimple predominantly selects the skewed class leading to a poor performance.

In Fig. 2(b), we plot the performance of SPOTgreedy for different choices of s (which specifies the number of elements chosen simultaneously in each iteration). We consider the setting where the target has 50% skew of one of the ImageNet digits. Increasing s proportionally decreases the computational time as the number of iterations $\lceil \frac{k}{s} \rceil$ steadily decreases with s. However, choosing few elements simultaneously generally leads to better target representation. We note that between $s = 1$ and $s = 10$, the degradation in quality is only marginal even when we choose as few as 110 prototypes and the performance gap continuously narrows with more prototype selection. However, the time taken by SPOTgreedy with $s = 10$ is 5.7s, which is almost the expected 10x speedup compared to SPOTgreedy with $s = 1$ which takes 55.0s. In this setting, we also compare the qualitative performance of the proposed algorithms in solving Problem (7). Figure 2(c) shows the objective value obtained after every selected prototype on ImageNet. SPOTgreedy consistently obtains a better objective than SPOTsimple, showing the benefit of the greedy and incremental selection approach.

Identifying Criticisms for MNIST. We further make use of the prototypes selected by SPOTgreedy to identify *criticisms*. These are data points belonging to the region of input space not well explained by prototypes and are farthest away from them. We use a witness function similar to [30, Section 3.2]. The columns of Fig. 3(b) visualizes the few chosen criticisms, one for each of the 10 datasets containing samples of the respective MNIST digits. It is evident that the selected data points are indeed outliers for the corresponding digit class. Since the criticisms are those points that are maximally dissimilar from the prototypes, it is also a reflection on how well the prototypes of SPOTgreedy represent the underlying class as seen in Fig. 3(a), where in each column we plot the selected prototypes for a dataset comprising one of the ten digits.

5.2   Prototype Selection from Different Domains

Section 5.1 focused on settings where the source and the target datasets had similar/dissimilar class distributions. We next consider a setting where the source and target datasets additionally differ in feature distribution, e.g., due to covariate shift [41].

Figure 2(c) shows examples from the classes of the Office-Caltech dataset [20], which has images from four domains: Amazon (online website), Caltech (image dataset), DSLR (images from a DSLR camera), and Webcam (images from a webcam). Images from the same class vary across the four domains due to several factors such as different background, lighting conditions, etc. The number of data points in each domain is: 958 (A: Amazon), 1123 (C: Caltech), 157 (D: DSLR), and 295 (W: Webcam). The number of instances per class per domain ranges from 8 to 151. DeCAF6 features [14] of size 4096 are used for all the images. We design the experiment similar to Sect. 5.1 by considering each domain, in turn, as the source or the target. There are twelve different tasks where task $A \rightarrow W$ implies that Amazon and Webcam are the source and the target domains, respectively. The total number of selected prototypes is 20.

Results. Table 1 reports the accuracy obtained on every task. We observe that our SPOTgreedy significantly outperforms MMD-Critic and ProtoDash. This is because SPOTgreedy learns both the prototypes as well as the transport plan between the prototypes and the target set. The transport plan allows the prototypes to be transported to the target domain via the barycentric mapping, a characteristic of the optimal transport framework. SPOTgreedy is also much better than SPOTsimple due to its superior incremental nature of prototype selection. We also empower the non-OT based baselines for the domain adaptation setting as follows. After selecting the prototypes via a baseline, we learn an OT plan between the selected prototypes and the target data points by solving the OT problem (2). The distribution of the prototypes is taken to be the normalized weights obtained by the baseline. This ensures that the prototypes selected by MMD-Critic+OT, and ProtoDash+OT are also transported to the target domain. Though we observe marked improvements in the performance of MMD-Critic+OT and ProtoDash+OT, the proposed SPOTgreedy and SPOT-simple still outperform them.

6   Conclusion

We have looked at the prototype selection problem from the viewpoint of optimal transport. In particular, we show that the problem is equivalent to learning a sparse source distribution w, whose probability values $\mathbf{w}_i$ specify the relevance of the corresponding prototype in representing the given target set. After establishing connections with submodularity, we proposed the SPOTgreedy algorithm that employs incremental greedy selection of prototypes and comes with (i) deterministic theoretical guarantees, (ii) simple implementation with updates that are amenable to parallelization, and (iii) excellent performance on different benchmarks.

Future Works: A few interesting generalizations and research directions are as follows.

- Our k-prototype selection problem (7) may be viewed as learning a ℓ_0-norm regularized (fixed-support) Wasserstein barycenter of a single distribution. Extending it to learning sparse Waserstein barycenter of multiple distributions may be useful in applications like model compression, noise removal, etc.
- With the Gromov-Wasserstein (GW) distance [35,40], the OT distance has been extended to settings where the source and the target distributions do not share the same feature and metric space. Extending SPOT with the GW-distances is useful when the source and the target domains share similar concepts/categories/classes but are defined over different feature spaces.

References

1. Arjovsky, M., Chintala, S., Bottou, L.: Wasserstein generative adversarial networks. In: ICML (2017)
2. Bien, J., Tibshirani, R.: Prototype selection for interpretable classification. Ann. Appl. Stat. **5**(4), 2403–2424 (2011)
3. Bien, J., Tibshirani, R.: Hierarchical clustering with prototypes via minimax linkage. J. Am. Stat. Assoc. **106**(495), 1075–1084 (2011)
4. Canas, G., Rosasco, L.: Learning probability measures with respect to optimal transport metrics. In: NeurIPS (2012)

5. Caruana, R., Lou, Y., Gehrke, J., Koch, P., Sturm, M., Elhadad, N.: Intelligible models for healthcare. In: SIGKDD (2015)
6. Courty, N., Flamary, R., Habrard, A., Rakotomamonjy, A.: Joint distribution optimal transportation for domain adaptation. In: NeurIPS (2017)
7. Courty, N., Flamary, R., Tuia, D., Rakotomamonjy, A.: Optimal transport for domain adaptation. TPAMI 39(9), 1853–1865 (2017)
8. Crammer, K., Gilad-Bachrach, R., Navot, A., Tishby, N.: Margin analysis of the LVQ algorithm. In: NeurIPS (2002)
9. Csiszár, I.: A class of measures of informativity of observation channels. Period. Math. Hung. 2(1), 191–213 (1972)
10. Cuturi, M.: Sinkhorn distances: lightspeed computation of optimal transport. In: NeurIPS (2013)
11. Cuturi, M., Doucet, A.: Fast computation of Wasserstein barycenters. In: ICML (2014)
12. Das, A., Kempe, D.: Submodular meets spectral: greedy algorithms for subset selection, sparse approximation and dictionary selection. In: ICML (2011)
13. Dhurandhar, A., Gurumoorthy, K.S.: Classifier invariant approach to learn from positive-unlabeled data. In: IEEE ICDM (2020)
14. Donahue, J., et al.: DeCAF: a deep convolutional activation feature for generic visual recognition. In: ICML (2014)
15. Dua, D., Graff, C.: UCI machine learning repository (2017)
16. Elenberg, E., Khanna, R., Dimakis, A.G., Negahban, S.: Restricted strong convexity implies weak submodularity. Ann. Stat. 46, 3539–3568 (2018)
17. Feydy, J., Séjourné, T., Vialard, F.X., Amari, S., Trouvé, A., Peyré, G.: Interpolating between optimal transport and MMD using Sinkhorn divergences. In: AISTATS (2018)
18. Frogner, C., Zhang, C., Mobahi, H., Araya-Polo, M., Poggio, T.: Learning with a Wasserstein loss. In: NeurIPS (2015)
19. Fujishige, S.: Submodular Functions and Optimization. Elsevier (2005)
20. Gong, B., Shi, Y., Sha, F., Grauman, K.: Geodesic flow kernel for unsupervised domain adaptation. In: CVPR (2012)
21. Gretton, A., Borgwardt, K.M., Rasch, M., Schölkopf, B., Smola, A.J.: A kernel two-sample test. J. Mach. Learn. Res. 13(25), 723–773 (2012)
22. Gurumoorthy, K.S., Dhurandhar, A., Cecchi, G., Aggarwal, C.: Efficient data representation by selecting prototypes with importance weights. In: IEEE ICDM (2019)
23. Gurumoorthy, K.S., Jawanpuria, P., Mishra, B.: SPOT: a framework for selection of prototypes using optimal transport. Technical report, arXiv preprint arXiv:2103.10159 (2021)
24. He, K., Zhang, X., Ren, S., Sun, J.: Deep residual learning for image recognition. In: CVPR (2016)
25. Hull, J.: A database for handwritten text recognition research. TPAMI 16(5), 550–554 (1994)
26. Idé, T., Dhurandhar, A.: Supervised item response models for informative prediction. Knowl. Inf. Syst. 51(1), 235–257 (2017)
27. Jawanpuria, P., Dev, S., Mishra, B.: Efficient robust optimal transport: formulations and algorithms. Technical report, arXiv preprint arXiv:2010.11852 (2020)
28. Jawanpuria, P., Meghwanshi, M., Mishra, B.: Geometry-aware domain adaptation for unsupervised alignment of word embeddings. In: ACL (2020)
29. Kantorovich, L.: On the translocation of masses. Doklady Acad. Sci. USSR 37, 199–201 (1942)

30. Kim, B., Khanna, R., Koyejo, O.: Examples are not enough, learn to criticize! criticism for interpretability. In: NeurIPS (2016)
31. Kim, B., Rudin, C., Shah, J.: The Bayesian case model: a generative approach for case-based reasoning and prototype classification. In: NeurIPS (2014)
32. Knight, P.A.: The Sinkhorn-Knopp algorithm: convergence and applications. SIAM J. Matrix Anal. Appl. **30**(1), 261–275 (2008)
33. Koh, P.W., Liang, P.: Understanding black-box predictions via influence functions. In: ICML (2017)
34. LeCun, Y., Bottou, L., Bengio, Y., Haffner, P.: Gradient-based learning applied to document recognition. Proc. IEEE **86**(11), 2278–2324 (1998)
35. Mémoli, F.: Gromov-Wasserstein distances and the metric approach to object matching. Found. Comput. Math. **11**(4), 417–487 (2011)
36. Mirzasoleiman, B., Karbasi, A., Sarkar, R., Krause, A.: Distributed submodular maximization. J. Mach. Learn. Res. **17**(235), 1–44 (2016)
37. Nath, J.S., Jawanpuria, P.: Statistical optimal transport posed as learning kernel mean embedding. In: NeurIPS (2020)
38. Nemhauser, G.L., Wolsey, L.A., Fisher, M.L.: An analysis of approximations for maximizing submodular set functions. Math. Program. **14**, 265–294 (1978)
39. Peyré, G., Cuturi, M.: Computational optimal transport. Found. Trends Mach. Learn. **11**(5–6), 355–607 (2019)
40. Peyré, G., Cuturi, M., Solomon, J.: Gromov-Wasserstein averaging of kernel and distance matrices. In: ICML (2016)
41. Quionero-Candela, J., Sugiyama, M., Schwaighofer, A., Lawrence, N.: Dataset Shift in Machine Learning. The MIT Press, Cambridge (2009)
42. Ribeiro, M., Singh, S., Guestrin, C.: Why should I trust you? Explaining the predictions of any classifier. In: SIGKDD (2016)
43. Rousseeuw, P.J., Kaufman, L.: Finding Groups in Data: An Introduction to Cluster Analysis. Wiley, Hoboken (2009)
44. Rubner, Y., Tomasi, C., Guibas, L.J.: The earth mover's distance as a metric for image retrieval. IJCV **40**(2), 99–121 (2000)
45. Russakovsky, O., et al.: ImageNet large scale visual recognition challenge. Int. J. Comput. Vis. **115**(3), 211–252 (2015). https://doi.org/10.1007/s11263-015-0816-y
46. Schubert, E., Rousseeuw, P.J.: Faster k-Medoids clustering: improving the PAM, CLARA, and CLARANS algorithms. In: International Conference on Similarity Search and Applications (2019)
47. Smola, A., Gretton, A., Song, L., Schölkopf, B.: A Hilbert space embedding for distributions. In: International Conference on Algorithmic Learning Theory (2007)
48. Solomon, J., et al.: Convolutional Wasserstein distances: efficient optimal transportation on geometric domains. ACM Trans. Graph. **34**(4), 66:1–66:11 (2015)
49. Thomee, B., et al.: YFCC100M: the new data in multimedia research. Commun. ACM **59**(2), 64–73 (2016)
50. Tibshirani, R., Hastie, T., Narasimhan, B., Chu, G.: Diagnosis of multiple cancer types by shrunken centroids of gene expression. PNAS **99**(10), 6567–6572 (2002)
51. Villani, C.: Optimal Transport: Old and New. Springer, Heidelberg (2009)
52. Wei, K., Iyer, R., Bilmes, J.: Submodularity in data subset selection and active learning. In: ICML (2015)
53. Weiser, M.: Programmers use slices when debugging. Commun. ACM **25**(7), 446–452 (1982)
54. Wohlhart, P., Köstinger, M., Donoser, M., Roth, P., Bischof, H.: Optimizing 1-nearest prototype classifiers. In: CVPR (2013)
55. Yeh, C.K., Kim, J., Yen, I.E.H., Ravikumar, P.K.: Representer point selection for explaining deep neural networks. In: NeurIPS (2018)

Author Index

Printed in the United States
by Baker & Taylor Publisher Services